Social Interaction in Learning and Development

Studying social interaction in human mind and activities is highly relevant for different epistemological and theoretical approaches (e.g., individual constructivism, social constructivism, dialogical approach). Consequently, there is a growing number of social interaction studies in various contexts (family, educational, professional, clinical, institutional, social, political, and cultural settings) which are based on different theoretical perspectives and methodological approaches. This produces a multiplicity of findings which are highly relevant, both theoretically and practically—although weakly interrelated and seldom discussed together. The main aim of this book series is to create a space for continuous and systematic critical reflection of social interaction studies and their integration with a special focus on: (1) a detailed account of actors and processes involved in different types of situated social interaction, (2) situatedness of social interaction within sociocultural and sociomaterial contexts and how social interaction and contexts constitute and transform each other; (3) how properly designed social interactions can provide opportunities for learning and development (in formal, informal, non-formal education), and (4) how the individual person navigates within these social interactions.

The book series aims to support an argumentative and productive dialogue among different theoretical and methodological traditions, in order to enable a better understanding of their strengths and weaknesses.

For more information on how to submit your proposal, please contact the publisher:
Amy.taylor-snyman@springernature.com

Cintia Rodríguez · Pedro Palacios ·
Iván Moreno-Llanos · Irene Guevara
Editors

The Social Life of Objects in Early Development

New Perspectives on the Pragmatics of the Object

Springer

Editors
Cintia Rodríguez
Faculty of Psychology
Universidad Autónoma de Madrid
Madrid, Spain

Pedro Palacios
Departamento de Psicología
Universidad Autónoma de Aguascalientes
Aguascalientes, Ags., Mexico

Iván Moreno-Llanos
Faculty of Psychology
Universidad Autónoma de Madrid
Madrid, Spain

Irene Guevara
Department of Psychology
Universidad Antonio Nebrija
Madrid, Spain

ISSN 2662-5512 ISSN 2662-5520 (electronic)
Social Interaction in Learning and Development
ISBN 978-3-031-87675-2 ISBN 978-3-031-87673-8 (eBook)
https://doi.org/10.1007/978-3-031-87673-8

This Springer imprint is published by the registered company Springer Nature Switzerland AG
The registered company address is: Gewerbestrasse 11, 6330 Cham, Switzerland

Acknowledgments

The list of researchers with whom we have discussed many of the ideas presented in this volume over the years is vast. Without them, this volume would not be what it is. Here, we will acknowledge some of them. The full list would require a chapter all by itself.

Starting with our dear colleges from the School of Geneva. First, Christiane Moro. Without her, the Pragmatics of the Object would not have been born. The support and enthusiasm of Eduardo Martí has been constant. In the School of Geneva the support offered throughtout the years by Madelon Saada-Robert, Edith Ackermann, Jean Paul Bronckart, Bernard Schneuwly, Mercè Pujol, Valérie Tartas, Anne-Nelly Perret-Clermont, Marc Ratcliff, and Christiane Gillièron, has been essential. The debates on autism and "other capacities" have been rich in Geneva with Pilar Blanco, and in Madrid with Ángel Rivière, Amaya Sterner, Teresa Miguel, Pedro González, Alex Pardos, and Ermila Luna. With Ermila, the debates have also come and gone between Madrid and México.

The semiotic analysis and what it means for the interaction have been rich with our dear colleagues from Colombia, Miralba Correa, Elda Cerchiaro, Lilian Patricia Rodríguez, Mariela Orozco, María Eugenia Villalobos, Milton Eduardo Bermúdez, and Rebeca Puche. We have to mention our dear colleagues from Argentina, Tono Castorina and Nora Scheuer, and from Brazil, Angela Branco and Dominique Colinvaux; our colleagues from the Jean Piaget Society, such as Ulrich Müller, Jeremy Carpendale, Nancy Budwig, Cynthia Lightfoot, Tom Bidell, Alejandra Contreras, Mauricio García-Barrera, Beau Wallbridge, and Violet Cieslik; and our colleagues from Portsmouth University, Alan Costall, Chris Sinha, Vasu Reddy, and Vera da Silva, who have contributed with intense debates on the relation between the affordances and the pragmatics of the object.

The presence of Jaan Valsiner has been constant since the kitchen seminar at Clark University in the late 90s. Jaan's influence in socio-cultural theory has opened the door to the material culture. We must also mention from Neuchâtel University, Antonio Iannaccone, Martina Cabra, and Tania Zittoun.

The meetings over the years with the research group Vocapi, from France, have enriched the meaning of interaction: Christine Sorsana, Annick Well-Barais, Alain Trognon, Felice Carugati, Patrizia Selleri, and Audrey Barthelemy-Musso.

The students from the Universidad Autónoma de Madrid (UAM), who have participated in our research in early years schools, have contributed to develop the Pragmatics of the Object. First, Luisa Estrada, who made us understand better the teacher's educative interventions. Later, thanks to Lilian Contin, Alejandra Flores, and Lucía Romero, we were able to analyze gestures and the indisputable interest of children on their teachers' book reading activities.

Other colleagues that were part of the Universidad Autónoma de Madrid, like Alberto Rosa, Laura Quintanilla, María Núñez, and Carlos Hernández Blasi. And those who continue being part of the UAM, like Nacho Montero, Floor van Alphen, Marta Casla, Eva Murillo, Marga Diges, Manolo Monroy, and Nacho Montorio.

The members and participants of our research group DETEDUCA have fostered many of the ideas discussed in this book. First, we have to mention Marisol Basilio. Her research on self-regulation, has been essential for our research about the early development of Executive Functions. Other members of DETEDUCA have fostered the dialogue between the early years school and early childhood intervention, like José Luis de los Reyes, Alejandro Arrillaga, Alessia Macagno, Ángeles Medina, María López, Alicia Vallejo, Gabi Moura, and Mayte Rebollo.

We thank the early years schools and their teachers and principals. In Madrid, we would like to thank specially the following public early years schools: La Cigüeña María, Antonio Mercero (La Cabina), La Patria Chica, La Jara, La Cornisa, Títeres and La Ardilla. We would like to thank also the fathers and mothers, and the children who participated in the different studies. Without them, this book would not have been possible.

Finally, all our gratitude goes to Aleksander Baucal, the co-director of the collection *Social Interaction in Learning and Development*, for his support and enthusiasm.

Part of the realization of this book is supported by Grants:

PID2020-119147GB-I00 funded by Ministerio de Ciencia e Innovación/Agencia estatal de Investigación (Spain)/10.13039/501100011033.

PRE2021-097423 funded by Ministerio de Ciencia e Innovación/Agencia estatal de Investigación (Spain) and European Social Fund+

Crédito Beca Fundación Colfuturo – Programa Crédito Beca 2021, cofunded by Ministerio de Ciencia, Tecnología, e Innovación (Colombia).

CHAMADA INTERNA PPGEMP Nº002/2022 de Apoio Financeiro Educação – Modalidade Profissional (Brasil).

EDITAL PGPDE Nº 012/2024 Apoio à execução de projetos de pesquisas científicas – Docentes da Pós-Graduaçao Stricto Sensu do Programa de Pós-graduação em Psicologia do Desenvolvimiento e Escolar (Brasil).

Introduction. On the Life of Objects in Early Development

Objects have often remained invisible in Developmental Psychology—overlooked and reduced to their "physical" attributes such as size, color, texture, or shape. This tendency is perhaps most evident during infancy. Our aim in *The Social Life of Objects in Early Development* is to highlight the "social life of objects" in everyday life. As Piaget noted, knowledge is rooted in action *with* objects. Humans do not live in a vacuum, a material void; instead, we are immersed in a material universe whose meanings are shared and public (Zittoun & Perret-Clermont, 2009). This *common ground* enables us to communicate with others, collaborate, think, regulate our own behavior, and adapt to our environment. Artifact objects serve as signs and are integral to daily life. For instance, a spoon conveys its purpose: it is used for eating. The spoon acts as a sign of what is done with it. Objects are indispensable when children act upon and transform their reality independently. They are also present in the caregiving routines—whether for hygiene, feeding, or general care from birth onward. Objects are equally significant in interactions between children and adults, facilitating an understanding of communicative intent even before children begin to speak. Objects play a key role in the earliest manifestations of executive functions, starting at the end of the first year of life when children set challenging goals and work to achieve them through their own means. They are also vital actors in the educational efforts of early childhood educators. In *The Social Life of Objects in Early Development*, we aim to show how children's use of objects evolves in remarkable ways during the early years of life.

Artifact objects, as material culture, belong to a semiotic and normative universe whose rules of use are publicly shared within specific communities of users. Considering objects as material culture implies that they carry collective meaning (De Los Reyes, 2022). Art historian Jules Prown states, "material culture is the study through artifacts of the beliefs—values, ideas, attitudes, and assumptions—of a particular community or society at a given time." Material culture rests on an obvious fact: "that the existence of a man-made object is concrete evidence of the presence of a human intelligence operating at the time of fabrication" (1982, p. 1). Material culture encompasses a wide range of objects known as artifacts: objects created or modified by humans, such as hammers, teapots, microscopes, houses, or paintings. This excludes natural objects like trees, mountains, or rivers, although natural objects altered by humans are included (Prown, 1993). For the subject of this book, it is particularly significant to consider the disciplines that, according to Prown, place artifacts at the center of their study and those that do not. Among the former are archaeology, cultural geography, folklore, history, art history, and social and cultural anthropology. Psychology and Linguistics, however, are explicitly excluded.

The philosopher Karen Barad challenges traditional distinctions between organic, inorganic, animated, or inanimate. She argues that laboratory practices are inherently social. Drawing on Foucault and Judith Butler, Barad explores how the material instruments used for measuring and documenting data in physics become entangled with specific discursive practices that shape how the data is interpreted (Freitas, 2016). Barad asks, "Why are language and culture granted their own agency and historicity while the matter is figured as passive and immutable?" (2003, p. 801). In the field of the history of science, British scholar Simon Schaffer highlights a recent shift toward examining overlooked or ignored aspects of science, including objects and the study of material culture. In *The Material Cultures of Enlightenment Arts and Sciences*, Adriana Craciun and Simon Schaffer suggest that the term "things" might be misleading—"the wrong term." They argue: "We might as well speak of objects, artifacts, waste, commodities, specimens, ephemera, relics, artworks, instruments, souvenirs. Each of these terms is bound up with specific economic models of making, seizure, collection, appropriation, storage, and exchange. Such characteristic economies all possess their own remarkable histories" (2016, p. 2).

In a 1994 article titled *"Une sociologie sans objet? Remarques sur l'interobjectivité"* [A sociology without an object? Notes on interobjectivity], French sociologist Bruno Latour lamented that, as in many human sciences, "sociology too often remains without an object [...]" (Latour, 1994, p. 598, *translation ours*). Objects remain invisible, perceived as asocial, marginal, and incapable of engaging in the construction of society. Latour addressed the status of action in its relationship with knowledge, asserting that objects are social actors. He advocated for recognizing "the activity of thought situated in practices, in places, in a world of objects" (1994, p. 587), arguing that we must "treat things as social facts" (p. 606). Latour introduced the concept of the "parliament of things," through which sociology could decenter humans and study the role of objects in interaction (Freitas, 2016). Both Latour and Barad view sciences as cultural practices "in order to think differently about culture and social-material relationships" (Freitas, 2016, p. 150).

In another text published 20 years later, Michalis Kontopodis (2014) also lamented Psychology's lack of interest in how people and things mutually constitute one another.

The lack of interest in the social dimension of objects was a consistent feature of the Geneva School (Perret-Clermont, 1996). Paradoxically, it was also a feature present in Vygotsky's cultural-historical psychology, as objects were disconnected from semiotics and culture. The distinction between material tools and signs, and between instrumental mediation (separate from signs) and semiotic mediation (through intentional signs, with language as the primary example), has left a lasting impact on cultural-historical psychology to this day—though this is beginning to change. Moro (2011) masterfully summarizes this critique of Vygotsky: "I consider that, in effect, culture has a tendency to be identified with a particular class of artifacts, those that support ideality or symbolism, and does not include that class of artifacts related to the material world" (p. 60).

Sinha also highlights the lack of interest in acknowledging the semiotic nature of objects (2014). However, creating an artifact requires starting with a plan and responding to a goal, where the conceptual or imaginative representation of the creator is involved. Artifacts have a canonical function, defined as their "*socially standardized* function." For example, the socially organized function of a knife is to cut, and that of a spoon is to eat. "[…] The canonical function that defines an artifact is both *normative* and *cognitive*" (Sinha, 2014, p. 123, emphasis in the original, translation ours). Drawing on Searle, Sinha compares artifacts to "institutional facts": "If one person is another's sister-in-law, this is a social relationship that cannot be reduced to the physical properties of that person's body…" (p. 124). This argument challenges one of the most common dichotomies in psychology: the distinction between the "social world," made up of people and their institutions, and the so-called "non-social world", composed of objects reduced to their "physical" attributes. This perspective strips objects of their social function, normative status, and semiotic role (Rodríguez & Moro, 1998), effectively excluding them from material culture.

Nevertheless, significant changes have been emerging in recent years. Psychology is beginning to reconsider objects' classical status as passive, obvious, banal, and inert entities. For example, various voices challenge the traditional perspective stemming from Gibson, which has framed *affordances* as objective properties directly offered by the environment. According to Naddei Grasso et al. (2024), affordances are not limited to motor skills but also encompass aesthetic experiences involving cognitive and emotional aspects. From ecological perspectives, Brinck and Reddy (2020) also highlight the emotional dimension of relationships with material objects. Alan Costall (2012) further distinguishes between *affordances* "in general" and *canonical affordances*, the latter referring to the socially agreed-upon, conventional uses of objects in their contexts. This distinction reveals a critical difference between what an object physically offers as a possibility for action and what is conventionally expected to be done with it. While this difference may seem trivial from the perspective of an experienced adult familiar with their cultural context, it is fundamental for children who have yet to acquire such knowledge. This distinction becomes even more critical for children with visual impairments (Chibaudel et al., 2022) or those on the autism spectrum, given their difficulties in using everyday objects for their conventional purposes (Williams et al., 2005) and the subsequent challenges this poses for adapting to their environment and communicating with others (Sterner & Rodríguez, 2012). In other fields, particularly those related to early childhood education (Tapparel, 2013/2022; Kontopodis, 2014), from infant classrooms (De los Reyes & Rodríguez, 2021) to primary and secondary education (Bisault et al., 2022; Bernier & Brossard, 2013/2022), or even in primary school settings where students create new artifacts (Kumpulainen & Kajamaa, 2021), the materiality of objects and artifacts is increasingly gaining recognition for its importance in educational practices and pedagogy.

The Contents of this Volume: The Pragmatics of the Object Today

Our theoretical perspective, which we have called "The Pragmatics of the Object," (PO) originated in Geneva in the 1980s. However, its consolidation and development occurred, as often happens, in the diaspora, when the Geneva School was unable or unwilling to ensure the continuity of a significant number of researchers who had been part of the institution (see discussion in Rodríguez & Martí, 2012).

In *The Social Life of Objects in Early Development*, new lines of research emerging in recent years are brought together under the framework of the Pragmatics of the Object. While the epicenter has been located in Madrid, these studies have also developed in Mexico, Chile, Brazil, Colombia, and Argentina[1].

The object and the subject's action as a source of knowledge were constant themes in the Geneva School. However, objects were not considered part of material culture nor included in human communication; they were regarded as part of "physical reality." These two factors—the importance of action with objects for psychological development and their positioning outside any social dimension—were pivotal in the origin of the Pragmatics of the Object (Moro & Rodríguez, 1989; Rodríguez & Moro, 1998). From the outset, we questioned the cognitive isolation in which the Geneva School had placed the child (and the object) during infancy—a period when the child most needs the presence, care, and guidance of others! Our aim was to bring a pragmatic and semiotic shift to the concept of object, rescuing it from the marginal position it had been placed.

This led us to the idea that objects carry public meanings, are part of material culture, and are used in everyday life according to rules of use. Our initial goal was to analyze how children acquire this shared knowledge within their community of users. In this way, objects became part of communicative acts, ceasing to be mute and interchangeable referents. This pragmatic dimension—focused on the types of uses developed during the first year of life—was not a research topic in Geneva at the time, even though action with objects is essential for the adaptation to the environment.

This volume includes new lines of research on the "social life of objects" in early development—a life that becomes evident when children use objects to accomplish tasks, communicate with others, and collaborate with adults and peers

[1] Another epicenter of the Pragmatics of the Object has been established at the University of Lausanne through research conducted under the direction of Christiane Moro.

in pursuit of shared goals in everyday situations. In addressing how such different individuals achieve a shared understanding of objective reality, we offer our answers here.

The common thread among the chapters of this book lies in the construction of object use within a semiotic network of cultural meaning. While early studies in the Pragmatics of the Object focused on how and when children consider everyday objects as signs of their social function (Moro & Rodríguez, 1989, 2005; Rodríguez & Moro, 1998, 1999; Costall & Dreier, 2006), this volume expands on the development of new types of cultural uses beyond functional or canonical ones. The chapters include investigations into *rhythmic-sound uses* of objects at home, in schools, and hospital settings; *symbolic uses* in neurotypical development, children with Down syndrome, and in peer interactions in the early years school; *numerical uses* in triadic interactions at home; and *communicative uses* of objects among children on the autism spectrum in everyday and therapeutic contexts. Additionally, new lines of research explore the origin and early development of gestures, as well as Executive Functions and self-regulation from a pragmatic perspective. This approach promotes a paradigm shift, situating executive functions in everyday contexts rooted in children's development. All studies were conducted in everyday settings—such as homes, early years schools, hospitals, and therapeutic environments—where children, parents, teachers, and caregivers were free to act and communicate as the intentional agents they are.

All the studies on early childhood included in this volume align with the idea that: "Objects only speak about themselves to those who can integrate them into a network of pre-existing knowledge" (Dujovne, 1995, as cited in De los Reyes, 2022, p. 217). This implies that objects are constructed throughout development. In this sense, we are far removed from the dominant "non-developmental nativist approach" described by Karmiloff-Smith (2010), which disregards the child's developmental history.

The Social Life of Objects in Early Development is divided into four parts.
Part I *Historical, Theoretical, and Methodological Roots of the Pragmatics of the Object* consists of three chapters. This section takes the reader on a journey through the 1970s–1980s' Geneva, the birthplace of the Pragmatics of the Object. It explores its theoretical, epistemological, and methodological foundations, its continuities and breaks with the Geneva School, as well as the early studies on the construction of canonical or functional object uses, and the baby-object-adult communication dynamic during the first year of life. This part concludes with a third chapter dedicated to the research method guiding the studies included in this volume.

In Chapter 1, *Pragmatics of the Object: Roots in the Geneva School*, Cintia Rodríguez provides a retrospective account of her experiences, first as a student and later as a *professeure assistante [assistant professor]* in the Geneva School during the 1970s and 1980s—a fascinating era marked by significant innovations. The chapter begins with the functionalist shift initiated by Piaget, Inhelder, and the *Groupe de stratégies et résolution de problèmes [Strategies and problem solving Group].* Rodríguez describes this period as a moment of "fermentation." The

Geneva *functionalist turn* brought a reevaluation of the status of objects and functional processes in studying the subject. Piaget introduced a novel focus on the functional aspects of development, functioning dynamics, and change mechanisms. Bärbel Inhelder, another central figure of this functionalist shift, led the *Groupe de stratégies et résolution de problèmes*, which, as Inhelder noted, "did not fear breaking with certain aspects of the past to observe and explore children's discovery processes in new ways" (1992, p. 15). The *Groupe* included influential figures such as Guy Cellérier, Annette Karmiloff-Smith, Alex Blanchet, Edith Ackermann, and Madelon Saada-Robert. Their critique of Piaget and their emphasis on capturing the dynamics of subject-object interaction, children's strategies for solving specific problems, microgenetic analysis, and the pursuit of creative solutions, were pivotal in the birth of the Pragmatics of the Object. Cintia Rodríguez reflects on the profound impact of these developments and highlights three key ideas: (1) The subject must be studied as an *intentional agent* who *acts* and *self-corrects* in *real time*; (2) Microgenetic analyses are essential for capturing underlying *processes* and their *creativity*; and (3) Understanding the subject requires taking the *object* seriously. These three axes have continued to guide her research ever since.

The chapter also explores the arrival of Vygotsky's ideas in Geneva during the 1970s (at a time when no French translations of the Soviet author's works were available), along with the introduction of cultural and social perspectives. This period also saw the emergence of the nativist theses on the "competent baby" from the Anglo-American world, which gained significant traction in subsequent decades and continue to influence contemporary thought. The author then delves into the various influences underpinning the Pragmatics of the Object. She highlights the Piaget's functionalist perspective on sensorimotor development, the *Groupe's* research, the arrival of Vygotsky's ideas on semiotic mediation, and Bruner's pragmatism from the linguistic turn, which focused on the practical goals of everyday life when adults and infants communicate.

In Chapter 2, *The Uses of Objects and Their Social Construction in Infancy*, Cintia Rodríguez continues the exploration of the Geneva School of the 1970s and 1980s. She addresses the foundational question of the Pragmatics of the Object: How do infants begin to use objects according to their function during the first year of life? Two key events occurred to answer this question. First, the Pragmatics of the Object became firmly rooted in the epistemological, theoretical, and methodological pillars of Geneva's *constructivism*. There was continuity with constructivist theses, particularly the non-negotiable status of the active subject in constructing their own knowledge, with the source of knowledge found in the subject's actions on the object rather than in the object itself. Other continuities included using observation as a method, microgenetic analyses, and longitudinal designs, all aimed at capturing the child's psychological development.

On the other hand, the break with Geneva occurs in two central aspects: the reduction of objects to their "physical" attributes and their systematic exclusion from communicative acts. From there, three sections are presented that form the backbone of the Pragmatics of the Object: (i) Artifact objects from everyday life are part of *material culture*; (ii) The *types* of *uses* children make of objects *develop* spectacularly during the first and second years of life, according to levels of *increasing semiotic complexity*. The construction of the *functional permanence* of objects marks the entry into the cultural uses of materiality in infancy and constitutes a turning point in development; (iii) In the last section, Cintia Rodríguez presents the interactive triangle of child-object-adult (the magical number three) as the minimal unit of construction of the human psyche. Children appropriate the public meanings of objects through *communication* with others, according to *levels of increasing semiotic complexity*.

Chapter 3, *Methodological Approach to the Study of Early Development from the Pragmatics of the Object*, concludes the first part of the book. In this chapter, Pedro Palacios, Iván Moreno-Llanos, Irene Guevara, and Cintia Rodríguez present the methodology used in the various studies within the Pragmatics of the Object framework. Systematic, detailed microgenetic observation of children's actions in their everyday contexts takes center stage. However, microgenetic observation is not limited to describing observed behaviors but extends to interpreting the cognitive processes inferred from them. The authors summarize the theoretical foundations of their approach: i) the observation of the subject as an agent in everyday situations, ii) the triadic interaction and the semiotic mediation of subjects in interaction, and iii) the longitudinal designs. These principles translate into studies where children actively participate in solving problems they encounter in daily life. Importantly, children are not observed in isolation. Interaction with adults—such as parents or teachers—is essential for constructing the conventional and public meanings characteristic of their culture or social group. Moreover, no controlled or structured activities are proposed. Instead, the researchers observe the spontaneous actions and interactions of participants. This approach contrasts with traditional research, which often relies on highly structured and arbitrary tasks. Although microgenetic observation is labor-intensive, it allows researchers to identify how children behave in everyday interactions, how these behaviors change over time, and how increasingly complex semiotic forms are constructed. Additionally, this methodology can uncover unexpected behaviors, leading to new research questions.

Semiotic observation categories are created to account for this development. While all studies share a standard corpus of categories, each expands or narrows the subcategories based on specific research questions. Palacios, Moreno-Llanos, Guevara, and Rodríguez argue that observation and microgenetic analysis of children's everyday activities provide a solid foundation for understanding the processes and dynamics of early socio-cognitive development, also at a macrogenetic level.

Part II *Types of Uses of Objects and Gestures. A Semiotic and Social Development* consists of four chapters, focusing on more recent research into the development of three types of cultural uses of objects and instruments that go beyond canonical uses: rhythmic-sound, symbolic, and numerical uses. This section concludes with a chapter on the development of gestures and the role of objects in constructing these early tools of communication and meaning-making.

In Chapter 4, *The Pragmatics of Music: Rhythmic-Sound Uses in Early Development at Home, in the Hospital, and in the Early Years School*, Iván Moreno-Llanos, María Jáñez-Álvarez, Miren Pérez-Eizaguirre, and María Jesús del Olmo present research on the development of rhythmic-sound uses of sound-producing objects and musical instruments in three contexts: at home, in interaction with parents; in the hospital, with preterm infants; and in early years schools, in interaction with teachers.

Objects are often relegated to dyadic interactions between infant and object, which begin around 5 months of age, or to the first triadic interactions, where infants communicate with adults about an object, typically around 9 months. However, adults organize triadic interactions that include infants in communicative niches much earlier. From the very beginning of life, adults mediate infants' relationships with objects, making their conventional use and meaning understandable. Objects thus become mediators of communication between adults and infants. In these triadic interactions organized by adults, the rhythm and sound of objects play a significant role in structuring early agreements with infants.

The authors describe two types of uses in the actions of infants and adults. *Rhythmic-sound uses* involve employing material objects to produce sound and rhythm. Any object used to create sound is referred to as a *sound-producing object*. On the other hand, *canonical rhythmic-sound uses* pertain to the structured use of *musical instruments* specifically designed to produce certain sounds. Both types of uses represent infants' first effective and conventional actions with objects, forming the foundation for their understanding of materiality's functions and public meanings. Rhythm and sound function as semiotic systems that enable the establishment of early agreements. The rhythm and pauses in the adult's actions serve as interaction organizers, fostering the infant's attention and participation. During pauses, the adult demonstrates and offers the object, sharing the referent. In this way, the adult "lends their intentions" to the infant, who will gradually take the initiative in the interaction.

These studies have also served as a foundation for hospital interventions. In neonatal care units, preterm infants find themselves in an atypical, disorganized environment that can become aversive due to noise or clinical procedures. Additionally, parents often face significant challenges in interacting with their newborns because of the anxiety and concern for their survival. In this context, the authors analyze music therapy interventions in which the music therapist conducts musical improvisations to support and guide parents in their interactions with their baby. This approach has been shown to improve the baby's vital signs while also enabling parents to engage meaningfully with their infant. Surprisingly, it also has a positive impact on the staff in the neonatal unit.

Finally, the authors present findings from research conducted in the first year of early years school (0–1 classrooms). They analyzed the rhythmic patterns of children during musical activities, focusing on the *rhythmic-sound uses* and *canonical rhythmic-sound uses* they produced. Children actively explored the sound properties of sound-producing objects and musical instruments. Their actions displayed a distinct rhythmic pattern characterized by frequent pauses and silences.

This indicates that their actions are organized and structured, resembling those of adults. However, their tempo tends to be slower, suggesting that these uses are still developing.

Overall, these findings highlight the importance of rhythm and sound in early development as fundamental semiotic systems that enable the first agreements between infants and adults around an object. These agreements provide a foundation for the development of more complex skills.

In Chapter 5, *Development of the First Symbols in Triadic Communicative Contexts*, Pedro Palacios, Karina Cárdenas, and Noemí Yuste explore the development of symbolic uses of objects. They investigate *how* children begin to use everyday objects symbolically within triadic communicative contexts—child-object-adult. The authors review various perspectives on symbolic development. In the first section, They start with approaches, such as Piaget's, that argue symbols originate from individual processes. They also address modularist and nativist theories regarding the origins of symbols. The following section focuses on social theories of the origin of symbols, particularly those of Vygotsky, as well as the work of Tomasello and his research group.

This section incorporates the Pragmatics of the Object, organized around several core ideas: Symbols form a semiotic system that precedes language and can be used not only for play but also for thinking, and as a means of communication and interaction with others. Symbolic meanings are built upon already conventional meanings, resulting from prior agreements anchored in the rules governing the canonical uses of objects. Another key idea is that adults play an educational role in symbolic development. First symbols emerge around 11 or 12 months of age during interactions with adults or peers. From there, the chapter is further divided into three sections. The first addresses neurotypical symbolic development. Here, Palacios, Cárdenas, and Yuste outline various levels of symbolic use according to their semiotic complexity. A key focus is on the first level of symbolic meaning. Level 1 comprises symbolic uses that represent the canonical use of the *same object* being used symbolically but *outside its usual context*. At this stage, decontextualization and the evocation of something absent are already observable. Children begin to detach from immediate circumstances, bringing absent realities into the here and now, rooted in the functional, canonical meanings of objects (e.g., using an empty spoon out of context to "eat" or "feed someone"). Other symbolic levels include substitution symbols (Level 2) and symbols in absence (Level 3). The chapter's second section focuses on symbolic development in children with Down syndrome. It confirms that the uses of objects are not self-evident. Mothers played a crucial role in fostering symbolic behaviors in their children, and the signs used by the children included material elements. The final section examines symbolic development among peers in early years schools. In each part, Palacios, Cárdenas, and Yuste present microgenetic observations that reveal the processes at play and the dynamics of interaction between adults and children or between peers. These detailed observations capture the "life of objects" in symbolic communicative situations.

In Chapter 6, *Early Development of Number: Semiotic and Social Construction*, Silvia Cavalcante and Eduardo Martí evaluate key contributions in psychology related to early numerical knowledge. They highlight the limitations of these contributions and advocate for the relevance of the Pragmatics of the Object by offering a critical perspective on recent studies in the field. The authors reference Piaget, who proposed that understanding numbers involves a long process of construction facilitated by children's operations with objects. Criticism of this view of late acquisition led to research on innate numerical abilities and the importance of counting, with contributions from authors such as Carey, Dehaene, and, more recently, Hirschfeld and Gelman. Cavalcante and Martí, engaging with the Pragmatics of the Object, critique the nativist perspective, which posits the existence of innate numerical knowledge. They argue that this perspective raises controversial and debatable questions. Number, they assert, is not an inherent property of objects but rather emerges through an active construction process by the subject in interaction with others. Moreover, as numbers are inherently symbolic, their construction and expression require symbolic treatment. The authors also critique studies on counting for failing to analyze in depth the critical role of social interaction, and for overlooking the variety of semiotic systems that underpin and enable numerical development. Based on these points, Cavalcante and Martí emphasize the semiotic nature of numbers and the importance of distinguishing this view from the nativist conceptualization of numbers. They illustrate their arguments with findings from a microgenetic study analyzing mother-child interactions in three dyads participating in a number-related game. They conclude that studies of numerical development cannot ignore the semiotic, social, and cultural nature of its construction.

In Chapter 7, *Gesture Development in the Early-Years-School: The Role of Early Interactions with Objects and Adults*, Irene Guevara reflects on the defining role of objects in early communicative development, challenging their traditional view as passive "referents" or mere contexts for early communicative acts. Drawing on ideas such as Clark's (2003) assertion that "much of what is currently called context is really acts of communication" (p. 244), Guevara analyzes the triple role of objects in early development: As first communicative signs, providing children with initial tools for expression; as early shared referents, offering a *common ground* for the first social interactions; and as active contexts, creating a variety of opportunities and communicative demands, which drive the development of new communicative forms and functions.

The author highlights *ostensive gestures* as the first intentional gestures, in which objects are not merely referred to but become an integral part of the gesture itself, forming part of the sign. These initial gestures enable the creation of shared meanings with minimal prior agreements, laying the foundation for developing more complex gestures, such as pointing. Guevara positions ostensive gestures as a critical window into understanding the process through which intentional communication emerges.

The chapter emphasizes the deeply recursive relationship between early gestures and initial object uses. Early uses are communicated through gestures, while the meanings of these gestures are anchored and derived from the conventional uses of objects. This close connection facilitates the progressive development of children's semiotic abilities, from ostensive gestures to indexical and representational ones, following a continuum of increasing semiotic complexity.

The chapter also highlights that early interactions with objects enable the understanding of others' intentions, a crucial step in interpreting the early communicative functions of infant gestures. These functions include widely studied purposes, such as sharing interests and making requests, but also encompass less explored functions, such as seeking help, evaluating achievements, informing about the unknown, and regulating actions. These dynamics are illustrated by longitudinal research conducted in 0–1-year-old classrooms at various public early years schools in the Community of Madrid, which provides a rich and situated empirical framework.

Finally, gesture development is analyzed not only through children's productions but also by considering the interaction contexts and adult mediation, particularly that of early childhood educators. Teachers play a key role in modeling, enriching, and correcting children's early gestural productions through multimodal strategies tailored to each child's needs. This process facilitates the gradual transformation of instrumental actions into intentional gestures, passing through transitional behaviors that reveal the construction process of shared meanings. Through these interactions, children develop not only gestures with diverse forms and functions but also increasingly rich, complex, and prolonged interactions. Overall, this chapter demonstrates how the recursive relationships between objects, gestures, and interactions shape one of the earliest communicative tools, driving cognitive, social, and communicative development in early childhood.

Part III: *Executive functions and their development in everyday situations: Toward a paradigm shift* includes four chapters. Numerous voices today advocate for a paradigm shift in the study of Executive Functions (EF). This shift is particularly critical in infancy, given the scarcity of research in this area, which is central to the construction of the psyche. The chapters in this section challenge standardized tasks in early development, offering an alternative theoretical and analytical framework rooted in the everyday contexts of early years schools. The section concludes with a chapter based on data from schools in Brasília, reflecting on the positive and negative influences of educational practices on the development of EF in the classroom.

In Chapter 8, *Executive Functions and Material Objects: What Is the Role of Materiality in Early Executive Functions Research?* Iván Moreno-Llanos and Julieth Barreto present a critical review of the tasks used in studies on the early development of Executive Functions with children aged 6 to 36 months. The analysis focuses on the characteristics of the objects included in the tasks, their status in tasks' objectives, and children's expected responses. Moreno-Llanos and Barreto find that most tasks present children with external goals involving abstract, arbitrary, and unfamiliar difficulties, which also require a solid understanding of spoken language. Tasks often aim to locate hidden objects for children aged 6–18 months. Between 18 and 24 months, tasks adapted from those designed for adults begin to appear. A significant volume of tasks is applied starting at 2–3 years of age, leaving a limited number of studies focusing on EF development before children begin to speak.

Moreno-Llanos and Barreto organize the tasks they analyzed into three broad categories based on their focus on the following dimensions of objects: i) physical, ii) perceptual, or iii) practical. In the first group, objects are conceived as "attractive physical entities," interchangeable and not representing conceptual or practical demands for children. This includes, among others, tasks inspired by Piaget's *A-not-B error*, designed to study the development of object permanence, and delay of gratification tasks based on Mischel's classic *Marshmallow Test*. *A-not-B* tasks are the most common in research with children under 12 months, as neither the experimenter's instructions nor the children's responses require language. The second group includes tasks originally designed for adults and adapted for children, such as *Day and Night* and *Dimensional Change Card Sort* (DCCS). Objects are considered based on perceptual characteristics, such as shape, color, and size. The final group includes tasks in which the practical dimension of objects is relevant, such as materiality to provoke changes in the world or achieve a compelling goal. Overall, these tasks tend to be more complex and less common. This group includes, for example, *detour tasks*, where children must *inhibit* the impulse to obtain an attractive object immediately and instead find the correct way to get it, or the *grasping task*, based on how children use a spoon to eat. The chapter concludes with a critical discussion of the physical and perceptual dimensions as the central focus of objects incorporated in tasks. Moreno-Llanos and Barreto debate the absence of cultural aspects in research on early Executive Function development. In most tasks, objects are merely a "means" or a "supporting element" and are not a significant part of the objective. Moreno-Llanos and Barreto join critical voices emphasizing the need to situate materiality and children's actions in meaningful, cultural, and pragmatic everyday contexts where challenges are not necessarily imposed, responses are far less arbitrary, and "errors" are considered children's adjustments and approximations to their goals.

In Chapter 9, *Is a Paradigm Shift Necessary Today in the Approach to Executive Functions?* Cintia Rodríguez, Iván Moreno-Llanos, and Irene Guevara organize their arguments into four sections. In the first section, the authors emphasize the growing criticism of standardized tasks as the predominant method for assessing Executive Functions. They highlight several aspects that have been overlooked by the dominant approach to studying EF over the past decades: ecological validity; the need to consider cultural aspects both in the design of tasks and in the conceptualization of EF; the progressive neglect of social factors in EF studies, such as the influence of family and school on their development; and the debate on domain-general *versus* domain-specific approaches to EF; among other issues.

A crucial step in this paradigm shift involves revisiting classical developmental theorists, particularly Piaget and Vygotsky, who positioned self-regulation as central to the construction of the subject. This review is presented in the second part of the chapter. Rodríguez, Moreno-Llanos, and Guevara revisit the debate between Vygotsky and Piaget on egocentric speech to emphasize action and the role of others as anchors of self-regulation in early development. They propose two key aspects for understanding early EF. First, they place at the center the prelinguistic constructions of children as they face their own challenges—actions involving the materiality of their everyday contexts and self-directed as well as other-directed gestures. Second, they consider social interactions as an essential factor in enabling children to construct and use semiotic tools for self-regulation.

In the third section of the chapter, the authors examine Piaget's perspectives in greater detail to understand self-regulation processes during the first year of life. They begin by revisiting his equilibration model from the 1970s, then refer to his earlier work on sensorimotor development in the 1930s and 1940s. While the equilibration model does not explicitly address the first year of life, the authors analyze its contributions to explaining the early development of EF. They highlight the role of children's awareness of the goals they set for themselves and the means to achieve them as key aspects of equilibration. This process results from regulatory responses to disequilibrium, driving children toward creative processes and novel solutions. Thus, equilibration occurs concerning the challenges and goals that children establish for themselves. Additionally, Rodríguez, Moreno-Llanos, and Guevara emphasize, as a central issue in studying EF during infancy, Piaget's distinction between *achieving* a goal and *understanding* why achievement occurs.

From Piaget's studies on sensorimotor development, the authors highlight the *origin and early development* of cognitive control in everyday situations, which Piaget examined with remarkable detail. Particularly noteworthy is stage IV, when children begin setting goals that require differentiated means. Since these challenges are not easily achievable, they necessarily involve equilibration processes. For this reason, the authors place the first manifestations of EF toward the end of the first year of life. They also identify that within the goals children set for themselves, it is possible to analyze components of EF, such as inhibition, flexibility, and working memory.

In the final section of the chapter, Rodríguez, Moreno-Llanos, and Guevara strongly advocate for a paradigm shift in the study of EF, mainly when focusing on their origins and early manifestations. They propose five fundamental ideas to address some of the challenges faced in this field: (1) Acknowledge children's agency, which is often obscured by contexts that place them in passive, arbitrary, and abstract situations; (2) Consider prelinguistic semiotic systems, challenging the notion that children who have not yet sufficiently developed language lack self-regulation; (3) Position a developmental perspective on children as the starting point, moving away from adult-centric perspectives to focus on what children are capable of achieving; (4) Understand EF as processes shaped by dialectic of *bottom-up* and *top-down* processes; and (5) Conduct longitudinal studies to capture the developmental trajectory of EF.

In Chapter 10, *Action and Communication in the Origin of Executive Functions: A Pragmatic Perspective*, Cintia Rodríguez, Iván Moreno-Llanos, Irene Guevara, and Gonzalo Flecha continue the arguments introduced in Chapter 9 by presenting a pragmatic approach to the study of Executive Functions from the end of the first year of life, focusing on children's everyday activities in early years schools. They base their analysis on children's actions, the significant challenges they set for themselves, and how they overcome their difficulties. The authors identify seven basic executive components evident in children's actions when they face meaningful challenges: the challenge itself (which organizes the action), the means to achieve it, inhibition, flexibility, action monitoring, persistence despite difficulties, and sustained attention toward their goal. During the second year of life, they observe the emergence of additional components, such as evaluation, seeking help, involving others in their activity, and planning. All these elements operate in a coordinated manner through semiotic systems.

The first challenges observed in early years schools emerge around 8–9 months of age. These challenges primarily relate to learning to use everyday objects and instruments according to their conventional, public, and social uses. These challenges are highly motivating for children, as they are meaningful in their daily lives. Initially, children aim to produce sound effectively through *rhythmic-sound* and *canonical rhythmic-sound uses* of sound-producing objects and musical instruments. Around 10 months of age, they begin to engage in *conventional uses* of various everyday objects. Only toward the end of the first school year, around 17 months, are the first challenges involving the *symbolic use* of objects observed. This progression illustrates the increasing semiotic complexity of the challenges faced by children, from basic forms such as sound production to more complex functional and symbolic forms.

To achieve these challenges, children employ a variety of *means* to organize and direct their actions. The authors highlight the use of objects and gestures as key tools. Through their use of objects, children explore actions with varying levels of effectiveness, progressively building their understanding. Gestures, on the other hand, act as forms of "external thinking." Children momentarily pause their actions and perform private gestures directed toward themselves to adjust their subsequent actions. These private gestures also develop over time. The earliest and most common are *private ostensive gestures*, where children show themselves and "study" the object causing them difficulty, seeking potential solutions—such as changing hands, position, or grip. By the end of the first year, children also begin to produce *private pointing gestures*, directing their attention and actions toward the object or location where they need to act. Finally, private symbolic gestures emerge during the second year of life, serving more complex functions. For instance, children may clap for themselves upon achieving a goal, positively evaluating their own actions. This dynamic interplay between the use of objects and gestures as means of self-regulation contrasts with traditional perspectives on the study of Executive Functions. Children's self-regulatory processes occur within action through a dialectical *bottom-up/top-down* dynamic. Through action, children construct representations, which they subsequently use to regulate future actions.

In Chapter 11, *Early Childhood Schools in Brasília: I Show You, and You Observe. Executive Functions, Educational Situations, and Object Use*, Francisco Rengifo and Gabriela Mietto present the results of their research on the development of Executive Functions in early years schools in Brazil. They analyze how teachers' educational practices either promote or hinder children's ability to set challenges for themselves and organize their behavior intentionally. The authors studied the types of educational situations created by teachers in the classroom, categorizing them as semi-structured, structured, or directed. In these Brasílian schools, they found that the educational focus often centers on developing skills typically associated with primary school, with activities involving objects that have a distinctly academic character. These findings stand in contrast to the results of studies conducted in Madrid.

What stands out is the high level of control and restriction that teachers impose on children's activities. Rather than fostering and guiding participation, teachers often limit children's opportunities to engage actively in the activities. Teachers specify the goal and the sequence of actions children are expected to perform. As a result, children have little control over the situation, with their actions restricted to executing the steps prescribed by the teachers.

On the other hand, teachers also frequently allow children to engage in activities with minimal support or to interact in loosely structured settings. In these cases, children face very open-ended tasks without a clear objective, and their actions unfold without the teacher's involvement. The authors present two educational scenarios illustrating this type of activity: sticking paper flags and reading a book. However, the observed children organized their actions creatively and autonomously. They sought to take control of the activity by setting their own goals, transforming it into a meaningful and challenging experience for themselves.

These activities contrast with the observations in the previous chapter, where teachers actively engaged with children in constructing conventional meanings and promoting intentional actions. In those cases, teachers were always part of the activity, offering children new challenges and alternatives, correcting inappropriate actions, and co-constructing conventional meanings. However, the authors emphasize that the way teachers in Brasília organize activities is not the result of negligence. Instead, it reflects a professional training system oriented toward primary education and the "know-how" cultural practices teachers bring into early childhood classrooms. Consequently, the authors discuss considerations for early childhood education in Brasília, suggesting that it could benefit from insights gained in prior studies.

Part IV *Psychoeducational Intervention in Everyday Situations in the Context of Autism* is the conclusion to *The Social Life of Objects in Early Development.* This section consists of a single chapter dedicated to the condition of Autism Spectrum Disorder (ASD).

In Chapter 12, *Construction of Shared Meanings from the Pragmatics of the Object. Psychoeducational Experiences in the Field of Autism*, Julia Benassi and Karina Cárdenas take on the challenge of supporting children with Autism Spectrum Disorder (ASD) and their families. As they demonstrate throughout the chapter, this support is carried out through semiotic mediation tools and carefully designed experiences to construct shared meanings that enable participation in various contexts of everyday life.

In this chapter, Benassi and Cárdenas analyze key aspects of socio-cognitive development in children with ASD. The chapter is divided into three sections.

First, they address general aspects of autism, exploring early development from a perspective based on the dimensional continuum. In the second section, the authors compare the communicative dimensions in children with ASD and those with neurotypical development. Here, they analyze the role of objects and semiotic mediations as they occur in interactions. In the third section, Benassi and Cárdenas examine the semiotic qualities of educational environments designed in educational practices. The objective is to promote children's participation in the world of objects and the construction of shared meanings. They describe various psychoeducational experiences conducted during a longitudinal follow-up with a child with ASD. The authors show how they use diverse semiotic systems, including artifact objects, gestures, images, words, rhythm, and music. These semiotic dynamics enable the construction of shared meanings in the everyday contexts of school, home, and therapy centers. The authors present a wide variety of detailed illustrations of the processes and semiotic systems used in psychoeducational experiences to generate shared meanings about the organization of daily time, the organization of space (zones, corners, or learning centers), and the visual cues and semiotic mediations that help "envelop" the spaces.

Throughout *The Social Life of Objects in Early Development*, it becomes evident that the lens through which objects are viewed inevitably shapes what is said about the subject. The ways humans use objects in daily life are embedded in and form the very core of material culture. These uses often also play a role in communication between individuals. The development of object uses during the early years of life, with their rapidly growing semiotic complexity, is closely linked to the semiotic systems at play in communication with others. The cultural uses of objects also contribute to the early forms of cognitive self-regulation, the development of intentionality, agency, and self-control. All of this facilitates increasingly complex forms of adaptation to the environment. It is striking how little attention developmental psychology has paid to the development of children's *types of object use* and how this essential construction for daily life both impacts and is impacted by communication with others.

This book fills a gap in a fundamental aspect of early development: the development of the traits that define us as human beings, specifically our relationship with the material culture that nurtures and shapes development. This book offers, at least in part, an answer to how different individuals come to share an understanding of objective reality.

Cintia Rodríguez
Pedro Palacios Salas
Iván Moreno-Llanos
Irene Guevara

References

Barad, K. (2003). Posthumanist performativity: Toward an understanding of how matter comes to matter. *Signs: Journal of Women in Culture and Society*, *28*, 3, 801–831. https://www.jstor.org/stable/10.1086/345321

Benassi, J., & Cárdenas, K. (this volume). Construction of shared meaning from the Pragmatics of the Object. Psychoeducational experiences in the field of autism.

Bernier, J.-P., & Brossard, M. (Eds.) (2013/2022). *Vygotski et l'école. Apports et limites d'un modèle théorique pour penser l'éducation et la formation* [Vygotsky and the school: contributions and limitations of a theoretical model for rethinking education and training]. Presses Universitaires de Bordeaux. DOI:10.4000/books.pub.47607

Bisault, J., Le Bourgeois, R., Thémines, J-F., Le Mentec, M., & Chauvet-Chanoine, C. (Eds.) (2022). *Objects to Learn About and Objects for Learning 2. Which Teaching practices for which issues?* Wiley Online Library.

Brinck, I., & Reddy, V. (2020). Dialogue in the making: emotional engagement with materials. *Phenomenology and the Cognitive Sciences*, *19*, 23–45. https://doi.org/10.1007/s11097-019-09629-2

Cavalcante, S., & Martí, E. (this volume). Early development of number: semiotic and social construction.

Chibaudel, Q., Dimitrov, L., Oriola, B., Jouffrais, C., Fibigerova, K., & Tartas, V. (2022). Professional report: From tangible objects to interactive maps for moving around and learning an area – Two examples with people with visual impairments. In J. Bisault, R. Le Bourgeois, J-F Thémines, M. Le Mentec, & C. Chauvet-Chanoine (Eds.), *Objects to Learn About and Objects for Learning 2.* Which Teaching practices for which issues? (pp. 95-110). Wiley Online Library.

Clark, H. (2003). Pointing and placing. In S. Kita (Ed.), *Pointing: Where language, culture and cognition meet* (pp. 243–268). New Jersey: Lawrence Erlbaum.

Costall, A. (2012). Canonical affordances in context. *AVANT*, *vol. III*, *2*, 85–93. http://hdl.handle.net/20.500.12424/142464

Costall, A. y Dreier, O. (2006). *Doing things with things. The Design and use of erveryday objects.* Hampshire: Ashgate.

Craciun, A. & Schaffer, S. (2016). Introduction. In A. Craciun & S. Schaffer (Eds.), *The Material Cultures of enlightenment arts and sciences* (pp. 1–11). London: Palgrave Macmillan.

De Freitas, E. (2016). Karen Barad. In E. de Freitas & M. Walshaw, *Alternative Theoretical Frameworks for Mathematics Education Research*, (pp. 149–173). Springer.

De los Reyes, J. L. (2022). A cultural viewpoint about objects: Objects that narrate cultures and emotions. In J. Bisault, R. Le Bourgeois, J-F. Thémines, M. LeMentec & C. Chauvet-Chanoine (Eds.), *Objects to Learn About and Objects for Learning 2* (pp. 213–227). Wiley Online Library.

De los Reyes, J. L., & Rodríguez, C. (2021). El reto de observar la acción educativa a través de los usos de la materialidad [The challenge of observing educational action through the uses of materiality]. In C. Rodríguez & J. L. de los Reyes (Coords.), *Los objetos sí importan. Acción educativa en la escuela infantil* (pp. 9–20). Horsori.

Guevara, I. (this volume). Gesture development in the early years school: The role of early interactions with objects and adults.

Karmiloff-Smith, A. (2010). From constructivism to neuroconstructivism. In P. Y. Brandt, J. Czellàr, D. Desbiez-Piat, H. Kilcher-Hagedorn, J. Reymond, & J. Vonèche (Eds.), *Des Signes et des orders. Hommage à Christiane Gillièron Paléologue*, (pp. 79–94). Labor et Fides.

Kontopodis, M. (2014). De l'importance des choses dans la vie quotidienne des enfants d'âge préscolaire. Enquêtes ethnographiques en psychologie du développement et en éducation [The importance of things in the daily lives of preschool children: ethnographic investigations in developmental psychology and education]. In C. Moro & N. Müller Mirza (Eds). *Sémiotique, culture et développement psychologique* (pp. 195-205). Presses Universitaires du Septentrion.

Kumpulainen, K., & Kajamaa, A. (2021). Makerspaces as tertiary artifacts? The meaning of material artifacts in students' social interaction during technology-Rich creative learning. In N.

Muller-Mirza & M. Dos Santos Mamed (Eds.), *Dialogical Approaches and tensions in learning and Development. At the Frontiers of the Mind*, (pp. 105–121). Springer.

Latour, B. (1994). Une sociologie sans objet? Remarques sur l'interobjectivité [A sociology without objects? remarks on interobjectivity]. *Sociologie du travail*, *4*, 94, 587-607. https://www.jstor.org/stable/43149969

Moreno-Llanos, I., & Barreto, J. (this volume). Executive Functions and material objects: What is the role of materiality in early Executive Functions research?

Moreno-Llanos, I., Jáñez-Álvarez, M., Pérez-Eizaguirre, M., & Del Olmo, M. J. (this volume). The pragmatics of music: Rhythmic-sound uses in early development at home, in the hospital, and in the early years school.

Moro, C. (2011). Material culture, semiotics and early childhood development. In M. Kontopodis, C. Wulf & B. Fichtner (Eds.), *Children, Development and Education. Cultural, Historical, Anthropological Perspectives* (pp. 57–70). Springer. https://doi.org/10.1007/978-94-007-0243-1

Moro, C., & Rodríguez, C. (1989). L'interaction triadique, bébé-objet-adulte durant la première année de la vie de l'enfant [Triadic interaction, baby-object-adult in the first year of life]. *Enfance*, *42*, 1–2, 75–82. https://doi.org/10.3406/enfan.1989.1881

Naddei Grasso, E., Strappini, F., Borghi, A. M., & Scorolli, C. (2024). Affordances, aesthetics, and sustainability: on the relationship between materials, language and space in everyday object perception. Preprint. Research Square. https://doi.org/10.21203/rs.3.rs-4143401/v2

Palacios, P., Cárdenas, K., & N. Yuste (this volume). Development of the first symbols in triadic communicative contexts.

Palacios, P., Moreno-Llanos, I., Guevara, I,. & Rodríguez, C. (this volume). Methodological approach to the study of early development from the Pragmatics of the Object.

Perret-Clermont, A.-N. (1996). Piaget parmi ses aînés et ses pairs [Piaget among his elders and peers]. In J. M. Barrelet & A. N. Perret-Clermont (Eds.), *Jean Piaget et Neuchâtel. L'apprenti et le savant*, (pp. 255–286). Lausanne: Payot.

Prown, J. D. (1982). An Introduction to Material Culture Theory and Method. *Winterthur Portfolio*, *17*, 1, 1–19. The University of Chicago Press. https://www.jstor.org/stable/1180761?origin=JSTOR-pdf

Prown, J. D. (1993). The truth of material culture: History or Fiction? In S. Lubar & W. D. Kingery (Eds.), *History from things. Essays on Material culture*, (pp. 1–19). Smithsonian Institution Press.

Rengifo-Herrera, F., & Mietto, G. (this volume). Early childhood schools in Brasília: I show you, and you observe. Executive Functions, educational situations, and object use.

Rodríguez, C. (this volume). Pragmatics of the Object: Roots in the Geneva School.

Rodríguez, C. (this volume). The uses of objects and their social construction in infancy.

Rodríguez, C., Moreno-Llanos, I., & Guevara, I. (this volume). Is a paradigm shift necessary today in the approach to Executive Functions?

Rodríguez, C., Moreno-Llanos, I., Guevara, I., & Flecha, G. (this volume). Action and communication in the origin of Executive Functions: A pragmatic perspective.

Rodríguez, C., & Moro, C. (1998). El uso convencional también hace permanentes a los objetos [Objects are made permanent also by their conventional use]. *Infancia y Aprendizaje*, *84*, 67–83. http://dx.doi.org/10.1174/021037098760378793

Sinha, C. (2014). Signification et matérialité. Le langage au fondement des artefacts symboliques [Meaning and materiality: language as the foundation of symbolic artifacts]. In C. Moro & N. Müller Mirza (Eds), *Sémiotique, culture et développement psychologique*, (pp. 117–138). Presses Universitaires du Septentrion.

Sterner, A., & Rodríguez, C. (2012). Valoración de Signos de Alarma entre los 9 y los 16 meses de edad [Evaluation of waring signs in autism spectrum disorders at the age of 9 to 16 months]. *Psicología Educativa*, *18*, 2, 145–158. http://dx.doi.org/10.5093/ed2012a15

Tapparel, S. (2013/2022). Micro-rupture et développement psychologique en situation educative dans un Centre de vie enfantine. L'objet 'brosse à dents' comme outil pour peindre en situation peinture [Micro-Rupture and psychological development in an educational setting at a childcare center: The toothbrush as a tool for painting during art activities]. In J.-P. Bernié & M. Brossard (Eds.), *Vygotski et l'école. Apports et limites d'un modèle théorique pour penser l'éducation et la formation*, (pp. 141-152). Presses Universitaires de Bordeaux. https://books.openedition.org/pub/47607

Williams, E., Kendell-Scott, L., & Costall, A. (2005). Parents' experiences of introducing everyday object use to their children with autism. *Autism, 9* (5), 495–514. https://doi.org/10.1177/1362361305057869

Zittoun, T., & Perret-Clermont, A.-N. (2009). Four social psychological lenses for dverlopmental pscyhology. *European Journal of Psychology of Education, 24*, 3, 387–403. https://doi.org/10.1007/BF03174768

Contents

Contributors

Julieth Barreto Universidad Libre, Cali, Colombia

Julia Benassi Escuela Superior de Sanidad "Ramón Carrillo", Facultad deBioquímica y Ciencias Biológicas, Universidad del Litoral, Santa Fe, Argentina

Karina Cárdenas Pontificia Universidad Católica de Chile, Villarrica, Chile

Sílvia Cavalcante Universitat de Lleida, Lleida, Spain

Gonzalo Flecha Early Years School Antonio Mercero, Madrid, Spain

Irene Guevara Department of Psychology, Universidad Antonio de Nebrija, Madrid, Spain

María Jesús del Olmo Universidad Autónoma de Madrid, Madrid, Spain

María Jáñez-Álvarez Centro de Salud Mental Puente de Vallecas, Madrid, Spain

Eduardo Martí Universitat de Barcelona, Barcelona, Spain

Iván Moreno-Llanos Universidad Autónoma de Madrid, Madrid, Spain

Pedro Palacios Universidad Autónoma de Aguascalientes, Aguascalientes, Mexico

Miren Pérez-Eizaguirre Universidad Autónoma de Madrid, Madrid, Spain

Francisco Rengifo-Herrera Universidade de Brasília, Brasília, Brasil

Cintia Rodríguez Universidad Autónoma de Madrid, Madrid, Spain

Gabriela Sousa de Melo Mietto Universidade de Brasília, Brasília, Brasil

Noemí Yuste Universidad Internacional de La Rioja, La Rioja, Spain

Part I

Historical, Theoretical, and Methodological Roots of the Pragmatics of the Object

Pragmatics of the Object: Roots in the Geneva School

1

Cintia Rodríguez

> Partager les *valeurs* du quotidien silencieux (gérer la cuisine, la propreté, les vêtements, l'esthétique et comme le passé des objets), c'était ma manière (silencieuse) de converser avec elle.-Et c'est ainsi qu'elle n'étant plus là, je peux encore le faire.[1]
>
> Roland Barthes. *Journal de deuil.* (2009, p. 205)

The Pragmatics of the Object (PO) took its first steps in the 1980s, during the Geneva School's *functional turn*. The focus of these works lies in the processes of psychological construction, where the subject-object interaction and action manifest in their full splendor. This movement included contributions from the later Piaget, his most loyal collaborator, Bärbel Inhelder, and many of their disciples. However, despite Geneva being the developmental psychology school that has emphasized objects and action the most in the construction of the psyche, it showed little interest in or outright ignored the social and cultural dimensions of objects. This lack of interest remains evident today in early childhood psychology.

How do infants begin to use objects canonically by their function in everyday life during their first year of life? [55, 76]. This was the question we, Christiane Moro and myself, posed. In doing so, we introduced a pragmatic dimension to objects within infancy. This approach implies that objects, beyond obeying causal relationships, are also situated within a *normative* universe and possess *public rules*

[1] Sharing the *values* of silent everyday life (manage cooking, cleanliness, clothing, aesthetics and like the past of objects), it was my (silent) way of conversing with her. And that's how now that she is no longer there, I can still do it. Roland Barthes *Mourning Diary* (Translated by us).

C. Rodríguez (✉)
Universidad Autónoma de Madrid, Madrid, Spain
e-mail: cintia.rodriguez@uam.es

C. Rodriguez Garrido et al. (eds.), *The Social Life of Objects in Early Development*,
Social Interaction in Learning and Development,
https://doi.org/10.1007/978-3-031-87673-8_1

of use *shared* by a community of users. Through this construction, infants gain the ability to functionally engage with the material world, while also communicating with others using the *common ground* offered by this shared knowledge. It was striking that a topic we considered foundational to socio-cognitive development was not part of the leading research themes in infancy studies. Even Piaget had not shown interest in this duality of objects in their cognitive and communicative dimensions. In fact, objects are rarely included today in communicative situations between individuals.

To answer the question we posed, we first focused on a key protagonist: *objects*. What do children do with objects, how do the meanings they assign to them develop, and how do they use them? Everyone knows that the first thing children do when they manage to grab an object is to put it in their mouth and suck on it. We were interested in studying when and how the gradual transition occurs from these initial undifferentiated (non-canonical) uses to the *functional*, socially specific uses of objects (canonical uses). From the beginning, we ruled out the idea of considering the child acting in isolation. Objects are part of material culture, they are complex, and they do not directly reveal to children what they mean, what they are, or what they are for. Adults, however, are so accustomed to interacting with objects that it seems obvious what should be done with them. For children, the situation is very different. They are not born knowing what objects are, what they are for, or how to use them in daily life. This means that to answer the question of how children come to use objects by their function, focusing solely on their actions in isolation was insufficient. It was necessary to also consider how the ways adults use everyday objects involve and influence children.

The decision to include adults in the equation also introduced another key protagonist: *communication* between adults and children, which significantly complicated the investigation. Studying two domains—*action and communication*—and constructing categories based on this duality posed a major challenge. We had no referents to guide us, either within Geneva or beyond it. Moreover, these areas of infancy research were largely disconnected. A characteristic example of this disconnection can be seen in Piaget's work. Action is the indisputable protagonist of psychological development, and although others are often present, communication is never considered a cause of development [14]. The other paradigmatic example is Bruner's work from the 1970s, inspired by Vygotsky, which focused on mother-infant communication to explore the origins of language. Here, action on objects is deemed irrelevant (Vergnaud [94] notes Vygotsky's disinterest in action and Piaget's disinterest in language). Our challenge was to transcend this dichotomy and integrate communication (adult-infant interaction *about* and *with* objects) and action (with objects and tools) into a single communicative act. This integration implies that specific objects play a significant role—they cease to be mere referents.

Thus, although our interest was initially focused on objects, we analyzed *communication* between children and adults from the very beginning. We considered that communication *with* and *about* objects would shed light on the psychological construction that begins during the first year of life. The triad of adult–child-object held the keys to the cultural construction of the meanings of the material reality surrounding children from birth. Within this triad, intersubjective agreements regarding the functional meanings of the material world are established.

Embarking on this research agenda meant walking a complex path for two reasons. The first was that it implicitly challenged core aspects of Piaget's exceptional work on sensorimotor development. The second reason was that in Geneva during the 1970s and 1980s, Piaget's work on infant development was not only unquestioned but actively celebrated, as it aligned well with the functionalist approaches of the time.

In contrast, during the 1970s and 1980s, the defenders of the "competent baby" in the Anglo-American world were questioning Piaget's sensorimotor framework. These ideas reached Geneva through figures like Pierre Mounoud [56, 57]. The concept of the "competent baby" and nativist theses marked a new direction in early cognitive development research that remains hegemonic today [10, 90]. This shift impacted both the research methods—very different from those used by the Geneva School— and the very conception of the subject. Piaget's constructivist epistemology was challenged by innatist theses (see discussions in Karmiloff-Smith [45], and Allen & Bickhard [3]). The radically active child, who takes creative initiatives, as well as the longitudinal designs and the articulation between microgenesis and macrogenesis—hallmarks of the Geneva School—gave way to cross-sectional designs and a "child who reacts to stimuli" in highly controlled experimental settings. The child was reduced to "an eye looking stimuli" without acting [77], becoming, as Eleanor Gibson said, "the poor child bombed by stimuli" with no possibility of movement [36, p. 14].

For our part, rather than adhering to the innatist theses of the competent baby, we went in the opposite direction. We delved deeper into constructivist theses, focusing on children's actions as agent subjects and on communication with adults around complex everyday objects. The social and normative construction of objects from daily life—a subject we considered central to the foundations of early socio-cognitive development—was not a research topic in Geneva at the time. Nor was it a focus for the proponents of the competent baby. Neither then nor now.

This was precisely what we wanted to investigate.

Below, I present the theoretical sources that inspired us to varying degrees and which, in the 1970s and 1980s, coexisted and shaped the Geneva School. I highlight Piaget and Inhelder's works on the functional turn, Inhelder, Sinclair, and Bovet's research on learning, and the *Groupe de stratégies et résolution des problèmes* [Problem-Solving and Strategies Group] studies on real-time problem-solving strategies and microgenesis. During this period, intercultural and social perspectives, notably influenced by Vygotsky, also began to arrive in Geneva. I will then address the strengths and limitations of three direct influences on the Pragmatics of the Object (PO): Piaget's sensorimotor development framework, Bruner's work on early development inspired by Vygotsky and the pragmatism of the linguistic turn, and the semiotics of American philosopher Charles S. Peirce, the founder of pragmaticism.

Let us begin with Geneva during the functional turn of the 1970s and 1980s.

1.1 Geneva in the 1970s: The Functional turn of Piaget, Inhelder, and the Groupe

I arrived in Geneva in the summer of 1979. That fall, I began my specialization in Psychologie Génétique (Developmental Psychology). Piaget's ideas had scarcely been disseminated in Spain, where I had trained as a psychologist in the 1970s. The dominant paradigm at the time was behaviorism. However, José Luis de la Mata, one of the professors in the Faculty of Psychology in Madrid who left a profound impression on many of us, spoke passionately about Piaget's epistemology and psychology. This had a significant impact on me. It is worth noting that Miguel Siguán and Juan Delval were influential in promoting Piaget's work in the Spanish-speaking world, but I met them many years later, after I had already been living in Geneva for several years.

The Geneva School fascinated me from the very first day. Reality exceeded the high expectations I had built up. I was fortunate to arrive at a time when it was "overflowing" with ideas and activity. As I mentioned earlier, it was in the midst of its *functional turn*. From the late 1960s through the 1970s and 1980s, substantial changes were underway (see discussion in Rodríguez & Martí [78]). These changes were palpable and directly influenced those of us who were there. At that time, Piaget was re-evaluating the status of *objects* and the *processes of functioning* to study the subject. The Centre International d'Épistémologie Génétique (CIEG) was entering its "second period" [33]. It moved away from studying the genesis of the major structures of the subject—such as the large stages (concrete and formal operations)—which had been the most widely disseminated part of Piaget's work. The focus now shifted to the *functional* aspects of development, the *dynamics of cognitive functioning*, and the mechanisms of *change*. Key works from this period include *Les explications causales* [Understanding Causality] [68], *La prise de conscience* [The grasp of consciousness][62], *Réussir et comprendre* [Success and understanding] [63], and *L'équilibration des structures cognitives, problème central du développement* [The equilibration of cognitive structures: the central problem of intellectual development] [64], considered the most significant text of this period. In Chap. 10 of this volume, we will delve deeper into the contribution of this part of Piaget's work to our research on self-regulation and Executive Functions (EF).

One of my earliest discoveries was that the Geneva School was not just about Piaget. While Piaget's theory was the backbone of the institution and provided a shared common ground—a solid, unifying framework—the Geneva School was much richer and more diverse.[2] It hosted significant debates and included other

[2] When Jaan Valsiner proposed in 2010 that Eduardo Martí and I write *After Piaget*, we decided against offering our own version of Geneva during that time. Instead, we chose to let diverse voices share their personal trajectories, which originated in Geneva during the 1970s and 1980s and evolved afterward—most of them during the diaspora. Even today, multiple *After Piaget* books could be written to capture the wide range of trends that emerged from Geneva during those years.

major figures. One of these was Bärbel Inhelder, Piaget's closest collaborator since the 1930s.

1.1.1 Inhelder's Influence on the Functional Turn

It would be incomplete and unfair to attribute the functional turn solely to Piaget. Inhelder played a central role. In 1974, Inhelder, Hermine (Mimi) Sinclair, and Magali Bovet published *Apprentissage et Structure de la Connaissance* [Learning and the Structure of Knowledge]. This work was a bold move to study the "psychological subject" rather than only the "epistemic subject" [35]. Christiane Gillièron summarized it as follows: "It is the psychological subject that must be taken seriously when psychology is used to answer epistemological questions" [38, p. 126]. They argued that learning could promote the development of operational structures—a novel emphasis in Geneva at the time.

In reality, Inhelder's functional concern with subjects was not new; it had been part of her project for many years [7]. She noted in the preface to *Le cheminement des découvertes de l'enfant* [40] that her interest in functional aspects had always been present, dating back to her early works on the development of quantities published in 1941. However, she had always prioritized structural research conducted with Piaget.

It wasn't until the 1960s that her interest in procedures of discovery gained momentum. The arrival of cybernetics and artificial intelligence in Geneva, introduced by figures like Seymour Papert and Guy Cellérier, was pivotal. In 1968, they published *Cybernétique et épistémologie* with Voyat. Inhelder later noted, "I was able to move from a structural analysis of general categorical thought to an analysis of the procedures involved in solving specific problems" [40, p. 14]. Inhelder was not alone in this endeavor. She had young collaborators in the *Groupe de Stratégies et Résolution de Problèmes* (commonly referred to as the *Groupe* in Geneva) who, as she put it, "were not afraid to break with certain aspects of the past to observe and explore children's discovery procedures in a new way" [40, p. 15]. They elevated the role of action and objects in psychological construction [41]. Who Were These Collaborators?

The *Problem solving and strategies Group* was formed in the early 1970s and was in full bloom when I arrived. It was led by Bärbel Inhelder and included members such as Annette Karmiloff-Smith, Alex Blanchet, Edith Ackermann, Helga Kilcher, Madelon Saada-Robert, and André Boder (though by 1979, Karmiloff-Smith had already joined Geneva's diaspora). César Coll participated briefly.

Guy Cellérier was another key figure in the *Groupe.* He taught courses in *Épistémologie* and *Cybernétique.* His lectures, filled with passion, were as dynamic as his ideas. He had the exceptional ability to think while teaching. In addition to undergraduate students, members of the *Groupe* often attended his classes, partly because no course ever repeated the same content. Cellérier captivated us all. In one of his elegant reflections, he argued that the source of knowledge lies in the subject's activity: "[If] the subject acts on the environment (for example, modifying the position of objects or their own), the inputs from the environment may include a subset O' that originates from the subject's action [...]. From then on, the engine of knowledge no longer belongs strictly to the environment [...]." ([23, pp. 14–15]; translation ours). Placing the subject's action as the engine of knowledge, rather than merely the *inputs* from the environment, is highly significant for research with infants today, given that much of it focuses not on their actions but on their *reactions* to stimuli.

Edith Ackermann

Guy Cellérier

Madelon Saada-Robert

Compared to Piagetian research on general cognitive structures (macrogenesis), the *Groupe's* work on the procédures of discovery while solving tasks (microgenesis) represented a 180-degree shift. They went far in their critique of Piaget: "The time has come to focus above all on the *processes of invention* or *discovery* of the subject in their search for solutions to specific, well-differentiated problems" ([42, pp. 58–59]; translation and emphasis ours). They sought to understand how children made sense of specific tasks and how they "made objects speak" [46, 48]. The focus now shifted to microgenesis, which involved narrowing the temporal scope to minutes and seconds and broadening the level of detail in studying behavior: what children do here and now to solve a problem [5]. Experimental situations had to capture the development of the subject's thinking by observing their actions. The *Groupe* analyzed the means children invented to use what they knew rather than merely describing the different levels of their cognitive development [1, p. 192]. For more details on this approach, see Chaps. 10 and 11 of this volume, which discusses Executive Functions.

Capturing the dynamics of children's actions while solving challenging tasks through microgenetic analysis was incredibly time-consuming, as the protocols were essentially detailed descriptions of their actions. These studies were applied to a limited number of subjects, and a single experimental session could last an hour [6, 49]. Despite these difficulties, the *Groupe* produced extraordinary research. In *The Microgenetic Method: Legacy of Bärbel Inhelder* [69], Rebeca Puche and Julio César Ossa analyze the enduring contribution of Inhelder and her team to psychology—a contribution that continues to this day.

How did these innovations affect Piaget? Piaget seemed to accept one key idea from the work of Inhelder et al. [43]: that learning could influence the development of structures. However, it is less clear whether he accepted the *Groupe's* criticism of his relative disinterest in objects and action in parts of his work.

The *Groupe's* critique of Piaget's relative neglect of action and the secondary status of objects in some of his writings left a deep impression on us. It was a key factor in the birth of the Pragmatics of the Object.

1.1.2 My Experience With Three Genevas: Piaget's Structures, the Functional Turn, and the Groupe

I found myself immersed in these three Geneva perspectives simultaneously. While they all shared a common Piagetian foundation, they differed in ways that were far from minor.

As a specialization student, I attended courses taught by Inhelder and Sinclair and visited schools to conduct the classic operational conservation tests (see Ducret's excellent article [32], on Piagetian clinical interviewing and its origins). All of this was framed within the classic structuralist theses of major developmental stages—macrogenesis, measured over years of construction.

In 1983, I began working as a *research assistant* under the direction of Magali Bovet on a study of causality and learning with children aged 9–12. This research aligned with *Apprentissage et Structure de la Connaissance* [Learning and the Structure of Knowledge], developed with Inhelder and Sinclair. Magali conveyed to me her deep respect for children, and from her, I learned much about conducting clinical interviews. Unlike the classic operational tests, which sought to identify children's developmental levels without providing tools to help them advance further, this approach assumed that the learning situation could influence their operational structures. Participating in this research allowed me to explore this new, more functional approach, that linked learning with development.

As I mentioned earlier, the influence of the *Groupe de Stratégies et Résolution de Problèmes* was crucial for the emergence of the Pragmatics of the Object. I was incredibly fortunate to participate in the research led by Madelon Saada-Robert from the moment I arrived in Geneva. This experience left an indelible mark on me. We visited schools weekly. With admirable delicacy and respect, Madelon presented children with a task: building a ramp to allow a car to ascend to a "parking lot" situated at the top of a "building." The children, who quickly felt comfortable and engaged, were given blocks and wooden planks to construct the ascending ramp (see Saada-Robert [81, 82]). We collected data—Madelon meticulously recorded the protocol, noting every detail of the children's process: their actions, corrections, hesitations, trial-and-error attempts, strategy shifts, pauses, and more. I was in awe of how quickly she captured all this in handwritten notes, often without using video recordings, though filming was sometimes employed. She wasn't looking for errors. Every action the children performed held meaning, revealing how they represented the task, how they adjusted their representations through action, and how new actions stemmed from those revised representations. The children's performances illuminated their discovery processes as they solved tasks.

Through this research, I learned that to understand the subject, one must take the object seriously—not merely as a referent. Objects here acquired a new status, absent in Piaget's classic conservation research, where interactions with experimental materials did not produce significant changes and primarily served to indicate developmental levels. In contrast, in Madelon's work, children's interaction with objects became a source of knowledge and creativity. This necessitated detailed analysis—microgenesis, the intricate process of back-and-forth movements between goals and means, starting again and iterating (see Chap. 3 on Methods in this volume). Ackermann [1] highlighted that one of the *Groupe*'s objectives was to uncover the "heuristics" children invented to build upon what they already knew. This marked a sharp difference from Piaget's classic work, which focused on "describing their knowledge at different levels of cognitive development" [1, p. 192].

Madelon also conveyed her skepticism toward Piaget's normative subject and his structural framework. Children of different ages often used the same strategies to solve problems, while children of the same age employed different strategies. She taught me how to observe (to look with a theoretical lens) and conveyed me the passion for observing real subjects in real time—fully engaged in what they were doing and discovering. Through Madelon, I learned that observation could be as rigorous a scientific method as experimentation. She placed me in a position of freedom as a researcher, which is not always the case in infancy studies. Thanks to her, I discovered the beauty of interactions between subjects and objects.

The research with Madelon coincided with my involvement as student in "Practical Work," where we conducted classic operational tests using the clinical interview method. One anecdote stands out: while conducting *the three-mountain task* on spatial representation and perspective-taking, a child immediately gave the correct answer. Lacking spatial orientation myself, I kept probing with clinical interview techniques—"Are you sure?" "How can you tell?" The girl must have wondered why I insisted so much when her answer, which never wavered, was clearly correct. It surprised me that I hadn't yet reached the operational level myself. Madelon would have been proven right! I hid my confusion as best I could to avoid detection by the course assistant.

The experience with Madelon strengthened my view of Geneva as a place where alternative yet complementary perspectives were debated. For all of us undergraduate students, it was fantastic to witness how Piaget's disciples, who were deeply familiar with his theory, critiqued his relative disinterest in action with objects as a source of knowledge. This meant that from the very beginning while developing immense respect for Piaget's theory, I also viewed it through the critical lens of the *Groupe*.

However, The *Groupe*'s critique of Piaget did not apply equally to all his work. They upheld his functional turn of the 1970s, particularly his studies on causality, consciousness, and equilibration, as well as his 1930s work on sensorimotor development. The latter's functional and dynamic analysis of behavior, emphasis on microgenesis, true subject-object interaction, relevance of objects, constructivist thesis, equilibration processes, longitudinal dimension, were more aligned with their constructivist focus. However, this alignment might explain why the *Groupe* never investigated early development. They took Piaget's sensorimotor findings as established and focused instead on children aged four and older.

When Christiane Moro and I began our research with children as young as seven months, we could not directly draw upon the *Groupe's* work. At the time, they were uninterested in the role of communication in cognitive construction. Nonetheless, their influence was decisive for three main reasons: (1) The necessity of studying the subject as an *intentional agent acting* and *correcting* in *real time.* (2) The utility of *microgenetic* analysis in capturing ongoing *processes* and *creativity.* (3) The importance of taking the *object* seriously to understand the subject. These three pillars have always shaped my work and continue to do so today.

1.2 Vygotsky Arrives in Geneva in the 1970s. Cultural and Social Perspectives

The growing interest in the role of culture and social interaction became evident across various domains of research of the Faculty in the 1970s. Vygotsky's arrival in Geneva—albeit through the "back door"—played a crucial role in this shift. Two research groups were influential in disseminating his ideas. The first was the Social Psychology group, composed of Willem Doise, Anne-Nelly Perret-Clermont, and Gabriel Mugny. They challenged the solitude in which Piaget typically situated the subject while advocating for the tradition of G.H. Mead and Vygotsky [30]. One of their most widely recognized research lines demonstrated that children achieve better results in Piagetian conservation tasks when working cooperatively compared to working alone [31]. Doise encouraged us, his students, to broaden the concept of cognitive conflict into the notion of socio-cognitive conflict, shifting from Piaget's individual equilibrium to the role of social regulation in shaping reasoning processes in children. As Perret-Clermont noted: "[In] certain phases of development, the joint actions of multiple individuals, who must resolve conflicts between their differing viewpoints, lead to the construction of new individual coordinations" ([60, p. 39]; see also Perret-Clermont [61]).

In 1979, Anne-Nelly, already part of the Geneva diaspora, described how the presence of other individuals compels newborns "to coordinate their actions with those of others" [60, p. 36]. She urged a move beyond the subject-object interactions characteristic of Piagetian tradition to consider triadic interactions: "the interdependence between the knowing subject, other knowing subjects, and the object to be known" [60, p. 35]. This aligns with Vygotsky's thesis that from the beginning of life, children relate to the world through another person [95], a topic discussed extensively in Chap. 2 of this volume.

The second pathway for Vygotsky's ideas in Geneva came through Jean-Paul Bronckart's team in the Didactics of Language, which included members like Bernard Schneuwly, Daniel Bain, Mercè Pujol, and Joaquim Dolz. They developed the paradigm of socio-discursive interactionism [14], positing that human behavior results from a historical process of socialization enabled by the development of semiotic tools. Our introduction to Vygotsky partially occurred through them when we encountered Jean-Paul Bronckart and Madeleine Ventouras-Spycher's chapter "The Piagetian Concept of Representation and the Soviet-Inspired View of Self-Regulation," published in 1979 [15]. It was the first text we read from the socio-cultural tradition that challenged some of Piaget's assumptions. We read it with great interest, as it helped us begin to rethink early development from a Vygotskian perspective—a perspective that was not self-evident at the time, given that the socio-cultural tradition's primary interest in infants was largely tied to language development.

Vygotsky's ideas spread among many Geneva researchers. At the First Sociocultural Congress held in Madrid in 1992, numerous contributions from Geneva, including members of the *Groupe*, were presented. Four years later, the Second Congress of Sociocultural Psychology was held in Geneva in 1996, with the inaugural conference delivered by Bärbel Inhelder and Jerome Bruner. Inhelder pronounced the famous sentence: "I know many post-Piagetians, but I don't know any post-Vygotskians" (though I quote it, it may not be literal). The Jean Piaget Archives Foundation devoted its 14th advanced course to comparing Piaget and Vygotsky's theories on the occasion of their shared centenary [53, 92].

The combination of Vygotsky and Piaget in Geneva was, I would say, unique. Despite adopting Vygotsky's new ideas, Piaget's influence remained ever-present. His focus on the subject as an agent, the undeniable status of objects and interactions, psychological construction, strategies and microgenesis, self-regulation processes, equilibration, and the development of consciousness persisted [2, 54, 75, 83]. Bronckart aptly described this as a paradox: "[…] we, the Vygotskyans, criticize Piaget for his lack of real consideration of social and semiological aspects. On the other hand, it is because Piaget left aside these aspects that his theory constitutes an indispensable complement to the social interactionism movement today" [14, p. 57].

Vygotsky's theory helped us distance ourselves from the solitary subject characteristic of Geneva's psychology, including that of Piaget, Inhelder, Sinclair, Bovet, and even the *Groupe*.

I will not elaborate much further on those who brought new cultural and communicative perspectives to Geneva. I will mention only Pierre Dasen and the french psychologist Henry Wallon. Dasen introduced an intercultural approach in 1979 through his course *Psychologie interculturelle* [Intercultural Psychology], based on his work with children in Africa, Aboriginal children in Australia, and Inuit children in Canada.[3] His course profoundly impacted me, challenging the notion that the Western model is the sole reference for psychological development [27]. In a more recent text, Dasen summarized this perspective: "If cognition is a universal feature of the human species, its organization depends on external memories (symbolic or technical tools) [...]. Its nature is therefore both neural and contextual/cultural" ([25, p. 130]; translation ours).

I remember several anecdotes. One of them is that during his research in Africa, following "the Geneva way of investigating," he focused solely on children's behavior. He never considered the possible influence of the mothers. When he later decided to examine their influence, he could not use his videos because they had been damaged (Personal Communication, Geneva, 1987). Dasen's legacy endures to this day. Instead of the spiral used by Piaget to represent universal psychological development, Dasen used the metaphor of a tree full of branches. Different cultures likely emphasize certain "branches" more than others. I use this metaphor every year with my undergraduate students.

I have always been interested in psychological development with consideration for cultural diversity. I wish I had been able to work more closely with Pierre Dasen. The dimension of cultural diversity is missing in the Pragmatics of the Object, and I feel it should be further developed.

Despite the geographic proximity, the shared French language, the ongoing debates with Piaget, and the convergence with Vygotsky, it cannot be said that Wallon's ideas had significant influence in Geneva. One exception was André Bullinger and his team. Social exchanges and postural development begin at birth, encompassing tonic-postural and emotional aspects that are part of the mechanisms of equilibration [20, 74].

Bullinger distinguished between the organism and the body, defining the body as a product of development that the child must come to know, like any other object in the environment [19]. I have always had immense respect for this work, and it strikes me that contemporary perspectives on embodiment do not give it the attention it deserves.

I will conclude this overview by referring to Christiane Gillièron, whose influence on the Geneva School, and particularly on us, was significant [9]. She taught

[3] I had the privilege of conducting the research *"Les enfants de la deuxième génération d'immigrants à l'école genevoise (Suisse)"* [Children of the second generation of immigrants at Geneva schools (Switzerland)] under his direction during the 1981–1982 academic year. This preliminary work led to a series of studies on intercultural education in Geneva's primary education system between 1987 and 1991. In a text published in 1995 (co-authored by Anne-Nelly Perret-Clermont), Dasen advocated for respect for heritage languages and stated that "intercultural education is concerned both with the well-being of foreign children entering our schools and with raising the awareness of all students about respecting diversity" [26, p. 235], further emphasizing that "it is the school that should adapt to the new pluricultural reality rather than forcing children to conform to a monocultural school culture" [26, p. 236]. He emphasized the importance of taking the individual within the broader cultural context as the unit of analysis and viewed education as encompassing all phenomena of cultural transmission, whether occurring inside or outside the school [24].

"Methodology" in the fourth year. A notable feature of her approach was her departure from those who viewed observation merely as a preliminary step to validation, which they believed could only come from experimentation. Gillièron held great respect for observation as a research method, considering it not a substitute or fallback when experimentation was impossible but a valid approach in its own right. For Gillièron, "observation begins with hypotheses, and as long as these are explicitly and clearly articulated, nothing prevents the use of planned observation to test their plausibility" [37, p. 152]. Experimentation and observation, she argued, are two possible strategies (see Chap. 3 in this volume on Methodology), and neither guarantees absolute truth. "Unrefined observation carries undeniable risks, but they are no greater than those posed by poor experimentation. It is far too easy to compare studies where observation is flawed with others where experimentation is elegant, and conclude the superiority of the latter" ([37], p. 152; translation is ours). She also emphasized, for instance, that in experimentation, "the experimenter is more concerned with controlling the situation and presenting themselves as the one who orchestrates the process than with offering the subject a genuine opportunity to act as an agent" [37, p. 242].

1.3 The First Steps of the Pragmatics of the Object: Influences

1.3.1 The Functionalist Turn in Geneva: Piaget's Sensorimotor Development and its Paradoxes

I was deeply immersed in early development while teaching the Seminar of Developmental Psychology to first-year students. The seminar gave substance to my interest in studying phenomena from their origins. Infant development is the perfect domain for this exploration. It was a privileged space, both for discovering an exceptional theory and for highlighting some significant gaps. It was here that my collaboration with Christiane Moro began—a partnership that lasted over two decades and became the foundation for the Pragmatics of the Object.

The trilogy that constitutes Piaget's sensorimotor development—*La naissance de l'intelligence chez l'enfant* [The Origins of Intelligence in children] [65], *La construction du réel* [The Construction of reality in the child] [66], and *La formation du symbole* [Play, dreams and imitation in childhood] [67]—has inspired the majority of research topics in early cognitive development to this day [10, 29, 39, 51, 58, 59, 73, 87–91]. For Rochat [73], what will transcend time, beyond Piaget's impactful theory, "[...] are Piaget's observations and the groundbreaking clinical attunement, the feel and genius it took to collect them" (p. 80).

I have returned to these texts by Piaget time and again. If I had to explain why they have impacted and continue to impact me so profoundly, I would need to compile a long list that includes both the topics and the way they are addressed. Piaget delves into the foundations of the human psyche: the origin of the subject as an agent, the origin and formation of the permanent object, of causality, the origin of intentionality, the establishment of early goals, the origin of tool use, the origin of symbols, of problem-solving, and self-regulation—what we now refer to as Executive Functions. Piaget considers equilibration to be the fundamental problem of any theory of development.

Another exceptional aspect concerns the *method*. Piaget and his wife, Valentine Piaget, collected data in their home with their three children over more than seven years. Although this involved a sample size of N = 3 (a point frequently criticized), the corpus includes approximately 10,000 observations, many of which are "experiments" [70]. The observations are so detailed that behaviors can be "seen" with considerable precision, allowing for alternative interpretations—for instance, Clairelise Bonnet's reinterpretation of Piaget's observations on the origins of symbols [8]. The longitudinal nature of the study allows us to witness the progressive construction of intelligence. This gives Piaget's notion of stages a dynamic quality—nonlinear, without rigid boundaries—very far from the over-simplified, encapsulated stages often presented in psychology textbooks. In the sensorimotor stage, Piaget achieves something exceptional: establishing bridges between microgenesis (the level of detailed, successive observations with small variations) and macrogenesis (stages marked by qualitative changes). Microdevelopment captures, as Karmiloff-Smith put it, "how very young, prelinguistic children learn about their worlds" [47, p. 49]. The object Piaget presents in the sensorimotor stage is "alive." It exists within the perimeter of the transformative and creative action of the active subject. By focusing on action, Piaget transcends the subject-object dualism.

However, the deeper we delved into Piaget's sensorimotor stage, the more apparent certain paradoxes became, challenging the constructivist thesis itself. The solitude in which Piaget places the subject also extends to the object. In the construction of the object, others do not play a role. This aligns with his view of the object, which primarily focuses on its physical attributes. He neglects the development of the object's public meanings and its function in daily life, despite the fact that his observations of his children were conducted in a home environment. In fact, the emphasis on the physical attributes of objects has persisted in the literature on early development to this day [80].

It is worth noting that, albeit cautiously, some aspects of Piaget's sensorimotor development that affect the object were questioned in Geneva. For instance, Inhelder et al. [44] did tangentially refer to the *function* of objects. In a study conducted with children aged 9–21 months, they observed a progressive functional adaptation of objects. Initially, children used objects in an undifferentiated manner, as if "they could do anything with any object." Gradually, a principle of differentiation emerged, and ultimately, the children used the objects appropriately, according to their conventional use. They explicitly mentioned *conventional uses*, noting that these *significant*, appropriate *acts* precede the emergence of symbols and are a prerequisite for the appearance of deferred signifiers. Inhelder et al. [44] concluded that, beyond object permanence, a degree of "functional pertinence" is necessary as a precursor to symbols, representation (in the strict sense), and language. With "functional pertinence," children begin to "organize the world" through "spontaneous behaviors" (p. 241; see Chap. 2 on functional permanence of the object in this volume). We found it striking that they discussed conventions while overlooking the role of others in their construction (see discussion in Rodríguez [77]). Nevertheless, this work was highly significant for Christiane Moro and me because it introduced a promising pragmatic analysis within the Piagetian paradigm.

In *Les bébés et les choses ou la créativité du développement cognitif* [Babies and things or the creativity of cognitive development], Sinclair et al. [85] continued to investigate children's interaction with objects in a school context. Over the years, I consider that this work has gained relevance, both in terms of psychological development and in relation to schooling and early childhood education. Today, few question the importance of objects and materiality for educational action [84], particularly in infant education (see Chap. 10 on early Executive Functions and Chap. 11 on Early Childhood Education in Brazil in this volume).

Although I was not one of his regular students, and despite his work focusing on language and linguistic activity, Bronckart has been a key reference for me since the early 1980s for several reasons. First, he has always shown a particular interest in Piaget's sensorimotor studies [11, 13 14]. He explicitly acknowledges that "[...] social interactionism offers a critical reinterpretation of Piaget's considerable work, particularly the three fundamental texts *La naissance de l'intelligence* [65], *La construction du réel* [66], and *La formation du symbole* [67]" [13, p. 22]. Additionally, Bronckart questions the relevance Piaget places on representation in the origins of language, where the represented world is exclusively physical, ahistorical, and asocial [12, p. 13]. Drawing on De Saussure, he criticizes Piaget for ignoring why and how, in language, the two mental images—sound (which becomes the signifier) and meaning (which becomes the signified)—are connected. In linguistic signs, the relationship between the signifier and the signified is arbitrary, as concepts can be represented by any sequence of sounds. Bronckart argues that it is, therefore, necessary to "move beyond individual reference and refer to the society that has made a particular segmentation of constructed images into content *conventional*. The child's access to designation, to the ability to create [linguistic] signs, is, in reality, the child's insertion into this social convention" ([11, p. 61]; translation ours).

Another critique of Piaget's sensorimotor theory comes from Wallon. In *De l'acte à la pensée* [From action to thought], Wallon questions the idea that the signifier/signified relationship in semiotic function is the automatic result of practical activity [96] as an individual process without the intervention of others [28]. Both critiques of Piaget—Wallon's and Bronckart's—regarding the lack of a social basis in the origins of semiotic function in general and linguistic signs, in particular, were highly useful. These critiques could be extended to other constructions of prelinguistic development. We began to question whether children could recognize themselves as agents transforming their environment, capable of intentional behavior, distinguishing means from ends, pursuing increasingly complex goals, using tools, or producing symbols (see Chap. 5 in this volume on Symbols), all while acting in solitude, independent of others and without normative frameworks to rely on. Producing gestures (see Chap. 7 in this volume on Gestures) or using objects also requires a shared consensus with others about their meanings. Gradually, we came to the conclusion that it was necessary to introduce a social dimension into prelinguistic development that included objects.

Moreover, as I mentioned earlier, participating in the *Groupe's* research also contributed to questioning the status of the object in Piaget's sensorimotor stage. We adopted their lens when considering some of its limitations. Although the Groupe's influence was "indirect," given that they did not work with infants, its impact remains to this day.

The Pragmatics of the Object has always studied the subject as an agent acting (and communicating) in real time. We have consistently focused on behaviors through microgenesis to capture processes, the dynamics of interaction, and the creativity implied. Another lasting lesson from the *Groupe* since the 1980s is that to understand the subject, one must take the object seriously.

1.3.2 Vygotsky and the Pragmatism of Bruner's Linguistic Turn

In our critique of the cognitive solitude of the child in Piaget's work, the arrival of Vygotsky's ideas in Geneva was pivotal. On the one hand, it allowed us to expand the subject-object dyad characteristic of the Geneva School to include the adult. For Vygotsky, the unit of analysis in psychological construction is triadic: adult-baby-object, aligning with thinkers like Wallon, Charlotte, and Karl Bühler. On the other hand, it introduced semiotic mediation in early development, with signs serving as tools for both communication and thought [71]. Vygotsky's thesis on the semiotic organization of consciousness was likely his most significant contribution. However, his influence was indirect, as his focus on signs was primarily on language, which prevented him from exploring nonverbal forms of communication [93]. The infant was not the focus of his theory nor of those who brought his work to Geneva. Regarding early development, Vygotsky's theory presents significant gaps, neither action nor objects were central to his interest. My hypothesis is that if Vygotsky (who died in 1934, before *The Origin of Intelligence* was published in 1936) had known Piaget's sensorimotor trilogy, he might not have maintained the division between lower and higher psychological processes—a division that has hindered the introduction of a cultural perspective into prelinguistic development, precisely when children most need others, as Vygotsky himself recognized! This highlights why Piaget retains a clear advantage over Vygotsky in understanding early development to this day.

Bruner's Vygotskian-inspired work, developed during his time at Oxford in the 1970s, on the origins and development of language from its prelinguistic phase, was highly valuable to us. Drawing on the *pragmatism of the linguistic turn* influenced by the later Wittgenstein and John Austin, which had a profound impact on the human sciences, Bruner's work contributed significantly to the study of adult-infant interaction during the prelinguistic phase (see discussion in Rodríguez [79]). This approach introduced a pragmatic "everyday life" perspective on communication and language, moving away from the formalism of Chomsky's grammar and syntax as a focus and toward analyzing the practical goals of everyday communication between adults and infants. As Bruner noted, "[T]he acquisition of a first language is very context-sensitive, [...] it progresses far better when the child already grasps in some *prelinguistic* way the significance of what is being talked about or of the situation in which the talk is occurring" ([17, p. 71]; emphasis in the original). Austin's pragmatic maxim, "how to do things with words," deeply influenced early development research, and for Bruner, the child does not simply learn what to say, "but how, where, to whom, and under what circumstances" [17, p. 71]. Language, he argued, is acquired through use, not passively as a spectator. This pragmatic perspective helps bridge the gap between prelinguistic communication and language, between gesture and word, and between the structure of action and language ([18]; see discussion in Rodríguez [77]).

This pragmatic turn applied to mother-infant interaction opened a highly productive field of research in the United Kingdom (see, for example, the book edited by Lock [50]), in the USA, and in Europe, with the work of Bates et al. [4] on the functions of gestures, whose influence persists to this day. In Geneva, it impacted teams such as those led by Bronckart and Mimi Sinclair. In *Symbolisme et interaction interpersonnelle* [Symbolism and interpersonal interaction], published in 1987 [86], Sinclair definitively incorporates communication and social interaction into the early stages of development, referencing the work of Andy Lock, Mary Bateson, and Bruner on mother-infant exchanges.

This pragmatic perspective on adult-infant interaction was pivotal for us. If language is *used* in everyday life, so too are objects. Just as Bruner had distanced himself from Chomsky's formalism regarding language, we could also move away from the formalism that considers objects solely for their "physical" attributes while ignoring their functional ones. This was precisely what we were seeking for objects: to introduce them into a pragmatic perspective that acknowledged their everyday uses. If mother-infant interaction could be studied, then we could do the same—but by including objects.

However, Bruner's impact was also indirect. Similar to Vygotsky on another level, Bruner was not interested in objects. His pragmatic orientation toward the origins of language excluded the material world (see discussion in Rodríguez [79]). For this reason, we had to distance ourselves from Bruner at a certain point. As Castañares [21] ([see also Castañares and Manneti [22]) asserts, language is too powerful, it is the semiotic system par excellence. As Eco notes, it is the semiotic system into which other systems can be translated, for better or worse [34]. If language were to take center stage, there would be no room for action, for objects, or for the semiotic systems that operate beneath language. In Bruner's perspective at the time, the tree of language obscured the forest of other, less "powerful" semiotic systems.

The authors of the linguistic turn at the time were centered on language, showing little interest in what operates "beneath" it. And that was precisely what interested us: what lies beneath language—the uses of objects. We had to make a significant effort to introduce a *pragmatic* dimension into the *development of object use*. Here, the semiotics of the American philosopher Charles Sanders Peirce proved invaluable. This required us to move away from Saussure's semiology, the dominant reference in Geneva for those studying language [11]. Saussure also significantly influenced Piaget's sensorimotor development framework, particularly in his distinction between the types of signifier/signified relationships found in signals, indices, symbols, and linguistic signs (see discussion in Rodríguez [77]). Peirce's semiotics complemented Vygotsky's semiotic perspective and Saussure's semiology, as Peirce did not limit his analysis to verbal language but considered all forms of signification. This was, and remains, essential for the Pragmatics of the Object, as it allowed us to incorporate objects into a theory of signification that could help explain the processes underlying the construction of early functional uses during the first year of life, taking into account both action and communication in a prelinguistic phase of development.

To conclude this section, I will refer to two aspects related to Bruner. First, Peirce's semiotics also influenced him: Peirce's general theory of signs enabled Bruner to understand Vygotsky and distance himself from Piaget ([16]; see discussion in Rodríguez [79]). We took the reverse path from Bruner. We approached Peirce after realizing that semiotic mediation was a key contribution of Vygotsky to constructing the human psyche. The second point concerns an opportunity I had to discuss with Bruner, during one of his visits to Madrid in the 1990s, the risk that his position on the hegemony of language in early development might overshadow earlier semiotic constructions. His response was masterful. I recall it from memory, so his words are not verbatim: "I have studied language. One cannot investigate everything at once."

Since not everything can be investigated at once, everyday objects will play a central role in the next chapter. Objects will not be considered interchangeable nor merely external referents to the communicative act. Instead, objects will become key protagonists in action when children use them and in communication when adults and children interact *with* and *about* them.

1.4 Conclusions

Through this journey into the Geneva School of the 1970–1980s, I hope to have shed some light on what it represented for Developmental Psychology at the time and the profound impact it left on several generations of contemporary researchers [9, 52, 69, 72].

The Geneva School of the 1970–1980s was a fascinating place. A series of circumstances converged internally, including the evolution of Piaget's theses as he embraced more functional approaches, allowing him to move away from the relative "rigidity" of his structuralist works on major developmental stages. The "late"

Piaget of the 1970s displayed a vigor, clarity, and vision that remain striking to this day. But, as highlighted throughout this chapter, the Geneva School was more than just Piaget. Other key figures included Bärbel Inhelder, Mimi Sinclair, and Magali Bovet, who consolidated a more psychological approach in Geneva without abandoning their work's epistemological foundations. Their proposal to consider learning and its influence on development marked a turning point in understanding structures and major developmental stages. Another major internal shift occurred with the *Problem solving and strategies Group* questioning one of Piaget's foundational concepts: What was, in fact, the status of action, objects, and subject-object interaction in the construction of the psyche?

One of the reasons the Geneva School of the 1970s–1980s was so exceptional was the arrival of Vygotsky's sociocultural theses, which significantly impacted the institution and marked a turning point for many researchers of the time [54, 61, 83].

The Pragmatics of the Object has its roots in and was nourished by Piaget's work on sensorimotor development, his functional orientation of the 1970s, and the debates between Piaget and his closest disciples, who advocated for a greater role of action and objects in psychological construction. It was also influenced by the arrival of Vygotsky in Geneva and, with him, Bruner's pragmatic theses on the origins of language. Bruner opened a solid pathway for analyzing mother-infant communication in everyday life. Our task was to extend the pragmatic and cultural dimension to objects and the semiotics that operate beneath language. We thus gave a "pragmatic turn" to the work of the *Groupe* and their focus on what real subjects do in real-time to solve problems with objects. We added a social and cultural dimension to objects in infancy, which meant incorporating communication between children and adults.

Beyond the innovations introduced by the Pragmatics of the Object (see Chapter 2 of this volume), I must emphasize the deep impact that the Geneva School of those years left on my work. As I mentioned at the beginning, the questions I have always asked as a researcher have been guided by the premise that children must be able to take the initiative, find creative solutions at their level, act, and make sense of the situations they encounter. I have preferred to observe what children do—a practice I confess fascinates me. Analyzing the processes of behavior in detail, their microgenesis, is endlessly engaging and deeply beautiful.

I have always focused on objects and material instruments. Far from being mere referents to be taken lightly, objects often form part of the communicative act. From the children's perspective, objects are complex, opaque, and far less obvious than psychology often assumes. They serve as tools for accomplishing tasks in daily life—far more than we, as adults, can imagine.

I have always analyzed communication between adults and children, ensuring that children have the opportunity to demonstrate their agency in everyday life. I have never been interested in "correct behaviors" but rather in understanding the children's logic when they act and communicate in their daily lives.

I have adopted one of the key principles of the *Groupe*: to understand the subject, one must take the object seriously as a substantial part of action and communication, particularly in the early years of life. And it has been worth it.

References

1. Ackermann, E. (1992). Reconstruire la même quantité ailleurs: comment procèdent les jeunes enfants? [Reconstructing the same quantity elsewhere: how do young children proceed?]. In B. Inhelder, G. Cellérier, E. Ackermann, A. Blanchet, A. Boder, D. De Caprona, J.-J. Ducret, & M. Saada-Robert. *Le cheminement des découvertes de l'enfant. Recherche sur les microgenèses cognitives* (pp. 177–192). Delachaux et Niestlé.
2. Ackermann, E. (2015). Give me a place to stand and I will move the world! Life-long learning in the digital age. *Infancia y Aprendizaje, 38*(4), 689–717.
3. Allen, J., & Bickhard, G. (2022). Emergent constructivism: theoretical and methodological considerations. *Human Development, 66*, 276–294. https://doi.org/10.1159/000526220
4. Bates, E., Camaioni, L., & Volterra, V. (1975). The acquisition of performatives prior to speech. *Merril-Palmer Quarterly, 21*(3), 205–226.
5. Blanchet, A. (1994). Microgenesis, cognitive and social control. In N. Mercer & C. Coll (Eds.). *Teaching, learning and interaction* (pp. 17–23). Fundación Infancia y Aprendizaje.
6. Blanchet, A., Ackermann-Valladao, E., Kilcher, E., & Robert, M. (1978). Une hypothèse sur les connaissances utilisées en situation de résolution de problème [A hypothesis about the knowledge used in problem-solving situations]. *Cahiers de Psychologie, 21*, 111–117.
7. Bond, T. G., & Tryphon, A. (2024). The experimental method of adolescents: Bärbel Inhelder's Unfinished Symphony. *History of Psychology*. https://doi.org/10.1037/hop0000269
8. Bonnet, C. (1980). *L'enfant et le symbolique* [The child and the symbolic]. J. Vrin.
9. Brandt, P.-Y., Czellàr, J., Desbiez-Piat, D., Kilcher, H., Reymond, J., & Vonèche, J. (2010). *Des signes et des ordres. Hommage à Christiane Gillièron Paléologue* [Signs and orders: a tribute to Christian Gillièron Paléologue]. Labor et Fides.
10. Bremner, G., Dunn, K., & Tham, D. S. Y. (2017). Perception, knowledge and action in infancy. In A. Slater & G. Bremner (Eds.), *An introduction to developmental psychology* (3rd ed., pp. 143–181). Wiley.
11. Bronckart, J. P. (1977). *Théories du langage. Une introduction critique* [Theories of language. A critical introduction]. Pierre Mardaga.
12. Bronckart, J. P. (1992). El discurso como acción. Por un nuevo paradigma psicolingüístico [Discourse as action. For a new psycholinguistic pradigm]. *Anuario de Psicología, 54*, 3–48.
13. Bronckart, J. P. (1996). *Activité langagière, textes et discours. Pour un interactionisme socio-discursif* [Language activity, texts, and discourse. For socio-discursie ineractionism]. Delachaux et Niestlé.
14. Bronckart, J. P. (2012). Contributions of Piagetian constructivism to social interactionism. In E. Martí & C. Rodríguez (Eds.), *After Piaget* (pp. 43–58). Transaction Publishers.
15. Bronckart, J.-P., & Ventouras-Spycher, M. (1979). The Piagetian concept of representation and the Soviet inspired view of self-regulation. In C. Zivin (Ed.), *The development of self-regulation through private speech* (pp. 991–131). Wiley.
16. Bruner, J. (1978). Foreword. In A. Lock (ed.). *Action, gesture and symbol. The emergence of language* (pp. vii–viii). Academic Press.
17. Bruner, J. (1983). Préface [Preface]. In J. Bruner. *Le développement de l'enfant. Savoir faire, savoir dire* (pp. 7–9). P.U.F. Texts translated and presented by Michel Deleau.
18. Bruner, J. (1990). *Acts of meaning*. Harvard University Press.
19. Bullinger, A., & Millán, R. (1993). Le développement moteur: une perspective instrumentale [Motor development: an instrumental perspective]. In V. Pouhas & F. Jouen (Dir.). *Les comportements du bébé: expression de son savoir?*, (pp. 95–103). Mardaga.

20. Bullinger, A. (2012). Clinical approach of the premature infant, evaluations and developmental care. In E. Martí & C. Rodríguez (Eds.), *After Piaget* (pp. 83–94). Transaction Publishers.
21. Castañares, W. (2002). Signo y representación en las teorías semióticas [Sign and representation in semiotic theories]. *Estudios de Psicología, 23*(3), 339–357.
22. Castañares, W. & Manetti, G. (2001). Presentación [Presentation]. In W. Castañares & G. Manetti (Coords.). Historia de la Semiótica. Homenaje a Umberto Eco [History of Semiotics. In honor to Umberto Eco]. *deSigniS, 25*, 15–18.
23. Cellérier, G. (1968). Modèles cybernétiques et adaptation [Cybernetic models and adaptation]. In G. Cellérier, S. Papert, & G. Voyat (1968). *Cybernétique et épistémologie*, (pp. 5–91). Presses Universitaires de France.
24. Dasen, P., Inhelder, B., Lavallée, M., & Retschitzki, J. (1978). *Naissance de l'intelligence chez l'enfant baoulé de Côte d'Ivoire* [Birth of intelligence in the Baoulé child in Côte d'Ivoire]. Hans Huber Berne.
25. Dasen, P. (1995). École et éducation interculturelle. Introduction [School and intercultural education. Introduction]. In E. Poglia, A.N. Perret-Clermont, A. Gretler, & P. Dasen (Ed.). *Pluralité culturelle et éducation en Suisse. Etre migrant II*, (pp. 235–238). Peter Lang.
26. Dasen, P. (2002). Développement humain et éducation informelle [Human development and informal education]. In P. R. Dasen & C. Perregaux (Eds.), *Pourquoi des approches interculturelles en sciences de l'éducation?* (pp. 107–123). De Boeck Université.
27. Dasen, P. (2011). Psychologies et cultures (Note de lecture) [Psychologies and cultures (Reading note)]. *Alterstice, 1*(2), 129–132.
28. Deleau, M. (1990). *Les origines sociales du développement mental. Communication et symboles dans la première enfance* [The social origins of mental development. Communication and symbols in early childhood]. Armand Colin.
29. Diamond, A. (2006). The early development of EFs. In E. Bialystok & F. I. M. Craik (Eds.), *Lifespan cognition. Mechanisms of change* (pp. 70–95). Oxford University Press.
30. Doise, W. (1979). Introduction. In A. N. Perret-Clermont (Ed.), *La construction de l'intelligence dans l'interaction sociale* (pp. 1–2). Peter Lang.
31. Doise, W., Mugny, G., & Perret-Clermont, A.N. (1975). Social interaction and the development of cognitive operations. *European Journal of Social Psychology, 5*(3), 367–383.
32. Ducret, J. J. (2000). *Jean Piaget 1968–1979: Une décennie de recherches sur les mécanismes de construction cognitive* [Jean Piaget 1968-1979: A decade of research on the mechanisms of cognitive construction]. Service de la Recherche en Éducation.
33. Ducret, J.-J. (2016). Jean Piagt et la méthode "clinico-critique" [Jean Piaget and the clinical-critical method]. *Journal Français de Psychiatrie, 2*(44), 79–84. https://doi.org/10.3917/jfp.044.0079
34. Eco, U. (1984/1990). *Semiótica y Filosofía del lenguaje* [Semiotics and philosophy of language]. Lumen.
35. Enesco, I., & Sebastián, C. (2012). Viaje en la nave de Teseo: La noción de artefacto en el niño (y el uso animal de herramientas) [Journey in Theseus' ship: The notion of artifact in the child (and the animal use of tools)]. In J. A. García Madruga, R. Kohen, C. del Barrio, I. Enesco, & J. L. Linaza (Eds.). *Construyendo mentes. Ensayos en homenaje a Juan Delval* (pp. 45–68). UNED.
36. Gibson, E. J., & Pick, A. (2000). *An ecological approach to perceptual learning and development*. Oxford University Press.
37. Gillièron, C. (1985). *La construction du réel chez le psychologue. Epistémologie et méthodes en sciences humaines* [The construction of reality in the psychologist. Epistemology and methods in science]. Peter Lang.
38. Gillièron, C. (1997). *In memoriam* Bärbel Inhelder (1913–1997). *Anuario de Psicología, 74*, 125–127.
39. Gómez, J.C. (2012). Del simio al niño y del niño al simio: Historias de Psicología Evolutiva [From ape to child, and from child to ape: Developmental psychology histories]. In J.A. García Madruga, R. Kohen, C. del Barrio, I. Enesco, & J. L. Linaza (Eds.). *Construyendo mentes. Ensayos en homenaje a Juan Delval* (pp. 29–44). UNED.

40. Inhelder, B. (1992). Avant-Propos. In B. Inhelder, G. Cellérier, E. Ackermann, A. Blanchet, A. Boder, D. De, J.-J. Ducret, & M. Saada-Robert. *Le cheminement des découvertes de l'enfant. Recherche sur les microgenèses cognitives* (pp. 13–16). Delachaux et Niestlé.
41. Inhelder, B., & De Caprona, D. (1992). Un parcours de recherche [A trail of research]. In B. Inhelder, G. Cellérier, E. Ackermann, A. Blanchet, A. Boder, D., J.-J. Ducret, & M. Saada-Robert. *Le cheminement des découvertes de l'enfant. Recherche sur les microgenèses cognitives* (pp. 51–92). Delachaux et Niestlé.
42. Inhelder, B., Ackermann-Valladao, E., Blanchet, A., Karmiloff-Smith, A., Kilcher-Hagedorn, H., Montangero, J., & Robert, M. (1976). Des structures cognitives aux procédures de découverte [The cognitive structures in the processes of discovery]. *Archives de Psychologie,* XLIV(171), 57–72.
43. Inhelder, B., Lézine, I., Sinclair, H., & Stambak, M. (1972). Les débuts de la fonction symbolique [The origins of symbolic function]. *Archives de Psychologie, 41*, 187–243.
44. Inhelder, B., Sinclair, H., & Bovet, M. (1974). *Apprentissage et structures de la connaissance* [Learning and the Structure of Knowledge]. PUF.
45. Karmiloff-Smith, A., & Inhelder, B. (1975). If you want to get ahead, get a theory. *Cognition, 3*(3), 195–212.
46. Karmiloff-Smith, A. (1992/1994). *Más allá de la modularidad* [Beyond the modularity]. Alianza.
47. Karmiloff-Smith, A. (2012). From constructivism to neuroconstructivism: The activity-dependent structuring of the human brain. In E. Martí & C. Rodríguez (Eds.), *After Piaget* (pp. 1–14). Transaction Publishers.
48. Karmiloff-Smith, A. (2013). 'Microgenetics': No Single Method Can Elucidate Human Learning. Commentary on Parnafes and diSessa. *Human Development, 56*, 47–51.
49. Kilcher, H., & Saada-Robert, M. (1977). Procédures d'actions lors de constructions de ponts et d'escaliers [Action procedures for bridge and stairs construction]. *Archives de Psychologie, 45*(173) 53–83.
50. Lock, A. (1978). The emergence of Language. In A. Lock (ed.). *Action, gesture and symbol. The emergence of language* (pp. 3–18). Academic Press.
51. Marcovitch, S., & Zelazo, P. (2009). A hierarchical competing systems model of the emergence and early development of executive function. *Developmental Science, 12*(1), 1–25. https://doi.org/10.1111/j.1467-7687.2008.00754.x
52. Martí, E. (1996/2000). Los mecanismos de internalización y externalización del conocimiento en las teorías de Piaget y Vygotski [The mechanisms of internalization and externalization of knowledge in Piaget's and Vygotsky's theories.]. In A. Tryphon & J. Vonèche (Eds.), *Piaget-Vygotski: la genesis social del pensamiento* (pp. 81–114). Paidós.
53. Martí, E. (2012). Thinking with signs: From symbolic actions to external systems of representation. In E. Martí & C. Rodríguez (Eds.), *After Piaget* (pp. 151–170). Transaction Publishers.
54. Martí, E., & Rodríguez, C. (Eds.). (2012). *After Piaget*. Transaction Publishers.
55. Moro, C., & Rodríguez, C. (2005). *L'objet et la construction de son usage. Une approche sémiotique du développement préverbal* [The object and the construction of its use. A semiotic approach to preverbal development]. Peter Lang.
56. Mounoud, P. (1976). Les révolutions psychologiques de l'enfant [Children's psychological revolutions]. *Archives de Psychologie, 44*(171), 103–114.
57. Mounoud, P., & Bower, T. G. R. (1974). Conservation of weight in infants. *Cognition, 3*(1), 29–40.
58. Nelson, K. (1996). *Language in cognitive development. The emergence of the mediated mind*. Cambridge University Press.
59. Pascual-Leone, J. (2012). Piaget as a pioneer of dialectical constructivism: Seeking dynamic processes for human science. In E. Martí & C. Rodríguez (Eds.), *After Piaget* (pp. 15–41). Transaction Publishers.
60. Perret-Clermont, A. N. (1979). *La construction de l'intelligence dans l'interaction sociale* [The construction of intelligence in social interaction]. Peter Lang.

61. Perret-Clermont, A. N. (2012). "Choose two or three scapegoats and make your point!" Should I? Critical thoughts on a fabulous experience and its heritage. In E. Martí & C. Rodríguez (Eds.), *After Piaget* (pp. 207–225). Transaction Publishers.
62. Piaget, J. (1936/1977). *La naissance de l'intelligence chez l'enfant* [The origins of Intelligence in children]. Delachaux et Niestlé.
63. Piaget, J. (1937/1977). *La construction du réel chez l'enfant* [The Construction of reality in the child]. Delachaux et Niestlé.
64. Piaget, J. (1945/1976). *La formation du symbole chez l'enfant* [Play, dreams and imitation in childhood]. Delachaux et Niestlé.
65. Piaget, J. (1971). *Les explications causales* [Understanding Causality]. Presses Universitaires de France.
66. Piaget, J. (1974). *La prise de conscience* [The grasp of consciousness]. Presses Universitaires de France.
67. Piaget, J. (1974). *Réussir et comprendre* [Success and understanding]. Presses Universitaires de France.
68. Piaget, J. (1975). *L'équilibration des structures cognitives. Problème central du développement* [The equilibration of cognitive structures: the central problem of intellectual development]. Presses Universitaires de France. Version électronique réalisée sous l'égide de la *Fondation Jean Piaget.*
69. Puche, R., & Ossa, J. C. (2024). *The microgenetic method. Legacy of Bärbel Inhelder.* SpringerBriefs in Psychology.
70. Ratcliff, M. (2018, 31 May–June 2). *Only three subjects, but 10.000 observations. Jean and Valentine Piaget's notebooks on infants.* Communication presented at the Discussion Session. Have development, the world, and everyday life disappeared from today's psychology of early development? Lessons from Jean and Valentine Piaget's notebooks on infant development. 48th Annual Meeting, JPS Society, Amsterdam.
71. Rivière, A. (1985). *La Psicología de Vygotski* [Vygotsky's psychology]. Visor.
72. Rochat, P. & Bullinger, A. (1994). Posture and Functional Action in Infancy. In A. Vyt, H. Bloch, & M. H. Bornstein (Eds.). *Early child development in the French tradition: contributions from current research* (pp. 15–34). Erlbaum Associates.
73. Rochat, P. (2012). Baby assault on Piaget. In E. Martí & C. Rodríguez (Eds.), *After Piaget* (pp. 71–82). Transaction Publishers.
74. Rochat, P. (2023). The evolution of developmental theories since Piaget: A metaview. *Perspectives on Psychological Science, 19*(6), 921–930. https://doi.org/10.1177/17456916231186611
75. Rodríguez, C., & Moro, C. (1999). *El mágico número tres. Cuando los niños aún no hablan* [The magic number three. When children do not speak yet]. Paidós.
76. Rodríguez, C. (2006). *Del ritmo al símbolo. Los signos en el nacimiento de la inteligencia* [From rhythm to symbol. Signs in the origin of intelligence]. Horsori.
77. Rodríguez, C. (2007). Object use, communication and signs: The triadic basis of early cognitive development. In J. Valsiner & A. Rosa (Eds.), *The Cambridge handbook of socio-cultural psychology* (pp. 257–276). Cambridge University Press.
78. Rodríguez, C. (2012). The functional permanence of the object: A product of consensus. In E. Martí & C. Rodríguez (Eds.). *After Piaget* (pp. 123–150). Transaction Publishers.
79. Rodríguez, C., & Martí, E. (2012). Introduction. The fertility of Piaget's legacy. In E. Martí & C. Rodríguez (Eds.). *After Piaget* (pp. xix–xxxviii). Transaction Publishers.
80. Rodríguez, C., Benassi, J., Estrada, L., & Alessandroni, N. (2017). Early social interactions with people and objects. In A. Slater & G. Bremner (Eds.), *An introduction to developmental psychology* (3rd ed., pp. 211–257). John Wiley & Sons.
81. Saada-Robert, M. (1985). Changements de significations et de guidage de l'action chez l'enfant en situation de résolution de problème [Changes in meaning and action guidance in children in problem-solving situations]. *Archives de Psychologie, 53*(207), 395–398.

82. Saada-Robert, M. (1992). La construction microgénétique d'un schème élémentaire [The microgenetic construction of an elementary schema]. In B. Inhelder, G. Cellérier, E. Ackermann, A. Blanchet, A. Boder, D. De Caprona, J.-J. Ducret, & M. Saada-Robert. *Le cheminement des découvertes de l'enfant. Recherche sur les microgenèses cognitives* (pp. 119–137). Delachaux et Niestlé.
83. Saada-Robert, M. (2012). From individual to didactic microgenesis: Studies on situated knowledge transformations. In E. Martí & C. Rodríguez (Eds.). *After Piaget* (pp. 187–206). Transaction Publishers.
84. Sanchidrián, C. (2013). Tres modelos de espacios educativos y de materiales pedagógicos: Infants Schools, Kindergarten y Casas de Niños [Three models of educational spaces and pedagogical materials: Infants schools, kindergarten and houses of the children]. *Tabanque. Revista Pedagógica, 26*, 15–37.
85. Sinclair, H., Stambak, M., Lezine, I., & Verba, M. (1982). *Les bébés et les choses ou la créativité du développement cognitif* [Babies and things or the creativity of cognitive development]. PUF.
86. Sinclair, H. (1987). Symbolisme et interaction interpersonnelle [Symbolism and interpersonal interaction]. In J. Montangero, A. Tryphon, & S. Dionnet (Eds.), *Symbolisme et connaissance,* Cahier 8 (pp. 155–168). Fondation Archives Jean Piaget.
87. Slater, A., Johnson, S. P., & Muir, D. (2017). The scope and methods of developmental Psychology. In A. Slater & G. Bremner (Eds.). *An introduction to developmental psychology* (3rd ed., pp. 3-40). Wiley.
88. Smith, L. B., Thelen, E., Titzer, R., & Dewey, M. (1999). Knowing in the context of acting: The task dynamics of the A-not-B error. *Psychological Review, 106*(2), 235–260.
89. Spelke, E. S. (2017). Core knowledge, language and number. *Language, Learning and Development, 13*(2), 147–170. https://doi.org/10.1080/15475441.2016.1263572
90. Spelke, E., & Kinzler, K. D. (2007/2014). Core knowledge. In J. G. Bremner & A. M. Slater (Eds.), *Psychology of infancy. Vol. 4. Cognitive development: From Piaget to the developing theory of mind* (pp. 121–134). Sage.
91. Thelen, E., & Bates, E. (2003). Connectionism and dynamic systems: are they really different? *Developmental Science, 6*(4), 378–391.
92. Tryphon, A., & Vonèche, J. (1996/2000). *Piaget-Vygotski: la genesis social del pensamiento* [Piaget-Vygotsky: the social genesis of thought]. Paidós.
93. van der Veer, R. (2021). Vygotsky's legacy: Understanding and beyond. *Integrative Psychological and Behavioral Science, 55*, 789–796.
94. Vergnaud, G. (2009). Activité, developpement, représentation [Activity, development, representation]. In *Colloquium Didactique des Mathématiques. Conférence Plénière Invitée* [Key note]. Paris. www.gerard-vergnaud.org
95. Vygotski, L. (1984/1996). El primer año [The first year]. In L. Vygotski (Eds.), *Obras escogidas IV. Psicología infantil* (pp. 275–318). Visor.
96. Wallon, H. (1942/1970). *De l'acte à la pensée* [From act to thought]. Flammarion.

2 The Uses of Objects and Their Social Construction in Infancy

Cintia Rodríguez

Often, the most obvious things are those that require the most explanation.

Castañares and Manetti ([13]; our translation).

How do children begin to use objects by their functions during the first year of life? This was the question Christiane Moro and I posed in the 1980s when we were Research Assistants at the Geneva School. To answer this, we first had to acknowledge that artifact objects are not limited to their physical properties, such as size, texture, shape, or color. They also have social attributes; they are used in everyday life, and these uses are known and shared by the community of users surrounding the children. Second, we started with something evident: Children are not born knowing what objects are, how to use them, or even which ones are essential for survival. These skills must be constructed (see Chap. 1 of this volume).

It is not difficult to conclude that, with this premise, we distanced ourselves from the Geneva School. The divergence—or the break—arose from the pragmatic perspective we applied to objects. Objects are part of material culture, a normative and public universe that children access through communication with

C. Rodríguez (✉)
Universidad Autónoma de Madrid, Madrid, Spain
e-mail: cintia.rodriguez@uam.es

C. Rodriguez Garrido et al. (eds.), *The Social Life of Objects in Early Development*,
Social Interaction in Learning and Development,
https://doi.org/10.1007/978-3-031-87673-8_2

others. Therefore, it was necessary to remove both the subject and the object from the isolation the Geneva School had placed them in.

However, the Pragmatics of the Object also represented continuity with our teachers. From the outset, it was anchored in the epistemological and methodological foundations of the Geneva School. This continuity has remained constant to this day.

I will begin with the aspects that signify *continuity* with the Geneva School—elements that were far from minor. The Pragmatics of the Object is rooted, first and foremost, in the epistemological principles of Genevan *constructivism.* What exactly does this mean? The meanings attributed to objects, to oneself, or others, are not *pre-existing* truths. Instead, they must be constructed [46] throughout development.

For Piaget, studying knowledge meant moving away from any isolated consideration of the "here and now." Knowledge can only be understood through its *construction*, tracing its *development over time.* It was essential to study knowledge as a psychological *construction* and to view all knowledge as relative to a particular stage of that construction [68]. Determining how knowledge grows and is constructed required considering "all knowledge from the perspective of its *development over time*, that is, as a *continuous process* for which neither a definitive beginning nor an ultimate end could ever be reached" ([68, p. 18], translation and emphasis ours).

Christiane Moro and I assumed that children are not born knowing what objects are or how to use them. Nor did it seem reasonable to think that such knowledge could suddenly emerge. We needed to approach the social construction of objects by children through their development and the processes involved over time.

The central status of the agent, the active subject, in constructing their own knowledge—a hallmark of the Geneva School—led us to distance ourselves from the simplistic idea (still widespread today) that knowledge is merely a copy of reality. On the contrary, we considered that analyzing the dynamics of children's actions would provide significant insights into the constructive processes involved in the meanings of objects. We have always been interested in analyzing *processes* and *action* rather than focusing solely on outcomes.

The Piagetian and Genevan principle that we adopted as our own—and which has accompanied me throughout my career as a researcher—is the consideration that all psychology must address the *relationships* between the *subject* and the *object.* The *source of knowledge* is not found in the object but in the *subject's activity with the object.* The subject is an agent who constructs themselves by acting upon and transforming their environment. Therefore, thought arises from action; it is the internalization and representation of experience. Elementary actions are progressively internalized and mentalized [68].

Another hallmark of the Geneva School is that objectivity is not an immediate fact, a starting point, but a product. This concept was central to distancing ourselves from the widely held belief in psychology that objects directly reveal what they are and what they mean. That is, they directly reveal what they allow—their *affordances*. As we will see later, the results of successive investigations do not support this idea.

The Pragmatics of the Object also aligns with the Geneva School's methodological aspects. We placed great importance on observation from the beginning, which we have always considered a research method rather than a precursor to experimentation. One of the advantages of observation as a research method is that it allows for the emergence of original, unexpected, and unpredictable behaviors in children—behaviors that were not anticipated or that fell outside the scope of strict research questions. In fact, surprising behaviors from children enabled us to open new lines of research, such as the development of symbols [81], the development of private gestures as tools for self-regulation [82], and the development of executive functions from the end of the first year of life in early-years-schools [80]. Qualitative analyses of behavior have been a constant in all our research, though we have also considered quantitative aspects [4, 54]. We never worked in a laboratory. Our data always come from the everyday contexts in which children develop—at home or in early years school. Our designs have always been longitudinal, and our analyses are microgenetic. For this reason, the number of participants in all our studies has been limited. The approaches of the *Groupe de stratégies et résolution de problèmes* [87, 88] [Problem solving and strategies group] provided the epistemological foundation for taking children's actions with objects seriously as a source of knowledge and cognitive development (see discussion in Chap. 1 of this volume). The microgenetic method, one of the *Groupe's* most notable contributions, allowed us to delve into the processes involved in the social construction of objects. Through microgenesis, we were able to capture, in detail, the dynamics of interaction within the adult-infant-object triangle.

An important advantage of microgenetic analyses in early development is the close connection between the subtlety of microgenesis and the establishment of milestones characteristic of macrogenesis. This is mainly because the most remarkable developmental changes occur within the brief span of the first two years of life. The articulation between microgenesis and macrogenesis becomes much more challenging in later stages of development.

We have always studied children as the agents they are, who act and seek creative solutions. We adopted Gillièron's [32] maxim: without providing the subject with a genuine opportunity to act as an agent, psychological development does not occur and may not even be worth studying (see Chap. 3 of this volume for details on the Method used in home and early years school research).

The divergence—or distance, depending on how one prefers to frame it—from the Geneva School arose in two core aspects, which we have already hinted at. We questioned (i) the reduction of objects to their *physical properties* and (ii) their *systematic exclusion from communicative acts*. What, then, are the central tenets of the Pragmatics of the Object? These can be summarized in three main premises:

(1) Everyday artifact objects are part of *material culture*; they are social and cannot be reduced to "physical reality."

(2) Objects are *used* in daily life for practical, public purposes. Children's *uses* of objects *develop* spectacularly during the first 18 months of life. For this reason, it is necessary to analyze the *types of uses* according to levels of *increasing semiotic complexity*.
(3) Children appropriate the public meanings of objects through *communication* with others, which develops according to levels of *increasing semiotic complexity*.

Let us now delve into these aspects, beginning with the social dimension of the material world.

2.1 Everyday Artifact Objects as Part of Material Culture

Stating that artifact objects and tools are part of material culture, are social constructions, and serve purposes related to the daily activities of humans is now widely accepted across numerous disciplines. In the *Handbook of Material Culture*, Tilley et al. [96] argue that studies on material culture emphasize the dialectical and recursive relationship between people and things: people create and use things, and things shape people. Subjects and objects are indelibly interconnected.

Several aspects of material culture highlighted by Tilley et al. [96] are particularly relevant here. For instance, things are created by people—they are artifacts. Producing them requires technology, and they are exchanged and consumed. Things are connected to conscious ideas and intentions held by people and to unconscious structures of thought and emotion, habitual experiences, and the consequences of social life, which transcend individual intentional awareness. Material culture relates to society: things are integral to being human and living with others. Things are tied to emotions and personal and social identities. They are linked to individual and collective history and tradition. Moreover, things interact with the human body, influencing, constraining, extending, and limiting its capacities.

Over the past 30–35 years, studies on material culture as an integral dimension of culture have proliferated. The idea that studying material culture is essential for understanding social relationships has gained traction. As Sophie Woodward states, "Culture and society are seen as being created and reproduced by the ways in which people make, design, and interact with objects. [...] Objects symbolize or represent aspects of a pre-existing culture or identity" [106, p. 1]. This perspective challenges the traditional dichotomy between what is "material" and what is "cultural" [96] and challenges the historical division between the natural sciences, focused on the study of the material world, and the social sciences, which aim to understand society and social relations. It also confronts "the assumption, perpetuated by disciplinary divisions and also philosophical trajectories, that the object and subject are separate, wherein the latter is assumed to be immaterial, and the former is assumed to be *inert* and *passive*" ([106, p. 1], emphasis ours).

Historically, two disciplines—archaeology [34, 35, 51] and anthropology—have been the primary domains for studying material culture [96]. Material culture is the primary source of evidence in prehistoric archaeology concerning the human past. However, material culture is also studied by disciplines such as geography, history, design, and sociology. In sociology, Bruno Latour [43] introduces the concept of *interobjectivity*, challenging the notion of intersubjectivity by asserting the significance of objects in human action and interaction. This body of work marked a turning point not only in sociology but also in some areas of the human sciences. Latour criticized sociology, arguing that "[l]ike many human sciences, it has constructed itself to resist attachment to objects" [43, p. 236].

From sociology, Ian Woodward also argues that objects shape material culture: "[...] The term 'material culture' emphasizes how apparently inanimate things within the environment act on people, and are acted upon by people, for the purpose of carrying out social functions, regulating social relations and giving symbolic meaning to human activity" [105, p. 3]. Sophie Woodward and Cornelia Mayr [107] argue that materiality is integral to everyday social life. Among other topics, these authors explore how secrets are kept—or sustained—through and with objects. This approach sheds light on how people relate to objects at home and provides a framework for studying what remains hidden within material culture.

Other fields, such as history [24] or pedagogical and educational practices ranging from early childhood education to university [8], also endorse material objects' cultural and social status.

Since its origins in antiquity, semiotics has also included material reality, acknowledging that objects have meaning and can serve as signs [14]. During the twentieth century, semiotics explored the meanings conveyed by materiality in areas as diverse as everyday life [27], space and architecture [28], and fashion or advertising [2]. For Barthes, "Any system of signs, whatever their substance and limits, images, gestures, musical sounds, objects, and the complex associations of all these, which form the content of ritual, convention, and public entertainment: these constitute, if not *languages*, at least systems of signification" (Barthes, 1967, cited by Layton [44, p. 31], emphasis in the original). Similarly, for the semioticians of *Group* μ, "at its foundation, the notion of object is not essentially separable from the notion of sign" ([36, p. 81], our translation). I will return later to the semiotic dimension of objects. In summary, many scientific disciplines regard artifact objects as material culture, and a segment of semiotics readily considers them as signs.

Traditionally, the situation in psychology has been quite different. It is not common for psychology to be included among the disciplines interested in material culture, and even less so for it to establish a connection between object and sign. As we have already seen, this was the case with the Geneva School. Similarly, and despite their differences, the same can be said of the sociocultural school. Neither Vygotsky nor Luria assigned material objects a notable status. Christiane Moro described this lack of interest as follows:

> Although over the past decades culture can be said to have re-entered psychology, one can only be puzzled by the fact that material culture did not receive the same attention and has been neglected by both 'mainstream' and cultural-historical traditions. To counter-balance this strange absence, the assumption I start from [...] is that material culture and material objects are at the heart of human development processes, conditioning our everyday relationship to the world, and influencing how we live, act, think and develop as human beings from an early age. [58, p. 172]

It is true that Vygotsky and Luria consider both material tools (instrumental mediation) and signs (semiotic mediation) as mediators [71]. These two forms of mediation are distinguished by their orientation: while signs are internally directed and influence one's own psyche or that of others through communication, material tools are externally oriented, focusing on action, and are not connected to communication.

The dichotomy between signs on the one hand and material tools on the other excludes material tools and objects from any semiotic dimension. This distinction has profoundly influenced sociocultural theory, which is not without its issues, as acknowledged by Miettinen and Paavola [48]. According to these authors, the distinction between sign and material tool should be reconsidered: "Mediational means tend to form complex constellations of artifacts or instrumentalities in which semiotic and practical functions are fused and intertwined in many ways" (p. 148). This perspective aligns with the approaches of semioticians such as Group μ, Castañares, Roland Barthes, and Peirce, opening the door to considering objects through their semiotic dimension—a concept that, as we have seen, lies at the core of the Pragmatics of the Object.

As noted, part of psychology's difficulty in incorporating objects and material tools into a semiotic network stems from the sociocultural orientation's lack of interest in material culture. However, increasing voices advocate for the cultural status of artifact objects as social constructions [59, 86, 100] governed by norms [21]. According to Miller, "the concept of artifact refers to a human-made object that has a meaning and constitutes a part of our culture" (2011, cited by Miettinen & Paavola [48, p. 153]). Artifacts encompass intentionality, as they are created according to intended uses. They are not "found" but rather the result of fabrication [90]. Domains such as children's play and gender differentiation [11], creativity [33], learning in early childhood institutions [62], typical and atypical development [40], autism ([45, 104], see also Chap. 12 of this volume on autism), and visual impairments [17] are some examples of the growing interest in objects as material culture.

Although I previously alluded to Vygotsky's lack of interest in objects, the following quotes suggest that he may have been expanding the scope of what he considered social toward the end of his life. He references Durkheim, who "deduces from human social life both space and time, as well as all objective reality" ([101, p. 91], translation ours). Inspired by Bogdanov, he further states: "The objectivity of the physical bodies with which we interact in our experience ultimately rests on the mutual control and concordant judgment of different individuals. More generally, the physical world is socially agreed-upon experience, socially harmonized experience—in a word, *socially organized experience*" (pp. 91–92, emphasis in the original, translation ours).

I will now address object permanence, one of the foundational aspects of human psychology in infancy. Analyzing how psychology has approached object permanence offers a paradigmatic view of the status of objects within the discipline, particularly in early development. Despite the diversity of perspectives regarding its origin, development, or the methods used to study it, there is a common denominator: other people do not play a role in object permanence. Children are left alone, and objects are not identified with material culture but solely with what is referred to as "physical reality."

2.1.1 Object Permanence: A Paradigmatic Example in Infant Studies

If action upon the material world, whether in solitude or through interaction with others, is fundamental to psychological development, the lens through which objects are viewed inevitably shapes what is said about the subject. A paradigmatic domain illustrating how objects have been considered in early developmental psychology is the body of research on object permanence.

As everyone knows, object permanence has been one of the cornerstones of early development since Piaget's work, and it continues to have a significant influence today. An object is considered permanent when children know it still exists even when it has disappeared from their sight. Piaget himself provides a compelling reason for its importance: "Something must be conserved; otherwise, the reasoning is impossible" (in Bringuier [10, pp. 40–41], translation ours). Piaget proposed two key ideas to support his thesis against nativist perspectives on object permanence: "Nothing suggests that the universe of the first weeks is truly *segmented* into 'objects,' into things conceived as permanent [...]" ([69, p. 11], translation ours). The segmentation of the universe into objects must be constructed: "The notion of an object, far from being innate or ready-made through experience, is constructed little by little" ([69, p. 10], translation ours). His starting point on *La construction du réel chez l'enfant* [The construction of reality in the child] on the notion of the object and its construction is masterful and succinctly summarizes his perspective:

> The first question to ask in order to understand how the newborn *intelligence constructs the external world* is whether, during the first months, the child conceives and perceives things as we do—in the form of *substantial, permanent objects with constant dimensions*. If we assume they do not, then we must explain how *the notion of an object is constructed*. ([69, p. 9], emphasis and translation ours)

For Piaget, object permanence involves a lengthy construction process throughout sensorimotor development. It constitutes the first invariant, one that is independent of the social world and culture: "It is not the cultural environment that allows [the child] to discover [...] the permanence of the object" (in Bringuier [10, p. 40], translation ours). Furthermore, it is "the foundation of our representation of the material world" (ibid., p. 41).

Object permanence has significant implications for development. For example, it enables the emergence of the first symbols, and of linguistic signs: if objects lacked consistency in the subject's thought, they could not be evoked in the form of words or gestures ([41]; discussion in Rodríguez [72]). Other forms of permanence develop later, such as the conservation of substance, weight, volume, number, and many others.

According to Piaget, the earliest forms of object permanence appear in the III stage of sensorimotor intelligence, around 6–7 months of age, when children retrieve a partially hidden object. This process concludes in the VI stage, around 18 months.

Around 11–12 months, Piaget describes the A-not-B error. He observed this phenomenon at first with an error made by his cousin at that age when Piaget, still very young, was taking care of him. The child was repeatedly playing with a ball, throwing it, and retrieving it. On one occasion, the ball rolled under an armchair (A), and the child successfully retrieved it. Later, however, the ball rolled under a fringed sofa (B), partially obscuring its visibility. Instead of persistently searching for the ball where it had disappeared (B), the child went straight to the armchair (A), where it had initially disappeared.

Inspired by Piaget's work, many laboratory experiments have been conducted on object permanence, particularly the A-not-B error. This task has become popular as a way to investigate the earliest manifestations of Executive Functions ([25, 49]; see Chaps. 8–10 on Executive Functions in this volume).

As noted in Chap. 1, over the past few decades, nativist and modularist theories of the "competent baby" have become dominant [9]. For example, Spelke, one of its most prominent advocates, refers to *objects* as one of the nuclear types of knowledge, "core knowledge." She describes objects as "nonliving bodies" and focuses on "their motion. It is the foundation for our commonsense understanding of the physical world" [93, p. xviii]. According to Spelke, object permanence (or the concept of number) does not require a lengthy construction process, which is why it manifests much earlier than the ages proposed by Piaget [47]. In Spelke's view, children do not need to act to find a disappeared three-dimensional object. Instead, observing their reactions to the appearances and disappearances of "objects" typically presented on screens with self-generated motion is sufficient. Piaget's three-dimensional object is often replaced by images to which children respond. This paradigm emphasizes the naturalization of objects, focusing exclusively on their "physical" dimension.

Dynamic systems theory represents another highly influential approach in early development today. I will highlight the nuanced work of Esther Thelen and collaborators. They firmly oppose the nativist theories of the "competent baby," arguing that children do not require a "preexisting 'knowledge' of what properties define and delimit objects" [95, p. 175]. In alignment with Piaget, they assert that objects are constructed through experience, enabling environmental adaptation. Regarding object permanence, they draw inspiration from Gibson: "From a Gibsonian perspective, *movement* is what allows *discrimination* and *discovery* of the *invariants* in the environment—the common and correlated properties of flow, movement, edges, textures—that are necessary for adaptive actions" (p. 194, emphasis ours). Movement, they argue, enables children to discriminate and discover the invariants of their environment. Unlike proponents of the "competent baby" perspective, and in alignment with Piaget, object segregation is constructed. It results from the interaction of two perceptual systems: "a 'what' and a 'where' systems. The "what" mechanisms are concerned with categorizing and identifying objects and using the *static properties of objects—edges, colors,* and *shapes.* The "where" mechanisms situate perception and make use of movement-generated and dynamic information in visual displays" ([95, pp. 173–174], emphasis ours). When discussing the dynamic exploration children must undertake, they emphasize: "contours, edges, backs of objects, sources of sounds, textures, weights, and surfaces [...] They must move—their eyes, their heads, their hands, the soles of their feet—to provide the same 'takes' on the objects and events, and their own activities within the stimulus array [...]" (p. 194). These texts highlight, on the one hand, the essential activity required of the child in constructing object permanence and, on the other, the emphasis on the strictly physical dimensions of object invariance (see also Smith [92]). In this sense, they are not far from Piaget's perspective.

In conclusion, Spelke's nativist perspective eliminates both the role of action and the gradual construction of object permanence. This is not the case with Piaget or dynamic systems theory [92, 95]. However, despite their marked epistemological differences, two common denominators exist among all these perspectives: (i) Object permanence does not include normative or functional aspects. It concerns strictly "physical" invariants. (ii) Children achieve object permanence in isolation, without communication or the involvement of others' actions (see discussion in Rodriguez [83]).

Despite the years that have passed, the debate about what object permanence is, when it manifests, and its implications for other psychological constructs remains unsolved [9, 52, 61]. When I introduce the social dimension of objects as material culture, this uncertainty increases farther. Left in the shadows is the construction of object invariants as material culture—artifacts used in daily life, with specific functions recognized and shared by members of the culture to which children belong. These functions are indispensable for their survival.

Tilley [97] also highlights this absence in anthropology, pointing out the lack of detailed ethnographic studies on the importance of objects in early childhood socialization.

Particularly noteworthy is a text published over 80 years ago by the French psychologist Henri Wallon, where he refers to the cultural dimension of objects. Wallon questioned the notion that a child is born into an unchanging, eternal world. On the contrary, the world is composed of concrete objects from a specific era that are embedded within institutions.

> *The child cannot be considered apart from the environment* in which their growth takes place and which envelops them from birth. The universe to which they must adapt [...] *is not a kind of universe in itself, unchanging and eternal*; it is the collection of *objects specific to the era*: their cradle, their bottle, their swaddling clothes, the fire, artificial light; later, the *furniture* whose structures they manipulate, the tools that shape their habits or teach them to craft things; the *institutions* into which their existence is embedded; and also the techniques of *language*, explanation, and understanding that govern their thoughts, imposing upon them—through conceptual or logical frameworks—the segmentation of forces and objects that populate the world. This world is made available today by *millennia of civilization and material and intellectual elaboration*". ([103, p. 77], emphasis and translation ours)

From this perspective, I will address in this chapter, at the end of the next section, the construction of another form of permanence: the *permanence of the uses of objects according to their function.* This functional permanence is socially shared in daily life, linked to material culture, and begins to be gradually constructed throughout the first year of life.

2.2 Types of Uses and Their Development: Functional Permanence of Objects in Daily Life

If we consider the arguments of those who assert that objects are part of material culture, and we accept that, beyond "physical" attributes such as substance, contours, edges, textures, weight, surface, or color, objects *also* possess social properties and are defined by *what can be done* with them, then it becomes essential to focus on *what children do* with objects during their process of adaptation to a specific cultural environment. Since we assume that children are not born knowing what objects are or what they are for, we must account for this construction and development. In this process, children are not alone—they become users long before they are aware of it, thanks to adults who include them in their own objectives related to feeding, hygiene, comfort, or care [76]. Adults lend their intentions to children long before children realize it themselves. It is, therefore, necessary to explain *how the notion of object* is constructed according to its *function*, how the *use* of objects in daily life *develops*, how what children do with objects changes throughout development, and how this affects their relationship with the world, with themselves, and with others. Ultimately, this process impacts their constitution as agent subjects.

It is universally acknowledged today that the early years of life are an ideal period for investigating the foundations of psychological development. There is extensive literature on the development of emotional expression, phonetics, language, gestures, memory, perception, object permanence, categories, numbers, motor development, and neurodevelopment, to name a few examples [91]. However, it is striking how little attention has been given to the development of *types of actions and uses* children engage in with objects and how this construction—essential for daily life—affects other developmental domains.

When discussing actions with objects, the generic and imprecise term *exploration* is often used: "The child explores objects." This term typically encompasses the period from around 4–5 months, when children begin to manipulate objects independently, to the emergence of the first symbols, which the literature places around 18 months (see Chap. 5 on symbols in this volume). However, using the broad term "exploration" to describe very different abilities over such a long period does not seem very rigorous. This is a time of spectacular development, encompassing everything from the origins of intentional communication and the first manifestations of Executive Functions to tool use and the beginnings of language. It is, therefore, essential to specify what children do with objects, for what purpose, and how. An account must be given of how all this develops.

How do children come to *use* everyday objects according to their canonical functions during childhood? What specific *types of uses* do they engage in with objects before assigning them their socially recognized functions? How do these uses *develop*? What role do adults play in this crucial construction? And what are the implications of this development for their daily lives?

To address these questions, we initially conducted two longitudinal studies with 12 children (6 boys and 6 girls) aged 7–13 months. We observed their interactions with their mothers at home and with two complex, everyday objects suited to their interests and action abilities. Details of the results can be found in two books: one in Spanish, *El mágico número tres. Cuando los niños aún no hablan* [The magic number three: When children do not speak yet] [81], and another in French, *L'objet et la construction de son usage. Une approche sémiotique du développement préverbal* [The object and the construction of its use: A semiotic perspective of preverbal development] [60]. Neither has been translated into English. The main results are summarized in English in Rodríguez [79]. Next, I will discuss the development of types of uses.

2.2.1 The Object and What is Done with It are Two Different Things. Types of Uses

When observing what children did at 7 months with the objects provided to their mothers in both studies—a toy truck with fitting pieces that could be inserted through holes on the top and a replica telephone—something became evident that is not intuitive from an adult perspective: object and use do not coincide. What does this mean? It means an *object* is one thing, and what is *done* with it is another. With any given object, many things can be done. That is what the children (and their mothers) in the study taught us.

As expected, none of the children at 7 months used the everyday objects we presented to them according to their intended functions. Overall, the mothers' efforts to involve the children in their own use of the objects did not seem to help much, either. There was a significant discrepancy between what the mothers did with the objects and what the children themselves did.

Based on their semiotic complexity, this led us to organize the vast array of actions performed by the children with the objects between 7 and 13 months. Peirce's semiotics were invaluable in this process, as they allowed us to classify and bring "order" to the enormous diversity of actions. We analyzed their development in terms of how far the children's uses were from the public function of the objects. We identified three types of uses, arranged from least to most complex: (1) Non-canonical uses, (2) Proto-canonical uses, and (3) Canonical, conventional, or functional uses.

(1) *Non-canonical uses*: These are called non-canonical because they are unrelated to the norms or intended functions of the objects. What did children do, and what do non-canonical uses consist of? Essentially, children sucked, shook, or banged the objects together with varying degrees of accuracy. Strictly speaking, children performed a considerable number of actions whose common denominator was that they were undifferentiated uses. They applied similar actions to very different objects, regardless of their function in daily life or what their mothers did with them. Both boys and girls engaged in the *same* undifferentiated uses, resulting in an overgeneralization that ignored the specific nature of the object. They interacted with objects based solely on what the objects physically allowed them to do. We called these primitive types of uses *non-canonical* because they fall outside the canon—the social function for which the objects were designed [90]. Non-canonical uses represent the first level of meaning: iconicity (or Firstness in Peirce's semiotic theory). To suck on an object, children do not need to rely on extensive prior knowledge, establish categories, or agree on meanings with others. Nor does sucking an object invite communication with others.

What is interesting about *non-canonical*, undifferentiated uses is that they were observed across all ages. Children sucked on the objects at 7, 10, and 13 months, although the frequency was highest at 7 months and decreased at 10 months, and even more so at 13 months. What does this mean? It means that the "abandonment" of non-canonical uses, which are the furthest from the canon, was gradual and did not occur suddenly. From this, it can be inferred that children were not imitating their mothers, as no mother sucked on any object. Nor did they "suddenly" imitate their mothers when they used the objects according to their intended functions. Children required time to construct and appropriate meanings in line with their own developmental trajectories before performing uses analogous to those of their mothers.

In more recent studies, which will be discussed in this volume, all children engaged in non-canonical uses [16, 65] (see Chaps. 5 on symbols and 6 on numerical development). This pattern was also observed in studies on Executive Functions ([39], see Chap. 10 on EF). A common denominator in these studies is that non-canonical uses were also progressively abandoned, as children became more "experts" in canonical, symbolic, numerical uses, or pursuing their objectives involving everyday materiality.

(2) *Proto-Canonical Uses*: These are more elaborate and specific than non-canonical uses, as they begin to align with the canonical use or convention, though without fully achieving it. Following Peirce's semiotics and the progression of meanings, proto-canonical uses correspond to the second level of signification (Secondness). Proto-canonical uses occupy an intermediate level between iconicity and symbolism (convention), as per Peirce's framework. Occasionally, children achieve these uses by "riding on" the actions of adults—a phenomenon observed sporadically at 7 months but more frequently at 10 months [81].

Proto-canonical uses are highly varied depending on the objects. As with non-canonical uses, they reveal two very important points. First, the abandonment of the most basic uses does not happen suddenly. Second, neither does the acquisition of the conventional use of objects occur abruptly. Instead, we observe a gradual progression—a progressive conquest of meanings. By analogy with synaptic pruning, which predominantly occurs during infancy [29], we can refer to a "pruning" of non-canonical uses, where less effective uses are gradually abandoned in favor of more effective ones, facilitating better adaptation to the environment.

Proto-canonical uses can serve as a "springboard," gradually facilitating the transition to more complex and specific uses of particular objects. Children can eventually achieve canonical uses by building on proto-canonical uses and making progressive adjustments. Proto-canonical uses can also act as excellent tools for self-regulation [53, 80] and provide insights into the *processes* implicated, including the shift in beliefs about what can be done when interacting with the material world.

(3) *Canonical or Functional Uses:* All children in both studies used the objects according to their function—or attempted to—by 13 months of age [60, 81]. They all succeeded, or more precisely, made efforts to use the objects in line with their socially shared function, the same functions that adults attribute to everyday objects almost "automatically." This automaticity arises because we no longer recall the steps we followed in our early years to recognize and use everyday material culture according to its function. Using an object according to its function—engaging in its canonical or conventional use—means that an item, previously open to undifferentiated uses (as was mostly the case at 7 months), transforms into a specific object with a defined function. It ceases to be interchangeable and becomes part of a class. Canonical uses do not originate from an individual decision by the child or their mother. The objects included in the study are part of collective material culture, transmitted from generation to generation [106]. However, what occurs on the individual level, within each child, is the appropriation and specific construction that must be undertaken—and this is something no one else can do on their behalf.

Canonical or functional uses occupy the third level of signification, thirdness, and convention, according to Peirce. The relationship connecting the representamen with its immediate object is conventional, the result of a rule or law. At this stage, children began to use objects according to their specific function. These are *canonical uses, whose rules of use are socially shared and understood*. They are uses recognized and agreed upon by the community of users, reflecting a consensus regarding the meaning of materiality.

In both studies [60, 81], all children engaged in canonical uses at 10 months (Fig. 2.1) on some occasions (44.2% of cases). However, as mentioned earlier, they sometimes "lowered the level" and reverted to sucking the objects (non-canonical, undifferentiated uses). By 13 months, canonical uses predominated (86.8%), with only occasional instances of sucking the objects. This indicates that, by this age, the two everyday objects used in the study had already become signs of their functional use. Children knew what the objects were for and shared this knowledge with adults, reflecting their grasp of the material culture of their time. Nevertheless, precisely controlling how to use the objects still required a long process of refinement and self-regulation, potentially spanning months or even years. For example, using a telephone fully functionally demands some mastery of language, illustrating how the complexity of the objects influences the required developmental trajectory.

In conclusion, both studies demonstrated a significant *development* in the *types of uses* performed by children. The three types of uses emerged in an orderly sequence, from the least to the most complex. All children began "at the beginning," with undifferentiated, non-canonical uses. No 7-month-old used the objects at the most complex level. As noted earlier, conventional meanings were the last to appear. A kind of "pruning" of non-canonical uses occurred, as these were gradually replaced by proto-canonical and canonical uses. *Undifferentiated* uses applied to any object were abandoned in favor of *specific* uses for each object. This transition was *gradual*. At times, all three types of uses coexisted within a single sequence, particularly around 10 months of age. Thus, changes in representations and beliefs followed a gradual process, unfolding step by step rather

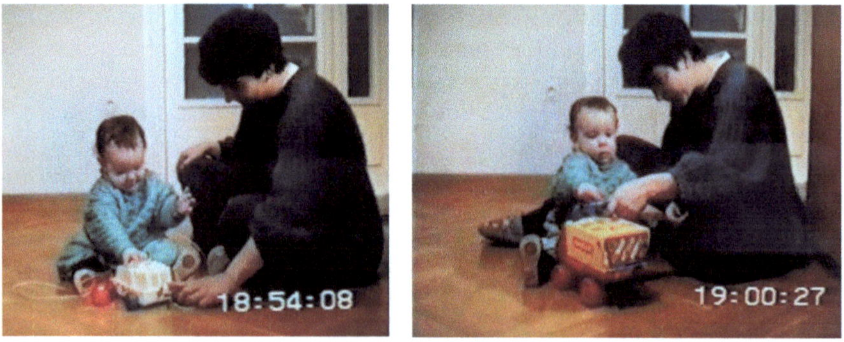

Fig. 2.1 The adult and J, aged 10 months, interact with a telephone and a truck with fitting pieces. By this age, J already took the initiative to use both objects according to their function on several occasions [81]

than suddenly. This makes sense: a mastered use is not abruptly replaced by an emerging one.

Had children remained anchored in their initial undifferentiated uses, such as sucking or shaking everything, their adaptation to the environment would have been compromised. It would be very difficult to reach agreements with others about what materiality is and what it means. This would impact communication, the ability to establish shared goals, and the understanding of others' actions and intentions. As we will see later, adults played a decisive role in this process of establishing consensus. Another interesting aspect is that no two children were the same, nor were any two dyads identical. Strictly speaking, each dyad was unique and followed "its own path."

Before concluding this section, I will refer to the findings of Dimitrova [26] in a longitudinal study conducted with children aged 8–16 months. Dimitrova found a positive relationship between mastery of object uses and children's production of gestures. Greater production of undifferentiated, non-conventional uses was associated with a lower tendency to produce communicative gestures directed toward adults. Conversely, there was a positive correlation between conventional uses and both explicit gestures and ambiguous gestures (although the latter showed a statistically weaker relationship). For Dimitrova, these results suggest that "when children begin to share common meanings with others regarding the referent (i.e., the object), they are already able to communicate intentionally through gestures" (p. 96). Thus, there appears to be a relationship between the shared meanings associated with object uses and the early communicative competencies of children (see Chap. 7 on gesture development).

This implies that constructing a *common ground*—a shared basis of understanding about the meaning of materiality—directly impacts intentional communication between adults and children. It becomes much easier to interpret the intentions of others when there is a *common ground* regarding the functions of material culture, compared to when such understanding has not yet been established.

To conclude this section, the distinction between object and use, along with evidence of different types of uses with varying levels of semiotic complexity in early development, challenges the notion of *affordance*, one of the most popular concepts in psychology since James Gibson [31] introduced it in his studies with adults. For Gibson, perception is direct, allowing individuals to see what objects enable (*afford*) without requiring representations. Let us now examine the limitations of *affordances* in early development.

2.2.2 Object and Use Do Not Coincide: Limits of the Concept of Affordance

No one today would argue that names naturally emanate from objects. The relationship between a name and its referent relies on convention, as Saussure argued in *Cours de linguistique générale* [Course in General Linguistics] [89] with his principle of the radical arbitrariness of the linguistic sign. However, a fusion often occurs between object and use, as if the object directly communicated its meaning and, consequently, how it should be used— as if it inherently carried its own instructions for use.

One of the central ideas of the Pragmatics of the Object, which has guided all research conducted to date, is that *object* and *use* do not coincide [60]. Objects do not inherently reveal how they should be used. The participation of others who possess this pragmatic knowledge is essential. Without this input, children would not be able to access the public meanings of objects or rely on the *common ground* we just discussed in relation to intentional communication. It is crucial to differentiate between what *can literally be done* with any object and what, by convention, *should be done* with it. These two aspects do not coincide, yet this distinction seems absent in the concept of *affordance*.

However, as we have been indicating, the distinction between what can physically be done with an object and what should be done is not intuitive for adults. An illustration of the "natural" and "obvious" consideration of objects can be found in Gallagher's [30] defense of enactivism. Drawing on Gibson, he asserts: "When, for example, I perceive something, I perceive it as actionable. That is, I perceive it as something I *can* reach, or not, something I *can* pick up, or not; something I *can* hammer with, or not, and so forth. If I perceive an event rather than an artifact, I perceive it as something I can intervene in, or not. Such affordances for potential actions (even if I am not planning to take action) shape the way that I actually perceive the world" [30, p. 33].

The difficulty with this argument is that the event Gallagher refers to pertains to what an adult with consolidated knowledge perceives as a potential for action. For adults, it is evident that objects have functional uses in daily life: a glass is a glass, and it is for drinking; a spoon is a spoon, and it is for eating. However, this is not obvious to children, as we can see when analyzing their behavior (whether acting alone or interacting with an adult).

In this regard, it is worth mentioning Alan Costall, a well-known author associated with Gibson's ecological traditions. However, Costall critiques Gibson by distinguishing between what he calls *affordances* "in general" and *canonical affordances*, the latter referring to the cultural and conventional dimensions of objects [21]. *Canonical affordances* are particularly relevant to artifacts and are both conventional and normative. This distinction is very useful in understanding that children lack the certainty adults have, as shown by the results just presented. To begin with, children do not perceive an artifact as such. This is why they start by doing what they physically can with objects, such as sucking on them. Children are not born pre-equipped to identify what objects are or what their functions might be—they must construct this understanding.

Therefore, the distinction between *object* and *object use* challenges the concept of *affordance*. It is true that Gibson's work brought a "breath of fresh air" by introducing dynamism into what he called the organism-environment relationship, which was of great interest to us at the time [81]. Perhaps this was partly due to his proximity to Piaget, as Alan Costall suggests when he states that "both Piaget and Gibson challenged the unworldliness of modern psychology by insisting on the primacy of being in the world or sensorimotor intelligence" [20, p. 85]. However, we encounter a significant problem: objects do *not* "speak." They do not tell children *directly what* they are, *how* they should be used, or *what* they are *for*. To paraphrase Piaget, objectivity is a result, attaining this pragmatic knowledge, essential for daily life, is not a starting point but a endpoint. In light of our data, objects seemed much more "opaque" than the concept of *affordance* suggests. One thing is what *can* physically be done with an object (like sucking on a telephone receiver), and another is what *should* conventionally be done (placing it to the ear to listen to someone speaking from a distance). These two types of uses often do not coincide and imply that children change their beliefs (as Peirce might say), make new inferences, and construct new representations of the shared meaning of objects. Using an object according to its function is a construction that involves representational changes—a representation that is the product of action and communication with others, as we will see later.

Valsiner [100] also critiques *affordances*, emphasizing the intentional subject with goals that are necessarily imaginary and represented: "Cultural psychology considers the affordances of objects not as givens, but as results of functional fit with future goals. The latter are necessarily imaginary. I make a tool now in order to act with it upon something in the future when the tool is ready, and assuming that the function it needs to fulfill is still actual at that time" (p. 152).

The distance that Moro and I initially took from the concept of affordance is further supported by symbolic uses, precisely because in symbols, the gap between object and use can expand as much as the subject decides. It is the subject, with their representations and specific goals, who determines what the object becomes—not necessarily its *affordances*. The case of a 15-month-old child pretending to drink from a replica horse [64] is a paradigmatic example (see Chap. 5 on symbols in this volume). It seems bizarre to claim that the "horse invites drinking" without acknowledging the child's representations, which led him to transform the horse into a cup.

The distinction between what can physically be done and what should conventionally be done with artifact objects [81] becomes evident when analyzing what children do with objects during their first year of life. This distinction is confirmed in later studies, as explored in various chapters of this volume, including rhythmic-sound uses (see Chap. 4), numerical uses (see Chap. 6), and uses in the context of autism spectrum conditions (see Chap. 12). An object is one thing, what is done with it is another. This creates a certain analogy between the names and the canonical uses of objects: neither emerges directly from the object itself. Both are mediated by a convention (obviously, to a greater extent in the case of names).

2.2.3 Canonical or Functional Uses: Objects as Signs of their Use

As mentioned earlier, semiotics has been of great help. Roland Barthes, the semioticians of *Group* μ, Umberto Eco, Wenceslao Castañares, and, of course, Peirce, have all shown interest in the significance of materiality within various aspects of daily life. This marks a significant distinction from Vygotsky, who focused primarily on intentionally produced signs, with language as the highest expression. Indeed, psychology has historically been, and continues to be, primarily interested in intentionally produced signs. As noted earlier, for *Group* μ, the notion of an object cannot be separated from the notion of sign, defined as a "*stable configuration* whose pragmatic role is to enable anticipations, calls, or substitutions" ([36, p. 81], emphasis ours).

Another advantage of Peirce's semiotics, or semiotics inspired by Peirce [27, 12], is that signs trigger inferences. Signs allow interpretations to extend beyond the sign itself, opening a highly suggestive realm for the subject's activity. Viewed this way, the sign becomes a starting point. Both ideas—the sign as inference and the object as sign—proved very useful in our research. What does this mean? In summary, I can say that the meanings children attribute to the objects used in our study change markedly when considering the progression of their uses at 7, 10, and 13 months. From the beginning, objects point to possible uses for a subject capable of achieving them. They trigger inferences that vary greatly in children depending on their developmental level, experience, and knowledge.

At the first level of signification, the object is "under construction." With non-canonical uses, children do not go very far. For example, as noted, they might suck on any object. These uses are undoubtedly important because they are the first to emerge and occur systematically. However, they do not rely on social rules; they are undifferentiated and can be applied to any object without considering its function as shared by the community. These uses do not invite communication with others. The inferences generated at this level would be of the following type:

If *any* object,
Then suck it, shake it. *Non-canonical* uses

The situation is very different when children already know what objects are for. The inferences they make are mediated by the knowledge they have acquired through experience. The inference they draw considers the object's public function. For instance, the inference triggered by a telephone begins to activate around 10 months and consolidates by 13 months (though not always): *If* telephone, *then* "I bring it to my ear to 'talk'" or "I hand it to my mother so she can talk." This use relies on a rule shared by users of telephones with receivers (even though modern mobile phones no longer have receivers separate from the main body). The function and meaning of the receiver as a receiver crystallize, becoming permanent. Once users understand the function of an object, the object becomes a *sign of its canonical use* (conventional or functional). It thus evokes a purpose for use—a set of practical goals that everyone understands and shares.

If that object,
Then, use it for its public function. *Canonical uses*

This aligns with the maxim of *Group* μ: "If our perception isolates *invariants* from the mass of sensory information, it is evidently based on *practical objectives*: these invariants serve as *a guide for the subject's action.* The properties of the object then become decision-making factors" [36, p. 80]. Objects thus become signs of their functional use for children, following specific rules. This means they no longer do just anything with an object. The certainty children gradually gain—that a receiver is used as a receiver—results from action and interaction with others about what that object signifies. It does not come from the object itself. This process involves a lengthy journey of adjustments, revisions, and back-and-forth transitions from undifferentiated uses to specific uses with precise objectives. As noted earlier, the change is significant but gradual.

In light of all this, I dare to assert that when an object first elicits the option, and later the necessity, for children to *use it according to its function*, it is because that object has already become a sign of its use (public and shared with others). This is a form of permanence that includes practical objectives of daily life and can be referred to as *functional permanence.* It differs from the classical concept of object permanence (which I will call "physical") so extensively studied in infancy. Without a doubt, physical (classical) permanence and functional permanence are fundamentally different in nature, and it would be essential to investigate the relationship between them. Let us now explore what functional permanence adds to this discussion.

2.2.4 Functional Permanence of Objects, Classes, and Cognitive Control

As discussed earlier, significant attention has been devoted to object permanence, partly because it forms, as Piaget noted, the foundation of our representation of the material world. We also observed that the various perspectives studying object permanence have largely overlooked the functional aspects of objects [83].

Another perspective on objects involves considering the permanence of their functional and pragmatic dimension. This idea is not new. For *Group* μ, the notion of an object is described as a "permanent and functional sum" [36, p. 79]. The functional and pragmatic nature of an object entails invariance—a permanence of "what objects are for" in daily life. For us, this requires investigating how the *functional permanence* of objects develops during infancy. This means identifying and analyzing when and how an object becomes a sign of its use, which is to say when it becomes a stable configuration for children. This has significant pragmatic consequences. As *Group* μ states, it opens the door to anticipation and facilitates interaction with others around a materiality whose meanings are shared. It also aids in understanding others' intentions when they act and communicate with children.

The sign prompts inferences that require the development of a system. Compared to the "physical" object permanence studied in psychology, the novelty of *functional permanence* lies in its foundation on practical objectives and the shared meanings of objects within human groups at specific moments in their cultural history. Functional permanence becomes the basis of our *representation of the material world in daily life*—its pragmatic aspects that enable setting objectives. It is rooted in the conventions constructed during the first year of life through agreements with others and reaches a critical point when consensus is established about *how to use the material world*. The progression into functional permanence is gradual.

With the objects used in the study [60, 81], functional permanence emerges around 10 months and stabilizes by 13 months. However, this process happens earlier for "less complex" or more frequently used everyday objects. For example, according to Baldwin [1], children recognize the bottle by around 4 months. They also recognize and use sound objects from 4 months [84], some basic musical instruments from 8 months ([77]; see Chap. 4 in this volume), and spoons for eating from 11 months ([80]; see Chap. 10 on EF in this volume).

Functional permanence is essential in daily life. It accounts for two key aspects: (1) Our relationship with materiality—what to do with it and for what purposes, (2) Our relationship with others—functional permanence provides *common references with shared meanings* (Latour calls it interobjectivity). This eliminates the problem of trivializing the referent and addresses Wittgenstein's difficulties regarding the subject's radical solipsism. The meanings related to the material world and possibilities for action are constructed in consensus with others. It could be argued that in addition to language, objects and their uses are also part of the "shared forms of life" Wittgenstein referred to—an idea that proved so valuable in the pragmatic turn of the second half of the twentieth century (see discussion in Rodríguez [73]).

As adults, we are so certain of belonging to a community of users that we do not feel the need to make it explicit. Having shared knowledge about the material world is indispensable not only for managing practical goals in daily life but also—and equally importantly—for interpreting the intentions of others as they act and communicate with us. Social psychologist Moghaddam [50] also discusses *interobjectivity* and posits a normative system that preexists individuals. To his question of how different individuals come to share an understanding of objective reality, we are, at least partially, providing an answer.

Another important consequence of entering a universe of socially shared rules regarding objects (and tools) is that when children use objects according to their function, they cease to interact with unique exemplars and begin relating to *members of classes*. These are the same classes that adults recognize. For example, if what defines a chair is that it serves for sitting, the stability of that possibility constitutes its *functional permanence*. It is the function— "it serves for sitting"—that unifies all chairs, regardless of their physical attributes such as shape, size, volume, color, texture, height, width, etc. Chairs were constructed with that purpose in mind. Thus, a relationship should be established between functional permanence and the origin of at least some types of concepts [83]. As Wallon stated: "*The origin of concepts* must not be sought in the schemas related to *immediate reactions that circumstances* provoke in any living being according to its level of organization. Concepts are not a *simple intellectual replica of these schemas. They belong to another system whose evolution is tied to the existence of human societies*" ([103, p. 72], emphasis and translation ours).

Functional permanence also necessarily impacts cognitive control and early executive functions. Once children know what an object is for, even if they struggle to use it effectively, the representation of the goal they are pursuing serves as a guide for their own actions. This enables them to persist, overcome difficulties, and maintain their objective—an objective that others can also understand. Thus, the functional permanence of objects (and tools) influences the emergence of symbols (see Chap. 5 in this volume), concepts, executive functions, and self-regulation (see Chap. 10 in this volume).

I will now address the influence of adults on children's development of functional and cultural uses of objects.

2.3 The Early Triangle. Children Acquire and Internalize the Function of Objects through Communication with Adults

As I mentioned earlier, one of our first decisions was to bring the child and the object out of the isolation in which Piaget and the Geneva School had placed them. By questioning the concept of *affordance*, we dismissed the idea that objects "directly tell how they should be used." If we wanted to investigate how children acquire the public meanings of objects, it was essential to consider the influence of adults. Although our focus was on the uses of objects and their development, we needed to broaden the scope of the subject-object interaction to include the adult as well. For this reason, we chose to study *triadic interactions—baby-object-adult* (the magic number three). The baby-object-adult triad became the unit of analysis at that time and has remained so, with some variations depending on new research questions, in studies conducted at home and, more recently, in early-years-schools.

The premise was clear: if objects do not inherently convey how they should be used, children acquire their public meanings through communication with others who act as custodians of material culture. If objects represent aspects of a culture that preexist individuals [50, 106], adults bring that tradition to life, facilitating its appropriation by children. Since the function of objects is not self-evident (even the simplest objects pose challenges when their purpose is unknown), children require the intentional actions of others who, to varying degrees and through diverse behaviors, act as guides. In this *early* triangle, the object becomes part of the communicative act between the adult and the child (see Clark [18], on redefining the communicative act). This means that *communication* and *joint action*, *with* objects and *about* them, are necessary for children to ascribe the social and public meanings shared by the community of users in which they live. The meaning of objects is constructed through communication and joint action, which is especially crucial in early development before language becomes the primary tool for communication.

The *early triangle* baby-object-adult, which we adopt as the unit of analysis, precedes and does not coincide with the so-called *triadic interactions* of the end of the first year when children intentionally communicate with others about events or objects [5, 98, 99].

Strictly speaking, the interaction between the baby, objects, and the adult begins at birth, when the adult lends their intentions to the child and incorporates them into their own intentional actions related to practical goals in contexts such as hygiene, caregiving, feeding, or play [72]. The child becomes part of an interactive triangle as a *user* of the material world long before they are aware of it, thanks to the adult's intentional actions [76].

Thus, despite focusing on the pragmatic turn of objects, we addressed communication from the beginning. The uses of objects were positioned at the intersection of communication between children and adults. The aim was to investigate the life that objects acquire when two subjects use them and communicate *with* and *through* them. Objects ceased to be external referents to the communicative act and instead became instruments of the communicative act itself. This occurred even though the knowledge of the adult and the baby was radically asymmetrical.

Without the arrival of Vygotsky's ideas in Geneva, I don't think we would have been able to make that leap and include the adult as a second protagonist. His thesis—that the path from the child to the world passes through another who acts as a mediator, a guide—partially represented a break with the hegemonic epistemological position in Geneva:

> [...] *the child's first contact with reality (even when fulfilling the most elementary biological functions) is socially mediated.* [...] *Objects appear and disappear from the child's visual field at the will of adults; the child is carried through space in the arms of others. Any change in posture, or even simply being turned over, is interwoven with the social situation.* Disturbing stimuli are removed, just as the child's basic needs are satisfied (through the same means), by others. ([102, p. 285], emphasis ours)

It would be unfair not to mention Wallon. Although his influence in Geneva was, paradoxically, much less than that of Vygotsky, Wallon also conceived of psychological development within the framework of the interactive triangle. According to Wallon, the "physical environment" and the "social environment" are, in fact, inseparable in an individual's perception; the former is perceived and "constructed" through "social frameworks" (Wallon, 1941, cited by Tap [94]), while the latter plays an intermediary or hinge-like role between the internal world and the concrete world of the environment. New voices from ecological traditions also reference the interactive triad. For instance, Costall and Leudar [22] critique the common image found in psychology textbooks of dyadic baby-adult interactions (where the adult is often depicted as the mother, not the father) as occurring in an artificial vacuum—without objects or context. They argue that adult-baby communication does not occur in a void but is situated in, and transformative of the surrounding world. More recently, Williams et al. [104] have focused on triadic interactions involving children on the autism spectrum.

As I mentioned in Chap. 1, we would not have been able to make much progress without Vygotsky (and Wallon). Both provided the epistemological foundations to expand the scope of the subject-object interaction characteristic of Geneva in the 1980s and to include the adult.

From the earliest investigations [60, 81], we examined situations in which objects became part of the communicative act between adults (referred to as A) and children. In these initial studies, A's interventions were numerous and highly adapted to each specific situation and the children's ages. The range of interventions included *preparing* materials before the children acted, *adjusting* in response to incomplete uses by the children, *distant demonstrations* (serving as a model of use), and *immediate demonstrations* (less frequent), such as guiding a child's hand to introduce them to a specific use. All adults communicated through *language*, accompanied by abundant *gestures*, which varied significantly depending on what the children were or were not capable of doing. The interventions of A were consistently effective in capturing the children's *attention*. Observing A's actions was well-established by 7 months. However, observing A did not guarantee that children correctly interpreted A's gestures or assigned the same meaning to the object as A, based on what the children *subsequently* did.

The effectiveness of A's attempts to involve children in object use or to encourage them to take the initiative varied significantly across the three ages studied. At 7 months, these efforts were largely ineffective. Children struggled greatly to interpret A's gestures when the adult tried to guide them toward functional uses. Only with strong support from A were children occasionally introduced to canonical and proto-canonical uses. At this age, A always took the initiative in using objects for their function; no child initiated such actions. By 10 months, however, children sometimes began taking the initiative themselves. They interpreted A's gestures more accurately and had a better understanding of practical objectives and what A expected of them—such as when an object was handed to them or pointed out. At 13 months, A's interventions increased and became more effective in eliciting canonical uses from the children. By this age, children interpreted A's gestures regarding expected uses much better and more frequently took the initiative than A (in 60% of cases).

The most frequent gestures produced by A were object ostensive gestures (primarily to give). These were followed by pointing gestures. A often exaggerated gestures, making them "attention-keeping" and redundant. For example, this included moving the object shown to the child, touching the referent while pointing at it (touch-pointing gesture), or repeating the pointing gesture multiple times (multiple pointing).

Objects progressively became *signs of their functional use*. At 7 and 10 months, once children took the object offered by A, they performed non-canonical uses, such as sucking on it. By 10 months, however, they also began to inhibit these non-canonical uses to engage in canonical uses (40.7%). By 13 months, when A handed them the objects, they no longer sucked on them. Functional, *canonical* uses had become consolidated (62%), along with a smaller proportion of *proto-canonical* uses (20.6%). This indicates that children shared the social meaning of objects with A to a greater extent, illustrating the progressive "pruning" of non-canonical uses mentioned earlier.

Another highly significant finding was that children in both studies did not appear to mechanically repeat what the adults did. What we observed instead was a progressive appropriation of meanings increasingly aligned with usage norms. Children only "imitated" A occasionally after a distant demonstration at 13 months. Before that age, imitation was very rare. This challenges the notion of "learning through imitation." Instead, the opposite seems to occur: children imitate only after reaching a certain level of understanding of the meanings.

Objects also lead to different forms of communication. The interaction between adults and babies varied depending on the referent object. This suggests that specific types of uses may require equally specific semiotic communication systems. For instance, with a telephone, verbal communication was more common, whereas touch-pointing gestures were more frequently produced when introducing fitting pieces into holes.

In conclusion, if objects have already become signs of their functional, canonical use, communicative gestures also become functional. Both developments indicate that children gain access to the semiotic systems related to artifacts with public meanings through intentional communicative semiotic systems in which objects are included as referents (see Chap. 7 on Gestures in this volume). These objects, in turn, are used within communicative situations. All of this occurs as the result of a constructive process that requires the active participation of both children and their mothers.

2.4 Conclusions

In this chapter, I have presented a brief synthesis of the core principles that structure the Pragmatics of the Object, tracing its origins to the Geneva School in the 1980s. We distanced ourselves from Piaget and our mentors in three essential aspects. First, we shifted the focus of objects toward pragmatics. This involved challenging the reduction of material objects to their physical properties by incorporating their social dimension and their public functions shared by a community of users. Objects are used to accomplish tasks in daily life, and navigating the material universe is essential for survival. Our adaptation to the environment depends on this ability. I have also referred to perspectives from anthropology, sociology, history, and semiotics that consider artifact objects as material culture and shared social knowledge. In early developmental psychology, this view of objects remains largely absent, even today. Our starting point was to ask how children come to attribute the public meaning objects hold in the specific contexts they inhabit. How do they come to use them according to their function? We assumed that children are not born knowing what objects are, what they mean, or how to use them.

Another central principle of the Pragmatics of the Object is that children progressively appropriate the social meanings of objects through communication with others who possess that knowledge. From the beginning, this led us to move away from the isolation in which the Geneva School had placed children (and objects) and to focus on the semiotic mediators implied in child–adult communication. We also distanced ourselves from the concept of *affordance*. Objects do not reveal everything. Objects are not self-evident. They do not inherently convey how they should be used functionally. To acquire such knowledge, another person must intervene to some degree. Thus, even though our focus was on the development of children's uses of objects, we became deeply involved in examining the communication between adults and children *with* and *about* objects. The triadic interaction of adult–child-object became our unit of analysis.

I have discussed the *functional permanence* of objects to add a pragmatic and social dimension to object permanence (which I have called "physical"), a concept extensively studied in infancy. As children begin to use certain everyday objects canonically, according to their function, during their first year, they stop treating them as unique exemplars. Objects become members of classes. For instance, "If I use *this* spoon for eating, I can use *any* spoon because it serves the *same* function." This shift has significant implications, marking an initial entry into the conceptualization of objects based on their shared uses. Objects become signs of their use (*if* this object, *then* I *use* it for its *function*). This knowledge is shared with other members of the community. Seeing objects as signs of social use not only enables effective navigation in the material world (I know what I can do) but also facilitates communication with others and understanding their intentions. This is based on a *common ground* that has been gradually constructed.

The early studies analyzed here highlighted that object and use do not coincide. An object is one thing, and the use made of it is another. Rodríguez and Moro [81], Moro and Rodríguez [60] identified three *types* of uses based on their semiotic complexity. Non-canonical uses, indiscriminate uses unrelated to the object's function. Proto-canonical uses that approximate the canonical function but do not fully achieve it, lying somewhere in between. Canonical or functional uses are when children identify both the meaning and the function of *that* object. Achieving canonical use can require a lengthy process of construction, depending on the complexity of the object. However, its origins are in everyday objects that occur within the first year of life. Using an object canonically or functionally means that it becomes permanent through its function.

Over the past 25 years, we have focused on studying other types of object (and tool) uses (see an initial synthesis in Rodríguez et al. [75]), which go beyond the canonical uses presented in this chapter. These new types of uses have opened up new lines of research. Their common denominators are the semiotic systems that account for the development of different types of uses and the communication surrounding them, the longitudinal designs, and microgenetic analyses, which focus on processes and allow for detailed observations of change, and the data collection in everyday settings, home or early-years-schools, and, in some cases, hospital and treatment contexts for children on the autism spectrum. Children and adults (parents, teachers, therapists) were always free to behave as the active and intentional subjects they are, even when specific studies required participation in certain "games." Another shared feature was the use of observation as a method, enabling us to understand the processes, the "life" of interactions, and child development. Below, I provide a brief summary of the new lines of research, which include the study of the development of new types of object (and tool) uses, the development of gestures, and the origins and early development of Executive Functions:

(i) *Rhythmic-sound uses* in hospital settings [63], at home [56, 57, 84], with premature infants in hospital environments [42], and in early-years-schools [19], (see Chap. 4 in this volume).
(ii) *Symbolic uses* at home in typical development [64, 66, 67] and atypical development [23], (see Chap. 5 in this volume).
(iii) *Metacanonical uses* in early-years-schools. These uses are midway between conventional uses (effective and functional) and symbolic uses (performed with an "inappropriate" object as a substitute). Metacanonical uses are highly creative, originating from functional permanence and, in the absence of the "appropriate" object, utilizing a substitute object while maintaining effectiveness and alignment with the goals of functional uses [74, 85].
(iv) *Numerical uses.* These represent a much more complex semiotic system that builds on the previous types of uses. Longitudinal studies conducted at home in triadic interactions involve children aged 24–36 months [16, 15], (see Chap. 6 in this volume).
(v) *Uses of objects in the autism spectrum* during triadic communicative situations [6, 7], (see Chap. 12 in this volume).

The origin and development of intentional communication through *gestures*, both at home [55, 73, 78] and in early-yesars-schools [37, 38], constitutes another area of research where objects are incorporated into the communicative act, (see Chap. 7 in this volume).

Finally, another line of research explores the origins of *self-regulation and Executive Functions*, both at home [3, 4, 82] and in early-years-schools [39, 53, 54, 70, 77]. Private gestures and the use of objects play a central role in the early manifestations of executive control, starting at the end of the first year of life (see Chaps. 8, 9, 10 and 11 in this volume) .

As noted earlier, over more than 20 years, a diverse group of researchers has expanded the Pragmatics of the Object with new areas of inquiry. The purpose of this book is to provide an account of these lines of research.

References

1. Baldwin, J. M. (1894/1968). *Mental development in the child and the race*. Augustus M. Kelley.
2. Barthes, R. (1957). *Mythologies*. Éditions du Seuil.
3. Basilio, M., & Rodríguez, C. (2011). Usos, gestos y vocalizaciones privadas: de la interacción social a la autorregulación [Private Uses, Gestures and Vocalizations: from Social Interaction to Self-regulation]. *Infancia y Aprendizaje, 34*, 181–194. https://doi.org/10.1174/021037011795377593
4. Basilio, M., & Rodríguez, C. (2017). How toddlers think with their hands: Social and private gestures as evidence of cognitive self-regulation in guided play with objects. *Early Child*

Development and Care, 187(12), 1971–1986. https://doi.org/10.1080/03004430.2016.1202944
5. Bates, E., Camaioni, L., & Volterra, V. (1975). The acquisition of performatives prior to speech. *Merril-Palmer Quarterly, 21*(3), 205–226.
6. Benassi, J. (2012). *Las concepciones de signo en los estudios de detección y desarrollo temprano de los Trastornos del Espectro Autista: Revisión teórica a la luz de una perspectiva pragmática del desarrollo temprano del niño* [Conceptions of Sign in Studies on the Detection and Early Development of Autism Spectrum Disorders: A Theoretical Review in Light of a Pragmatic Perspective on Early Childhood Development].(Master's Thesis). FLACSO–UAM, Bs.As. Retrieved from https://repositorio.flacsoandes.edu.ec
7. Benassi, J., & Rodríguez, C. (2020). The genesis of shared reference. A pragmatic perspective of autism. *Infancia y Aprendizaje, 43*(4), 779–792. https://doi.org/10.1080/02103702.2020.1814600
8. Bisault, J., Le Bourgeois, R., Thémines, J-F., Le Mentec, M., & Chauvet-Chanoine, C. (Eds.). (2022). *Objects to learn about and objects for learning 2.* Which Teaching practices for which issues? Wiley Online Library.
9. Bremner, G., Dunn, K., & Tham, D. S. Y. (2017). Perception, knowledge and action in infancy. In A. Slater & G. Bremner (Eds.), *An introduction to developmental psychology* (pp. 143–181, 3rd ed.). Wiley.
10. Bringuier, J.-C. (1977). *Conversations libres avec Jean Piaget [Informal Conversations with Jean Piaget].* Robert Laffont.
11. Cabra, M. (2021). *Gender differentiation in children's play: A sociocultural perspective.* Doctoral Thesis. Institute of Psychology and Education of the Faculty of Humanities. Université de Neuchâtel.
12. Castañares, W. (2002). Signo y representación en las teorías semióticas. [Sign and Representation in the Semiotics Theories] *Estudios de Psicología, 23*(3), 339–357.
13. Castañares, W. (2014). *Historia del pensamiento semiótico. 1 La Antigüedad grecolatina.* [History of Semiotic Thought. 1 The Greco-Roman Antiquity] Trotta.
14. Castañares, W., & Manetti, G. (Coord.) (2001). *Historia de la Semiótica. Homenaje a Umberto Eco* [History of Semiotics. In honnor to Umberto Eco]. DeSignis Serie Transformaciones. Editorial Una historia necesaria.
15. Cavalcante, S., & Rodríguez, C. (2015). La comprensión del dado como objeto con funciones numéricas. Un estudio longitudinal con dos niños de los 24 a los 36 meses en interacción con un adulto [The Understanding of the Die as an Object with Numerical Functions: A Longitudinal Study with Two Children from 24 to 36 Months in Interaction with an Adult]. *Estudios de Psicología, 36*, 48–70.
16. Cavalcante, S., Rodríguez, C., & Martí, E. (2019). Early understanding of cardinal number value: Semiotic, social, and pragmatic dimensions in a case study with a child from 2 to 3 years old. *Integrative Psychological and Behavioral Science, 53*, 397–417. https://doi.org/10.1007/s12124-018-9464-4
17. Chibaudel, Q., Dimitrov, L, Oriola, B., Jouffrais, C., Fibigerova, K., & Tartas, V. (2022). Professional report: From tangible objects to interactive maps for moving around and learning an área—Two examples with people with visual impairments. In J. Bisault, R. Le Bourgeois, J-F. Thémines, M. LeMentec, & C. Chauvet-Chanoine (Eds.), *Objects to learn about and objects for learning 2* (p. 95–110). Wiley Online Library.
18. Clark, H. (2003). Pointing and placing. In S. Kita (Ed.), *Pointing: Where language, culture and cognition meet* (pp. 243–268). Lawrence Erlbaum.
19. Correa, M., Villalobos, M. E., Cárdenas, K., Moreno-Llanos, I., Del Olmo, M. J., & Moreno-Nuñez, A. (2021). Usos rítmico-sonoros de objetos e instrumentos musicales en las aulas 0–1 y 1–2 [Rhythmic and Sound Uses of Objects and Musical Instruments in 0–1 and 1–2 Classrooms]. En C. Rodríguez & J. L. de los Reyes (Coords.) *Los objetos sí importan. Acción educativa en la escuela infantil* (pp. 57–82). Horsori.

20. Costall, A. (2004). From direct perception to the primacy of action: A closer look at James Gibson's ecological approach to psychology. In G. Bremner & A. Slater (Eds.), *Theories of infant development* (pp. 70–89). Blackwell.
21. Costall, A. (2012). Canonical affordances in context. *AVANT, III*(2), 85–93. http://hdl.handle.net/20.500.12424/142464
22. Costall, A., & Leudar, I. (2007). Getting over "the problema of other minds": Communication in context. *Infant Behavior & Development, 30*, 289–295.
23. Cárdenas, K., Rodríguez, C., & Palacios, P. (2014). First symbols in a girl with Down syndrome: A longitudinal study from 12 to 18 months. *Infant Behavior and Development, 37*, 416–427. https://doi.org/10.1016/j.infbeh.2014.06.003
24. De los Reyes, J. L. (2022). A cultural viewpoint about objects: Objects that narrate cultures and emotions. In J. Bisault, R. Le Bourgeois, J-F. Thémines, M. LeMentec, & C. Chauvet-Chanoine (Eds.), *Objects to learn about and objects for learning 2* (Chapter 10, pp. 213–227). Wiley Online Library.
25. Diamond, A. (1985). Development of the ability to use recall to guide action, as indicated by infants' performance on A-no-B. *Child Development, 56*, 868–883.
26. Dimitrova, N. (2014). L'usage de l'objet, un lieu privilégié d'émergence de la communication intentionnelle chez l'enfant [The Use of Objects as a Privileged Site for the Emergence of Intentional Communication in Children]. In C. Moro & N. Muller Mirza (Eds.), *Sémiotique, culture et développement psychologique* (pp. 79–98). Presses Universitaires du Septentrion.
27. Eco, U. (1973/1988). *Signo [Sign]*. Labor.
28. Everaert-Desmedt, N. (2000). *Sémiotique du récit [Semiotics of Narrative]*. DeBoeck Université.
29. Faust, T. E., Gunner, G., & Schafer, D. P. (2021). Mechanisms governing activity-dependent synaptic pruning in the developing mammalian CNS. *Nature Reviews, 22*, 657–673. https://www.nature.com/articles/s41583-021-00507-y
30. Gallagher, S. (2020). *Action and interaction*. Oxford University Press.
31. Gibson, J. J. (1979). *The ecological approach to visual perception*. Houghton-Mifflin.
32. Gillièron, C. (1985). *La construction du réel chez le psychologue. Epistémologie et méthodes en sciences humaines [The Construction of Reality in the Psychologist: Epistemology and Methods in the Human Sciences]*. Peter Lang.
33. Glaveanu, V. P. (2018). The sociocultural study of creative action. In A. Rosa & J. Valsiner (Eds.), *Cambridge handbook of sociocultural psychology* (2nd ed., pp. 163–177). Cambridge University Press.
34. González-Ruibal, A. (2004). Artistic expression and material culture in Celtic Gallaecia, *e-Keltoi: Journal of Interdisciplinary Celtic Studies, 6*, 113–166. https://dc.uwm.edu/ekeltoi/vol6/iss1/3
35. González-Ruibal, A., Hernando, A., & Politis, G. (2011). Ontology of the self and material culture: Arrow-making among the Awá hunter-gatherers (Brazil). *Journal of Anthropological Archaeology, 30*, 1–6. https://doi.org/10.1016/j.jaa.2010.10.001
36. Groupe μ (1992). *Traité du signe visual. Pour une réthorique de l'image* [Treatise on the Visual Sign: Toward a Rhetoric of the Image]. Seuil.
37. Guevara, I., Moreno-Llanos, I., Romero, L., Zapardiel, L., & Rodríguez, C. (2022). Challenges in first-years school: Early manifestations of executive function. In J. Bisault, R. Le Bourgeois, J. F. Thémines, M. Le Mentec, & C. Chauvet-Chanoine (Eds.), *Objects to learn about and objects for learning 2. Which teaching practices for which issues?* (pp. 193–209). ISTE-Wiley.
38. Guevara, I., & Rodríguez, C. (2023). Developing communication through objects: Ostensive gestures as the first gestures in children's development. *Developmental Review, 68*, 101076. https://doi.org/10.1016/j.dr.2023.101076
39. Guevara, I., Rodríguez, C., & Núñez, M. (2024). Developing gestures in the infant classroom: From showing and giving to pointing. *European Journal of Psychology of Education, 39*, 4671–4702. https://doi.org/10.1007/s10212-024-00895-6

40. Iannaccone, A., Savarese, G., Manzi, F., & Mollo, M. (Eds.). (2021). Sociomateriality in children with typical and/or atypical development. Frontiers Media SA. https://doi.org/10.3389/978-2-88966-434-4
41. Inhelder, B., Lézine, I., Sinclair, H., & Stambak, M. (1972). Les débuts de la fonction symbolique [The Beginnings of the Symbolic Function]. *Archives de Psychologie, 41*, 187–243.
42. Jáñez-Álvarez, M., Moreno-Llanos, I., Santacatalina-Pulido, C., De León-Barrios, Y. J., García-Laredo, E., Del Olmo, M. J., & Rodríguez, C. (2024). Analysis of triadic interaction between parents, their preterm infants, and a sonorous object. *Psychology of Music*. https://doi.org/10.1177/03057356231225673
43. Latour, B. (1996). On interobjectivity. *Mind, Culture and Activity, 3*(4), 228–245.
44. Layton, R. (2006). Structuralism and semiotics. In C. Tilley, W., Keane, S. Küchler, M. Rowlands, & P. Spyer (Eds.), *Handbook of material culture* (pp. 29–42). Sage.
45. Manzi, F., Savarese, G., Mollo, M., & Iannaccone, A. (2020). Objects as Comunicative Mediators in children with autism spectrum disorder. *Frontiers in Psychology, 11*, Article 1269. https://doi.org/10.3389/fpsyg.2020.01269
46. Martí, E. (2022). *Comportamientos que nos hacen humanos. Una mirada desde la Psicología Evolutiva.* [Behaviors That Make Us Human: A Perspective from Developmental Psychology]. Horsori.
47. Martí, E., Salsa, A., & Scheuer, N. (2024). *Cuando los niños se encuentran con los primeros números. Investigaciones en clave constructivista.* [When Children Encounter Their First Numbers: Research from a Constructivist Perspective]. Miño y Dávila.
48. Miettinen, R., & Paavola, S. (2018). Beyond the distinction between tool and sign: Objects and artifacts in human activity. In A. Rosa & J. Valsiner (Eds.), *Cambridge handbook of sociocultural psychology* (2nd ed., pp. 148–162). Cambridge University Press.
49. Miller, S. E., & Marcovitch, S. (2015). Examining executive function in the second year of life: Coherence, stability, and relations to joint attention and language. *Developmental Psychology, 51*(1), 101–114. https://doi.org/10.1037/a0038359
50. Moghaddam, F. M. (2003). Interobjectivity and culture. *Culture & Psychology, 9*(3), 221–232.
51. Montoya, R. (2024). *Pompeya. Una ciudad romana en 100 objetos.* [Pompeii. A Roman City in 100 Objects]. Crítica.
52. Moore, K., & Meltzoff, A. (1999). New findings on object permanence: A developmental diferente between two types of occlusion. *British Journal of Developmental Psychology, 17*, 563–584.
53. Moreno-Llanos, I., Guevara, I., Palacios, P., & Rodríguez, C. (2024). How to study the early development of executive function? Let's put control back in the hands of children. *New Ideas in Psychology*. https://doi.org/10.1016/j.newideapsych.2023.101049
54. Moreno-Llanos, I., Zapardiel, L., & Rodríguez, C. (2021). Children's first manifestations of cognitive control in the early years school: the importance of the educational situation and materiality. *European Journal of Psychology of Education*. https://doi.org/10.1007/s10212-020-00505-1
55. Moreno-Núñez, A., Rodríguez, C., & Miranda-Zapata, E. D. (2020). Getting away from the point: The emergence of ostensive gestures and their functions. *Journal of Child Language, 47*(3), 556–578. https://doi.org/10.1177/03057356231225673
56. Moreno-Núñez, A., Rodríguez, C., & Del Olmo, M. J. (2015). The rhythmic, sonorous and melodic components of adult–child–object interactions between 2 and 6 months old. *Integrative Psychological and Behavioral Science, 49*(4), 737–756. https://doi.org/10.1007/s12124-015-9298-2
57. Moreno-Núñez, A., Rodríguez, C., & Del Olmo, M. J. (2017). Rhythmic ostensive gestures: How adults facilitate infants' entrance into early triadic interactions. *Infant Behavior and Development, 49*, 168–181. https://doi.org/10.1016/j.infbeh.2017.09.003
58. Moro, C. (2015). Material culture: Still 'Terra Incognita' for psychology today? *Europe's Journal of Psychology, 11*(2), 172–176. https://doi.org/10.5964/ejop.v11i2.995

59. Moro, C. (2016). To encounter, to build the world and to become a human being. Advocating for a Material-Cultural turn in developmental psychology. *Integrative Psychological and Behavioral Sciences, 50*, 586–602.
60. Moro, C., & Rodríguez, C. (2005). *L'objet et la construction de son usage. Une approche sémiotique du développement préverbal.* [The Object and the Construction of Its Use: A Semiotic Approach to Preverbal Development]. Peter Lang.
61. Munakata, Y., McClelland, J. L., Johnson, M. H., & Siegler, R. S. (1997/2014). Rethinking Infant Knowledge: Toward an adaptive process account of successes and failures in object permanence tasks. In J. G. Bremner & A. M. Slater (Eds.), *Psychology of infancy. Vol. 4. cognitive development: From Piaget to the developing theory of mind* (pp. 53–112). Sage.
62. Munch, A. M. (2014). Apprendre et "faire ouvre" dans les institutions de la petite enfance [Learning and "Creating" in Early Childhood Institutions]. In C. Moro & N. Müller-Mirza (Eds.), *Sémiotique, culture et développement psychologique* (pp. 159–176). Presses Universitaires du Septentrion.
63. Del Olmo, M. J., Rodríguez, C., & Ruza, F. (2010). Music therapy in the PICU: 0 to 6 month-old babies. *Music and Medicine, 2*(3), 158–166.
64. Palacios, P., & Rodríguez, C. (2015). The development of symbolic uses of objects in infants in a triadic context: A pragmatic and semiotic perspective. *Infant and Child Dvelopment, 24*, 23–43. https://doi.org/10.1002/icd.1873
65. Palacios, P., Rodríguez, C., & Méndez-Sánchez, C. (2018). Communicative mediation by adults in the construction of symbolic uses by infants. *Integrative Psychological and Behavioral Science.* https://doi.org/10.1007/s12124-018-9422-1
66. Palacios, P., Rodríguez, C., Méndez-Sánchez, C., Hermosillo, A. E., Sahagún, M. A., & Cárdenas, K. (2016). Desarrollo de los primeros usos simbólicos en niños mexicanos desde la Pragmática del Objeto [The development of the first symbolic uses in Mexican children from the pragmatics of object]. *Estudios de Psicología, 37*, 59–89. https://doi.org/10.1080/02109395.2015.1122437
67. Palacios, P., Yuste, N., & Cárdenas, K. (2021). Los símbolos en la escuela infantil [Symbols in Early Childhood Education]. In C. Rodríguez & J. L. de los Reyes (Eds.), *Los objetos sí importan. Acción educativa en la Escuela Infantil* (pp. 109–132). Horsori.
68. Piaget, J. (1937/1977). *La construction du réel chez l'enfant [The Construction of Reality in the Child].* Delachaux et Niestlé.
69. Piaget, J. (1949/1973). *Introduction à l'épistémologie génétique. [Introduction to Genetic Epistemology]1/La pensée mathématique.* PUF.
70. Rengifo-Herrera, F. J., Mietto, G., Nascimento-Dias, P. Gerbassi. T., & De Melo, C. (2024) Os objetos, a mediação de adultos e seu papel nos processos de desenvolvimento e educação em crianças pequenas. [Objects, Adult Mediation, and Their Role in the Development and Education of Young Children]. En F. Negreiros, & J. F. Patiño (Orgs.), *Psicologia escolar na América Latina: rumos e desafios* (pp. 18). Átomo & Alínea.
71. Rivière, A. (1985). *La Psicología de Vygotski [Vygotsky's Psychology.].* Visor.
72. Rodríguez, C. (2006). *Del ritmo al símbolo. Los signos en el nacimiento de la inteligencia [From Rhythm to Symbol: Signs in the Birth of Intelligence.].* Horsori.
73. Rodríguez, C. (2009). The 'circumstances' of gestures: Proto-interrogatives and private gestures. *New Ideas in Psychology, 27*, 288–303.
74. Rodríguez, C. (2022). The construction of executive function in early development: The pragmatics of action and gestures. *Human Development, 66*, 239–259. https://doi.org/10.1159/000526340
75. Rodríguez, C., Basilio, M., Cárdenas, K., Cavalcante, S., Moreno-Núñez, A., Palacios, P., & Yuste, N. (2018). Objects pragmatics: Culture and communication—The bases for early cognitive development. In A. Rosa & J. Valsiner (Eds.), *The Cambridge handbook of sociocultural psychology* (2nd ed., pp. 223–244). Cambridge University Press.
76. Rodríguez, C., Benassi, J., Estrada, L., & Alessandroni, N. (2017). Early social interactions with people and objects. In A. Slater & G. Bremner (Eds.), *An introduction to developmental psychology* (3rd ed., pp. 213–257). Wiley.

77. Rodríguez, C., & Moreno-Llanos, I. (2023). A pragmatic turn in the study of early executive functions by object use and gestures. A case study from 8 to 17 months of age at a nursery school. *Integrative Psychological and Behavioral Science, 57*, 607–654. https://doi.org/10.1007/s12124-020-09578-5
78. Rodríguez, C., Moreno-Núñez, A., Basilio, M., & Sosa, N. (2015). Ostensive gestures come first: Their role in the beginning of shared reference. *Cognitive Development, 36*, 142–149.
79. Rodríguez, C. (2007). Object use, communication and signs: The triadic basis of early cognitive development. In J. Valsiner & A. Rosa (Eds.), *The Cambridge handbook of socio-cultural psychology* (pp. 257–276). Cambridge University Press.
80. Rodríguez, C., Estrada, L., Moreno-Llanos, I., & De los Reyes, J. L. (2017). Executive functions and educational actions in an Infant School: Private uses and gestures at the end of the first year. *Studies in Psychology, 38*(2), 385–423. https://doi.org/10.1080/02109395.2017.1305061
81. Rodríguez, C., & Moro, C. (1999). *El mágico número tres. Cuando los niños aún no hablan [The Magic Number Three: When Children Still Do Not Speak]*. Paidós.
82. Rodríguez, C., & Palacios, P. (2007). Do private gestures have a self-regulatory function? A case study. *Infant Behavior and Development, 30*(2), 180–194. https://doi.org/10.1016/j.infbeh.2007.02.010
83. Rodríguez, C. (2012). The functional permanence of the object: A product of consensus. In E. Martí & C. Rodríguez (Eds.), *After Piaget* (pp. 123–150). Transaction Publishers.
84. Rodríguez, C., & Moro, C. (2008). Coming to agreement: Object use by infants and adults. In J. Zlatev, T. Racine, C. Sinha, & E. Itkonen (Eds.), *The shared mind: Perspectives on intersubjectivity* (pp. 89–114). John Benjamins. https://doi.org/10.1075/celcr.12
85. Rodríguez, C. (2023). La acción y los gestos, protagonistas en el origen de las Funciones Ejecutivas [Action and Gestures: Key Players in the Origin of Executive Functions]. In M. Orozco-Hormaza, E., Cerchiaro-Ceballos & J.C. Ossa (Eds), *¡Sí hubo futuro en el pasado! Aportes de Rebeca Puche-Navarro a la construcción de la psicología en Colombia* (pp. 92–131). Editorial ASCOFAPSI.
86. Rosa, A., & Valsiner, J. (Eds.). (2018). *The Cambridge handbook of sociocultural psychology* (2nd ed.). Cambridge University Press.
87. Saada-Robert, M. (1985). Changements de significations et de guidage de l'action chez l'enfant en situation de résolution de problème [Changes in Meaning and Guidance of Action in Children During Problem-Solving Situations]. *Archives de Psychologie, 53*(207), 395–398.
88. Saada-Robert, M. (1992). La construction microgénétique d'un schème élémentaire [The Microgenetic Construction of a Basic Scheme]. In B. Inhelder, G. Cellérier, E. Ackermann, A. Blanchet, A. Boder, D. De Caprona, J.-J. Ducret, & M. Saada-Robert. *Le cheminement des découvertes de l'enfant. Recherche sur les microgenèses cognitives* (pp. 119–137). Delachaux et Niestlé.
89. Saussure (De) F. (1916/1985). *Cours de linguistique générale [Course in General Linguistics]*. Edition critique préparée par Tullio de Mauro. Payot.
90. Sinha, C. (2014). Signification et matérialité: Le langage au fondement des artefacts symboliques [Meaning and Materiality: Language as the Foundation of Symbolic Artifacts]. In C. Moro & N. Muller Mirza (Eds.), *Sémiotique, culture et développement psychologique* (pp. 117–138). Presses Universitaires du Septentrion.
91. Slater, A., & Bremner, G. (Eds.). (2017). *An introduction to developmental psychology* (3rd ed.). Wiley
92. Smith, L. (2005). Cognition as a dynamic system: Principles from embodiment. *Developmental Review, 25*, 278–298. https://doi.org/10.1016/j.dr.2005.11.001
93. Spelke, E. S. (2022). *What babies know* (Vol. 1). Oxford University Press.
94. Tap, P. (1981). La socialization de l'enfant selon Wallon [The Socialization of the Child According to Wallon]. In H. Wallon (Ed.), *Hommage à Henri Wallon, pour le centenaire de sa naissance*. Université de Toulouse-Le Mirail (pp. 81–96). http://www.pierretap.com/pdfs/39.pdf

95. Thelen, E., & Smith, L. (1994/1998). *A dynamic systems approach to the development of cognition and action*. The MIT Press.
96. Tilley, C. (2006). Objectification. In In C. Tilley, W., Keane, S. Küchler, M. Rowlands, & P. Spyer (Eds.), *Handbook of material culture* (pp. 60–73). Sage.
97. Tilley, C., Keane, W., Küchler, S., Rowlands, M., & Spyer, P. (Eds.). (2006). *Handbook of material culture*. Sage.
98. Tomasello, M. (2014). *A natural history of human thinking*. Harvard University Press.
99. Trevarthen, C., & Hubley, P. (1978). Secondary intersubjectivity: Confidence, confiding and acts of meaning in the first year. In A. Lock (Ed.), *Action, gesture and symbol: The emergence of language*. Academic Press.
100. Valsiner, J. (2014). *An invitation to cultural psychology*. Sage Publications.
101. Vygotski, L.S. (1934/1985). *Pensée et Langage*. [*Thought and language*]. Editions Sociales.
102. Vygotski, L. (1984/1996). El primer año [The First Year]. In L. Vygotski (Ed.), *Obras escogidas IV. Psicología infantil* (pp. 275–318). Visor.
103. Wallon, H. (1942/1970). *De l'acte à la pensée [From Action to Thought]*. Flammarion.
104. Williams, E., Costall, A., & Reddy, V. (2018). Autism and triadic play: An object lesson in the mutuality of the social and material. *Ecological Psychology, 30*(2), 143–173. https://doi.org/10.1080/10407413.2018.1439140
105. Woodward, I. (2007). *Understanding material culture*. Sage Publications.
106. Woodward, S. (2013). *Material culture*. Recuperado Noviembre 2024, de https://www.oxfordbibliographies.com/display/document/obo-9780199766567/obo-9780199766567-0085.xml; https://doi.org/10.1093/OBO/9780199766567-0085
107. Woodward, S., & Mayr, C. (2023). Secret objects in the home: Potency, (in)visibility and everyday relationships. *Cultural Sociology, 18*(3) 354–369. https://doi.org/10.1177/17499755231151203

3 Methodological Approach to the Study of Early Development from the Pragmatics of the Object

Pedro Palacios, Iván Moreno-Llanos, Irene Guevara, and Cintia Rodríguez

Methodology is a crucial aspect for scientific research. The method employed by a researcher to collect and analyze obtained data involves an exercise in transparency, reliability, and replicability. Theory and method go hand in hand and enrich each other.

The Pragmatics of the Object, as a theoretical and epistemological perspective, proposes a research method primarily (but not exclusively) based on the methodology developed at the Geneva School since Piaget's studies [15, 16]. Our methodological proposal to understand development is based on microgenetic, situated, and longitudinal observation. This means the systematic and longitudinal observation of children's actions in their everyday contexts. In this sense, the child is conceived as an active agent, interacting spontaneously with their reference figures (parents, teachers), solving everyday problems, and building knowledge and skills through these experiences.

This methodology permeates the various investigations conducted from the Pragmatics of the Object, adapting specifically to the particularities of each study. Adjustments are made based on the research questions and the contexts in which we have studied early development. Throughout this chapter, we will present and

P. Palacios (✉)
Universidad Autónoma de Aguascalientes, Aguascalientes, Mexico
e-mail: pedro.palacios@edu.uaa.mx

I. Moreno-Llanos · C. Rodríguez
Universidad Autónoma de Madrid, Madrid, Spain

I. Guevara
Department of Psychology, Universidad Antonio Nebrija, Madrid, Spain

C. Rodriguez Garrido et al. (eds.), *The Social Life of Objects in Early Development*, Social Interaction in Learning and Development,
https://doi.org/10.1007/978-3-031-87673-8_3

elaborate on the epistemological foundations of our methodology, detailing the decisions they involve for data collection and analysis.

3.1 Epistemological Foundations

In this first part, we will present the epistemological foundations that inform our methodological proposal. Specifically, we will outline the considerations regarding research that we have taken into account to design the procedures for data collection and analysis. We will emphasize the role of the child as an active agent who interacts and develops through triadic interactions and the role of semiotics in designing our observation categories.

3.1.1 The Active Subject

The cornerstone of our research lies in considering the child as an active agent subject who acts in the real world with specific objects. In the microgenetic methodology, the child is seen as a subject with initiative, actively participating in situations and seeking solutions to encountered problems. During development, particularly during the sensorimotor stage (0–24 months), the relationship between the child's transformative actions in the world and their cognitive development is very tight. What children do nourishes their knowledge structures, which in turn guide their subsequent actions [15].

To understand children as agents means studying them in their everyday situations. Gould [9] takes this a step further, arguing that removing the subject from their daily contexts and designing laboratory-based studies destroys the subject of investigation. To study the child as an active subject, we do not impose external or arbitrary objectives based on equally arbitrary instructions that rigidly organize children's actions [2]. Instead, we observe their actions within a material proposal or in spontaneous situations, with their usual caregivers. In our studies, these caregivers are typically their parents or teachers.

In studies conducted at home, everyday objects are presented that can be used to investigate the cognitive process of interest, creating *structured observations*. For example, the maraca is a musical instrument that facilitates early triadic interactions starting at two months of age (see Chap. 4 in this volume). Telephones and shape-sorting trucks enable studies of the development of conventional uses of objects ([19], see Chap. 2 in this volume). To study the development of symbolic uses, sets of replica objects, such as a toy horse or artifacts such as a wooden spoon, are introduced (see Chap. 5 in this volume). For studying numerical uses, a game was organized with a replica horse that moves according to the number indicated by a die (see Chap. 6 in this volume). These are just a few examples.

In the early years school, by contrast, we aimed to observe what happens during daily activities organized by the teachers. Therefore, we did not propose specific material objects that needed to be used. This *semi-structured* observation allowed us to explore the richness of the teachers' material proposals and the developmental objectives they work on in the classroom. This approach opened the door to studying a variety of developmental processes, such as rhythmic-sound uses (see Chap. 4 in this volume), symbolic uses among peers (see Chap. 5 in this volume), gestures (see Chap. 7 in this volume), and executive functions (see Chaps. 10 and 11 in this volume).

In both contexts—home and early years school—we maintained the premise that children should have the opportunity to act and interact spontaneously, setting their own goals and interests and guiding interactions accordingly. For this reason, we consistently used instructions such as "act with your child as you normally would" or "act with the children as you normally would." This approach avoided situations where children were required to respond to externally imposed stimuli by researchers. Instead, we observed the process of knowledge construction through their actions and interactions with others.

To minimize reactivity [12], we spent time ensuring that the child became familiar with the presence of the researcher and the camera, so they felt comfortable with us. At home, this involved organizing one or two visits before starting the observation. In early years schools, we utilized the first month of the school year—considered an adaptation period—for children to familiarize themselves with us and the camera. Lastly, we aimed to be "boring" to the child, remaining as inconspicuous as possible, so as not to interfere with their activity.

3.1.2 Triadic Interaction: Action and Communication with and Through Objects

Although Piaget's constructivist theory has been fundamental to our understanding of early development, Piaget tends to present the child as a lone, epistemic subject, who interacts with the world to build formal knowledge structures. In contrast, Vygotsky's sociocultural theory [23, 24] highlights the important role of interaction with others in early development. From the perspective of the Pragmatics of the Object, we also find it essential to include objects within social and cultural frameworks, where their shared functions and meanings become evident. Children's development cannot be understood separately from the social interactions in which they participate. The role of adults as mediators is fundamental in enabling children to access these shared meanings.

Therefore, the child should not be considered a subject that develops in isolation, but rather in constant social interaction. Children develop through social interactions with significant others, such as parents or teachers, around a common referent. This also entails understanding the child as an active participant in the interaction—capable of initiating actions, interacting, communicating, and pursuing goals.

Child-object-adult interactions are referred to as triadic interactions (explored in detail in Chap. 4 of this volume). As noted by Palacios et al. [14], communication and educational processes are essentially triadic. They require active subjects in interaction, who emit and interpret signs related to a specific referent. These signs are produced, updated, and transformed during the interaction.

Rodríguez and Moro [19] argue that the triadic unit of analysis refers to a methodological unit that defines the boundaries of observation. This unit aligns with the epistemological stance presented earlier, in which the construction of meanings (and knowledge) results from the semiotic mediation that occurs within communication with others about a shared referent. In other words, the adult mediates the relationship between the child and the object. Adults play a crucial role in creating activities in which children encounter objects and regulate their participation with those objects. For example, adults may redirect, adjust, promote, complete, or even inhibit a child's actions, thereby enabling (or hindering) their development.

Using the triadic unit of analysis in our research implies analyzing the child-object-adult interaction as a unified whole. The triadic nature of this unit allows us to observe the dynamics of relationships between its components at any given moment, as well as the transformations of these elements and their relationships throughout development. A consistent feature of our studies is that the adult and child have asymmetrical positions regarding their knowledge and use of semiotic mediators. This asymmetry influences the configuration and dynamics of triadic interactions, as well as the type of participation each one assumes within the triad. Such asymmetry creates the conditions for the adult to provide mediation or guide the child's development [14]. For instance, the communication and interaction between the adult and child around an object will vary depending on the object in question and the developmental stage of the shared meaning-making process [14]. These relationships will, in turn, differ at subsequent stages of development.

At home, the child-object-adult triad is relatively constant and stable. Therefore, in our studies, we exclude sequences in which children act in dyads, either solely with their parent or solely with an object, without coordinating both elements. However, in eary years schools, the triad is more diffuse. In Madrid, Spain, early childhood education spans the first six years of life and is regulated by law. In the first cycle of early childhood education (0–3 years), each teacher is responsible for eight children in the 0–1-year-old classroom and twelve children in the 1–2-year-old classroom.[1] This presents a significant challenge. Studying only "pure" triadic interactions, in which all three elements are active simultaneously, would result in a limited number of very brief sequences restricted to specific moments.

In early years schools, we had to acknowledge that the teacher's influence is constant. The organization of space, available materials, and planned activities are integral parts of the teacher's educational actions, alongside their "online"

[1] The terms 0–1, 1–2, and 2–3 years are colloquial but widely accepted. They refer to the first, second, and third years of the first cycle of early childhood education in Spain, respectively, rather than the actual ages of the children. Children can begin the first year in September at ages ranging from 4 months (those born in April or May of the previous school year) to 8 months (those born in January). Additionally, children born between May and December may start the first year at any time (with some exceptions), always beginning at a minimum age of 4 months.

educational interactions with children. Therefore, it is common to observe and analyze children's actions with objects in dyads (with objects or teachers), while recognizing the teacher's educational influence throughout the session. This has been particularly relevant in studies on gestures and executive functions (see Chaps. 7–11 in this volume).

Thus, in our studies, we always consider the triadic relationship. Even when the child occasionally acts alone in seemingly dyadic situations, we account for the adult's educational and communicative influence on their development. Next, we address signs as the mediators enabling triadic interaction.

3.1.3 Semiotics

Triadic interactions occur through semiotic mediation, meaning through the use of sign systems. The ability to use signs is closely linked to representation and communication [10]. Assigning meaning to the world around us allows us to establish a relative stability [19]. Without meaning, we would navigate a chaotic, disordered, and unpredictable world. Therefore, in our studies, we have included the analysis of meaning within the processes of early communication and cognitive development. Peirce's semiotics (see [10]) has been a source of inspiration, as it allows us to include objects in the processes of communication and thought. Unlike other semiotic theories, Peirce developed a theory encompassing all forms of meaning-making—not only language but also less conventional and structured forms, such as action, gestures, emotions, and material reality.

However, a detailed exploration of Peirce's semiotics is beyond the scope of this chapter. For now, suffice it to say that, according to Peirce, every sign is anchored, in some sense, in reality. That is, the sign relates to a known object, situation, or phenomenon that it represents. Moreover, every sign exists as such only when a mind assigns it meaning—that is, interprets it. Peirce's perspective enables us to study the signs children and adults use throughout development in their triadic interactions, based on increasingly complex and arbitrary semiotic relationships.

In the framework of the studies presented in this volume, semiotics plays a key role in developing our categories of observation. These semiotic categories are sensitive to children's development [12], progressing from more "general" forms, closely tied to material reality—such as ostensive and indexical gestures—to increasingly complex, abstract, and conventional forms, such as symbols and language (see Chap. 7 in this volume). In the uses of the objects, we also observe a progression from non-conventional uses, detached from social rules, to conventional, symbolic, and even meta-canonical uses (see Chaps. 2, 4–6 in this volume). In other words, rules for using objects become established during development, eventually detaching from the object itself, representing it, and being used in creative and novel ways. These categories (see Table 3.1), which will be detailed in various chapters of this volume, have been developed, adapted, and expanded to address diverse research questions.

Table 3.1 General categories of the Pragmatics of the Object

1. Attention. The child (C) focuses their attention on the object (O) or the adult (A)
2. Emotional expressions. External manifestation of an emotion. Smile
3. Uses of objects and tools **Non-canonical uses**. Undifferentiated uses. Sucking, bitting, throwing **Protocanonical uses.** Approximations to canonical uses. Moving the spoon in the plate **Rhythmic-sound uses.** Using objects to produce sound or rhythm. Hitting the table rhythmically with the spoon **Rhythmic-sound canonical uses**. Using musical instruments by their rules of use. Shaking a bell **Canonical uses.** Using an object by its social and public function. Eating with a spoon **Symbolic uses.** Using an object to represent something absent. Pretending to eat with an empty spoon **Metacanonical uses.** Effective uses with objects that were not designed to fulfill that specific function **Numerical uses.** Uses of the object with a numerical function. Advancing a replica horse through a board according to the number indicated by a die
4. Non-linguistic semiotic mediators **Demonstrations of object uses.** Uses of the objects by the adult for the child **Gestures** **Ostensive gestures.** Sing and referent coincide **Showing** an object **Giving** an object **Indexical gestures.** Gestures that direct attention towards an object, situation, or event in the distance **Touch-pointing.** Touching the referent with the finger **Pointing.** Indicating the referent with the extended finger in the distance **Others.** Indicating with the hand, or with an object in the distance **Symbolic gestures.** Gestures that represent something absent
5. Vocalizations and Language **Vocalizations**. Children's vocal productions **Language**

3.2 Microgenetic, Situated, and Longitudinal Observation

In this second part, we will outline the fundamental aspects of our methodological design: the microgenetic, situated, and longitudinal observation. We will examine each term, delving into the theoretical foundations that support this methodology.

3.2.1 Observation as a Research Method

Observation involves recording and/or coding the observable actions of research subjects—that is, what the researcher can see and hear of the subject's behavior [1]. According to Bunge [4], observation is the basic empirical procedure of scientific research. He characterizes scientific observation as selective and interpretative. It is selective because it is an intentional and deliberate perception guided by a specific objective, explicitly defining what, how, when, who, and where to observe [12]. It is interpretative because it is illustrated, informed, or guided by a theory or prior knowledge (Table 3.1).

Far from being a mere description of what occurs over a period of time, observation focuses on interpreting the dynamics of what is observed, as well as the underlying structures and processes, to answer a previously formulated scientific question [1]. To achieve this level of analysis, the researcher requires a solid theoretical foundation upon which to develop the necessary categories for rigorous observation and guide the interpretation of the results. This approach has been central in developmental psychology, as demonstrated by the work of classical authors like Piaget, Vygotsky, and Wallon, who were excellent observers. Their careful and detailed observations of children's behaviors formed the basis of their theoretical legacies and underscored the importance of robust observational and qualitative methodologies for understanding early development.

However, in recent decades, observation as a method has often been considered merely a "prelude" or an "exploratory" phase before traditional research [1, 8, 18]. Some journals even reject observational studies outright. This tendency, coupled with an emphasis on ever-larger population samples, has fueled the rise of standardized tasks and measures. These developments have distanced research from the everyday situations and dynamics in which development occurs, posing a challenge to the ecological validity of contemporary research.[2] Authors like Tamis-LeMonda [22], Rogoff et al. [20], and De Barbaro and Fausey [6] argue that observation in everyday contexts not only complements experimental methods, but is essential to capturing the complexity of human development in real-world settings.

In line with these ideas, the Pragmatics of the Object emphasizes the importance of observation in science in general and in developmental psychology in particular, offering a wealth of data from everyday situations. After all, children do not develop in a laboratory by solving specifically designed tasks. Instead, they develop in a material, social, and cultural world full of complex interactions and dynamics. These dynamics cannot be fully understood solely through scores on standardized tasks conducted in laboratory settings.

This does not mean abandoning experimental methodologies—quite the contrary. These arguments aim to recognize the interdependence of both approaches, depending on the research question. Observation offers a close connection to reality, generating novel ideas and hypotheses for experimental study design and greater validation of laboratory studies [18].

María Teresa Anguera, an influential methodologist, has spent decades defending and developing observational methodology to meet the necessary criteria of systematicity, objectivity, and formalization to be considered a scientific method

[2] At this point, it is important to highlight the significant role of Jane Goodall in the field of ethology. Goodall demonstrated how prolonged observation in natural contexts reveal unexpected behaviors, such as tool use by chimpanzees. We might mention also the names of Darwin, Köhler in primatology, or Bates, Camaioni and Volterra in early development.

[1]. She has explored how to use observational data not only in qualitative studies (via descriptions of observed sequences) but also to create databases for quantitative analysis (e.g., [3]). Anguera highlights the complementarity of qualitative and quantitative approaches in observational methodology.

In summary, we consider observational methodology a fully-fledged research method, not a mere "description" of reality or a preliminary "exploration" preceding traditional research. Systematic and rigorous observation allows for the extraction of data from everyday situations in which subjects act. For this, observation must be based on solid theoretical foundations that establish observation levels and categories and guide data interpretation.

3.2.2 Microgenetic Observation: A General Overview

Microgenesis refers to a form of observational recording of subject behavior. This methodology focuses on studying the origins and development of cognitive processes [23]. Unlike standardized tasks, where children's behavior is quantified through dichotomous success/failure measures or total numerical scores, microgenetic observation recognizes and records behavior as it naturally occurs throughout the observation period. It entails a detailed study of development in real-time, examining microchanges that unfold during the observed situation [19].

This methodology begins with recording children's behavior, followed by an interpretative process grounded in theory to make sense of the observations. Describing behavior or counting frequencies is the initial step. Subsequent inferences based on theory are necessary to understand the observed changes in behavior, addressing questions such as: Why do children do what they do? Why do they stop? How do they transition from one behavior to another? It is crucial to draw conclusions from the observational record and the description of observed behaviors.

Although various authors have proposed diverse microgenetic methodologies (e.g., [13, 23]), our approach is inspired by methodologies developed at the Geneva School, specifically by the Problem Solving and Strategies Group (see Chaps. 1 and 2 in this volume).

To study the development of pre-verbal children under two years old, Piaget developed the "naturalistic observation." This methodology involves describing children's actions in structured situations to test pre-established hypotheses. Piaget employed this method in his studies of his three children, resulting in his work on the sensorimotor period, such as *La naissance de l'intelligence chez l'enfant* (1936/1948). On the other hand, Bärbel Inhelder, Piaget's closest collaborator, focused on children's problem-solving processes rather than their underlying logical knowledge structures. She developed the so-called "microgenetic method," based on detailed analyses of children's actions when faced with problems presented by the researcher (for a more detailed historical review, see [17]). Today, this methodology continues to yield remarkable results, such as the variety of strategies children use to solve the Tower of Hanoi [5].

Madelon Saada-Robert, a collaborator of Inhelder, integrated Piaget's "naturalistic observation" and Inhelder's "microgenetic observation" to develop her own methodology, termed "situated microgenetics" [17]. Unlike her mentors, Saada-Robert studied children's development in their everyday contexts, where they act and communicate as active subjects [21]. This is the approach upon which we have built our microgenetic methodology.

Following Saada-Robert's lead, the Pragmatics of the Object has gone beyond the laboratory and standardized tasks to study children's development in their everyday contexts, specifically at home and in the early years schools. Everyday contexts provide new insights into the daily dynamics of children's interactions with peers, adults, and material culture. These contexts also offer unique information about the sociocultural experiences shaping children's development. This approach has enabled us to challenge theoretical positions and the timing of key psychological skills, such as object uses, intentional communication, or self-regulation, as explored in this book's chapters. It has also allowed us to build and refine new approaches to the Pragmatics of the Object.

The process of coding, once done using "pen and paper", is now facilitated by software tools that enable continuous recording [12] and greater control over data quality, along with the creation of databases for quantitative analysis [1]. These tools are also useful for verifying observations through reliability measures, such as inter-rater agreement using Cohen's Kappa (see [12]).

In our case, we use ELAN Linguistic Annotator software. Although originally designed for coding verbal behavior, its flexibility supports rigorous and systematic observation across multiple levels, coordinating hierarchical inputs (see [7, 11]). The software links video recordings with observation protocols, enabling review, modification, and the extraction of descriptive data such as frequency, duration, and latency of observed behaviors. These protocols can also be used for quantitative data analysis (see [3]).

Figure 3.1 illustrates the different levels of categories we commonly use: attention, object uses, and gestures of a child in the 1–2-year-old classroom using a flashlight. At a glance, we can identify their attention to the object and the canonical uses performed: (a) illuminating, and (b) repeatedly turning the flashlight on and off.

3.2.3 Longitudinal Studies

Although the value of longitudinal designs is widely recognized in early development literature, most studies in developmental psychology rely on cross-sectional designs. Cross-sectional studies compare differences between groups of children of different ages, typically using quantitative analyses of task performance scores. However, discussing early development solely in these terms is risky. While cross-sectional designs are accessible and cost-effective, they do not provide insight into the dynamics of development. Instead, they offer a "snapshot" of one or more

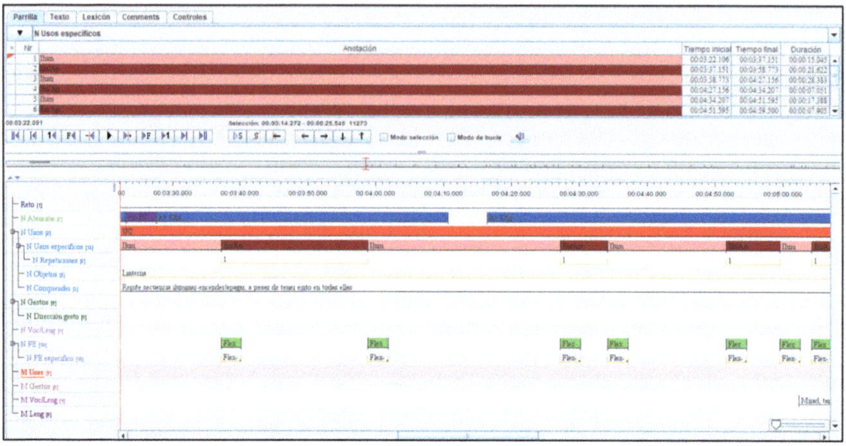

Fig. 3.1 Coding example of a microgenetic observation using ELAN

groups of children at specific points in time. Comparisons between different groups do not reveal the processes of change that explain development.

By contrast, longitudinal designs involve observing (or measuring) the same subjects at two or more points in time [3, 25]. This approach transforms data into a narrative about the developmental process itself. Longitudinal studies focus on analyzing progressive changes over time, emphasizing not only what children do but also the *processes of change*—how behaviors and underlying psychological structures transform during development.

These designs enable researchers to observe and explain changes or evolution in individuals over time, making them especially relevant in developmental psychology despite their associated costs in time and resources. The Pragmatics of the Object embraces longitudinal designs precisely because their greatest strength lies in observing processes of developmental change in triadic communicative contexts. They also enable the coordination of macro- and microgenetic dimensions, which are particularly relevant during infancy, when significant changes occur in very short periods of time.

3.3 Conclusions

Throughout this chapter, we have presented the theoretical and epistemological foundations guiding the development of our microgenetic, situated, and longitudinal methodology, which characterizes our studies. We have reviewed the importance of observation as a legitimate research method, demonstrating how it can be conducted systematically and formally. Furthermore, we have emphasized the significance of conducting microgenetic observations in everyday contexts, focusing on children's spontaneous actions in interactions with their parents and/ or teachers.

This methodological approach allows us to analyze the progressive development of inferences made about children's underlying psychological processes, grounded in the theoretical bases we have been developing for years. In our case, methodology and theory are inseparably intertwined. This synergy has enabled us to explore development in real-world contexts, thereby enriching both our theoretical understanding and the practical implications of our research.

By combining observational rigor with longitudinal design, we are able to capture the dynamics of development over time, offering unique insights into the processes of change that underpin children's growth. The triadic perspective—including the child, adult, and object—has provided a valuable framework for examining the sociocultural and material dimensions of early development.

As we continue to refine and adapt our methodologies, our work highlights the importance of integrating observational and semiotic approaches to better understand the complexity of early childhood development. This chapter has served as a foundation for the studies detailed in the subsequent chapters of this volume, offering a cohesive overview of the methodological innovations driving our research.

References

1. Anguera, M. T. (2010). Posibilidades y relevancia de la observación sistemática por el profesional de la psicología [Possibilities and relevance of systematic observation by the psychologist]. *Papeles del Psicólogo, 31*(1), 122–130. ISSN 0214-7823.
2. Baker, S. T., Friedman, O., & Leslie, A. M. (2010). The opposites task: Using general rules to test cognitive flexibility in preschoolers. *Journal of Cognition and Development, 11*(2), 240–254. https://doi.org/10.1080/15248371003699944
3. Belza, H., Herrán, E., & Anguera, M. T. (2023). Keys to responsive feeding in early education: Systematic observation of Pikler-Lóczy's educators' behaviour during breakfast. *International Journal of Early Childhood, 56*, 605–623. https://doi.org/10.1007/s13158-023-00366-x
4. Bunge, M. (1967/1984). L'observation [The observation]. In M. P. Michiels-Philippe (Dir.) *L'observation.* (pp. 47–59). Delachaux et Niestlé.
5. Cerchiaro-Ceballos, E., Ossa, J. C., Cabas-Manjarréz, M. F., Bustamante-Meza, L. (2023). Qué nos dicen las trayectorias sobre la planificación cognitiva en niños prescolares? [What do trajectories tell us about preschool children's cognitive planing?]*Revista Interamericana de Psicología, 57*(1), e1804. https://doi.org/10.30849/ripijp.v57i1.1804
6. De Barbaro, K., & Fausey, C. M. (2022). Ten lessons about infants' everyday experiences. *Current Directions in Psychological Science, 31*(1), 28–33. https://doi.org/10.1177/09637214211059536
7. ELAN (Version 6.9) [Computer software]. (2024). Nijmegen: Max Planck Institute for Psycholinguistics. Retrieved from https://archive.mpi.nl/tla/elan
8. Gillièron, C. (1985). *La construction du réel chez le psychologue. Epistémologie et méthodes en sciences humaines* [The construction of reality in the psychologist. Epistemology and methods in human sciences]. Peter Lang
9. Gould, P. (1996). Space, time and the human being. *International Social Science Journal, 48*(150), 449–460.

10. Houser, N. (2010). Peirce, phenomenology and semiotics. In P. Cobley (Ed.), *The Routledge companion to semiotics* (pp. 89–100). Routledge. ISBN 0-203-87415-3
11. Lausberg, H., & Sloetjes, H. (2009). Coding gestural behavior with the NEUROGES-ELAN system. *Behavior Research Methods, 41*, 841–849. https://doi.org/10.3758/BRM.41.3.841
12. León, O. G., y Montero, I. (2015). *Métodos de investigación en psicología y educación: las tradiciones cuantitativa y cualitativa* [Research methods in psychology and education: quantitative and qualitative traditions] (4th ed.). McGraw Hill.
13. Luria, A. R. (1959). The directive function of speech in development and dissolution. *Word, 15*(2), 341–352. https://doi.org/10.1080/00437956.1959.11659703
14. Palacios, P., Rodríguez, C., Méndez-Sánchez, C., & Hermosillo-de la Torre, A. E. (2013). Contextos comunicativos e interactivos triádicos: la unidad básica de la educación [Communicative and interactive triadic contexts: the educational basic unit]. En P. Palacios, M. C. Farfán, E. Navarrete, & S. C. Miramontes (Comp.), *Psicología educativa: reflexión, práctica e intervención* (pp. 14– 40). UAEM.
15. Piaget, J. (1936/1948). *La naissance de l'intelligence chez l'enfant*. [The origins of intelligence in children]. Delachaux et Niestlé. (version ´electronique, Fondation Jean Piaget).
16. Piaget, J. (1974). Réussir et comprendre [To succeed and to understand]. Presses Universitaires de France.
17. Puche-Navarro, R., & Ossa, J. C. (2024). Following the path of Inhelderian method. In R. Puche-Navarro & J. C. Ossa (Eds.), *The microgenetic method. Legacy of Bärbel Inhelder* (pp. 5–29). SpringerBriefs. https://doi.org/10.1007/978-3-031-68748-8
18. Rai, T. S., & Fiske, A. (2010). ODD (observation- and description-deprived) psychological research. *Behavioral and Brain Sciences, 33*(2/3), 106–107. https://doi.org/10.1017/S0140525X10000221
19. Rodríguez, C., & Moro, C. (1999). *El mágico número tres. Cuando los niños aún no hablan* [The magic number three. When children still do not talk]. Paidós.
20. Rogoff, B., Dahl, A., & Callanan, M. (2018). The importance of understanding children's lived experience. *Developmental Review, 50*(Pt. A), 5–15. https://doi.org/10.1016/j.dr.2018.05.006
21. Saada-Robert, M. (2012). From individual to didactic microgenesis: Studies on situated knowledge transformations. In E. Martí & C. Rodríguez (Eds.), *After Piaget* (pp. 187–205). Transaction Publishers.
22. Tamis-LeMonda, C. S. (2023). The mountain stream of infant development. *Infancy, 28*, 468–491. https://doi.org/10.1111/infa.12538
23. Vygotski, L. S. (1931/1995). *Obras escogidas III. Historia del desarrollo de las funciones psíquicas superiores* [Selected Works III. History of the development of higher psychic functions]. Visor.
24. Vygotski, L. S. (1934/1994). *Obras escogidas II. Pensamiento y lenguaje. Conferencias sobre psicología* [Selected works II. Thought and language. Conferences in psychology]. Machado.
25. White, R., & Arzi, H. (2005). Longitudinal studies: Designs, validity, practicality and value. *Research in Science Education, 35*(1), 137–149. https://doi.org/10.1007/s11165-004-3437-y

Part II

Types of Uses of Objects and Gestures. A Semiotic and Social Development

The Pragmatics of Music: Rhythmic-Sound Uses in Early Development at Home, in the Hospital, and in the Early Years School

4

Iván Moreno-Llanos, María Jáñez-Álvarez, Miren Pérez-Eizaguirre, and María Jesús del Olmo

In this chapter, our goal is to explore the influence of two musical elements, rhythm and sound, through the uses of sound objects and musical instruments in early development.

Music and its musical elements, rhythm, melody, harmony and form elicit physical, emotional and behavioral responses, which influence our interactions with others, whatever the age and specific circumstances (see, for example, [15, 100]). Most of the research conducted in the musical field on infant-adult interaction has focused on the vocal component of infant-adult interactions [5, 48]. In infant cries, we can observe *glissandos* and a melodic contour. Similarly, we adults vocalize for infants in a melodic, "singing" manner. However, there are few studies that have analyzed how infants begin to use sound objects and musical instruments throughout the first year of life, and what their influence is on psychological development.

With this objective in mind, the chapter is divided into two main blocks. In the first block (Sects. 4.1 and 4.2), we will briefly review the origins of research on infant-adult communication and the current status of dyadic (infant-adult) and triadic (infant-adult-object) interactions. In the second block we will present the theoretical bases of the Pragmatic of the Object in the study of the rhythmic-sound

I. Moreno-Llanos (✉) · M. Pérez-Eizaguirre · M. J. del Olmo
Universidad Autónoma de Madrid, Madrid, Spain
e-mail: ivan.moreno@uam.es

M. Jáñez-Álvarez
Centro de Salud Mental Puente de Vallecas, Madrid, Spain

C. Rodriguez Garrido et al. (eds.), *The Social Life of Objects in Early Development*, Social Interaction in Learning and Development,
https://doi.org/10.1007/978-3-031-87673-8_4

uses of sound objects and musical instruments (Sects. 4.3 and 4.4). Then, we will present some studies that we have carried out at home, in the hospital, and in the early years school (classroom 0–1 years).

First, we will deal with typically developing infants at home (Sect. 4.5). We will observe how the use of sound objects and musical instruments by the adult provides the bases for the organization of the first interactions with the infant, in which the material world is included. From these first triadic infant-adult-object interactions, the adult introduces the infant to the shared meanings and uses of objects.

Next, we will present how this research has been used in the hospital context, with premature infants (Sect. 4.6). The structure offered by music and musical instruments favors the interaction between parents and their baby in an at-risk situation. It also provides developmental benefits for infants, such as a reduced heart rate and increased oxygen saturation. In addition, it helps to better organize the hospital environment in general, demonstrated in the reduction of hustle and bustle and ambient noise. This had an improvement in the well-being not only of the infant, but also of his or her parents, and the other people in the neonatal care unit.

Thirdly, we will present some observations that highlight the importance of sound objects and musical instruments in the 0–1 year old early years school classrooms, with infants whose ages range from 4 or 5 months at the beginning of the school year to 17–18 months at the end. We observed that the use of sound objects and musical instruments by infants plays a very prominent role in the educational situations planned by teachers [18]. These are the first conventional uses observed in the early years school, through which infants begin to exercise their intentionality from a very early age. In their uses, they show a constant rhythm, which allows them to participate in the first triadic interactions with the teacher and even with other infants.

We will close the chapter with some conclusions and reflections on the role of sound objects and musical instruments in early development.

4.1 Infant-Adult Communication

Wallon [102] was one of the first to propose how the first encounters between the infant and the adult take place. Wallon emphasizes the importance of emotions as the nexus that makes possible the encounter and communication between individuals. Later, during the 1970s, there was a boom in research on infant-adult communication. The term “mother-infant dialogue” (see, for example [86]) emerged to describe these interactions, a metaphor that we consider not entirely appropriate, since it draws attention on language skills that develop later [41].

Bruner [12], on the other hand, gave a notable impulse to research on early infant communication, studying the communicative aspects prior to and necessary for later language development. Among the infants’ prelinguistic abilities, rhythmic skills are those that first emerge and develop [85]. Authors such as Fraisse

[28] and Stern [89], Stern et al. [91] emphasize the importance of rhythm in early infant-adult interactions. Rhythm, as an early semiotic system, allows the organization of the interaction, makes possible the expression and understanding of emotions ([51], see also [102]), and favors interactive synchrony between the adult and the infant [7, 11, 26, 58, 88, 90].

The variety of terms used to refer to this synchrony shows the multiplicity of nuances and approaches: *co-regulation* [27], *mutual influence* [16], *mutual regulation* [29], *affect attuned* [89], *contingency* [57], *coordination* [36]. These studies show that the analysis of rhythm in interaction is becoming more and more important, as well as recognizing the infant as an active agent from the first interactions with the adult. This theoretical approach has been widely used to assess aspects of parent-infant interactions such as the general style of approach, the possibilities of interaction, and the particularity of the bond [6, 26, 88, 95, 97]. For example, Kaye [40] discusses the infant's rhythmic singularities during breastfeeding:

> The infant has a suck-pause pattern at feeding time that is different from that of other mammals, with preintentional pauses whose circularity is supported by the interaction with the adult based on repetition, rhythm, and systematicity, qualities that are the prelude to the conversational human communicative pattern ([40], pp. 52–56).

Pauses in breastfeeding allow the regulation of the tempo of the interaction ([62], see also [64]), creating the first spaces of interaction between mother and baby [2]. During breastfeeding, we can observe moments of reciprocity and recursivity. The infant's readiness is important to activate sucking, but without the adult's help, the infant will not reach the breast or the bottle. In turn, the infant's sucking will determine his/her posture and the sequence of rhythms of his/her action, as well as the adult's responses. Papousek and Papousek [59] emphasize the intuitive character and the mutual influence of this interaction between mothers and infants, highlighting the adjustment of the adult's language prosody to the infant's perceptual sensitivity.

4.2 Dyadic and Triadic Interactions

The most widely accepted perspective in early development literature considers that, during the first 8–9 months of life or so, the infant interacts mainly in dyads, either with adults or with objects. In infant-adult interactions "proto-conversations" take place (note, again, the linguistic load of this term), which are characterized by a turn-taking structure and a clear emotional content ([8, 17], cited in [34, 82]). Trevarthen [94, 96] calls these infant-adult interactions *primary intersubjectivity*.

On the other hand, infant-object interactions begin when infants are able to grasp close objects, at about 5 months of age. Piaget [64], analyzing *in extenso* the infant-object interaction, emphasizes the active position of the infant and the importance of habit and repetition in cognitive development, which implies a rhythmic pattern [22].

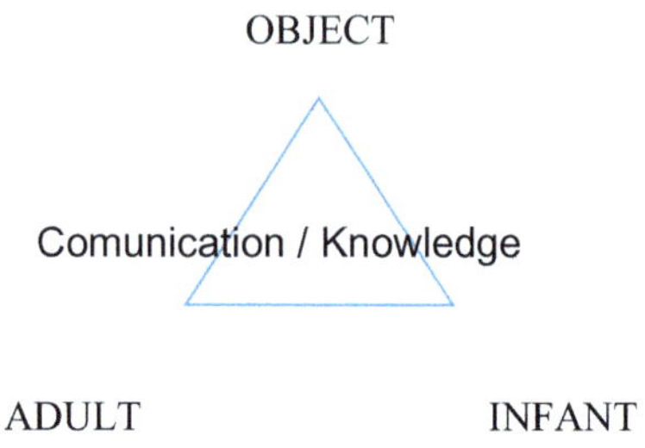

Fig. 4.1 Triadic interaction

Around 9 months of life, the infant begins to communicate intentionally with others about an external referent, organizing *triadic interactions*, infant-adult-object, intentionally. This ability is called *secondary intersubjectivity* [94].

However, from this perspective we can appreciate a "material void", in which infant-adult interactions during the first 9 months of life are devoid of material referents. Objects do not seem to be part of infants' development until 5 months of age, when they begin to grasp them. On the other hand, we also observe a "social void" in infant-object interactions, in which the infant interacts alone with objects devoid of shared meanings. This "disconnection" of materiality from any social and communicative dimension would imply a spontaneous development of infants' cognitive and intentional communication skills towards the end of the first year [56]. Therefore, the scarcity of studies on infant-adult-object triadic interactions in the first months of life as a unit of analysis is striking.

Since the 1980s, with the arrival of Vygotsky's [98] ideas in the West, the importance of the adult as a mediator in the relationship of infants with the world has gained ground. Triadic interactions (see Fig. 4.1) thus become the unit of analysis of learning, development, and semiotic mediation, through which adults introduce infants to the conventional meanings and knowledge of their culture.

In developmental psychology, these ideas have been developed from the Pragmatics of the Object paradigm [72]. According to this perspective, objects are part of the material culture, which determines their functions and rules of use that give meaning to the actions performed with them. Their uses and meanings are not immediately accessible to infants. Instead, they are constructed in the interaction between subjects, as "the result of semiotic mediation; [...] where the object itself is situated within the communication with others" ([76], p.125). That is, the adults make the use and meaning of objects comprehensible to the infant [73]. Thus, the adult acts as a mediator between the infant and the conventional meanings and uses of objects. The object, therefore, also becomes an "instrument" that the adult uses as a mediator in communication with the infant.

From this perspective, triadic interactions would be present from a very early age. At first, organized and directed by the adult, who approaches and demonstrates the world to the infant, lending their intentions to the infant, creating communication niches. Although it is not until two months of life that infants can voluntarily direct their body towards the source of a sound, their hearing is functional from the fifth month of gestation [9]. At around two months of life, thanks to their increased body control, their capacity to respond to adult actions is multiplied. They become able to look attentively at what the adult shows them, maintaining eye contact, and responding emotionally through smiles and body movements. Between 2 and 6 months, the infant will progressively take more initiative in interaction. Objects will become "things to grasp", and later, "things to use" (see [55, 56, 78]). The infant, therefore, takes an active role in these interactions, rather than being a passive recipient of the adult's actions [79].

In these interactions, the adult uses objects as instruments for communication, "lending his/her intentions" to the infant [74]. The ostensive gestures with objects, the rhythm, and the sonority, make up the first semiotic systems through which the adult and the infant construct the first shared meanings. According to Paz [61], "what we call culture is rooted in rhythm" (p. 14). Therefore, objects are powerful instruments of communication, especially during the first years of life.

4.3 Sound Objects and Musical Instruments

From the Pragmatics of the Object, we are interested in studying how infants use sound objects and musical instruments. However, distinguishing what is a sound object or a musical instrument is a conceptual challenge. Establishing a clear difference is a complex debate that involves philosophical and anthropological aspects. For example, in some areas, musical instruments are understood as *processes* rather than devices, while musicians and performers are considered agents of musical ecologies, that is, of the expression and nonverbal communication they perform through them [71].

However, it is worth reflecting on this, and trying to establish appropriate categories for the objects that infants use with the intention to communicate in social interactions. Therefore, we will establish key differences between both elements from the Pragmatics of the Object. Likewise, although these objects serve to produce multiple elements necessary for musical interpretation, such as melody and harmony, in this chapter we will focus on their rhythmic and sound characteristics, which are the closest to the infant's understanding at a semiotic level.

If we begin with the question of what is a *sound object*, Pierre Schaeffer offers an interesting definition. According to this author, a sound object is *one that can be used to produce sound* (Schaeffer, 1992, cited in [30]). This definition is pragmatically broad. It assumes that any object can reach the status of *sound object*, as long as it is used with the intention of producing sound. It is the use that determines its status as a *sound object*.

However, the definition of *musical instrument* is much more restrictive. According to the Spanish Royal Academy (RAE): "A musical instrument is an object composed of one or more parts arranged in such a way that it serves to produce musical sounds".[1] In other words, a musical instrument is an object *intentionally designed with the function of producing sound*, and which is considered suitable for use in musical compositions by the community of users. In addition, *musical instruments* have a history. Users modify their physical structure (even creating new musical instruments altogether), modes of interpretation, sound ideals, and meanings, depending on the musical communicative needs and purposes for which they have been designed [66]. Ontologically, the *musical instrument* is singularized, and in a certain way enriched, thanks to the works written for them by different composers of all styles and historical periods [84].

In summary, the fundamental difference between a *sound object* and a *musical instrument* lies in their shared meanings and functions. *Sound objects* can be used to produce sound given their physical characteristics, with a clear communicative and interactive intention, but they do not have a conventional musical function. In contrast, a *musical instrument* is an object designed to produce musical sounds, and is part of the material culture of a social group, which gives it a public, conventional, and shared function and meaning. Next, we will review how infants begin to use sound objects and musical instruments.

4.4 The Pragmatics of the Object. The Uses of Sound Objects and Musical Instruments

In the beginnings of the Pragmatics of the Object [77], the focus was situated on "how infants come to use objects for their conventional function". To this end, three types of uses were established (see also Chap. 2, this volume):

- *Non-Canonical Uses*, uses that do not follow the conventional rules of objects and tools, which are not used for their function. They are undifferentiated uses, independent of the specific object or tool. An example would be sucking any object.
- *Proto-canonical uses* (or premises to canonical uses) are approximations to the canonical or functional use. At this point, infants have some understanding of the object's intended use, but have difficulty performing the canonical use effectively or completely.
- And finally, *canonical or functional uses* are uses based on conventional, socially shared rules for objects and tools.

At 7 months of age, non-canonical uses of materiality, such as sucking, hitting, or throwing, predominate. These uses are based on what infants can physically do with objects. Between 10 and 13 months, infants begin to use everyday objects that

[1] This definition would lead us to consider what is or is not a *musical sound*, but we would enter a broad, extensive, and certainly exciting debate, that musicology, archeology and ethnomusicology contemplate in their studies and research.

are accessible for their function (conventional uses), thanks to triadic interactions with adults [77].

However, before 7 months, some uses initially considered non-canonical, such as tapping, shaking, rubbing, are in fact "coated" with rhythm and sonority. We have observed that infants actively explore the rhythmic and sound characteristics of objects from the time they are able to grasp them, between 4 and 6 months [55, 78]. When infants perform rhythm, it does not necessarily imply that they are "making music". However, in contexts of triadic interaction, the object and its rhythmic-sound uses become means that the infant around 8 months of age employs with a clear communicative and social interaction intention [23, 54, 72]. These lead us to rethink how we considered the categories of object uses in relation to sound objects and musical instruments. As we previously commented, rhythm and sound constitute the first semiotic systems through which the adult and the infant reach the first agreements. Therefore, we decided to include two new types of uses to our categories: *rhythmic-sound uses* and *rhythmic-sound canonical uses.*

Rhythmic-sound uses are similar to non-canonical uses in several aspects. They are undifferentiated uses, not based on conventional rules and meanings, which can be produced independently of the object. That is, any object is susceptible of being used to produce sound and rhythm (following Schaeffer's definition of sound object). However, unlike non-canonical uses, rhythmic-sound uses have external efficacy. Sound and rhythm are perceptible by both the infant who produces them, and the adult that perceives them. When the infant makes an object sound, the adult can intervene in this action.

These uses represent the infant's first effective actions with objects and tools. When the infant becomes the agent of their own actions, they comprehend that changes in objects are brought about by their own action (see [64], Stage III of sensorimotor development). This promotes the development of early agency and intentionality. They also involve the construction of the understanding of material objects as *functional* elements, that is, objects serve to do things in the world, although infants do not yet understand their conventional meanings and functions.

Rhythm and sound, therefore, are constituted as general elements that infants can produce with any object. Nonetheless, through the production of rhythm and sound, infants enter into the first conventional uses of sound objects and musical instruments. Because of this, we have called the later *rhythmic-sound canonical uses.* From 8 to 9 months infants make *rhythmic-sound canonical uses* with very simple musical instruments such as rattles, jingle bells, or bells. At 10–11 months, we begin to observe more complex *rhythmic-sound canonical uses*, such as playing tambourines or metallophones with drumsticks [53].

Thus, *rhythmic-sound uses* and *rhythmic-sound canonical uses* bridge the gap between earlier *non-canonical uses* and later *canonical uses.* These uses, therefore, occupy a privileged place in early development, forming part of the first infant-adult agreements around the material world. For example, in the actions and interactions between infants and their parents and in the construction of shared meanings [55, 56, 78], as well as in peer interactions [18]. They also give rise to the first manifestations of goal-directed action in the early years schools classrooms ([53, 75], see also Chap. 10, this volume). In the following sections, we will show some results of research conducted at home, in the hospital, and in the early years school, regarding the uses of sound objects and musical instruments in early development. We will begin with the studies carried out at home, with normotypical infants and with premature infants.

4.5 Triadic Interactions at Home. The Adult Introduces the Infant to Shared Meanings Through Rhythmic-Sound Uses

As we previously commented, the infant begins to communicate intentionally with others about an object at around 9 months of age [93, 94]. However, how this skill develops has been much less studied. From the Pragmatics of the Object, we consider that the origin of intentional communication must be sought in the interactions initiated, controlled, and directed by the adult [72]. Before the infant is able to communicate intentionally, the adults communicate and interact intentionally with them, and makes sense of objects and events in the world [74]. To this end, we have studied how the adult introduces the infant in niches of interaction through the use of a musical instrument such as the maraca [21, 39, 56].

The first infant-adult-object triadic interactions and the construction of shared referents in the first months of life take place through non-linguistic semiotic systems, such as the *uses of objects* and *gestures.*[2] Adult's *demonstrations of use* take various forms. They can be *distant*, when the adult acts as a model, placing the maraca between them and making it sound. They can also be *immediate*, when the adult places the maraca in the infant's hand and moves it to sound it together. In this way, the adult shows the infant the necessary hand movement to use the object, with the infant's own body. With premature infants, which we will see in more depth in the next section, in addition to distant and immediate, the adult's demonstrations with the maraca also occur closer to the body, through *immediate demonstrations on the hand* (touching the infant's hand with the maraca) or *immediate demonstrations on the body* (touching the infant's body with the maraca) [39].

The adult, in addition, brings *structure* to these demonstrations. It incorporates a certain rhythm and frequent pauses.[3] The rhythm and pauses are elements that structure the adult's action [56]. Pauses can be understood as moments of listening, of invitation to participate in the interaction and of coordination among participants [81]. In short, pauses in the adult's action open spaces for the infant

[2] Adult language, although always present, is not the semiotic system through which the infant understands the meanings of objects and interaction. Instead, the infant is able to understand, to some extent, the adult's uses of objects and gestures.

[3] Pauses are considered when they last more than 3 s. If they last less, they are considered "silences" within the same use.

to intervene. In contrast, when the adult's action is prolonged in time, when it is very brief, or when it has few pauses, infants tend to withdraw their attention [38, 43]. With premature infants, we observed that adult demonstrations tend to be less *structured* during the second and third month of life. Pauses tend to be very short or nonexistent. In certain cases, parents may be playing for several minutes without pausing. However, we observed a progressive increase in the frequency and duration of pauses, which consolidate *structured demonstrations* [38, 39].

During pauses, adults tend to produce gestures, mainly *ostensive gestures.* For example, the adult *shows*, placing the maraca in the midline between them and the infant, at a distance. With this gesture, the adult seeks to attract the infant's attention to the object, intentionally sharing the referent [55, 56]. Less frequently, we observed ostensive gestures of *giving*, which requires the infant to take the maraca that the adult yields. Finally, some adults also invite the infant to explore the object through *placing* gestures, placing the object within the infant's reach, with the intention that the infant took it by themselves. Despite their prevalence in the literature, *pointing gestures* and *symbolic gestures*, both by the adult and the infant, appear later in development than ostensive gestures ([13, 32, 39], see also Chap. 7, this volume).

In these interactions, both typically developing infants and premature infants progressively increase their participation. Through demonstrations of uses and gestures, the adult promotes the infant's agency in the use of the maraca by lending their intention. From the second month of life, the infant begins to actively participate through their orientation of their gaze and their first smiles in response to the adult's actions [56]. The premature infant seems to start responding a little later, from the third month [39]. Between the second and fourth month of life, the infant progressively develops its ability to use the maraca, beginning with *adult-prompted grasping attempts*, moving through *self-initiated grasping attempts*, and culminating with their own *canonical rhythmic-sound uses* of the maraca [39, 55, 56]. Premature infants, however, usually show a small delay of one or two months in this process [39].

So far we have shown the development of the first triadic interactions at home, organized by the parents, with typically developing infants and preterm infants. In the following section, we will show how these studies have been applied in clinical situations with preterm newborns.

4.6 Intervention in Hospital Contexts Through Rhythm and Sound. The Case of the Premature Infant

In recent years, the survival rate of preterm infants has increased considerably, due to recent advances in neonatology [60, 67, 92]. However, the premature infant presents early developmental risks. Generally, their level of alertness, activity, and responsiveness is lower [10], although these delays usually disappear over time [4, 19, 68]. Other studies consider that the difficulties shown by premature infants have their origin in medical complications or interaction difficulties shown by their caregivers [31, 35, 50, 83]. These difficulties in infant-adult interaction can be explained, in part, by the context of risk in which premature infants are born into, and by the stress of parents who fear for their infant's life.

The neonatal unit, with its clinical instruments, staff, and operating rules, is an atypical setting for the premature newborn. In these contexts, the stimulation packages perceived by the baby are not usually organized. The levels of stimulation (light, noise, bustle, etc.) may exceed the thresholds appropriate for the baby's well-being. These include the beeping of the monitors where vital signs are recorded, the bustle caused by the movement of cribs, the presence and movement of people working in and visiting these units, and the aversive situations to which the baby is frequently subjected, such as cures, X-rays, or painful and invasive interventions [47].

On the other hand, the sensitivity of premature infants to manipulation and external stimuli, as well as their short periods of wakefulness, can generate frustration in the parents, who may feel alienated or even rejected by their baby. These elements hinder the newborn's sensory-motor opportunities [64] and the spontaneous interactions with their parents [70]. To cope with these potential difficulties, Neonatal Units have incorporated different elements to attenuate noise, intense light, stress, and aversive experiences. In our closest case, the Hospital de la Paz (Madrid) has implemented a project to improve the quality of life of the premature baby. For example, they have placed the noisiest clinical apparatus outside the room, soundproofed the rooms, and even placed elements to signal an increase in decibels (volume) in the room, so that the people present can identify and self-regulate the environmental noise [20, 42, 99]. Among these, interventions with music therapy have also been proposed:

> Music-therapy experiences act as a support for hospitalized babies that *normalize the context and give coherence to their new situation*; by doing (with active music therapy techniques) or listening to music (with passive techniques), *the child receives a coherent and organized multimodal stimulation where not only the senses but also the emotions are involved* ([22], p. 34, emphasis added).

Music-therapy acts as a "bridge" linking (i) clinical intervention, which improves the vital signs and, therefore, the survival of the premature infant, and (ii) psychological intervention, which favors the early development of the infant, and the interaction between parents and their baby. This mediation is possible through the music played by the music therapist, who takes into account the baby's rhythms, from the most basic ones (physiological and behavioral) to the most complex ones (specific to the relationships, structures, etc. in which the infant finds themselves).

The infant's familiarity with the sonority of his environment will help them to achieve a sense of consistency, security, and well-being, a domain that given the circumstances of prematurity may be altered [46, 65, 85]. In addition, music functions as a semiotic mediator in the infant-adult interaction. These experiences mediate the interaction of parents with their baby, facilitating the expression of emotions and shared experiences [85]. Intervention with music-therapy serves to maintain the infant's level of alertness, promotes their attachment and its development, and reduces parental stress [23, 38]. To this end, the music therapist must be attentive to the particular sound quality of the baby and the environment, share these observations, and encourage the parents to experience them and integrate them into their interactions with their newborn. In the succession of these pleasurable experiences, new and increasingly complex experiences will be created [45].

Joanne Loewy et al. [46] demonstrated the beneficial effect of including parents in music-therapy interventions when they are encouraged to sing lullabies to their babies. To this proposal, we add the possibilities provided by a musical instrument such as the maraca, as an invitation to participate in a broader triadic context [56]. Next, we illustrate with an example (Fig. 4.2), the type of interventions that we have been performing in the Neonatal Intermediate Treatment Units (UTIs) of Hospital La Paz (Madrid) (see, for example, [24]). This intervention was divided into 3 parts:

1. After a first contact and presentation with the families, the music therapist begins with an instrumental improvisation based on a melody chosen by the parents and adjusted to the sound characteristics of the room (see Fig. 4.2, image 2.1).
2. Next, the parent holding the baby is invited to sing a song chosen by them and adapted in lullaby form. When there is more than one family member, the participating family member can invite the rest to participate (see Fig. 4.2, image 2.2).
3. Within 5 min of starting the lullaby, a maraca is offered to the parents to accompany the interpretation of the song and encourage interaction with their infant (see Fig. 4.2, image 2.3).

These musical interventions in communicative situations result in decreased heart rate, increased oxygen saturation, and increased physiological well-being in the premature infant, as well as reduced emotional stress in the adult [3, 14, 22, 25, 33, 46, 87,37].

In the case of the parents, some were moved at the beginning of the musical intervention, and once they relaxed, they interacted with their infants more naturally. Others, less frequently, remained tense in front of the cameras throughout the session, especially when they became active performers. However, the presence of other family members favored a more relaxed participation. When the adult caregiver was able to incorporate singing into the session, their degree of involvement in the musical joint action increased, as did the infant's satisfaction and comfort. This in turn increased the frequency of the adult's attempts at interaction and their attention towards the infant's responses [37]. This is of utmost importance because, once the parents calms down, they begin to consider the infant beyond the initial concerns of survival. Instead, they begin to consider the infant "positively", starting from what the infant is capable of doing, and to connect psychologically and emotionally with them [101].

2.1

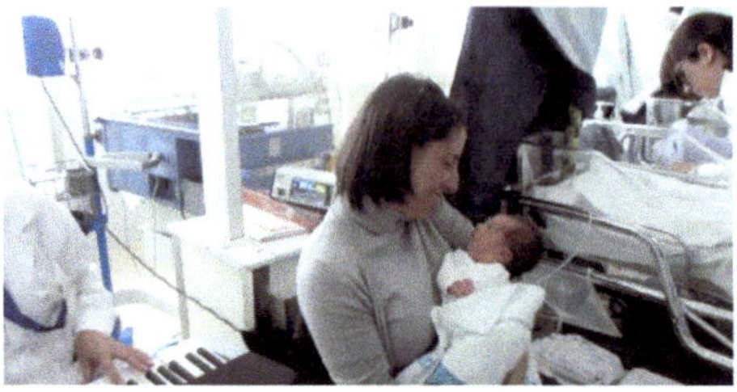

Musical improvisation
Duration: 5 min.

The music therapist performs a musical improvisation with a keyboard, adjusting to the sonority of the room.

The infant is awake. He directs his gaze towards his mother and the other sound sources.

2.2

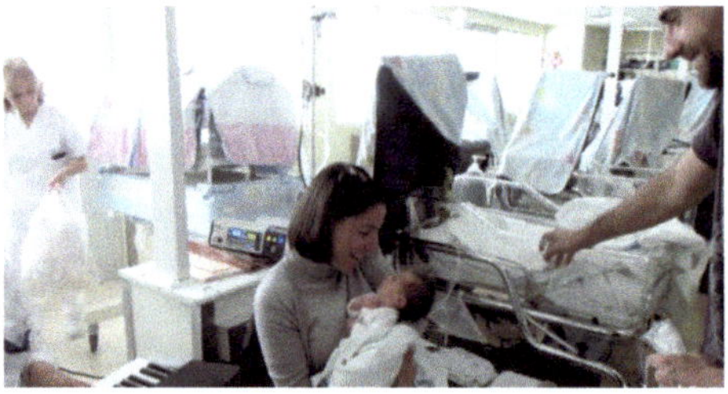

Lullaby singing
Duration: 5 min.

The mother sings a lullaby, accompanied by the music therapist's interpretation.

2.3

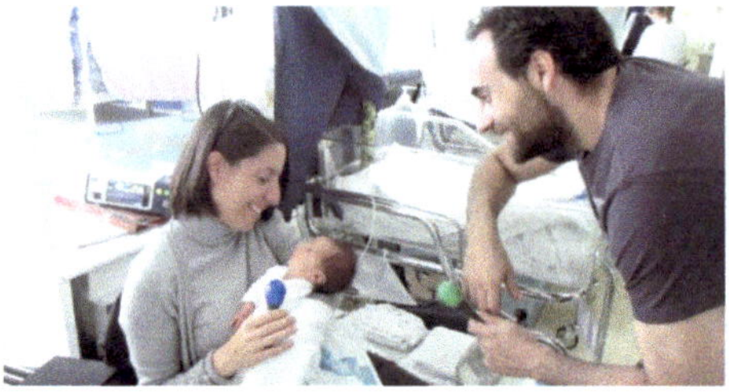

Use of the maraca
Duration: 5 min.

The mother uses the maraca in triadic interaction with instrumental accompaniment by the music therapist.

In this particular intervention, the mother insisted that the father joined in the interaction with his own maraca.

Fig. 4.2 Musical intervention with therapeutic intent in a late preterm infant seen at 36 weeks and 5 days of gestation, in interaction with his mother and father

The musical intervention, surprisingly, also affects the other people in the room. After the intervention, the ambient noise and bustle was significantly reduced. For example, the doctors and nurses were calmer. Their movements were more delicate, with greater care not to make noise in their daily tasks [38].

Therefore, the music therapy session offers the infant and the adult a rhythmic-sound-musical space of interaction through music [22, 24]. Although in the first months the newborn's responses to the music therapy intervention are still automatic, like the reflex of orientation, this will be the first step for the development of more complex triadic interactions [21].

So far, we have discussed infant-adult-object interactions, and how the adult introduces the infant to conventional uses and meanings. In the next section, we will discuss the role of rhythm and music in early years school classrooms, where the adult is a teacher. We will present some results of observational studies we have carried out in early education classrooms in public schools in Madrid.

4.7 Rhythm, Sonority, and Musicality in the 0–1 Classroom of the Early years School

In Spain, infants can start attending early years school at 4 months of age, although schooling is not mandatory until they are 6 years old. The first course, 0–1 year, usually begins at 4–8 months of age, and ends at around 12–16 months.

Despite the acknowledged importance of music in early development, there is a striking lack of studies analyzing the presence of music in early childhood education, which typically covers the first 6 years of life (for a study with children aged 5 years and older, see [103]). This may be because, in the better part of the world, early childhood education is not mandatory. In the case of the United States, public early childhood education 3–5 years is a recent concept, which poses new challenges for music teachers working with these ages. In particular, an adjustment is needed to bring traditional music teaching closer to earlier ages [49]. On the other hand, in some countries, the increasing focus on reading and arithmetic from the age of 3 has led to the reduction of artistic aspects in the early childhood education curriculum. This is the case, for example, in Australia [1].

Before the age of 3 early childhood education has received even less attention. This is due to the fact that not all countries offer a regulated and publicly funded early childhood education, and instead offering early childcare. However, there are some cases where the 0–3 years is considered part of the education system, although it is not mandatory. Even so, we find certain differences in the relationship with music and musical expression. In Chile, early childhood education teachers must have musical training by law. In Cali (Colombia), however, musical activities come from the teachers' own cultural practices [18]. Public early years schools in Spain, which work with infants from 4 months of age, must present a curricular program regulated by law, with specific developmental objectives that teachers must implement in the classroom. Among them, "musical language" is mentioned as a means of communication, expression and enjoyment, with the aim of promoting cultural awareness and the artistic development of infants [69]. However, musical competencies are not mandatory in the initial training of early childhood education teachers in Spain [18].

The development of musical competencies, therefore, is not usually an explicit part of the classroom activities. Instead, they tend to be focused on specific activities, such as singing songs in the welcome activity, the presentation of musical instruments during the "basket of treasures",[4] or at significant cultural moments,

[4] The "basket of treasures" is a common activity in early childhood classrooms, which consists of presenting the children with a set of various objects (the "treasures") inside a basket, a box, etc. The children have free access to this basket and to the objects inside it. In some cases, we have observed

such as Christmas. Even so, we find it interesting to highlight these musical activities, however punctual they may be, in which we can analyze how infants are able to begin to use sound objects and musical instruments in intentional and complex manner. These activities allow access to the first shared meanings through rhythm and sonority. This development regarding the use of sound objects and musical instruments is directly related to important psychological skills such as intentional communication, or the early development of Executive Functions ([52, 73, 75], and Chaps. 8–10 in this volume).

In the following section, we will present some results that are part of an ongoing study on the analysis of the musical characteristics of infants' action. This study is part of a larger project involving five public early years schools in Madrid (Spain). Based on the observations made monthly during an academic year in the 0–1 year-old classroom, we selected those activities in which the teachers proposed to the infants to use sound objects and musical instruments.

To analyze the musical activities in the classroom, we developed specific categories of observation aimed at identifying pauses, accent, dynamics, tempo of the performance, and uses of the sound object or musical instrument. In this chapter, we will present two microgenetic observations that illustrate the types of analyses we performed, second-by-second, using ELAN software (v5.2, [44, 80]). We paid special attention to the reiteration of musical elements of the uses of objects and the structure of the musical patterns. We used the program MuseScore 4 to write and represent the rhythm.

4.7.1 The Rhythmic-Sound Canonical Use of the Musical Instrument: Bell

This activity took place during the second month of the academic year. The teacher provided the infants with previously selected musical instruments and sound objects. Among others, she presented a bell, a maraca, different rattles and jingle bells, and shakers.

Ils (8 months, 7 days) is very interested in these musical instruments. From the beginning of the activity, he uses, more or less effectively, some rattles that are within his reach. At one point, his teacher proposes him a challenge. She performs a *distant demonstration of the canonical use* of the bell: she takes it by the handle with two fingers and shakes it in the air, from left to right, in front of him (see Fig. 4.3, image 3.1), and then gives the bell to Ils. Thus, the teacher creates a triadic interaction that facilitates Ils' interest in using the bell. The teacher's action (distant demonstration and giving gesture) is an invitation to Ils.

Ils takes the bell that his teacher offers him and begins to use it. Thus, he becomes an intentional agent by using the bell to produce sound. We should note that he does not try to use the bell as his teacher did. That is, picking it up with

that these baskets are organized according to a specific theme, for example, musical instruments (see [18]).

his fingers and shaking it in the air. Instead, he adjusts his action progressively, looking for the most effective way to produce sound. During the sequence that follows, Ils performs three distinct uses:

- Rhythmic-Sound Protocanonical Use (Fig. 4.3, image 3.3): Ils grasps the bell by the skirt, and strikes it against the floor. It is a very general approach to the sound of the bell. It is a use of low efficiency.
- Rhythmic-Sound Canonical Use 1 (Fig. 4.3, image 3.2): Ils grasps the bell by the handle, skirt down, and "pins" it against the floor. With this use, Ils approaches the canonical use of the bell. It is a use of intermediate effectiveness.
- Rhythmic-Sound Canonical Use 2 (Fig. 4.3, image 3.6): Ils grasps the bell by the handle, skirt up, and shakes it up and down, striking it against the floor. This is the closest use to the canonical use that we adults typically make. We consider this use to be the most effective.
- Ils also performed some Non-Canonical Uses, sucking the bell.

This variety of Ils' uses demonstrates his progressive development towards more effective and conventional forms.

At a general level, during the sequence, Ils and his teacher produced a large number of pauses in their uses. The presence of pauses indicates that the uses were structured. In the teacher's initial demonstration, the pauses also serve to attract Ils' attention, as well as to invite him to participate in the interaction. The dynamic was always given in *mezzoforte* (hereafter *mf*), an intensity meaning "moderately loud." That is, the sound produced is of intermediate intensity. The teacher and Ils marked the accent every fourth pulse. That is, each fourth pulse had a slightly higher intensity than the rest (as a visual example, we could represent it as a-a-a-A), which also denotes a certain organization in their action. The tempo, or beats per minute of the action (speed), was faster in the teacher, who performs 120 beats per minute, while in Ils it was 80. Since the bell is a typical musical instrument, not a replica object, it has weight, and playing it is more difficult for Ils than for his teacher. In terms of development, the infants's tempo denotes his experience with different sound objects and musical instruments (see Table 4.1).

Taken together, these data allow us to infer the development of Ils' uses of the bell. Ils requires more effort to get sonority out of the bell. This can be seen in his tempo, which is slower than that of his teacher, and in the variety of uses he produces. Ils strikes the bell against the floor, with 3 grips of varying effectiveness, while his teacher waves it in the air. On some occasions, he reverts to non-effective, non-canonical uses by sucking on the bell.

Next, we will show the rhythm analysis of Ils and his teacher during the sequence. The indication ♩= 60 indicates that each quarter note, (♩) is equivalent to, approximately, one second. The joined sixteenth notes (♬) correspond to two quarter-second beats. On the other hand, quarter rests (𝄽) are equivalent to 1 s pauses, while half rests (𝄼) are equivalent to two second pauses.

It is notated in G,[5] on the second line of the staff from the bottom (), because the bell used is tuned to that note. The time signature denotes the organization and structure of the score. They serve to specify how many beats are in

3.1 00:00-00:02

*Ils looks at the teacher when she rings the bell (*distant demonstration*). She plays 4 sixteenth notes (a quarter second each) and a quarter note (a second), twice, in a 2/4 time signature.

Then, she gives the bell to Ils.

Teacher's Distant Demonstration:

Duration: 2 seconds

3.2 00:09-00:13

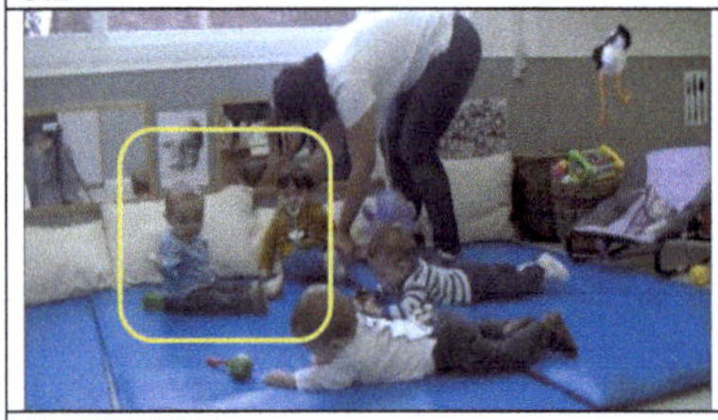

*Ils rings the bell, holding it by the handle with the skirt down, and striking it against the floor (*rhythmic-sound canonical use 1*).

The figuration corresponds to five quarter notes. We complete the measure with three rests (one half rest, and one quarter rest).

Ils' RSCU 1

Duration: 4 seconds

Ils then shows the bell to himself (*private ostensive gesture*), changing hands and adjusting his grip. 00:13-00:21

3.3 00:23-00:27

*Ils rings the bell, grabbing it by the skirt (*rhythmic-sound proto-canonical use*).

The figuration corresponds to 2 quarter notes, 1 quarter note rest (1 second pause) and 1 quarter note.

Ils' RSPCU

Fig. 4.3 Uses of the musical instrument bell. Duration 1′10″

[5] Sol, in latin notation.

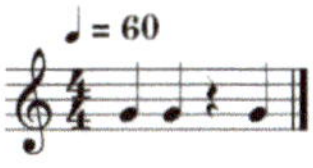

Duration: 4 seconds

After this use, he switches hands again, and sucks on the bell handle (*non-canonical use*).
00:31-00:36

3.4 00:42-00:58

*Ils returns to ringing the bell holding it by the handle and with the skirt down (*rhythmic-sound canonical use 1*).

In this case, he performs 6 quarter notes and a rest of half note, that is to say a pause of two seconds.

Ils' RSCU 1

Duration: 8 seconds

3.5 00:48-00:58

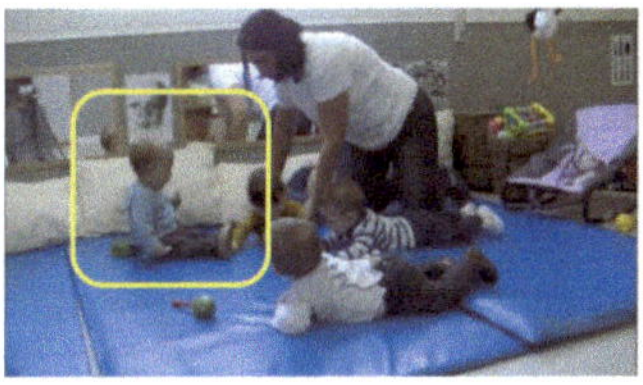

*After the half rest, Ils strikes the bell again against the floor (*rhythmic-sound canonical use 1*).
M tells him: "Slowly", to regulate the intensity of his use, since a partner, Y, was nearby.

His rhythm remains the same, but in this case it corresponds to 12 quarter notes. The tempo also remains one quarter note (one beat) per second approximately.

Ils' RSCU 1

Duration: 12 seconds

3.6 01:02-01:12

Ils adjusts his grip of the bell. We can see that he is looking for further refinement. In this case, he lays the bell down and grasps it with the skirt up, *to shake it in the air and hit it against the floor (*canonical rhythmic-sound use 2*). He makes it sound better, the bell vibrates more. This is important since the bell is an instrument that prolongs the sound. When it is used properly, the duration of the sound is longer.

In the last block of the selected sequence, he makes 10 quarter notes, that is to say 10 strokes per second approximately.

Ils's RSCU 2

Duration: 10 segundos

Fig. 4.3 (continued)

Table 4.1 General indicators of observation 1

	Teacher	Infant
Uses	Rhythmic-sound canonical use	Non canonical uses Rhythmic-sound protocanonical uses Rhythmic-sound canonical uses (1 and 2)
Pauses	Yes	Yes
Dynamic	mf	mf
Accent	Every 4 pulses	Every 4 pulses
Tempo	120 aprox	80 aprox

each block and their duration. The time signature of the teacher (Fig. 4.3) was 2/4, i.e., each block of the staff is equivalent to two seconds. On the other hand, Ils' time signature was 4/4, each block equals four seconds.

However, Ils' sequence of uses with the bell does not end here. Ils continues to perform rhythmic-sound canonical uses for more than a minute and a half, alternating between different uses for maximum effectiveness (see complete sequence in [75]).

During this activity, we also observed how musical instruments and sound objects enable the interaction between subjects. In the case of the interaction between Ils and his teacher, the uses of the bell provide common ground for interaction and regulation of action. The teacher intervenes to guide Ils' action at specific moments (see Fig. 4.4).

On the other hand, we have observed an incipient form of peer interaction. Ils and Y (0;8,3) begin to interact through sound objects and musical instruments (see Fig. 4.5). While one uses the objects to produce sounds, the other waits, watching attentively.

Although we cannot confirm the communicative intention between the two infants, it is interesting to observe how the action of one influences the action of the other, reaching an approximation to "turn-taking" thanks to the sound and rhythm when playing musical instruments and sound objects.

From these observations, we can highlight the importance of rhythmic-sound aspects from an early age. The use of the bell allows Ils not only to exercise his agency and intentionality (see Chaps. 8–11 on Executive Functions), but also to start building the first agreements with his teacher, and possibly with Y, through the mediation of the sound objects and musical instruments. Peer interaction through the sonority of objects, therefore, opens up as a very attractive line of research to be explored.

4.7.2 The Rhythmic-Sound Use of Everyday Objects: Cans

This activity took place in the eighth month of observation, in the same classroom. The teacher organized an activity with everyday objects such as cans of different

	*Ils produces a *rhythmic-sound canonical use 2* (the most effective).
	M, who is attentive to his action, recognizes a potential danger: Ils is waving the bell too hard near his face and could hurt himself. *Therefore, she regulates Ils' action through language: "Slowly Ils, slowly, you may hit yourslef". Ils looks at her attentively and stops his action.
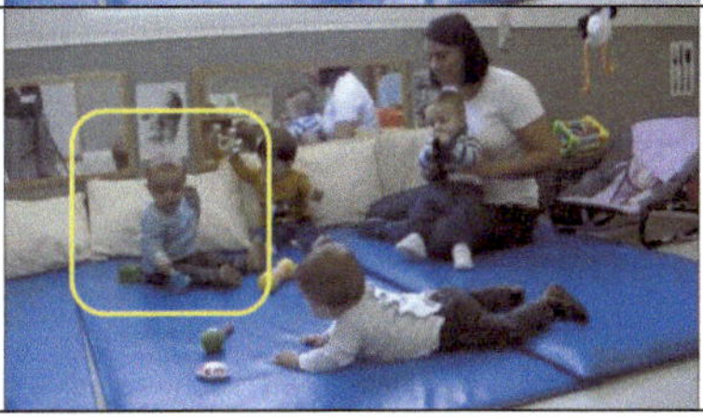	*Ils adjusts his grip, returning to rhythmic-sound canonical uses of level 1, of intermediate effectiveness, but more secure. For the remainder of the activity, he does not return to level 2 uses.

Fig. 4.4 The teacher regulates Ils' uses of the bell

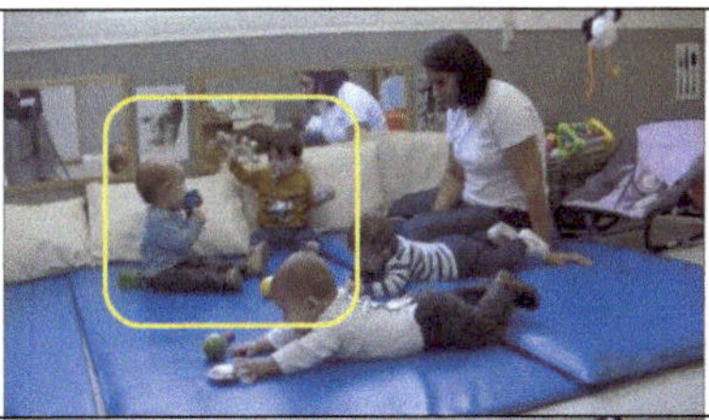	*While Y uses the rattles (*rhythmic-sound canonical use*), Ils watches him attentively. Somehow, he seems to be waiting for his turn to perform, sucking on the bell (*non-canonic use*).
	* When Y stops his uses and looks at the rattles (*private ostensive gestures*), Ils resumes his *rhythmic-sound canonical uses* with the bell.

Fig. 4.5 Interaction between Ils and Y around sonority

shapes and sizes. The infants could use the proposed objects freely, while the teacher intervened at specific moments.

In this sequence, we observed how Ar (1 year, 27 days), uses cans of different sizes in a coordinated way to produce sound, that is, as *sound objects.* From the beginning of the activity, he is very interested in the cans. At first, he tries to put a large can inside another one of the same size, which is impossible, as they do not fit (*protocanonical use*, as the cans are used to store other things inside). The teacher continues placing smaller cans around the infants. Ar picks up two and immediately puts them inside a large can (*canonical use*). This shows that Ar knows the canonical use of cans, as objects to keep things inside (in his case, smaller cans). However, he puts a twist on his activity.

He starts shaking the cans, producing sound. From this moment on, he orients his activity towards the objective of exploring the sonority of the cans. During the sequence, we identify Ar's *rhythmic-sound uses.* These uses consist of producing sound with the cans, objects that were not designed for this purpose. Ar introduces variations to these uses, combining different objects and adjusting his action to produce specific sounds. The fact that Ar initially uses the cans according to their *canonical use*, as well as the variations he introduces to his *rhythmic-sound uses*, allow us to conclude that the latter were not fortuitous, but intentionally pursued.

During the sequence, Ar repeats the same rhythmic pattern approximately every 5–10 s. We observe a large number of pauses, which organize his action. His moment of shaking the cans lasts, approximately, the same time as the pauses. The dynamics always occurred in *mezzoforte*. However, unlike Ils and the teacher in the previous sequence, Ar did not mark accents. Finally, his tempo was approximately 120 beats per minute (see Table 4.2).

Next, we will show the analysis of Ar's rhythm during the sequence. Again, we mark ♩ = 60, indicating that each quarter note (♩) equals approximately one second. In Ar's uses, we mark two conjoined eighth notes (♫), which represent two pulses of half a second each (not to be confused with the sixteenth notes present in the previous observation). In this case, they are crossed out (x), since the figures do not indicate a specific musical note, but simply mark the duration of each pulse. This is usual for percussion musical instruments, such as drums, which do not produce medody (see Fig. 4.6).

Table 4.2 General indicators of observation 2

	Ar
Uses	Rhytmic-sound uses Protocanonical uses Canonical uses
Pauses	Yes
Dynamic	mf
Accent	Not regular
Tempo	120 aprox

At the beginning of the sequence, Ar stores and takes out different cans (*canonical uses*).	00:00- 00:35
6.1	00:36- 02:08
	Ar stores a small can into the large can (*canonical use*). He then shakes the large can looking for it to rattle. However, the cans get stuck. When shaken, they do not produce sound. Ar recognizes this situation. He looks into the can (*private ostensive gesture*) as if asking “why doesn't it rattle?” *Then, he reaches in to try to pull out the stuck cans, unsuccessfully. He repeats these strategies (shaking, looking inside, and trying to pull the cans out) for more than a minute and a half, until he succeeds in retrieving the small cans.
6.2	2:08-2:14
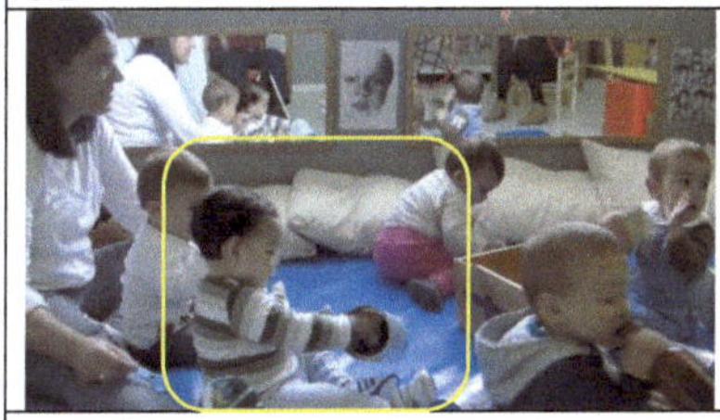	*Next, he shakes the small can inside the large one to produce sound (*rhythmic-sound use*). He performs 12 pulses, in a rhythm of two eighth notes per second.
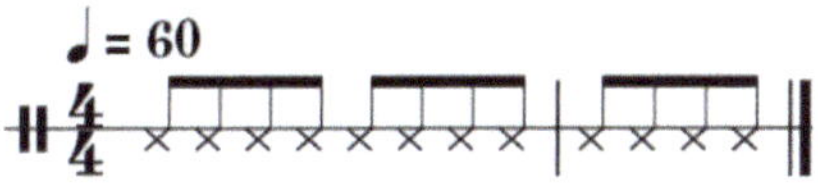 Duration: 6 seconds	
Ar stores the small cans and transfers them from one large can to another (*canonical use*).	02:29-02:48
6.3	02:51-02.56
	He then inserts his hands into both large cans and begins to shake them at the same time, and banging them together (*rhythmic-sound use*). He produces a rhythm of approximately 8 eighth-note figures, two per second.
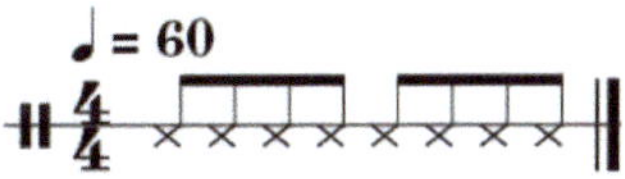 Duration: 4 seconds	
During the next minute, Ar stores and takes out the cans (*canonical use*), and tries to produce sound, unsuccessfully.	03:02- 4:06
6.4	04:07-07:43

Fig. 4.6 Uses of cans as sound objects. Duration 7′43″

From this moment until the end of the sequence, Ar gets to sound the cans, repeating a steady rhythm of approximately 8 eighth-note figures, two per second, followed by a pause.

He repeats this rhythmic pattern 18 times. He also adds variations, combining different objects:

- On repetition 15, he introduced a spoon.
- On repetition 16, he added an additional can.
- In repetition 17, he hit the can from the outside with a spoon.
- In repetition 18, he introduces a wooden piece of cutlery, which he shakes from inside the can.

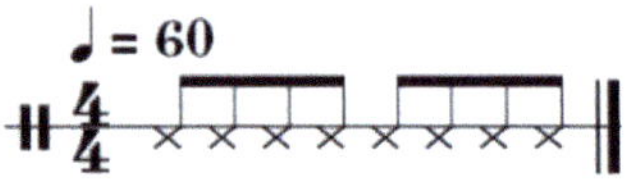

Duration: 4 seconds (approximately, for each repetition)

Fig. 4.6 (continued)

From this sequence, we can conclude that Ar shows a clear rhythmic pattern linked to the *rhythmic-sound use* of the cans. His action becomes directed and intentional, with the goal of producing sound. Although we cannot confirm or deny the teacher's previous educational influence in the origin of these uses, we do find certain significant elements. Ar understands that the large can sounds when it has smaller cans inside. We can confirm that Ar performs an intentional process of searching for the sonority with different objects. We can also observe elements of self-regulation and executive functioning: Ar sets a difficult, non-immediate goal, before which he organizes his action in a flexible way, and inhibits non-effective uses. When he drops the small cans and the large one stops rattling, instead of giving up, he persists in his goal: he stops his action and retrieves the small can, putting it back in the large can. We also observe that he searches flexibly for possible variations to the sonority. He uses one or two small cans, a plastic spoon, and a wooden spoon. This implies that *rhythmic-sound uses* are related to the manifestations of Executive Functions in the classroom (see Chaps. 8–11, this volume).

It is important to emphasize that the rhythmic of the infants in school, in the sequences we have shown, has been binary. That is, with one accent every two (a-A) or four beats (a-a-a-A).[6] It is also important to note that both infants repeat

[6] Although in the presented sequence Ar did not show a specific accent, in later uses he showed an accent every two beats.

certain rhythmic patterns, which, together with the pauses and silences they perform, shows that there is a rhythmic sound structure in the use of the musical instrument and sound object.

4.8 Conclusions

Throughout this chapter, we have analyzed the importance of rhythm and sonority in early development. Not only through listening to music (cds, radio, background music), but also through infants' musical production with sound objects and musical instruments. The research we have shown represent a promising first step in considering the role of musical uses of objects in early development.

From a very early age, the rhythm and sonority of materiality act as one of the first semiotic mediators between infants and adults. That is, sound objects and musical instruments enable early triadic interactions between adult and infant. First, from the adult's intention, who introduces the infant in meaningful situations of interaction, organized and structured, in which the infant constructs the first shared meanings with the adult. Thanks to these organized, adult-controlled interactions, the infant will progressively take the initiative in the interaction [55]. This lays the foundation for the development of more complex skills, such as intentional communication and language (see Chap. 7, on the development of gestures).

In addition, we have observed one of the first interactions between peers. Ils and Y, at 8 months, organize their action according to the uses of the other. Although this interaction is very simple, it opens a space to study peer interaction from a very early age. In triadic interactions, both with adults and peers, pauses, silences, and the rhythm of the participants organize the interaction, opening spaces for intervention. The adult has to take into account these pauses in the rhythmic-sound interaction that they establish with the infant, to promote the infant's action in the interaction.

In this sense, sound objects and musical instruments are very attractive for infants from the middle of the first year of life. Likewise, some of the first functional uses that infants make on their own initiative are rhythmic-sound ones [78]. Thanks to these uses, infants develop their initiative in action, that is, their intentionality and agency. Infants begin to consider objects based on what they can functionally do with them. In a very general way, they constitute a first access to the rules of uses of the objects. The infant will progressively construct and appropriate the uses and cultural meanings of the everyday objects, also thanks to the mediation of the adult. In this case, the first canonical uses we have observed are clearly rhythmic-sound, with musical instruments such as bells and metallophones [53, 75], objects with culturally and socially defined rules of use.

The use of sound objects and musical instruments can also be of benefit for clinical or therapeutic purposes. Intervention with music therapy in neonatal treatment rooms offers important benefits for the development of the baby in risk situations, such as prematurity [39]. The music therapist mediates the interaction between the adult and the baby, creating a coherent and structured space of interaction through music. This is of vital importance, not only for the baby, but also for the rest of the people close to him. For the baby, music therapy offers an organized stimulation in an environment that is often disorganized and noisy. This results in increased well-being for the baby, as well as a reduced heartbeat and increased oxygen saturation.

For parents, who often face serious difficulties, fears and doubts about their newborn, given their concern for their survival, the music therapist organizes a series of musical activities that allow them to approach the baby in an organized way. Thanks to the music therapy intervention, parents can begin to interact with their baby, develop an emotional bond, and feel more capable as parents. It also offers them the opportunity to express their emotions and doubts in a safe environment.

Finally, the effects of music therapy also extend to the hospital setting in general. After the intervention, the climate of the pediatric units becomes more organized, calmer, which promotes the well-being not only of the premature baby, but also of the other people present, both parents and hospital staff. All these benefits, both in isolation and as a whole, act as protective factors for the development of the babies, reducing the risks inherent to their preterm condition.

On the other hand, in the early years school, we have observed how sound objects and musical instruments are among the first objects that infants begin to use in a functional way. The teachers present and demonstrate how to use these objects, with the aim of promoting the infants' agency and autonomy, as well as their intentional communication, throughout the academic year. Rhythmic-sound uses and canonical rhythmic-sound uses are the first effective, functional, and even conventional (in the case of musical instruments) uses that infants begin to produce intentionally in the first year of the early years school. This is connected, in part, with the development of Executive Functions (see Chaps. 8–11, this volume; see also [53, 75]).

We have observed that infants maintain a constant rhythmic pattern, establish accents, mainly binary, and mark their own tempo. This means that the infants structure their action in an intentional way, not by chance. This organization, as we commented previously, allows the encounter with others, be it the teacher or a peer.

However, the scarcity of studies on music in early childhood education (0–6 years) is striking. Currently, music in schools has been linked to the previous experience of teachers, or to their cultural knowledge, and only in some cases is it considered part of the initial training of teachers (see [18]). This issue is of great importance, since, in Spain, the subject of music is established in the LOMLOE (*Ley Orgánica de Modificación de la Ley Orgánica de Educación*) as a compulsory subject. Royal Decree 95/2022 includes the musical expression as a key objective for the first cycle of early childhood education.

We consider it necessary, therefore, to consider seriously the role of music, and of rhythmic-sound aspects of sound objects and musical instruments, as key elements in early childhood education. This would imply a serious discussion of the early childhood education curriculum, as well as the initial training of teachers in musical knowledge. Rhythm, being one of the first musical manifestations of human beings, should be observed and supported throughout the process of development and learning, from the first cycle of early childhood education (0–3 years). For all these reasons, we consider that the professionals who develop their work in the early years school should have sufficient competences in music education to be able to successfully lead the musical development of infants at an early age. It is very important for their general development to provide infants with musical experiences with sound objects and musical instruments appropriate in sonority and size in order to consolidate one of the first semiotic systems present in early development, such as rhythmic and sound interaction with peers and adults.

References

1. Acker, A., & Nyland, B. (2018). Music as a platform for intercultural understanding: early childhood curriculum and a growing neoliberal imperative. In C. Roofe & C. Bezzina (Eds.), *Intercultrual studies of curriculum. Theory, policy and practice* (pp. 85–104). Palgrave Macmillan. https://doi.org/10.1007/978-3-319-60897-6
2. Ajuriaguerra, J. (1978). Neuropsicología del desarrollo [Neuropsychology of development]. *Journal for the Study of Education and Development, 1*(2), 5–22.
3. Arnon, S., Shapsa, A., Forman, L., Regev, R., Bauer, S., Litmaanovitz, I., & Dolfin, T. (2006). Live music is beneficial to preterm infants in the neonatal intensive care unit environment. *Birth, 33*, 131–136.
4. Bakermans-Kranenburg, M. J., van Ijzendoorn, M. H., & Juffer, F. (2003). Less is more: Meta-analyses of sensitivity and attachment interventions in early childhood. *Psychological Bulletin, 129*(2), 195–215. https://doi.org/10.1037/0033-2909.129.2.195
5. Barbosa, M., Vences, M., Rodrigues, P. M., & Rodrigues, H. (2023). Babies' engagement in music theater performances: A microanalytical study of the aesthetic experiences in early childhood. *Psychology of Aesthetics, Creativity, and the Arts, 17*(1), 118.
6. Beebe, B. (1982). Micro-timing in mother-infant communication. In *Nonverbal communication today: Current research* (pp. 169–195).
7. Beebe Beebe, B., & Lachmann, F. M. (1988). The contribution of mother-infant mutual influence to the origins of self- and object representations. *Psychoanalytic Psychology, 5*(4), 305–337. https://doi.org/10.1037/0736-9735.5.4.305
8. Belinchón, M., Rivière, A., & Igoa, J. M. (1992). *Psicología del lenguaje. Investigación y teoría*, 4 [Psychology of language. Research and theory]. Trotta.
9. Boulch, J. (1983/1995). *El desarrollo psicomotor desde el nacimiento hasta los seis años* [Psicomotor development from birth to six years]. Doñate.
10. Boyle, E., Draper, E., Evans, T., Field, D., Manktelow, B., Marlow, N., Seaton, S., Smith, L. K., & Johnson, S. (2014). Infant neurodevelopmental outcomes following late and moderately preterm birth. *Archives of disease in childhood. Fetal and Neonatal Ed., 99*, Suppl. 1.
11. Brazelton, T. B., Koslowski, B., & Main, M. (1974). The origins of reciprocity: The early mother-infant interaction. In M. Lewis & L. A. Rosenblum, *The effect of the infant on its caregiver* (pp. 49–76). Wiley-Interscience.
12. Bruner, J. S. (1975). From communication to language—A psychological perspective. *Cognition, 3*(39), 255–287. https://doi.org/10.1016/0010-0277(74)90012-2
13. Butterworth, G. (2003). Pointing is the royal road to language for babies. In S. Kita (Ed.), *Pointing: Where language, culture, and cognition meet* (pp. 9–33). Lawrence Erlbaum Associates Publishers.
14. Cassidy, J. W., & Standley, J. M. (1995). The effect of music listening on physiological responses of premature infants in the NICU. *Journal of Music Therapy, 32*(4), 208–227.

15. Ciccone, A. (2013). Rhythmicity in infants' experiences and their development. *Journal of Physiology-Paris, 107*(4), 286–290. https://doi.org/10.1016/j.jphysparis.2013.03.003
16. Cohn, J. F., & Tronick, E. Z. (1988). Mother-infant face-to-face interaction: Influence bidirectional and unrelated to periodic cycles in either partner's behavior. *Developmental Psychology, 24*(3), 386–392. https://doi.org/10.1037/0012-1649.24.3.386
17. Condon, W. S., & Sander, S. L. (1974). Neonate movement is synchronized with adult speech interactional participation and language acquisition. *Science, 183*, 94–101.
18. Correa, M., Villalobos, M. E., Cárdenas, K., Moreno-Llanos, I., Del Olmo, M. J., & Moreno-Nuñez, A. (2021). Usos rítmico-sonoros de objetos e instrumentos musicales en las aulas 0-1 y 1-2 [Rhytmic-sound uses of objects and musical instruments in classroom 0-1 and 1-2]. In C. Rodríguez & J. L. de los Reyes (Coords.) *Los objetos sí importan. Acción educativa en la escuela infantil* (pp. 57–82). Horsori.
19. Crnic, K. A., Greenberg, M. T., Ragozin, A. S., Robinson, N. M., & Basham, R. B. (1983). Effects of stress and social support on mothers and premature and full-term infants. *Child Development, 54*(1), 209–217. https://doi.org/10.2307/1129878
20. D'Souza, S. R., Lewis, L. E., Kumar, V., Kamath, A., Nayak, B. S., Noronha, J. A., & George, A. (2015). Noise in neonatal intensive care unit: Effects on hospitalized preterm infants. *Manipal Journal of Nursing and Health Sciences (MJNHS), 1*(1), 57–62.
21. De León, Y. J. (2020). *La influencia de la musicoterapia en procesos neurobioquímicos del desarrollo temprano* [The influence of music therapy on neurobiochemical processes in early development]. [Unpublished PhD dissertation]. Universidad Autónoma de Madrid.
22. Del Olmo, M. J. (2009). *Musicoterapia con bebés de 0 a 6 meses en cuidados intensivos pediátricos* [Music therapy with infants 0 to 6 months in pediatric intensive care] [Unpublished PhD dissertation]. Universidad Autónoma de Madrid.
23. Del Olmo, M. J. (2021). Musicoterapia hospitalaria I. Características neonatología y pediatría. Situaciones de alarma sanitaria [Hospital music therapy I. Neonatology and pediatrics characteristics. Health alarm situations]. In M. Pérez-Eizaguirre & M. J. Del Olmo (Eds.), *Musicoterapia* (pp. 53–82). Paraninfo.
24. Del Olmo, M. J., Rodríguez, C., & Ruza, F. (2010). Music therapy in the PICU: 0- to 6-month-old babies. *Music and Medicine, 2*(3), 158–166. http://mmd.sagepub.com
25. Ettenberger, M., Odell-Miller, H., Cárdenas, C. R., Serrano, S. T., Parker, M., & Camargo Llanos, S. M. (2014). Music therapy with premature infants and their caregivers in Colombia—A mixed methods pilot study including a randomized trial. *Voices: A World Forum for Music Therapy, 14*(2). https://doi.org/10.15845/voices.v14i2.756
26. Feldman, R. (2007). Parent-infant synchrony and the construction of shared timing: Physiological precursors, developmental outcomes, and risk conditions. *Journal of Child Psychology and Psychiatry, 48*(3–4), 329–354. https://doi.org/10.1111/j.1469-7610.2006.01701.x
27. Fogel, A. (1993/97). *Developing through relationships: Origins of communication, self, and culture.* University of Chicago Press.
28. Fraisse, P. (1976). *Psicología del ritmo* [Psychology of rhythm]. Ediciones Morata.
29. Gianino, A., & Tronick, E. Z. (1988). The mutual regulation model: The infant's self and interactive regulation and coping defense capacities. In T. Field, P. McCabe, & N. Schneiderman (Eds.). *Stress and coping across development* (pp. 47–68). Erlbaum.
30. Godøy, R. I. (2006). Gestural-sonorous objects: Embodied extensions of Schaeffer's conceptual apparatus. *Organised Sound, 11*(2), 149–157.
31. Greenberg, M. T., & Crnic, K. A. (1988). Longitudinal predictors of developmental status and social interaction in premature and full-term infants at age two. *Child Development, 59*(3), 554–570. https://doi.org/10.1111/j.1467-8624.1988.tb03216.x
32. Guevara, I., & Rodríguez, C. (2023). Developing communication through objects: Ostensive gestures as the first gestures in children's development. *Developmental Review, 68*, 101076. https://doi.org/10.1016/j.dr.2023.101076

33. Hartling, L., Shaik, M. S., Tjosvold, L., Leicht, R., Liang, Y., & Kumar, M. (2009). Music for medical indications in the neonatal period: A systematic review of randomised controlled trials. *Archives of Disease in Childhood-Fetal and Neonatal Edition, 94*(5), F349–F354. https://doi.org/10.1136/adc.2008.148411
34. Holt, S., Fogel, A., & Wood, R. (1998). Innovation in social games. In M. Lyra & J. Valsiner (comp.), *Child development within culturally structured environment* (Vol. IV, pp. 35–51). Ablex.
35. Ionio, C., Colombo, C., Brazzoduro, V., Mascheroni, E., Confalonieri, E., Castoldi, F., & Lista, G. (2016). Mothers and fathers in NICU: The impact of preterm birth on parental distress. *Europe's Journal of Psychology, 12*(4), 604–621. https://doi.org/10.5964/ejop.v12i4.1093
36. Jaffe, J., Beebe, B., Feldstein, S., Crown, C. L., Jasnow, M. D., Rochat, P., & Stern, D. N. (2001). Rhythms of dialogue in infancy: coordinated timing in development. *Monographs of the Society for Research in Child Development, 66*(2), i–149. http://www.jstor.org/stable/3181589
37. Jáñez-Álvarez, M. (2019). *Valoración de la intervención musical en su función terapéutica en recién nacidos preteérmino moderados-tardíos* [Evaluation of musical intervention in its therapeutic function in moderate-tardy preterm newborns]. Unpublished PhD dissertation. Universidad Autónoma de Madrid.
38. Jáñez-Álvarez, M., Del Olmo, M. J., & Rodríguez, C. (2021). The impact of music therapy in late-moderate premature infants, on their parents and their environment, in a Spanish neonatal intermediate care unit. *Music & Medicine, 13*(4), 272–283. https://doi.org/10.47513/mmd.v13i4.764
39. Jáñez-Álvarez, M., Moreno-Llanos, I., Santacatalina-Pulido, C., De León-Barrios, Y. J., García-Laredo, E., Del Olmo, M. J., & Rodríguez, C. (2024). Analysis of triadic interaction between parents, their preterm infants, and a sonorous object. *Psychology of Music.* https://doi.org/10.1177/03057356231225673
40. Kaye, K. (1982/1986). *La vida mental y social del bebé. Cómo los padres crean personas* [The mental and social life of babies How parents create persons]. Paidós.
41. Kaye, K., & Wells, A. J. (1980). Mothers' jiggling and the burst—pause pattern in neonatal feeding. *Infant Behavior and Development, 3*, 29–46. https://doi.org/10.1016/S0163-6383(80)80005-1
42. Khajeh, M., Bahramnezhad, F., Dehghanzadeh, S., Aghdam, N. F., Bagheri, H., & Baha, R. (2021). The effect of moderating noise pollution on premature infants' behavioral and physiological responses in neonatal intensive care unit. *International Journal of Health Studies*, 1–6.
43. Kiepura, E., Niedźwiecka, A., & Kmita, G. (2022). Silence matters: The role of pauses during dyadic maternal and paternal vocal interactions with preterm and full-term infants. *Journal of Child Language, 49*(3), 451–468. https://doi.org/10.1017/S030500092100012X
44. Lausberg, H., & Sloetjes, H. (2009). Coding gestural behavior with the NEUROGES-ELAN system. *Behavior Research Methods, 41*, 841–849. https://doi.org/10.3758/BRM.41.3.841
45. Licastro, L. (2010). *Comunicación y lenguaje. Perspectiva de la intervención tempana* [Communication and Language. Early intervention perspective]. http://www.musiterapiaenlainfancia.com/comunicación-y-lenguaje/
46. Loewy, J., Stewart, K., Dassler, A. M., Telsey, A., & Homel, P. (2013). The effects of music therapy on vital signs, feeding, and sleep in premature infants. *Pediatrics, 131*(5), 902–918. https://doi.org/10.1542/peds.2012-1367
47. Madden, S. L. (2005). *El Gran Libro del Prematuro* [The big book of preemies]. Medici.
48. Malloch, S., & Trevarthen, C. (2018). The human nature of music. *Frontiers in Psychology, 9*, 364981.
49. May, B. N. (2013). Public school early childhood music education: Challenges and solutions. *General Music Today, 27*(1), 40–44. https://doi.org/10.1177/1048371313494783

50. Minde, K. K., Marton, P., Manning, D., & Hines, B. (1980). Some determinants of mother-infant interaction in the premature nursery. *Journal of the American Academy of Child and Adolescent Psychiatry, 19*(1), 1–21. https://doi.org/10.1016/s0002-7138(09)60649-x
51. Miroudot, L. (2000). *Structuration mélodique et tonalité chez l'enfant* [Melodic structuration and tonality of the child]. L'Harmattan.
52. Moreno-Llanos, I., Guevara, I., Palacios, P., & Rodríguez, C. (2024). How to study the early development of executive function? Let's put control back in the hands of children. *New Ideas in Psychology, 72*, 101049. https://doi.org/10.1016/j.newideapsych.2023.101049
53. Moreno-Llanos, I., Zapardiel, L. A., & Rodríguez, C. (2021). Children's first manifestations of cognitive control in the early years school: The importance of the educational situation and materiality. *European Journal of Psychology of Education, 36*, 903–922. https://doi.org/10.1007/s10212-020-00505-1
54. Moreno-Núñez, A., Rodríguez, C., & Miranda-Zapata, E. D. (2019). Getting away from the point: The emergence of ostensive gestures and their functions. *Journal of Child Language, 47*(3), 556–578. https://doi.org/10.1177/03057356231225673
55. Moreno-Núñez, A., Rodríguez, C., & Del Olmo, M. J. (2015). The rhythmic, sonorous and melodic components of adult-child-object interactions between 2 and 6 months old. *Integrative Psychological and Behavioral Science, 49*(4), 737–756. https://doi.org/10.1007/s12124-015-9298-2
56. Moreno-Núñez, A., Rodríguez, C., & Del Olmo, M. J. (2017). Rhythmic ostensive gestures: How adults facilitate infants, entrance into early triadic interactions. *Infant Behavior and Development, 49*, 168–181. https://doi.org/10.1016/j.infbeh.2017.09.003
57. Nichols, K., Gergely, G., & Fonagy, P. (2001). Experimental protocols for investigating relationshipsamong mother-infant interaction, affect regulation, psysiological markers of stress responsiveness, and attachment. *Bulletin of the Menninger Clinic, 65*, 371–379.
58. Papousek, H. (1996). Musicality in infancy research: Biological and cultural origins of early musicality. In I. Deliège & J. Sloboda (Eds.), *Musical beginnings: Origins and development of musical competence* (pp. 37–55). Oxford University Press.
59. Papousek, H., & Papousek, M. (1989). Intuitive parenting: Aspects related to educational psychology. *European Journal of Psychology of Education, 4*(2), 201–210. https://doi.org/10.1007/BF03172602
60. Partnership for Maternal, Newborn and Child Health [PMNCH]. (2011). *Essential interventions, commodities, and guidelines for reproductive, maternal, newborn, and child health.* The Partnership for Maternal Health, Newborn and Child Health and the Aga Khan University.
61. Paz, O. (2006). *El arco y la lira* [The arc and the lyre]. Fondo de Cultura Económica.
62. Perinat, A. (1993). *Comunicación animal, comunicación humana* [Animal communication, human communication]. Siglo XXI.
63. Pérez-Eizaguirre, M., & Del Olmo, M. J. (coords., 2021). *Musicoterapia* [Music theapy]. Paraninfo.
64. Piaget, J. (1936/1948). *La naissance de l'intelligence chez l'enfant*. [The origins of intelligence in children]. Delachaux et Niestl´e. (version ´electronique, Fondation Jean Piaget).
65. Provasi, J., Blanc, L., & Carchon, I. (2021). The importance of rhythmic stimulation for preterm infants in the NICU. *Children (Basel, Switzerland), 8*(8), 660. https://doi.org/10.3390/children8080660
66. Racy, A. J. (1994). A dialectical perspective on musical instruments: The east-mediterranean Mijwiz. *Ethnomusicology, 38*(1), 37–57. https://doi.org/10.2307/852267
67. Raju, T. N. K. (2017). "Late preterm" birth—Ten years later. *Pediatrics, 139*. Article e20163331. https://doi.org/10.1542/peds.2016-3331
68. Ravn, I. H., Smith, L., Lindemann, R., Smeby, N. A., Kyno, N. M., Bunch, E. H., & Sandvik, L. (2011). Effect of early intervention on social interaction between mothers and preterm infants at 12 months of age: A randomized controlled trial. *Infant Behavior and Development, 34*(2), 215–225. https://doi.org/10.1016/j.infbeh.2010.11.004
69. Real Decreto 95/2022, de 1 de febrero, por el que se establece la ordenación y las enseñanzas mínimas de la Educación Infantil. Ministerio de Educación y Formación Profesional [Royal

Decree 95/2022, of February 1st, which establishes the organization and minimum teaching requirements for Early Childhood Education. Ministry of Education and Professional Training].
70. Rochat, P., & Hespos, S. J. (1997). Differential rooting response by neonates: Evidence for an early sense of self. *Infant and Child Development, 6*(3–4), 105–112.
71. Rodger, M., Stapleton, P., Van Walstijn, M., Ortiz, M., & Pardue, L. (2020, July). What makes a good musical instrument? A matter of processes, ecologies and specificities. In *Proceedings of the international conference on New Interfaces for Musical Expression, NIME 2020* (pp. 405–410). https://doi.org/10.5281/zenodo.4813438
72. Rodríguez, C. (2006). *Del ritmo al símbolo. Los signos en el nacimiento de la inteligencia* [From rhythm to symbol. Signs in the birth of intelligence]. Horsori.
73. Rodríguez, C. (2022). The construction of executive function in early development: The pragmatics of action and gestures. *Human Development, 66*(4–5), 239–259. https://doi.org/10.1159/000526340
74. Rodríguez, C., Basilio, M., Cárdenas, K., Cavalcante, S., Moreno-Núñez, A., Palacios, P., & Yuste, N. (2018). Objects pragmatics: Culture and communication as the bases for early cognitive development. In J. Valsiner & A. Rosa (Eds.), *The Cambridge handbook of sociocultural psychology* (pp. 223–244). Cambridge University Press.
75. Rodríguez, C., & Moreno-Llanos, I. (2023). A pragmatic turn in the study of early executive functions by object use and gestures. A case study from 8 to 17 months of age at a nursery school. *Integrative Psychological and Behavioral Science, 57*, 607–654. https://doi.org/10.1007/s12124-020-09578-5
76. Rodríguez, C., & Moro, C. (1998). El uso convencional también hace permanentes a los objetos [Conventional use also makes objects permanent]. *Journal for the Study of Education and Development, 21*(84), 67–83. https://doi.org/10.1174/021037098760378793
77. Rodríguez, C., & Moro, C. (1999). *El mágico número tres. Cuando los niños aún no hablan* [The magic number 3. When children still do not talk]. Paidós.
78. Rodríguez, C., & Moro, C. (2008). Coming to agreement. Object use by infants and adults. In J. Zlatev, T. P. Racine, C. Sinha, & E. Itkonen (Eds.) *The shared mind: Perspectives on intersubjectivity* (pp. 89–114). John Benjamins Publishing Company. https://doi.org/10.1075/celcr.12
79. Rosmanith, N., Costall, A., Reichelt, A. F., López, B., & Reddy, V. (2014). Jointly structuring triadic spaces of meaning and action: Book sharing from 3 months on. *Frontiers in Psychology, 5*, 1390. https://doi.org/10.3389/fpsyg.2014.01390
80. Saada-Robert, M. (1985). La construction microgénétique d'un schème élémentaire [The microgenetic construction of an elementary schema]. In B. Inhelder, G. Cell´erier, E. Ackermann, A. Blanchet, A. Boder, D. De Caprona, J. J. Ducret, & M. Saada-Robert (Eds.), *Le cheminement des d´ecouvertes de l'enfant. Recherche sur les microgen'eses cognitives* (pp. 119–137). Delachaux et Niestlé.
81. Santacatalina, C. (2017). *La sesión de musicoterapia en Neonatología. Patrones rítmicos en la interacción adulto-bebé* [The music therapy session in neonatology. Rhythmic patterns in the adult-baby interaction.]. Unpublished Mastery Thesis. Universidad Autónoma de Madrid.
82. Schaffer, H. R. (1984). The child's entry into a social world. *Behavioural Development: A Series of Monographs*, 236.
83. Schappin, R., Wijnroks, L., Uniken Venema, M. M., & Jongmans, M. J. (2013). Rethinking stress in parents of preterm infants: A meta-analysis. *PLOS ONE, 8*(2), Article e54992. https://doi.org/10.1371/journal.pone.0054992
84. Sève, B. (2018). *El instrumento musical. Un estudio filosófico* [The musical instrument. A philosophical study]. Acantilado
85. Shenfield, T., Trehub, S. E., & Nakata, T. (2003). Maternal singing modulates infant arousal. *Psychology of Music, 31*(4), 365–375. https://doi.org/10.1177/03057356030314002
86. Spitz, R. A. (1965). *The first year of life: A psychoanalytic study of normal and deviant development of object relations.* International Universities Press, I.

87. Standley, J. M. (2002). A meta-analysis of the efficacy of music therapy for premature infants. *Journal of Pediatric Nursing, 17*(2), 107–113. https://doi.org/10.1053/jpdn.2002.124128
88. Stern, D. N. (1974). Mother and infant at play: The dyadic interaction involving facial, vocal, and gaze behaviors. In M. Lewis & L. A. Rosenblum (Eds.), *The effect of the infant on its caregiver* (pp. 177–202). Wiley-Interscience.
89. Stern, D. (1985/1995). *The interpersonal world of the infant. A view from Pshycoanalisis and developmental Psychology*. Basic Books.
90. Stern, D. (1995/1997). *La constelación maternal* [The maternal constellation]. Paidós.
91. Stern, D. N., Beebe, J., Jaffe, J., & Bennett, S. L. (1977). The infants' stimulus 'world' during social interaction: A study of the structure, timing and effects of caregiver behaviors. In R. Schaffer (Ed.), *Interactions in infancy, The Loch Lomond symposium* (pp. 177–203). Academic Press.
92. Stoll, B. J., Hansen, N. I., Bell, E. F., Shankaran, S., Laptook, A. R., Walsh, M. C., Hale, E. C., Newman, N. S., Schibler, K., Carlo, W. A., Kennedy, K. A., Poindexter, B. B., Finer, N. N., Ehrenkranz, R. A., Duara, S., Sánchez, P. J., O´Shea, T. M., Goldberg, R. N., Van Meurs, K. P., ... Eunice Kennedy Shriver National Institute of Child Health Human Development Neonatal Research Network. (2010). Neonatal outcomes of extremely preterm infants from the NICHD Neonatal Research Network. *Pediatrics, 126*, 443–456. https://doi.org/10.1542/peds.2009-2959
93. Tomasello, M. (2008). *Origins of human communication.* MIT Press.
94. Trevarthen, C. (1974). Cerebral embryology and the split brain. In M. Kinsbourne & W. L. Smith (Eds.), *Hemispheric disconnection and cerebral function* (pp. 208–237). Charles C Thomas.
95. Trevarthen, C. (1979). Communication and cooperation in early infancy: A description of primary intersubjectivity. *Before Speech: The Beginning of Interpersonal Communication, 1*, 530–571.
96. Trevarthen, C. (2008). Shared minds and the science of fiction: Why theories will differ. In J. Zlatev, T. P. Racine, C. Sinha, & E. Itkonen (Eds.) *The shared mind: Perspectives on intersubjectivity* (pp. VII-XIII). John Benjamins Publishing Company. https://doi.org/10.1075/celcr.12
97. Tronick, E. D., Als, H., & Brazelton, T. B. (1977). Mutuality in mother–infant interaction. *Journal of Communication, 27*(2), 74–79. https://doi.org/10.1111/j.1460-2466.1977.tb01829.x
98. Vygotsky, L. (1931/1995). El problema del desarrollo de las funciones psíquicas superiores [The problem of the development of higher psychic functions]. In L. S. Vygotsky, *Obras Escogidas*, (3), (pp. 11–46). Visor.
99. Wachman, E. M., & Lahav, A. (2011). The effects of noise on preterm infants in the NICU. *Archives of Disease in Childhood-Fetal and Neonatal Edition, 96*(4), F305–F309.
100. Wallin, N. L., Merker, B., & Brown, S. (Eds., 1999). *The origins of Music.* The MIT Press.
101. Wallon, H. (1951/1985). *El desarrollo psicológico de la primera infancia. Manual para el seguimiento del desarrollo infantil desde el nacimiento hasta los seis años* [The psychological development of early childhood. A manual for monitoring child development from birth to six years of age]. Visor.
102. Wallon, H. (1942). *De l'acte á la pensée* [From act to thougth]. Editions Flammarion. ISBN 9782082101660.
103. Zachariou, A., & Whitebread, D. (2019). Developmental differences in young children's self-regulation. *Journal of Applied Developmental Psychology, 62*, 282–293. https://doi.org/10.1016/j.appdev.2019.02.002

Development of the First Symbols in Triadic Communicative Contexts

5

Pedro Palacios, Karina Cárdenas, and Noemí Yuste

5.1 Introduction

The development of symbols or symbolic uses of objects (referred to in the psychological literature as symbolic, representational, or pretend play) has long been a central topic in developmental psychology. In this chapter, we address the development of symbols during infancy from the Pragmatics of the Object. One of the questions we started with was *how* infants begin to use everyday objects symbolically in triadic communicative and interactive contexts, adult–object–infant. We assume, from the perspective we adopt here, that *cultural materiality*, the rules of canonical uses of objects linked to *communication and participation of others*, especially adults, should be considered at the basis of the development of the first symbols.

One of the first problems we encounter when entering the fascinating and, at the same time, complex world of symbols is knowing *what they are* and *what their origin is*. Both Peirce [77, 78], recognized as "the father" of semiotics, and Eco [23, 24], who continued and disseminated Peirce's semiotics, point out that symbols have so many meanings, and have been defined in so many ways, that in the end we do not know what they are (see discussion in Palacios, [69]). In relation to the origin of the symbol, it is enough for the moment to mention that Saussure

P. Palacios (✉)
Universidad Autónoma de Aguascalientes, Aguascalientes, Mexico
e-mail: pedro.palacios@edu.uaa.mx

K. Cárdenas
Pontificia Universidad Católica de Chile, Villarrica, Chile

N. Yuste
Universidad Internacional de La Rioja, La Rioja, Spain

C. Rodriguez Garrido et al. (eds.), *The Social Life of Objects in Early Development*, Social Interaction in Learning and Development,
https://doi.org/10.1007/978-3-031-87673-8_5

[94], recognized as "the father" of semiology, and Peirce [77, 78] agree on the social and conventional origin of the symbol, but not on its arbitrary character.[1] In the field of developmental psychology, as we will see, we also find this social and conventional origin of symbols in some approaches, while not in others.

In this chapter, we are going to use the criterion of the origin of the symbol to group the different approaches that we present. First, we deal with the positions assuming an individual origin of the symbol, whose basic idea is that symbols are private meanings that infants create for themselves. After that, we address the approaches of the social origin of the symbol, where the infant is no longer alone, but is accompanied by the other, whose participation is important in the development process of symbols. We place the Pragmatics of the Object as part of the latter, since the meaning of symbolic uses is based on shared practices and public rules of the uses of objects. Uses that the infant constructs in situations in which he/she communicates and interacts with the other. Later, we present some results of our longitudinal studies in everyday contexts on symbolic development at home with normotypical infants, with infants with Down syndrome and, finally, in an early years school among peers.

Next, we begin with two representative positions on the individual origin of the symbol: Piagetian constructivism, and the modular and innatist approach. First, we will refer to Piaget because of the great legacy and influence he has had to date in studies on the development of symbols.

5.2 Individual Origin of the Symbol

5.2.1 Piagetian Individual Constructivism

Piaget [80] defines symbols as motivated signifiers, that is, there is a relationship of similarity or resemblance between the symbol and its meaning. They are private products of the child's individual thought, thus stripping them of any hint of agreement or convention with other people.

According to the Piagetian approach, symbols are part of, and emerge with, the development of representation or symbolic function around 18–24 months of age [8, 42, 67, 80]. Piaget proposes that the symbol comes from play (understood as the repetition of deforming assimilation schemes, for pure pleasure). Piaget considers play the conduit from action to representation, to the extent that it evolves from sensorimotor play to symbolic play. In Piagetian jargon, the terms symbol, symbolic play and playful symbol are equivalent.

Piaget assigns to the symbol a merely representative function, alien to communication and social conventions. However, this conception of the Piagetian

[1] According to Sausure, arbitrary refers to the fact that the relationship between the signifier and the signified is unmotivated. That is, that the signifier does not have any natural link with the signified.

symbol, which emphasizes the individual and solitary action of the child, has been questioned by different authors [11, 12, 26, 71, 69, 86, 88, 122].

In the first studies of symbol development, the other was absent. This situation arose from the Piagetian and Geneva School vision, focused on the lone child, playing symbolically with physical objects with his/her own means, (e.g., Belsky & Most, [8]; Inhelder et al., [42]; Piaget, [80]). Under this approach, the adult, specifically the mother, although present in research on symbolic development, is instructed not to participate or make any kind of suggestion to her child (e.g., Hill & McCune-Nicolich, [38]; McCune, [62]; Nicolich, [67]).

5.2.2 Modularist and Innatist Posture

The modularist and innatist approach, whose epistemological bases are very different from Piagetian individual constructivism, nonetheless agrees with it in that symbols concern only the child, by placing them as mental representations. The emergence of symbolic play, from a modularist and innatist perspective, is an early manifestation of the Theory of Mind (ToM). The development of ToM requires a specialized and innate neurocognitive mechanism, called the Theory of Mind Mechanism (ToMM), which begins to mature during the second year of life [3, 33, 50, 52, 54, 95, 96]. The ToMM is the one that makes possible the emergence of symbolic play, between 18 and 24 months [32, 50, 51].

This perspective also assume that infants possess an innate concept of "pretending" or symbolic play. This concept, along with other innate basic concepts of propositional attitudes such as "believing" and "desiring", are conceived as mechanisms (ToMM) that exist before knowledge and that are free of meanings [33]. The innate concept of "pretending" simultaneously enables both the production of solitary symbolic play and the understanding of symbolic play in others (see Friedman & Leslie, [32]).

In symbolic play, according to Leslie [50], there are simultaneously two types of representations: one corresponds to primary representations and the other to meta-representations. Primary representations, he says, have a direct semantic relationship with the world and are, by definition, transparent. That is, they represent objects, events and situations of the world in a precise, true and literal manner. Leslie assumes that infants have the capacity for "primary representation" from birth. Symbols, on the other hand, are meta-representations, opaque, suspended -quarantined- and decoupled copies of the primary representations generated by ToMM [51, 53].

This approach has been widely questioned (e.g., Harris, [35]; Kim et al., [45]; Lillard, [56, 57]; Palacios, [69]; Perner, [79]; Sobel, [102]; Wellman, [123]). Here we draw attention to two issues. First, it is a paradox to speak of concepts free of meaning. This may reflect a failure to consider that all meaning and knowledge is based on use, on shared practices with others [77, 86, 90, 125]. It also reflect the assumption on transparency and literality in mental representation, instead of taking into account that all knowledge or thought is mediated by signs [77, 88,

120]. Second, they also leave aside the role that agreement, or convention, has in the formation of meanings (e.g., Bruner, [12]; Palacios, [69]).

In contrast to these approaches, there are conceptions that maintain that the development of symbols has a social origin, which we will discuss shortly. The Vygotskian semiotic position is a pioneer of this group. It has been a source of inspiration and support for the other two approaches that we are reviewing. One of them is that of Tomasello and his group. Following Vygotsky very closely, they make the distinction between natural sensorimotor *affordances* (individual line of cognitive development) and intentional *affordances* (cultural line of cognitive development) of objects in their approach to symbolic play (see Tomasello, [108]). As we will see, the social origin of the symbol is the starting point of this approach, although at some point they seem to question it. The other approach is the Pragmatics of the Object. Inspired by Vygotsky (and Peirce's semiotics), it introduces semiotic mediation in early development before speech, as well as the adult–object–child triadic interactions (see Chap. 1 of this book).

5.3 Social Origin of the Symbol

5.3.1 Vygotskian Semiotics

The Vygotskian semiotic conception proposes that a nuclear aspect in the psychological development of the child is the mediation of others through signs. It places the origin of the signs in communication and interaction with other people. Vygotsky [118], for example, in his work *"The first year"* refers to the child's relationship with the surrounding reality as social from the beginning. Any relationship of the child with things is carried out with the help of, or through, another person.

When Vygotsky refers specifically to symbolic play, we find three important aspects to consider: (1) in symbolic play, some objects substitute others, becoming their signs. But what is of greatest importance is not the perceptual similarity between the physical object and the designated or signified object, but rather *its functional use.* That is, the possibility of carrying out with the help of the physical object *the representative gesture of the designated object* [120]. (2) *There is no symbolic play without rules.* Any imaginary situation of any type of play entails certain rules of behavior, and such imaginary situations are understandable under the rules of real situations [119]. (3) The child, from *preschool age*, assigns a different meaning to a specific object during symbolic play. That is, the child looks at an object, but acts (representative gesture) disregarding what he or she is looking at [119].

The use of rules, non-perceptual similarity and the functional use of the object (the representative gesture) are aspects that we share and that are at the base of our conceptualization of symbols [69, 86]. Instead, we question the age at which symbolic productions begin. In our studies, as we will see later, we have found the first symbolic uses of objects at 11–12 months of age in infants. Among them, some symbolic uses by substitution [19, 74, 71, 75, 128].

5.3.2 Approach of Tomasello and His Group

According to Tomasello and his group, infants learn the intentional *affordances* of objects (the specific functions of objects) in their sociocultural environment through imitative learning [6, 7, 13, 108–111, 113, 110]. However, contradicting themselves, they have also come to express that infants can individually acquire the intentional *affordances* of objects [82, 112], calling into question the social origin of the symbol and, therefore, assigning it an individual origin.

They propose that, in symbolic play, infants *decouple* the intentional *affordances* of objects to exchange them and use them with other objects [108, 112]. It is not until after 2 years of age that children begin to use objects symbolically. They consider that many of the first symbolic productions of infants under 2 years of age are not symbolic. They simply imitate (repeat or copy literally) the actions that they have seen adults do with those objects [83, 104, 108, 114, 110]. Here, as we did with Vygotsky earlier, we question the age at which these authors claim that children begin to use objects as symbols. It is also highly questionable their claim that these activities are "not symbolic" before the age of 2 and that infants carry them out without understanding them. This idea is contrary to what we, and they themselves, have proposed. That is, that infants need to first know the canonical uses, or in their terms, the intentional *affordances* of objects in order to be able to make symbolic uses.

They have also suggested that the infant's previous knowledge and meanings of an object come into competition or conflict with each other, in such a way that they make it difficult for the child to use the object as a symbol at a given moment. According to Striano et al. [103] and Tomasello et al. [114], the knowledge of the physical attributes of the object that infants under 2 years of age have makes it difficult for them to use it as a symbol. They could not inhibit their sensorimotor schemes (natural sensorimotor *affordances*) when faced with the object entering their "apprehensible" or action space.

It is worth mentioning that, a few years earlier, DeLoache [20, 21] had reported that the representation of the physical object, a miniature model of a furnished room, creates difficulties for children under 3 years of age to use it as a symbol. She claims that children have a dual representation problem, caused by the presence of two simultaneous mental representations: (1) the representation of the object as a physical entity, which can be explored or manipulated, and (2) the representation of the object to represent something different than itself. In this case, that the miniature model represents the real room. These representations conflict with each other, so that the physical object representation of the miniature furnished room makes it difficult for the child to use it as a symbol to search for an object hidden in the real room. In contrast, when the real room is "shrunken by a magic machine" (in reality, the room is hidden and the miniature model is placed without the child seeing it), the child can actually find the hidden object [22]. In this case, the child would not perceive a conflict between the two objects, since they would be considered "the same object", eliminating the need for dual representation.

This difficulty of two simultaneous representations is further aggravated when it implies the presence of three simultaneous representations. When a cup is used as a hat, the difficulty for the child is that at the same time there is competition between: (1) the representation of the cup as an object with sensorimotor *affordances* (physical characteristics), (2) the representation of the cup as an object with well-defined intentional *affordances* (it is used for drinking) and (3) the representation of the cup as an object that represents a hat [104, 108]. In this case, prior knowledge of the physical characteristics and functional uses makes it difficult to acquire the new meaning of the object as a symbol.

This interpretation of a possible conflict or competition between the different meanings attributed to an object contradicts again their own approach, which states that the child must first know the intentional *affordances* of the objects so that he/she can subsequently decouple the *affordances* [108, 112]. Likewise, it seems that they do not consider the detachment of the rules of the canonical uses of objects as a gradual and progressive process. Instead, it is considered an all-or-nothing phenomenon that appears at a certain age [71]. In the case of the cup as a symbol of a hat, the child must be very clear about how cups and hats are used (which may not happen at the same time in the child's life), so that he/she can have the possibility of *transferring* and *applying* the rule of the canonical use of hats to cups.

5.3.3 Pragmatics of the Object

From the perspective of the Pragmatics of the Object, symbols or symbolic uses of objects are considered a type of sign that represents something absent. Therefore, they are more complex signs than those whose meaning refers to something present. For example, there would be no symbol if a child eats efficiently with a spoon (canonical use). However, there would be a symbol if a child "pretends to eat" with an empty spoon representing the missing food. Later we will look at this example in more detail. With the first symbols, infants gain access to new systems of meaning, different from canonical uses, and a different way of relating with others and with themselves [69, 86, 88]. Symbolic uses allow them to begin to operate with absent realities, or that are beginning to be absent, related to public and shared meanings of objects.

The first symbols form a semiotic system prior to language, or the linguistic sign. In addition to being used for playing (symbolic play), they can be used for thinking, when infants do not have verbal language yet. Symbols can also serve as a means of communication and interaction with others. For example, infants can use them to ask for something or to respond to the adult [74, 71, 88]. We have found that infants begin to make their first symbols from 11 to 12 months of age, when they are interacting with an adult [19, 71, 75], or even with their peers [128].

From the Pragmatics of the Object, we locate the social origin of the first symbolic meanings of objects in two elements. On the one hand, they are based on meanings that are already conventional, the product of previous consensus, anchored in the rules that govern the canonical uses of objects. And on the other, in the educational role that is mainly played by the adult. Symbolic uses require a long construction process assisted by the adult. They are not transparent, nor do they emerge spontaneously and directly from objects. Instead, they need to be shown, produced, suggested and taught by someone else. Adults seek to communicate to infants that objects can be used in symbolic ways. Adults give them "life", bringing absent meanings to the here and now, through a series of communicative mediators. We are going to dedicate a moment to each of these aspects, which are at the basis of the social origin of symbols.

In general terms, we can establish that there are currently two conceptions of the material object. In one of these, the object is conceived in terms of its physical properties. In the other, in addition, the object is conceived as having shared public meanings, or rules of use in everyday life. In the first case, we speak of a physical materiality or physical object, while in the second we speak of cultural materiality or cultural material object. In the Piagetian constructivist approach, the symbol originates from the action of the child with the physical object. In innatist and modularist positions, the physical object and the cultural material object are absent. The innate primary representations are the origin of the symbol.

On the other hand, in the Pragmatics of the Object, the symbolic uses of objects are based on the rules of the canonical or conventional uses of objects. This means that symbolic uses are transferred from the shared practices of the canonical uses of objects, giving another meaning of a symbolic nature to the object, transforming it, turning it into something else, bringing the absent to the present [74, 71, 88, 91]. It is almost impossible for a child to make symbolic uses with an object unless he or she understands and knows, to some extent, the canonical use represented by the symbol. Likewise, the symbol is understood by reference to the canonical use of the object it represents, so that the similarity can be established between uses, not between objects [69, 86, 92], as proposed, for example, by Piaget.

In the symbolic use in which Guille, at 15 months, uses a plastic horse to "drink" [71], the relationship is not in the perceptual similarity. The horse and the cups do not look physically similar. What they have in common is the use. When using the horse as if it was a cup (symbolic use), he is giving it the function of cups in real life (canonical use). It is sufficient for the child to use the horse in a different way for it to stop representing cups and to attribute another meaning to it. Let us remember what Vygotsky [120] said: the motivated nature of the symbol is not relevant, what is essential is the functional use or the representative gesture. Furthermore, objects, like signs, do not have meanings in themselves. Meanings are, in any case, the result of interpretation, of reconstruction [77].

Infants construct the canonical use, the social meaning assigned to the object, within its sociocultural context, in everyday triadic adult-object-child interactions

[64, 69, 90], see Chap. 2 of this volume). The moment when the object becomes a sign of its use for the child, he/she assigns it a *functional permanence*, a meaning based on its public use [87]. For example, *any* spoon can be used to eat and *any* telephone to talk. This functional permanence of the object allows the child not only to represent it as an existing entity (the classical object permanence of Piaget), but to know the functional meaning of the object within its sociocultural environment.

Prior learning creates and increases the possibility that the rules of canonical uses become *detached* from the material objects where they were born, and are *transferred* and *applied* to a) the same object, in circumstances different from those of the canonical use (e.g., "eating" or "feeding" with an empty spoon), b) other objects (e.g., using a spoon as a telephone to "talk") or c) to evoking it in the absence of the object (e.g., making the gesture of holding a spoon in the hand and bringing it to the mouth to "eat" or "feed"). This continuum has given rise to establishing certain levels of symbolic uses of objects that we present later. Therefore, the entry to symbolic uses is a matter of degree, evolution and change. That is, the development of the first symbolic uses is a gradual and progressive process as infants enter the levels of symbolic uses of objects. Likewise, the different levels seem to be more the result of familiarity and knowledge of the rules for using objects, as well as the situations in which they are usually presented, than of age [74, 71].

In a recent publication, Hashmi [36] highlights, based on other publications, that the familiarity that infants have with structured and replica toys (which he calls "realistic") promote more symbolic play. Striano et al. [104] found that infants produced more symbolic actions to represent a person with replica objects, a doll, compared to a stone or pencil. We also found, as we will see later, that participants (adults and infants) preferred replica objects for symbolic uses. Ban and Uchiyama [2] point out that this preference for replica objects varies as the infant develops. They found that 18-month-olds significantly more often selected brightly colored tableware replica toys to use symbolically, while 30-month-olds chose real tableware. They state that a likely reason for these preferences is the familiarity that children have with these objects in their daily lives, at different times in their lives.

As we pointed out before, in the social origin of the symbol there is also the other. Communication and participation of the other are necessary for the child to be able to use an object as a symbol. The place of the other can be occupied by any person who knows this type of meaning and use of the object (such as parents, teachers, siblings, classmates, etc.) and is the one who guides and provides the necessary opportunities for the child to be able to construct the symbolic meanings and uses. Or in other words, the child requires the semiotic communicative mediation of the other, to understand and use an object as a symbol.

From the Pragmatics of the Object, the educational role of the adult in the development process of the first symbolic uses is produced through semiotic communicative mediators, or the communicative and intentional signs that the adult uses to communicate something to the child in relation to the uses of objects (Rodríguez and Moro, [90], see Chap. 3, this volumen). The changes observed in the communicative mediation of the adult will be described in the following section.

We have observed that, initially, when infants do not yet produce or understand symbolic uses, adults have total control in the creation of symbolic scenarios. They choose the objects, delimit the contents, the plot, the roles of each one, etc. When infants begin to produce their first symbolic uses, adult participation remains very active and diverse, and is clearly related to the child's level of symbolic development. Adults allow infants to be the ones who create symbolic scenarios, carry out symbolic uses that children do not yet produce, create opportunities for infants to initiate symbolic uses, accompany infants' symbolic uses with similar but exaggerated symbolic gestures, imitate infants' symbolic uses to emphasize, complete, prolong or provide feedback on infants' symbolic actions, etc. And they do all the above through communicative mediators [72, 69].

Some studies on symbolic play took up the role of the adult as a guide or model in the 1980s, when Vygotsky's ideas permeated the West. They began to include the adult to analyze their participation in symbolic play research, while at the same time questioning studies of solitary symbolic play [70]. In these first studies, symbolic play is investigated in free play situations with the participation of mothers (e.g., Fiese, [30]; Slade, [100]; Tamis-LeMonda & Bornstein, [107]).

Research has consistently shown that mothers' involvement facilitates symbolic play in children who are already of an age where they can already engage in symbolic play with objects. It has been found that: (1) the episodes of symbolic play are of longer duration [60, 100], (2) the number of episodes also increases [30], (3) the levels of symbolic play are more complex [30, 60, 100, 126] and (4) more diverse [68] compared to solitary symbolic play. These studies account for the effect of the participation of mothers in the production of symbolic play, but not the importance that should be given to the adult to understand the process of construction of the first symbols in triadic contexts [72], which we present in the next section.

Mothers encourage symbolic play with a wide variety of behaviors that have been named, defined, and grouped in different ways across studies [1, 29–31, 46, 61, 100, 105, 107]. Among the range of behaviors referred to in these publications we find demonstrations, maternal verbalizations (with two subcategories: indications and elaborations), turn-taking, maternal sensitivity, maternal involvement (distinguishing three levels: non-involvement, verbal comment and interaction), suggestions, requests, reciprocity (distinguishing three different degrees of participation: low participation, spectator and high participation), maternal intrusion (with subcategories such as elaborating or extending symbolic play, among others), direction of maternal attention (with three subcategories: maintaining, extending, and redirecting symbolic play), comments, supporting the child's effort (offering feedback, praising, encouraging independence, etc.), explicit guidance (directing play, correcting the child, providing a model, etc.), implicit guidance (requesting or giving help, joining in the child's play, describing the child's behavior or one's own behavior), etc.

This wide and diverse range of behaviors makes it almost impossible to compare the results of different studies, despite the similarities that could be established between categories or between categories and subcategories. Likewise, the results of the correlations reported by some of these studies between some categories and subcategories are inconsistent and even contradictory (see Palacios et al., [72] for a review).

An attempt has also been made to investigate what mothers' behaviors could be indicators for the child that it is a symbolic play [58, 59]. In these studies, it was found that mothers look and smile more frequently and for longer periods in the symbolic play situation. The mother's modification in looking and smiling serves as a key to symbolic play for infants aged 15 to 24 months old.

Finally, it has been reported that the participation of the mother versus siblings and peers has a different effect on the child's symbolic play. Youngblade and Dunn [126] compared infants' symbolic play with their mothers and with their siblings and found that infants participated more in symbolic play with their siblings than with their mothers. On the other hand, Markova and Legerstee [60], when comparing the symbolic play of 15-month-old infants with their mothers and with their peers, found that mothers facilitated their infants' symbolic play. With peers, on the other hand, parallel social symbolic play was the one that had the highest frequency and duration.

Below we will present some results of our studies on the development of early symbolic uses during infancy. We begin with longitudinal studies in infants with normotypical development.

5.4 Symbolic Development in Infants with Normotypical Development

In the studies on the origin and evolution of symbols in triadic situations between *adult, object and infant*, we had many questions. Mainly because it had not been investigated until that moment, in a systematic way, *how* infants construct uses and meanings of the first symbols in triadic situations. We asked ourselves: When do infants begin to use objects as symbols? How does this process of development of symbolic uses occur? Is knowledge of the rules of canonical uses, which are social and public, in fact the basis of symbolic uses? What is the role of the adult in this process? Do adults make symbolic uses of objects before infants understand or produce them by themselves? And, if so, at what level of complexity and with what function do they do so? What are the communicative mediators that the adult uses? What changes occur in the mediators and what effects do they have on the child during the process of symbol construction? Among others.

To answer this series of questions, we have longitudinally investigated the development of the first symbols in infants in triadic communication and interaction with the mother or father. We proposed 10 objects in a semi-structured situation, when infants were 9, 12 and 15 months old [71], and when they were 9, 12, 15 and 18 months old [74]. The objects used are an empty bottle of body cream, an empty cardboard box with a string tied to the front, a child's toothbrush, a wooden kitchen spoon, a plastic lighter, a white cloth, a plastic horse, a cloth doll with a cap, a toy mobile phone and a small oval stone.

Let us remember that, for the Pragmatics of the Object, the triad *adult, object and infant* constitutes the basic unit of observation, which is studied in micro genetic analysis (see Chap. 3, this volume). This methodological approach allows us to observe in detail the changes in the process of construction of symbols by the infant, as well as the changes or modifications in the communication and interaction between the adult and the child throughout the development process. Let us see what we have found.

5.4.1 Some General Data

In both studies, we observed that no infant made symbolic uses of objects at 9 months. 100% of the symbolic uses observed at this age were made by adults in both studies. Adults are the ones who intentionally and deliberately encourage infants to be not only spectators of the symbolic uses made in front of and for them. They make infants participants in these symbolic practices so that they become the owners of the symbolic uses and meanings. For example, adults pretend to "talk" on the phone using a replica phone or a real phone (symbolic distant demonstration), and then put the phone to the infant's ear to have the infant "talk" (symbolic immediate demonstration). However, the infant eventually takes the phone away from his/her ear because he/she does not yet understand this action by the adult (see Table 5.2 below). In the case of the doll, as another example, the adult often moves it towards the infant's face to have the infant kiss it, producing the onomatopoeic sound of the kiss in a prolonged and exaggerated manner. The infant only reacts with a smile or brings his/her hands towards the doll, but does not kiss it.

Infants make the first symbolic uses of objects at 12 months. These uses are very similar to those made by parents, which does not mean that infants "make literal copies" of the productions of adults as claimed by Tomasello and his group, as we described earlier. Continuing with the previous examples, infants "talk" on the phone, and kiss the doll. We also found, in both investigations, that the duration of the symbolic episodes and the total frequency of symbolic uses increased as the infants developed. When comparing the percentage of the total frequency of symbolic uses by adults and infants with each other, in both studies we found that this percentage increases in infants, while in adults decreases as infants develop. This shows that infants demonstrate increasing competence in using and understanding objects symbolically. Consequently, the support provided by adults decreases, but becomes more aligned with the infants' development in using objects as symbols.

Adults and infants increased the number of objects used symbolically throughout the studies. In one of the studies, with a Spanish population, only 8 of the 10 objects were used symbolically at the end of the study [72, 71]. Neither the stone nor the white cloth were used symbolically. In the other study, with a Mexican population, all 10 were used symbolically [74]. In addition, in both studies, both adults and infants showed a preference for three replica objects for symbolic use, in the following order: the doll, the telephone, and the horse.

These findings are very suggestive regarding the possible cultural differences in the symbolic practices of adults with objects, which in turn have a relationship with daily life practices in each culture. For example, in the case of the white cloth, in the practices of caring for and raising infants from birth, Mexicans tend to wrap them up a lot. From the first observation, adults used the cloth to cover and rock the doll. On the other hand, in Madrid it is not a common practice to cover infants as much as in Mexico, and the participants in the study never used the cloth to cover the doll [74].

5.4.2 Levels of Symbolic Uses

In the development process of the first symbols, we have identified four levels of symbolic uses (see Table 5.1). The first symbolic uses made by infants had a very close relationship with the canonical use of the object. Only later do they transfer these rules of canonical uses to other objects, or even to a purely imagined object. This progressive detachment from the rules of canonical use of the object implies greater abstraction and complexity. The degree to which symbols are detached from the original material support represents differentiated symbolic levels.

Level 1 is made up of symbolic uses that represent the canonical use of the *same object, outside of its usual context.* There is decontextualization, but there is also evocation of something absent. With these symbolic uses, infants begin to detach themselves from current and present circumstances, to bring here and now absent realities related to canonical meanings (e.g., using the spoon to "eat" or "feed" when there is no food involved), or they attribute properties to an object that lacks them (e.g., using the plastic horse and pretending that it is galloping; the horse becomes an animated object and is attributed the galloping ability of a real horse). At this level, two sublevels are distinguished: 1.1, if the symbolic use is directed at oneself (e.g., the infant "eats") and 1.2, if it is directed at the adult or another object (e.g., the infant "feeds" the adult).

Symbolic uses of level 1 have been considered as functional play (see Sidhu et al., [98] for a review), as pre-symbolic play [62] and as transitional play [9, 107]. For example, if a infant puts the phone to his/her ear without vocalization or brings an empty cup to his/her mouth, these are not considered symbolic play because, in the first case, according to Bentenuto et al. [9] and Tamis-LeMonda and Bornstein [107], there is no confirmatory evidence that it is symbolic play, as the vocalization would be missing. In the second case, McCune [62] considers that the signifier (the gesture of drinking using the object) is merely a part of the meaning ("literal drinking").

The above may indicate that, since play theorization, it has been difficult and complicated to have a criterion that unequivocally marks when an action is a symbol and when it is not, as well as when it is a canonical or functional use and

Table 5.1 Levels of symbolic uses of objects

Level/ sublevel	Type of symbolic uses	Example
1	Symbolic uses that represent the canonical use of the *same object outside of its usual context*	
1.1	Symbolic uses that evoke the absent canonical use directed at oneself	"Talking" on the phone – putting the phone to one's ear with or without vocalization or language
1.2	Symbolic uses that evoke the absent canonical use directed to the other or another object	Putting the phone to the adult's or doll's ear
2	Symbolic uses by *substitution*, which represent the canonical use of a different object	
2.1	Symbolic uses by *substitution* directed at oneself	Using the stone as a telephone to "talk"
2.2	Symbolic uses by *substitution* directed at the other or another object	Using the toothbrush as a spoon to "feed" the adult
3	Symbolic uses made *without the material support* of any object (*in absentia*)	Placing one hand on one's ear as if it was a telephone
4	*Symbolic narratives in action* or sequenced symbolic uses	
4.1	Symbolic narratives of symbolic uses of level 1	Wrapping the doll in the cloth and rocking it
4.2	Symbolic narratives of levels 2 or 3	Putting the stone—food—in the spoon and "feed" the adult and the horse
4.3	Symbolic narratives that involve the transformation of the object as an agent	"Dialing" and giving the phone to the doll so that it "talks" by saying "here"

This table has been reworked from Palacios et al. [74]

when it is not. From the Pragmatics of the Object, as has already been said, the type of use at a given time is what gives meaning to the object and is what marks the difference, in this case, between the canonical and the symbolic. The use of the empty cup, without liquid, is like the use of the empty spoon, without food. The cup is not being used to drink some liquid (canonical use), as it is usually used, but rather to simulate drinking some absent liquid (symbolic use). Using a cup with liquid and drinking is not the same as using an empty cup and simulating drinking. The same can be said of the telephone.

Level 2 groups symbolic uses by *substitution.* They represent the canonical use of an object *other than* the one being used. As in the previous level, the same two sublevels are differentiated: 2.1 when directed at oneself and 2.2 when directed at another or an object. In symbolic uses by substitution there is also decontextualization and evocation of something absent, but in a more elaborate way. With them, infants distance themselves from the canonical use of the object itself, to use it as if it were another, thus assigning it a new meaning.

At this level 2, the meaning of the object changes depending on the creativity and imagination with which infants can multiply and make flexible the rules of canonical uses that can be applied to the object. For example, the meaning of the stone is different when it is used as food (you "eat" the stone or "feed" it to the horse or the adult) than when it is used as a telephone (you use the stone to "talk" or to make the doll "talk"). We have also observed that, on occasions, adults express their disagreement and put limits on some symbolic uses by substitution. For example, when infants pretend to drink using the horse or when they use the toothbrush to comb their hair (see observations in Palacios & Rodríguez, [71]), or when they use the doll as a telephone or the lighter as a hairbrush, among others [69].

Level 3 consists of symbolic uses made *without the material support* of an object. At this level, what remains is the *objectless gesture* representing the rule of canonical use. For example, simulating holding a glass or cup in one's hand and bringing it to one's mouth to "drink" or bringing an absent telephone to one's ear to "speak."

Finally, *level 4* groups *symbolic narratives in action*, or sequenced symbolic uses, where two or more symbolic acts are linked together in a complex symbolic action, or where a symbolic act is applied to more than one agent. At this level there are three sublevels: 4.1, groups symbolic narratives of level 1 of symbolic uses; 4.2, symbolic narratives of levels 2 and/or 3 and 4.3, symbolic narratives that imply the transformation of the object as an agent.

It has been proposed that symbolic play progresses based on the trends that occur in three development processes: decentration, decontextualization and integration. The *decentering* process refers to infants first performing symbolic actions directed at themselves and later directing them at others. The *decontextualization* process is characterized by the substitution of one object for another, using non-realistic objects in symbolic play. And finally, the *integration* process involves chaining or combining more than one symbolic action in a sequence (see Ha, [34] for a review).

In our levels of symbolic uses, the process of decentration is observed in levels 1 and 2 with their two sublevels. In 1.1 and 2.1 when the symbolic use is directed at oneself, and in 1.2 and 2.2 when it is directed at the other or another object. The process of decontextualization is present from level 1 and not from level 2, with substitution, as has been commonly conceived. In fact, levels 1, 2 and 3 represent different degrees of decontextualization and show the tendency of this process in the development of symbolic uses of objects. And finally, the integration process is observed at level 4, where different symbolic actions are coordinated in a narrative.

Our results show that, at 12 months, the highest percentage of the total frequency of infants' symbolic uses was that of symbols representing the canonical use of the *same object outside its usual context* (level 1), such as "talking" with a replica phone, or "eating" with an empty spoon. This higher percentage is maintained at later ages observed in the two studies [74, 71].

In relation to the process of decentralization of symbolic uses, we have found that the percentage of the frequency of symbolic uses of level 1.1 (directed to oneself) decreases as the infants develop, while level 1.2 (directed to the adult or another object) increases [74].

The percentages of the frequency of symbolic uses by *substituting* one object for another (level 2) and in the *absence* of the object (level 3) were low at the same ages reported in both studies [74, 71], with the percentage for level 3 being even lower. These data show the gradual detachment of the place of origin of the rules of canonical uses, and the difficulty that infants have in applying these rules to other objects or in the absence of an object. They also show, together with those of level 1, the tendency of the process of decontextualization of symbolic uses, where the degree of decontextualization that is most present in all the ages observed is that of the symbolic uses of level 1.

In one of the studies [74] we found that the percentages of symbolic uses of level 4 infants were progressively increasing. There is a predominance of symbolic narratives in action of infants of sublevel 4.1, followed by those of sublevel 4.2 and then by those of sublevel 4.3, which shows that infants rely on the symbolic uses they master best to create short stories. They also show the tendency of the integration process in the development of the symbolic uses of objects.

The percentages of the total frequency of symbolic uses by adults and infants at each level are very similar. In both studies [74, 71] we found that the highest percentage of the total frequency of symbolic uses by adults was, as in infants, level 1 at all ages observed (9, 12, 15 and 18 months) and, likewise, the percentages of the total frequency of uses of levels 2, by substitution, and 3, in absence, by adults were low at all ages. Finally, the percentages of symbolic uses of level 4 by adults also progressively increased.

5.4.3 Adult Communicative Mediation

In the origin and evolution of the first symbolic uses, communication and support from the adult, through semiotic communicative mediators, play a very important role, as we have been highlighting. Adult communicative mediation changes during the development process of the first symbolic uses of objects [72]. At earlier ages, adults direct and provide greater support, which is why they resort more frequently to symbolic demonstrations and the orchestration of different semiotic mediators. Orchestration refers to the configuration and chaining of different non-verbal communicative mediators (e.g., ostensive gesture of showing-demonstration of symbolic use-ostensive gesture of offering, demonstration of symbolic use-ostensive gesture of offering, etc.) accompanied by language. The progressive withdrawal of the adult's communicative mediation is adjusted as infants understand and produce symbolic uses with greater ease. In Figures 5.1 and 5.2 a sequence of symbolic uses of the telephone is presented that together illustrate the changes in the type of adult communicative mediation. Figure 5.1 is from 9 months and Figure 5.2 from 15 months of age of the infant.

Guille 0;9,0. Sequence 7 — Duration: 39 seconds

The sequence begins when the adult (A) shows the phone to the infant (N), while asking him "Shall we call daddy?" N looks at the phone.

Image 1

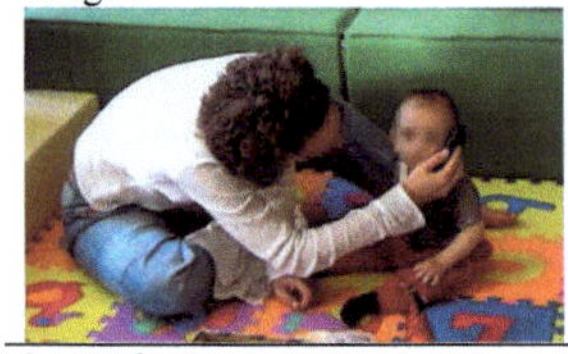

A presses the keys, puts the phone to her ear and says "Helloooo, is Guillermo there?" N looks at A's action.
Then A puts the phone to N's ear*: "Do you want to talk? Do they want to tell you something?"
N takes the phone away from his ear with his hand.

Image 2

A presses the keys again and puts the phone to N's ear. Then she puts the phone to her ear and says, "are you there, dad?" N looks at A's action.
Then on two more occasions, A places the phone to N's ear. On both occasions N removes it*.

Fig. 5.1 Adult communicative mediators during symbolic uses of the telephone at 9 months of age of the infant * Exact moment represented in each image
The first part of the sequence has been published in Palacios and Rodríguez [60] and has been reworked here

Guille 1;3,4. Sequence 2 — Duration: 28 seconds

The sequence begins with N looking and walking towards the phone and picking it up.

Image 1

N looks at the phone and presses a key repeatedly while A says "call grandma, aren't you going to call grandma?" N presses a key several times and then takes the phone to his ear saying "eeee"*.
A accompanies him: "helloooo".

Image 2

While N presses a key several times, A brings her head closer to N and pointing to her ear, touching it several times*, says "put it on me, let's see if I can hear it".

Image 3

N puts the phone to A's ear* and A says "Hello Grandma, hello". N then takes the phone away from A's ear, looks at it, and puts it down.

Fig. 5.2 Adult communicative mediators during symbolic uses of the telephone at 15 months of age of the infant * Exact moment represented in each image

At 9 months, the way in which the mother has orchestrated the communicative mediators shows the persistence with which she tries to make the infant become a co-protagonist in the symbolic uses of the telephone. However, the infant is still a long way from using this object in a symbolic way. Two orchestrations of the adult are clearly distinguished: (1) *ostensive gesture of showing-symbolic distant demonstration-symbolic immediate demonstration* (shows the phone to the infant- "dials" and "speaks" on the phone-puts the phone to the infant's ear so that he "speaks") (Fig. 5.1. See Image 1) and (2) *symbolic immediate demonstration-symbolic distant demonstration-symbolic immediate demonstration on two occasions* ("dials" and puts the phone to the infant's ear so that he "speaks"-puts the phone to her ear and "speaks"-puts the phone to the infant's ear so that he "speaks" on two occasions) (Fig. 5.1. See Image 2). The infant behaves consistently and differently when faced with alternating distant and immediate demonstrations from the mother. He looks attentively at the former and moves the phone away from his ear during the latter, indicating that he does not yet possess the knowledge that allows him to understand and use the phone symbolically.

At 15 months, we find a very different situation. Now it is the infant who is interested in the telephone. He presses the keys and "talks" (Fig. 5.2. See Image 1), although it is true that this symbolic use is preceded by the mother's suggestion that he calls his grandmother. As for the non-linguistic communicative mediators used by the adult, there is no orchestration here, she only makes the gesture of immediate pointing (touches the ear) redundantly (does it several times) (Fig. 5.2. See Image 2). The infant understands this gesture and puts the phone to his mother's ear so that she can "speak" (Fig. 5.2. See Image 3).

The different communicative mediators used by adults were very effective in attracting the attention of infants of all ages and, from 12 months onwards, in making symbolic uses of objects. Likewise, the communicative mediators also provoked different emotional expressions in the infants, mainly smiling, laughing, general body movements as a sign of happiness, and clapping [72].

Analysis of the *functions* of demonstrations shows that, at 9 months of age, all adult demonstrations of symbolic uses have a *demonstrative function.* That is, they serve the predominant function of *showing the infant how to use the object symbolically.* This demonstrative function diminishes at later ages, while other functions come into play. At 12 months, they perform symbolic demonstrations to *evaluate* and *provide feedback* on the infants' symbolic uses, to *respond* to the infants' ostensive gestures of giving, and to *complete* the infants' symbolic uses. At 15 months, in addition to the above, they perform symbolic demonstrations for the first time to *correct* the infants' symbolic uses. These various functions account for (1) the adjustment that occurs in the communicative exchange around the use of objects as symbols and (2) that the adult always acts in tune with the performance and knowledge of the infants [72].

In the next section, we describe the results of the longitudinal studies carried out in infants with Down syndrome from the Pragmatics of the Object.

5.5 Symbolic Development in Infants with Down Syndrome

The symbolic development of infants with Down syndrome has been studied, as in infants with normotypical development, through various methodologies. In particular, from play situations, either the infant alone with objects or with the participation of an adult. The focus has been on analyzing infants' symbolic play, but also on other types of play such as exploratory and functional play [5, 9, 27, 38, 44, 81]. Studies have mainly focused on, as in normotypical development (e.g., Aksoy et al., [1]), the relationship between cognitive development and the level of complexity of play [63], the association between language -both expressive and comprehensive- and symbolic play [44], or the relationship between the quality and level of play with affective aspects [65].

In research where symbols are analyzed in the context of solitary interaction between the infant and the object, it is noted that the level of symbolic play correlates more with mental age than with chronological age [38] and with higher levels of cognitive development. Infants with high levels of symbolic play not only had higher levels of cognitive development, but also showed more enthusiasm and more thorough exploration of objects during play [65].

Studies on symbolic play usually compare infants with Down syndrome with normotypical developing infants of the same mental age, as measured by some developmental scale. The ages of infants with normotypical development usually start at 12 months of chronological age, so in infants with Down syndrome they can range from 18 to 20 months (e.g., Beeghly & Cicchetti, [5]; Hill & McCune-Nicolich, [38]; Lalueza, [47]), with a difference of approximately 9 months when matching them by mental age [49]. This implies that, in some cases, infants with Down syndrome already perform symbolic behaviors, and it is not possible to determine at what point in their development, their chronological age, the first symbolic uses of objects appear or what type of symbols they can make at different times in their development. Despite this, various studies maintain that the course and content of symbolic play in infants with Down syndrome is very similar to that observed in infants with normotypical development, but that it emerges at a delayed rate.

The symbolic play of infants with Down syndrome progresses following the same developmental sequence observed in infants with normotypical development, which is characterized by decentering, decontextualization and integration [5, 16, 38, 65, 116]. Decentering implies that infants first create self-directed symbols and then direct them to others, which implies a more complex level (e.g., sublevels 1.2 and 2.2, see Table 5.1). Regarding decontextualization, some authors refer to what characterizes it as the substitution of one object for another. That is, the use of objects that are less and less appropriate or realistic to carry out a symbolic use (e.g., Bretherton et al., [10]; Elder & Pederson, [25]; Fein, [28]). However, as we have already mentioned, decontextualization also occurs when symbols are made with the same object as conventional use, but in circumstances different from those of said use. For example, when a infant "eats" or "feeds" his/her mother with an empty spoon (sublevels 1.1 and 1.2, see Table 5.1). In this situation, without food or a plate, for example, the effectiveness and necessary steps required when one really wants to use the spoon effectively to feed oneself are not required [89].

Integration can be observed when the infant is able to chain more than one symbolic action, generating what Palacios et al. [74] call symbolic narratives in action (level 4, see Table 5.1).

As we mentioned in the previous section, symbolic uses are another semiotic system that serves communication with others and with oneself when we think. These become more complex with development, the simplest being those in which the same object with which the conventional use is carried out is used as a support for the symbolic use. Within this level 1, the most basic, infants can direct the uses to themselves, but also to others. The most complex ones would be those in which the symbols imply symbolic narratives where the object is treated as an agent (see Table 5.1, level 4.3).

Cárdenas et al. [17] conducted a longitudinal single-case study to analyze whether this progression in the appearance of symbolic uses also occurred in a girl with Down syndrome, whom they studied from 12 to 18 months. The results indicate that the infant made the first symbolic uses when she was 13½ months of chronological age. From that age until 18 months, the most frequent uses were those of level 1. For example, using the spoon to "eat." The infant also made more complex uses, but less frequently, such as when she used the toothbrush as a comb (use by substitution, level 2) and other uses *in absentia* (level 3), such as "washing her hands" after the mother "put soap" on them. Her symbolic uses were mainly directed at the object and herself, never at the mother, even though her mother was interacting with her daughter and was part of the triadic interaction.

The objects most used by the girl were the telephone, the spoon and the doll. Two of them, the doll and the telephone, coincide with the most used by infants with normotypical development [74, 71]. Both objects are very present in the daily life of infants.

In another longitudinal study with infants with Down syndrome between 12 and 21 months of chronological age, in interaction with their mothers, Cárdenas [19] and Cárdenas et al. (*submitted* [18]) found that infants also mostly make symbolic uses of level 1 at 12, 15, 18 and 21 months. In addition, they observed that some infants made more complex symbolic uses, for example, of sublevel 4.1 which involves symbolic narratives in action of uses of level 1. For example, "eating" with the spoon, and then "feeding" the doll and the adult. Some of the participants make symbolic uses that involve replacing one object with another (level 2). Faced with this type of symbolic use, such as "feeding" the doll with the mobile or using the spoon to "comb one's hair", the mothers express their disapproval. Adults consider this type of use as "inappropriate". They encourage the infants to represent this use using the "appropriate" object, for example, the spoon to "feed" the doll. From our point of view, these more complex symbolic uses show a greater capacity for abstraction and transfer of the rules of canonical uses by infants. Disapproval of this type of symbolic uses by substitution has also been found in mothers and fathers of infants with normotypical development [69].

For example, as indicated above, Palacios and Rodríguez [71] found that adults correct certain symbolic uses that are further from convention, such as when they use the horse to "drink" or "comb" their hair with the toothbrush.

Something similar is reported by Lalueza and Perinat [48], who found that mothers of infants with Down syndrome put more emphasis than mothers of infants with normotypical development on their infants mastering the correct use of objects and are less concerned about symbolic uses.

During triadic interactions, both in the study by Cárdenas [19] and in Cárdenas et al. [17], mothers assume a role that can be considered educational, teaching infants the symbolic use of objects, using various sign systems: words, songs, gestures, demonstrations of symbolic uses of objects, among others. They configure multimodal educational scenarios that support the progressive construction of symbolic meanings by infants.

Next, in Figure 5.3 [17], it is illustrated how the construction of meanings and symbolic uses of objects requires the mediation of the adult through signs.

Victoria's mother has set herself the goal of getting her daughter to use the box as if it were a plate. That is, to use it in a more complex symbolic way than she has been using the spoon up to now, which involves the substitution of one object for another. This is a challenge for Victoria because it is a use she has never realized before. In Vygotskian terms, we could say that the infant's real development zone is using the spoon to "eat" and to "feed" the doll or adult. And from our point of view, being able to use the box as if it were a plate means reaching a new level of development.

Furthermore, in this interaction we can observe several aspects that we consider important to highlight: (1) how the girl, through various systems of signs, mainly non-verbal, manages to communicate with her mother with and through the objects that are part of the interaction (spoon, doll, box) (Fig. 5.3. See Image 1). (2) That the uses of the objects are not transparent or obvious to Victoria. The meaning of the uses of the spoon and the box are diverse and depend on the use that is made of them (Fig. 5.3. See Image 2). Initially, Victoria and her mother do not share the same meaning regarding the use of the box (Fig. 5.3. See Image 1 and 2). Despite the mother's various invitations to "take food" from the box, Victoria does not immediately understand this request, but instead uses the simpler symbolic uses that she already understands: "eating" with the spoon (level 1.1) and "feeding" the doll and then "eating" (level 4.1).

(3) The mother remains attentive and adjusts her interaction, produces signs that are less complex than language, demonstrates the symbolic use she expects the infant to make (Fig. 5.3. See Image 5), and shows herself as a model of this use. However, Victoria does not immediately understand this either. Seeing that this does not work, her mother adapts her mediation again, carrying out the symbolic demonstration of the use, but this time taking Victoria's hand to "take food" from the box (Fig. 5.3. See Image 4), linking it with another use, "feeding" the doll, while producing onomatopoeia (Fig. 5.3. See Image 5). Finally, after all these symbolic uses and demonstrations by the mother, Victoria "takes food" from the box (Fig. 5.3. See Image 6) and "eats". Victoria has understood the meaning attributed

Victoria (V) 18 months		Duration: 1 minute 48 seconds
Image 1	Image 2	Image 3

Mother (M) says "you feed it [the doll]. We don't have a plate. Look here, with this (brings the box closer to V), it acts as a plate". And M touches V's leg to get her attention. V does not respond to M's invitation and hits the floor with the spoon*. M says "how it sounds".	M hits the ground with his fist and V goes to that place and hits it with the spoon. M turns the box over, hits it and says "it makes a sound here too". V hits the box several times and vocalizes "ah". M also says "ah". V "eats" with the spoon* and then "feeds" the doll. M says "to feed it, of course".	M turns the box: "take the food from here, take the food" -points to the inside of the box-. V puts the spoon in the box. M picks up the spoon and says "like this," while "picking up food" from the box with the spoon and offering it to V. V watches M's action, but does not take the spoon, so M says "for you" and "feeds" her with the spoon*, accompanying her demonstration with onomatopoeia.

Image 4	Image 5	Image 6
		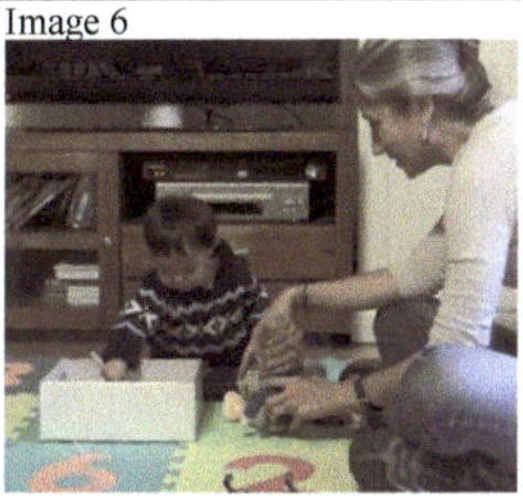
M takes V's hand, takes "food from the box"*, says "we feed it" and they "feed" the doll: "Mmmm, how delicious. Mmm, how delicious. Look, should we take the food from here?" pointing with the spoon to the inside of the box.	M says "you take it – "take food" from the box" and give it to it like this". "They feed" the doll*. "Mmmm, how it eats". V "feeds" the doll and M accompanies "oh, how delicious". Immediately, V "eats" with the spoon" and M says "and for you. Oh how delicious, mmm how delicious".	M says "get more food, get, get" pointing twice at the box. V "gets food" from the box* and "eats" with the spoon. M accompanies her: "Here, for you and now get food", V "gets" food again, M says "and for it [the doll]".

Fig. 5.3 Semiotic mediation for the construction of symbolic meanings and uses of the box as a plate * Indicate the moment that each image represents

to the box, which is shared by both: the box acts as a plate from which "we take the food".

(4) The mother is sensitive to the infant's interest in making sounds by hitting the spoon (Fig. 5.3. See Image 1). She goes from hitting the floor with her fist to hitting the box, an object that she wants Victoria to use to "pick up" the food because there are no plates. The mother does not lose sight of her objective and from these more basic uses that Victoria makes of the spoon, she manages to involve her daughter in more complex uses.

(5) The communicative signs used by Victoria included materiality. Victoria's own agency, her looks, gestures, and uses of objects give valuable information to the mother, who adjusts her own action based on what the girl did. This highlights the reciprocal and dynamic nature of these interactions that involve materiality [72, 124]. Therefore, not only does the adult have an important role in managing the interaction. Infants, with their active role, contribute to the communicative exchange as well. In the words of Sastre and Pastor [93], the infant guides the tutor, in this case the mother, while being guided by her.

Although studies on symbolic play in infants with Down syndrome do not focus on the sign systems used by adults, findings show that adults, through their scaffolding, can support the development of infants' play. Roach et al. [85] indicate that the most complex symbolic play achieved by infants with Down syndrome is associated with facilitating or supportive behaviors of mothers, such as giving or receiving a toy or bringing it to the infant. When the infant's solitary play with the object is compared with that involving the adult, the quality of the play increases both in infants with Down syndrome and in infants with normotypical development [14].

Another aspect that is linked to the effect that the mother's presence has on the symbolic play of infants with Down syndrome is related to the sensitivity that they show. Symbolic play is greater in infants whose mothers were highly sensitive compared to mothers who showed low sensitivity [117]. Along with maternal sensitivity, adult directiveness is an aspect that is analyzed when observing the symbolic play of infants with normotypical development and infants with Down syndrome. Crawley and Spiker [15] found large individual differences between mothers in aspects such as directiveness and sensitivity for both groups of infants. While some mothers were highly directive, others followed the infant's initiative or spent most of their time observing and commenting on the activities carried out by their infants. They emphasize that sensitivity is not sufficient, because if the interaction is characterized by being sensitive to the infants' initiative but does not provide a minimum level of direction, or if no further details are given about the play, an optimal environment is not provided to stimulate a infant with Down syndrome. Mothers considered highly stimulating were those who combined high sensitivity and directivity in their interactions, with their infants showing more advanced development. They also point out that directivity may be necessary when infants show limited attentional skills or difficulties in sustained attention during the interaction.

In the following section, we focus on the development of the first symbolic productions in a usual institutional context for infants, the early years school, while they interact with a partner and different objects.

5.6 Symbolic Development Among Peers

Early years school is another area in which we have explored the development of early symbols. It is an institution that, among other things, offers and expands the world of social relationships for infants. On a day-to-day basis, it enables increased experiences of interaction with adults other than parents and family members, as well as exchanges with peers or equals. It makes it possible to investigate this development when a infant interacts with a teacher, or with an equal and objects.

In a previous work [75] we have pointed out (1) that the study of the development of symbolic uses in the first years of early infanthood education 0–2 years has received little attention, (2) that the curricular plans of early infanthood education in Spain, Chile and Mexico contemplate working with symbols as learning content from 18 to 24 months of age of infants, continuing the widespread idea in psychological literature, that the beginning of symbols occurs at that age. And (3) that there is a gap between the curricular proposals and what happens in the classroom. For example, we found that infants make symbolic uses of objects in interaction with the teacher long before 18 months.

In Palacios et al. [75], two observations are presented that draw a lot of attention precisely because of the age that the boy and girl were at the time of carrying out the symbolic use. In the first of them, a Spanish boy of almost 8 months of age pretends to eat while the teacher brings the spoon to his mouth without food and in the second, a Mexican girl of 10 and a half months pretends to fly a paper plane that the same teacher has created. Therefore, there is no doubt that the curricular plans ignore that infants are capable of understanding and using objects symbolically even before the first year.

In the early years school, infants are encouraged to understand the world in which they live, its norms and social rules. Symbolic activities help infants to understand the reality that surrounds them, to understand the world. Through "acting as if", infants can represent different objects or characters in their environment. Vygotsky [121] highlights that symbolic play allows them to represent real-life situations, which helps them to develop abstract thinking skills and to practice social roles. Valles Medina and Rios Arriaga [115] point out that symbolic play is essential in learning strategies. It allows infants to express what they want, acquire knowledge and skills, and it is a mediator between the teacher and the student. In the same sense, Párraga and Meza [76] indicate the benefits of symbolic productions in early education, expressing that infants act without fear of error, allow the rehearsal of behaviors, in such a way that self-confidence increases.

One of the great potentials offered by early years school is the company of peers. The first social contacts and interactions between infants of similar ages often take place in classrooms. The "others", the "equals", are essential in social development and a great model for learning. Peer interaction, conceived as a process of communication and interaction initiated and maintained by infants themselves, evolves gradually. In its early stages, it includes a series of basic interactive behaviors, such as establishing eye contact, maintaining proximity to peers, making ostensive gestures of showing, offering and receiving objects, making verbal or nonverbal requests, among others [4, 66, 84, 99, 128]. Symbolic play in interaction with peers has numerous benefits for the psychological development and social skills of infants [37, 43, 55, 97, 101, 106].

Bauminger-Zviely et al. [4] highlight that experiences of engaging in social play and symbolic play with peers in early infanthood contribute significantly to the development of infants' skills. Symbolic play among peers provides the opportunity to learn to share the meanings of symbolic actions, to negotiate and resolve conflicts, and to meta communicate. Research shows that, as early as 14–16 months, infants engage in symbolic productions when interacting with peers [39–41]. These productions basically consist of making "as if" (level 1 of symbolic complexity) with replica objects [40].

From the Pragmatics of the Object, Yuste [127] conducted a study with infants aged 9 to 21 months to investigate whether they engaged in symbolic interactions with peers from 12 months onward, similar to how they interact with adults. This research was carried out at the early years school attended by the infants. They were offered three kits of replica objects. These are miniature objects, similar to real objects that the infants are familiar with (kit 1 *tableware*: plates, forks, spoons, cups and glasses; kit 2 *hairdressers*: dolls, hairbrushes, combs and hairdryers; kit 3 *telephones*). The results show that, as early as 12 months, infants perform symbolic productions with a miniature replica object, at level 1, and symbolic narratives at level 4.1 (see Table 5.1) in triadic interaction with another partner 6 months older. Furthermore, no infant performs symbolic uses of level 2, by substitution, and 3, *in absence*, with these replica objects, even at 21 and 24 months of age. This means that the replica objects seemed to hinder the production of symbols of greater complexity. We will return to this issue later.

Figure 5.4 shows how the youngest 12-month-old infant (Hugo, wearing a blue and white striped jumper) performs a symbolic narrative in action at level 4.1: he "dials the numbers" and "talks on the phone". Meanwhile, his 18-month-old partner (Israel, wearing a dark green jumper) performs a more complete symbolic narrative in action at the same level: "he dials the numbers", "talks" and "hangs up".

In this observation (Fig. 5.4), the influence that the symbolic use of the telephone made by Hugo, the youngest, has on the symbolic use of his partner is very striking and evident. Without having the intention of influencing his partner, Hugo ends up doing it. Israel only had to look at Hugo's symbolic use of the telephone to understand this symbolic use and then do it himself. The results show that infants make symbolic uses with replica objects from the age of 12 months. These results coincide with previous research (e.g., Palacios et al., [74]) regarding the age at which infants make their first symbolic productions in triadic interactions with an adult.

Hugo (1;0,7) and Israel (1;6,1)			Duration: 17 seconds
Image 1	Image 2	Image 3	Image 4

1. Hugo (striped jumper) has touched the buttons on the phone pretending to *dial*. 2. He then puts on the handset pretending to "talk", without making any vocalizations. 3. Israel (dark green shirt) has observed the scene and approaches one of the phones.	4. Hugo has thrown the phone he was using onto the tatami (non-canonical use). 5. Israel presses the keys on the phone "dialing the number" before "speaking".	6. Israel "talks" on the phone with the receiver in his ear, vocalizing: "hello". 7. Hugo looks again at the phone he had thrown on the tatami.	8. Israel "hangs up" the phone after finishing "talking". 9. Hugo has observed his partner and approaches to take the phone that Israel drops.

Fig. 5.4 Symbolic narrative in action at level 4.1 with the telephone in peer interaction

A second study [128] analyzed whether infants in peer interaction make symbolic uses of more complex levels. The dyads are composed of a infant of 11, 13 and 15 months with another infant six months older (17, 19 and 21 months respectively). In this investigation, two sets of objects were presented. One comprised of miniature replica objects (like the kits used in the first study) and the other comprised of everyday artifact objects (empty water bottles, spoons, empty yogurt containers, cardboard boxes with a string tied to the front, toothbrushes, stuffed dolls, universal remote controls, syringes without a needle, and old iron keys). The results show that all 11-month-old infants make symbolic uses of level 1 with miniature replica objects (plate, glass, spoon or comb). Something similar happens with artifact objects that are very familiar to infants (spoon and empty yogurt container). Familiarity favors the realization of symbolic uses of levels 1 and 4.1 from 11 months.

In this study it was also found that with the artifact objects the infants made symbolic uses by substitution of level 2 (see Fig. 5.5). This marks a substantial difference with the replica objects, with which the infants never reached level 2 by substitution. 50% of the sample (5 of the 10 dyads) of 13 months made symbolic productions of level 2, by substitution, with the artifact objects. However, with the artifact objects they never made symbolic uses *in absence*, of level 3.

In Fig. 5.5 we can see that while Neo, 13 months old, uses the toothbrush as if it were a hairbrush (symbolic use of level 2.1), Dario, who simulates "drinking" from the empty bottle (symbolic use of level 1.1), looks at how his partner "combs" his hair. In the literature on peer play, this type of situation is often referred to as "parallel social symbolic play" [41, 60].

Neo (1;1,2) and Darío (1;7,3)	Duration: 13 seconds
	1. Neo, who has picked up the toothbrush, switches it from one hand to the other. He then "combs" his hair, using the toothbrush as if it were a hairbrush. 2. Dario "drinks" from the empty bottle while watching his partner's action.

Fig. 5.5 Symbolic use level 2: toothbrush used as a hairbrush

In the first study [127], infants from 12 to 21 months carry out, on most occasions, symbolic uses in parallel and, on very few occasions, shared symbolic uses, although in 55, 97% of the time they were together they looked at their partner's action. This does not happen when an adult is involved in the interaction. Markova and Legerstee [60] conducted a comparative study between infants' symbolic productions with their mothers and peers and showed that 15-month-old infants produced more complex and longer symbolic productions with adults than with peers. They engaged in parallel symbolic play with their peers. These symbolic productions in the company of a peer were accompanied by eye contact, the other did not invite his/her peer to share symbolic behaviors, nor did they engage in shared symbolic play, but they observed each other. The authors conclude that performing symbolic productions in the company of a peer is probably more balanced and motivating for infants than participating in symbolic productions with adults. Howes et al. [41] also reported that mothers facilitate more complex symbolic play, whereas parallel symbolic play is more frequent and lasts longer with peers.

In summary, when accompanied by a peer, all infants perform level 1 symbolic uses with replica objects at 11 months and half of the 13-month-old infants perform level 2 symbolic productions, by substitution, with artifact objects. These symbolic productions were not shared between the infants, but there were occasions in which the symbolic uses of one of them were the starting point for the peer to also perform similar symbolic uses, and, on numerous occasions, they observed each other and shared the objects.

These results show that there is a gap between the curricular proposals in early infanthood education and the daily activities that arise from these proposals and then occur within the classroom. These results also suggest that offering infants one or another type of object implies promoting different learning. With replica objects, symbolic productions would be promoted from an earlier age than indicated by the literature and curricular proposals. While with artifact objects, more complex symbolic productions would be promoted. It would therefore be necessary to rethink the materials and organization in the classrooms of the first year of early infanthood education (level 0–1 years), where only exceptionally infants' symbolic productions are promoted [75]. Schools should strive to establish a symbolic play corner in these classrooms from the beginning of the course with suitable materials (for example, replica objects, materials not marked by function, recycled material, etc.), where teachers encourage, promote and teach plural uses at first and then let infants themselves, in the company of their peers, share this space.

5.7 Conclusions

The study of the development of the first symbols has been carried out from different theoretical-methodological approaches that defend an individual or social origin of the symbol. We propose that accounting for the process of development of the first symbolic uses of objects in dyadic infant–object contexts is not the same as accounting for the process of development of the first symbolic uses of objects in triadic communicative contexts adult–object–infant. When studied in different contexts, they yield different results and, therefore, lead to accounting for this process in a different way [71, 69].

Research in dyadic situations has led to conceive symbols as play, to locate their origin in the solitary action of the infant himself/herself, to explain them in terms of mere mental representation, to define objects based on their physical characteristics (e.g., Belsky & Most; [8]; Inhelder et al., [42]; McCune, [62]; Piaget, [80]) and to consider that the infant's symbolic play is motivated unidirectionally by the mother (see Fein and Fryer, [29]). Instead, research carried out in contexts of triadic communication and interaction has allowed, among other things, to understand symbols as means of communication and thought (not only as a play), to locate their origin in previously agreed meanings, to understand that their origin is semiotically mediated, to explore the educational role of the adult, to conceive that objects have agreed rules of use and not only physical attributes and to show that the motivation to create shared symbolic meanings of objects is bidirectional [17, 72–73, 87–88].

For a infant to use an object as a symbol in his/her daily interactions with others, the participation of others is necessary, as well as having knowledge of the cultural materiality, the rules of the canonical uses of objects. This is supported by the following facts that emerge from our research.

In relation to the *importance of adult participation* in the origin and evolution of symbolic uses, we have found that when infants *do not yet perform or understand* the symbolic uses of objects, (1) adults perform them for and with infants with normotypical development and Down syndrome. And, as might be expected, all the symbolic uses we observe are made by adults. (2) Adults direct and provide further support by using communicative mediators, which they adjust and change as required, to engage infants in the symbolic meanings of the objects displayed in front of and for them. As noted above, adults use the orchestration of different communicative mediators and use all demonstrations of symbolic uses to teach or show infants how the object is used symbolically.

When infants *begin to make and understand* symbolic uses, which occurs, as we have observed, from 11 months of age among peers or 12 months in infants with normotypical development and with Down Syndrome, (1) adults begin to decrease the total frequency of symbolic demonstrations more and more as infants show greater competence and ease in using objects symbolically, observing that infants increase the total frequency of symbolic uses throughout their development. 2) Adults also begin to decrease the support and direction they provide, showing a progressive withdrawal of communicative mediators that corresponds to the infants' increasing capacity to understand and produce symbolic uses. Adults progressively resort less to the orchestration of different communicative mediators and use symbolic demonstrations less to teach the symbolic use of the object, but instead, they begin to use symbolic demonstrations to provide feedback, complete, correct, etc., the infants' symbolic uses.

Regarding the *importance of objects*, specifically the rules of canonical uses, in the origin and evolution of the first symbols we have consistently found that (1) the highest percentage of symbolic uses of adults and infants (with normotypical development and with Down syndrome), in triadic interactionswas that of level 1 symbols. This is also true for peer interactions (see levels in Table 5.1). In other words, adults most frequently produce symbolic uses of level 1, where there is a very close relationship between the present symbolic use evoking the absent canonical use. Therefore, infants' first symbols, as well as those they most frequently produce during their development, are of level 1.

(2) The highest percentage of symbolic uses of sublevel 4.1, which groups the symbolic narratives of the symbolic uses of level 1, of adults and infants (with normotypical development and with Down syndrome) in triadic interactions highlights the importance of canonical uses as the basis for the origin and creation of symbolic narratives. These symbolic uses are also dominant in peer interactions.

(3) The low percentage of levels 2, and lower percentage of levels 3 (symbols by substitution and in the absence of the object, respectively) in adults and infants (with normotypical development and with Down syndrome)indicate that the rules of canonical uses are gradually detached from their place of origin. It also indicates the difficulty of infants to transfer and apply these rules to another object or to represent them through a symbolic gesture without an object. In peer interactions, level 2 symbolic uses have minimal presence, while levels 3 are absent.

The path we have taken in the research we have carried out on the early development of the first symbols puts us in perspective of looking forward and realizing that future studies are required on the evolution of the symbolic uses of objects at later ages than those observed. We also consider it necessary to continue researching to expand our knowledge on the development of symbolic uses in triadic situations in infants with other developmental trajectories, especially if we consider that the symbolic uses of objects make up a type of semiotic system that is used to communicate and think.

If we assume symbolic uses as a semiotic system, mediated by others, a great space opens up for research, regarding the possible functions of the first symbols in infants with normotypical and atypical development. It also offers the possibility to study the semiotic mediation carried out by adults who interact daily with neurodivergent infants and how the construction of these symbolic meanings can be supported in populations with atypical development.

In our studies we have left aside the analysis of the use of language by adults and infants (when language is present) and between peers. This opens another space to study the relationship between symbolic uses and more complex and abstract semiotic systems, delving into the characteristics of the sign systems used by adults and infants with typical and atypical development and by infants among peers.

Finally, the results shown in this chapter on the development of symbols have practical implications in the educational, clinical and developmental fields, for example, as well as in the daily life of the infant. Knowing the process and the moment of development in which infants with normotypical development usually begin to make their first symbolic uses and the materiality that is used for the construction of symbolic meanings allows (1) to guide the pedagogical decision-making of early infanthood education professionals regarding the materiality that they can offer to infants in educational environments from 0 to 1 year classrooms, as well as the starting age to work on this type of curricular content, (2) to detect atypicalities in the early communicative development of infants who attend or do not attend the early years school, (3) to guide early care and early infanthood education professionals on the diversity of signs that they can put into action, considering the multimodality of semiotic systems and (4) to consider the first symbolic uses of objects as a system of signs that allows the infant not only to play and participate in playful interactions with others, adults or peers, but also to communicate when the language acquisition process is still in development.

References

1. Aksoy, A. B., Kunduracı, H. K. O., & Aksoy, M. (2022). Symbolic play: Mother and child behaviours. *Early Child Development and Care, 192*(8), 1257–1269. https://doi.org/10.1080/03004430.2020.1865337
2. Ban, M., & Uchiyama, I. (2022). Developmental changes in toy preferences during pretend play in toddlerhood. *Early Child Development and Care, 192*(7), 1069–1078. https://doi.org/10.1080/03004430.2020.1838497
3. Baron-Cohen, S., Leslie, A. M., & Frith, U. (1985). Does the autistic child have a "theory of mind"? *Cognition, 21*(1), 37–46. https://doi.org/10.1016/0010-0277(85)90022-8
4. Bauminger-Zviely, N., Eytan, D., Hoshmand, S., & Ben-Shlomo, O. R. (2021). *Preschool peer social intervention in autism spectrum disorder*. Springer. https://doi.org/10.1007/978-3-030-79080-6
5. Beeghly, M., & Cicchetti, D. (1987). An organizational approach to symbolic development in children with Down syndrome. *New Directions for Child Development, 36*, 5–29.
6. Behne, T., Carpenter, M., Gräfenhain, M., Liebal, K., Liszkowki, U., Moll, H., Rakoczy, H., Tomasello, M., Warneken, F., & Wyman, E. (2008). Cultural learning and cultural creation. In U. Müller, J. I. M. Carpendale, N. Budwig & B. Sokol (Eds.), *Social life and social knowledge. Toward a process account of development* (pp. 65–101). LEA.
7. Bellagamba, F., & Tomasello, M. (1999). Re-enacting intended acts: Comparing 12- and 18-months-olds. *Infant Behavior and Development, 22*(2), 277–282. https://doi.org/10.1016/S0163-6383(99)00002-8
8. Belsky, J., & Most, R. K. (1981). From exploration to play: A cross-sectional study of infant free play behavior. *Developmental Psychology, 17*, 630–639. https://doi.org/10.1037/0012-1649.17.5.630

9. Bentenuto, A., de Falco, S., & Venuti, P. (2016). Mother-child play: A comparison of Autism spectrum disorder, Down syndrome, and typical development. *Frontiers in Psychology, 7*. https://doi.org/10.3389/fpsyg.2016.01829
10. Bretherton, I., O'Connell, B., Shore, C., & Bates, E. (1984). The effect of contextual variation on symbolic play: Development from 20 to 28 months. In I. Bretherton (Ed.), *Symbolic play and the development of social understanding* (pp. 271–298). Academic Press.
11. Bronckart, J.-P. (1997). Semiotic interaction and cognitive construction. *Archives de Psychologie, 65*, 95–106.
12. Bruner, J. (2002). *Actos de significado. Más allá de la revolución cognitiva* (J. C. Gómez Crespo & J. Linaza, Trans.) [Acts of Meaning. Four Lectures on Mind and Culture]. Alianza Editorial. (original work published in 1990).
13. Carpenter, M., Call, J., & Tomasello, M. (2005). Twelve- and 18-month-olds copy actions in terms of goals. *Developmental Science, 8*(1), F13–F20. https://doi.org/10.1111/j.1467-7687.2004.00385.x
14. Cielinski, K. L., Vaughn, B. E., Seifer, R., & Contreras, J. (1995). Relations among sustained engagement during play, quality of play, and mother–child interaction in samples of children with Down syndrome and normally developing toddlers. *Infant Behavior and Development, 18*, 163–176.
15. Crawley, S. B., & Spiker, D. (1983). Mothers-child interaction involving two-year-olds with Down syndrome: A look at individual differences. *Child Development, 54*, 1312–1323.
16. Cunningham, C. C., Glenn, S. M., Wilkinson, P., & Sloper, P. (1985). Mental ability, symbolic play and receptive and expressive language of young children with Down syndrome. *Journal of Child Psychology and Psychiatry, 26*, 255–265.
17. Cárdenas, K. (2012). *Primeros usos simbólicos de niños con síndrome de Down en contextos de interacción triádica: un estudio longitudinal entre los 12 y 21 meses de edad* [First symbolic uses in children with Down syndrome in triadic interaction contexts: a longitudinal study between 12-21 months]. [Doctoral dissertation, Universidad Autónoma de Madrid]. https://repositorio.uam.es/handle/10486/11758
18. Cárdenas, K., Rodríguez, C., Miranda-Zapata, E., & Palacios, P. (Manuscript submitted for publication). First symbolic uses of objects in children with Down syndrome between the ages of 12 and 21 months: A longitudinal study in context of triadic interactions child-adult-object.
19. Cárdenas, K., Rodríguez, C., & Palacios, P. (2014). First symbols in a girl with Down syndrome: A longitudinal study from 12 to 18 months. *Infant Behavior and Development, 37*(3), 416–427. https://doi.org/10.1016/j.infbeh.2014.06.003
20. DeLoache, J. S. (1995). Early symbol understanding and use. In D. Medin (Ed.), *The psychology of learning and motivation* (Vol. 33, pp. 65–114). Academic Press.
21. DeLoache, J. S. (2000). Dual representation and young children's use of scale models. *Child Development, 71*(2), 329–338. https://doi.org/10.1111/1467-8624.00148
22. DeLoache, J. S., Miller, K. F., & Rosengren, K. S. (1997). The credible shrinking room: Very young children's performance with symbolic and nonsymbolic relations. *Psychological Science, 8*(4), 308–313. https://doi.org/10.1111/j.1467-9280.1997.tb00443.x
23. Eco, U. (1994). *Signo* (F. Serra Cantarell, Trans.) [Sign]. Labor. (original work published in 1973).
24. Eco, U. (2000). *Semiótica y filosofía del lenguaje* (R. P., Trans.) [Semiotics and the philosophy of language]. Lumen. (original work published in 1984).
25. Elder, J. L., & Pederson, D. R. (1978). Preschool children's use of objects in symbolic play. *Child Development, 49*, 500–504.
26. El'konin, D. B. (1966). Symbolics and its functions in the play of children. *Soviet Education, 8*(3), 35–41.
27. de Falco, S., Esposito, G., Venuti, P., & Bornstein, M. H. (2010). Mothers and fathers at play with their children with Down syndrome: Influence on child exploratory and symbolic activity. *Journal of Applied Research in Intellectual Disabilities, 23*(6), 597–605.

28. Fein, G. G. (1975). A transformational analysis of pretending. *Developmental Psychology, 11*(3), 291–296.
29. Fein, G. G., & Fryer, M. G. (1995). Maternal contributions to early symbolic play competence. *Developmental Review, 15*(4), 367–381. https://doi.org/10.1006/drev.1995.1014
30. Fiese, B. H. (1990). Playful relationships: A contextual analysis of mother-toddler interaction and symbolic play. *Child Development, 61*, 1648–1656. https://doi.org/10.2307/1130772
31. Fletcher, K. K., Cates, C. B., Mendelsohn, A. L., & Tamis-LeMonda, C. S. (2020). Play in Mexican-American mothers and toddlers is frequent, multimodal, and rich in symbolic content. *Infancy, 25*(5), 535–551. https://doi.org/10.1111/infa.12344
32. Friedman, O., & Leslie, A. M. (2007). The conceptual underpinnings of pretense: Pretending is not "behaving-as-it." *Cognition, 105*(1), 103–124. https://doi.org/10.1016/j.cognition.2006.09.007
33. German, T. P., & Leslie, A. M. (2001). Children's inferences from "knowing" to "pretending" and "believing." *British Journal of Developmental Psychology, 19*, 59–83. https://doi.org/10.1348/026151001165967
34. Hà, T. A. (2022). Pretend play and early language development—Relationships and impacts: A comprehensive literature review. *Journal of Education, 202*(1), 122–130. https://doi.org/10.1177/0022057420966761
35. Harris, P. L. (1994). Understanding pretense. In C. Lewis & P. Mitchell (Eds.), *Children's early understanding of mind: Origins and development* (pp. 235–259). Lawrence Erlbaum Associates.
36. Hashmi, S. (2023). How do children play with toy trains and for what benefits? A scoping review. *European Journal of Investigation in Health, Psychology and Education, 13*, 2112–2134. https://doi.org/10.3390/ejihpe13100149
37. Hermann, S. (2017). *Evaluation of a simulation based on a fairy tale. Playful intervention to promote skills socioemotional disorders in preschool children* [Doctoral dissertation, Westfälische Wilhelms-Universität Münster].
38. Hill, P. M., & McCune-Nicolich, L. (1981). Pretend play and patterns of cognition in Down's Syndrome children. *Child Development, 52*, 611–617. https://doi.org/10.2307/1129181
39. Howes, C. (1985). Fantasy sharing: Social pretend play in young children. *Child Development, 56*(5), 1253–1258. https://doi.org/10.2307/1130240
40. Howes, C., & Matheson, C. C. (1992). Sequences in the development of competent play with Peers: Social and social simulation play. *Developmental Psychology, 28*(5), 961–974.
41. Howes, C., Unger, O., & Seidner, L. B. (1989). Social pretend play in toddlers: Parallels with social play and with solitary pretend. *Child Development, 60*(1), 77–84. https://doi.org/10.2307/1131073
42. Inhelder, B., Lézine, L., Sinclair, H., & Stambak, M. (1972). Les débuts de la fonction symbolique [The origins of symbolic function]. *Archives de Psychologie, 41*, 187–243.
43. Jaggy, A.-K., Kalkusch, I., Bossi, C. B., Weiss, B., Sticca, F., & Perren, S. (2023). The impact of social pretend play on the social development of preschool children: Results of an experimental study. *Early Childhood Research Quarterly, 64*, 13–25. https://doi.org/10.1016/j.ecresq.2023.01.012
44. Joginder Singh, S., Gan, B., & Shu, S. Y. (2021). Association between symbolic play and language: A comparison between typically developing children and children with Down syndrome. *Journal of Developmental & Behavioral Pediatrics, 42*(2), 146–151. https://doi.org/10.3390/children8090801
45. Kim, S., Kristen-Antonow, S., & Sodian, B. (2021). A longitudinal study of early pretense: Metarepresentational or not. *International Journal of Behavioral Development, 45*(4), 345–354. https://doi.org/10.1177/0165025421992868
46. Laakso, M. L., Poikkeus, A. M., Eklund, K., & Lyytinen, P. (1999). Social interactional behaviors and symbolic play competence as predictors of language development and their associations with maternal attention-directing strategies. *Infant Behavior and Development, 22*(4), 541–556. https://doi.org/10.1016/S0163-6383(00)00022-9

47. Lalueza, J. L. (1991). *Desarrollo del símbolo en el juego interactivo en niños con síndrome de Down y niños sin disminución* [Symbol development in interactive play in children with Down syndrome and typical children]. [Doctoral dissertation, Universidad Autónoma de Barcelona]. https://ddd.uab.cat/record/63209
48. Lalueza, J. L., & Perinat, A. (1994). Desarrollo de los significados compartidos en el juego entre adultos y niños con síndrome de Down [Shared meaning development in play between adults and children with Down syndrome]. *Infancia y Aprendizaje, 67–68*, 133–146.
49. Layton, T., Chuang, M. C., & Hao, G. (2014). Play behaviors in Chinese toddlers with Down syndrome. *J Psychol Abnorm Child, 3*, 131. https://doi.org/10.4172/2329-9525.1000131
50. Leslie, A. M. (1987). Pretense and representation: The origins of "theory of mind." *Psychological Review, 94*, 412–426. https://doi.org/10.1037/0033-295X.94.4.412
51. Leslie, A. M. (1994). Pretending and believing: Issues in the theory of ToMM. *Cognition, 50*, 211–238. https://doi.org/10.1016/0010-0277(94)90029-9
52. Leslie, A. M., German, T. P., & Polizzi, P. (2005). Belief-desire reasoning as a process of selection. *Cognitive Psychology, 50*, 45–85. https://doi.org/10.1016/j.cogpsych.2004.06.002
53. Leslie, A. M., & Thaiss, L. (1992). Domain specificity in conceptual development: Neuropsychological evidence from autism. *Cognition, 43*, 225–251. https://doi.org/10.1016/0010-0277(92)90013-8
54. Leslie, A. M. (1992). Pretense, autism, and the theory-of-mind module. *Current Directions in Psychological Science, 1*, 18–21. https://www.jstor.org/stable/20182118
55. Li, J., Hestenes, L. L., & Wang, Y. C. (2016). Links between preschool children's social skills and observed pretend play in outdoor childcare environments. *Early Childhood Education Journal, 44*(1), 61–68.
56. Lillard, A. S. (1993). Pretend play skills and the child's theory of mind. *Child Development, 64*(2), 348–371. https://doi.org/10.2307/1131255
57. Lillard, A. S. (2001). Pretend play as twin earth. *Developmental Review, 21*, 1–33. https://doi.org/10.1006/drev.2001.0532
58. Lillard, A., Nishida, T., Massaro, D., Vaish, A., Ma, L., & McRoberts, G. (2007). Signs of pretense across age and scenario. *Infancy, 11*, 1–30. https://doi.org/10.1207/s15327078in1101_1
59. Lillard, A. S., & Witherington, D. C. (2004). Mothers' behavior modifications during pretense and their possible signal value for toddlers. *Developmental Psychology, 40*(1), 95–113. https://doi.org/10.1037/0012-1649.40.1.95
60. Markova, G., & Legerstee, M. (2012). Social pretence with mothers and peers at 15 months. *European Journal of Developmental Psychology, 9*(6), 711–722. https://doi.org/10.1080//17405629.2012.671714
61. Markova, G., & Legerstee, M. (2015). The role of maternal behavior in children's pretense during the second year of life. *Cognitive Development, 34*, 3–15. https://doi.org/10.1016/j.cogdev.2014.12.011
62. McCune, L. (1995). A normative study of representational play in the transition to language. *Developmental Psychology, 31*, 198–206. https://doi.org/10.1037/0012-1649.31.2.198
63. McCune-Nicolich, L. (1981). Toward symbolic functioning: Structure of early pretend games and potential parallels with language. *Child Development, 52*, 785–797.
64. Moro, C., & Rodríguez, C. (2005). *L'objet et la construction de son usage chez le bébé* [Object and the construction of its use in babies]. Peter Lang.
65. Motti, F., Cicchetti, D., & Sroufe, L. A. (1983). From infant affect expression to symbolic play: The coherence of development in Down syndrome children. *Child Development, 54*, 1168–1175.
66. Mundy, P. (2018). A review of joint attention and social-cognitive brain systems in typical development and autism spectrum disorder. *European Journal of Neuroscience, 47*, 497–514. https://doi.org/10.1111/ejn.13720
67. Nicolich, L. M. (1977). Beyond sensorimotor intelligence: Assessment of symbolic maturity through analysis of pretend play. *Merrill-Palmer Quarterly, 23*, 89–99.

68. O'Connell, B., & Bretherton, I. (1984). Toddler's play alone and with mother: The role of maternal guidance. In I. Bretherton (Ed.), *Symbolic play: The development of social understanding* (pp. 337–366). Academic Press.
69. Palacios, P. (2009). *Origen de los usos simbólicos de los objetos en los niños en contextos de comunicación e interacción triádicos* [The origin of symbolic uses of objects in children in communicative contexts and triadic interactions] [Doctoral dissertation, Universidad Autónoma de Madrid]. https://repositorio.uam.es/handle/10486/4029
70. Palacios, P., & Rodríguez, C. (2006). Los símbolos en los contextos de interacción triádica [Symbols in triadic interaction contexts]. In P. Palacios (Ed.), *Memoria. Primer congreso internacional de psicología del desarrollo. Primer encuentro de egresados* (pp. 1–9). Universidad Autónoma de Aguascalientes.
71. Palacios, P., & Rodríguez, C. (2015). The development of symbolic uses of objects in infants in a triadic context: A pragmatic and semiotic perspective. *Infant and Child Development, 24*, 23–43. https://doi.org/10.1002/icd.1873
72. Palacios, P., Rodríguez, C., & Méndez-Sánchez, C. (2018). Communicative mediation by adults in the construction of symbolic uses by infants. *Integrative Psychological and Behavioral Science, 52*, 209–227. https://doi.org/10.1007/s12124-018-9422-1
73. Palacios, P., Rodríguez, C., Méndez-Sánchez, C., & Hermosillo-De-La-Torre, A. E. (2013). Contextos comunicativos e interactivos triádicos: la unidad básica de la educación [Communicative contexts and triadic interactions: the basic unit of education]. In P. Palacios, M. A. Farfán-García, E. Navarrete-Sánchez & S. C. Miramontes-Zapata (Comp.), *Psicología educativa: reflexión, práctica e intervención* (pp. 15–40). Universidad Autónoma del Estado de México.
74. Palacios, P., Rodríguez, C., Méndez-Sánchez, C., Hermosillo-De-La-Torre, A. E., Sahagún, M. Á., & Cárdenas, K. (2016). The development of the first symbolic uses in Mexican children from the pragmatics of object / Desarrollo de los primeros usos simbólicos en niños mexicanos desde la pragmática del objeto. *Estudios de Psicología, 37*(1), 59–89. https://doi.org/10.1080/02109395.2015.1122437
75. Palacios, P., Yuste, N., & Cárdenas, K. (2021). Los símbolos en la escuela infantil [Symbols in early years schools]. In C. Rodríguez & J. L. de los Reyes (Coord.), *Los objetos sí importan. Acción educativa en la escuela infantil* (pp. 109–131). Horsori.
76. Párraga, J. M. T., & Meza, A. K. T. (2022). Metodología lúdica en la construcción de la identidad y autonomía de los niños de educación inicial [Playful methodology in the construction of children's identity and autonomy in early childhood education]. *Revista EDUCARE-UPEL-IPB-Segunda Nueva Etapa 2.0, 26*(Extraordinario), 459–475.
77. Peirce, C. S. (1987). Collected papers of Charles Sanders Peirce. In A. S. Sercovich (Ed.), *Obra lógico-semiótica* (R. Alcalde y M. Prelooker, Trans.). Taurus. (original work published in 1965).
78. Peirce, C. S. (1988). *El hombre, un signo. El pragmatismo de Peirce* (J. Vericat, Trans.) [The man, a sign. Peirce's pragmatism]. Crítica. (original work published in 1965).
79. Perner, J. (1991). *Understanding the representational mind: Learning, development, and conceptual change.* MIT Press.
80. Piaget, J. (1976). *La formation du symbole chez l'enfant* [Play, dreams, and imitation in childhood]. Delachaux & Niestlé. (original work published in 1945).
81. Quinn, S., & Kidd, E. (2018). Symbolic play promotes non-verbal communicative exchange in infant-caregiver dyads. *British Journal of Developmental Psychology, 37*, 33–50. https://doi.org/10.1111/bjdp.12251
82. Rakoczy, H., Tomasello, M., & Striano, T. (2005). On tools and toys: How children learn to act on and pretend with "virgin objects." *Developmental Science, 8*(1), 57–73. https://doi.org/10.1111/j.1467-7687.2005.00393.x
83. Rakoczy, H., Tomasello, M., & Striano, T. (2005). How children turn objects into symbols: A cultural learning account. In L. Namy (Ed.), *Symbol use and symbolic representation* (pp. 69–97). LEA.

84. Rice, C. E., Adamson, L. B., Winner, E., & McGee, G. G. (2016). A cross-sectional study of shared attention between children with autism and typically developing children in an inclusive preschool setting. *Topics in Language Disorders, 36*(3), 245–265. https://doi.org/10.1097/TLD.0000000000000099
85. Roach, M. A., Stevenson Barratt, M., Miller, J. F., & Leavitt, L. A. (1998). The structure of mother-child play: Young children with Down syndrome and typically developing children. *Developmental Psychology, 34*, 77–87.
86. Rodríguez, C. (2006). *Del ritmo al símbolo. Los signos en el nacimiento de la inteligencia* [From rhythm to symbol. Signs in the birth of intelligence]. Horsori.
87. Rodríguez, C. (2012). The functional permanence of the object: A product of consensus. In E. Martí & C. Rodríguez (Eds.), *After Piaget* (pp. 123–150). Transaction Publishers.
88. Rodríguez, C., Basilio, M., Cárdenas, K., Cavalcante, C., Moreno-Nuñez, A., Palacios, P., & Yuste, N. (2018). Object pragmatics: Culture and communication – the bases for early cognitive development. In A. Rosa & J. Valsiner (Eds.), *The Cambridge handbook of sociocultural psychology* (2nd ed., pp. 223–244). Cambridge University Press. https://doi.org/10.1017/9781316662229
89. Rodríguez, C., Estrada, L., Moreno-Llanos, I., & de los Reyes, J. L. (2017a). Executive functions and educational actions in an infant school: Private uses and gestures at the end of the first year / Funciones ejecutivas y acción educativa en la escuela infantil: Usos y gestos privados al final del primer año. *Estudios de Psicología, 38*(2), 385–423. https://doi.org/10.1080/02109395.2017.1305061
90. Rodríguez, C., & Moro, C. (1999). *El mágico número tres. Cuando los niños aún no hablan* [The magic number three. When children do not talk yet]. Paidós.
91. Rodríguez, C., & Moro, C. (2002). Objeto, comunicación y símbolo. Una mirada a los primeros usos simbólicos de los objetos [Object, communication and symbol. A look at the first symbolic uses of objects]. *Estudios de Psicología, 23*, 323–338. https://doi.org/10.1174/021093902762224416
92. Rodríguez, C., Palacios, P., Cárdenas, K., & Yuste, N. (2017b). Los símbolos: ¿formas de segundo o tercer sentido? In C. Moro & N. Müller Mirza. *Semiótica, cultura y desarrollo psicológico* (pp. 105–122). Antonio Machado Libros.
93. Sastre, S., & Pastor, E. (1999). Rol del ajuste en la interacción temprana en bebés trisómicos y normales [The role of adjustment in the early interaction with trisomic and normotypical babies]. *Revista Interuniversitaria de Formación del Profesorado, 36*, 71–81.
94. Saussure, F. D. (2001). *Curso de lingüística general* (A. Alonso, Trans.)[Course in general linguistics]. Losada. (original work published in 1916)
95. Scholl, B. J., & Leslie, A. M. (1999). Modularity, development and "theory of mind." *Mind and Language, 14*(1), 131–153. https://doi.org/10.1111/1468-0017.00106
96. Scholl, B. J., & Leslie, A. M. (2001). Minds, modules, and meta-analysis. *Child Development, 72*(3), 696–701. https://doi.org/10.1111/1467-8624.00308
97. Schwebel, D. C., Rosen, C. S., & Singer, J. L. (1999). Pretend play and preschool children's theory of mind: The role of co-constructed simulation. *British Journal of Developmental Psychology, 17*(3), 333–348.
98. Sidhu, J., Barlas, N., & Lifter, K. (2022). On the meanings of functional play: A review and clarification of definitions. *Topics in Early Childhood Special Education, 42*(2), 189–201. https://doi.org/10.1177/0271121420951859
99. Siposova, B., Tomasello, M., & Carpenter, M. (2018). Communicative eye contact signals a commitment to cooperate for young children. *Cognition, 179*, 192–201. https://doi.org/10.1016/j.cognition.2018.06.010
100. Slade, A. (1987). A longitudinal study of maternal involvement and symbolic play during the toddler period. *Child Development, 58*, 367–375. https://doi.org/10.2307/1130513
101. Smits-van der Nat, M., van der Wilt, F., Meeter, M., & van der Veen, C. (2024). The value of pretend play for social competence in early childhood: A meta-analysis. *Educational Psychology Review, 36*(2), Article 46. https://doi.org/10.1007/s10648-024-09884-z

102. Sobel, D. M. (2023). Understanding pretense as causal inference. *Developmental Review, 68*, 1–15. https://doi.org/10.1016/j.dr.2023.101065
103. Striano, T., Rochat, P., & Legerstee, M. (2003). The role of modeling and request type on symbolic comprehension of objects and gestures in young children. *Journal Child Language, 30*, 27–45. https://doi.org/10.1017/S0305000902005524
104. Striano, T., Tomasello, M., & Rochat, P. (2001). Social and object support for early symbolic play. *Developmental Science, 4*, 442–455. https://doi.org/10.1111/desc.2001.4.issue-4
105. Stuart, A. C., Gufler, S. R., Tharner, A., & Væver, M. (2023). Story stems in early mother-infant interaction promote pretend play at 30 months. *Infant Behavior and Development, 73*, 1–10. https://doi.org/10.1016/j.infbeh.2023.101893
106. Talavera-Sánchez, R. (2023). Juego simbólico en el desarrollo de las habilidades de interacción social en niños de 5 años de dos instituciones educativas públicas del distrito de Ate-Lima [Symbolic play in the development of social interaction skills in 5 year old children in two public educational institutions in the district of Ate- Lima]. *593 Digital Publisher CEIT, 8*(1–1), 348–369. https://doi.org/10.33386/593dp.2023.1-1.1671
107. Tamis-LeMonda, C. S., & Bornstein, M. (1991). Individual variation, correspondence, stability, and change in mother and toddler play. *Infant Behavior and Development, 14*, 143–162. https://doi.org/10.1016/0163-6383(91)90002-A
108. Tomasello, M. (1999). *The cultural origins of human cognition*. Harvard University Press.
109. Tomasello, M. (2000). Culture and cognitive development. *Current Directions in Psychological Science, 9*(2), 37–40.
110. Tomasello, M. (2004). Learnig throug others. *Daedalus Winter, 133*(1), 51–58. https://www.jstor.org/stable/20027896
111. Tomasello, M., Kruger, A. C., & Ratner, H. H. (1993). Cultural learning. *Behavioral and Brain Sciences, 16*(03), 495–552. https://doi.org/10.1017/S0140525X0003123X
112. Tomasello, M., & Rakoczy, H. (2003). What makes human cognition unique? From individual to shared to collective intentionality. *Mind and Language, 18*(2), 121–147. https://doi.org/10.1111/1468-0017.00217
113. Tomasello, M., Savage-Rumbaugh, S., & Kruger, A. C. (1993). Imitative learning of actions on objects by children, chimpanzees, and enculturated chimpanzees. *Child Development, 64*(6), 1688–1705. https://doi.org/10.2307/1131463
114. Tomasello, M., Striano, T., & Rochat, P. (1999). Do young children use objects as symbols? *British Journal of Developmental Psychology, 17*(4), 563–584. https://doi.org/10.1348/026151099165483
115. Valles Medina, V. M., & Rios Arriaga, J. C. (2022). Estrategia del juego simbólico y la expresión oral una revisión bibliográfica [Symbolic play strategy and oral expression: a literature review]. *EduSol, 22*(80), 80–95.
116. Vendrell, R. (2003). *La capacitat representativa dels nens petits amb síndrome de Down. Anàlisi de casos a través del joc* [Representative capacity of young children with Down syndrome]. [Doctoral dissertation, Universidad Ramón Llull].
117. Venuti, P., De Falco, S., Giusti, Z., & Bornstein, M. H. (2008). Play and emotional availability in young children with Down syndrome. *Infant Mental Health Journal, 29*(2), 133–152.
118. Vygotsky, L. S. (1996). El primer año [The first year]. In L. S. Vygotsky, *Obras escogidas IV. Psicología infantil* (pp. 275–318) (L. Kuper, Trans.). Visor. (original work published in 1931).
119. Vygotsky, L. S. (1996). El papel del juego en el desarrollo del niño [The role of play in child development]. In L. S. Vygotski, *El desarrollo de los procesos psicológicos superiores* (pp.141–158) (S. Furió, Trans.). Critica. (original work published in 1933).
120. Vygotsky, L. S. (2000). Historia del desarrollo de las funciones psíquicas superiores [History of development of higher-order psychological functions]. In L. S. Vygotski, *Obras escogidas III. Problemas del desarrollo de la psique* (pp. 11–340) (L. Kuper, Trans.). Visor. (original work published in 1931).
121. Vygotsky, L. S. (2004). Imagination and creativity in childhood. *Journal of Russian and Eastern European Psychology, 42*(1), 7–97.

122. Wallon, H. (1970). *Del acto al pensamiento* (E. Dukelsky, Trans.) [From act to thought]. Psique. (original work published in 1942).
123. Wellman, H. M. (1990). *The child's theory of mind*. MIT Press.
124. Williams, E., Costall, A., & Reddy, V. (2018). Autism and triadic play: An object lesson in the mutuality of the social and material. *Ecological Psychology, 30*(2), 146–173. https://doi.org/10.1080/10407413.2018.1439140
125. Wittgenstein. L. (1967). *Investigaciones filosóficas* (A. Rossi, Trans.) [Philosophical investigations]. UNAM. (original work published in 1953).
126. Youngblade, L. M., & Dunn, J. (1995). Individual differences in young children's pretend play with mother and sibling: Links to relationships and understanding of other people's feelings and beliefs. *Child Development, 66*(5), 1472–1492. https://doi.org/10.2307/1131658
127. Yuste, N. (2012). *Producciones simbólicas en la escuela infantil en interacción entre iguales* [Symbolic productions in the early years school in peer interaction]. [Unpublished Advanced Studies Diploma]. Universidad Autónoma de Madrid.
128. Yuste, N. (2017). *Primeros usos simbólicos con objetos réplica y artefacto con niños/as de 9 a 24 meses* [First symbolic uses with replica and artifact objects with children 9-24 months of age]. [Doctoral dissertation, Universidad Autónoma de Madrid]. https://repositorio.uam.es/handle/10486/680694

Early Development of Number: Semiotic and Social Construction

6

Sílvia Cavalcante and Eduardo Martí

In this chapter we will first review the main contributions made in psychology related to early numerical knowledge. We will start with the classical studies of the Geneva school and the nativist proposal, followed by studies on counting, highlighting the limitations that we consider pertinent. Finally, we will highlight the importance of taking into account the social and semiotic component in studies concerning numerical knowledge, thus emphasizing the relevance of the Pragmatics of the Object perspective for this approach. We will illustrate our position through a longitudinal study conducted from this perspective on the numerical understanding displayed by mother–child dyads in a play situation involving numerical uses of objects. We hope that this chapter offers a critical view on the directions that studies on the development of number should consider when analyzing the processes of change in childhood.

Number, the essential foundation of mathematics, has been a recurrent subject of analysis and study by philosophers and scientists. In psychology, one of the contributions that proved decisive for its novelty and scope was the proposal of Piaget and the Geneva School. Based on the essential logical structure of number (which combines cardinal and ordinal aspects), Piaget understands number as a progressive construction of the subject, a construction that results from the synthesis of the operations of classification and seriation. Thus, for example, the number

S. Cavalcante (✉)
Universitat de Lleida, Lleida, Spain
e-mail: silvia.cavalcante@udl.cat

E. Martí
Universitat de Barcelona, Barcelona, Spain
e-mail: eduard.marti@ub.edu

C. Rodriguez Garrido et al. (eds.), *The Social Life of Objects in Early Development*, Social Interaction in Learning and Development,
https://doi.org/10.1007/978-3-031-87673-8_6

3 evokes the class of all numbers 3, different from the class of 1's and 2's; at the same time, each class can be ordered considering that 3 is greater than 2, and 2 is less than 3. One of the indications that children really understand number, according to Piaget, is when they are able to judge that two collections of elements placed in correspondence one by one continue to have the same number of elements (i.e., the same cardinal value) even if their appearance changes, for example, when the elements are separated or joined together. This is the well-known conservation of number test, designed by Piaget and Szeminska in 1941.

By giving crucial importance to the operative synthesis, Piaget understands that children's operations on objects are essential for the understanding of number. Number is not a property of objects; it is a construct resulting from the activity of the subject. In fact, the agency of the child is a central point in Piaget's theory as the main element in the developmental processes in childhood. The problem is that, in the case of numbers, the operative synthesis is late, and we know that long before this happens, children develop numeracy-related understanding, as we will see below. Research in recent decades points in two main directions: innate numerical knowledge and counting activities as a means of knowing the cardinal value of a collection.

6.1 The Nativist Proposal

In the 1980s, a perspective that argued that babies, from very early on, present important nuclear knowledge ("cognitive primitives") about different aspects such as space, language, objects, social relations, and also number, was gaining ground. A body of experimental research, sometimes very ingenious, showed that the starting point of infants' knowledge about different aspects of reality was richer and more organized than Piaget had supposed [18, 27, 35].

In the case of number, most of the research was experimental in nature, conducted in the laboratory mainly following techniques based on gaze duration using, above all, the technique of habituation or violation of expectations and cross-modal visual preference, in which visuospatial and perceptual skills predominate. The stimuli presented (in most cases, images projected on a screen) varied in the number of elements. Taken together, the results corroborate the idea that, from very early on, a few months after birth, infants are able to discriminate stimuli on the basis of the number of elements (independently of other characteristics of the stimuli). Such discrimination occurs when comparing collections of few items (up to 4 or 5) and also with larger collections. In this case, for discrimination to be possible, the difference must be greater in terms of the number of items in the collections: for example, it is possible to discriminate a collection of eight from a collection of four items, but not a collection of 30 from a collection of 34 [7, 48, 51]. This capacity for perceptual discrimination applied to number has led many authors to argue that humans are born with nuclear numerical knowledge. As Dehaene points out, we would have at birth "an immediate, automatic and unconsciously controlled perception of number" [10], p. 235. Thus, the consideration that gaze fixation is an indicator of innate characteristics and allows us to detect early cognitive skills lies in the fact that the duration of gaze implies attention and a certain level of processing, being a relatively spontaneous behaviour with little cognitive demand [25].

In our view, the nativist perspective, which defends the existence of innate numerical knowledge, has substantial limitations. Although our approach here is not to deny the interest of nativist studies, we consider that it is necessary to reflect on the importance of intentional action on objects when thinking about numerical development. Studies that focus on basic (predominantly perceptual) knowledge do not address the semiotic nature of numbers, and do not consider the interaction between cognition and communication, which means that there is no specific look at the place of the child's agency and of adults in their educational actions with the child. That said, there is an issue that is relevant to this topic and that is the importance of reflecting on the extent to which we can consider innate core knowledge—'basic number knowledge' or 'number sense'—to be related to the development of children's understanding of number.

For this discussion, some aspects may be relevant, such as the difference between the methodologies used in different studies aiming at detecting 'number sense', and studies focusing on number development. The experimental paradigm used in number sense studies places infants in front of visual stimuli displayed on screens; only the perception of these stimuli and the reaction of the subjects to this perception are of interest. Thus, we could say that knowledge is measured in terms of reaction (and not action); and perceiving dots or other representations of two-dimensional objects is not the same as operating on three-dimensional objects in the real world. Consider, for example, that real-world objects do not tend to move intrinsically, nor are they naturally segmented (like two-dimensional objects presented on screens, in methods based on gaze duration).

A first problem in relation to this is that it is not certain that the visual acuity of infants at this age is good enough to clearly distinguish the elements that make up the collections [20]. But, more importantly, it is not clear that the subject has been able to perform adequate segmentation of the parts of the visual stimulus, which is necessary for the number of items to be appreciated. In the absence of any reference to the subject's actions (whether motor or perceptual actions linked to eye movements), it is difficult to be sure that infants are reacting to the number of elements in the stimuli and not to other aspects. And as the strictly numerical aspects of the stimuli correlate with other information related to continuous quantities (occupied space, density, total perimeter, etc.), it is likely, as some authors argue, that the discriminations made by subjects are based on all these continuous cues and not on the number of elements [24, 32]. It is therefore necessary to incorporate study designs in which the actions of the infants with the objects play a greater role, as well as the adults who interact with the infant and the object, thus establishing a triadic interaction.

Moreover, if babies possess some kind of numerical knowledge from the first months of life, we may question why it is so long and costly for children to show numerical knowledge, not only taking into account the late demands proposed by

Piaget (until 6–7 years, according to him, there is no real concept of number) but the numerous works that show slow progress in the knowledge of the cardinal value associated with the first number words between 2 and 4 years of age [41]. A counter-argument to this criticism could be that innate number knowledge is perceptual and non-semiotic in nature, whereas the number knowledge to which Piaget alludes or that which results from work on cardinal value is semiotic in nature [15]. But does it make sense to talk about number when the knowledge in question is not semiotic in nature? Number is semiotic by nature and requires a semiotic approach for its construction and expression, whether through language (words-number), gestures (showing a quantity with the fingers), notations, groups of objects placed in correspondence with the elements of another collection or areas of the body (the body as a referent, for example, consider the system devised by the Papuans of New Guinea) [19, 23, 28, 36]. We may be born with a capacity for perceptual discrimination of quantities (both continuous and discontinuous), which is also present in many other animal species—but this capacity is by no means strictly numerical.

We consider that the nativist perspective on number seems to rest on an empiricist epistemology of number insofar as number is considered, like shape or colour, a property of reality and not a construct of the subject. Moreover, when the stimuli that the experimenter presents to the subject are supposed to be 'numerical', they are in fact 'numerical' for the observer, but not so from the child's point of view, as we have just seen. It is not a knowledge that is constructed by the subject's actions. Nor is it constructed jointly with other people.

6.2 Counting to Know How Many There Are

It is suggestive that Piaget devised a numerical task (the conservation of discrete quantities) independently of counting. In fact, he sought children's numerical knowledge outside the influence of adults and considered that knowing how to count does not guarantee that the child will apply it adequately to appreciate the numerical equivalence of two sets. However, some authors from the same Geneva school pointed out the importance of counting before being able to solve the conservation task. According to Morf et al. [30], the fact of counting elements can favour the resolution of the conservation task, since the serial aspect of counting linked to enumeration has the function of determining classes of numerical equivalences, an achievement prior to the operative invariants. Later, Sophian [47] also explored the relationship between counting and conservation task and Bryant [5] related the principles of counting to Piaget's proposal.

Counting has been studied systematically by several authors, including Briars and Siegler [4], Fuson [11], Gelman and Gallistel [13]. Although the child easily learns to recite the number series correctly (at least the first numbers), it is not until some years later, around the age of 4–5 years, that he or she is able to count any collection of items properly in order to know how many there are, although before that he or she may be able to count smaller collections [50]. Counting is not easy as each item has to be assigned an appropriate and different verbal label. And it has to be understood that any kind of items can be counted and that the order in which the items are chosen is irrelevant. These 5 principles (one-to-one correspondence, stable order, cardinality, abstraction, irrelevant order) are what guarantee error-free counting.

Of particular importance is the cardinal value principle, whereby it is known that the last number word pronounced in a count applied to a collection of items corresponds to the cardinal value of the whole collection, thus corresponding to the symbolic value of the number. This principle is particularly relevant because, as suggested by Piaget and corroborated by several authors, it is possible for young children to correctly apply the number words to a set of items, but when asked to give an exact number of items they do not always use the result of their count [3, 47, 49].

Therefore, a set of studies were deployed that analysed the comprehension of first number words by means of purposefully designed tasks. Among the tasks used, two stand out. In the first ('What's-on-this-Card'), children have to choose the number of items drawn on a card. The subject has to pronounce the appropriate number word. In another task, ('Give-a-Number'), faced with a large collection of objects, children are asked to say a certain number of objects. The subject has to choose only the number of objects indicated by the number word pronounced by the experimenter. This task is more cognitively complex than the previous one and is the one that has been most widely used to study the development of the cardinal value of number words. These tasks do not necessarily involve the child counting; he or she can also appreciate the cardinal value of a collection without counting, which is known as subitizing and is frequent in collections of few items (up to 3–4 items) [7, 21].

The results of this research conclude that 24-month-old children need approximately two years to progressively understand the cardinal value associated with the first number words, and from a certain point (around the age of 4), they understand that any number word indicates a certain cardinal value. The first level would be that of the youngest children who do not manage to coherently attribute any number word to a given cardinal value ('no-knowers'). Then would come the 'one-knowers' level, where they succeed only with the number word 'one', but fail with collections of two or more items. Then comes the 'two-knowers' level, then 'three-knowers' and finally 'four-knowers'. At this level (between three and four years), children are able to understand that any number word corresponds to a given cardinal value ('cardinal-principle-knowers') [7, 50].

This proposal for levels of knowledge arises from a large body of experimental studies carried out in the laboratory. It is interesting in showing how slowly and progressively young children understand cardinal value, but in our opinion, it has a problem: it addresses these aspects of numeracy far from the contexts in which children develop. These results, therefore, do not take into account the diversity of activities and social contexts that convey numerical knowledge and that may give rise to different developmental pathways that do not necessarily fit into such a strict model of levels. Nor do they take into account the functional component of numeracy (what is the purpose of counting? how is it integrated into the demands of the task?); moreover, they focus exclusively on a semiotic register (verbal), leaving aside other forms of communication and expression of number.

6.3 The Social and Semiotic Component

Although most research on the early development of number (both Piaget's and much of the research on counting and levels of knowledge) has focused on a subject's responses to particular tasks set in a laboratory context, children are introduced to number knowledge in a variety of social contexts (mainly family and school) in which they interact with others in activities involving numbers [43]. Several studies conducted in children's families have shown the variety of numerical activities in which young children (from one to five years of age) engage and which allow the most basic numerical knowledge to be built—and have also shown the impact of these activities on children's knowledge development [2, 17, 22, 26]. Some of these studies have focused on longitudinal researches that allows for a precise analysis of the type of interactions that take place between adults and children in activities involving numbers, which is necessary to understand the very process of constructing numerical knowledge (e.g., [46]).

One last important aspect is the variety of the semiotic systems in the way children and adults approach numerical mastery. In general, language has been given priority as a vehicle of communication and as a way of expressing numerical values (number words), forgetting that there are forms which take on great importance in numerical activities, especially when it comes to early development: uses of objects, gestures, images. Several studies have pointed out the importance of taking into account this semiotic diversity [8, 9, 14, 36, 42].

When we think of numbers, and their semiotic character, beyond the reactions to quantities, we must take into account the cultural elements that are involved in developing the child's understanding of them. Talking about numbers means producing numerical words, numerical gestures, object counting-developing understanding of what is counted and for what. Moreover, taking into account all this diversity of semiotics, we cannot disregard the fact that all these forms of expression take place within interactions, so it is necessary to consider the role of the adult or others more competent, and the agency of children on cultural material objects, where they live and act. We also cannot miss the developmental character of these elements, before knowing how to count, the boy and girl already know, for example, the numerical words and gestures that support them in this task.

6.4 The Development of Numbers from the Pragmatics of the Object

As discussed in Chaps. 1 and 2, the perspective of the Pragmatics of the Object is a theoretical proposal by Rodríguez and Moro [38] that includes studies on the development processes that occur before language. These studies focus on the development of semiotic systems such as gestures and the uses of objects that, from preverbal stages, are used intentionally by children as thought tools to regulate their action, and which, in addition, constitute a basis for the development of later and more complex semiotic systems [1, 6, 29, 39, 40], among others). In the proposal by Rodríguez and Moro of the Pragmatics of the Object, the communicative-educational and cultural influences are considered in the early stages of cognitive development, during the first years of life.

Adopting this perspective helps address many of the limitations in studies on early numerical knowledge that we have just highlighted. For a start, this approach distances itself from nativist explanations that overlook the subject's actions and the constructive nature of knowledge. Similar to the perspective of the Geneva School, we emphasise children's actions and the constructive nature of development. However, unlike that perspective, which focuses on the structural and logical aspects of number, independent of everyday activities like counting, our emphasis is on analysing children's activities in context. We consider the interaction process between the child and the adult, the functional aspects of numerical knowledge, and pay attention to the semiotic diversity of these activities. This is because we consider that more complex semiotic systems, such as numerical ones, are built upon earlier semiotic systems that serve as their foundation, such as gestures and the use of objects.

Number holds a semiotic status in its own right, which means that studies analysing its development must take this into account. As is common sense, number is not a property of objects but rather knowledge derived from an active process of construction by the subject when interacting with objects. With this in mind, any study on number in childhood should inherently consider the agency of the child, the adult, and the socially constructed uses of objects involved in the development of numerical knowledge.

The Pragmatics of the Object helps us understand the necessary process of change to deeply analyse numerical development, considering the earlier semiotic systems that underpin it. Gestures, the use of objects, and language are semiotic systems constructed from the earliest months of a child's life, and they contribute to understanding later semiotic systems, such as the numerical one. This perspective allows us to see how semiotic systems produced during interactions interrelate and form the foundation for new systems. Recognising that number is a semiotic construction that cannot be acquired in isolation is essential; in fact, understanding numbers involves a complex process of semiotic (re)construction before children can fully grasp them. Within this process, the triad of child–adult–object is central.

Thinking about the analysis of numerical development requires considering the role of all those systems that precede number to understand how this new system of signs has emerged (or could emerge). For instance, what role do ostensive gestures, pointing gestures, and symbolic gestures play in the development of children's understanding of numbers? And how have the uses of objects evolved until they are finally employed in a numerical way?

By order of complexity, we know that children understand and produce ostensive gestures first, followed by pointing gestures, and finally symbolic gestures [33, 37]. For a thorough analysis of the semiotic and pragmatic nature inherent to numbers, it is important to understand how these gestures contribute to numerical comprehension. As mentioned earlier, when children count objects in the material world, a segmentation process is required to treat objects as distinct elements. This segmentation emerges early on from interactions with objects, for instance, through ostensive gestures. These gestures, used in adult–child–object interactions from the first days of a baby's life, serve to share attention on the presented object. Ostensive gestures continue to play a significant role in interactions across various situations throughout childhood development, including during counting and the use of numerical information, as we will illustrate later.

On the other hand, we also know that pointing gestures play a very important role in counting processes. Adults and children use these gestures to touch objects, helping to manage some of the basic principles of counting, such as one-to-one correspondence and stable order.

Fuson [11] comments that counting objects requires the person counting to establish a relationship between the object and the number words; the number words would be on a temporal plane, while the objects would be on a spatial plane. The connection between these planes requires some form of mediator, which is usually the pointing gesture. In this case, the pointing gesture establishes the temporal and spatial correspondence between the number labels and the objects in question. Thus, counting using pointing gestures can be difficult for children, as it requires coordination between two actions, each belonging to different semiotic systems: performing the gesture and also labelling the objects with number words. Additionally, another difficulty is added to this action, concerning the understanding that each entity to be counted must be treated as a single element. In this regard, it is common to see children around two years old counting in a disorganised manner, touching the objects without establishing correspondences between gestures and number words, likely because they are still unable to treat the elements as unitary in these counting situations.

Saxe and Kaplan [44] also argue that at four years old, pointing gestures (touching the object) are related to counting accuracy. Similarly, Gelman [12] verified that accuracy in counting actions increases when children are allowed to touch or manipulate the items they are counting. In fact, Schaeffer et al. [45] observed a discrepancy in the counting accuracy of children when they were prohibited from using pointing gestures to count. It seems, therefore, that pointing gestures by touching the objects, rather than just pointing at them from a distance, help improve the accuracy of the counting process [16]. Ultimately, we could say that immediate pointing gestures [38]—when the index finger touches the indicated object—can help link each element to a numerical label sequentially and also assist in keeping track of the elements that have already been counted and those that still need to be counted. Finally, they can facilitate the treatment of objects as discrete units.

With this, we can see that the pointing gesture is a key element in the early stages of counting. However, children understand and produce this gesture much earlier than they are able to comprehend and use it for numerical functions—and this only occurs if the child is interacting with an adult who, in the case of counting, teaches them which portion of reality should be segmented according to the chosen criterion.

What about numerical gestures? From their first year, adults make an effort to show children how to represent their age with gestures, encouraging them to use their index finger as a form of expression: for the number one, the number two, and so on during these early years of life. Of course, these forms of expression are part of the process of symbolic understanding of numbers and lay the groundwork for future numerical comprehension. Similarly, symbolic gestures also involve other ways of representing something not physically present, such as moving fingers as if placing food on a plate, for example. From an early age, children perform these gestures, which will, in some way, appear in simple board games or symbolic games that involve numerical practices in the early stages. Understanding numerical development, therefore, must also address the question of what role symbolic scenarios created during playful contexts have in the display of numerical practices in childhood. Indeed, numbers do not appear in a vacuum; they emerge in a context where *something is being counted and for some purpose*. It is through interactions with others and generally in playful contexts that children discover what to count, how to count, and why.

On the other hand, we cannot overlook the rhythmic component in counting situations, particularly when establishing correspondences between gestures and the objects being counted. Nunes and Bryant [31] specifically point out that some mathematical activities, such as counting, are rhythmic activities. The correspondence discussed by Fuson [11] between the gesture and the counted object also relies on a rhythmic component for its execution. This rhythmic component is another semiotic system that should be considered in studies of numerical development, in addition to the other systems we have previously described. In fact, Moreno-Núñez et al. [29] propose that the first semiotic systems to emerge in development are rhythmic-sound systems. Through the baby's sustained attention at two months and the increasing use of objects until six months, the authors suggest that this is likely where the first canonical uses of objects are found, so rhythmic-sound components may constitute the first semiotic systems observed in development.

Early understanding and use of numbers often refer to different elements of reality (people, events, actions, sounds, but especially material objects). In this regard, we cannot think about the early understanding of numbers without considering the objects to which these numbers are applied. The complexity of numbers is also related to the fact that they can be applied to any collection of objects around us—and those around children in their routines. Any and every object can receive a numerical label (for example, during counting) that represents it as a unit and as part of a set. These objects, in themselves, before being countable, have other functions and uses, which also develop within the context of interactions. It is necessary to consider early numerical development in light of the cultural uses of the objects to which these numbers are applied. From the perspective of the Pragmatics of the Object, we conclude that understanding numerical development cannot disregard the uses children make of objects before they use them numerically; and this is crucial if, in addition to understanding numerical development, we wish to promote educational actions to foster it. How can we encourage the numerical use of an object that already has another canonical or conventional use? Considering how objects are conventionally used seems central to developing their numerical use once the numerical use becomes rooted in these prior functions.

6.5 An Illustration: The Little Horse Game

We can illustrate our line of reasoning with a longitudinal study we conducted with three dyads to explore the early numerical development of children aged between 2 and 3 years [8, 9]. During the interactions, the dyads had to move the little horse along a segmented path (with 10 squares) until the little horse reached its food plate (Fig. 6.1). We observed how the children gradually transitioned from using the objects in a non-numerical and non-conventional way to eventually using them in a conventional numerical manner within the context of the situation we proposed.

The act of performing symbolic gestures and using objects symbolically was not at all complex for the children at these ages. In other words, for a 2-year-old, moving a replica horse to a bottle cap that represents a food plate and making it "eat" are common actions that reflect their familiarity with the semiotic systems involved in this situation. The novelty for the children was that they had to follow a rule: in order for the horse to move, they had to roll a die, then count the dots and move the horse accordingly, step by step, in line with the dots indicated by that unfamiliar object. On one hand, it was a game with simple rules, where the die was a conditioning object that underpinned the game's rules: to move the horse,

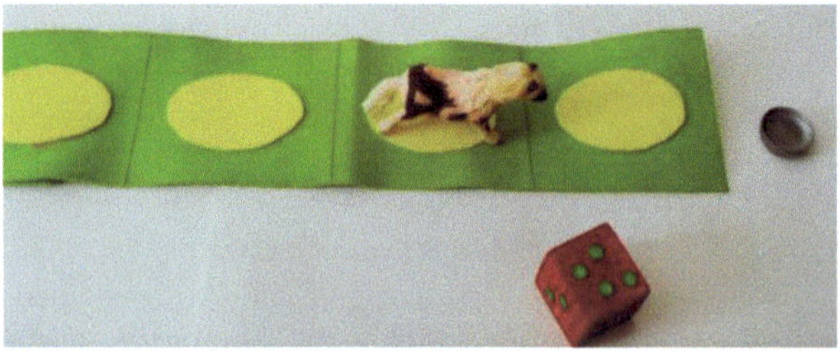

Fig. 6.1 Materials used (die, horse, path, "food plate")

the numerical information from the die had to be respected. As one can imagine, this was not an easy rule for the children to accept, considering that, in a playful role they were already familiar with, they wanted to feed the horse—something that was, after all, the main objective of the game.

Thus, in this game situation, we observed that the children initially understood (1) the objective of the game—to feed the horse, then (2) they gradually understood the rules of the game (rolling the die, counting the dots, although incorrectly at first, and moving the horse, not necessarily in exact alignment with the numerical information on the die, especially at the beginning of the game), and finally, (3) they used the objects in a numerical and precise way, by counting the dots accurately and moving the horse according to the numerical information on the die. This progression towards conventional use of numbers took place in the final sessions.

We observed that the support from adults, the active role of the children, and the cultural history of the objects interacted dynamically, leading to a slow and gradual process of numerical understanding by the participants. During the interactions, both adults and children relied on a wide variety of semiotic systems familiar to them. It was evident that both the adults and the children made an effort to make sense of the situation, drawing on prior resources that intertwined with the new demands of the game related to numbers.

Initially, the children used the objects based on functions they already knew: for example, they moved the horse directly to its food and fed it, ignoring the die; they rode the horse off the path, not respecting the boundaries of the squares; they used the die as a seat for the horse and even as a projectile to knock it down (Fig. 6.2).

At the same time, the adults' efforts to transform the children's non-conventional numerical uses of the objects into conventional numerical uses were remarkable: they used ostensive gestures to show the die (Fig. 6.3), pointing gestures to count the dots and squares on the path (Fig. 6.4), as well as more direct demonstrations, guiding their index fingers to the dots or their hands with the horse to ensure they followed the steps on each square of the path (Fig. 6.5). They also

Fig. 6.2 Continuous advancement (after rolling the die, the girl abandons the path, stands up, and runs with the horse in hand, heading towards the food plate. She immediately feeds the horse)

Fig. 6.3 Ostensive gesture of the die by the adult

used a variety of symbolic gestures, such as interrogative gestures and others representing the act of putting food on the horse's plate, with the clear intention of providing context for the game: the horse should reach its food, and that's why numbers were used.

They also used verbal mediators to offer cognitive assistance (explaining the game rule, for example), metacognitive assistance (insisting that the child recap the

Fig. 6.4 Adult's pointing gesture to indicate the squares on the "path"

Fig. 6.5 Adult's demonstration (guiding the girl's hand) as the horse moves forward

counting done, informing the cardinal value of the collection), as well as affective assistance (accepting some counting mistakes, for example, with the clear goal of maintaining the children's motivation, initially focusing on understanding the rule—and later emphasizing the precise and accurate counting of the dots on the die). We were able to observe how the adults took advantage of the children's prior object uses as a basis for introducing new uses, making a great effort to connect the numerical uses of objects with the previous, non-canonical (or non-conventional) uses by the children.

6.6 Conclusions

In conclusion, we can clearly see how the numerical system is anchored in previous semiotic systems, through the agency of both the adult and the children during interactions in their daily lives. In our view, results like those from the study we mentioned highlight the importance of not overlooking the semiotic nature of numbers, and thus the semiotic and cultural foundations of their development, particularly the importance of the triadic analysis (child–adult-object) for understanding it. To use a numerical system of signs, children must actively participate in a communicative-educational interaction with an adult. Studies on number comprehension should include analysis of the semiotic systems that the child could rely on to act and develop numerical understanding. This understanding occurs through processes of change in which the adult plays a key role, once early numerical knowledge is rooted in previously shared semiotic systems. From our perspective, future research on numbers should take into account that numbers, as a cultural construction, are related to cultural objects.

Thus, from our perspective, when discussing numerical knowledge, we cannot separate the fact that thinking about numbers means thinking about a semiotic system that is culturally constructed. Therefore, from our point of view: (1) studies in the field of numerical knowledge need perspectives that take into account the child's actions on objects in functional everyday contexts; (2) in order to learn how to use a numerical sign system, the child must participate in a communicative-educational interaction with an adult; and (3) it is necessary to analyze the semiotic systems on which children could rely to act and develop numerical understanding, as we assume that basic numeracy is rooted in prior semiotic systems, such as the use of objects, including rhythmic-sound uses.

References

1. Basilio, M., & Rodríguez, C. (2011). Usos, gestos y vocalizaciones privadas: De la interacción social a la autorregulación [Private Uses, Gestures, and Vocalizations: From Social Interaction to Self-Regulation]. *Infancia y aprendizaje, 34*, 181–194. https://doi.org/10.1174/021037011795377593
2. Benavides-Varela, S., Butterworth, B., Burgio, F., Arcara, G., Lucangeli, D., & Semenza, C. (2016). Numerical activities and information learned at home link to the exact numeracy skills

in 5–6 years-old children. *Frontiers in Psychology, 7*, 94. https://doi.org/10.3389/fpsyg.2016.00094
3. Bermejo, V. (1996). Cardinality development on counting. *Developmental Psychology, 32*, 263–268. https://psycnet.apa.org/doi/10.1037/0012-1649.32.2.263
4. Briars, D., & Siegler, R. S. (1984). A featural analysis of preschoolers' counting knowledge. *Developmental Psycholoy, 20*, 607–618. https://psycnet.apa.org/doi/10.1037/0012-1649.20.4.607
5. Bryant, P. (1997). Mathematical understanding in the nursery school years. In T. Nunes & P. Bryant (Eds.), *Learning and teaching mathematcis: An international perspective* (pp. 53–67). Psychology Press.
6. Cárdenas, K., Rodríguez, C., & Palacios, P. (2014). First symbols in a girl with down syndrome: A longitudinal study from 12 to 18 months. *Infant Behavior and Development, 37*, 416–427. https://doi.org/10.1016/j.infbeh.2014.06.003
7. Carey, S. (2009). *The origins of concepts*. Oxford University Press.
8. Cavalcante, S., & Rodríguez, C. (2015). The understanding of die as an object that has numerical functions. A longitudinal study using two children from the ages of 24 to 36 months interacting with an adult. La comprensión del dado como objeto con funciones numéricas. Un estudio longitudinal con dos niños de los 24 a los 36 meses en interacción con un adulto. *Estudios de Psicología, 36*, 48–70. https://doi.org/10.1080/02109395.2014.1000028
9. Cavalcante, S., Rodríguez, C., & Martí, E. (2019). Early understanding of cardinal number value: Semiotic, social, and pragmatic dimensions in a case study with a child from 2 to 3 years old. *Integrative Psychological and Behavioral Science, 53*, 397–417. https://doi.org/10.1007/s12124-018-9464-4
10. Dehaene, S. (2016). *El cerebro matemático* [The number sense](Original published in 2007). Siglo Veintiuno Editores.
11. Fuson, K. (1988). *Children's counting and concept of number*. Springer Verlag.
12. Gelman, R. (1980). What young children know about numbers. *Educational Psychologist, 15*, 54–68. https://doi.org/10.1080/00461528009529216
13. Gelman, R., & Gallistel, C. R. (1978). *The child's understanding of number*. Harvard University Press.
14. Gibson, D. J., Gunderson, E. A., Spaepen, E., Levine, S., & Goldin-Meadow, S. (2019). Number gestures predict learning of number words. *Developmental Science, 22*, e1279. https://doi.org/10.1111/desc.12791
15. Gilmore, C. K., McCarthy, S. E., & Spelke, E. S. (2010). Non-symbolic arithmetic abilities and mathematics achievement in the first year of formal schooling. *Cognition, 115*, 394–406. https://doi.org/10.1016/j.cognition.2010.02.002
16. Graham, T. (1999). The role of gesture in children's learning to count. *Journal of Experimental Child Psychology, 74*, 333–355. https://doi.org/10.1006/jecp.1999.2520
17. Gunderson, E. A., & Levine, S. C. (2011). Some types of parent number talk count more than others: Relation between parents' input and children's number knowledge. *Developmental Science, 14*, 1021–1032. https://doi.org/10.1111/j.1467-7687.2011.01050.x
18. Hirschfeld, L. A., & Gelman, S. A, (2002). *Cartografía de la mente. La especificidad de dominio en la cognición y en la cultura* [Mapping the Mind: Domain Specificity in Cognition and Culture]. *Vol 1. Orígenes, procesos y conceptos*. Gedisa.
19. Ifrah, G. (1981). *Histoire universelle des chiffres* [Universal History of Numbers]. Robert Laffont.
20. Kellman, P. J., & Arterberry, M. E. (2006). Infant visual perception. In D. Kuhn y R. S. Siegler (Eds.), *Handbook of child psycholoy. Vol. 2. Cognition, perception and language* (pp. 109–160). Wiley.
21. LeCorre, M., Brannon, E. M., Van de Walle, G. A., & Carey, S. (2006). Re-visiting the competence/performance debae in the acquisition of the counting principles. *Cognitive Psychology, 52*, 130–169. https://doi.org/10.1016/j.cogpsych.2005.07.002

22. LeFevre, J., Skwarchuk, S., Smith-Chant, B., Fast, L., Kamawar, D., & Bisanz, J. (2009). Home and children´s math performance in the early school years. *Canadian Journal of Behavioural Science, 41*, 55–66. https://doi.org/10.1016/j.jecp.2022.105578
23. Leibovich, T., & Ansari, D. (2016). The symbol-grounding problem in numerical cognition: A review of theory, evidence, and outstanding questions. *Canadian Journal of Experimental Psychology, 70*, 12–23. https://doi.org/10.1037/cep0000070
24. Leibovich, T., Katzin, N., Harel, M., & Henik, A. (2017). From sense of number to sense of magnitiude: The role of continous magnitudes in numerical cognition. *Behavioral and Brain Sciences, 40*, 1–16. https://doi.org/10.1017/S0140525X16000960
25. Mariscal, S., Casla, M., Rujas, I., & Aguado-Orea, J. (2012). Los métodos basados en la duración de la mirada ¿una ventana a la cognición temprana? [Methods Based on Gaze Duration: A Window into Early Cognition?] *Estudios de psicología, 33*, 277–292. https://psycnet.apa.org/doi/10.1174/021093912803758219
26. Mazzocco, M. M. M., & Claessens, A. (2020). Introduction to the special issue: Parents supporting early mathematical thinking. *Early Childhood Researxh Quarterly, 50*, 1–3. https://doi.org/10.1016/j.ecresq.2019.07.007
27. Mehler, J., & Dupoux, E. (1992). *Nacer sabiendo. Introducción al desarrollo cognitivo del hombre* [Born Knowing: Introduction to Human Cognitive Development]. Alianza Editorial.
28. Mix, K. S., Sandhofer, C. M., & Baroody, A. J. (2005). Number words and number concepts: The interplay of verbal and nonverbal quantification in early childhood. *Advances in child development and behavior, 33*, 305–346. https://doi.org/10.1016/S0065-2407(05)80011-4
29. Moreno-Núñez, A., Rodríguez, C., & del Olmo, M. J. (2015). The rhythmic, sonorous and melodic components of adult-child-object interactions between 2 and 6 months old. *Integrative Psychological and Behavioral Science, 49*, 737–756. https://doi.org/10.1007/s12124-015-9298-2
30. Morf, A., Gréco, P., & Piaget, J. (1962). *Bibliothéque scientifique internationale: Structures numériques élémentaires*. Presses Universitaires de France.
31. Nunes, T., & Bryant, P. (1996). *Children doing mathematics*. Blackwell.
32. Núñez, R. (2017). Is there really an evolved capacity of number? *Trends in cognitive science, 21*, 409–424. https://doi.org/10.1016/j.tics.2017.03.005
33. Palacios, P., & Rodríguez, C. (2015). The development of symbolic uses of objects in infants in a triadic context: A pragmatic and semiotic perspective. *Infant and Child Development, 24*, 23–43. https://doi.org/10.1002/icd.1873
34. Piaget, J., & Szeminska, A. (1941). *La genèse du nombre chez l'enfant* [The Genesis of Number in the Child]. Delachaux et Niestlé.
35. Rochat, P. (2012). Baby assault on Piaget. In E. Martí & C. Rodríguez (Eds.), *After Piaget* (pp. 71–82). Transaction Publishers.
36. Rodríguez, J., Martí, E., & Salsa, A. (2018). Symbolic representations and cardinal knowledge in 3- and 4-year-old children. *Cognitive Development, 48*, 235–243. https://doi.org/10.1016/j.cogdev.2018.09.004
37. Rodríguez, C., Moreno-Núñez, A., Basilio, M., & Sosa, N. (2015). Ostensive gestures come first: Their role in the beginning of shared reference. *Cognitive Development, 36*, 142–149. https://doi.org/10.1016/j.cogdev.2015.09.005
38. Rodríguez, C., & Moro, C. (1999). *El mágico número tres. Cuando los niños aún no hablan.* [The Magical Number Three: When Children Still Do Not Speak] Paidós.
39. Rodríguez, C., & Palacios, P. (2007). Do private gestures have a self-regulatory function?: A case study. *Infant Behavior and Development, 30*, 180–194. https://doi.org/10.1016/j.infbeh.2007.02.010
40. Rodríguez, C., Palacios, P., Cárdenas, K., & Yuste, N. (2014). Les symboles: formes de second ou de troisième sens? [Symbols: Forms of Second or Third Meaning?]. In C. Moro & N. Muller Mirza (Eds.), *Sémiotique, culture et développement psychologique.* (pp. 99–116). Presses universitaires du Septentrion.

41. Rodríguez, C., & Scheuer, N. (2015). The paradox between the numerically competent baby and the slow learning of two-to four-year-old children. La paradoja entre el bebé numéricamente competente y el lento aprendizaje de los niños de dos a cuatro años de edad. *Estudios de Psicología, 36*, 32–44. https://doi.org/10.1080/02109395.2014.1000009
42. Salsa, A., & Martí, E. (2015). Objects, pictures and words. Effects of representational format on four-year-olds' quantity knowledge. *Studies in Psychology, 36*, 71–91. https://doi.org/10.1080/02109395.2014.1000031
43. Saxe, G. B., Guberman, S. R., & Gearhart, M. (1987). Social processes in early number development. *Monographs of the Society for Research in Child Development, 52*, i–162. https://doi.org/10.2307/1166071
44. Saxe, G. B., & Kaplan, R. (1981). Gesture in early counting: A developmental analysis. *Perceptual and Motor Skills, 53*, 851–854. https://doi.org/10.2466/pms.1981.53.3.851
45. Schaeffer, B., Eggleston, V. H., & Scott, J. L. (1974). Number development in young children. *Cognitive Psychology, 6*, 357–379. https://doi.org/10.1016/0010-0285(74)90017-6
46. Scheuer, N., & Sinclair, A. (2009). From one to two. Observing one child's early mathematical steps. In C. Andersen, N. Scheuer, M. del P. Pérez Echeverría, E. Teubal (Eds.), *Representational systems and practices as learning tools* (pp. 19–37). Sense Publishers.
47. Sophian, C. (1988). Limitations on children's knowledge about counting: Using counting to compare two sets. *Developmental Psycholy, 24*, 634–640. https://doi.org/10.1037/0012-1649.24.5.634
48. Van Loosbroek, E., & Smitsman, A. W. (1990). Visual perception of numerosity in infancy. *Developmental Psychology, 26*, 916–922. https://psycnet.apa.org/doi/10.1037/0012-1649.26.6.911.b
49. Wynn, K. (1990). Children's understanding of counting. *Cognition, 36*, 155–193. https://doi.org/10.1016/0010-0277(90)90003-3
50. Wynn, K. (1992). Children's acquisition of number words and the counting system. *Cognitive Psychology, 24*, 220–251. https://doi.org/10.1016/0010-0285(92)90008-P
51. Xu, F., & Spelke, E. (2000). Large number discrimination in 6-month-old infants. *Cognition, 74*, B1–B11. https://doi.org/10.1016/S0010-0277(99)00066-9

Gesture Development in the Early-Years-School: The Role of Early Interactions with Objects and Adults

7

Irene Guevara

Gestures, alongside language, are essential elements in our everyday interactions, functioning as fundamental tools for communication [26, 47, 72]. Even in contexts where a common language is absent, such as second-language learning, gestures have proven to be an invaluable resource that facilitates both communicative comprehension and production [61, 127]. Moreover, research has highlighted that gestures not only serve communicative functions but also play a critical role in processes such as thinking, self-regulation, and learning [2, 3, 54, 55, 135]. Recognizing gestures' relevance for sociocognitive development has sparked growing academic interest in recent years, transcending psychology to integrate into disciplines such as psycholinguistics [61, 87], semiotics [45, 98], anthropology [46, 62], cognitive neuroscience [52, 105], and even technological fields such as robotics and artificial intelligence [13, 64].

Much research on gestures has focused on their role as accompaniments to verbal discourse, known as "co-verbal gestures" [71, 87]. These studies emphasize that gestures not only visually complement linguistic content but also synchronize the rhythm of discourse and emphasize its meanings. Far from being mere accessories to speech, gestures, and language are considered to form an integrated multimodal system crucial for communication, cognition, and learning [74, 95, 96]. However, gestures emerge earlier than first words [7], suggesting possible distinct semiotic origins that eventually converge and coordinate throughout development. This highlights the importance of gestures as essential meaning-making tools in

I. Guevara (✉)
Department of Psychology, Universidad Antonio Nebrija, Madrid, Spain
e-mail: iguevara@nebrija.es

C. Rodriguez Garrido et al. (eds.), *The Social Life of Objects in Early Development*, Social Interaction in Learning and Development,
https://doi.org/10.1007/978-3-031-87673-8_7

the early stages of communication, making them a key topic in developmental psychology.

Research on early gestures has shown that they act as precursors and predictors of language in both typical and atypical development [36, 121]. Factors such as gestures' onset age, frequency, and variability predict the production and content of first words [21, 119] and influence lexical, grammatical, and syntactic development [8, 27]. Furthermore, in atypical development, the absence or alteration of early gestures can be an early indicator of communicative disorders, such as Autism Spectrum Disorder (ASD) [33, 67]. Gestures are also valuable tools for facilitating communication in speech delays, such as Down syndrome [28, 126] or sensory disabilities [104].

However, the importance of studying early gestures extends beyond their relationship with language or their role in atypical development. Gestures represent one of the first intentional meaning-making tools children use from the final third of their first year of life to communicate and make sense of their surroundings [7, 26]. This makes them a privileged window into understanding how communicative intentionality emerges, a fundamental aspect of socio-cognitive development [22, 79]. While research has shed light on *when* and *to what extent* gestures begin to be used, debates persist regarding their exact definition (the "*what*"), particularly concerning gestures involving objects (a topic addressed in Sect. 7.3). Likewise, fundamental questions about the origin (the "*how*") and functions (the "*why*") of these early gestures remain open, underscoring their importance as a cornerstone of early development.

In this chapter, we adopt a theoretical-methodological approach based on the Pragmatics of the Object (PO, from here on) to explore how early gestures are progressively constructed in everyday interaction contexts. We illustrate this approach with data from our longitudinal observational research conducted in early-years-schools' classrooms, an environment rich in interactive situations, objects, and communicative peers. Although underexplored in the existing literature, this setting is a privileged space to analyze how gestures transform into increasingly complex meaning-making tools, facilitating more varied, prolonged, and sophisticated communicative exchanges. This chapter, therefore, seeks not only to synthesize recent empirical evidence but also to highlight the relevance and value of the PO framework in understanding the role of gestures in the construction of shared meanings during the early stages of development.

7.1 The Pragmatics of the Object in the Study of Early Gestures

A significant part of research from the PO perspective focuses on analyzing the role of objects and their uses in early communicative development. At first glance, linking communicative development—traditionally associated with social interaction between individuals (the social domain)—with objects —typically tied to exploration of the physical environment— may seem contradictory. However, this apparent paradox forms the guiding thread of this chapter. Far from being mere material elements, objects act as symbolic mediators in human interactions from the earliest stages of life, creating spaces for communication and the construction of shared meanings.

Rodríguez and Moro [114] argue that understanding the role of objects in early development requires a *pragmatic shift* in their conceptualization, similar to Bruner's [14] explanation of the origin of language. This means considering objects not just as interchangeable "physical realities" with evident meanings and individual uses but as social elements whose meanings are shaped by social, cultural, and historical consensus within user communities. Objects are not understood solely by their perceptual features but also by their possibilities of use. For example, a spoon is not merely a metal utensil but an instrument for eating. As Castañares [30, p. 37] states, "*acting as a sign is one of the many functions objects acquire.*" Thus, objects become signs of their uses, enabling communication and representation through and about them. The uses of objects provide a shared sociocultural framework of meanings, making it possible to interpret communicative intent when individuals act and interact with objects 39. This implies that knowledge about the purposes and uses of objects—their "functional permanence"—is not innate for children, just as names do not naturally emerge from the things they represent [140]). Children need to construct and internalize the uses of toys, tools, or utensils through interactions with adults who are expert users of objects. In this way, the uses of objects are built in early communicative interactions.

Communication does not occur in a vacuum; it is always tied to a referent (we communicate *about* something), whether an object, event, action, or concept. While dyadic interactions in early infancy have been widely studied—for example, tonic-postural dialogue [138], gaze exchanges [133], or mutual smiles 75—the process of building agreements around objects has received less attention. In early triadic interactions, adults introduce the world to infants who are not yet capable of acting or intentionally communicating about it. Objects emerge as niches of shared interest for communicating, joint acting, and joint attending. Although it has traditionally been assumed that triadic interactions between child-adult-object emerge at the end of the first year of life, when children communicate *intentionally* [129, 133], evidence suggests these interactions begin much earlier. From the first months of life, adults facilitate access to the material world through gestures and other semiotic mediators, such as words or gaze, presenting objects, and demonstrating their uses. These early triadic interactions, initiated and sustained by adults, allow children to familiarize themselves with the conventional uses of objects and the various semiotic mediators—gestures, words, gaze, or expressions—that adults use to communicate them, laying the foundation for developing communicative intentionality.

A central topic in PO has been identifying the semiotic mediators that allow children to integrate into the social realities of objects. Gestures are one of the first semiotic mediators that adults use to introduce the world to infants and regulate their actions, combining them with other systems of signs, such as gaze, smiles, demonstrations of use, and spoken language (as part of communicative streams—see [48]. Adults segment reality to make it accessible for children through gestures—for example, *showing* objects of interest, *placing* objects within their interactive spaces, offering or *giving* objects to facilitate their use, *pointing* to relevant aspects of an object, or even *representing* absent objects, extending the child's possibilities for action beyond the here and now.

In this sense, the relationship between early object uses and gestures is inherently bidirectional and recursive. Objects facilitate the emergence of early gestures by functioning as initial referents for communication between adults and children. First gestures are anchored in objects and their uses, creating a network of shared meanings that allows for some understanding of each other's communicative intentions [42, 111]. At the same time, acquiring conventional uses of objects does not result solely from children's individual and solitary actions. The uses of objects are consolidated through participation in interactions with others, who demonstrate these uses through semiotic mediators like gestures. The child must interpret and internalize these mediators to play an increasingly active role in these exchanges (see, for example, Table 7.5, where the teacher introduces the child to the use of storing objects through gestures, language, and actions).

Our research on gesture development in early-years-schools classrooms supports this idea. Observations revealed that as children gained greater knowledge about objects, their uses, and their embedded contexts, their gestures acquired more abstract meanings and more complex functions. For example, at 10 months old, a child might show a book to the teacher to share an interest in that particular book (a declarative function). By 12–13 months, the same gesture had acquired a more complex meaning related to *using* the book (its referent) within the classroom context. Showing the book no longer referred to a particular object but to a joint reading activity, indicating a more complex and conventional understanding of the object.

In this sense, participation in joint action practices with objects not only promotes knowledge about objects but also supports the development of basic referential skills. Furthermore, increasing knowledge of object uses creates a shared reference framework between children and teachers, enabling communication to emerge and diversify into increasingly complex forms (see also [42]).

Thus, objects serve a triple function in the early years of life: (1) they act as the first referents of children's initial gestures, (2) they configure their first communicative signs when they extend them or offer them to share meanings, and (3) they establish a common framework of meanings that enables their first interactions with others. Therefore, talking about objects necessarily involves discussing their uses, and understanding these uses requires exploring the communicative interactions in which they are constructed. In this process, gestures emerge as key protagonists in early communicative development.

Table 7.1 Changes in children's uses of objects inform about changes in their gestures' functions and meanings

December—Semi-structured activity: Books *Participant (age): Ils (0;10;7)*	

Ils shows a book to the teacher *(Ostensive gesture of showing—Declarative function)*	The teacher looks at him and smiles. Seconds later, he sucks the book *(non-conventional use)*
Frebruary. Semi-structured activity with books *Participant (age): Ils. (0;15; 12)*	
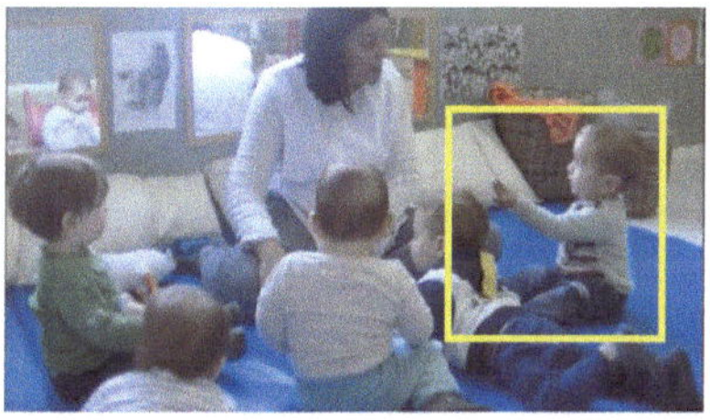	
Ils shows a book to the teacher *(Ostensive gesture of showing—Imperative function)*	The teacher takes the book and begin to read it. Ils looks at the book (shared conventional use of the book)

7.2 A Semiotic Order in the Development of Early Gestures: *Types* of Gestures

During the first year of life, gestures become increasingly frequent and diverse communicative tools [58]. However, not all gestures are equally effective across developmental stages. Different types of gestures, often grouped under umbrella terms such as "deictic gestures" [7], emerge at distinct developmental moments, serve specific functions, and vary in their impact on atypical development and associated cognitive processes [59]. For instance, while 7-month-old infants often fail to respond to pointing gestures—focusing instead on the finger itself rather than the referenced object [15, 114]—they readily engage with ostensive gestures like giving and showing, acting directly on the referenced objects by looking, reaching, or exploring their possible uses [91, 66]. Similarly, children's early attempts to share references often involve extending an object toward an adult rather than pointing at it [26, 82]. This leads us to question: *What distinguishes pointing from*

Table 7.2 Extended index fingers in the classroom

October—Semi-structured activity: Balls *Participant (age): S (0;7;12)*	

S extends his hands and his index finger while lying on his chair. He does not look at the teacher or tries to reach any object. He moves his index in circles	

ostensive gestures, and how can these differences be explained within communicative development?

From the perspective of the PO, the answer lies beyond the morphology of gestures (e.g., whether or not the index finger is used) in their semiotic complexity. A gesture is not merely a hand movement; it is an intentional representational action that connects a sign (what the child does with their body) to a referent (the gesture's meaning, often an object in early development). From this standpoint, referents are not merely the gesture's context but defining elements. Without a referent, it is impossible to speak of a gesture (see example in Table 7.2), as its meaning emerges from its reference to something specific and its purposeful use. The relationship between the sign and the referent—its proximity, level of conventionality, or arbitrariness—determines the gesture's complexity and provides a developmental progression.

Building on the semiotic framework proposed by Umberto Eco [45], Rodríguez [110] categorizes early gestures into three main levels of complexity (see Fig. 7.1):

1. *Ostensive Gestures*: Gestures where the child's hand holds an object that they extend, offer, or place in another's interactive space to refer to that object [100]. Here, the sign and the referent coincide—the object itself is part of the communicative act. Without the object, the gesture and its communicative intent disappear. This group includes gestures such as showing, giving [7], and placing [32], although placing has been less studied in early development [116].
2. *Indexical Gestures*: Gestures where the sign and referent are differentiated but linked through a directional relationship that indicates a distant referent. Pointing gestures are the most representative of this group, but reaching gestures are also included. Indexical gestures require greater inferential abilities to connect the sign to the referent—for instance, understanding that the relevant content lies in the object being pointed to, not the finger itself [131].
3. *Representational Gestures*: Gestures that represent absent referents in time or space, either through resemblance (iconic gestures) or social convention

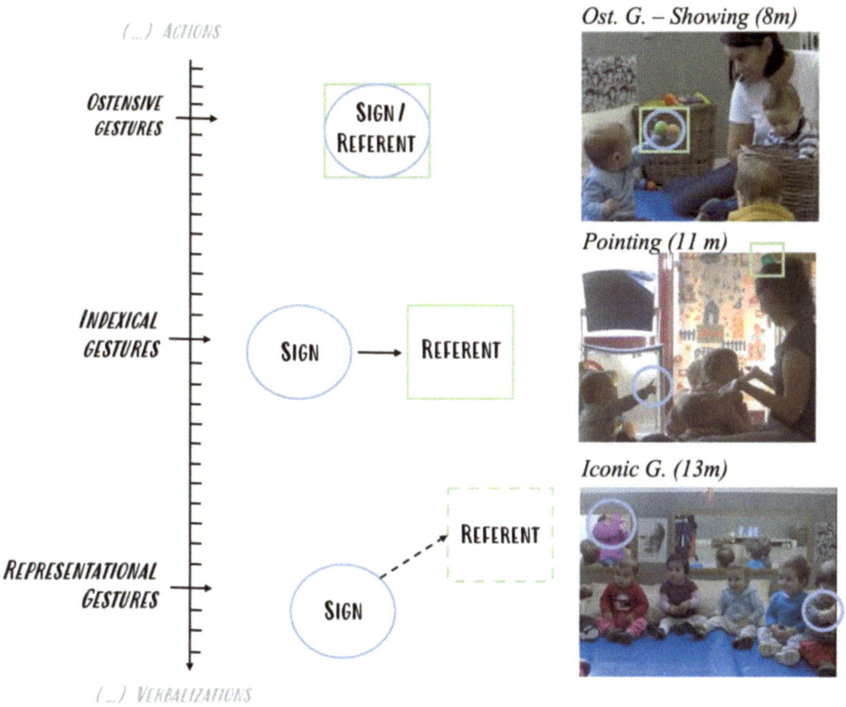

Fig. 7.1 Levels of semiotic complexity in gestures. *Figure taken from Guevara* [57]

(arbitrary gestures). These gestures require more inferential understanding and contextual awareness to connect the sign to its represented meaning [1, 65].

Since this classification is a continuum, certain gestures combine features from different levels. For example, touch-pointing, where the finger touches the referenced object directly, lies between ostensive gestures and distal pointing (see Fig. 7.2). By incorporating elements of ostensive gestures, touch-pointing reduces the ambiguity of traditional pointing and directs attention more precisely to specific aspects of the referent [91]. This decreased complexity may explain its frequent use by both adults and children in contexts such as problem-solving, shared reading, or cognitively demanding situations [35, 136]. Observations from our classroom research [60] show that children frequently use this gesture to self-direct attention during their interactions with classroom objects, highlighting its role in private regulatory functions (see Chaps. 9 and 10 of this volume for more details).

The proposed classification suggests that increasing the distance between sign and referent introduces greater ambiguity, requiring advanced referential and inferential skills for gesture production and interpretation. Ostensive gestures, typically emerging between 8 and 10 months, are the first gestures in children's communicative repertoire because they allow for the construction of shared meanings

Fig. 7.2 Private touch-pointing. * *The complete sequence regarding the private function (self-regulation) of this gesture has been published in Rodríguez and Moreno-Llanos* [117]

with minimal prior agreements. In contrast, indexical and representational gestures appear later, as they depend on a more sophisticated understanding of the socio-material context and intersubjective agreements surrounding the gesture and its referent [109]. For instance, pointing, observed between 9 and 13 months, requires understanding that the relevant content is in the object being pointed to and discerning which specific dimension of the object is being referenced [131]. Thus, the most complex gestures rely on both advanced referential abilities and coordination between communicative partners. This perspective is also useful to analyze how teachers adjust their interventions when trying to stablish their first agreements with children about object uses (see Table 7.5).

Considering this semiotic approach leads to the idea that gesture development follows an ostensive-indexical-representational progression, where communication through ostensive gestures forms the foundation for more complex semiotic systems. These systems progressively move children beyond their immediate environment toward more distant, absent, and abstract referents. However, our research in early-years-schools' classrooms nuance this linear perspective by showing that gesture development is neither strictly linear nor cumulative. More complex gestures do not replace earlier ones; rather, they coexist and adapt flexibly to the communicative demands of the context. For example, in activities where children had free access to objects (e.g., treasure baskets or musical instruments), ostensive gestures predominated. However, when there was a need to indicate details (e.g., turning book pages) or when the referenced object was not easily manipulable, children adjusted their communicative tools, producing touch-pointing gestures in the former case or distal pointing in the latter. Additionally, gesture development is dynamic: as soon as ostensive gestures emerge, prototypical forms of other gestures, such as proto-pointing, can also be observed (see Sect. 7.6.1). These early gestures coexist with more consolidated forms in emotionally or cognitively challenging contexts.

Following a semiotic theoretical framework to study gesture development provides a continuity perspective, viewing different types of gestures not only as distinct elements with specific forms, functions, and developmental processes but also as semiotic mediators. These gestures are interrelated tools for creating and exchanging meanings in interactive settings such as classrooms, where their complexity increases with the evolving relationship between the sign and the referent.

7.3 First Gestures in Early Development: The Current State of the Literature

Pointing gestures have been, by far, the most extensively studied during the first years of life. This gesture represents a significant milestone in early development [23, 84], marking a critical shift in how children interact with the world as they transition from dyadic to triadic intentional communicative interactions [15, 134]. Pointing is fundamental for joint attention [94] and is closely associated with language development [34], symbolic abilities [139], and theory of mind [17]. Additionally, its importance stems from its role as an early indicator of communicative developmental issues [4, 107], its multiple communicative functions [11, 125], and its universality across cultures [18, 81, 123].

However, pointing is not the first gesture to appear in development. Before responding to pointing, infants already react to ostensive gestures, such as adults showing or offering objects, by looking at or reaching for the offered object [69, 92]. Furthermore, infants begin producing ostensive gestures intentionally before using pointing for similar purposes, such as sharing references or regulating their own behavior [67]. Ostensive gestures are also the first communicative tools used by adults to introduce the material world to infants during the first months of life, even before infants can explore objects independently [91, 106, 111].

Although ostensive gestures have played a central role in the PO framework—describing how intentional action with objects leads to intentional communication *with* and *through* objects—these gestures have been underexplored in the psychological literature. As a result, little is known about their developmental trajectories.

The limited research on ostensive gestures can be attributed to different methodological and theoretical challenges. Methodologically, some authors [9, 99, 122] highlight the difficulty of identifying these gestures due to their ambiguous morphology and the challenge of distinguishing between gestures and actions, as both involve object manipulation. Additionally, many experimental studies restrict object interactions, limiting the observation of ostensive gestures [53, 73]. Theoretically, ostensive gestures' status as gestures has been questioned because traditional criteria associate gestures with an empty hand, excluding them from being considered inherently communicative. However, the PO framework [115] emphasizes that objects, as socially and historically meaningful realities, serve as effective tools for creating and exchanging meanings. In this sense, ostensive gestures of showing or giving objects represent the first intentional signs in infants' communicative repertoire.

Increasingly, critical voices are recognizing the communicative and referential role of early ostensive gestures [10, 19, 32, 124]. These gestures not only enable infants to place objects within a shared attentional framework but also reflect their emerging social motivation to interact with others about the surrounding world. Our classroom observational research supports these findings, revealing that, like other gestures, ostensive gestures may initially emerge as "ritualized behaviors," highly context-dependent with limited functions [14, 108]. However, they soon evolve into clearly intentional gestures with specific forms and meanings, generalizing across diverse contexts (see examples of this progression in [56]. Children persistently and flexibly employ ostensive gestures to achieve a range of communicative functions, such as sharing interests, displaying achievements, soliciting help, or regulating their own actions (see [25] with giving gestures development).

From the PO perspective, objects are not merely referents in joint action situations but also tools for communication, allowing children to construct meaning intentionally [114]. In this way, ostensive gestures are consolidated as fundamental gestures in early communicative development.

7.4 Ostensive Gestures as Precursors to Pointing

Recent studies have highlighted the relationship between ostensive gestures' frequency and onset age and the subsequent development of pointing [19, 85], as well as their indirect connections to language development [31]. These findings suggest that ostensive gestures not only emerge earlier in development but also act as precursors to pointing by allowing infants to engage in social interactions mediated by objects from an early age (see Table 7.3).

These findings support the idea that ostensive and pointing gestures, despite appearing distinct in form and complexity, are interconnected and play a critical role in the origins of intentional communication, helping to build the referential foundations necessary for the later development of more complex forms of communication.

7.4.1 Ostensive Gestures in Early Childhood Education Classrooms

Observations conducted in early-years-schools provide empirical evidence of the role of ostensive gestures as precursors to pointing gestures in a context that has been underexplored in previous literature (see [56]). Ostensive gestures were identified as the first gestures in the communicative repertoire of young children, enabling their active participation in triadic interactions from the final third of the first year of life. These gestures were the most frequent and performed by the largest number of children, serving both communicative functions with others and self-regulatory functions.

Table 7.3 Evidence supporting ostensive gestures' role as precursors to pointing

Evidence	Previous literature
Children produce ostensive gestures before pointing and respond earlier to adults' ostensive gestures compared to their pointing gestures	Bates et al. [7], Butterworth [15], Dimitrova and Moro [42], Iverson and Wozniak [67], Juvrud et al. [69], Rodríguez and Moro [114]
Adults use ostensive gestures to communicate and regulate infants' actions from the earliest months, long before using pointing for similar purposes	Contin and Rodríguez [35], Jáñez et al. [70], Moreno-Núñez et al. [92], Rader and Zukow-Goldring [106]
The frequency and onset age of ostensive gestures significantly correlates with pointing gestures and, indirectly, with language	Cameron-Faulkner et al. [19], Choi et al. [31], Donellan et al. [44], McGillion et al. [86], Manwaring et al. [85]
Ostensive gestures are less complex gestures than pointing from a semiotic perspective, explaining their earlier emergence	Eco [45], Rodriguez [112, 113]
Ostensive gestures fulfill communicative (phatic, declarative, imperative, interrogative, evaluative) and private self-regulatory functions later observed in pointing gestures	Basilio and Rodríguez [5], Bates et al., [7], Dimitrova et al. [41], Moreno-Llanos et al., [90], Rodríguez [112], Parladé and Iverson [102]
Both ostensive and pointing gestures are altered in early communication disorders, such as ASD, though each retains distinct characteristics	Clements and Chawarska [33], Heymann et al. [63], LeBarton and Iverson [78], Mishra et al. [89]
Ostensive and pointing gestures appear in early parent–child interactions across various cultures, reflecting their role as basic forms of communication	Fernández-Flecha et al. [50], Lieven and Stoll [81], Kwon et al. [76], Salomo and Liszkowski [123], Cameron-Faulkner et al. [18]

* *Table taken from Guevara* [57] *summarizing conclusions of Guevara and Rodríguez* [59]

No child began pointing in the classroom without first performing ostensive gestures. Positive and moderate correlations between the frequencies and onset ages of both gestures suggest that ostensive gestures lay the foundations for the later development of pointing. These correlations acquired even more significance when additional pragmatic relations were analyzed. The communicative functions observed in children's early ostensive gestures during communicative acts were the same later observed in their pointing gestures (see example in Table 7.4).

However, we do not claim that the knowledge acquired through ostensive gestures is directly transferred to pointing gestures. This knowledge must be *reconstructed*, as evidenced by initial difficulties in producing indexical gestures and the coexistence of ostensive gestures with proto-pointing gestures. Ostensive gestures prepare children not only to develop more complex gestures but also to acquire fundamental social norms, such as turn-taking, anticipation of responses, and the ability to capture others' attention. Furthermore, ostensive gestures facilitate the internalization of conventional uses of objects, creating shared reference frameworks that are essential for interpreting and participating in communicative actions.

Table 7.4 Different gestures with similar functions

January—Semi-structured activity: Musical instruments *Participant (age): A (0;12;11)*	

A shows a musical instrument to the teacher for her to make it sound *Ostensive Gesture—Imperative Function*	A points to the box of musical instruments to ask the teacher for them *Pointing Gesture—Imperative Function*
December—Semi-structured activity: Free Play *Participant (age): Y. (0;11;8)*	
	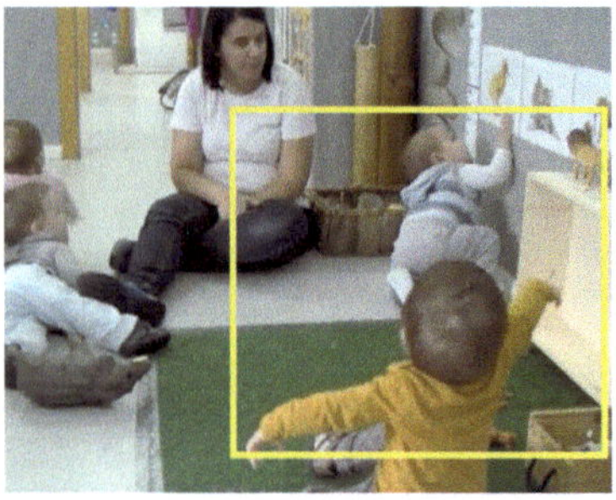
Y shows an animal toy to the teacher to share it with her (he holds it back when she tries to grab it) *Ostensive Gesture—Declarative Function*	Y points to the animals in the shelf to share them with the teacher *Pointing Gesture—Declarative Function*

Ostensive gestures are not only precursors to pointing but also retain their significance within the gestural repertoire throughout the first year of life, even as this repertoire diversifies into more complex forms of signification. Their persistence over time, observed in both children and the communicative repertoire of adults, underscores their central role in the construction of shared meanings and the development of intentional communication in everyday social contexts.

7.5 Taking a Pragmatic Turn in the Study of Early Gestures

From the PO perspective, gestures are inherently pragmatic. This means that their meaning emerges based on the intention or purpose with which they are performed in a particular context [112]. Following Peirce (1987, cited in [114], a gesture cannot be considered outside of its function, which is determined by the interactive context that frames it: the other person, the referent and the shared meanings surrounding that referent. For example, Basilio [6] describes a child extending a wooden block toward an adult. This action may function as a *request* for help if it follows a failed attempt to fit the blocks together and if the child understands the conventional use of the object (*imperative* function). In contrast, if the child is unfamiliar with the object's use and simply sucks on the blocks, the gesture may carry a more ambiguous function to keep the interaction going (*phatic* function). Studies like those of Liebal et al. [80] further emphasize how interpreting early gestures, such as pointing, heavily depends on the context in which they occur.

It is crucial to understand that the meaning of gestures is not predetermined but rather constructed and negotiated in daily interactions. Identifying the functions of gestures requires a shift in the analytical perspective toward an interactive analysis. This perspective moves beyond examining gestures in isolation or focusing solely on their morphology. Instead, it considers the full framework of the interaction, including elements such as the preceding and subsequent events, the material objects involved and how the child uses them, the context in which the gestures occur (home, school, park) and their cultural norms, and the meanings the objects acquire within those environments. Additionally, the interpretation of gestures by the interlocutor and the child's subsequent reaction—whether they accept, persist, or modify their communicative attempt—provide key indicators of the gesture's function.

Thus, the functions and meanings of children's gestures depend on several interconnected factors: (1) the gesture itself, (2) the referent and the shared knowledge about it, (3) the specific interactional situation, including prior and subsequent actions of the participants, and (4) the context of production, which shapes the meanings attributed to the referent (see Fig. 7.3).

This comprehensive approach allows us to understand gestures not as isolated actions but as fundamental components within the dynamic fabric of early human communication.

7.5.1 The *Functions* of Gestures

(a) *Declarative and imperative functions*

Since the foundational studies of Bates et al. [7], the declarative and imperative functions have dominated research on early gestures. These functions, proposed by analogy to language, represent two of the many possible ways in which children

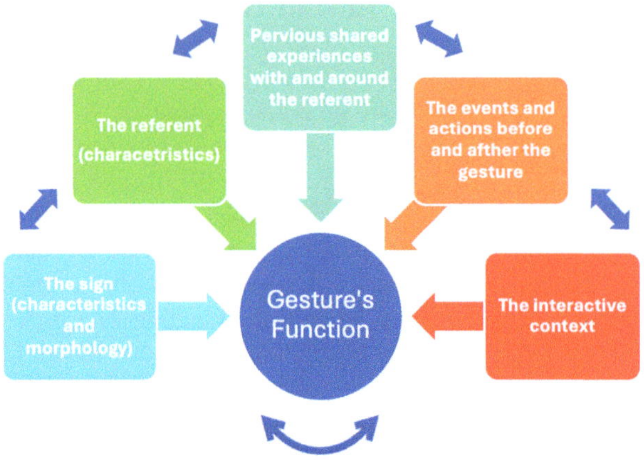

Fig. 7.3 Elements needed to interpret a child's gesture function

use gestures. The declarative function, regarded in later studies as the more complex and inherently communicative function, involves a child producing a gesture to share information or interest with another person [34]. In contrast, the imperative function is associated with instrumental goals, where the gesture is performed to influence the other person's behavior in order to achieve a specific objective [16].

Our classroom data support these findings, highlighting that declarative and imperative functions are the earliest and most common functions in children's gestural repertoire. These functions were observed in both ostensive and indicative gestures, with no clear pattern regarding which function emerges first (see example in Table 7.4). From our perspective, both declarative and imperative gestures are part of a polysemous repertoire, where a single gesture can fulfill different functions depending on the communicative context in which it occurs [58, 56]. This approach underscores the functional flexibility of early gestures in the process of constructing shared meanings.

(b) *Beyond declarative and imperative functions*

Although declarative and imperative functions have been the primary focus of the literature, children's gestures, like language, can serve multiple functions depending on the context. Southgate et al. [125] describe an *interrogative* function in pointing gestures, while Moro and Rodríguez [93] identify a similar function in the ostensive gestures of a 15-month-old girl. Basilio and Rodríguez [5] propose an *evaluative* function in children's ostensive and representational gestures when they successfully achieve an objective, a finding corroborated by Moreno-Llanos et al. [90]. Likewise, Liszkowski et al. [83] have suggested an *informative* function in early pointing gestures. However, their laboratory-based studies leave open questions about how these gestures manifest in everyday situations (see discussion in [56]. For their part, Moreno-Núñez et al. [92] propose a *phatic* function in initial ostensive gestures, analogous to the phatic function of language described by Jakobson [68].

In our classroom observations, we identified these same functions in children's gestures from 11 months of age:

(1) *Interrogative Function*: Children used gestures (ostensive, indicative, and representational) to request help when experiencing difficulties with the conventional use of an object, seeking the teachers' intervention while maintaining control over the action. This interrogative function was also observed during negotiations between teachers and children about joint actions and object uses (see Table 7.5) or when teachers corrected the children's gestures and the children attempted to clarify the expected behavior (see example in [58].

(2) *Evaluative Function*: Children performed ostensive and representational gestures with evaluative functions after successfully completing actions related to the conventional use of objects, typically as a form of positive self-assessment. For instance, they clapped toward the teacher after putting bottles into a box (Fig. 7.4) or smiled while showing a block to the teacher after successfully building a tower (see example in [90]. Evaluative gestures were also observed at the end of joint activities, such as reading books or singing songs, where they were often encouraged and scaffolded by the teachers from the early months of the school year (see Table 7.5).

(3) *Informative Function*: Children also produced gestures to provide information that teachers *appeared* to lack, particularly in response to specific questions about the location of objects in the classroom. This function was observed exclusively in pointing gestures once children had acquired experience with the indicated referent and the routine in which it was embedded. For example, before the shared reading routine, the teacher asked, "Where is 'Pollo Pepe'?" [the title of a book], the children pointed to the bookshelf where the book was kept (see another example in Table 7.6).

Children's gestures were not solely directed at others for communicative purposes. Once children began producing gestures in the classroom (around 8 months), they also performed similar gestures without an intended recipient other than themselves. Even with the teacher present, there was no evidence that these gestures aimed to attract her attention (e.g., no eye contact, body posture adjustments, or gesture persistence). These gestures mirrored those previously used by teachers to communicate with and regulate the children's actions, suggesting their social origin through interaction with others and objects. By the end of the first year, children produced a comparable proportion of gestures directed at others and self-directed gestures. The latter were categorized into two main groups:

Table 7.5 Establishing agreements about object uses in the classroom: storing objects to tide up

December—Semi-Structured Activity: Free Play
Participants: A—Child (11;18;11)/T—Teacher

T adjusts her gestures, decreasing their semiotic complexity, to transmit the child the expected use of the box.

T. points to the box to instruct A to store the tray she is sucking. She says, "Put it here"	A does not respond. T produces a touch-pointing and repeats the instruction This time A looks at the tray but does not take it	M. produces an ostensive gesture and offers the tray to A. She looks at it and then takes it

The child makes an interrogative gesture to reach an agreement with T about the objects' use

A looks at T and shows her the tray (ostensive gestures—interrogative function). T smiles and nods while saying "yes, put it in the box" (representational gesture)	A persists in her gesture (ostensive gestures—interrogative function). T adjusts her gesture complexity to a *pointing* while saying "put it here."	A lets the tray fall into the box. M claps and says, "Very Good!" (representational gesture—evaluative function)

(continued)

Table 7.5 (continued)

T scaffolds the child's entrance into a new gesture form and function

M. holds her palm up in front of A while saying, "Give me five!"	A places her hand on T's palm and smiles. T makes their hands clap and says, "Very good, high five!"	

Fig. 7.4 Arbitrary representational gesture (clapping) with an evaluative function after a successful conventional use: placing bottles into a box

(1) *Attentional Control*: Gestures used by children to focus their attention on objects of interest within the classroom (see Fig. 7.5), fulfilling a function similar to what the literature calls "self-declarative" gestures [39, 40]. For example, children looked toward the playground and pointed to the door (self-directed pointing) just before walking toward it to attempt to open it. Similarly, they presented a book to themselves (self-directed ostensive gesture) before opening it and turning its pages.

(B) *Cognitive Self-Regulation (Private Gestures):* These gestures were observed in situations where children faced a difficult goal, typically related to performing the functional (or conventional) use of objects in the classroom. In such circumstances, children coordinated their gestures and actions with objects to

Table 7.6 Informative functions in early pointing gestures in the classroom

November—Semi-structured activity: Free play *Participants: D (10;12;10)/Teacher (T)*	
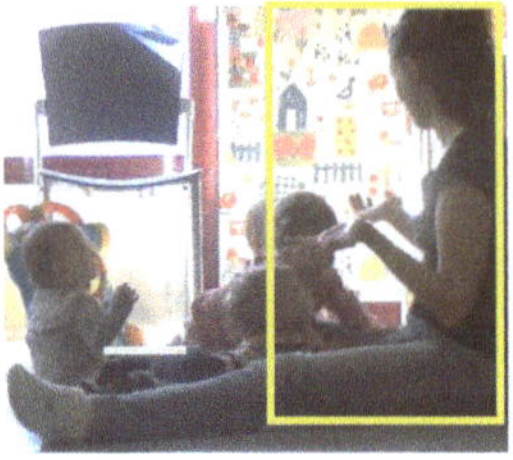	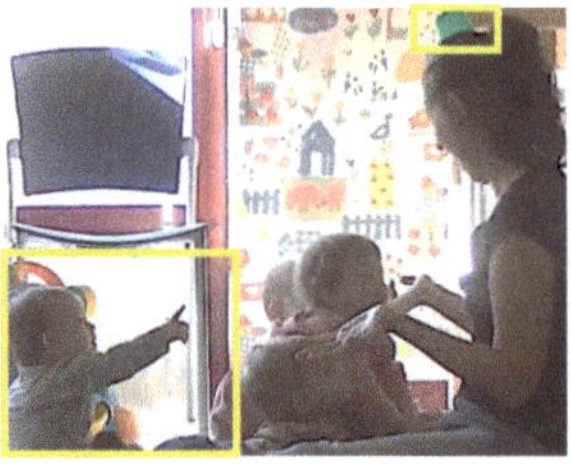
T places a cup on top of her head. She waits a few seconds and asks "Where is the cup" while gesturing (*representational gesture—arbitrary*)	D points to the place where the cup is in response (*informative function*)

Fig. 7.5 Self-directed attentional pointing gesture

achieve their intended goal. These gestures will be described in further detail in Chaps. 9 and 10 in this volume.

7.6 The Progressive Construction of Gestures

If we were to pinpoint the origins of communication in development, it would begin well before the first gestures emerge. Children exhibit expressive bodily and vocal behaviors from birth that others interpret as communicative signs, even if they are not performed intentionally. For instance, adults derive information from a newborn's crying, even though this behavior is viewed more as an expressive response than as an intentional act aimed at influencing adults. The term "gestures" is only applied when children demonstrate communicative intentionality, typically between 9 and 12 months.

From a cognitive perspective, this fundamental shift in communicative ability is seen as a sudden behavioral change resulting from an internal development in socio-cognitive skills. Children begin producing gestures and engaging in joint attention behaviors at this stage, based on an understanding that others are intentional agents whose attention can be influenced [130, 132]. In this view, early gestures are conventional productions that emerge from the child's prior knowledge of social relationships.

In contrast, the constructivist perspective argues that thought and communicative abilities are not pre-existing in the child's mind but are progressively constructed through meaningful interactions with objects and people. Applying this idea to gesture development, perspectives like the PO and similar approaches suggest that the meanings of actions and gestures are not predefined; instead, they are co-constructed within communicative social practices [20, 140]). From this viewpoint, gestures are built through active participation in social contexts, with their meanings developing and transforming as children gain social experience with others and objects.

A clear example of this approach is the development of the pointing gesture recently described by the relational perspective. Various authors have described how the child's early movements of the index finger—such as failed attempts to reach for objects 136 or tactile exploration [101]—are interpreted by adults as intentional communication [24, 103]. During these interactions, adults attribute meaning to the child's actions, enabling them to anticipate the consequences of their behavior and progressively act more referentially. Thus, the early gestures observed in development are better understood as processes rather than outcomes. These gestures do not initially reflect an adult-like understanding of their meaning or social function but acquire significance as children participate in increasingly complex social practices.

The qualitative and microgenetic analysis of interactions in early childhood classrooms provided similar findings regarding the development of ostensive gestures (showing and giving) throughout the school year. Changes were observed in both the morphology and functions of these gestures, which became progressively more conventional and specific (see Table 7.7).

Additionally, changes were observed in the interactions in which ostensive gestures occurred. Initially, ostensive gestures occurred in highly structured exchanges, predominantly initiated, guided, and concluded by the teachers. These interactions were brief and focused more on the interpersonal exchange than on the objects or specific themes to which they referred (the objects served primarily as mediators for the social interaction).

By the end of the observations, these interactions had evolved into clear intentional and conventional "social acts," often extended over time, which could be initiated and/or guided by the child. These interactions frequently included multiple gestures in succession—whether several ostensive gestures or other types of gestures—that were flexibly coordinated and alternated. Additionally, adjustments to ostensive gestures were observed based on the child's specific goals and interests, where the referent objects and their joint uses with the teacher became central

Table 7.7 Changes in the morphology and functions of ostensive Gestures over the school year

Changes in morphology (forms)	
Ostensive Gestures—GIVING	*Ostensive Gestures—SHOWING*
• Fine-tuning object release: Fewer difficulties releasing objects into the other person's hand or lap • Improved directionality: Better aiming of objects towards the receiver's hand • Positioning objects attentively: Placing objects within the other person's field of attention before extending them to their hand • Gaze alternation: Switching gaze between the receiving hand and the other person's face or eyes • Vocal coordination: Coordinating vocalizations to direct others' attention towards the gesture	• Clear arm extension: Full extension of the arms towards the other person • Height alignment: Object is extended at the level of the other person's field of attention or gaze • One-handed manipulation: Improved ease in extending the object, transitioning from holding it with both hands to alternating freely between one hand and the other • Prolonged extension time: Gradual increase in the time spent extending the object based on the other person's response • Gaze alternation: Alternating gaze between the other person and the object being shown • Vocal coordination: Synchronizing gestures with vocalizations
Changes in functions	
• Transition from phatic functions—where the goal was to prolong the interaction rather than exchange meanings about specific referents—to ostensive gestures (both showing and giving) with a wide range of communicative functions, such as sharing interest in particular referents, initiating joint actions, obtaining information or changes in the immediate environment, and sharing achievements • Initial polysemic ostensive gestures, where the meaning of the gesture depended on adult responses (the child appeared to accept the adult's interpretation of their gestures), evolved into ostensions with specific meanings in particular contexts. In these cases, the gesture persisted until the expected response was achieved	

* *Table taken from Guevara* [57] *summarizing the data presented in Guevara et al.* [56]

elements of the communicative act. In these exchanges, the child persisted in their efforts to create and exchange meanings, adapted their productions to overcome challenges, and even decided when to conclude the interaction.

In this sense, gestural development is a process rather than an outcome; it is not linear but gradual across all dimensions: the forms and functions of gestures, intentionality, and the understanding of others as intentional agents. The development of gestures involves a progressive construction process shaped by the particular circumstances in which children operate and the specific interactional contexts in which they participate.

7.6.1 Halfway Between Action and Gestures: Proto-Gestures

Considering gestural development as a progressive construction allowed us to analyze how children's actions and interactions gradually give rise to gestures. The first intentional communicative instances observed in the classroom progressively involved transforming children's instrumental actions with objects into increasingly complex referential actions with and about these same objects. In this process, it is possible to identify intermediate behaviors, which we have termed *proto-gestures*: actions in which the child already has some communicative experience with the gesture but whose form or function is not yet fully consolidated. For example, a proto-gesture may lack the clarity in morphology or purpose of a conventional gesture, but through practice and interaction, it becomes more refined and acquires unquestionable intentionality. These early gestural productions often serve undifferentiated functions, which diversify and become more precise with experience in different social contexts.

In the classroom, the first observed gestures were mostly "proto-gestures." These transitional behaviors between actions and gestures were characterized by: (1) Having an ambiguous function, (2) occurring outside the expected social contexts, and (3) lacking morphology aligned with conventional standards. For instance, many early pointing gestures were characterized by difficulties in achieving the conventional form of the gesture. Children often pointed with an open or semi-open hand, alternated between extending the index finger and using an open palm, or struggled to keep their arm steady in a specific direction (see example in Table 7.8).

Similarly, "proto-symbols" were identified when certain early representational gestures, such as clapping, had a conventional morphology but occurred at any point during the school day without clearly fulfilling an evaluative function or marking the completion of an activity (see Fig. 7.6). Likewise, early waving gestures revealed difficulties in both executing the lateral hand movement [58] and identifying whom to greet, when, or under what circumstances it was appropriate to greet (see Table 7.9).

From our perspective, the origins of intentional communication cannot be fully understood without analyzing these proto-gestural productions within progressively more complex triadic interactions. These interactions not only build

Table 7.8 Proto-pointing gesture

December—Directed activity: Puppet show *Participant (age): Ils (0;12;11)*	

Ils proto-points to a puppet to share it with T (*declarative function*). He moves his arm in circles due to the excitement	Ils proto-points to the puppet to share it with T, alternating between little extensions of his index finger and an open-hand extension

Fig. 7.6 Scaffolding an arbitrary proto-symbol: High-five. T puts her hands up in front of the child. When he reaches for them, she celebrates by smiling and saying, "High five!"

Table 7.9 Correction of children gestures' communicative direction

November—Semi-structured Activity: Free Play *Participanst: V (0;11;10) / Teacher: T*	
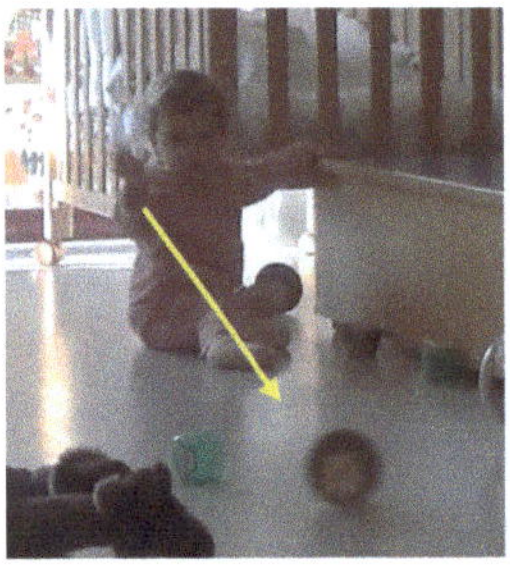	
V waves towards a metallic cup that fell and rolled away (Proto-symbol– arbitrary)	
	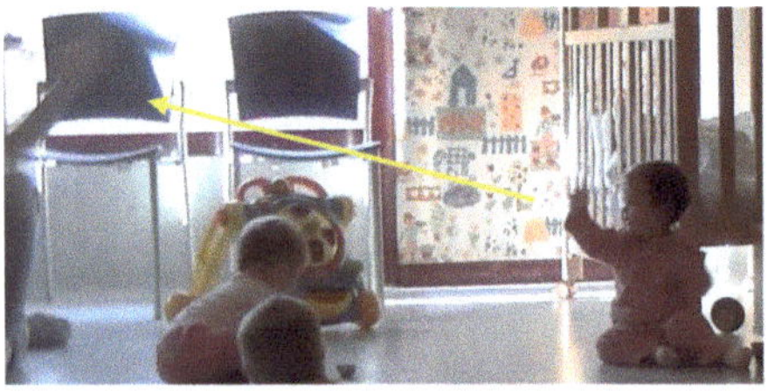
T mirrors V's gesure correcting her communciative direction: She waves at V while saying "Bye bye V."	V looks at M, smiles and repeats her waving, this time directed to M

shared meanings but also establish the foundations for developing intentionality and children's communicative abilities [22, 58].

7.7 The Role of Adults in the Emergence and Development of Early Gestures

As outlined throughout this chapter, children are immersed in a social environment where adults play a crucial role as semiotic mediators from birth. Adults employ various communication systems—such as gestures, objects' uses, tools, and language—to interact with children, make the surrounding world more accessible, and regulate their behavior (see Fig. 7.7).

The role of adults is fundamental for the development of early gestures. There are two main perspectives regarding how adults influence this process. On the one hand, research has documented the importance of modeling, that is, how adults' verbal and gestural productions influence those of children [51, 97]. On the other hand, emphasis is placed on the responsiveness of adults—their ability to respond contingently and coherently to the child's attentional focus—which facilitates the development of intentional communication [24, 128].

Research on language development has demonstrated that infant-directed speech or motherese, characterized by short, repetitive phrases, elongated vowels, and synchrony between speech, gestures, and objects, is essential for linguistic learning [49, 120]. Regarding gestures, it has been observed that adults adapt their communicative productions when interacting with children, using gestures that are more concrete, slow, and repetitive, synchronized with gaze and verbalizations, and with consistent meanings between gestures and words [38, 66]. These adaptations not only facilitate children's comprehension but also increase their attention and object exploration [12, 75].

Furthermore, the adult's interactive style directly influences the frequency and complexity of children's gestures. Studies such as those by Miller & Lossia [88] and Dimitrova et al. [43] demonstrate that contingent responses and adults'

Fig. 7.7 Elements of the triadic communicative interaction unit of analysis

adjustments to children's gestural productions enhance communicative development. For instance, strategies like "translating" children's gestures into words and "contingent imitation" are effective in enriching these interactions [73, 119].

The importance of adults in the development of children's gestures has led to the design of intervention programs, particularly for cases of atypical development or socioeconomic disadvantage. Examples such as the MORE program (Modeling, Opportunities, and Respond/Expand) by Romano & Windsor [118] aim to promote deictic gestures through strategies like environmental arrangements, gesture modeling, and contingent responses. These programs also highlight the importance of tailoring interventions to the child's interests and creating meaningful environments that motivate communicative participation [29]. The goal is not merely to teach specific forms of communication but to promote challenging and enriching experiences that stimulate their development.

7.7.1 Adults as Mediators in Early Childhood Education

Although most studies have focused on the role of parents at home or of professionals in therapeutic settings, it is essential to investigate how other significant adults, such as teachers, mediate children's communicative development in educational contexts. At home, it has been shown that parents are fundamental mediators, helping children progressively appropriate their communicative intentions until they internalize and use them autonomously [37]. It is reasonable to assume that in early childhood education, where teachers plan their actions based on explicit educational objectives, this process intensifies and diversifies, offering unique opportunities for early communicative development.

In our research in early-years-schools' classrooms, we observed that teachers' educational actions around children's gestures included interventions before and after the gestures were produced. These actions were categorized into six main types (see summary in Table 7.12):

(1) *Contingent responses*: Despite the asymmetrical ratio in classrooms, where there are approximately eight children per teacher, observations showed that teachers responded contingently to about half of the gestures directed at them. These responses:
   - Occurred primarily in situations of joint action with objects, aligning with the children's attentional focus and interests (i.e., they were coherent).
   - Included chains of semiotic mediators of varying complexity (multimodal communication): gestures (ostensive, indexical, and representational), verbalizations, object uses (immediate or distant demonstrations of conventional uses), directive gaze, facial expressions, prosody changes, and others. Teachers adjusted the complexity of these mediators when comprehension difficulties arose—for instance, transitioning from pointing to an ostensive gesture of showing the same object (see Table 7.5).

- Incorporated redundancies that made the semiotic mediators more salient or explicit for the children, such as onomatopoeias, movements or shaking of objects, exaggerated facial expressions, repetitions, or melodic components.
- Focused not only on children's gestural productions but also on their connection with specific referents (objects and their uses) and their communicative directions.

  In this way, teachers' responses made sense and had meaning for children's gestures based on the specific contexts in which they occurred, the referents involved, and the prior history of interactions in the classroom. These responses promoted greater knowledge acquisition about objects and their uses, creating shared reference frameworks from which new communicative interactions could emerge.

(2) *Correction of proto-gestures*: Teachers "corrected" children's gestures when their forms or functions differed from conventional or contextually expected ones (considered, in these cases, as proto-gestures). Teachers mirrored children's gestures in conventional forms or redirected them to more appropriate contexts (see Table 7.9).

(C) *Enrichment of gestures*: When children produced gestures with conventional forms and functions, teachers: (i) Imitated them, building on the children's initial proposals and complementing them with the multimodal use of other coordinated semiotic mediators, such as verbalizations or gazes (Table 7.10). These actions often led to the repetition of the gesture by the children, or (ii) "Translated" the gestures into words analogous to the inferred meaning of the gesture.

(D) *Referential Models:* Before children produced their first gestures, teachers already included gestures in their daily interactions, both in ritualized activities (such as songs or book reading) and in more flexible and dynamic ways during their everyday interactions.

(E) *[Over]Interpretation*: From children's earliest months in the classroom, teachers interpreted their instrumental actions or movements as intentional gestures, giving them meaning based on the context. For example, teachers interpreted children's attempts to reach objects as reaching gestures or their emotional expressions as greeting gestures. As noted in previous literature, these instances of "overinterpretation" can help children understand the effects of their actions on the world and anticipate the responses of others (Table 7.11).

(F) *Scaffolding*: Teachers scaffolded children's engagement in interactive gestures that required another person's response to be completed, such as gestures of giving or high-fiving (the latter with specific evaluative functions)—See example in Table 7.5.

Table 7.10 Enrichment of early gestures

October—Structured activity: Sound making objects *Participant: Ils (0;8;3)*	
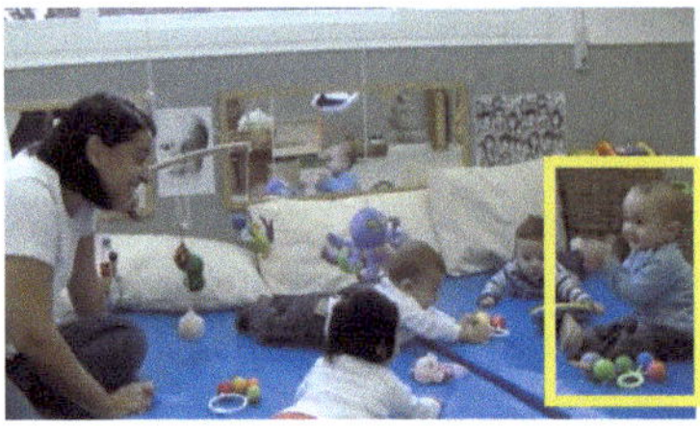	Ils looks at M, smiles, and claps *(Representational gesture—Arbitrary. Phatic function)*
	T mirrors Ils' gesture and enriches it: she combines it with a verbalization: "Great!", providing an evaluative function
	Ils smiles and repeats the gesture *(Representational gesture—Arbitrary. Phatic function)*

Table 7.11 Giving meaning to children's early actions and vocalizations

October—Structured activity: Free play *Participant: Ils (8;3;8)/Teacher (T)*	

Ils smiles, vocalizes and raises his arm toward the camera	T says, 'Say hello, yes, are you waving?' Ils looks at T

Table 7.12 Immediate actions by teachers concerning children's gestures

Before Gestures	After Gestures
Promotion	*Respones, Enrichment, and Correction*
• Consistently interpreted and responded to children's instrumental actions as if they were intentional communicative acts • Acted as a reference model for the use of gestures with various functions during structured activities, where the use of redundancies to emphasize gestures stood out, but also during everyday interactions • Explicitly prompted children to perform certain gestures, allowing time for their responses, scaffolding their actions when necessary, and reinforcing proto-gestures through positive expressions • Performed immediate demonstrations of gestures	• Provided contingent responses to children's gestures, following their focus of attention and interests • Imitated children's gestures, assigning meaning and expanding them with multimodal elements • Modeled the use of gestures in coordination with other semiotic mediators (such as language and gaze), emphasizing them through redundancies • Corrected the morphology of proto-gestures by reflecting them in their conventional forms • Corrected the functions of gestures and proto-gestures by interpreting them differently and assigning varying meanings according to the context

Overall, it is noteworthy that the educational actions observed in the classrooms spontaneously included activities across all intervention areas suggested in programs designed to promote deictic gestures in early childhood [118]: adjustments to the environment to create communicative opportunities, gesture modeling during daily interactions, and identifying, responding to, and enriching children's communicative productions. Additionally, the teachers' actions incorporated strategies previously associated with language promotion in the literature, such as repetitions [29], providing children with choices and sufficient time for their responses, using communicative prompts, and anticipating upcoming activities. These similarities between the observed educational action and the strategies recognized as promotive of both gestures and language could explain why early-years-school's classrooms are considered environments that generate equal learning opportunities for children in socially disadvantaged situations.

7.8 Conclusion

The Pragmatics of the Object perspective underscores the foundational role of early interactions with others and the socio-material world in shaping children's first communicative acts. This perspective challenges traditional views of gestures and context by positioning objects as active agents in the construction of shared meanings. In the classroom, objects function as first communicative tools (early signs), first referents (shared knowledge that anchors joint activities), and first contexts for shared interactions, mediating opportunities, and demands for communication.

One advantage of this perspective is the possibility of study the foundational role of ostensive gestures (showing and giving) as the first intentional gestures observed in development. These gestures not only facilitate proximal interactions with objects but also serve as precursors to more complex gestures like pointing marking critical milestones in early communicative development.

Furthermore, by applying a semiotic framework, this chapter organizes gestures into levels of complexity based on the relationship between signs and referents, revealing a developmental trajectory from proximal gestures to more complex, distal, and representational ones. This approach also illuminates the gradual transformation of instrumental actions into intentional communicative gestures, highlighting transitional behaviors such as proto-gestures. Teachers play a critical role in this process, mediating, promoting, expanding and correcting gestural communication through planned activities, responsive interactions, and demonstrations. Both their actions in the classroom and their planning of material objects and structured environments support the gradual transformation of instrumental actions into intentional gestures, enhancing children's cognitive, social, and communicative growth.

Finally, this chapter illustrated the different functions that early gestures have during communicative interactions, opening the door to the possibility of gestures not only as "communicative tools" but as "semiotic mediators." In this sense, we consider that, depending on their communicative direction, gestures have specific functions: those that relate to others about objects and private gestures that are self-directed to help children organize and coordinate their own actions and attention when confronted with everyday challenges. The private functions of gestures will be described in detail in Chaps. 9 and 10 of this volume.

References

1. Acredolo, L., & Goodwyn, S. (1988). Symbolic gesturing in normal infants. *Child Development, 59*(2), 450–466. https://doi.org/10.2307/1130324
2. Alberto, R., Shvarts, A., Drijvers, P., & Bakker, A. (2022). Action-based embodied design for mathematics learning: A decade of variations on a theme. *International Journal of Child-Computer Interaction, 32*, 1–23. https://doi.org/10.1016/j.ijcci.2021.100419
3. Alibali, M. W., Spencer, R. C., Knox, L., & Kita, S. (2011). Spontaneous gestures influence strategy choices in problem solving. *Psychological Science, 22*(9), 1138–1144. https://doi.org/10.1177/0956797611417722
4. Baron-Cohen, S., Cox, A., Baird, G., Swettenham, J., Nightingale, N., Morgan, K., Drew, A., & Charman, T. (1996). Psychological markers in the detection of autism in infancy in a large population. *The British Journal of Psychiatry, 168*(2), 158–163. https://doi.org/10.1192/bjp.168.2.158
5. Basilio, M., & Rodríguez, C. (2017). How toddlers think with their hands: Social and private gestures as evidence of cognitive self-regulation in guided play with objects. *Early Child Development and Care, 187*(12), 1971–1986. https://doi.org/10.1080/03004430.2016.1202944
6. Basilio, M. (2014). *Los signos preverbales como herramientas de pensamiento: El origen social de la autorregulación cognitiva en niños de 14 a 18 meses de edad* [Preverbal signs

as tools of thought: The social origin of cognitive self-regulation in children from 14 to 18 months of age. Unpublished Doctoral Thesis]. Universidad Autónoma de Madrid, Spain.
7. Bates, E., Camaioni, L., & Volterra, V. (1975). The acquisition of performatives prior to speech. *Merrill-Palmer Quarterly of Behavior and Development, 21*(3), 205–226.
8. Bavin, E. L., Prior, M., Reilly, S., Bretherton, L., Williams, J., Eadie, P., Barrett, Y., & Ukoumunne, O. C. (2008). The early language in Victoria study: Predicting vocabulary at age one and two years from gesture and object use. *Journal of Child Language, 35*(03), 687–701. https://doi.org/10.1017/S0305000908008726
9. Boundy, L., Cameron-Faulkner, T., & Theakston, A. (2016). Exploring early communicative behaviours: A fine-grained analysis of infant shows and gives. *Infant Behavior and Development, 44*, 86–97.
10. Boundy, L., Cameron-Faulkner, T., & Theakston, A. (2018). Intention or attention before pointing: Do infants' early holdout gestures reflect evidence of a declarative motive? *Infancy, 24*(1), 228–248. https://doi.org/10.1111/infa.12267
11. Bourdais, C., Danis, A., Bacle, C., Santolini, A., & Tijus, C. (2013). Do 10- and 13-month-old infants provide informative gestures for their mothers in a hiding game? *Infant Behavior and Development, 36*(1), 94–101. https://doi.org/10.1016/j.infbeh.2012.11.006
12. Brand, R. J., & Shallcross, W. L. (2008). Infants prefer motionese to adult-directed action. *Developmental Science, 11*(6), 853–861. https://doi.org/10.1111/j.1467-7687.2008.00734.x
13. Breazeal, C. (2003). Emotion and sociable humanoid robots. *International Journal of Human-Computer Studies, 59*(1–2), 119–155. https://doi.org/10.1016/S1071-5819(03)00018-1
14. Bruner, J. S. (1974). From communication to language: a psychological perspective. *Cognition, 3*(3), 255–287. 16/0010-0277(74)90012-2
15. Butterworth, G. (2003). Pointing is the royal road to language for babies. In S. Kita (Ed.), *Pointing. Where language, culture and cognition meet* (pp. 9–33). Lawrence Erlbaum Associates.
16. Camaioni, L. (1993). The development of intentional communication: A re-analysis. In J. Nadel & L. Camaioni (Eds.), *New perspectives in early communicative development* (pp. 82–96). Routledge.
17. Camaioni, L., & Perucchini, P. (2010). The role of declarative pointing in developing a theory of mind. *Infancy, 5*(3), 291–308. https://doi.org/10.1207/s15327078in0503_3
18. Cameron-Faulkner, T., Malik, N., Steele, C., Coretta, S., Serratrice, L., & Lieven, E. (2021). A cross-cultural analysis of early prelinguistic gesture development and its relationship to language development. *Child Development, 92*(1), 273–290. https://doi.org/10.1111/cdev.13406
19. Cameron-Faulkner, T., Theakston, A., & Tomasello, M. (2015). The relationship between infant holdout and gives and pointing. *Infancy, 20*(5), 576–586. https://doi.org/10.1111/infa.12085
20. Canfield, J. V. (1995). The rudiments of language. *Language and Communication, 15*(3), 195–211.
21. Capobianco, M., Pizzuto, E. A., & Devescovi, A. (2017). Gesture-speech combinations and early verbal abilities. *Interaction Studies, 18*(1), 55–76.
22. Carpendale, J. I., Kettner, V. A., & Guevara, I. (2023). A genealogy of gestures: On the nature and emergence of gestural communication within shared routines. *Human Development*. https://doi.org/10.1159/000533645
23. Carpendale, J. I., & Lewis, C. (2004). Constructing an understanding of mind: The development of children's social understanding within social interaction. *Behavioural and Brain Sciences, 27*, 79–96.
24. Carpendale, J. I., & Lewis, C. (2021). *What makes us human*. Routledge.
25. Carpendale, J., Müller, U., Wallbridge, B., Boesch, T., Cameron-Faulkner, T., & Ten Eycke, K. (2021). The development of giving forms of object exchange: Exploring the roots of communication and morality in early interaction around objects. *Human Development, 65*(3), 166–179. https://doi.org/10.1159/000517221

26. Carpenter, M., Nagell, K., & Tomasello, M. (1998). Social cognition, joint attention, and communicative competence from 9 to 15 months of age. *Monographs of the society for research in child development, 63*(255), 1–174.
27. Cartmill, E. A., Hunsicker, D., & Goldin-Meadow, S. (2014). Pointing and naming are not redundant: Children use gesture to modify nouns before they modify nouns in speech. *Developmental Psychology, 50*(6), 1660–1666. https://doi.org/10.1037/a0036003
28. Caselli, M. C., Vicari, S., Longobardi, E., Lami, L., Pizzoli, C., & Stella, G. (1998). Gestures and words in early development of children with down syndrome. *Journal of Speech, Language, and Hearing Research, 41*(5), 1125–1135.
29. Casla, M., Moreno-Núñez, A., Alam, F., & Rosemberg, C. (2024). How teachers emphasize their speech: Gestures and self-repetitions during group interaction with toddlers. *Language and Education.* https://doi.org/10.1080/09500782.2024.2312983
30. Castañares, W. (2007). Cultura visual y crisis de la experiencia [Visual culture and crisis of experience]. *Cuadernos de Información y Comunicación, 12*, 29–48.
31. Choi, B., Wei, R., & Rowe, M. (2021). Show, give, and point gestures across infancy differentially predict language development. *Developmental Psychology, 57*(6), 851–862. https://doi.org/10.1037/dev0001195
32. Clark, H. (2003). Pointing and placing. In S. Kita (Ed.), *Pointing: Where language, culture and cognition meet* (pp. 243–268). Lawrence Erlbaum.
33. Clements, C., & Chawarska, K. (2010). Beyond pointing: Development of the "Showing" gesture in children with autism spectrum disorder. *Yale Review of Undergraduate Research in Psychology, 2*, 1–11.
34. Colonnesi, C., Stams, G., Kister, I., & Noom, M. (2010). The relation between pointing and language development: A meta-analysis. *Developmental Review, 30*, 352–366.
35. Contin, L., & Rodríguez, C. (2021). La lectura del libro en la escuela infantil como facilitador de la atención en bebés [The book-reading in the early-years-school as an enabler of attention in babies] (Chapter 3). In C. Rodríguez & J.L. De los Reyes (Eds.), *Los objetos sí importan. Acción educativa en la escuela infantil* [Objects matter. Educational action in the early-years-school]. Horsori Editorial.
36. Crais, E., Douglas, D. D., & Campbell, C. C. (2004). The Intersection of the development of gestures and intentionality. *Journal of Speech, Language and Hearing Research, 74*, 678–694.
37. Cuevas, I. (2006). *Desarrollo humano y educación* [Human development and education. Unpublished Manuscript]. Universidad Autónoma de Madrid, Spain.
38. Cárdenas, K., Rodríguez, C., & Palacios, P. (2014). First symbols in a girl with down syndrome: A longitudinal study from 12 to 18 months. *Infant Behavior & Development, 37*(3), 416–427.
39. Delgado, B., Gómez, J. C., & Sarriá, E. (2009). Private pointing and private speech: Developing parallelisms. In A. Winsler, C. Fernyhough, & I. Montero (Eds.), *Private speech, executive function, and the development of verbal self-regulation* (pp. 153–162). Cambridge University Press.
40. Delgado, B., Gómez, J. C., & Sarriá, E. (2010). Early functions of the gesture of private pointing: Contemplation and self-regulation through the gesture of pointing. *Action Psychological, 7*(2), 59–70.
41. Dimitrova, N., Mohr, C., Ozçaliskan, S., & Adamson, L. B. (2020). Early lateralization of gestures in autism: Right-handed points predict expressive language. *Journal of Autism and Developmental Disorders, 50*, 1147–1158. https://doi.org/10.1007/s10803-019-04347-9
42. Dimitrova, N., & Moro, C. (2012). Common ground on object use associates with caregivers' gestures. *Infant Behavior and Development, 36*, 618–626. https://doi.org/10.1016/j.infbeh.2013.06.006
43. Dimitrova, N., Özcalıskan, S., & Adamson, L. (2016). Parents' translations of child gesture facilitate word learning in children with autism, down syndrome and typical development. *Journal of Autism & Developmental Disorders, 46*(1), 221–231. https://doi.org/10.1007/s10803-015-2566-7

44. Donellan, E., Bannard, C., McGillion, M. L., Slocombe, K. E., & Matthews, D. (2019). Infants' intentionally communicative vocalizations elicit responses from caregivers and are the best predictors of the transition to language: A longitudinal investigation of infants' vocalizations, gestures, and word production. *Developmental Science.* https://doi.org/10.1111/desc.12843
45. Eco, U. (1992). *La production des signes* [Production of signs] Le Livre de Poche.
46. Enfield, N.J. (2009). *The anatomy of meaning. Speech, Gesture, and Composite Utterances.* Cambridge University Press.
47. Español, S., & Rivière, Á. (2000). Gestos comunicativos y contextos interpersonales: Un estudio con niños de 10 a 16 meses / Communicative gestures and interpersonal contexts: A study with 10 to 16 months old infants. *Estudios de Psicología, 21*(1–2), 225–245. https://doi.org/10.1174/021093900320380785
48. Estrada, L. (2021). Tipos de situaciones educativas en la escuela infantil: el rol mediador de los maestros. In C. Rodríguez & J.L. De los Reyes (Eds.), *Los objetos sí importan. Acción educativa en la escuela infantil* [Objects matter. Educational action in the early-years-school]. Horsori Editorial.
49. Fernald, A., & Kuhl, P. (1987). Acoustic determinants of infant preference for motherese speech. *Infant Behavior and Development, 10,* 279–293. https://doi.org/10.1016/0163-6383(87)90017-8
50. Fernández-Flecha, M., Blume, M., Junyent, A., & Tijero-Neyra, T. (2021). Gesture development in Peruvian children and its relationship with vocalizations and vocabulary. *Gesture, 20*(1), 1–29.
51. Fusaro, M., Vallotton, C. D., & Harris, P. L. (2014). Beside the point: Mothers' head nodding and shaking gestures during parent–child play. *Infant Behavior and Development, 37*(2), 235–247. https://doi.org/10.1016/j.infbeh.2014.01.006
52. Gallese, V., & Lakoff, G. (2005). The brain's concepts: The role of the sensory-motor system in conceptual knowledge. *Cognitive Neuropsychology, 22*(3–4), 455–479.
53. Ger, E., Altinok, N., Liszkowski, U., & Küntay, A. (2018). Development of infant pointing from 10 to 12 months: The roles of relevant caregiver responsiveness. *Infancy, 23*(5), 708–729. https://doi.org/10.1111/infa.12239
54. Goldin-Meadow, S. (2003). *Hearing gesture: How our hands help us think.* Belknap Press.
55. Goldin-Meadow, S., & Alibali, M. W. (2013). Gesture's role in speaking, learning, and creating language. *Annual Review of Psychology, 64*(1), 257–283. https://doi.org/10.1146/annurev-psych-113011-143802
56. Guevara, I. (2025). El origen y desarrollo de los primeros gestos y sus funciones en la escuela infantil [The origin and development of first gestures and their functions in the early years school. Unpublished Thesis Dissertation]. Universidad Autónoma de Madrid.
57. Guevara, I., Moreno-Llanos, I., & Rodríguez, C. (2020). The emergence of gestures in the first year of life in the Infant School classroom. *European Journal of Psychology of Education, 35,* 265–287. https://doi.org/10.1007/s10212-019-00444-6
58. Guevara, I. & Rodríguez, C. (2023). Developing communication through objects: Ostensive gestures as the first gestures in children's development. *Developmental Review, 68,* 101076. https://doi.org/10.1016/j.dr.2023.101076
59. Guevara, I., Rodríguez, C., & Núñez, M. (2024). Developing gestures in the infant classroom: From showing and giving to pointing. *European Journal of Psychology of Education.* https://doi.org/10.1007/s10212-024-00895-6
60. Guevara, I., Moreno-Llanos, I., Romero, L., Zapardiel, L., & Rodríguez, C. (2022). Challenges in first-years schools: Early manifestations of executive function (Chapter 9). In J. Bisault, R. Le Bourgeois, J.-F. Thémines, M. LeMentec, & C. Chauvet-Chanoine (Eds.), *Objects to learn about and objects for learning 2.* Wiley Online Library.
61. Gullberg, M. (2006). Some reasons for studying gesture and second language acquisition (Hommage à Adam Kendon). *International Review of Applied Linguistics in Language Teaching, 44*(2), 103–124.

62. Haviland, J. B. (1993). Anchoring, iconicity, and orientation in Guugu Yimithirr pointing gestures. *Journal of Linguistic Anthropology, 3*(1), 3–45.
63. Heymann, P., Northrup, J. B., West, K. L., Parlad´e, M. B., Leezenbaum, N. B., & Iverson, J. (2018). Coordination is key: Joint attention and vocalization in infant siblings of children with autism spectrum disorder. *International Journal of Language & Communication Disorders, 53*(5), 1007–1020. https://doi.org/10.1111/1460-6984.12418
64. Huang, C., & Mutlu, B. (2016). Anticipatory robot control for efficient human-robot collaboration. In *Proceedings of the 2016 ACM/IEEE International Conference on Human-Robot Interaction* (pp. 83–90).
65. Iverson, J. M., Capirci, O., & Caselli, M. C. (1994). From communication to language in two modalities. *Cognitive Development, 9*(1), 23–43. https://doi.org/10.1016/0885-2014(94)90018-3
66. Iverson, J. M., Capirci, O., Longobardi, E., & Caselli, M. C. (1999). Gesturing in mother-child interactions. *Cognitive Development, 14*(1), 57–75. https://doi.org/10.1016/S0885-2014(99)80018-5Iverson
67. Iverson, J., & Wozniak, R. (2007). Variations in vocal-motor development in infant siblings of children with autism. *Journal of Autism and Developmental Disorders, 37*, 158–170.
68. Jakobson, R. (1960). Linguistics and poetics. In T. Seboek (Ed.), *Style in language* (pp. 350–377). Cambridge.
69. Juvrud, J., Bakker, M., De Valk, J., Kaduk, K., Gredebäck, G., & Kenward, B. (2019). Longitudinal continuity in understanding and production of giving-related behavior from infancy to childhood. *Child Development, 90*(2), e182–e191. https://doi.org/10.1111/cdev.13131
70. Jáñez, M., Del Olmo, M. J., & Rodríguez, C. (2021). The impact of music therapy in late-moderate premature infants, on their parents and their environment, in a Spanish neonatal intermediate care unit. *Music & Medicine, 13*(4), 272–283.
71. Kendon, A. (2004). *Gesture: Visible action as utterance.* Cambridge University Press.
72. Kersken, V., Gómez, J.-C., Liszkowski, U., Soldati, A., & Hobaiter, C. (2019). A gestural repertoire of 1- to 2-year-old human children: In search of the ape gestures. *Animal Cognition, 22*(4), 577–595. https://doi.org/10.1007/s10071-018-1213-z
73. Kishimoto, T. (2017). In Japan, cross-sectional and longitudinal observations of pointing gestures by infants and their caregivers. *Cognitive Development, 43*, 235–244. https://doi.org/10.1016/j.cogdev.2017.06.001
74. Kita, S., Alibali, M. W., & Chu, M. (2017). How do gestures influence thinking and speaking? The gesture-for-conceptualization hypothesis. *Psychological Review, 124*(3), 245–266. https://doi.org/10.1037/rev0000059
75. Koterba, E. A., & Iverson, J. M. (2009). Investigating motionese: The effect of infant-directed action on infants' attention and object exploration. *Infant Behavior and Development, 32*(4), 437–444. https://doi.org/10.1016/j.infbeh.2009.07.003
76. Kwon, A. Y., Vallotton, C. D., Kiegelmann, M., & Wilhelm, K. H. (2018). Cultural diversification of communicative gestures through early childhood: A comparison of children in English-, German-, and Chinese- speaking families. *Infant Behavior and Development, 50*, 328–339. https://doi.org/10.1016/j.infbeh.2017.10.003
77. Lavelli, M., & Fogel, A. (2005). Developmental changes in the relationship between the infant's attention and emotion during early face-to-face communication: The 2-month transition. *Developmental Psychology, 41*(1), 265–280. https://doi.org/10.1037/0012-1649.41.1.265
78. LeBarton, E., & Iverson, J. M. (2016). Gesture development in toddlers with an older sibling with autism. *International Journal of Language & Communicative Disorders, 51*(1), 18–30. https://doi.org/10.1111/1460-6984.12180
79. Leavens, D., Russell, J. L., & Hopkins, W. D. (2005). Intentionality as measured in the persistence and elaboration of communication by chimpanzees (Pan troglodytes). *Child Development, 76*(1), 291–306. https://doi.org/10.1111/j.1467-8624.2005.00845.x
80. Liebal, K., Behne, T., Carpenter, M., & Tomasello, M. (2009). Infants use shared experience to interpret pointing gestures. *Developmental Science, 12*(2), 264–271.

81. Lieven, E., & Stoll, S. (2013). Early communicative development in two cultures: A comparison of the communicative environments of children from two cultures. *Human Development, 56*(3), 178–206.
82. Liszkowski, U. (2008). Before L1: A differentiated perspective on infant gestures. *Gesture, 8*(2), 180–196. https://doi.org/10.1075/gest.8.2.04lis
83. Liszkowski, U., Carpenter, M., Striano, T., & Tomasello, M. (2006). 12-and-18-months-olds point to provide information for others. *Journal of Child Language, 7*(2), 173–187.
84. Liszkowski, U., & Ruether, J. (2021). Ontogenetic origins of infant pointing. In N. Gontier, A. Lock, & C. Sinha (Eds.), *The Oxford handbook of human symbolic evolution.*
85. Manwaring, S. S., Mead, D. L., Swineford, L., & Thurm, A. (2017). Modelling gesture use and early language development in autism spectrum disorder. *International Journal of Language & Communication Disorders, 52*(5), 637–651. https://doi.org/10.1111/1460-6984.12308
86. McGillion, M., Pine, J. M., Herbert, J. S., & Matthews, D. (2017). A randomized controlled trial to test the effect of promoting caregiver contingent talk on language development in infants from diverse socioeconomic status backgrounds. *Journal of Child Psychology and Psychiatry, 58*(10), 1122–1131. https://doi.org/10.1111/jcpp.12725
87. McNeill, D. (2005). *Gesture and thought.* Chicago University Press.
88. Miller, J. L., & Lossia, A. K. (2013). Prelinguistic infants' communicative system: Role of caregiver social feedback. *First Language, 33*(5), 524–544.
89. Mishra, A., Ceballos, V., Himmelwright, K., McCabe, S., & Scott, L. (2021). Gesture production in toddlers with autism spectrum disorder. *Journal of Autism Developmental Disorders, 51*(5), 1658–1667. https://doi.org/10.1007/s10803-020-04647-5
90. Moreno-Llanos, I., Zapardiel, L., & Rodríguez, C. (2020). Children's first manifestations of cognitive control in the early years school: The importance of the educational situation and materiality. *European Journal of Psychology of Education, 36*, 903–922. https://doi.org/10.1007/s10212-020-00505-1
91. Moreno-Núñez, A., Rodríguez, C., & Miranda-Zapata, E. (2020). Getting away from the point: The emergence of ostensive gestures and their functions. *Journal of Child Language, 47*(3), 556–578. https://doi.org/10.1017/S0305000919000606
92. Moreno-Núñez, A., Rodríguez, C., & Del Olmo, M. J. (2017). Rhythmic ostensive gestures: How adults facilitate infants' _entrance into early triadic interactions. *Infant Behavior and Development, 49*, 168–181. https://doi.org/10.1016/j.infbeh.2017.09.003
93. Moro, C., & Rodríguez, C. (1991). Why does the child tend the object toward the adult? The social construction of the meaning of objects. *Childhood and Learning, 53*, 99–118.
94. Mundy, P., Block, J., Delgado, C., Pomares, Y., Van Hecke, A., & Venezia, M. (2007). Individual differences and the development of joint attention in infancy. *Child Development, 78*(3), 938–954. https://doi.org/10.1111/j.1467-8624.2007.01042.x
95. Murillo, E., & Casla, M. (2020). Multimodal representational gestures in the transition to multiword productions. *Infancy, 26*(1), 104–122.
96. Murillo, E., Montero, I., & Casla, M. (2021). On the multimodal path to language: The relationship between rhythmic movements and deictic gestures at the end of the first year. *Frontiers in Psychology, 12*, 1–8.
97. Namy, L. L., Acredolo, L., & Goodwyn, S. (2000). Verbal labels and gestural routines in parental communication with young children. *Journal of Nonverbal Behavior, 24*(2), 63–79.
98. Nöth, W. (1990). *Handbook of semiotics.* Indiana University Press.
99. Olson, J., & Masur, E. F. (2011). Infant's gestures influence mothers' _provision of object, action, and internal state labels. *Journal of Child Language, 38*, 1028–1054. https://doi.org/10.1017/S0305000910000565
100. Osolsobě, I. (1971). The role of models and originals in human communication (the theory of signs and the theory of models). *Language Sciences, 14*, 32–36.
101. O'Madagain, C., Kachel, G., & Strickland, B. (2019). The origin of pointing: Evidence for the touch hypothesis. *Science Advances, 5*(7). https://doi.org/10.1126/sciadv.aav2558

102. Parladé, M. V., & Iverson, J. (2010). *The reorganization of communicative behaviors around the onset of the vocabulary spurt.* In Rivista di psicolinguistica applicata (p. 3).
103. Paulus, M., Kammermeier, M., & Melzel, S. (2023). The emergence of pointing as a communicative gesture: Age-related differences in infants' non-social and social use of the index finger. *Cognitive Development, 65*, 101298.
104. Preisler, G. (1995). Development of communication in deafblind children. *Scandinavian Journal of Disability Research, 7*(1), 41–62. https://doi.org/10.1080/15017410510032145
105. Pulvermüller, F. (2013). How neurons make meaning: Brain mechanisms for embodied and abstract-symbolic semantics. *Trends in Cognitive Sciences, 17*(9), 458–470.
106. Rader, N., & Zukow-Goldring, P. (2015). The role of speech-gesture synchrony in clipping words from the speech stream: Evidence from infant pupil responses. *Ecological Psychology, 27*(4), 290–299. https://doi.org/10.1080/10407413.2015.1086226
107. Ramos-Cabo, S., Vulchanov, V., & Vulchanova, M. (2020). Different ways of making a point: A study of gestural communication in typical and atypical early development. *Autism Research, 14*(5), 984–996. https://doi.org/10.1002/aur.2438
108. Reddy, V., Markova, G., & Wallot, S. (2013). Anticipatory adjustments to being picked up in infancy. *PLoS ONE, 8*(6), 1–9.
109. Rodríguez, C. (2006). *Del ritmo al símbolo. Los signos en el nacimiento de la inteligencia* [From rhythm to symbol. Signs in the birth of intelligence]. Horsori.
110. Rodríguez, C. (2009). The «circumstances» of gestures: Proto-interrogatives and private gestures. *New Ideas in Psychology, 27*(2), 288–303.
111. Rodríguez, C. (2012). The functional permanence of the object: A product of consensus. In E. Martí & C. Rodríguez (Eds.), *After Piaget.* Transaction Publishers.
112. Rodríguez, C., Moreno-Núñez, A., Basilio, M., & Sosa, N. (2015). Ostensive gestures come first: Their role in the beginning of shared reference. *Cognitive Development, 36*, 142–149. https://doi.org/10.1080/02109395.2014.1000009
113. Rodríguez, C., & Moro, C. (2008). Coming to agreement: Object use by infants and adults. In T. Zlatev, C. Sinha, & E. Itkonen (Eds.), *The shared mind: Perspectives on intersubjectivity* (pp. 89–114). John Benjamins.
114. Rodríguez, C., & Moro, C. (1999). *El mágico número tres. Cuando los niños aún no hablan* [The magic number three. When children do not speak yet]. Paidós.
115. Rodríguez, C., Basilio, M., Cárdenas, K., Cavalcante, S., Moreno-Núñez, A., Palacios, P., & Yuste, N. (2018). Object pragmatics: Culture and communication, the bases for early cognitive development. In A. Rosa & J. Valsiner (Eds.), *Cambridge handbook of sociocultural psychology* (2nd Ed.). Cambridge University Press.
116. Rodríguez, C. (2022). The construction of executive function in early development: The pragmatics of action and gestures. *Human Development, 66*, 239–259. https://doi.org/10.1159/000526340
117. Rodríguez, C. & Moreno-Llanos, I. (2020). A pragmatic turn in the study of early executive functions by object use and gestures. A case study from 8 to 17 months of age at a nursery school. *Integrative Psychological and Behavioral Science.* https://doi.org/10.1007/s12124-020-09578-5
118. Romano, M. K., & Windsor, K. S. (2020). Increasing deictic gesture use to support the language development of toddlers from high poverty backgrounds. *Early Childhood Research Quarterly, 50*(1), 129–139. https://doi.org/10.1016/j.ecresq.2018.12.004
119. Rowe, M. L., & Goldin-Meadow, S. (2009). Early gesture selectively predicts later language learning. *Developmental Science, 12*(1), 182–187. https://doi.org/10.1111/j.1467-7687.2008.00764.x
120. Rowe, M. L., & Snow, C. E. (2020). Analyzing input quality along three dimensions: Interactive, linguistic, and conceptual. *Journal of Child Language, 47*(1), 5–21. https://doi.org/10.1017/S0305000919000655
121. Rowe, M. L., Özçalıskan, S., & Goldin-Meadow, S. (2008). Learning words by hand: Gesture's role in predicting vocabulary development. *First Language, 28*(2), 182. https://doi.org/10.1177/0142723707088310

122. Salo, V., Rowe, M., & Reeb-Sutherland, B. (2018). Exploring infant gesture and joint attention as related constructs and as predictors of later language. *Infancy, 23*(3), 432–452.
123. Salomo, D., & Liszkowski, U. (2013). Sociocultural settings influence the emergence of prelinguistic deictic gestures. *Child Development, 84*(4), 1296–1307. https://doi.org/10.1111/cdev.12026
124. Salter, G., & Carpenter, M. (2022). Showing and giving: From incipient to conventional forms. *Philosophical Transactions of the Royal Society B, 377*, 20210102. https://doi.org/10.1098/rstb.2021.0102
125. Southgate, V., van Maanen, C., & Csibra, G. (2007). Infant pointing: Communication to cooperate or communication to learn? *Child Development, 78*(3), 735–740. https://doi.org/10.1111/j.1467-8624.2007.01028.x
126. Stefanini, S., Caselli, M. C., & Volterra, V. (2007). Spoken and gestural production in a naming task by young children with down syndrome. *Brain and Language, 101*(3), 208–221. https://doi.org/10.1016/j.bandl.2007.01.005
127. Taleghani-Nikazm, C. (2008). Gestures in foreign language classrooms: A empirical analysis of their organization and function. In M. Bowles et al. (Eds.), *Selected proceedings of the 2007 second language research forum* (pp. 229–238). Cascadilla Proceedings Project.
128. Tamis-LeMonda, C., Kuchirko, Y., & Song, L. (2014). Why is infant language learning facilitated by parental responsiveness? *Current Directions in Psychological Science, 23*(121), 121–126.
129. Tomasello, M. (2008). *Origins of human communication.* The MIT Press.
130. Tomasello, M., Carpenter, M., Call, J., Behne, T., & Moll, H. (2005). Understanding and sharing intentions: The origins of cultural cognition. *Behavioral and Brain Sciences, 28*, 675–735.
131. Tomasello, M., Carpenter, M., & Liszkowski, U. (2007). A new look at infant pointing. *Child Development, 78*(3), 705–722. https://doi.org/10.1111/j.1467-8624.2007.01025.x
132. Tomasello, M., & Rakoczy, H. (2003). What makes human cognition unique? From individual to shares collective intentionality (review). *Mind and Language, 18*(2), 121–147. https://doi.org/10.1111/1468-0017.00217
133. Trevarthen, C. (1990). Signs before speech. In T. A. Sebeok & J. Umiker-Sebeok (Eds.), *The semiotic web.* Mouton de Gruyter.
134. Trevarthen, C. & Hubley, P. (1978). Secondary intersubjectivity: Confidence, confiding and acts of meaning in the first year. In A. Lock (Ed.), *Action. Gesture and symbol: The emergence of language.* Academic Press.
135. Tversky, B., & Jamalian, A. (2011). Thinking tools: Gestures change thought about time. *Topics in Cognitive Science, 13*(4), 750–776.
136. Valloton, C., Fusaro, M., Hayden, J., Decker, K., & Gutowski, E. (2015). Give me a hand: Differential effects of gesture type in guiding young children's problem-solving. *Instructional Science, 43*(6), 709–735. https://doi.org/10.1007/s11251-015-9357-6
137. Vygotski, L. S. (1978). *Mind in society: The development of higher psychological processes.* Harvard University Press.
138. Wallon, H. (1970). Del acto al pensamiento (E. Dukelsky, Traductor) [From act to though]. Buenos Aires: Psique. (Trabajo original publicado en 1942)
139. Werner, H. & Kaplan, B. (1963). *Symbol formation: An organismic developmental approach to language and the expression of thought.* Wiley.
140. Wittgenstein, L. (1953/2009). *Philosophical investigations.* Blackwell.

Part III

Executive Functions and Their Development in Everyday Situations. Toward a Paradigm Shift

8 Executive Functions and Material Objects: What Is the Role of Materiality in Early Executive Functions Research?

Iván Moreno-Llanos and Julieth Barreto

When children begin to control and regulate their behavior, attention, and thinking, and even emotions, in order to achieve goals remains a topic of much debate. This ability has been conceptualized as a set of cognitive processes related to the conscious and intentional control of behavior and thought, called the *Executive Functions* (EF). Alterations in EF have been linked to developmental disturbances such as Autism Spectrum Disorder [67] or Attention Deficit Hyperactivity Disorder [36], academic performance [18], and even poorer physical and mental health [25]. Recently, the proposal that infants begin to control their behavior towards the end of the first year of life, around 7–8 months, is gaining support [24, 43, 69, 86]. However, the development of EF during the first and second years of life remains underexplored (see, e.g. Miller & Marcovitch [61]). At these ages, infants' action with materiality occupies a major place. Therefore, we consider it necessary to conduct a critical review on the study of EF, paying special attention to the role of objects in research during the early ages.

I. Moreno-Llanos (✉) · J. Barreto
Universidad Autónoma de Madrid, Madrid, Spain
e-mail: ivan.moreno@uam.es

J. Barreto
Universidad Libre, Cali, Colombia

C. Rodriguez Garrido et al. (eds.), *The Social Life of Objects in Early Development*, Social Interaction in Learning and Development,
https://doi.org/10.1007/978-3-031-87673-8_8

8.1 The Executive Functions

The interest in the ability to control our behavior has been and remains a major focus of psychology since the mid-nineteenth century [41, 76]. In 1848, J. M. Harlow published the famous case of Phineas Gage, a construction worker who had his left frontal lobe pierced by an iron bar. Consequently, he became a person lacking direction and inhibition, unable to start, maintain, or adjust his action toward concrete goals [2]. This case sparked interest in understanding the frontal lobes' functions in controlling behavior.

Alexander R. Luria was a pioneer in studying the effects of frontal lobe damage in soldiers shot during World War II (1948/1963), and in people with acquired brain disorders ([55]; Luria, 1996, cited in [2]). Luria proposed that the frontal lobes comprise the system in charge of synthesizing perceived information and programming, controlling, and verifying goal-directed behavior. Because of this, Luria is considered the father of *Executive Functions* (EF), although he never used this term. A few years later, Muriel Lezak would define "Executive Functions" as "those mental capacities necessary for formulating goals, planning how to achieve them, and carrying out action plans effectively" [52, p. 281]. If Luria is the father of EF, we could consider Lezak to be their mother.

Although Luria began his studies on self-regulation processes in the field of neuropsychology and clinical psychology, on patients with brain damage, he was also a developmental psychologist who collaborated with, and continued the work of Lev S. Vygotski. As such, he was also interested in the early manifestations of self-regulation in children.

Vygotski and, later Luria developed a sociocultural approach to the so-called "higher psychological functions", including self-regulation, or the contemporary EF [82, 83]. Vygotski proposed the division between (i) "lower" biological psychological functions, such as perception or movement, and (ii) "higher" psychological functions, which develop in social interaction with other people, and are mediated through cultural semiotic (sign) systems, such as voluntary attention, logical memory, concept formation, and even self-regulation. He considers these functions as emergent, learnt, cognitive processes that arise from the integration and organization of other "fundamental" neural functions and networks (Luria, 1962/1980, cited in Mikadze et al., [59, 82], for a similar proposal, see [1]). These "higher" functions first occur at the "interpersonal" level, between people. Later, the function is reconstructed internally at the "intrapersonal" level. That is, it becomes self-oriented to control one's action [83]. In Luria's words: "what the child does today with help, he will tomorrow be able to do on his own" [54, p. 349].

However, Vygotski and Luria focused exclusively on language as the semiotic instrument of self-regulation. They did not study how other semiotic systems, prior to language, can fulfill these functions. In Chap. 10 of this volume, we will discuss how gestures and uses of objects also fulfill semiotic mediation and self-regulatory functions, long before the development of language.

Luria, in particular, studied how, from the age of 12 months, the language that adults address to children acquires the function of external regulation or hetero-regulation, and those children will later address themselves to self-regulate (see Luria [54]). The "deictic" function of language, or when the adult's words fulfill the function of indicating concrete objects to guide the child's action, is consolidated at 2 years of age. Previously, Luria says, children show significant difficulties in distinguishing which concrete object the adult is referring to. For example, they tend to reach for more attractive and distracting objects, or persist in reaching the same initial object, despite changes in instructions.

The development of comprehension of more complex instructions, which require the organization of action before its execution, occupies the third and part of the fourth year of life. For example, in the conditional instruction "When the light flashes, you will press the ball (rubber bulb)" (p. 346), children up to 2 years of age are not able to synthesize the different elements of the instruction. They tend to execute the response, "press the ball", as soon as they hear it. At 2:8–2:10, they begin to organize their action according to the instructions. However, they will tend to press the ball repetitively regardless of whether the light is on or off.

On the other hand, the use of self-directed language with self-regulatory function follows a similar development. At 2–2:6 years, faced with the condition "When the light comes on, press the ball," the experimenter instructs the child to say "Press!" when the light comes on. The child can say the word correctly each time the light comes on, but will not press the ball. By the age of 3, the child begins to coordinate self-instructions with the execution of the necessary motor response (Tikhomirov, 1958, cited in Luria [54]), but the *inhibitory* function of language is not sufficiently developed. Faced with the more complex condition "press in front of the red light, and do not press in front of the blue light", the experimenter instructs the child to say "Press!" in front of the red light, and "Do not press!" in front of the blue light. At 3–3:6 years, the child can say each word when appropriate. However, he/she presses the ball in front of both signals. The child's language will reach this level of inhibition through speech at 4–4:6 years.

Therefore, the epistemology developed by Vygotski and Luria adopts a developmental perspective, based on the analysis of the child's action. Their methodological position is based on the fact that tasks should offer the subject the ability to act freely to face difficulties that hinder his/her action, instead of being rigidly controlled by the experimenter. They seek to explain how cognitive processes develop through the detailed analysis of children's actions [20]. As we have shown, Luria analyzed not only children's successes but also their mistakes. He was concerned with identifying and describing children's concrete actions: what they do, how they do it, what they do it for, and what they achieve at each moment of development.

This methodology, which combines quantitative as well as qualitative aspects, contrasted with the dominant mechanistic view of the time, has continued to the present day. In his text, *The History of the Development of Higher Mental Functions*, Vygotski [82] announced his concern about this growing mechanicism in psychology, the segmentation and atomization of the subject's intentionality into a set of isolated elementary functions, biologically located in specific brain networks (see also Martin & Failows [57]). Luria, as his follower, highlighted the excessive use of tasks as the explanatory method. From his perspective, tasks, or the scores obtained on them, should not encompass the entire explanation of the subject's psychological functioning. Instead, task should be considered as an instrument to be able to explain the behavior, the cognitive functions, and the fundamental components of these functions [61]:

> I am inclined to strongly reject an approach in which *these auxiliary aids become the central method* and in which their role as servant to clinical thought is reversed so that *clinical reasoning follows instrumental data* as a slave follows its master. (Cole et al., 2006, p. 177, cited in [61, p. 3], emphasis added)

Lezak, as a clinical neuropsychologist, also addressed the epistemological trap in which the examiner finds themselves when using only standardized and highly structured tasks that presents an external objective to an intentional subject:

> [B]y its very nature the examination places the subject *within a structured situation* in which *the examiner dictates what the subject is to do, with what, and when.* ... Unless the patient demonstrates frank cognitive defects, *even the examiner who pays attention to the qualitative aspects of the patient's test performance may be as ignorant about the patient's capacity to take care of himself and be productive in the real world* at the end of a formal examination as he was at its beginning. ... Those who do not observe the patient *in situations in which he must act on his own behalf* may not be aware that something is missing from the patient's behavioral repertoire. ([52, pp. 283–284], emphasis added)

In this regard, Vygotski, Luria, and Lezak advocated in favor of a rigorous observation of the subject's activity, not only through tasks but also in everyday situations, in order to understand their psychological functioning. From this perspective, the goal, or the objective towards which the subject orients his behavior to, occupies a relevant place.

Despite the epistemological and methodological basis developed by Vygotski and Luria, the evolutionary perspectives based on the observation and explanation of the subject's behavior in meaningful situations have been relegated to the background (see Chaps. 9–11, this volume). Instead, the cognitivist and mechanistic positions they warned about, based on the identification and study of discrete "fundamental" cognitive processes, closely linked to biological and neuropsychological aspects, which are studied independently, have dominated in psychology.

8.2 The Executive Functions Today

The current dominant conception of EF arises from these perspectives. They consider that the intentional and voluntary control of behavior takes place from the coordination of a set of independent cognitive processes. EF are characterized as (i) "higher order" processes, which exert their influence on other "lower" cognitive processes, and (ii) as a general-domain, content-free, independent of the specific situation faced by the subject. EF, therefore, are considered intrinsic and universal cognitive processes of the human being, localized in discrete neural networks (see, e.g.Fiske & Holmboe [37]), independent of the culture in which they develop, of learning, and social interaction. Recently, however, this approach has received numerous theoretical as well as methodological criticisms, which we will expose in parallel throughout the following sections due to the close relationship between the two (in Chap. 9, this volume, Rodríguez, Moreno-Llanos and Guevara will defend the need for a paradigm shift in the study of EF).

Research on EF from a cognitivist perspective has been linked to the specific tasks used to study them. EF, as control processes, are not self-evident. That is, they cannot be observed and assessed directly [19, 52]. Instead, it is necessary to employ indirect measures. The most common way to study them has been through the development of standardized tasks that, theoretically, demand the subject's EF for accurate performance. For example, by imposing specific goals and constraints, adding difficulties and additional demands on familiar behaviors, or generating conflicts between a number of possible responses. The goal of this type of tasks is for the subject to intentionally control his or her actions according to the task demands.

However, the definition and conceptualization of the different processes that constitute EF have been imprecise [30]. Generally, it has been based on the description of specific behaviors that, subsequently, have been used to develop equally particular tasks, according to researchers' previous definitions and assumptions [3]. This has entailed a proliferation of conceptualizations of different executive processes, as well as tasks to assess them. Packwood et al. [68], in a review of the different definitions commonly mentioned in research to date, developed an index of 18 components of EF. To these, they add another 18 components that are mentioned only once. For example, they find the definitions of skills such as goal setting, strategy generation, inhibition, etc.

Furthermore, the intimate connection between control processes and controlled processes has given rise to a constraint known as the "task purity problem" [64, p. 52]. According to this limitation, to solve a particular task the subject requires a range of executive and non-executive processes. Therefore, it is not possible to extract a "pure" measure of the target EF from a single task, as these other processes may influence the subject's performance. Consequently, researchers tend to design unfamiliar and perception-based tasks, centered on the physical characteristics of objects. This includes tasks that involve sensory perception, with an emphasis on visual processing, such as recognizing dimensions like color, shape, and size. Researchers hypothesize that this kind of simplification of the tasks and the subject's action, separating them from everyday situations and social and cultural influences, will lead to more 'pure' measures of EF [38].

On the other hand, Miyake et al. [64] proposed using *Latent Factor Analysis.* This statistical methodology consists of analyzing a set of tasks for 'commonalities'. This approach enables researchers to categorize the diverse tasks by underlying psychological factors and obtain more 'pure' measures. In their study, they identified three discrete factors, which they designated as follows:

- *Inhibition or Inhibitory Control*. The ability to stop preponderant or automatic responses.
- *Alternation or Flexibility*. The ability to change the focus of attention, to switch between different tasks or registers, or to switch between different possible responses.
- *Maintain and Update* (although now commonly referred to as *Working Memory*). The ability to hold, update, and manipulate information in mind.

Although these factors are sufficiently dissociable, they also exhibit moderate correlations with one another. This led the authors to consider that EF share common elements and that they are not truly and totally independent. This has given rise to the contemporary conception of the *Unity and Diversity of Executive Functions*. This conception and methodology have become the current dominant perspective. The three factors of inhibition, flexibility, and updating have been considered the fundamental elements of EF, and have guided research in various fields of knowledge. In cognitivist psychology, through the study of cognitive control factors (e.g. Miyake et al. [64]). In neuropsychology, research of each function's neuroanatomical correlate has been a prominent area of investigation (e.g. Banich & Depue [5]; Bissonette & Roesch [10]). And even in developmental psychology, through the identification and development of identified factors (e.g. Brydges et al. [12]; Wiebe et al. [84]).

Nevertheless, this emphasis on identifying and examining 'pure factors', eliminating social and cultural influences from tasks, has led to the notion that EF are 'independent' of such influences. Instead, they are considered 'universal' to human behavior, as *top-down* control resources that apply equally in all situations faced by the subject, both in daily life and in the laboratory. These assumptions are contrary to the principles of evolutionary epistemology and to the foundations of the sociocultural psychology of Vygotski and Luria, as previously discussed. Conversely, an increasing number of researchers and theorists are calling for recognition of the influence of Western cognitivist psychology on these assumptions, methodologies, and interpretations, and the limitations they present. We will examine some of these issues below.

Starting from the beginning, in their seminal work on the *Unity and Diversity of Executive Functions*, Miyake et al. [64] were extremely cautious in interpreting the results obtained through latent factor analysis:

> In this article, we have taken a rather pragmatic approach, *focusing on three of the most frequently postulated functions in the literature*... Despite this success, *we are not claiming that the three investigated executive functions are the only executive functions, nor would we suggest that they are anything like the fundamental units or primitives of cognition*. Our exploration of the diversity of executive functions is only a first step, and there are a number of important issues that need to be addressed in future research... First, although our choice of the three target functions in this study seemed a reasonable one, *it is certainly not exhaustive and there are other important relatively basic functions that need to be added to the current list*... Second, the relationship between these relatively basic executive functions and more complex concepts like "planning" needs to be examined... Finally, although the current level of analysis might be the most useful at this moment, *it is also possible that*

> *the target functions we considered here can be decomposed into more basic component processes.* (pp. 89–90, emphasis added)

As they themselves indicate, the selection of functions and tasks to be studied was based on pragmatic considerations. It is important to consider the limitations that this approach generates. The objective of their research was to evaluate the suitability of latent factor analysis as a useful methodology for the study of EF. The selection of inhibition, flexibility, and maintenance/update was made because they were the most studied and represented functions in the literature. Miyake et al. [64], see also Doebel [31] highlight the necessity for further research in three key areas: (1) identify which are the elementary or basic functions of cognitive control, as their approach was not exhaustive, (2) study the relationship and dynamics between the different functions, and (3) study whether the proposed EF can be decomposed into simpler elements (see also Karr et al. [49]). These ideas align with Luria's proposal, which advocates studying the set of basic components that, in their interaction, give rise to higher psychological functions (see Mikadze et al. [59]).

However, at some point in the research on EF, these concerns have disappeared. Instead, inhibition, alternation, and maintenance/update have been elevated to the status of 'nuclear' or 'foundational' EF, considered universal and, according to some researchers, necessarily biological. On the other hand, other EF, such as goal setting and planning, have been considered 'higher order' EF that would develop later as a consequence of the interaction between the 'nuclear' EF [26].

The question of where EF are located in the brain has become a prominent topic in both cognitivist and developmental psychology. This has even resulted in studies attempting to elucidate the relationship between EF and genetics. EF are considered to be 'highly heritable' psychological traits [39]. Although the genetic explanation of EF is beyond the scope of this chapter, it could be argued that such studies show some limitations. First, they do not recognize the importance of macro-social and macro-cultural aspects underlying the social environment in which subjects of the same group develop, and which they necessarily share (language, values or norms, etc., see Doebel [31]; Gaskins & Alcalá [40]; Kotik-Friedgut & Ardila [51]). Instead, they diminish the significance of environmental variability to 'shared' or 'unshared situations', as if these were factors completely independent of the broader social and cultural framework in which children develop. Second, they fail to recognize or take into account the epigenetic interaction between genes and the environment. Biology recognizes that genes, by themselves, determine little or nothing. Instead, they necessarily require their expression in an environment that, in turn, determines how they will be expressed, forming a complex interaction that will result in the observed phenotype (see, for example, Lickliter & Moore [53]).

Therefore, although the task-based methodological approach to EF and latent factor analysis seeks to give more objectivity to EF-related concepts, the interpretations of these results are not unburdened by the theoretical assumptions and prior social and cultural values of the researchers.

8.3 Current Criticisms of the Study of Executive Functions

At present, some authors have revived the criticisms that Vygotski, Luria, and Lezak once directed at standardized tasks. The utilization of standardized tasks has resulted in the fragmentation of intentionality into discrete factors, simplifying and reducing reality into perceptual dimensions, in which socio-cultural aspects are overlooked. It is typical for tasks to require the subject to react to each item following the instructions of the experimenter, effectively reducing the subject's actions to a "stimulus–response mapping" [4, p. 242]. This focus on perception implies abandoning the intention of a subject in setting meaningful goals and organizing their action to achieve them. Consequently, the primary function of executive functioning, the capacity to establish and pursue meaningful goals, has disappeared from the focus of research. Furthermore, the everyday situations in which EF develop are ignored. The development of EF in children is mainly explained by what tasks they can solve (see, for example Carlson [14]), rather than how they find solutions or organize their action in the face of difficulties they encounter in their everyday activities (see, for example, Barker & Munakata [6]; Barker et al. [7]).

Some authors who are even more critical point out that the tasks, as well as the neuroanatomical correlates identified from them, are used as necessary and sufficient evidence that the proposed concepts constitute clearly differentiated functions [30, 68]. However, such interpretations fail to acknowledge the significance of highly sign-mediated social and cultural learning in solving the tasks. As an example, the 'Day and Night' task, in which the child must say 'night' when presented with a card representing a sun, and 'day' when presented with a moon, requires a level of symbolic and fictional, 'pretend' skill development that is not obvious or immediate to children. In contrast, the younger the child, the more important is the social convention he or she is learning, in which the sun is related to the word 'day' and the moon to the word 'night'. Saying the opposite is a more complicated skill, which cannot be explained solely based on a 'universal' factor, independent of the language and symbolic skills the child has developed.

Other critical authors have also identified significant limitations associated with the analysis of latent factors (see Doebel [31] and Martin & Failows [57]). Differences in the age of the groups studied, the number and diversity of tasks proposed, or the interpretation of the factors obtained make it difficult to compare studies and results. This is especially relevant during early development (0–6 years). At these ages, the tasks used tend to show floor and ceiling effects. Tasks must be adjusted to the level of motor, social, and linguistic development of the children [44]. Thus, tasks that may be challenging for a 3-year-old are typically no longer difficult for a 6-year-old. This results in a rather narrow age range for the application of the tasks. Therefore, different tasks are used for different ages (as we will see below). Secondly, research on the development of EF through latent factor analysis often underrepresents certain components of EF. It is common for these studies to use several tests of *inhibition*, but only a single test of *flexibility* (see, for example, Wiebe et al. [84]).

These critical authors further suggest that latent factor analysis may be revealing common aspects of task demands or the responses required to solve them, rather than the underlying structure of EF [31, 49]. Instead, they propose to conceive of EF as the ability to activate and use task-relevant information, which is semiotically mediated by social and cultural factors. To illustrate, the utilization of motor skills together with social values and rules, mnemonic (memory) forms, or other semiotic instruments that children employ to regulate their behavior.

Finally, it is notable that the majority of studies in the field of executive functions have been based on the seminal work of Miyake et al. [64]. However, the proposition that EF are 'universal' and 'content-free' processes does not recognize the influence that Western socio-cultural elements have had on their conception. The most commonly used tasks have been designed in WEIRD contexts (from 'Western', 'Educated', 'Industrialized', 'Rich', and 'Democratic' populations). In these cultures, the values that are often promoted are related to individual success, obedience to the adult, competitiveness, or speed of response, to name a few.

Using these tasks in culturally different contexts gives rise to deficit-based interpretations compared to Western cultures. Gaskins and Alcalá [40], who studied EF in Yucatec Mayan children, observed that children respond very differently from their peers in Western cultures. First, they are uncomfortable with lengthy verbal instructions, as it is unusual for them to receive instructions from adults. Moreover, during some tasks, they tend to spend a lot of time solving them correctly without making mistakes. In others, they directly reject some premises, as they clash with their cultural values. For example, in *delayed gratification* tasks, they leave the room because they do not understand why they have to wait without doing anything. Their culture values the correct use of time to help the community.

Similarly, Delgado et al. [22] highlight the environmental differences faced by children from different socio-economic backgrounds, despite their similar understanding of the tasks in question. Children from high socio-economic backgrounds tend to score better on a *gambling* task. In contrast, children who have developed in disadvantaged contexts tend to direct their behavior towards immediate rewards, choosing the riskier option and consequently losing more rewards in the long run. Delgado et al. propose that these differences are due to context. They consider it possible that children from disadvantaged backgrounds have learned to make quick decisions, due to the unpredictability and scarcity of resources they face in their daily lives.

Such studies undermine assumptions that EF are 'universal' and 'culture-free' processes. It also reminds us that macro data, such as quantitative analysis of tasks, is insufficient to explain individual behavior and development. We believe that EF should be situated within an evolutionary perspective, incorporating approaches to their origin and early development.

Nevertheless, despite the limitations associated with using standardized tasks, we cannot reject the considerable advancements made in this field. Conversely, it is essential to comprehend the characteristics and limitations of these tasks in order to ascertain the necessity for change and to define long-term research objectives. In the following sections of this chapter, we will delve into a topic that, to our knowledge, has not been part of the EF review: what is the role of objects in tasks?

8.4 In Search of the Grail: Early EF Tasks

It is common for the study of early EF development to be carried out with children from 2–3 years of age. As we have shown in the previous pages, standardized tasks usually present external, highly structured objectives that require verbal instructions from the experimenter. As such, tasks with infants before the age of 2 are less frequent [44, 63].

In contrast, at these ages, action is essential for the infant's development [69]. From their transformative action with objects, infants construct their knowledge and understanding of the world. And, in particular, for the development of EF [65, 72]. Therefore, from the thesis of the Pragmatics of the Object, we consider it crucial to perform an analysis of the role of objects, and of materiality in general, in the tasks most used in research on the early development of EF. Particularly between 6 and 36 months of life, when children are still developing their understanding of spoken language.

This work is part of an ongoing systematic review of standardized tasks used with children up to 3 years of age. We conducted a search in PsycARTICLES that included the following search terms, according to the controlled vocabulary MeSH (Medical Subject Headings):

- Executive function: executive function* OR Function, Executive OR Executive OR Executive Control* OR "Effortful Control" OR "Inhibition" OR "Flexibility" OR "Shifting" OR "Switching" OR "Working Memory" OR "Updating".
- Children: Infant OR Psychology, Child OR Child Development OR Child, Preschool.
- Tasks: Neuropsychological Tests OR Behavioral Assessment of Dysexecutive Function OR "Task" OR "Evaluation" OR "Task" OR "Evaluation".

This search yielded a total of 9782 articles. After filtering by defining specific ages ("preschool": 2–5 years, and "infancy": 2–23 months), and eliminating repeated results, we obtained a base of 443 articles. We then reviewed the abstracts of the articles to select those that would form part of the final sample, based on the following criteria. (1) The study must include at least one task to assess EF, explicitly stating the objectives, instructions, objects used (if any), and responses to be made by the children. (2) These tasks should include at least one typically developing group, no older than 36 months. In the case of presenting tasks for several age groups, we only took into account for this review those tasks that have a sample of typically developing children under 36 months of age. The results we present correspond to the tasks used in 55 articles.

In the following sections, we will analyze the role of objects in solving these tasks. We will briefly indicate what the objectives of the tasks are and what the expected responses of the children are. For this purpose, we group the tasks according to three general dimensions, depending on the status of the objects and the proposed objectives:

- The physical dimension: objects are considered by their status as a physical and attractive material for children, existing in a space.
- The perceptual dimension: objects are considered in terms of a set of perceptual characteristics, the most frequent being shape, color, and size.
- The practical dimension: objects are considered in terms of what can be done with them.

It is striking that, from 6 to 22–24 months of age, the task most used to assess EF in infants is the A-not-B error [24, 69]. This task occupies a predominant place, because it does not require verbal instructions, and the response required from the infant is quite simple: to reach for a hidden object. From 22–24 months, a select group of tasks based on the perceptual aspects of objects begins to appear. Materiality seems to occupy, mainly, a role based on its physical and perceptual aspects. Up to this point, objects are defined as a set of discrete perceptual dimensions that are used to guide the subject's action. Therefore, they are interchangeable [71]. The object and its function, its pragmatic value, are irrelevant. What is important is its shape, its color, or its size.

Only timidly have some researchers tried to present objects according to practical objectives, based on what children do with them instead of reacting to their physical characteristics. This is a novelty concerning previous standardized tasks, since they take into account, to some extent, the functional aspects of the objects, about concrete and meaningful objectives for the children.

At 36 months of age, we have observed an explosion in the variety of tasks. Although these ages are not part of our objective in this chapter, it is worth noting that, with the effective development of language and symbolic representation, the design of standardized tasks reaches its maximum expression, when children begin to understand more arbitrary objectives.

In the following, we will present the most common tasks according to the physical, perceptual, and practical dimensions of the objects.

8.4.1 Tasks Dealing with the Physical Dimension of Objects

In this first block of tasks, objects are considered in their most general and, we could say, "coldest" dimension. Objects are considered "physical entities", starting from their existence as physical materiality and their location in space. The object "is" a thing or "occupies a space", and is considered "intrinsically attractive" for children. That is, the child tends to the object, and, therefore, will seek to reach it or get it. In the classification of objects, we can find two opposite poles:

- The object as an "end". In these tasks, the child must reach or get an attractive object. However, the object or objects are hidden. The child must regulate their actions in order to get them.
- The object as "temptation". In these tasks, in contrast, the object is immediately available. However, the child must inhibit this temptation and, instead, wait for the experimenter to give permission.

We will discuss some of the tasks in detail below.

8.4.1.1 *The Object as an "End": Tasks in Which the Child Must Find Hidden Objects*

In object finding tasks we have identified two paradigms. Despite their apparent differences, they exhibit notable similarities. The objective of both A-not-B error-based tasks and self-ordered pointing tasks is to locate hidden objects. The chosen object or objects are considered intrinsically attractive to the child. In the A-not-B paradigm, the child must find a single object that is hidden by the experimenter in different places. On the other hand, in the Self-ordered Pointing tasks, the child has to find all the hidden objects, searching only once in all locations.

A-Not-B Error Tasks

Among the tasks for infants of early ages, i.e., under 12 months, the A-not-B Error task is perhaps the most common. It has been used with infants as young as 6 months. This task, which is inspired by the situation originally designed by Piaget [69], is widely taken up in its structure, demands, and difficulties, not only in research focused on EF, but also from different theoretical perspectives interested in the cognitive development of children before language (e.g., from dynamic systems, Sánchez et al., [87]).

The original study proposed by Piaget [69], considers the construction of object permanence. That is, how infants progressively understand that the object exists beyond their perception and action. Piaget rigorously monitors the infants' actions with objects during sensorimotor development. Through his meticulous observations, he explains the gradual development and construction of object permanence. However, as we will see later, in the versions of the task included in research on EF at early ages, infants' action is reduced to "finding the thing", an object that is also often interpreted as a reward.

In this way, we could consider that the interaction of the infant with the object is not taken into account. Rather, it is a question of how many times the infant searches for the object in the right or wrong place, focusing mainly on the mistakes the child makes [74].

The general objective of the A-not-B tasks is to find an object hidden in different places as many times as possible. Among the objects we observe, for example, toys, stickers, and even (although in decline, perhaps due to a greater concern for healthy eating) snacks or candies. Concerning the objects in which to hide the reward, it is common to use different formats and numbers of containers. The classic format uses two or three.

Various authors have suggested that the A-not-B error task satisfies the criteria necessary for studying or evaluating EF in infants [24, 29, 35, 56]. Generally, the task is structured as follows:

- First, an object attractive to the infant is hidden in a location A, next to another location B (and even C, D, etc., depending on the number of different locations presented by each variant of the task), and the infant is left to search. Here, the object also functions as a "reward". It is usual that, between approximately 6 and 12 months, the infant searches correctly in the first location A.
- After a number of repetitions, determined by the researchers (e.g., after a number of correct searches [29, 35]; or following a previously established protocol [23]), the object is hidden in location B (or C, D, etc.). It is usual that, at first, infants continue to search for the object in A. Between 12 and 18 months, children begin to be able to inhibit searching in A in favor of searching in B when they see the displacement. It is considered that for the infant to succeed in finding the object in B, they must maintain the representation and mentally update its new location. Consequently, the task enables the examination of working memory. In addition, children must inhibit the search in A and be flexible to search for the object in the new location. Between 18 and 24 months, they will be able to search in B, even if they have not seen the displacement.

Some variations of the task impose additional demands, such as including time delays between hiding the object and letting the infant search for it [27, 35]. Short delays seem to help infants inhibit the impulse to search for the object where it was found the first few times. In contrast, long delays seem to cause infants to be unable to maintain and update where the object is located, leading them to respond by chance. Other authors place additional demands on infants' working memory by hiding objects behind a screen or under a cloth [16, 24] so that they do not use their body orientation or gaze as a bias in their search.

Another task, which follows a similar pattern to the A-not-B task, uses an apparatus with drawers of varying colors [42] or marked with different symbols [16]. These, in turn, are usually covered by rags or screens, which the infant has to lift before reaching the hidden object [24, 28, 29].

Self-Ordered Pointing Tasks

The general objective of these tasks is to select each item from a set or collection only once. We have identified two main options depending on age. (1) From 14 months, the infant must find hidden objects in several different possible locations. (2) From 36 months onwards, the child must point to each picture in a set only once. Because the second option is designed for children 36 months and older, we will describe the task for children 14 months and older.

Similar to the A-not-B tasks, in self-ordered pointing tasks we differentiate between (a) objects "rewards" and (b) objects as places where these rewards are hidden. Most frequently, a collection of stickers is hidden in clearly distinguishable containers, such as boxes of different shapes or colors [29, 46, 47]. The infant must find as many stickers with as few attempts as possible. To do so, they must maintain and update their mental representation to remember where they have already searched and inhibit searching in those locations again. For infants between 14 and 15 months, the locations where objects are hidden are fixed [23, 29]. In contrast, for children aged 24 months and older, containers are covered and mixed using a rotary table [9, 11, 46, 47]. This version places additional demands on working memory.

8.4.1.2 *The Object as "Temptation"*

At the opposite pole to the object "as an end", we find a set of tasks where the object is "forbidden". These are commonly referred to as *Delay of Gratification* tasks and are characterized by being one of the most recognizable and extensive groups in the study of *inhibition.*

The most representative task of this type is the well-known *Marshmallow test*, designed by Walter Mischel in the 1970s [59, 60]. This task consists of offering the child a marshmallow. The experimenter tells the child that they will leave the room for a moment to look for something, and proposes the following: the child can (a) eat the marshmallow they have, or (b) wait for the experimenter to return and receive an additional marshmallow. Since then, a myriad of similar tasks have been proposed based on the same premise: wait and do not touch the "forbidden" object. In these tasks, the child must inhibit the temptation or impulse to touch the object, the "immediate reward", in favor of a greater reward later. The objects can be various: marshmallows, candies, stickers, etc.

In the different variations of this task, designed for children from 14 months of age, there are two distinct blocks:

Delay tasks. The child must wait for a set amount of time to access the object (see, for example, Carlson et al. [15]; Devine et al. [23]; Gottwald et al. [42]). Some variations of this task include additional demands, such as the experimenter making noise wrapping a gift, while the child must inhibit their impulse to look (*Gift task* [50]).

Choice tasks. The child must decide between (a) immediately taking a smaller number of "rewards" (e.g., a single candy or sticker) or (b) saving a larger amount of "rewards" (e.g., two/three/four/etc. candies or stickers) "for later," which means saving them until the end of the session [9, 45]. A very interesting variant of the choice task consists of having the child choose the rewards but for a third subject (e.g., for the experimenter [70]). Children tend to choose the greater long-term reward for the third subject, suggesting that the child's emotional involvement is less when choosing for someone else.

Similar to the A-not-B error tasks, the objects in the Delayed Gratification tasks are characterized by their physical dimension. They are, again, "attractive physical entities" for children, easily interchangeable, and do not offer conceptual or practical difficulties [19]. On the other hand, the correct response in this type of task is considered to be to resist temptation now in order to receive more later. In this sense, it could be argued that the correct choice, in addition to being arbitrary, is culturally mediated. In Western cultures, it is highly valued that children can resist this type of temptation. However, how they do it and for what purpose (understood in their everyday situations, beyond "receiving more of that temptation in a laboratory task") has received considerably less attention in developmental psychology. In addition, other cultures or specific developmental situations influence this ability (see Delgado et al. [22]; Gaskins & Alcalá [40]; Kotik-Friedgut & Ardila [51]).

8.4.1.3 *The Physical Dimension of Objects. Some Conclusions*

In this type of task, as we have shown, objects are defined by their "physical" dimension. That is, by the location they occupy in space and as "intrinsically attractive" to children. In this sense, they are reduced to the two poles we discussed at the beginning of the section. They are "things to find" or "things not to touch" without permission. These tasks, therefore, eliminate any hint of the practical or social value of the objects.

8.4.2 Tasks Dealing with the Perceptual Dimension of Objects. Objects as a Set of Discrete Features

In this section, we will present tasks that consider objects from their perceptual characteristics, especially those related to vision, such as color, shape, and size. The general goal of this type of tasks is to organize the action according to the perceptual dimensions of the objects shown. For example, (i) to classify or organize objects based on conflicting dimensions, such as color or shape, (ii) to inhibit responding according to a preponderant dimension in favor of a less usual dimension, (iii) to discriminate between different dimensions, and (iv) to recall and/or replicate the perceptual pattern. We present the tasks in more detail below.

8.4.2.1 *Classification Tasks by Dimensions*

Classification tasks have been part of the study of EF almost since their conception. The first tasks developed on perceptual feature classification date back to the mid-twentieth century [33]. The most representative task of this group, the *Wisconsin Card Sorting Task*, officially appears in the study of Grant and Berg (1948, cited in [33]). In this task, subjects must arrange a series of cards showing several shapes (forms) such as stars, crosses, triangles, and circles. These shapes can be presented in different colors, such as red, yellow, green, or blue. The subject must infer the classification rule according to the feedback received after each response (hit/miss). Patients with frontal lobe brain damage have serious difficulties in adjusting their behavior flexibly when changing the classification dimension.

The classic task for this group is known as the *Dimensional Change Card Sort* (DCCS) [88]). In this task, the relevant dimensions are reduced to two: shape

Table 8.1 The traditional version of DCCS: example of the pre-change organization (color)

Target card	(Rabbit) **Red**	(Boat) **Blue**
Correct answers	(Rabbit) **Red** (Boat) **Red**	(Rabbit) **Blue** (Boat) **Blue**

In bold: relevant dimension
In brackets: non-relevant dimension

Table 8.2 The traditional version of DCCS: example of the post-change organization (shape)

Target card	**Rabbit** (Red)	**Boat** (Blue)
Correct answers	**Rabbit** (Red) **Rabbit** (Blue)	**Boat** (Blue) **Boat** (Red)

In bold: relevant dimension
In brackets: NON-relevant dimension

(rabbit/boat) and color (blue/red). The task is organized into two moments. First, in a pre-change or learning moment, children must organize the cards into two blocks (represented by two model cards), for example, according to their color (see Table 8.1).

This first moment has the objective of creating a preponderant response in the child. Next, the child is told that the cards should now be grouped according to a second dimension (post-change). Following the previous example, by shape (see Table 8.2).

These types of tasks have been simplified for children from 24 to 27 months of age. For example, by separating the dimensions [9]. In these tasks, the color is presented as the background of the card, while the figure is presented in black (see Table 8.3). For example, a black truck on a red background, or a black car on a blue background. It is considered that children have less difficulty organizing the cards when the dimensions are clearly differentiated.

Other variations add "hot" or motivational features. For example, instead of cars or animals, the cards show two American snacks, "Goldfish" (shaped like a fish) and "Teddy Graham" (shaped like a bear). They were then asked to put them into buckets according to a label or card representing them. The experimenters instructed the children that if they did the task well, they could take the snacks home [9]. These objects are considered to pose more difficulties for children.

Table 8.3. Example of dimension separation for the DCCS task

Truck	**Car**
Truck	**Car**

Another variant of this type of task is based on the active identification by the child of the dimensions in which a set of images is equal [48]. In this task, the child is presented with blocks of three images, presenting objects (telephones, socks, or fish), in four dimensions (shape, color, size, number). The child must select, in the same set, two cards that are alike in one dimension, the greatest number of times. For example: two objects are socks, two are red, and two are big.

Some tasks, instead of presenting cards, present physical objects, such as blocks of two sizes (big/small) and two cubes (big cube, small cube). At first, the child must place the blocks in the corresponding cube according to their size, with larger blocks placed in the larger cube and smaller blocks placed in the smaller cube. In the second step, they should put them in the opposite cube [16]. In a similar case, the child is asked to put away large ("mommies") or small ("babies") animal figures [9].

For infants aged 14 months and older, we have identified a single task that resembles the classification tasks. In this task, the experimenter shows the infant that, when a red ball is put through the hole of the corresponding color, a music box sounds. The experimenter then offers the red balls to the child. In a second moment, the experimenter demonstrates the same with the green balls in the green hole [23]. In this task, therefore, color congruency is maintained, but the lengthy verbal instructions necessary to understand conventional sorting tasks are also eliminated.

8.4.2.2 *Preponderant Dimension Inhibition Tasks: Stroop Tasks*

Stroop tasks are named after J. R. Stroop [80], who studied interference effects on attention. These tasks are designed to suppress dominant responses in favor of non-habitual responses. The classic version of the task consists of presenting subjects with a series of colored words (such as "red", "blue", "green"), printed in a color different from the one they indicate. For instance, the word "red" is written in blue letters. The subject must say as quickly as possible the color in which the words are printed, inhibiting reading the word. The essence of this task lies in the challenge presented by requiring a response that opposes the subject´s typical reactions -indicating the color of the word, instead of simply reading the word- thereby increasing the demands for cognitive inhibition.

This task has been adapted for children aged 24 months and older, utilizing images representing everyday items. For example, when presented with large objects, children should say that they belong to "the baby," while small objects belong to "the mommy" [46, 47], say that the image of the sun is "night," while the image of the moon is "day" [13, 17, 21], that the green card is "snow," while the white card is "grass" [13, 17], that the image of the boy is "girl," while the girl is "boy" [62], or that the dog goes "meow," while the cat goes "woof" [85]. In these types of tasks, therefore, children need to use oral language to provide appropriate responses.

As previously noted, Stroop tasks require individuals to respond to situations by inhibiting automatic responses. In the case of the tasks adapted for children, we observe that they require them to "inhibit" everyday situations. This means that children must "lie" regarding what they know about the names, correspondences, or sounds of everyday elements. Therefore, the tasks may impose additional demands on children, who are still in the process of constructing an understanding of the world around them in infancy. Consequently, unlike adults, they do not have the same experience of social conventions and the arbitrariness of the dimensions involved in these task versions.

8.4.2.3 *Discrimination Tasks Between Dimensions: Go/No-Go*

In Go-no-Go tasks, children must discriminate between items that require giving a response ("Go") and those that require inhibinting a response ("No-Go"), according to the task criteria. These tasks are based on response schemes "If A → Go; If B → no-go." They draw inspiration from the traditional game of "Simon Says". In this game, one of the participants acts as "Simon," the game director, indicating different actions that the rest must follow. However, they must only act if the command begins with "Simon says…". For instance, "Simon says stand up" requires standing up ("Go"). On the other hand, "Stand up" requires players to *inhibit* their response ("No-Go"). Players who make an error are eliminated, and the last one standing is the winner. In this type of task, it is essential for children to stay attentive and avoid responding automatically.

In general, Go/no-Go tasks are used with children from 36 months onwards, as they require a good linguistic level to understand the verbal instructions of the task. However, there is a version for 32-month-olds called "Figure School" [34]. It consists of a storybook depicting a schoolyard where there are "characters" playing. The characters are shaped like geometric figures: squares and circles, with facial expressions (happy, sad) and colors (red squares and blue circles). The child is told that their names are their color. Subsequently, the characters appear in a line. The child must name each figure indicating its color. To do this, the following rules must be taken into account: Go: name the color of the happy figures, No-Go: inhibit naming the color of the sad figures.

The use of objects in Go/No-Go tasks has historically been limited. Since their inception, these have primarily been designed for implementation through computer programs (see, e.g. Miller et al. [62]; Wiebe et al. [84]). For example, the child should press the button only when the target animal appears, *inhibiting* responses to all other stimuli [62]. Conversely, in other variations, the child should press the button for all animals except the target [85]. Although the Figure School, a task for children aged 32 months and older, in its initial version involves a book in the application procedure, children do not have access to it or the opportunity to use it. In addition, the expected response from the children is verbal.

8.4.2.4 *Recall and Perceptual Pattern Replication Tasks: Working Memory*

Tasks that assess working memory have been part of psychological assessment since the first intelligence tests of the Binet-Simon scale [81] or the more recent *Wechsler Intelligence Scale for Children* (WISC-IV, see Baron [8]). The general objective of these tasks is to (a) maintain as much information as possible, or

(b) manipulate and update the information received to arrive at the correct answer. These classic tasks have been simplified for children, in which children must recall and repeat sequences of words or numbers (see Carlson et al. [17]; Miller et al. [60]; Willoughby et al. [85]). A less direct adaptation of tasks designed for adults is the Nebraska Farm task [84]. In this task, the child must remember the locations of various animals on a 3×3 grid. The sequences begin with 2 animals to locate, and the number of animals increases after every two successful attempts.

Although most of the tasks of this type are used with children at the upper end of the ages included in our analysis (36 months), there are versions for 24-month-old children, such as the *Truck Task* and the *Bead Task* [46, 47]. In the *Truck Task*, the child is required to remember the image of a truck and then, without seeing it again, select it from a set of cards with images of similar trucks. During a second moment of the task, the child must avoid selecting the initial image of the truck, and instead choose a different one. The *Bead Task* consists of two parts as well. First, the child must select the image that represents physical the beads previously presented to them by the experimenter. In a second moment, the child has to recreate, with physical beads, the pattern shown in an image.

In all these cases, the relevant information to solve the task consists of remembering and/or replicating the perceptual characteristics of the items presented. Objects such as animals, trucks, or colored beads are also reduced to the set of their perceptual dimensions of shape, color, or size, to the point of being replaced by images representing those objects.

8.4.2.5 *The Perceptual Dimension of Objects. Some Conclusions*

In this section, we have shown a set of tasks based on the perceptual criteria of materiality. The objectives of the tasks and the children's responses are subordinated to these dimensions, based on the introduction of arbitrary and external rules imposed by the researcher. Objects are defined by their shape (or, if we argue for a certain degree of conceptualization), color, or size. The objects themselves do not form a meaningful part of the task but act as stimuli to which the children have to react according to the experimenter's demands. They are not supported by meaningful relationships of everyday life or pragmatics.

8.4.3 The Practical Dimension of Objects. Material Objects with Which to Act and Achieve Concrete Objectives

In this final section, we will present tasks that involve using objects for practical objectives. Although these tasks may not be directly aligned with the Pragmatics of the Object because they do not emphasize objects as cultural materiality (see Chap. 2, this volume), they do recognize objects as materiality to provoke changes in the world or to achieve an efficacy goal. From a perspective rooted in the Pragmatics of the Object ([75], see also Chap. 2, this volume), objects are defined by their conventional and public functions. Consequently, they serve to do things. Doing things with objects implies higher levels of complexity compared to the tasks discussed in the previous two sections, where children must respond to physical or perceptual dimensions. Or, in the cases of *delayed gratification*, where children cannot exert any action on the objects. As we will see, appealing to practical characteristics indicates that objects are not so easily interchangeable. However, these types of tasks are the least frequent in our review. In the following, we will show three cases. First, the *Detour-reaching tasks*, in which children must *inhibit* reaching the object immediately and, instead, look for the right way to get it. Second, the *Grasping Task*, which examines how children use a spoon to eat. Finally, we will show a case of observing children's actions with a selection of objects.

8.4.3.1 *Detour-Reaching Task*

The goal of these tasks is to obtain an object-reward located inside a box. However, the child cannot immediately access or open this box. Instead, they must *inhibit* the immediate reaching impulse and "go around" to find a way to reach the object. We have identified two well-defined blocks of these tasks.

The first block is for infants between 6 and 12 months old and is similar to A-not-B tasks. Objects are defined by their mere physical dimension, as things "to reach". The child is presented with two objects: (i) a "reward" or attractive object, inside (ii) a box. The box has openings on two sides. In this case, the box can be (a) completely transparent or (b) completely opaque. The box is presented to the child with the front side always blocked. The child must *inhibit* the immediate reach and look for where they can access the object. The position of the open sides varies according to protocol [29].

In the second block, designed for children from 18 months old, we can observe the practical aspects of materiality in the study of the EF. The task becomes more complex and, we believe, more interesting. In this case, the box is completely closed. Its front side is transparent, while the rest of the box is opaque. Therefore, the child can see the "reward" inside. In addition, the box has additional mechanisms that the child must use to open it. These can be (a) *causal*, such as a lever to pull, or a knob to turn, or (b) *arbitrary*, such as a telephone that the child has to pick up. To get the object, the child must *inhibit* reaching directly and instead use such mechanisms.[1]

This task may involve additional requirements, coordinating different mechanisms in a sequence of steps. For instance, the child might need to (1) pick up the phone and then (2) pull the lever; or (1) remove a paper clip and then (2) pull the lever [58]. More complex rules can also be incorporated, such as differentiating the correct response from the color of a light: If a yellow light is illuminated, then the knob should be turned, if the light is green, the switch should be pressed [46]. This situation presents a conflict of responses. Children must be *flexible* to adjust their behavior based on the light cue.

[1] The experimenter opens the window via an electrical switch. Although the child's actions do nothing, the experimenters assume the child will believe it does.

The objects involved in the *Detour-reaching Tasks* have been designed specifically for their purpose, making them somewhat unfamiliar to the children. Nevertheless, they are considered according to their practical and causal value: the box containing an object and a mechanism that, when used correctly, enables it to be opened. In this context, we find that children's responses are close to (i) conventional uses in the case of causal situations (levers or knobs), or (ii) symbolic uses in arbitrary situations (telephones to "call").

McGuigan and Núñez [58], in their research using these tasks, found that children perform better in causal conditions than in arbitrary conditions. Specifically, they respond better when they are required to pull a lever or turn a knob to open a box compared to performing actions considered arbitrary, which are imposed by the experimenter and lack an intelligible relationship between the action and its outcome. However, in arbitrary tasks, children's performance improves when the instruction they receive incorporates a narrative that gives meaning to the arbitrary relationship between their actions and the result. For example, using the telephone to call "Mr. Cow/Sheep/Chicken" (the object to be obtained) and invite them to come out and play. In this way, the narrative transforms the situation, giving meaning to the child's action, and probably makes it more effective within the context of the task.

8.4.3.2 *The Grasping Task*

This task was designed by Neale et al. [66] for use with infants from 12 months old. The authors criticize the high linguistic demands of the standardized tasks most commonly employed to study EF in early childhood. They also indicate that, although the complexity of the stimuli is reduced in the tasks for children, the semiotic complexity of these tasks remains at a level of abstraction similar to the tasks used with adults. They consider it necessary, therefore, to reduce the need for language to understand the task objectives.

The objective of this task is, therefore, pragmatically oriented: using a spoon as a tool for eating. This, in terms that we have used throughout the book, consists of performing the canonical use of the tool, with an efficiency objective. The child is hungry and must use the spoon to eat. It is interesting to note the similarities with a case study we published from the Pragmatics of the Object perspective, regarding how a child, at 11 months, attempts to eat autonomously with a spoon in the Early Years School [73].

The Neale et al. [66] task is structured as follows. The parent feeds the infant a few times. Then, they place the spoon on top of two boxes, allowing the infant to pick it up and bring it to their mouth independently. For example, placing the bowl of the spoon to the infant's left, while the handle is placed to the infant's right. When the child eats from the spoon, the parent places it back on the boxes, but this time, changes the orientation. Following the previous example, the adult places the bowl to the right and the handle to the left. In this situation, the infant must adjust their grip, since, if they maintain the same approach, they will pick up the spoon by the bowl, losing efficiency. The difficulties of the task, therefore,

Table 8.4 Spoon grips in The Grasping Task

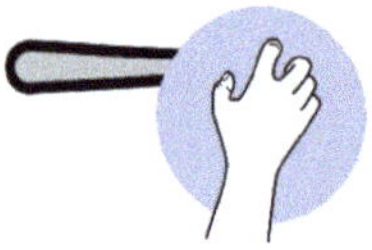		1. The infant grasps the spoon with the hand close to the bowl, without correcting their action
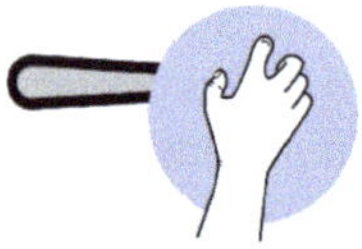	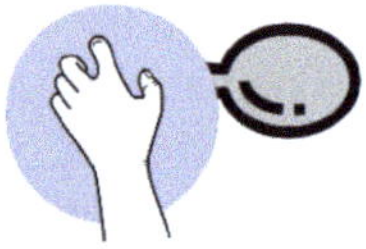	2. The infant first grasps the spoon with the hand near the bowl but corrects their action and switches the spoon to the other hand
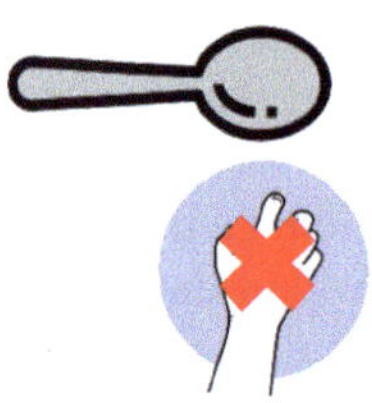		3. The infant begins to direct their hand closer to the bowl but inhibits their action and switches to the hand closer to the handle
		4. The infant grasps the spoon with the hand closest to the handle[2]

come from the parent's (guided by the experimenter) manipulation in changing the orientation of the spoon.

In this task, Neale et al. [66] identified and classified the various approaches of infants when using the spoon. These actions depended on which hand the infant used: the hand closest to the bowl or the hand closest to the handle. They identified the following possible actions as a function of their approach to the conventionality of spoon use (see Table 8.4).

In this task, therefore, the objective to be achieved is, to a large extent, pragmatic. More importantly, the infant's action in front of a meaningful and everyday object is emphasized. The difficulties come from the organization or orientation of the infant's action to the tool-spoon. The infant must adjust their action to achieve maximum efficiency.

[2] Icons: Spoon, by Pause08 (Flaticon.com); Hand, by Leremy (https://www.freepik.es/icono/mano_11434713#fromView=resource_detail&position=50).

8.4.3.3 *Systematic Observation of Spontaneous Behavior*

Thus far, our discussion has centered on how researchers use objects to design tasks to evaluate EF. However, Sastre-Riba and his collaborators [77–79] propose a twist in this paradigm. Instead of organizing a task with a specific goal, with specific objects, and with rules to follow, they organized a spontaneous activity situation for 15-month-old infants. They present the infants with a variety of objects, which they can use in different ways. For example: covering/uncovering, putting away/taking away, knocking, grouping, lining up, connecting/disconnecting, fitting, stacking, etc. To study EF, they analyze how many different ways they use objects, what difficulties they face, how they correct their errors, and what means they use. In this case, what predominates is the action of the children in facing their challenges (see Chap. 10, this volume).

8.4.3.4 *The Practical Dimension of Objects. Some Conclusions*

Although the tasks that take into account the practical value of objects are limited, they serve as a valuable example of how we can study children's EF based on their actions. As we indicated previously, the objectives that children face in these tasks are characterized by having a practical value. The child must regulate their action to change or achieve something in the world. That is to say, to achieve a concrete and defined end. In the cases we have seen, to open a box, or to eat efficiently with a spoon. However, children's actions are still quite understudied. In this tasks, children have little control over the situation and must solve the task according to the organization and rules of the task. In the systematic observations [77–79], in contrast, it is the children themselves who decide their goals and actions with the objects.

8.5 Discussion

8.5.1 Objects in FEs Tasks. Focus on Perceptual Dimensions

As we have observed, the predominant role of objects in the most common tasks for children up to 3 years of age is reduced to their perceptual elements. In this sense, objects act as a "means" or a "support" for the task, rather than being integral to the goals or challenges presented. Consequently, they are easily interchangeable, since they lack intrinsic value based on their identity or functions.

In A-not-B error tasks, the object is defined insofar as it can be found. In the Delay of Gratification tasks, objects are defined as a "temptation" that children must resist. "Don't look", "Don't touch", "Don't grab", or "Wait" are the correct actions (or, rather "non-actions"). In this context, any attractive object to the child can be used in an A-not-B error or a *Delay of Gratification Task*. The same principle applies to *Self-Ordered Search Tasks*. In this type of task, it does not matter what the *object presented is for*. Instead, the goals are defined by the physical characteristics or shape of the objects.

We can also observe this phenomenon in tasks focused on the perceptual dimension of objects. Objects are defined by attributes like color, size, or shape, and more complex concepts such as quantity, order, or orientation. Children must respond to these objects according to these discrete dimensions, not the object itself. In the case of sorting tasks, what defines the object is its resemblance to other stimuli according to separable dimensions. In Go/no-Go tasks, the shape of the stimulus defines the child's response. In working memory tasks, the child must remember the order of different perceptual elements.

This has resulted in the objects being disconnected from the pragmatic contexts and cultural meanings for which they were originally designed and utilized by the community of users [75]. Instead, their use in unfamiliar and arbitrary contexts has been prioritized, and this shift to "culture- and content-free" contexts could impact children's performance.

8.5.2 The Objectives and Rules Are Mostly External and Arbitrary

As previously mentioned, most of the tasks used to study the early development of EF come from studies with adults. Stroop tasks, dimension classification tasks, or working memory tasks have been employed for years to evaluate deficits or lesions in adult populations. For instance, the *Dimensional Change Card Sort* task is a simplified two-dimensional version of the *Wisconsin Card Sorting Test* (see, for example, Eling et al. [33]), which features up to five different dimensions. The original *Stroop* task, based on letters written in different colors, has been simplified to use two cards in two colors representing two items familiar to children (sun/moon; grass/snow; boy/girl; etc.).

In these cases, it is not frequent that the task goals are related to physical, real, or pragmatic difficulties of the objects or the child's effective action. Instead, they are abstract and arbitrary difficulties proposed by the experimenters so that the child has to learn to solve an unfamiliar task or activity, according to established instructions. To convey these goals and instructions, children also require a good understanding of spoken language. This assumes that the most commonly used tasks begin to be applied from 2 to 3 years of age, so we are largely unaware of the development of EF before the infant begins to speak. Between 6 and 18 months of age, the search for hidden objects predominates. Later, from 18 to 24 months of age, tasks adapted from studies with adults begin to be used.

This type of tasks, however, implies assuming a view from the adult's functioning, and stablishing an interpretation based of cognitive deficits [31]. In this case, an adult can understand the concepts and instructions necessary to solve the tasks from different perspectives and meaningful relationships, thanks to the vast experience accumulated throughout their life. In contrast, developing children are still in the process of constructing these concepts and experiences. Asking them to do "the opposite of the usual" introduces an additional difficulty, as it requires going against their understanding of the world and the meanings they have developed. It is less common for tasks to be designed from what children do in their daily lives.

On the other hand, children's actions are reduced to what the experimenter asks for at each specific moment, which is known as "stimulus–response mapping" [4]. In this framework, for each stimulus presented, the child must give a specific response indicated by the experimenter's instructions. In this sense, children's actions are often reduced to a binary classification of successes and errors. On the other hand, the analysis of errors, and how children understand and resolve them, has gone unnoticed. This raises the question: what do children do after making a mistake?

In contrast, in everyday situations and activities, self-regulation occurs in a dynamic, *online* process. First, daily goals and challenges involve less structured activities [7]. In this sense, they allow for a variety of possible responses, more or less effective, which are nevertheless acceptable. Moreover, children do not give up after making a mistake but insist and look for alternatives. "Mistakes" are therefore part of the dynamics of activity and self-regulation. Through action, children construct their understanding of the world and their cognitive self-regulation skills (see full discussion in Moreno-Llanos et al. [65]). However, this approach to children's actions has not been a significant part of the study of EF. We will elaborate on this idea in the following chapters.

8.5.3 Absence of Cultural Aspects

The attentive reader may have noticed that we have not mentioned any aspect related to cultural dimensions in the presentation of EF tasks. This is because, as we mentioned at the beginning of the chapter, EF are considered to be domain-general and universal processes in human behavior. They would act as a "universal resource" that can be applied to any context. This perspective has led to the assumption that EF are not influenced by cultural elements or children's learning experiences. That is, the tasks could be used to obtain objective measures of executive functioning regardless of the culture in which the child develops.

However, an increasing number of authors consider that tasks have no cultural validity [32]. Gaskins and Alcalá [40], who studied how traditional standardized tasks surprise, and even generate rejection among Yucatec children, have further explored this debate. They observed that these children scored considerably lower than their Western peers. However, in their day-to-day lives, they showed great autonomy in organizing their activities, which is atypical for Western children of the same age.

The discrepancy between the "objective" task scores and the observation of children's behavior is due to varying cultural values. For example, in the *Delay of Gratification Tasks*, they consider "waiting without doing anything" as something strange. Some even left the room where the task takes place to do something else. Moreover, these children spend much more time performing the task correctly, something that clashes with tasks based on processing speed or reaction times, so highly valued in Western culture. To consider that Yucatec children have worse EF solely based on their task performance is an interpretation from a Western point of view. This highlights the necessity of considering cultural contexts when attempting to understand executive functions and their application.

8.6 Conclusions

Throughout this chapter, we have discussed how the development of EF has primarily been examined through standardized tasks. These tasks tend to emphasize the perceptual dimensions of materiality, which are considered more accessible for children, allowing researchers to obtain more 'pure' measures of Executive Functions [38]. However, this approach shows important limitations. First, these tasks detach materiality and children from their everyday, pragmatic, and cultural activities. Instead, they introduce arbitrary and unfamiliar goals, demands, and instructions for children. Such tasks, therefore, require extensive control by the experimenter, who sets out the goal, the demands, and the responses that the children must make. This reduces the ecological validity of the tasks, making it difficult to interpret the scores (see full discussion in Moreno-Llanos et al. [65]).

Therefore, we should situate children's materiality and action in their everyday, cultural, and pragmatic contexts. In everyday situations, there is no such extensive, external, and arbitrary control over children's actions. Instead, the goals that children face concerning materiality are more open-ended, and they can approach them in much broader ways [4, 6, 7]. In addition, every action, be it successful, miss, error, approach, etc., has value for the child's intended goal. Each "mistake" informs the child about their current action and possible subsequent actions. That is, the consequences of their action serve as a foundation for children to adjust their subsequent behaviors, which is particularly vital during early developmental stages when action plays a crucial role.

From a perspective based on children's actions, and considering objects as part of cultural materiality, we can observe the development of EF through (i) the objectives children set for themselves with objects, (ii) the challenges they encounter in utilizing these objects, and (iii) the strategies they employ to overcome these challenges.

We believe that these aspects are crucial to understanding the origin and early development of EF, but that they have been overlooked by the standardized task-based approach. We will address these ideas in more depth in Chap. 10.

References

1. Ardila, A. (2008). On the evolutionary origins of executive functions. *Brain and Cognition, 68*(1), 92–99. https://doi.org/10.1016/j.bandc.2008.03.003
2. Ardila, A. (2018). Is intelligence equivalent to executive functions? *Psicothema, 30*(2), 159–164. https://doi.org/10.7334/psicothema2017.329

3. Baggetta, P., & Alexander, P. A. (2016). Conceptualization and operationalization of executive function. *Mind, Brain, and Education, 10*(1), 10–33. https://doi.org/10.1111/mbe.12100
4. Baker, S. T., Friedman, O., & Leslie, A. M. (2010). The opposites task: Using general rules to test cognitive flexibility in preschoolers. *Journal of Cognition and Development, 11*(2), 240–254. https://doi.org/10.1080/15248371003699944
5. Banich, M. T., & Depue, B. E. (2015). Recent advances in understanding neural systems that support inhibitory control. *Current Opinion in Behavioral Sciences, 1*, 17–22. https://doi.org/10.1016/j.cobeha.2014.07.006
6. Barker, J. E., & Munakata, Y. (2015). Developing self-directed executive functioning: Recent findings and future directions. *Mind, Brain, and Education, 9*(2), 92–99. https://doi.org/10.1111/mbe.12071
7. Barker, J. E., Semenov, A. D., Michaelson, L., Provan, L. S., Snyder, H. R., & Munakata, Y. (2014). Less-structured time in children's daily lives predicts self-directed executive functioning. *Frontiers in Psychology, 5*, article 593. https://doi.org/10.3389/fpsyg.2014.00593
8. Baron, I. S. (2005). Test review: Wechsler Intelligence Scale for Children—Fourth Edition (WISC-IV). *Child Neuropsychology, 11*(5), 471–475. https://doi.org/10.1080/09297040590951587
9. Beck, D. M., Schaefer, C., Pang, K., & Carlson, S. M. (2011). Executive function in preschool children: Test-retest reliability. *Journal of Cognition and Development, 12*(2), 169–193. https://doi.org/10.1080/15248372.2011.563485
10. Bissonette, G. B., & Roesch, M. R. (2017). Neurophysiology of rule switching in the corticostriatal circuit. *Neuroscience, 345*, 64–76. https://doi.org/10.1016/j.neuroscience.2016.01.062
11. Blakey, E., Visser, I., & Carroll, D. J. (2016). Different executive functions support different kinds of cognitive flexibility: Evidence from 2-, 3-, and 4-year-olds. *Child Development, 87*(2), 513–526. https://doi.org/10.1111/cdev.12468
12. Brydges, C. R., Fox, A. M., Reid, C. L., & Anderson, M. (2014). The differentiation of executive functions in middle and late childhood: A longitudinal latent-variable analysis. *Intelligence, 47*, 34–43. https://doi.org/10.1016/j.intell.2014.08.010
13. Carlson, S. M. (2003). Executive function in context: Development, measurement, theory, and experience. *Monographs of the Society for Research in Child Development, 68*(3), 138–151. https://doi.org/10.1111/j.1540-5834.2003.06803012.x
14. Carlson, S. M. (2005). Developmentally sensitive measures of executive function in preschool children. *Developmental Neuropsychology, 28*(2), 595–616.
15. Carlson, S. M., Mandell, D. J., & Williams, L. (2004). Executive function and theory of mind: Stability and prediction from ages 2 to 3. *Developmental Psychology, 40*(6), 1105–1122. https://doi.org/10.1037/0012-1649.40.6.1105
16. Carlson, S. M., & Moses, L. J. (2001). Individual differences in inhibitory control and children's theory of mind. *Child Development, 72*(4), 1032–1053. https://doi.org/10.1111/1467-8624.00333
17. Carlson, S. M., Moses, L. J., & Breton, C. (2002). How specific is the relation between executive function and theory of mind? Contributions of inhibitory control and working memory. *Infant and Child Development, 11*, 73–92. https://doi.org/10.1002/icd.298
18. Castellanos-Ryan, N., Parent, S., Chaput-Langlois, S., Rioux, C., Jacques, S., Simard, C., Tremblay, R. E., Séguin, J. R., & Zelazo, P. D. (2023). Modelling executive function across early childhood: longitudinal invariance, development from 3.5 to 7 years and later academic performance. *Cognitive Development, 68*, 101365. https://doi.org/10.1016/j.cogdev.2023.101365
19. Chévalier, N. (2010). Les fonctions executives chez l'enfant: concepts et développement. [Executive Functions in Children: Concepts and Development] *Canadian Psychology, 51*(3), 149–163. https://doi.org/10.1037/a0020031
20. Cole, M., & Scribner, S. (1978). Introduction. In L. S. Vygotski, *Mind in society. The development of higher psychological processes* (pp. 1–14; C. Cole, V. John-Steiner, S. Scribner, & E. Souberman, Eds.). Harvard University Press.

21. Cuevas, K., & Bell, M. A. (2014). Infant attention and early childhood executive function. *Child Development, 85*(2), 397–404. https://doi.org/10.1111/cdev.12126
22. Delgado, H., Aldecosea, C., Menéndez, Ñ., Rodríguez, R., Nin, V., Lipina, S., & Carboni, A. (2022). Socioeconomic status differences in children's affective decisión-making: The role of awareness in the children's gambling task. *Developmental Psychology, 58*(9), 1716–1729. https://doi.org/10.1037/dev0001382
23. Devine, R. T., Ribner, A., & Hughes, C. (2019). Measuring and predicting individual differences in executive functions at 14 months: A longitudinal study. *Child Development, 90*(5), e618–e636. https://doi.org/10.1111/cdev.13217
24. Diamond, A. (1985). Development of the ability to use recall to guide action, as indicated by infants' performance on AB. *Child Development, 56*, 868–883.
25. Diamond, A. (2012). Activities and programs that improve children's executive functions. *Current Directions in Psychological Science, 21*(5), 335–341. https://doi.org/10.1177/0963721412453722
26. Diamond, A. (2013). Executive functions. *Annual Review of Psychology, 64*, 135–168. https://doi.org/10.1146/annurev-psych-113011-143750
27. Diamond, A., & Doar, B. (1989). The performance of human infants on a measure of frontal cortex function, the delayed response task. *Developmental Psychobiology, 23*(3), 271–294. https://doi.org/10.1002/dev.420220307
28. Diamond, A., & Goldman-Rakic, P. S. (1989). Comparison of human infants and rhesus monkeys on Piaget's AB task: Evidence for dependence on dorsolateral prefrontal cortex. *Experimental Brain Research, 74*, 24–40.
29. Diamond, A., Prevor, M. B., Callender, G., & Druin, D. P. (1997). Prefrontal cortex cognitive deficits in children treated early and continuously for PKU. *Monographs of the Society for Research in Child Development, 62*(4). https://doi.org/10.2307/1166208
30. Dick, A. S., & Overton, W. F. (2010). Executive function: Description and explanation. In B. W. Sokol, U. Müller, J. I. M. Carpendale, A. R. Young, & G. Iarocci (Eds.), *Self-and social regulation* (pp. 7–34). Oxford University Press.
31. Doebel, S. (2020). Rethinking executive function and its development. *Perspectives on Psychological Science, 15*(4), 942–956. https://doi.org/10.1177/1745691620904771
32. Doebel, S., & Müller, U. (2023). The future of research on executive function and its development: An introduction to the special issue. *Journal of Cognition and Development, 24*(2), 161–171. https://doi.org/10.1080/15248372.2023.2188946
33. Eling, P., Derckx, K., & Maes, R. (2008). On the historical and conceptual background of the Winsconsin Card Sorting Test. *Brain and Cognition, 67*(3), 247–253. https://doi.org/10.1016/j.bandc.2008.01.006
34. Espy, K. A. (1997). The shape school: Assessing executive function in preschool children. *Developmental Neuropsychology, 13*(4), 495–499. https://doi.org/10.1080/87565649709540690
35. Espy, K. A., Kaufmann, P. M., McDiarmid, M. D., & Glisky, M. L. (1997). Executive functioning in preschool children: Performance on A-not-B and other delayed response format tasks. *Brain and Cognition, 41*, 178–199. https://doi.org/10.1006/brcg.1999.1117
36. Fatima, S., Jamil, M., & Ardila, A. (2019). Cognitive control and criminogenic cognitions in South Asian gamblers. *Journal of Gambling Studies, 35*, 501–516. https://doi.org/10.1007/s10899-018-9805-8
37. Fiske, A., & Holmboe, K. (2019). Neural substrates of early executive function development. *Developmental Review, 52*, 42–62. https://doi.org/10.1016/j.dr.2019.100866
38. FitzGibbon, L., Cragg, L., & Carroll, D. J. (2014). Primed to be inflexible: The influence of set size on cognitive flexibility during childhood. *Frontiers in Psychology, 5*, article 101. https://doi.org/10.3389/fpsyg.2014.00101
39. Friedman, N. P., Miyake, A., Young, S. E., DeFries, J. C., Corley, R. P., & Hewitt, J. K. (2008). Individual differences in executive functions are almost entirely genetic in origin. *Journal of Experimental Psychology: General, 137*(2), 201–225. https://doi.org/10.1037/0096-3445.137.2.201

40. Gaskins, S., & Alcalá, L. (2023). Studying executive function in culturally meaningful ways. *Journal of Cognition and Development, 24*(2), 260–279. https://doi.org/10.1080/15248372.2022.2160722
41. Goldstein, S., Naglieri, J. A., Princiotta, D., & Otero, T. M. (2014). Introduction: A history of executive functioning as a theoretical and clinical construct. In S. Goldstein & J. A. Naglieri (Eds.), *Handbook of executive functioning* (pp. 3–12). Springer Science+Business Media. https://doi.org/10.1007/978-1-4614-8106-5_1
42. Gottwald, J. M., Achermann, S., Marciszko, C., Lindskog, M., & Gredebäck, G. (2016). An embodied account of early executive-function development: Prospective motor control in infancy is related to inhibition and working memory. *Psychological Science, 27*(12), 1600–1610. https://doi.org/10.1177/0956797616667447
43. Hendry, A., & Holmboe, K. (2021). Development and validation of the early executive functions questionnaire: A carer-administered measure of executive functions suitable for 9- to 30-months-olds. *Infancy, 26*, 932–961. https://doi.org/10.1111/infa.12431
44. Hendry, A., Jones, E. J. H., & Charman, T. (2016). Executive function in the first three years of life: Precursors, predictors and patterns. *Developmental Review, 42*, 1–33. https://doi.org/10.1016/j.dr.2016.06.005
45. Hongwanishkul, D., Happaney, K. R., Lee, W. S. C., & Zelazo, P. D. (2005). Assessment of hot and cool executive function in young children: Age-related changes and individual differences. *Developmental Neuropsychology, 28*(2), 617–644. https://doi.org/10.1207/s15326942dn2802_4
46. Hughes, C., & Ensor, R. (2005). Executive function and theory of mind in 2 year olds: A family affair? *Developmental Neuropsychology, 28*(2), 645–668. https://doi.org/10.1207/s15326942dn2802_5
47. Hughes, C., & Ensor, R. (2007). Executive function and theory of mind: Predictive relations from ages 2 to 4. *Developmental Psychology, 43*(6), 1447–1459. https://doi.org/10.1037/0012-1649.43.6.1447
48. Jacques, S., & Zelazo, P. D. (2001). The flexible item selection task (FIST): A measure of executive function in preschoolers. *Developmental Neuropsychology, 20*(3), 573–591. https://doi.org/10.1207/S15326942DN2003_2
49. Karr, J. E., Areshenkoff, C. N., Rast, P., Hofer, S. M., Iverson, G. L., & García-Barrera, M. A. (2018). The unity and diversity of executive functions: A systematic review and re-analysis of latent variable studies. *Psychological Bulletin, 144*(1), 1147–1185. https://doi.org/10.1037/bul0000160
50. Kochanska, G., Murray, K. T., & Harlan, E. T. (2000). Effortful control in early childhood: Continuity and change, antecedents, and implications for social development. *Developmental Psychology, 36*(2), 220–232. https://doi.org/10.1037/0012-1649.36.2.220
51. Kotik-Friedgut, B., & Ardila, A. (2020). A.R. Luria's cultural neuropsychology in the 21st century. *Culture & Psychology, 26*(2), 274–286. https://doi.org/10.1177/1354067X19861053
52. Lezak, M. D. (1982). The problem of assessing executive functions. *International Journal of Psychology, 17*, 281–297.
53. Lickliter, R., & Moore, D. S. (2023). Molecular and systemic epigenetic inheritance: Integrating development, genetics, and evolution. *Human Development, 67*(5–6), 305–317. https://doi.org/10.1159/000533192
54. Luria, A. R. (1959). The directive function of speech in development and dissolution. *WORD, 15*(2), 341–352. https://doi.org/10.1080/00437956.1959.11659703
55. Luria, A. R., Pribram, K. H., & Homskaya, E. D. (1964). An experimental analysis of the behavioral disturbance produced by left frontal arachnoidal endothelioma (meningioma). *Neuropsychologia, 2*, 257–280.
56. Marcovitch, S., & Zelazo, P. D. (2009). A hierarchical competing systems model of the emergence and early development of executive function. *Developmental Science, 12*(1), 1–18. https://doi.org/10.1111/j.1467-7687.2008.00754.x

57. Martin, J., & Failows, L. (2010). Executive function: Theoretical concerns. In B. W. Sokol, U. Müller, J. I. M. Carpendale, A. R. Young, & G. Iarocci (Eds.), *Self-and social regulation* (pp. 35–55). Oxford University Press.
58. McGuigan, N., & Núñez, M. (2006). Executive functioning by 18–24-month-old children: Effects of inhibition, working memory demands and narrative in a novel detour-reaching task. *Infant and Child Development, 15*, 519–542. https://doi.org/10.1002/icd.477
59. Mikadze, Y. V., Ardila, A., & Akhutina, T. V. (2019). A. R. Luria's approach to neuropsychological assessment and rehabilitation. *Archives of Clinical Neuropsychology, 34*(6), 795–802. https://doi.org/10.1093/arclin/acy095
60. Miller, M. R., Giesbrecht, G. F., Müller, U., McInerney, R. J., & Kerns, K. A. (2012). A latent variable approach to determining the structure of executive function in preschool children. *Journal of Cognition and Development, 13*(3), 395–423. https://doi.org/10.1080/15248372.2011.585478
61. Miller, S. E., & Marcovitch, S. (2015). Examining executive function in the second year of life: Coherence, stability, and relations to joint attention and language. *Developmental Psychology, 51*(1), 101–114. https://doi.org/10.1037/a0038359
62. Mischel, W., & Metzner, R. (1962). Preference for delayed reward as a function of age, intelligence, and length of delay interval. *Journal of Abnormal and Social Psychology, 64*(6), 425–431.
63. Mischel, W., Shoda, Y., & Rodriguez, M. L. (1989). Delay of gratification in children. *Science, 244*, 933–938.
64. Miyake, A., Friedman, N. P., Emerson, M. J., Witzki, A. H., & Howerter, A. (2000). The unity and diversity of executive functions and their contributions to complex "frontal lobe" tasks: A latent variable analysis. *Cognitive Psychology, 41*, 49–100. https://doi.org/10.1006/cogp.1999.0734
65. Moreno-Llanos, I., Guevara, I., Palacios, P., & Rodríguez, C. (2024). How to study the early development of executive function? Let's put control back in the hands of children. *New Ideas in Psychology, 72*, 101049. https://doi.org/10.1016/j.newideapsych.2023.101049
66. Neale, D., Basilio, M., & Whitebread, D. (2018). The grasping Task: A 12-month predictor of 24-month delay task performance and BRIEF-P inhibition scores. *Infant and Child Development, 27*, e2092. https://doi.org/10.1002/icd.2092
67. Ozonoff, S., Pennington, B. F., & Rogers, S. J. (1991). Executive function deficits in high-functioning autistic individuals: Relationship to theory of mind. *Journal of Child Psychology and Psychiatry, 32*(7), 1081–1105. https://doi.org/10.1111/j.1469-7610.1991.tb00351.x
68. Packwood, S., Hodgetts, H. M., & Tremblay, S. (2011). A multiperspective approach to the conceptualization of executive functions. *Journal of Clinical and Experimental Neuropsychology, 33*(4), 456–470. https://doi.org/10.1080/13803395.2010.533157
69. Piaget, J. (1936/1948). *La naissance de l'intelligence chez l'enfant* [The origins of intelligence in children]. Delachaux et Niestlé (version électronique, Fondation Jean Piaget).
70. Prencipe, A., & Zelazo, P. D. (2005). Development of affective decisión making for self and other. *Psychological Science, 16*(7), 501–505. https://doi.org/10.1111/j.0956-7976.2005.01564.x
71. Rodríguez, C. (2012). The functional permanence of the object, a product of consensus. In E. Martí & C. Rodríguez (Eds.), *After Piaget* (pp. 123–150). Transaction Publishers.
72. Rodríguez, C. (2022). The construction of executive function in early development: The pragmatics of action and gestures. *Human Development, 66*(4–5), 239–259. https://doi.org/10.1159/000526340
73. Rodríguez, C., Estrada, L., Moreno-Llanos, I., & de los Reyes, J. L. (2017). Executive functions and educational actions in an infant school: Private uses and gestures at the end of the first year. *Studies in Psychology, 38*(2), 385–423. https://doi.org/10.1080/02109395.2017.1305061
74. Rodríguez, C., & Moreno-Llanos, I. (2023). A pragmatic turn in the study of early executive functions by object use and gestures. A case study from 8 to 17 months of age at a nursery

school. *Integrative Psychological and Behavioral Science, 57*, 607–654. https://doi.org/10.1007/s12124-020-09578-5
75. Rodríguez, C., & Moro, C. (1999). *El mágico número tres. Cuando los niños aún no hablan* [Magic number three. When children still don't talk]. Paidós.
76. Santa-Cruz, C. (2017). Introduction to a special issue on executive functions. *Studies in Psychology, 38*(2), 277–283. https://doi.org/10.1080/02109395.2017.1305076
77. Sastre-Riba, S. (2004). Observación sistemática en la cognición temprana: funciones ejecutivas, lógica e interacción [Systematic Observation in Early Cognition: Executive Functios, Logic and Interaction]. *Metodología de las Ciencias del Comportamiento, Volumen Especial, 2004*, 557–566.
78. Sastre-Riba, S., Fonseca-Pedrero, E., & Poch-Olivé, M. L. (2015). Early development of executive functions: A differential study. *Anales de Psicología, 31*(2), 607–614. https://doi.org/10.6018/analesps.31.2.180711
79. Sastre-Riba, S., & Poch-Olivé, M. L. (2007). Interactive formats and executive functions in early development. *Revista de Neurología, 44*(2), S61–S65.
80. Stroop, J. R. (1935). Studies of interference in serial verbal reactions. *Journal of Experimental Psychology, 18*(6), 643–662.
81. Terman, L. M. (1916/2007). *The measurement of intelligence. An explanation of and a complete guide for the use of the standard revisión and extensión of the Binet-Simon intelligence scale.* The Riverside Press.
82. Vygotski, L. S. (1931/1978). *Historia del desarrollo de las funciones psíquicas superiores [History of the Development of Higher Mental Functions].* Academia de Ciencias Pedagógicas de la URSS.
83. Vygotski, L. S. (1978). *Mind in society. The development of higher psychological processes* (C. Cole, V. John-Steiner, S. Scribner, & E. Souberman, Eds.). Harvard University Press.
84. Wiebe, S. A., Sheffield, T., Nelson, J. M., Clark, C. A. C., Chevalier, N., & Espy, K. A. (2011). The structure of executive function in 3-year-olds. *Journal of Experimental Child Psychology, 108*, 436–452. https://doi.org/10.1016/j.jecp.2010.08.008
85. Willoughby, M. T., Blair, C. B., Wirth, R. J., Greenberg, M., & The Family Life Project Investigators. (2010). The measurement of executive function at age 3 years: Psychometric properties and criterion validity of a new battery of tasks. *Psychological Assessment, 22*(2), 306–317. https://doi.org/10.1037/a0018708
86. Zelazo, P. D., & Müller, U. (2007). Executive function in typical and atypical development. In U. Goswami (Ed.), *Blackwell handbook of childhood cognitive development* (pp. 445–469). Blackwell.
87. Sánchez, H., Guevara, M., & Cerchiaro, E. (2013). Desarrollo y/o cambio de la noción de objeto permanente y causalidad operatoria: Evidencia empírica en el primer año de vida [Development and/or change in object permanence notion and operative causality: Empirical evidence in the first year of life]. *Avances en Psicología Latinoamericana, 31*(2), 291–309.
88. Zelazo, P. D., Frye, D., & Rapus, T. (1996). An age-related dissociation between knowing rules and using them. *Cognitive Development, 11*, 37–63. https://doi.org/10.1016/S0885-2014(96)90027-1

Is a Paradigm Shift Necessary Today in the Approach to Executive Functions?

9

Cintia Rodríguez, Iván Moreno-Llanos, and Irene Guevara

> I wanted a Psychology that would apply to real people as they live their lives, not an intellectual abstraction in a laboratory.
>
> (Luria, *The Making of Mind*, 1979)

Being able to act and control one's own behavior, to set meaningful personal goals, to form action plans, to carry them out, and to evaluate whether the proposed objectives have been achieved; being able to include and collaborate with others to reach those objectives; knowing oneself capable of all this—these are fundamental aspects of daily life of human beings. Knowing ourselves as the masters of our thoughts and actions defines us as the intentional subjects that we are. The capacity for self-regulation, for controlling one's own behavior and thoughts, constitutes what are known as Executive Functions (EF). These functions begin to manifest in the last third of the first year of life, when a baby starts to control their behavior intentionally. However, this is only the beginning, as EF take between twenty and twenty-five years to fully develop [67], although those involving verbal processing may continue to develop until around the age of 40 [29]. Self-control also plays a central role as life approaches its end [38]. Many of us would reject the idea of our days being artificially prolonged after losing control over our actions and/or thoughts.

C. Rodríguez (✉) · I. Moreno-Llanos
Universidad Autónoma de Madrid, Madrid, Spain
e-mail: cintia.rodriguez@uam.es

I. Guevara
Department of Psychology, Universidad Antonio Nebrija, Madrid, Spain

C. Rodriguez Garrido et al. (eds.), *The Social Life of Objects in Early Development*, Social Interaction in Learning and Development,
https://doi.org/10.1007/978-3-031-87673-8_9

Research on EF has flourished in recent decades. This success has led to a dramatic increase in standardized tasks in which the experimenter determines what the subject must do, when, and how. Typically, only correct responses are considered, while "errors" are disregarded (see Chap. 8 on tasks in this volume). However, there is a growing number of authors claiming for a paradigm shift [16, 26] that accounts for the ecological validity of the tests used. That thoughtfully considers the social and cultural characteristics of the subjects and takes in consideration the meaningful activities and goals of the subjects in their daily lives [58]. A perspective that moves away from the segmentation and atomization of the various cognitive processes into which EF are often subdivided [5], and incorporates a robust developmental perspective through longitudinal designs [45]. If a paradigm shift in the approach to EF is necessary, this need is even more urgent in infancy. One of the greatest challenges is precisely placing EF within a developmental perspective. To this end, in this chapter, we will (i) begin by reviewing the increasingly numerous voices advocating for a paradigm shift in the approach to EF—a new paradigm that incorporates pragmatic, social, and cultural dimensions, ecological validity, and the meaningfulness of everyday situations. Next, we will delve into some significant contributions to self-regulation and EF from classic authors in developmental psychology. Their insights remain highly relevant today for framing this paradigm shift. (ii) We will review with the Vygotsky/Luria debate with Piaget concerning the function of egocentric speech (now referred to as *private speech*). Some aspects of this debate are particularly useful today for understanding early EF development, as they emphasize the role of others through semiotic mediators in the origins of self-regulation. (iii) We will then turn to Piaget's work on equilibration and awareness (from the 1970s) and sensorimotor development (from the 1930s to 1940s). His developmental perspective may shed new light on the origins and development of EF today, as Piaget focuses on the actions and intentional goals of children as early as 7–9 months of age. (iv) Finally, we will close the chapter with notes on the central aspects at stake in the paradigm shift concerning the early development of EF.

9.1 Theoretical and Epistemological Challenges in Executive Functions: A Paradigm Shift on the Horizon

As mentioned earlier, in recent decades, EF have predominantly been assessed through standardized tasks in "culture-free" laboratory contexts, removed from everyday life. A recent special issue coordinated by Sabine Doebel and Ulrich Müller [16] highlights the urgent need to reconsider both the conceptual and empirical approach to EF research. A paradigm shift is necessary [26]. One of the issues raised concerns the excessive reliance on standardized tasks, whose ecological validity is highly questionable. According to Niebaum and Munakata [48], "lab-based assessments of EF are intentionally context-free, requiring participants to perform arbitrary tasks involving simple, static, and well-controlled stimuli in sterile lab settings with unfamiliar experimenters" (p. 242). Another increasingly prominent critique of standardized tasks is the need to incorporate the specific cultural aspects in which children live and develop [2]. For example, in a study conducted with Mayan children in Yucatán, Gaskins and Alcalá [21] questioned the utility of standardized tests. The children in the study demonstrated considerable initiative and responsibility in their daily chores, far surpassing their North American peers. However, they scored very low on specific standardized tests. For instance, they did not understand why they had to wait idly during the "Delay of Gratification" task, which clashed with their cultural values and daily expectations. Similarly, Lewis et al. [33] highlighted differences between Korean and English children in the "Day-Night" task. Korean children scored the highest starting at age 3, while English children did not achieve similar scores until age 5. These findings underscore the importance of considering how EF are embedded within specific cultural processes. Doebel and Lillard [15] advocate for the role of play in the development of EF. Play involves "[d]iverse skills requiring the regulation of cognitive processes in the service of goals that are fundamentally shaped by cultural knowledge, norms, and values" (p. 5).

Another critique stems from the relative lack of research on the influence of environment and social interactions on EF [25], despite the foundational impact of Vygotsky's and Luria's sociocultural approaches emphasizing the social origins of self-regulation. As noted by Lewis and Carpendale [32], "as work on EF progressed it became less social and more individualistic and located purely within neuropsychological pathways." However, there is considerable evidence on the influence of family in supporting or hindering the development of EF in children [27], as well as the impact of maternal attention on children's cognition, which predicts later executive processes [8]. Recent studies also explore the role of teachers' practices in EF development in two-year-old children, concluding that teachers' actions predict the development of selective attention [30]. Furthermore, Zelazo et al. [76] highlight that early childhood education settings actively promote the development of EF.

According to Lewis and Carpendale [32], the waning interest in the social influences on EF is partly attributable to the development of methods for measuring neurological activity (MRI, PET, and EEG). In an autobiographical text published in 1930, Edouard Claparède, one of Piaget's mentors, expressed a similar feeling:

> On one hand, my neurological education pushed me to reduce mental activity to a constellation of more or less localized brain centers; on the other hand, the most elementary observation of human behavior phenomena showed me the impossibility of reducing their infinitely flexible manifestations to this rigid and rudimentary scheme. [7, p. 34]

Claparède's words remain relevant today, underscoring the need to promote both neuropsychological approaches and the observation of human behavior in everyday life, in all its flexibility and creativity.

The ecological validity of clinical tests is also under scrutiny. Neuropsychological assessments, beyond contributing to diagnoses, aim to predict patients' challenges in daily life. However, the segmentation of cognitive sub-processes in these tests bears little resemblance to patients' real-world activities [5].

Another debate centers on the domain-general *versus* domain-specific nature of EF [75]. This issue ties into the criticism of using standardized tasks for improving EF in everyday life. Meta-analyses of decades of research have reached a pessimistic conclusion: EF training enhances performance on the specific task used during training but rarely leads to general improvements in EF capacities or significant academic or real-life outcomes. "Contemporary frameworks of EF development across childhood have shifted from viewing EF as domain-general cognitive processes to viewing EF as cognitive skills developed to meet specific demands in the environment" [48, p. 242]. In the educational sphere, Matthews [39] highlights how some adolescents report that when teachers help them apply mathematics to real-world situations, it enables them to think creatively and helps them "think outside the box," echoing a term popularized by Adele Diamond.

Another critical argument is the assumption, following the work of Miyake et al. [42], that executive skills consist of only three core EF: inhibition, flexibility, and working memory. It is striking that these three components are now regarded as the "fundamental" or even "core" aspects of executive functioning, given that the researchers themselves were, in fact, cautious about this conclusion. They viewed their study as a preliminary step in understanding the diversity of EF:

> *[W]e are not claiming that the three investigated executive functions are the only executive functions, nor would we suggest that they are anything like the fundamental units or primitives of cognition.* Our exploration of the diversity of executive functions is only a first step, and there are a number of important issues that need to be addressed in future research to better characterize the nature of separability or diversity of executive functions. ([42, pp. 89–90], emphasis ours)

Another significant topic is what Gaskins and Paradise [22] refer to as "open attention." This concept suggests that attention is distributed across a broad field in everyday life, in contrast to most attention models, which focus narrowly. The relevance of this type of attention lies in its divergence from EF research using standardized tasks, where once children divert their attention from the task, the experiment is considered over. This approach seems questionable in daily life, where individuals are constantly drawn to various engaging and meaningful stimuli that demand a response, even if they later return to pursuing their intended goal.

Another critical consideration comes from authors who emphasize the central role of activity and goals in EF. According to Chevalier, "Executive function is goal-directed in nature; it cannot be exerted without a goal to reach" [6, p. 363]. The goal is maintained in the prefrontal cortex and guides action. However, this is often overlooked or insufficiently considered in standardized tasks. Niebaum and Munakata consider that [48]: "EFs are inherently goal-driven cognitive processes. In the lab, goals are provided by an experimenter (e.g., to sort pictures by their shape or color). Outside of the lab, goals, an individual's motivation to achieve them, are also driven by personal, historical, social, and cultural contexts [...] EFs are not automatically engaged [...] Engaging EFs takes effort [...]" (p. 249). In clinical practice with adults, this critique has been raised for decades. Authors such as Elkhonon Goldberg [23], a student of Luria, and Stuss and Alexander [66] question the use of standardized tasks that remove patients' own goals. Similarly, Muriel Lezak [34] warned about the absurdity of researchers providing goals for studying EF (see discussion in Rodríguez and Moreno-Llanos [63]). Notably, the establishment of meaningful goals is often considered a "higher-order" EF that develops later and, thus, is not included among the core EF [13, 70]. This perspective has significantly influenced how the earliest manifestations of EF have been studied.

In contrast, the situation in the literature on self-regulation in the school context is quite different. For example, in Pintrich's model [57], children's goals in primary and secondary school play a central role. Self-regulation is described as "an active, constructive process whereby learners *set goals for their learning* and then attempt to monitor, regulate and control their cognition, motivation, and behavior, *guided and constrained by their goals* and the contextual features in the environment" ([57, p. 453], cited by [65, p. 85], underlined by us, see also [75], for examples of self-regulation, co-regulation, and socially-shared regulation in primary school music classes).

In summary, all the critiques mentioned above regarding the excessive reliance on standardized tasks, the lack of ecological validity, the need to include specific cultural factors, the debate over domain-general versus domain-specific EF in daily life, the absence of subjects' own goals, and the gradual disinterest in the influence of social interactions in EF research are equally applicable to early development. Despite its undeniable relevance, early EF development has been studied relatively little [36], as it was only recently acknowledged that self-regulation processes begin to emerge before age 8 [75].

Early EF have also been primarily evaluated using standardized tasks. The A-not-B task is the most commonly used for children under 12 months. For children older than 12 months, a significant number of tasks have been designed to assess the three core EF components—flexibility, inhibition, and working memory (or updating)—in a segmented way (in Chap. 8 of this volume, Moreno-Llanos and Barreto provide a detailed overview of the most commonly used laboratory tasks for children aged 6 months to 3 years). The standard procedure involves the experimenter presenting the task to the child, instructing them on what to do, and the child responding according to the given instructions.

While acknowledging the advancements achieved through research using standardized tasks, many influential voices, as noted earlier, have questioned this approach due to its inherent paradox. If the goal is to measure a subject's ability to set their own goals, plan their actions, flexibly find appropriate means, inhibit irrelevant behaviors, monitor the course of their actions, and evaluate outcomes, it seems counter-intuitive that the experimenter, rather than the child, determines the goals, the means, and their changes. The objections raised by Muriel Lezak, Elkhonon Goldberg, Stuss, and Alexander concerning adult patients are even more pronounced when such tests are administered to children under the age of 2.

If a paradigm shift in the approach to EF is imperative, it may be time to revisit the work of classical developmental theorists who placed the origins and development of cognitive control at the heart of their theories. Their developmental approaches can contribute to reformulating this crucial area of human cognition. The following two sections address this. We will begin with the debate between Vygotsky/Luria and Piaget on egocentric speech (private speech) and then explore Piaget's model of equilibration and self-regulation in early development.

9.2 Private Speech (Egocentric Language) Serves a Self-Regulatory Function: The Vygotsky-Piaget Debate

How the intentional and conscious control of one's own actions and thoughts arises and develops in childhood is one of the core topics of Developmental Psychology. The Geneva School, led by Piaget, and the sociocultural school of Vygotsky and Luria placed self-regulation at the center of the subject's activity. It is directly related to the ability to adapt to the environment. This is not a minor issue, as Luria, following Vygotsky's legacy, is considered the father of modern neuropsychology [41]. Luria proposed a hierarchical model of the brain in which the frontal and prefrontal lobes, along with their connections, constitute the third functional unit responsible for programming, regulating, and monitoring behavior. These functions correspond to what we now call EF, although Luria never used the term [3, 20].

As is widely known, Vygotsky and Luria were interested from the beginning in language as the semiotic tool that enables self-regulation. Their starting point is the language adults direct at children, which fulfills an external regulatory function during the second year of life. Some additional time must pass before the child begins to use their own language to self-regulate:

> This transition from impulsive responses to responses controlled by the meaning of an utterance occurred in children somewhere between the age of three-and-a-half and four, although the exact timing differs greatly, depending on subtle features of the experiment and the particular children involved. [35, p. 114]

To trace the origins of the Vygotsky-Piaget debate, we must go back a century, when a young Piaget, at just 26 years old, published *Le langage et la pensée chez l'enfant* [The Language and Thought of the Child] in 1923. In this work, he argued that the language children direct to themselves is egocentric, a reflection of "autistic" thought. It is a form of language that does not considers the interlocutor:

> [...] the child does not care to know to whom they are speaking or whether they are being heard. They speak either to themselves or for the pleasure of associating whatever comes to their immediate action. This language is egocentric, first because the child only talks about themselves but, above all, because they do not seek to adopt the interlocutor's point of view. [...] The child does not show the need to influence the interlocutor or to truly teach

> them something: it is somewhat like the conversation in certain salons, where everyone talks about themselves, and no one listens. ([50, p. 22], our translation)

Piaget distinguishes three types of egocentric language: (i) *Repetition* (echolalia). This involves the mere repetition of syllables or words for the pleasure of speaking, but without addressing anyone. Piaget considers these remnants of infant babbling not yet socialized. (ii) *Monologue*: Children speak to themselves as if thinking out loud without addressing anyone. There is an absence of the social function of words. (iii) *Collective monologue*. Children relate others to their own actions or thoughts but without concern for whether they are genuinely being heard or understood. "The interlocutor's point of view never intervenes: the interlocutor is merely a pretext, a stimulus" [50, p. 23].

According to Piaget, egocentric language reflects equally egocentric thought, not yet sufficiently socialized: "[...] All egocentric thought is, by its structure, intermediary between autistic thought, which is 'non-directed,' meaning it floats according to whims (as in daydreaming), and 'directed' intelligence" [50, p. 282]. Socialized language emerges only around the age of 7, through which children exchange their thoughts with others. There is "true exchange, discussion, or even collaboration in the pursuit of a common goal" [50, p. 23].

In contrast to the thesis of the child as an egocentric being, which significantly impacted developmental psychology throughout the twentieth century, Vygotsky proposes an alternative hypothesis in his seminal work *Thought and Language* [74]. In Chapter 2, titled "*The problem of speech and thought in the child in J. Piaget's theory*," he argues that egocentric speech is "in a transitional stage in the evolution from externalized speech to inner speech" (p. 72). Unlike Piaget, Vygotsky asserts that egocentric speech does not reflect egocentric thought but has a social basis and is connected to "the logic of action and rational, goal-oriented thought" (p. 74).

Today, we know that EF are only activated when the individual faces a difficulty. EF are unnecessary in response to what is "easy." Remarkably, the following text remains highly relevant despite the years that have passed. Here, Vygotsky draws on the arguments of Claparède, Piaget's mentor, regarding awareness in the face of difficulties: "The *difficulties* and *disturbances* that arise in an activity [...], lead to an awareness of this activity" ([74, p. 70], emphasis added). Building on Claparède, Vygotsky notes that Piaget shows that "this awareness follows action and only appears when automatic adaptation encounters difficulties" [74, p. 92]. Individuals become interested in causes only when their actions are not correctly adapted; "*it is necessity to overcome difficulties that creates awareness, consciousness*" (p. 92, emphasis in the original). Vygotsky continues this time in his own words: "When adaptation is automatic, instinctive, the mind does not consider categories. The execution of an automatic act poses no problem for our mind. Without difficulty, there is no need, and therefore no awareness" (p. 92).

Vygotsky contends that egocentric speech manifests as a response to children's difficulties when trying to find solutions to problems or anticipating subsequent actions. "[The child's egocentric speech] very easily becomes an *instrument of thought* in a true sense, that is, it begins to serve the function of *elaborating a plan* to solve the *problem* that has arisen" ([74, p. 70], emphasis added).

However, Vygotsky states that older children behave differently: "They *look attentively*, reflect (if significant pauses are considered), and find the solution" (p. 70, emphasis added). "[...] we assume that the operation the preschool child performs by speaking aloud, the school-aged child performs using inner, silent speech" (p. 70). According to Vygotsky, word and action are closely linked:

> Our experiments have shown how the *word*, which expresses the result of the action, is indissolubly *intertwined with this action*, precisely because it reproduces and reflects the most important structural elements of the practical intellectual operation, because [the word] itself begins to illuminate and *guide the child's action*, subjecting it to an *intention* and a plan, raising it to the level of appropriate activity. (p. 71)

Vygotsky refers to Piaget when linking awareness and language: "The emergence of language always certifies this process of awareness" (p. 70). The Piaget-Vygotsky debate continues almost 20 years after Vygotsky's death. Piaget responds, revising this idea in a text published in 1962 titled, "Commentaire sur les remarques critiques de Vygotski" (Comments on Vygotsky's critical remarks) concerning *Language and Thought in the child* and *Judgment and Reasoning in the Child*: "[...] It took me a long time to see that the roots of logical operations are deeper than linguistic relationships and that I studied thought too much initially at the level of language [...]" [53, p. 391].

Here, Piaget offers an alternative to Vygotsky's thesis linking language and awareness, as he opens the door to the idea that the earliest self-regulation processes are not anchored in language but in action. Piaget's work on sensorimotor development masterfully addresses this issue, which will be the focus of the next section.

Beyond the immense significance of the Piaget-Vygotsky debate on egocentric language (private speech), one conclusion is clear today: Piaget's thesis on the "non-social," "autistic" status of egocentric language as a mere reflection of egocentric thought has not withstood the test of time. However, since Vygotsky's work became widely known in the West in the 1970s and 1980s, there is broad consensus that language, beyond being a tool for communication with others, also functions as a tool for self-regulation when children face challenging tasks. An extensive body of literature continues to document the role of private speech in the transition from hetero-regulation to self-regulation [43]. Private speech helps the child "in becoming progressively more aware of their own behavior, goal-directed activity, and even emotions, enabling them to exercise gradually an executive control on their activity, thoughts, and feelings" [4, p. 4].

Furthermore, the Vygotskian perspective can be applied beyond language—or, more precisely, "below language." It opens the door to the transition from regulation by others to self-regulation through prelinguistic signs, such as gestures and the use of objects [45, 64]. This is an essential area for analyzing the origins of EF today.

9.3 The Origin of EF from the End of the First year of Life: The Relevance of Piaget Today

Eduardo Martí and Edith Ackermann succinctly summarize the importance of self-regulation processes for development in Piaget's work: "To Piaget, the autoregulation [self-regulation] processes are crucial to explain cognitive changes and the direction of development" [37, p. 209]. "[T]he construction of self as a center of decision and control is at the core of [Piaget's] concern" [1, p. 66].

The model of equilibration has significantly influenced dynamic systems theories. Concepts such as self-organization and emergence in early childhood owe much to Piaget's influence [49, 69, 73]. Two periods of Piaget's work stand out. The Piaget of sensorimotor development (second period, 1930s–1940s) and The Piaget of the equilibration model, with its focus on awareness and the distinction between success and understanding why (fourth period, 1970s).

9.3.1 The Equilibration Model in Piaget, 1970s

We begin with the later Piaget, focused on self-regulation processes, which he terms *equilibration.* Piaget's interest in equilibration, the dynamics of cognitive functioning in individuals' specific activities [17, p. 11], and the processes of change became central in the Geneva School in the late 1960s and especially during the 1970s (see discussion in [60 and 62]. Equilibration is, for Piaget, the central problem of development [68]. The seminal work of this period is *L'équilibration des structures cognitives, problème central du développement* [The Equilibration of Cognitive Structures: The Central Problem of Development] [56]. Piaget views equilibration as a process governing all aspects of knowledge development. It does not involve static forms of equilibrium. For this reason, Piaget speaks of *equilibration* as a process, rather than equilibrium as a state.

One source of progress in development is disequilibrium, which compels the individual to move beyond their current state "and to search for solutions in new directions" [56, p. 17]. Regulations in response to disequilibria lead to reequilibrations that improve prior structures. Without disequilibria, there would be no better forms of equilibrium—what Piaget calls *majorant reequilibration* (équilibration majorante). The focus of development is thus placed on processes that generate novelty, a hallmark of *majorant equilibration.* Equilibration functions based on the goals the individual sets for themselves. In seeking a new balance, the initial systems are completed or even replaced by others.

Other significant works from this period include *La prise de conscience* [The Grasp of Consciousness [54] and *Réussir et comprendre* [Success and Understanding] [55]. Here, objects and their material properties gain new importance. Consciousness, which involves making deliberate decisions, entails conceptualizations derived from the effects of one's own actions. Using an object according to a goal and noting the results achieved (whether success, failure, or approximation) are conscious acts. Consciousness is triggered when, in attempting to solve a problem, "automatic regulations are insufficient, and it is necessary to actively search for new means" ([54, p. 262], our translation). According to Piaget, consciousness requires recognizing the goals to be achieved, with intention providing the overarching direction of the act. Consciousness also involves identifying the means employed, the reasons for their selection, or modifications made along the way [54].

Although Piaget's equilibration model rarely refers to infants, these works provide a strong foundation for analyzing self-regulation processes in early development. For instance, the search for new means to achieve challenging goals involves degrees of awareness and flexibility in action, enabling better forms of equilibrium. Another of Piaget's brilliant ideas is the distinction between *achieving* something and *understanding why*. Interestingly, in the literature on EF, there is extensive discussion of "achieving" goals; however, little attention has been given to the need children sometimes express to go a step further and understand *why* they achieved their goal. This distinction seems to us a central topic for EF [61].

9.3.2 Sensorimotor Development in Piaget, 1930s

Piaget's interest in equilibration as a process was already evident in *La naissance de l'intelligence chez l'enfant* [The Origins of Intelligence in Children] [51] and *La construction du réel chez l'enfant* [The Construction of Reality in the Child] [52]. His model of intelligence development as adaptation to the environment constitutes his most significant contribution to the study of the early development of EF. The ability to intentionally control one's behavior, set goals, and seek solutions to obstacles until achieving them is one of the core themes of development and one of its central milestones, starting in the second half of the first year of life [59]. In his work on sensorimotor development, Piaget documented the origins and early development of cognitive control in everyday life situations. As Pascual-Leone points out, "To this day [Piaget's] sensorimotor theory is one of the most coherent, constructivist, and causal theories available about thinking and problem-solving in infancy" [49, p. 33].

For the first time, during the fourth stage of sensorimotor development, around 8 or 9 months of age, children set goals that are not directly accessible and must find the means to achieve those goals. According to Piaget, a goal involves an "investment in the highest degree of awareness, which constitutes intentionality" [51, p. 189]. To achieve a goal the child sets intentionally, they must overcome various difficulties requiring differentiated *intermediate means*. The resistances and difficulties the child encounters when acting on an object drive the search for solutions and, consequently, self-regulation.

To reach the goal, the child must "keep the pursued goal in mind and try different known means to eliminate the difficulty" [51, p. 189]. This involves intentionally coordinating means-ends schemes. Piaget incorporates into action the elements now considered core EF components: the initial *inhibition* of the goal in favor of implementing the necessary means to achieve it, *flexibility* in organizing and testing different "transitive or mobile" means (p. 194), and *monitoring progress* (updating and working memory). Notably, Piaget emphasizes the central role of the challenging goals that children set for themselves. These goals enable the progressive consciousness involved in self-regulation processes (or equilibration, as he called them).

Piaget has played an essential role in the growing consensus today that the earliest manifestations of EF begin in the fourth stage [12]. The A-not-B error made by children when, according to Piaget, the object has not yet become fully permanent has inspired many researchers. The A-not-B error, transformed into a task, includes all the elements of what are now considered core executive functions: flexibility, inhibition, and working memory [9, 11–12, 36, 71]. However, there is a paradox: Piaget's developmental perspective, which emphasizes children's initiative and intentional action in everyday life with increasingly complex equilibration processes, has largely gone unnoticed (see discussion in Rodríguez and Moreno-Llanos [63]). His approach contrasts sharply with the use of standardized tasks, where the goals are those of the experimenter, not the child. In these tasks, the experimenter takes the active role, while the child is asked merely to react. As noted at the beginning of the chapter, a growing number of authors are questioning the use of standardized tasks to assess EF. It is highly likely that Piaget would align with these critical voices.

In conclusion, we can affirm that Piaget and the sociocultural school of Vygotsky and Luria share important theoretical and epistemological assumptions that can shed new light on EF research today. (i) They adopt a developmental perspective, (ii) The ability to self-regulate behavior is constructed and placed at the center of the subject's constitution, (iii) Action and interaction with the environment provide the keys and tools for this construction, (iv) There is a movement from external action (*bottom-up* processes) to internal representation and thought (*top-down* processes), and vice versa.

Nevertheless, both perspectives have their weaknesses. On the one hand, today, it seems complicated to defend Piaget's thesis about the lengthy construction process of the subject as a center of control and decision-making occurring in isolation, without guidance or consensus with others. As Vygotsky and Luria assert, children appropriate [31], Lemétayer uses the term adhesion) the semiotic and cultural tools that adults use in interaction and communication to regulate their behavior. This idea has been recently revisited by several authors cited at the beginning of the chapter. For instance, according to Doebel [14], EF involve activating representations such as values, beliefs, and interests, in addition to motor skills and other knowledge, which children use to direct their behavior toward meaningful goals.

On the other hand, based on Piaget's contributions to sensorimotor development, it is unconvincing to argue that language is the first or the only tool for self-regulation, as Vygotsky and, to a great extent, Luria claimed. It should be noted, however, that Vygotsky had already passed away by the time Piaget published in 1936 *The Origins of Intelligence in Children.* We can hypothesize that Vygotsky might have reconsidered his thesis on the role of language as the first instrument of self-regulation had he read this text. It is also highly likely that he would have nuanced his statement that the so-called "lower psychological functions," lack semiotic processes.

It is worth noting that despite the absence of prelinguistic semiotic mediators in the sociocultural literature on the origins of EF, this gap has been gradually addressed over the past two decades, with the inclusion of private gestures [18, 24, 46, 72]. Some authors argue that prelinguistic mediators provide the semiotic foundation upon which private speech later emerges [10]. In this sense, other semiotic systems before language could perform analogous, though not identical, functions of representation, communication, and self-regulation in infancy.

9.4 Paradigm Shift in the Early Development of Executive Functions

Understanding how children begin to consciously and intentionally regulate their own behavior in everyday life, from the end of their first year, is a significant challenge in psychology. The Pragmatics of the Object, the perspective we adopt here, draws on the theories of Piaget and Vygotsky while offering elements to transcend their respective paradoxes. First, it is essential to focus on prelinguistic constructions. Two undeniable protagonists emerge when children set their own challenges: actions with objects and material instruments, and self-directed gestures as well as gestures directed at others. Moreover, without prior guidance and regulation from others, it is difficult to imagine that children would independently acquire the semiotic tools necessary to initiate their own self-regulation processes. This pragmatic perspective, rooted in children's actions and initiatives in everyday situations, aligns with those advocating for a paradigm shift in EF research.

If, as we have seen, a paradigm shift in EF research is necessary in general, this need is even more urgent regarding the earliest manifestations of EF. In addition to the critiques mentioned earlier, it is essential to consider the specific research challenges in early development. Let us briefly examine some of these difficulties:

1. *Agency.* At the starting point of EF research, it is essential to position children as the active agents they are. At their level, children have the ability to make decisions and transform reality. They set their own meaningful challenges and are capable of seeking solutions to address them [63]. However, the use of standardized tasks often places children in a passive role, where they are expected to respond to the experimenter's objectives and initiative in arbitrary, abstract situations with low ecological validity. This paradox is already evident when applied to adults [6, 23, 34], and it becomes even more pronounced when dealing with children under two years of age.
2. *It is necessary to start from prelinguistic semiotic systems.* Another significant consequence of using standardized tasks is what can be called the *language obstacle*, as children may not have sufficient linguistic ability to understand what is expected of them [40, 47], especially in situations that disrupt their

everyday life. We already saw in the Vygotsky-Piaget debate the difficulty of positioning language as the primary tool of self-regulation. Before the ages of 2–3, children do not possess language skills developed enough to use it for self-regulation. However, it cannot be conclusively stated that a child without language does not exhibit self-regulation. This connects to the next point.

3. *Development as a starting point: what children can do.* It is necessary to introduce a developmental perspective that considers what children are capable of doing. However, standardized measures used with children are often simplifications and adaptations of those designed for adults [44]. Moreover, the consideration of EF as universal skills has contributed to viewing children in comparison to adults, emphasizing what they lack ("deficit lens"). This adult-centric perspective does not recognize that children set their own goals but instead assumes they depend on the initiative of others [16, 19]. Therefore, it is necessary to shift the focus from the child's deficits to a positive perspective of what they can do, taking their development seriously.
4. *Top-down and bottom-up processes.* Cognitive perspectives have primarily emphasized the top-down nature of executive functioning, from thought to action. However, if the goal is to explain the origins and early development of EF, it is essential to consider the dialectical feedback between bottom-up processes that start from action and move toward representation, and top-down processes that start from representation and return to action in a continuous cycle.
5. *Longitudinal studies.* The relative lack of longitudinal studies that adopt a developmental perspective is not a recent critique. Claire B. Kopp raised this issue in an article published in 1982 titled "Antecedents of Self-Regulation: A Developmental Perspective," which includes adults' influence on children's self-regulation development (for a methodological overview, see Chap. 3 in this volume).

9.5 Conclusions

One central idea in this chapter is the need for a paradigm shift in the approach to Executive Functions [16, 26]. In recent decades, standardized tasks have become the hegemonic method of study, disregarding the views of highly influential classical voices such as Alexander Luria and Muriel Lezak, who emphasized that tasks are not the evaluation itself but merely an instrument of assessment. Among recent critical perspectives, various arguments are presented, such as the lack of ecological validity in the tests, the failure to consider the social and cultural characteristics of individuals, the atomization and segmentation of the processes involved in EF, or the lack of attention to the meaningful activities of individuals in their daily lives [5, 58].

If a paradigm shift is necessary, it becomes urgent when addressing the origin and early development of Executive Functions. In this chapter, we have reviewed the legacies of Piaget and Vygotsky. We consider that both approaches can shed significant light on this paradigm shift. Vygotsky and Luria emphasized that semiotic instruments, which initially operate externally in interactions with others and are progressively internalized, are central to self-regulation. Without the intervention of semiotic systems, self-regulation is impossible. Meanwhile, Piaget's theory of sensorimotor development provides a developmental perspective on the child's progressive acquisition of control, culminating in the intentional control of their actions by the last third of the first year of life. From our perspective, this developmental milestone marks the origin of executive functioning in an agentive, creative individual who transforms their environment. This occurs long before verbal language becomes the primary tool of self-regulation.

We conclude that it is essential to promote a developmental approach with longitudinal designs that account for the processes involved in constructing Executive Functions. Research must start from what children actively do in their daily lives. From around 8–9 months of age, children begin producing gestures—whether self-directed or directed at others—and acting intentionally with objects to achieve their practical goals. The starting point of research must focus on the semiotic systems already functional by the end of the first year, preceding language development. At this age, intentional action involves the everyday uses of materiality. The pragmatic, social and communicative dimensions of objects lie at the core of the processes involved in nascent cognitive control.

In Chap. 10, we will elaborate on this pragmatic and semiotic perspective on Executive Functions, rooted in children's intentional actions and socially constructed meanings (see also Chap. 11 in this volume). The focus will be on how Executive Functions develop, beginning with the intentional activity of children using meaningful objects and instruments in daily life. This pragmatic approach may contribute to the paradigm shift from the very first manifestations of Executive Functions during the first year of life.

References

1. Ackermann, E. (1990). Circular reactions and sensori-motor intelligence: When Piaget's theory meets cognitive models. *Archives de Psychologie, 58*, 65–78.
2. Alcalá, L. (2023). The developing of executive function skills through culturally organized autonomy and helping. *Infant and Child Development, 32*(6), Article e2460. https://doi.org/10.1002/icd.2460
3. Ardila, A. (2018). *Historical development of human cognition. A cultural-historical neuropsychological perspective*. Springer.
4. Bochicchio, V., Keith, K., Montero, I., Scandurra, C., & Winsler, A. (2022). Digital media inhibit self-regulatory private speech use in preschool children: The "digital bubble effect." *Cognitive Development, 62*, 101180. https://doi.org/10.1016/j.cogdev.2022.101180
5. Bombín-González, I., Cifuentes-Rodríguez, A., Climent-Martínez, G., Luna-Lario, P., Cardas-Ibáñeez, J., Tirapu-Ustárroz, J., & Díaz-Orueta, U. (2014). Validez ecológica y entornos multitarea en la evaluación de las funciones ejecutivas [Ecological Validity and Multitasking Environments in the Assessment of Executive Functions]. *Revista de Neurologia, 59*(2), 77–87.
6. Chevalier, N. (2015). Executive function development: Making sense of the environment to behave adaptively. *Current Directions in Psychological Science, 24*(5), 363–368. https://doi.org/10.1177/0963721415593724

7. Claparède, E. (1930). Autobiographie [Autobiography]. In E. Claparède (1909/1972), *Psychologie de l'enfant et pédagogie expérimentale* (11 ed., pp. 19–62). Neuchâtel: Delachaux et Niestlé.
8. Conway, A., & Stifter, C. A. (2012). Longitudinal antecedents of executive function in preschoolers. *Child Development, 83*(3), 1022–1036.
9. Cuevas, K., Rajan, V., & Bryant, L. J. (2018). Emergence of executive function in infancy. In S. A. Wiebe & J. Karbach (Eds.), *Executive function. Development across the life span* (pp. 11–28). Routledge.
10. Delgado, B., Gómez, J. C., & Sarriá, E. (2011). Pointing gestures as a cognitive tool in young children: Experimental evidence. *Journal of Experimental Child Psychology, 110*(3), 299–312.
11. Diamond, A. (1985). Development of the ability to use recall to guide action, as indicated by infants' performance on A-no-B. *Child Development, 56*, 868–883.
12. Diamond, A. (2006). The early development of EFs. In E. Bialystok & F. I. M. Craik (Eds.), *Lifespan cognition. Mechanisms of change* (pp. 70–95). Oxford University Press.
13. Diamond, A. (2013). Executive functions. *Annual Review of Psychology, 64*, 135–168. https://doi.org/10.1146/annurev-psych-113011-143750
14. Doebel, S. (2020). Rethinking executive function and its development. *Perspectives on Psychological Science*, 1–15. https://doi.org/10.1177/1745691620904771
15. Doebel, S., & Lillard, A. S. (2023). How does play foster development? A new executive function perspective. *Developmental Review, 67*, 101064. https://doi.org/10.1016/j.dr.2022.101064
16. Doebel, S., & Müller, U. (2023). The future of research on executive function and its development: An introduction to the special issue. *Journal of Cognition and Development, 24*(2), 161–171. https://doi.org/10.1080/15248372.2023.2188946
17. Ducret, J.-J., & Cellérier, G. (2007). *L'équilibration: concept central de la conception piagétienne de l'épistémogenèse* [Equilibration: A Central Concept in the Piagetian Conception of Epistemogenesis]. Fondation Jean Piaget pour recherches psychologiques et épistémologiques. http://www.fondationjeanpiaget.ch/fjp/site/crypt/index.php?DOCID=1289, consultado el 21/01/2021.
18. Español, S., & Rivière, A. (2000). Gestos comunicativos y contextos interpersonales: un estudio con niños de 10 a 16 meses [Communicative gestures and interpersonal contexts: A Study with Children Aged 10 to 16 Month]. *Estudios de Psicología, 21*(65–66), 225–245. https://doi.org/10.1174/021093900320380785
19. Frick, A., & Chevalier, N. (2023). A first theoretical model of self-directed cognitive control development. *Journal of Cognition and Development, 24*(2), 191–204. https://doi.org/10.1080/15248372.2022.2160720
20. García-Barrera, M. A., Contreras, A., & Moreno-Llanos, I. (2023). Contribuciones de Alfredo Ardila a nuestra comprensión de la Función Ejecutiva [Contributions from Alfredo Ardila towards our understanding of Executive Function]. *Revista Neuropsicología, Neuropsiquiatría y Neurociencias, 23*(1), 15–29.
21. Gaskins, S., & Alcalá, L. (2023). Studying executive function in culturally meaningful ways. *Journal of Cognition and Development, 24*(2), 260–279. https://doi.org/10.1080/15248372.2022.2160722
22. Gaskins, S., & Paradise, R. (2010). Learning through observation in daily life. In David F. Lancy et al., *The Anthropology of learning in childhood*. AltaMira Press. ProQuest Ebook Central. http://ebookcentral.proquest.com/lib/universidadcomplutense-ebooks/detail.action?docID=480070
23. Goldberg, E. (2001). *The executive brain. Frontal lobes and the civilized mind*. Oxford University Press.
24. Guevara, I., & Rodríguez, C. (2023). Developing communication through objects: Ostensive gestures as the first gestures in children's development. *Developmental Review, 68*. https://doi.org/10.1016/j.dr.2023.101076

25. Hughes, C. (2011). Changes and challenges in 20 years of research into the development of executive functions. *Infant and Child Development, 20*, 251–271. https://doi.org/10.1002/icd.736
26. Hughes, C. (2023). Executive functions: Going places at pace. *Journal of Cognition and Development, 24*(2), 296–306. https://doi.org/10.1080/15248372.2023.2187636
27. Hughes, C., & Ensor, R. A. (2009). How do families help or hinder the emergence of early executive function? In C. Lewis & J. I. M. Carpendale (Eds.), Social interaction and the development of executive function. *New Directions in Child and Adolescent Development, 123*, 35–50.
28. Kopp, C. B. (1982). Antecedents of self-regulation: A developmental perspective. *Developmental Psychology, 18*(2), 199–214.
29. Korzeniowski, C., Ison M. S., & Difabio de Anglat, H. (2021). A summary of the developmental trajectory of executive functions from birth to adulthood. In P. A. Gargiulo & H. L. Mesones Arroyo (Eds.), *Psychiatry and neuroscience update. From epistemology to clinical psychiatry* (Vol. IV, pp. 459–473). Springer.
30. Koskulu-Sancar, S., Blom, E., van de Weijer-Bergsma, E., Grandfield, E., Verhagen, J., & Mulder, H. (2023). Teachers matter in early childhood: The relation between teacher behaviours and executive function development in toddlerhood. *Infant and Child Development, 33*, e2474. https://doi.org/10.1002/icd.2474
31. Lemétayer, F. (2005). Le développement de l'autorégulation du comportement dans un contexte ineractionnel au cours de la deuxième année de vie [The Development of Behavioral Self-Regulation in an Interactional Context During the Second Year of Life]. *L'année psychologique, 105*, 573–590.
32. Lewis, C., & Carpendale, J. I. M. (2009). Introduction: Links between social interaction and executive function. In C. Lewis & J. I. M. Carpendale (Eds.), Social interaction and the development of executive function. *New Directions in Child and Adolescent Development, 123*, 1–15.
33. Lewis, C., Koyasu, M., Oh, S., Ogawa, A., Short, B., & Huang, Z. (2009). Culture, executive function, and social understanding. In C. Lewis & J. I. M. Carpendale (Eds.), Social interaction and the development of executive function. *New Directions in Child and Adolescent Development, 123*, 69–85.
34. Lezak, M. D. (1982). The problem of assessing executive functions. *International Journal of Psychology, 17*, 281–297.
35. Luria, A. R. (1979). *The making of mind. A personal account of Soviet psychology* (M. Cole & S. Cole, Eds.). Harvard University Press.
36. Marcovitch, S., & Zelazo, P. (2009). A hierarchical competing systems model of the emergence and early development of executive function. *Developmental Science, 12*(1), 1–25. https://doi.org/10.1111/j.1467-7687.2008.00754.x
37. Martí, E. (1994). Peer interaction in problem solving. A microgenetic analysis of interpsychological mechanisms. In N. Mercer & C. Coll (Eds.), *Teaching, learning and interaction* (pp. 209–216). Fundación Infancia y Aprendizaje.
38. Martínez, T., & Sancho, M. (2024). Cuidado de larga duración: una nueva mirada [Long-Term Care: A New Perspective]. *Conferencia Ateneo de Madrid. Sección de Psicología.* Sala Ramón y Cajal, 19 de Abril, 2024. Madrid.
39. Matthews, J. S. (2018). When am I ever going to use this in the real world? Cognitive flexibility and unban adolescents' negotiation of the value of mathematics. *Journal of Educational Psychology, 110*(5), 726–746. https://doi.org/10.1037/edu0000242
40. McClelland, M. M., Cameron, C. E., & Dahlgren, J. (2019). The development of self-regulation in young children. In D. Whitebread (Ed.), *The Sage handbook of developmental psychology and early childhood education* (pp. 471–486). Sage.
41. Mecacci, L. (1977/1979). *Brain and history. The relationship between neurophysiology and Psychology in Soviet research.* Brunner/Mazel.
42. Miyake, A., Friedman, N. P., Emerson, M. J., Witzki, A. H., & Howerter, A. (2000). The unity and diversity of executive functions and their contributions to complex "frontal lobe" tasks: A

latent variable analysis. *Cognitive Psychology, 41*, 49–100. https://doi.org/10.1006/cogp.1999.0734
43. Montero, I., & De Dios, M.J. (2006). Vygotsky was right. An experimental approach to the relationship between private speech and task performance. *Estudios de Psicología, 27*(2), 175–189. https://doi.org/10.1174/021093906777571709
44. Moreno-Llanos, I., Guevara, I., Palacios, P., & Rodríguez, C. (2024). How to study the early development of executive function? Let's put control back in the hands of children. *New Ideas in Psychology*. https://doi.org/10.1016/j.newideapsych.2023.101049
45. Moro, C. (2012). Heuristique des thèses sémiotiques vygotskiennes pour l'approche du développement des fonctions exécutives chez le jeune enfant [Heuristics of Vygotskian Semiotic Theses for Approaching the Development of Executive Functions in Young Children]. *RIFL, 6*(2), 210–223.
46. Moro, C., Dupertuis, V., Fardel, S., & Piguet, O. (2015). Investigating the development of consciousness through *ostensions toward oneself* from the onset of the use of object to first words. *Cognitive Development, 36*, 150–160.
47. Neale, D., Basilio, M., & Whitebread, D. (2018). The grasping task: A 12-month predictor of 24-month delay task performance and BRIEF-P inhibition scores. *Infant and Child Development, 27*, e2092. https://doi.org/10.1002/icd.2092
48. Niebaum, J. C., & Munakata, Y. (2023). Why doesn't executive function training improve academic achievement? Rethinking individual differences, relevance, and engagement from a contextual framework. *Journal of Cognition and Development, 24*(2), 241–259. https://doi.org/10.1080/15248372.2022.2160723
49. Pascual-Leone, J. (2012). Piaget as a pioneer of dialectical constructivism: Seeking dynamic processes for human science. In E. Martí & C. Rodríguez (Eds.), *After Piaget* (pp. 15–41). Transaction Publishers.
50. Piaget, J. (1923/1984). *Le langage et la pensée chez l'enfant* [Language and Thought in the Child]. Denoël/Gonthier.
51. Piaget, J. (1936/1977). *La naissance de l'intelligence chez l'enfant* [The Birth of Intelligence in the Child]. Delachaux et Niestlé.
52. Piaget, J. (1937/1977). *La construction du réel chez l'enfant* [The Construction of Reality in the Child]. Delachaux et Niestlé.
53. Piaget, J. (1962/1985). Commentaire sur les remarques critiques de Vygotski concernant le *Langage et la pensée chez l'enfant* et *le Jugement et le raisonnement chez l'enfant* [Commentary on Vygotsky's Critical Remarks on "Language and Thought in the Child" and "Judgment and Reasoning in the Child"]. In L. S. Vygotski (1934/1985), *Pensée et Langage*. (pp. 387–399). Editions Sociales.
54. Piaget, J. (1974). *La prise de conscience* [The Emergence of Consciousness]. Presses Universitaires de France.
55. Piaget, J. (1974). *Réussir et comprendre* [Success and Understanding]. Presses Universitaires de France.
56. Piaget, J. (1975). *L'équilibration des structures cognitives. Problème central du développement* [The Equilibration of Cognitive Structures: A Central Problem in Development]. Presses Universitaires de France. Version électronique réalisée sous l'égide de la *Fondation Jean Piaget*.
57. Pintrich, P. R. (2000). Multiple goals, multiple pathways: The role of goal orientation in learning and achievement. *Journal of Educational Psychology, 92*(3), 544–555. https://doi.org/10.1037/0022-0663.92.3.544
58. Rader, N., & Zukow-Goldring, P. (2010). How the hands control attention during early word learning. *Gesture, 10*(2), 202–221. https://doi.org/10.1075/gest.10.2-3.05rad
59. Rodríguez, C. (2006). *Del ritmo al símbolo. Los signos en el nacimiento de la inteligencia* [From Rhythm to Symbol: Signs in the Birth of Intelligence]. Horsori.
60. Rodríguez, C. (2022). The construction of executive function in early development: The pragmatics of action and gestures. *Human Development, 66*(4–5), 239–259. https://doi.org/10.1159/000526340

61. Rodríguez, C. (2023). La acción y los gestos, protagonistas en el origen de las Funciones Ejecutivas [Action and Gestures as Key Players in the Origin of Executive Functions]. In M. Orozco-Hormaza, E. Cerchiaro-Ceballos, & J. C. Ossa (Eds.), *¡Sí hubo futuro en el pasado! Aportes de Rebeca Puche-Navarro a la construcción de la psicología en Colombia* (pp. 92–131). Editorial ASCOFAPSI.
62. Rodríguez, C., & Martí, E. (2012). Introduction. The fertility of Piaget's legacy. In E. Martí & C. Rodríguez (Eds.), *After Piaget* (pp. xix–xxxviii). Transaction Publishers.
63. Rodríguez, C., & Moreno-Llanos, I. (2023). A pragmatic turn in the study of early executive functions by object use and gestures. A case study from 8 to 17 months of age at a nursery school. *Integrative Psychological and Behavioral Science*. https://doi.org/10.1007/s12124-020-09578-5
64. Rodríguez, C., & Palacios, P. (2007). Do private gestures have a self-regulatory function? A case study. *Infant Behavior and Development, 30*(2), 180–194. https://doi.org/10.1016/j.infbeh.2007.02.010
65. Schunk, D. H. (2005). Self-regulated learning: The educational legacy of Paul R. Pintrich. *Educational Psychologist, 40*(2), 85–94. https://doi.org/10.1207/s15326985ep4002_3
66. Stuss, D. T., & Alexander, M. P. (2000). Executive functions and the frontal lobes: A conceptual view. *Psychological Research, 63*, 289–298.
67. Tervo-Clemmens, B., Calabro, F. J., Parr, A. C., Fedor, J., Foran, W., & Luna, B. (2023). A canonical trajectory of executive function maturation from adolescence to adulthood. *Nature Communications, 14*, 6922. https://doi.org/10.1038/s41467-023-42540-8
68. Thelen, E., & Bates, E. (2003). Connectionism and dynamic systems: Are they really different? *Developmental Science, 6*(4), 378–391.
69. Thelen, E., & Smith, L. (1994/1998). *A dynamic systems approach to the development of cognition and action*. The MIT Press.
70. Tirapu-Ustárroz, J., Cordero-Andrés, P., Luna-Lario, P., & Hernáez-Goñi, P. (2016). Propuesta de un modelo de funciones ejecutivas basado en análisis factoriales [A Proposed Model of Executive Functions Based on Factor Analysis]. *Revista de Neurología, 64*(2), 75–84.
71. Topál, J., Gergely, G., Miklósi, A., Erdöhegyi, A., & Csibra, G. (2008/2014). Infants' perseverative search errors are induced by pragmatic misinterpretation. In J. G. Bremner & A. M. Slater (Eds.), *Psychology of infancy. Vol. 4. Cognitive development: From Piaget to the developing theory of mind* (pp. 113–118). Sage.
72. Vallotton, C. (2008, September). *Infants take self-regulation into their own hands* (pp. 29–34). ZERO TO THREE.
73. van Geert, P. (2000). The dynamics of general developmental mechanisms: From Piaget and Vygotsky to dynamic systems models. *Current Directions in Psychological Science, 9*(2), 64–68.
74. Vygotski, L. S. (1934/1985). *Pensée et Langage* [Thought and Language]. Editions Sociales.
75. Zachariou, A., & Whitebread, D. (2019). Developmental differences in young children's self-regulation. *Journal of Applied Developmental Psychology, 62*, 282–293. https://doi.org/10.1016/j.appdev.2019.02.002
76. Zelazo, P. D., Muller, U., Frye, D., & Marcovitch, S. (2003). The development of executive function in early childhood. *Monographs of the Society for Research in Child Development, 68(3)*, Serial No. 274.

10 Action and Communication in the Origin of Executive Functions: A Pragmatic Perspective

Cintia Rodríguez, Iván Moreno-Llanos, Irene Guevara, and Gonzalo Flecha

> L'intelligence, ce n'est pas ce que l'on sait, mais ce que l'on fait quand on ne sait pas (Piaget).[1]

10.1 Introduction

A paradigm shift is needed to study Executive Functions (EF). This was the conclusion of the previous chapter. Here, we present a functional and pragmatic proposal for understanding the origins and early development of EF in everyday situations from the end of the first year of life. We start with infants' actions, initiatives, and interests as they set goals for themselves—goals that motivate them but present challenges because they are difficult to achieve. As we will see throughout this chapter, learning to use everyday objects and tools functionally represents one of the earliest challenges for infants.

[1] Intelligence is not what we know, but what we do when we don't know (Piaget).

C. Rodríguez (✉) · I. Moreno-Llanos
Universidad Autónoma de Madrid, Madrid, Spain
e-mail: cintia.rodriguez@uam.es

I. Guevara
Department of Psychology, Universidad Antonio Nebrija, Madrid, Spain

G. Flecha
Early Years School Antonio Mercero, Madrid, Spain

C. Rodriguez Garrido et al. (eds.), *The Social Life of Objects in Early Development*, Social Interaction in Learning and Development,
https://doi.org/10.1007/978-3-031-87673-8_10

Mastering the functional use of objects and tools represents highly engaging challenges for infants at this age. While adults find objects and their uses self-evident and straightforward, infants do not experience them the same way. Just as words have public meanings that do not emanate directly from them, objects and tools also possess public meanings that infants must learn. Adapting to the environment involves agency—being aware of one's capacity for action, which includes mastering everyday materiality and understanding what to do with it and how to do it. This growing interest in objects coincides with the onset of the construction of the functional permanence of objects. Functional permanence [62] refers to the process by which infants begin to understand and share with adults the socially constructed and public meanings of the material world around them (see Chap. 2 of this volume).

Once an infant sets a challenging, motivating goal that cannot be achieved directly, they must "take a detour." This involves activating various executive components that work together as a coordinated "team," each supporting the others. This occurs as early as the first manifestations of Executive Functions (EF) around 8 or 9 months of age.

In this chapter, we provide an initial exploration of what we consider to be seven fundamental executive components. The first, which serves as an umbrella uniting the others, is the *challenge*, the motivating and demanding goal the infants set for themselves. The challenge organizes, coordinates, and directs the other components: the search for appropriate *means*, the *inhibition* and *flexibility* to overcome difficulties, the *monitoring* of the course of one's actions, the *persistence* when facing obstacles, and the sustained *attention* to the progression of one's actions. These components and their harmonious interplay are all necessary to achieve the difficult goals that children pursue.

This chapter also shows that later, during the first half of the second year of life more complex executive components emerge, such as *evaluating* one's actions, *including others* in one's objectives, and *planning* future actions.

The seven main executive components occur through action, interaction within specific and concrete situations, and semiotic systems (systems of signs) that are socially constructed. Locating the earliest manifestations of EF in action requires a dialectical approach that considers both *bottom-up* processes—originating from action and modifying representation—and *top-down* processes—originating from representation to modify action in a continuous and reciprocal cycle.

The first socially constructed semiotic systems involved in EF are the uses of materiality available to infants and the gestures they direct at themselves (*private gestures*) and at others.

The functional and pragmatic approach to EF we advocate aligns with the definition of intelligence promoted by the Geneva School. For example, Edith Ackermann stated that "intelligence is not so much about what we know or what we can do, but rather what we are capable of *inventing* or *constructing* to help us achieve *goals that are too difficult* for our current abilities" ([1], p. 177, emphasis and translation ours). This definition of intelligence closely reflects the functional activation of EF when individuals face challenging objectives.

Beginning to set intentional goals around 8 or 9 months, as Piaget suggests, represents the highest degree of conscious investment ([55], p. 189), a true Copernican shift. The reason is evident: while the goal mentally directs the infant's intentional behavior, the means to achieve that goal are activated first in the realm of action. Intentionality sets a pivotal turning point in infants' lives, influencing their behavior, relationship with themselves and others, and their interaction with the material world. It opens up possibilities for control, anticipation, and creativity, introducing new and enhanced opportunities for adaptation to their environment.

A glance at the literature on early development is enough to deduce a consensus regarding the timing of the first intentional behaviors. As discussed in Chapter 9, Piaget's sensorimotor development framework offers a meticulous and detailed view of the initial intentional goals set by his infants, starting from 7 to 9 months [55]. At this point, EF are already functional. While Piaget never explicitly used the term EF (the term was coined later), his in-depth analysis of his infants' behavior indicates that achieving "difficult" goals involves activating various skills recognized today as EF.

There is also broad agreement in early childhood psychology that infants intentionally communicate with others through gestures at this age. They can integrate both the other person and the referent within a single communicative act [6, 71, 72], see discussion in [60]. All of this establishes a secure foundation for exploring early EF: the certainty that infants are beginning to develop an awareness of their newfound abilities to control their immediate environment and to communicate with others intentionally.

In Chapter 9, we argued that Piaget's perspective on self-regulation, rooted in action (what he termed *equilibration*) must be complemented by the recognition that cognitive control significantly depends on the social world and cultural tools [2]. At the origins of self-regulation, communication, and guidance from others, mediated through semiotic tools, play a central role [73]. In a longitudinal study by Moro [49] from the perspective of the Pragmatics of the Object, a striking sequence of triadic interaction (adult-infant-object) was documented during the final session. In this interaction, a mother helped her 16-month-old daughter navigate a challenging task, thereby contributing to developing the infant's EF. The task involved placing a cat's head onto a series of rings stacked on a wooden pole. Moro highlights how the adult's intervention, through semiotic mediators—including gestures, uses of objects, and language—guides, supports, and regulates the infant's activity:

> The regulation of action by the adult, at the level of the executive function's development in the child, involves different components [...] (notably, the *planning* of actions to achieve the goal, mental *flexibility*, selective *attention*, focus on *priority information*, and the *regulation* of *emotions*). (2012, p. 220, emphasis and translation ours)

Infants progressively internalize semiotic mediators throughout their development [8, 35, 42]. This process marks the transition from externally directed regulation, or hetero-regulation, to self-regulation. Infants gradually take control of their own behavior by relying on the meanings and semiotic tools socially constructed through interaction with others.

10.2 Pragmatic Perspective on the Origin of Executive Functions

We acknowledge that starting from infants' initiative and actions in their daily lives poses a challenge because, as Ardila notes, "Executive functions... rarely are analyzed in natural ecological conditions. How, indeed, do people solve everyday problems? This is obviously a crucial question in understanding human behavior" ([3], p. 93). Observing the challenges infants set for themselves in their daily lives, the complexity of these challenges, and how infants attempt to solve them is central to our investigation of the early development of EF. Our aim is not to identify successes or failures. In fact, "errors" are valuable opportunities to analyze the processes involved. Every action infants undertake is meaningful in understanding how they tackle their self-imposed challenges.

This pragmatic position involves distancing from the concept of EF as "endogenous neural mechanisms," a characteristic of cognitive neuroscience research (see Hughes, [35]). It also rejects the widely accepted notion of "executive deficit" [23], which posits that children under 2 or 3 years of age have "worse EF" compared to adults. Furthermore, it contrasts with the modular and segmented view of EF that has gained popularity in recent decades. This approach also questions the relevance of defending the "purity of the task," a hallmark of tests designed to evaluate specific EF components such as flexibility or inhibition. Additionally, it moves away from Vygotsky and Luria's theses that position language as the primary tool for self-regulation—a notion that remains influential. For instance, Frick and Chevalier [27] argue that language enables the shift from external regulation to self-regulation. However, language, as the quintessential semiotic system for self-regulation in later developmental stages, is absent in these early executive manifestations.

The first three studies on self-regulation co-authored by the first author of this chapter were longitudinal and took place in the infants' homes, focusing on their interactions with their parents [4, 5, 70]. The infants' ages ranged from 11 to 18 months. A common feature across these studies was that infants and adults were always allowed to act with their own initiative using the objects and tools provided by the researchers.

Thanks to the longitudinal designs, the transition from hetero-regulation—where parents guided their infants—to self-regulation could be analyzed. The studies also examined how infants refined the means to functionally use objects and material instruments. All participants demonstrated self-directed private gestures, which helped them "to think" about regulating their behavior and improving their object use (see Rodríguez, [63] for a summary of these studies).

The case of A., a 15-month-old girl, is particularly noteworthy. In the study's final session [4], she specifically sought her father's help after repeatedly hitting

After several unsuccessful attempts to insert the ball into the box by hammering with the mallet,
*A. reaches out her hand to her father, holding the mallet (ostensive gesture), seeking his assistance to achieve her goal. A. does not relinquish control. She decides what her father should do, how, and when.

(Basilio & Rodríguez, 2011)

Fig. 10.1 A. (1;3). Ostensive gestures are directed at the adult with a self-regulation function. Canonical use of tools [4]

a ball with a hammer without inserting it into a box. She did something that caught our attention: she requested her father's help by performing an ostensive gesture with the hammer and vocalizing "ee" (Fig. 10.1). Her father understood what she was asking and assisted her in hitting the ball with the hammer until it was successfully placed into the box. We concluded that, despite being a gesture directed at an adult, it served a self-regulatory function, as the girl decided when, how, and with what her father should act. She always retained the hammer and, thus, the control of the situation.

These studies demonstrated that using objects for their intended function is motivating and challenging for infants. Self-directed gestures proved useful in seeking solutions, helping infants achieve their goals, and correcting incomplete or ineffective uses. These findings paved the way for further research into the origins of EF in school settings with infants under 12 months old. It became clear that focusing on actions and gestures was essential to understand the early forms of self-regulation.

10.3 Executive Functions in Early-Years-Schools

The questions we posed when analyzing the early manifestations of EF in early-years-schools from a pragmatic perspective were as follows: How can EF be characterized starting from 8 or 9 months of age, focusing on actions and the challenges infants set for themselves in everyday situations? What semiotic systems are involved? How do EF develop between the end of the first year of life and the first half of the second year?

To address these questions, we examined the challenging and meaningful goals infants set for themselves. These goals, being complex, present a challenge for the infant, yet remain attractive and engaging. Thus, we started with infants' actions and intrinsic motivation to achieve their goals in everyday contexts such as early-years schools [2, 11, 14, 24], preserving the ecological validity of these situations.

On occasions when the teacher initiates an activity, it is considered an executive sequence if infants adopt and internalize the goal proposed by the teacher.

We aim to capture the *dynamics* of interaction when infants try to solve their own challenges: what they *do* to achieve their *goals*, the *bottom-up* (from action to representation) and *top-down* processes (from representation to action) they follow, what *means* they use, the *semiotic* complexity of those means and objectives, and how these objectives and means evolve during these initial stages of executive development. Our focus is on action, uses of materiality, and gestures as the key elements in the earliest manifestations of EF.

To illustrate this pragmatic perspective, we will refer to several studies conducted during the first year of early childhood education across five early-years schools in the Community of Madrid [31, 32, 47, 48, 63, 64, 66–68, 76]. In Spain, early childhood education spans the 0–6 age range. Infants can begin attending school as early as 4 months old. Although this period is not mandatory, there has been a progressive increase in enrollment among infants in the cycle 0–3 years [15], reinforcing the importance of early-years schools as developmental contexts. Promoting autonomy—defined as the ability to direct one's behavior responsibly [13]—is a core goal of the early childhood education curriculum [59].

Infants' ages ranged from 4 to 17 months at the start and end of each study, respectively. The materials accessible to them depended on their respective teachers' (hereafter referred to as M) criteria, organization, and educational objectives and their centers. Throughout the school year, the teaching staff adjusted the materials based on the new skills that infants were developing. No external materials were introduced into the classroom, nor were there any suggestions regarding what to do or how to interact with the infants. Recordings were conducted monthly, beginning in October and ending in July, capturing the activities planned by the teachers. These recordings often included the arrival, main activitiy/ies, and finally, mealtime, ending with the meal's conclusion. The total filming time across the five participating schools was 54 h and 36 min.

We selected sequences in which it was evident that infants set challenging goals for themselves, leading them to seek effective solutions using the materials available. Since these goals were self-determined, we consider them all significant. These challenges motivated the infants, as reflected in their persistent efforts despite their difficulties. We imposed no external time limits on the sequences beyond the spontaneous flow of the activity. Achieving a goal could take as little as 15 s or more than 30 min, depending on the complexity of the goal, the gap between the infants' initial abilities and what they needed to accomplish, their developmental level, their persistence, or M's decision regarding when and how to intervene.

We have divided the chapter into four sections: First, we discuss the *executive processes* involved when infants set *significant*, non-directly accessible *challenges* for themselves in the classroom. Next, we address *the types of uses* observed, noting that the difficulties primarily revolved around using objects and tools effectively. We then examine private gestures as flexible tools for "thinking" about achieving these goals. Finally, we conclude the chapter with a summary of key findings.

10.4 Infants Set Meaningful Challenges: Executive Processes Implied

The starting point for EF arises from within and through action. To resolve the challenges they set for themselves, infants must act. Once an infant sets a meaningful, non-directly accessible challenge, they must activate specific means to achieve their goal [40]. However, despite the primacy of action, representation also plays a role from the earliest manifestations of EF. Goals are not "naturally" given in objects but emerge from the infant's intentional decision. This involves top-down processes originating from the goal and bottom-up processes stemming from the action. The object progressively transforms through the feedback generated by action, leading to new representations. These representations, in turn, influence subsequent actions, creating a dynamic interplay between action and representation.

The earliest challenges we identified in early-years school classrooms emerged around 8 to 9 months. Below this age, we did not observe any challenges involving intentional differentiation and coordination of means and ends.

Below are the seven executive components observed from the earliest EF manifestations. These can be considered as the essential executive components:

(1) *Goal:* The starting point of executive functioning and the cornerstone that "guides" the involvement of other components is the significant and challenging goal infants set for themselves, which is not directly accessible. Goals inherently include emotional and motivational aspects [2, 11, 14, 24]. Goal and motivation for the goal are two sides of the same coin.

(2) *Inhibition:* Once infants set a *motivating* challenge for themselves, other components are needed due to the "distance" separating infants from their goal. Inhibition is the first step in this process. Paradoxically, they must temporarily *inhibit* the goal—a necessary condition to begin solving the challenge. This does not occur with "easy" and immediate objectives, but is required when obstacles stand between the infant and their goal. The infant must "pause" or inhibit the ultimate goal to focus on the intermediate steps or means necessary to achieve it. Inhibition is also applied to ineffective actions that steer the infant away from the goal and to distractions, such as the actions of other infants in the classroom.

(3) *Means:* The temporary inhibition of the goal allows the infant to explore what to do next. This involves identifying specific means aligned with the desired goal, the situation, and the context. The necessary means for achieving the goal must be subordinated to the goal and require coordination. At these early ages, gestures and object use are the primary means infants employ.

(4) *Flexibility:* Activating different means requires flexibility, as the connection between means and goals is not rigid. The means may vary depending on the characteristics of the goal, the available material resources, the presence of other people, and other situational factors.

(5) *Persistence*: Achieving a meaningful goal requires *persistence*, even when infants do not succeed on their first attempt. This persistence is necessary when the means they use are insufficient or inadequate or when multiple means must be coordinated simultaneously.
(6) *Monitoring:* Infants must *control* and *adjust* (updating) their actions, ensuring that the means they employ effectively bring them closer to their goal. This involves continuously evaluating whether their actions are working or require modification.
(7) *Attention*: Sustained attention is crucial for both the goal and the means to achieve it. We distinguish between attention *ON* (focused on the goal) and attention *OFF* (when something in the classroom diverts the infant's attention momentarily). The alternation between on- and off-attention is particularly significant in everyday situations in early-years schools. The approach to attention presented here parallels what Gaskins and Paradise [29] describe as *open attention*: "In open attention, the scope of attention is distributed across a wide field, in contrast to most models of attention that presume a narrow focus applied sequentially to a number of objects or events" (p. 99). *Open attention* is ongoing and plays a central role in everyday activities, enabling infants to balance their focus on the task while remaining aware of their broader environment.

The seven executive components emerge around 8 months of age. They "work as a team," coordinated to support a significant yet challenging goal, fueled by the necessary motivation throughout the process. It seems unlikely that 8-month-old infants would set goals for themselves without motivation. The challenge and the emotions surrounding it are mutually reinforcing. This means hot EF, associated with the orbitofrontal cortex, and linked to emotions, are engaged [75].

Alfredo Ardila [2] similarly distinguishes between metacognitive and emotional/motivational EF, which coordinate cognition and emotion/motivation. He observes that: "Solving everyday problems (functional application of EF), however, mostly requires the second ability (emotional/motivational)" ([2], p. 92). As we will explore in the following pages, when infants engage with motivating challenges in their daily lives, both cognitive and emotional EF are necessary, working in coordination at these early ages. This contrasts with the traditional view, which separates hot and cold executive functions [75].

In addition to the seven core or essential executive components, we have identified new ones emerging during the first half of the second year of life [48, 67]. These include:

(8) *Evaluation*: Around 12–13 months, we observed the first instances of positive evaluation when infants completed an activity with satisfactory results. They sometimes applauded using private symbolic gestures, either with others or for themselves.
(9) *Involving others in challenging goals*: During the first year of life, we found no executive sequences where infants involved others in their own challenges. Nor did they seek help when encountering obstacles. They set the challenges

for themselves and either resolved or attempted to resolve them independently. However, in the second year, from around 13–15 months, we observed sequences in which infants involved their teacher (M) in their goals. This could be by incorporating her into their action plan or seeking her assistance to achieve particularly complex objectives.

(10) *Planning*: In one instance, a 17-month-old infant planned his actions by preparing classroom materials before using them in a symbolic executive sequence. For the first time, there was a temporal gap between the planning phase and the execution of the actions required to achieve the challenge.

As language—the most powerful semiotic system [25]—increasingly intervenes in self-regulation, EF will be organized over the medium and long term [2, 28, 43], transcending the here-and-now characteristic of infancy, as described in this chapter.

As we have noted, studying EF from the perspective of infants' intentional actions and interests requires analyzing the teamwork of the core executive components: significant and motivating goals, initial inhibition of the goal, coordination of different means to achieve the goal, flexibility in employing those means, monitoring the course of action, persistence despite difficulties, and sustained attention.

Furthermore, it is necessary to consider the *specific situations* in which EF are engaged, including the *nature of the goal* infants pursue, the materiality involved, the particular *means* available, the semiotic systems employed according to their developmental level, and the duration of the sequences.

This aligns partially with the proposal by Niebaum and Munakata [53]: "[…] EF training should incorporate stimuli that are relevant to the contexts in which EF are needed [….] For example, training children in cognitive flexibility tasks using mathematical operations as rules should benefit math performance more than interventions that train flexibility with shape and color rules" (p. 8). Castorina and Barreiro [12] similarly emphasize the importance of considering the specificity of each knowledge object in regulation:

> The exchanges between systems of action and the world stabilize systems of thought through regulations. Such stability can only be understood at its genesis as a succession of a series of unstable systems. The subject's cognitive action on the world encounters resistance due to the specific characteristics of each object of knowledge. Consequently, the subject carries out regulatory processes to react to these disturbances. (p. 205, translation ours)

Therefore, in early EF development, it is essential to consider infants' specific objectives. It is insufficient to state that infants act or "experiment." It is necessary to analyze what they do and the semiotic complexity of the goals they set for themselves. Thus, it is imperative to specify the *types of uses* they aim for and how these evolve from the end of the first year of life (see Chapter 2 on types of uses and their development). We will discuss this next.

10.5 Types of Uses: Challenging Objectives Involve Using Objects and Tools

A consequence of focusing on early EF in infants' initiative and actions in their daily lives is that objects take the center stage. Action entails the transformation of objects. What is said about the object directly impacts the subject. Therefore, bringing objects out of the shadow where they are often placed in EF literature is necessary. It is crucial to analyze *what infants do or attempt to do* with objects.

Psychology, in general, and EF literature, in particular, have emphasized objects' "physical properties" [51]. However, artifact objects are part of material culture, possessing pragmatic and semiotic properties that cannot be reduced to shape, size, or color (see Chapter 8 of this volume). Objects serve a purpose—they are tools to achieve things. Early data on EF development suggest that infants are deeply interested in using objects despite the challenges this entails. Everyday objects present numerous queries and serve as a rich source of activity. This is unsurprising when considering that a fundamental aspect of an individual's adaptation to their environment depends on mastering their immediate material world. While the uses of material culture are socially constructed, the challenging objectives infants set for themselves are personal decisions at specific moments. Individual choices and the social construction of materiality are intricately intertwined in EF development.

Analyzing what infants do with objects, how they use them, for what purposes, what interests drive them, and how this evolves with development can shed significant light on the processes underlying early EF. As discussed in Chapter 2, understanding and mastering objects' socially agreed-upon functional uses is essential for adapting to the environment [52, 69]. Infants must construct these meanings. A pivotal moment in development occurs around the final third of the first year of life when infants begin their first intentional and functional interactions with objects and tools. Objects and tools progressively become *permanent through their function* [62]. Understanding the function of objects marks a turning point, not only in how infants relate to the material world but also in their interactions with others [22].

If we now consider the challenges infants face, the majority revolve around how to use the available objects and tools. This involved various types of difficulties because uses are not homogeneous; they differ in their semiotic complexity, which is why we emphasize *types of uses*. Focusing on the semiotic complexity of the types of uses/challenges allows us to address one of the central aspects of EF development. Figure 10.2 presents the frequency of challenges based on the types of uses identified in the five early-years schools studied during the *main activity* [48].

Focusing on the increasing complexity and semiotic diversity of the types of uses that captured infants' interest and presented challenges from 8 months onward allows us to approach the development of EF through action. Below, we present some examples of these types of uses. We begin with *rhythmic-sound uses*, then move on to *functional or canonical uses*, and finally to *symbolic uses.*

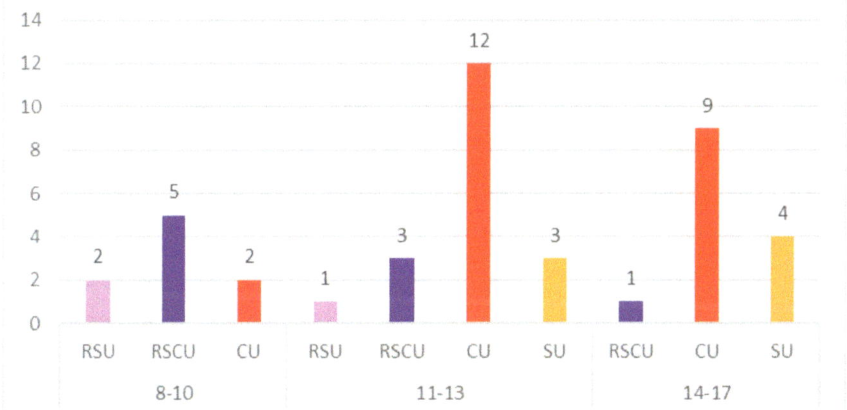

Fig. 10.2 Early childhood education. First course/challenges according to types of use and infants' age range in months during the main activity. RSU = Rhythmic-Sound Use; RSCU = Rhythmic-Sound Canonical Use; CU = Canonical Use; SU = Symbolic Use. Ages in months

10.5.1 Rhythmic-Sound Uses of Sound Objects and Musical Instruments

The most frequent and basic goals that infants set for themselves between 8 and 10 months involved using objects rhythmically to produce sound (Rhythmic-Sound Uses—RSU) and using musical instruments designed with a specific musical purpose (Canonical Rhythmic-Sound Canonical Uses—RSCU) (see Chapter 4 of this volume for the distinction between uses of sound objects and uses of musical instruments).

The first rhythmic-sound challenges we observed in early-years schools came from a girl, Ág. (0;8.9), and a boy, Ils. (0;8.7) (see Chapter 4, this volume, for the analysis of Ils.' rhythm using the bell). The common denominator is that both set meaningful objectives that captured their interest, even though achieving them required "taking a detour" because direct action was insufficient. We begin with Ág.'s sequence, which lasts 11 s. The girl sets herself an objective of making some inserted rings produce sound, a rhythmic-sound use (Fig. 10.3). The difficulty lies in the fact that she is standing unsteadily as she cannot yet stand independently. The rings are on a piece of furniture (3.1), requiring her to organize a sequence of intermediate actions to make them produce sound.

First, Ág. needs to *inhibit* her primary goal to focus on the *means she has determined*, which involves placing the rings on the ground within her reach (3.2). Once seated, she retrieves them (3.3–3.4). She then performs a *private ostensive gesture* (3.5), presenting the rings to herself to "think" before using them to produce sound (3.6), which was her initial objective. The entire process unfolds *flexibly*. She is *persistent* despite difficulties, *monitors* her actions, and maintains *attention* on her objective throughout the sequence [68].

At the start of the day, as infants arrive in the classroom, they have free access to the objects and spaces organized by M.

Activity Duration: 26'43"

Age: 0;8,9
Goal: To grab the rings and make them sound (rhythmic-sound use)
Difficulty: Ág. cannot use the rings on top of the table
Means: Placing the rings on the ground (ostensive gesture)
Attention ON (to goal): 11" (100%) Sequence Duration: 11"

3.1

Ág. steadies herself against a piece of furniture at her height.
*She grabs 4 stacked rings with her other hand.

3.2

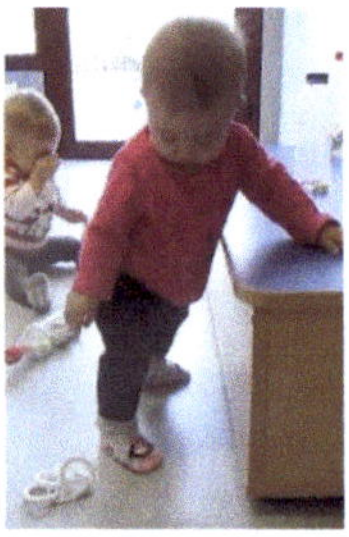

*She gently *drops-places* the rings on the floor, near her foot, while holding onto the furniture.

3.3

As she bends down, still holding onto the furniture, *she extends her *open* right hand toward the rings, *anticipating* her *intention* to retrieve them.

3.4

*As she sits down, she immediately retrieves the rings.

3.5

*Private ostensive gesture: She presents the rings to herself (centripetal orientation of her action), perhaps to "think" before acting.

3.6

*She makes the rings sound: *rhythmic-sound use.*
She finally achieves her goal. Ág. appears satisfied.

Fig. 10.3 Early manifestations of EF: How to make the rings sound. Rhythmic-sound uses. Complete Sequence in Rodríguez et al. [68]

Below, we can observe another challenge, set by J. (0;9,1), which involved ringing a bell (Fig. 10.4). This represents a rhythmic-sound canonical use of a musical instrument, embedded in cultural norms and rules of use, which implies greater semiotic complexity (see Chapter 4 in this volume). Rhythmic-sound uses evolve. As noted earlier, Ág., at 8 months (Fig. 10.3), successfully produced rhythmic sounds by shaking rings. These sound objects [17] do not present significant gripping challenges for 8-month-old infants. However, the situation is more complex with a musical instrument like a bell. At 9 months, J. had to make a series of adjustments to find the best grip (Fig. 10.4). Ringing a bell is more complex—its conventions of use are more challenging—than shaking rings. The *means* employed also varied, each objective and situation required specific means. *Monitoring* and *flexibility* differed between the ring and the bell. However, persistence and *focused attention ON* directed toward their respective objectives were evident in both cases.

10.5.2 Functional or Canonical Uses of Objects and Tools

The semiotic complexity of uses increased progressively, with functional uses following. Most challenges set by infants from 9 months onward were related to functional or canonical uses (Fig. 10.2): they sought ways to use objects and instruments according to their intended function.

We distinguish between rhythmic-sound canonical uses of musical instruments and overall functional uses of objects. Although strictly speaking, the uses of musical instruments *are* functional. However, given the specificity of the uses associated with musical instruments, we prefer to maintain the distinction (see Chapter 4 on rhythmic-sound uses).

Using accessible material in the classroom for its intended function was motivating and appealing to infants as young as 8 months, despite the difficulties they encountered. Their goals were highly varied. For example, infants attempted to remove pieces from a piggy bank, shake a ceiling-hung mobile that was difficult to reach, "read" a book, insert/retrieve balls from an "architecture," remove/insert walnuts into a hard-to-access can, eat with a spoon, insert/remove clips from a can, slide lids through a narrow slot in a container, fit blocks, and drink from a cup without assistance. The motivation of infants to pursue their goals with the available materiality was particularly noteworthy.

The spoon is a significant tool in infants' lives at this age. Many schools encourage infants to use spoons to eat, although mastering it requires a lengthy development process [8, 36]. In a study by Rodríguez et al. [66], an 11-month-old infant was observed eating with a spoon for the first time. The infant attempted this from the beginning of the meal with puree but only succeeded at the end with the dessert. The duration of this sequence was surprising, lasting over 30 minutes. The infant rejected any assistance offered by his teacher, as his challenge was to accomplish the task independently. This case is a paradigmatic illustration of persistence, sustained attention, flexibility in means, inhibition, and motivation to achieve a goal despite several obstacles (see discussion in Rodríguez, [63]).

As a cultural artifact, the spoon holds collective significance [18]. When infants use spoons to eat, they perform the same function as community members, giving continuity to a practice and sharing a meaning that humanity has carried out for millennia, guided initially by others. Using the spoon to eat or using other everyday tools effectively is fundamental to adapting to the environment.

M organizes an activity with musical instruments: bells, tambourines, rain sticks; and sound objects: jingles and rattles. She demonstrates their use and offers them in a way tailored to each infant according to their developmental stage.

Activity Duration: 19'24"

Age: 0;9,1
Goal: To use the bell effectively
Difficulty: Gripping the bell correctly
Means: Succesive approximations (canonical uses of diverse efficacy)
Attention ON (to goal): 1'07" (90,54%)

Sequence Duration: 1'14"

4.1

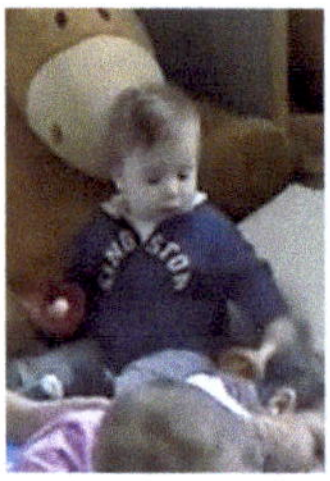

J shakes the yellow bell in the air and *strikes it on the floor (*canonical use* with intermediate efficacy).

4.2

Next, *he sucks on it (*non-canonical use*).
He then *inhibits* this use to make the bell ring.

4.3

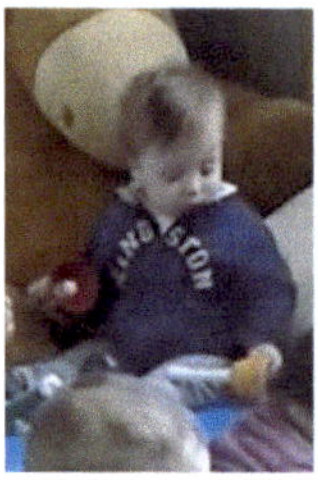

From the bell's base, *he strikes it against the floor (*protocanonical rhythmic-sound use*, with low efficacy).

4.4

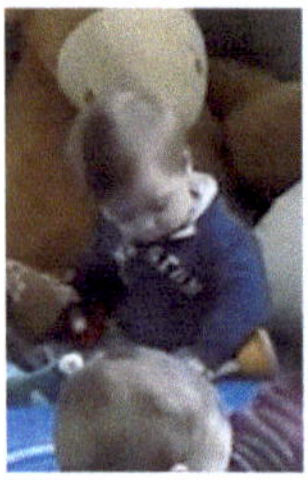

4.5

4.6

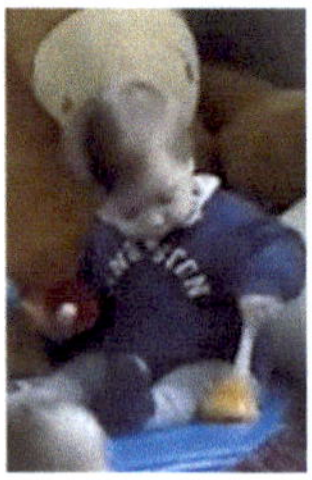

4.7

Gradually, he adjusts his grip *flexibly* (4.4 and 4.6), achieving increasingly effective *canonical uses*. First, he strikes the bell on the floor, "nailing it" (4.5), then shakes it in the air while striking it against the floor (4.7), resulting in greater effectiveness.

Fig. 10.4 How to effectively ring a bell: rhythmic-sound canonical uses. Unpublished Sequence

The complexity of infants' goals increased with age. For instance, P (1;1,22) set the goal of using a walker for its intended purpose: moving around the classroom (Fig. 10.5) [48]. In this sequence, all executive components reappear: a challenging goal, inhibition of ineffective uses, applying appropriate means, flexibility in the approach, monitoring of progress, persistence despite obstacles, and sustained attention.

While M is putting the younger infants to sleep, the older ones have free access to the objects and spaces in the classroom.

Activity duration: 20'03"

Age: 1;1,22
Goal: To move around the classroom using a walker (*canonical use of a tool*).
Difficulty: P must navigate various obstacles (*persistence*).
Means: Switches between walkers, adjusts direction, separates or arranges the walkers.
Attention ON: 6'51" (85,98%)

Sequence duration: 7'58"

5.1

5.2

P's *goal* is to move around the classroom using a walker. When unable to proceed due to obstacles such as the wall, an object, or *a peer (5.1), P explores various solutions (*flexibility in means*), which include *replacing the walker (*inhibition*) with another one (5.2).

5.3

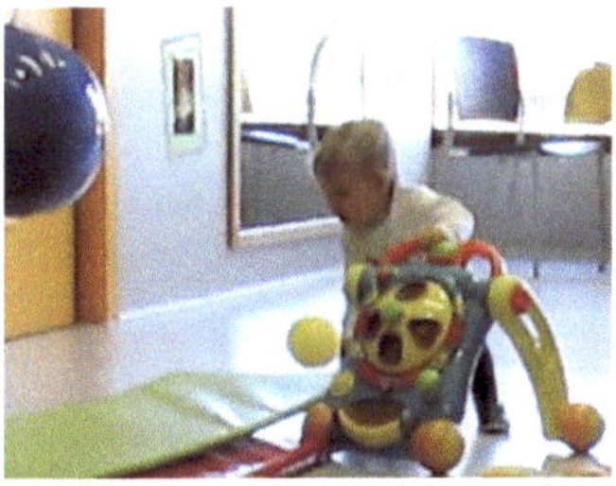

When unable to move forward due to the mat, *P tries to move it aside. When unsuccessful, P does not persist (*inhibition*) and pushes the walker along the side (*flexibility in means*).

5.4

*In another instance, unable to move forward due to a peer with another walker, P stops pushing (*inhibition*) and moves the walkers apart to the side (*flexibility*), allowing the continuation of his *goal* (*persistence*).

Fig. 10.5 How to move around the classroom with a walker: canonical use of a tool. Complete sequence available in Moreno-Llanos et al. [48]

10.5.3 Symbolic Uses of Objects and Tools

Infants also set challenges for themselves that involved the symbolic use of objects and tools. Symbolic uses were the last to emerge and were the least frequent in the first year of early childhood education (Fig. 10.2). This aligns with data on symbolic development. Symbols are partly rooted in functional uses detached from their original functional niche and applied (a) out of context, (b) with other objects through substitution, or (c) or in the absence of material support (see Chapter 5 in this volume on symbols) (Fig. 10.6). Compared to functional uses, symbols do not require efficacy. For example, successfully eating with a spoon requires significant time and effort from infants and their teachers. However, pretending to eat with a spoon is much "easier" in terms of efficacy, since it involves an abbreviated action performed with empty spoons outside of mealtime contexts (see Fig. 10.7). The first symbolic executive sequences appeared in schools around 12 or 13 months of age [48]. Infants typically involve their teacher (M) and only occasionally their peers. This may be because symbolic uses do not require efficacy and do not present difficulties when performed alone. The challenge arises when introducing another participant.

We now present a symbolic challenge. J.'s goal is to have "Drilo the Crocodile," a hand puppet, "eat" M and his peers (Fig. 10.6). However, he struggles to figure out how and where to insert his hand inside the puppet to "animate it."

In this sequence, all executive components are present. Notably, J. demonstrates *persistence*, spending two minutes trying to introduce the hand into the puppet. This persistence is also evident in his repeated attempts to find solutions. He also *inhibits* ineffective uses (Fig. 10.6, images 6.1 and 6.2) and *flexibly* explores different options until he discovers the opening for his hand (Fig. 10.6, image 6.3). Furthermore, there is an articulation between types of uses: the canonical use of inserting the hand into the puppet serves as a *means* to achieve his *symbolic goal* of "correctly eating" M using Drilo.

We now present another symbolic executive sequence (Fig. 10.7) of greater complexity because the symbolic uses emerge after an initial planning phase.

Planning Phase: The most notable aspect of this sequence is that Ils., a 17-month-old infant, begins with a *planning* phase before his symbolic activity. His challenge is to include M in his symbolic proposal. This is the only sequence we found where *planning* occurred before the action began [67].

The planning phase *before* his symbolic activity (Fig. 10.7) can be observed when Ils. gathers various kitchen utensils, containers, baskets, and spoons from the classroom (image 7.1), bringing them closer to M (image 7.2). The planning allows him to prepare the symbolic activity, which he *then* executes in several steps: he "cooks" himself (image 7.3), manages to involve M in the symbolic scenario with "his" utensils (image 7.47.4), "eats" using a spoon and several containers (image 7.5), and "feeds" M (image 7.6).

All of this demonstrates *flexibility* in symbolic uses. Ils shows significant *persistence* in gaining M's attention and involving her at different moments throughout

The teachers organize a welcome activity: they sing songs and tell stories using different puppets and replica animals.

Activity Duration: 10'00"

Age: 1;1,8
Goal: To "eat" M using "Drilo the Crocodile"
Difficulty: Figuring out how to insert his hand into the puppet (*canonical use*)
Means: Gradual approximations to symbolic use
Atención ON: 3'32" (64,04%)

Sequence Duration: 5'31"

From the start of the activity, J spends over two minutes trying to grab the crocodile (*persistence*). M does not allow him to take it. Once he succeeds, his goal becomes to have Drilo "eat" his peers and M (*symbolic use*). However, he encounters several difficulties in inserting his hand into the puppet's opening.

6.1

*J attempts to insert his hand through Drilo's mouth.
He is unsuccessful because it is not the correct place (*inhibition*).

6.2

*He places Drilo over his hand (*flexibility*). This also proves to be the wrong method (*inhibition*).
Nevertheless, Drilo "eats" his peers.

6.3

J successfully inserts his hand through the puppet's opening (*canonical use*).

*He achieves his goal: Drilo "eats" M (*symbolic use*).

Fig. 10.6 How to "eat" M with "Drilo the Crocodile." Symbolic use. Unpublished sequence

the sequence, as he must compete with his peers' proposals. It is also worth emphasizing Ils' high motivation and satisfaction upon successfully including M in his proposal.

The planning phase preceding the action indicates that *top-down* processes (stemming from representation) occur beforehand, with a temporal gap relative to *bottom-up* processes (use of objects and tools). This scenario introduces a novelty compared to the sequences presented so far, where *top-down* and *bottom-up* processes *co-occurred* during the action.

M organizes an activity around different kitchen utensils, such as spoons, cans, baskets, caps.
Activity Duration: 24'05"

Age: 1;4,28
Goal: "Eating" and "Feeding" M
Difficulty: *Planning* the scenario and capturing M's attention
Means: Organizing materials, various *symbolic uses*
Attention ON: 5'06" (74,63%)
Sequence Duration: 6'50"

7.1

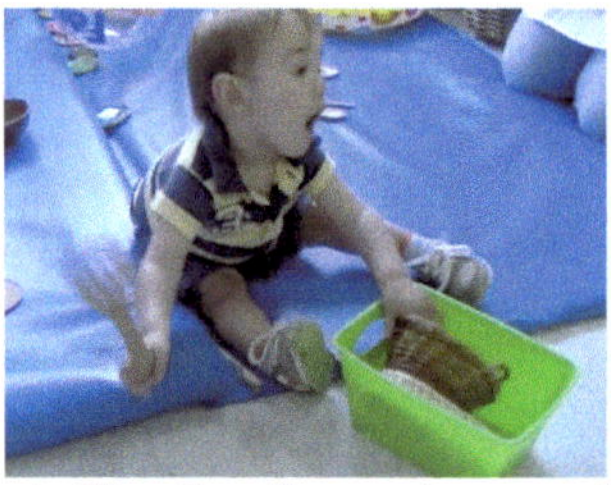

**Planning Phase:* Ils collects various utensils from the classroom to use for "cooking" and "eating" (*symbolic uses*).

7.2

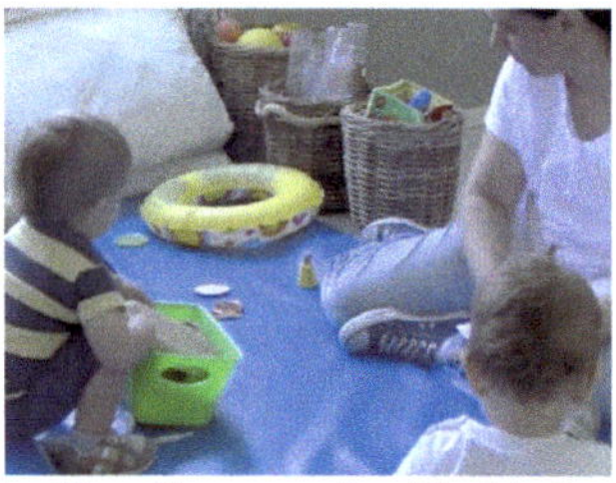

**Planning Phase:* Ils approaches M with the utensils he has gathered, *before* starting his symbolic action.

7.3

*Ils "cooks" with his utensils next to M (*symbolic uses*).

7.4

*Ils gets M to "cook" with his utensils. M accepts his symbolic proposal.

7.5

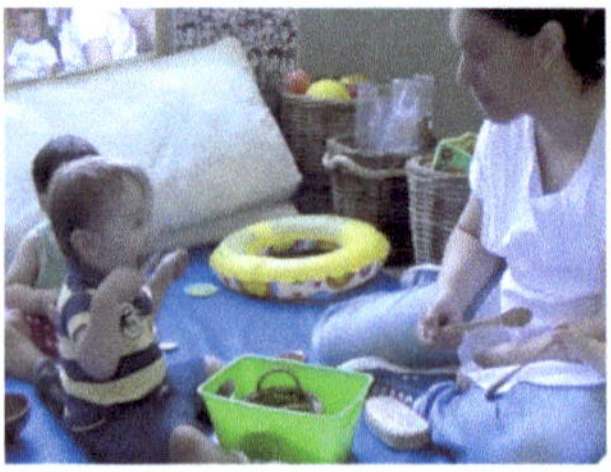

*Ils "eats" using a spoon and other utensils (*flexibility through symbolic uses*).

7.6

**Goal*: Ils successfully "feeds" M, competing with other classmates (*persistence*).

Fig. 10.7 Planning phase before "eating" and "feeding" M. Symbolic Uses. Complete Sequence in Rodríguez & Moreno-Llanos [67]

Before concluding this section on types of uses, we will briefly address *meta-canonical uses* [65]. These are effective uses, though carried out with objects not initially designed for that purpose. They share with canonical or functional uses the pursuit of efficacy and with symbolic uses the creative employment of objects for functions not intrinsic to them. We observed metacanonical uses in executive sequences among infants in their second year of early childhood education [64]. An example would be a girl, C. (1,5,27), who spends a sequence of 3′35″ attempting to stick wooden sticks into a bucket of sand, facing various difficulties yet persisting in her goal. This was a proposal by the teacher that the infant adopted as her own. The analysis of metacanonical uses is still exploratory, but these initial results are promising. They open pathways to explore the creative uses of materiality in development.

Next, we turn our attention to gestures, semiotic instruments that serve as means for achieving the challenging goals infants set for themselves. Similar to the use of objects and tools, gestures exhibit a progressively increasing semiotic complexity as development unfolds.

10.6 Self-directed Gestures as Means of Self-regulation

Before language becomes the primary system for communication and self-regulation, infants rely on earlier semiotic systems to interact with others and themselves. Among these systems, gestures stand out as flexible tools that allow infants not only to create and exchange meanings with others about the world around them (a function of gestures that has been widely studied) but also enable them to begin controlling their attention and behavior to achieve meaningful goals. This capacity emerges during the last third of the first year of life.

The notion that gestures, alongside language, not only serve to communicate but also play cognitive and problem-solving roles in everyday life is gaining increasing acceptance in psychology. There is growing evidence of these dual functions in studies conducted with school-aged infants, adults, or individuals with autism, among others [16, 26, 30, 34, 38, 44, 56]. However, how do these functions develop, and when can it be asserted that this dual role exists in infants' gestures? Furthermore, what is the relationship between the development of early gestures and the first manifestations of EF?

The earliest references in the literature to the role of gestures in early cognitive control trace back to studies by Bates et al. [7] focusing on the pointing gesture. The authors describe how, from the end of the first year of life and long before uttering their first words, infants begin performing self-directed pointing gestures in the absence of others. These self-directed pointing gestures have been linked to functions of control of attention toward objects and events of interest [10]. Additionally, Delgado et al. [19–21] attribute an "auto-declarative" function to these gestures: pointing to oneself allows infants to express and explore their understanding of the objects they interact with, thereby organizing their experience.

In line with these findings, Puche-Navarro [57, 58], in a study with infants aged 9 to 17 months on the origin of bimanuality in problem-solving situations (as activities that crystallize the means-end relationships), found that a 10-month-old girl *pointed* to the location of a ball inside a cylinder *before* continuing toward her goal. According to Puche-Navarro, pointing serves as a way to identify the steps needed for solving the task. This means that "before solving the task appropriately, [the infant] demonstrates pertinent indicators of their *understanding* of the proposed problem" (p. 120, emphasis ours). This gesture could be considered a *private pointing* in the service of comprehension, as Puche-Navarro suggests.

Subsequent studies show that infants also produce other types of private gestures, such as ostensive gestures of showing towards themselves or symbolic gestures [39, 41, 61]. According to Rodríguez and Palacios [70], when facing challenges -typically related to performing the functional use of objects- infants use gestures, as these have often been the same strategies adults previously employed to convey these uses and regulate their behavior. In this sense, the self-regulatory function of gestures likely has a social origin in early infant-adult interactions involving joint attention and action around attractive and challenging objects.

These self-directed gestures are referred to as "private gestures," analogous to the function of private speech (egocentric speech according to Vygotsky, 1934/1985 [73]; see discussion in Chapter 9 of this volume) as a key instrument for cognitive self-regulation [9, 74]. Infants pause their actions and provide themselves with external means to "think" about how to achieve a goal through self-directed private gestures [5, 33, 70]. We hypothesize that private gestures performed by infants when facing difficulties with the uses they are attempting serve as a form of "external thinking" [50]. This suggests that achieving a goal requires at least some *understanding* of what is being done, and private gestures fulfill this function by introducing moments of reflection and contemplation into the infant's interaction with the object. Private gestures prompt modifications in subsequent actions (a change in how the object is used) and, likely, in the representation of that use (a *bottom-up* process). This need for understanding is already evident in infants under 12 months of age.

We have observed that as the complexity of the classroom goals infants set for themselves increases, so does the semiotic complexity of the gestures they use to achieve these goals.

One of the main elements in the earliest self-regulatory behaviors is private ostensive gestures, which appear as early as 8 months of age [33]. At this stage, rather than continuing with the use of an object to resolve the difficulty they encounter (centrifugal orientation of their action), infants pause their activity to observe the object causing the problem carefully (centripetal orientation of their action) before resuming the activity with a somewhat altered or adjusted use of the object (see Fig. 10.8).

Later, around 11 months, infants also begin to incorporate private pointing gestures into their efforts to direct and maintain focus on their objectives. For instance, they use these gestures when objects fall outside their attentional frame, or when they require performing complex actions [66]. Private touch-pointing gestures are

The teachers organize an activity with containers and various objects for storing and removing, such as nuts and spoons.

Activity Duration: 12’23”

Goal: To store and remove nuts from a container (*canonical use*).
Difficulty: The container is opaque, so the infant cannot see what happens to the nuts once they are stored inside.
Age: 0;11;14
Means: Private ostensive and pointing gestures to guide her actions and attention.
Attention ON: 9’15” (79,06%)

Sequence Duration: 11’42”

8.1

After several attempts to grab the nuts from inside the container, Cn halts her action (*inhibition*) and
*shows herself the interior of the container (*private ostensive gesture*) to search for them (*flexibility*) before continuing (*persistence*).

8.2

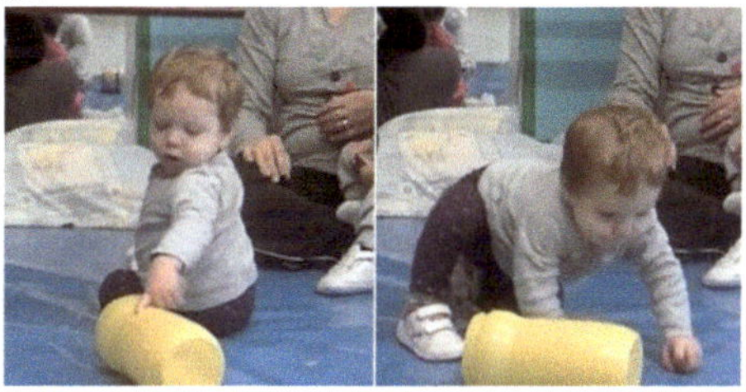

When the container falls and rolls away, Cn looks at it and
*touch-points it, before *turning to retrieve it (*persistence*).
She resumes removing the nuts from the container to store them again afterward.

Fig. 10.8 Private ostensive gestures and private pointing gesture. Complete sequence in Moreno-Llanos et al. [47]

observed more frequently to achieve their goals (Fig. 10.8). These gestures are particularly effective for directing the infant’s attention to relevant details of the objects they are interacting with, provided these objects are within the infant’s reach.

Finally, starting at 12 months, we have observed that infants perform private representational gestures, adding more complexity to their self-regulation processes. Through these gestures, such as clapping for themselves after successfully using an object, infants evaluate their own actions (see Fig. 10.9). Clapping highlights the close integration between cognitive and emotional/motivational components in EF: the satisfactory completion of a use aligns with the goal infants set for themselves. Positive evaluations are also a novelty in the second year. We did not observe evaluations in executive sequences before 12 months (see other examples in Basilio & Rodríguez, [5]; Guevara & Rodríguez, [33]; Moreno-Llanos et al., [48]).

Private gestures follow a proximal–distal-representational developmental trajectory, similar to gestures directed at others (as illustrated in Chapter 7 on the origins of intentional communication through gestures). Thus, the repertoire of private gestures becomes enriched based on infants’ growing signification skills in

M organizes an activity involving containers for storing and removing various objects, along with shape-sorting trucks.

Activity Duration: 20’10”

Goal: To insert wooden shapes into a shape-sorting truck.
Difficulty: To achieve the correspondence between the shape and the slot where it must fit on the truck. The truck has four sides with distinct slots.
Age: 1;0,1
Means: Private ostensive gesture to guide their action; private representational gesture to evaluate their action.
Attention ON: 4’24” (85,04%)

Sequence Duration: 5’11”

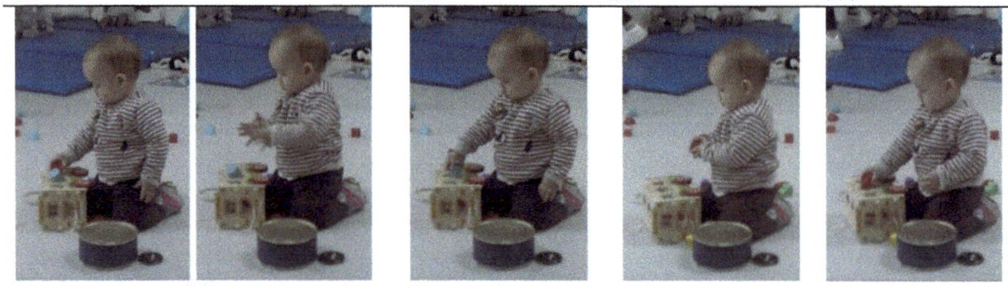

9.1	9.2	9.3	9.4
M tries to insert different shapes into the slots of the truck (*canonical use*). When she achieves her goal, *she claps for herself (*private representational gesture of evaluation*).	She continues with her objective *trying to insert other shapes (*persistence*).	After several failed attempts, she picks up another shape, *presents it to herself and rotates it in her hands (*private ostensive gesture*).	She proceeds with further attempts to insert different shapes into various slots (*persistence*).

Fig. 10.9 Private clapping gesture with evaluative function and private ostensive gesture for “thinking.”. Unpublished Sequence

their early years. Depending on their circumstances, they adjust their means to the properties of the objects they interact with. In other words, gestures are inherently pragmatic productions [54, 61, 69], acquiring meaning and significance insofar as they are performed with a function or purpose. Gestures’ forms and functions in the observed self-regulation sequences result from the complex interplay of various factors, such as the infant’s abilities, the characteristics of the referent (the object the gesture refers to), the infant’s knowledge and experience with that referent, and the specific interaction context. Including, for example, what infants and adults do before and after the gesture with the objects at hand.

In general, we have observed that infants produce private gestures to direct and maintain their attention on their goals, change strategies to overcome difficulties, prepare or anticipate their following action with the object, inhibit potential distractions, evaluate their performance, and involve others in their action plans (see Fig. 10.10).

M places books on the mat within the children's reach, who show evident interest. It is an activity they are familiar with.

Activity Duration: 20'22"

Age: 1;3,9
Goal: To get M to read the book.
Difficulty: Other children competing for M's attention.
Means: Variety of gestures (pointing, showing, clapping) and physical contact with the teacher (grabbing, touching, guiding her arm). Ils controls what M should do, when, and how.
Attention ON: 3'24" (86,81%)

Sequence Duration: 3'55"

10.1

* *Ils takes M's hand toward the book* to prompt her to read at the beginning of the sequence (*imperative function*).

10.2

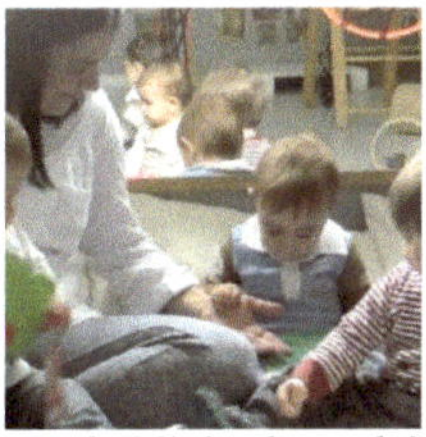

* *Ils guides M's hand toward the book* again after finishing the previous reading, when Ils closed the book. (*imperative function*).

10.3

* *Ils gives the book to M (ostensive gesture)* to encourage her to read it (*imperative function*).

10.4

* *Ils touch-Points the image* to prompt M to continue the reading (*imperative function*).

10.5

* *Ils gives the book to M (ostensive gesture)* to have her "make it disappear[1]" at the end of the reading (*imperative function*).

10.6

* *Ils claps (representational gesture)* after the book reading is finished (*positive evaluation function*).

Fig. 10.10 How to get M to read the book and accept my control of the situation.[2] Canonical Uses. Complete sequence in Rodríguez et al. [68]

[2] In this classroom, when finishing reading a book, M uses it as if it was "flying away", and hides it behind her back. Ils is demanding her to do so here.

As we noted in Chapter 9 of this volume, Piaget's work on equilibration provides a solid foundation for analyzing self-regulation processes. The search for new means to achieve challenging goals involves varying degrees of awareness and flexibility in action, allowing for better forms of equilibration. Piaget's distinction between *réussir* (succeeding) and *comprendre* (understanding), explored at various points in his work, sheds light on significant processes and highlights infants' active role when faced with their own challenges [64]. We have just seen how private ostensive gestures serve as a means to "think." This represents external thinking to explore solutions before returning to a corrected course of action. This demonstrates that infants are not automatons merely attempting to achieve their goals. Instead, they must *understand*, to some extent, where the difficulties lie and how to resolve them to succeed and reach their intended outcome.

In addition to private gestures, we have also identified, in some cases, *private uses of objects* in children over 13 months of age. These are the uses they perform after successfully achieving their goal. They repeat the use or modify some aspect of the procedure, retracing the previously completed path. Rather than seeking efficiency, it seems that infants aim to understand the process that led to the success of their actions [47, 67]. As if merely succeeding were not enough—they need to understand why they succeeded [4]. All evidence suggests that infants do not act blindly or mechanically. Instead, at their level, they need to *comprehend* how to achieve their objectives through private gestures and to consolidate them through repeated uses. Karmiloff-Smith argued for a similar phenomenon at other stages of development. She stated, "[c]hildren are not content simply to learn to talk or solve problems; they also want to understand how they do these things" ([37], p. 36). This significant distinction between succeeding (*réussir*) and understanding (*comprendre*), along with the corresponding development of awareness, has not, to our knowledge, been addressed in the literature on EF.

To conclude this section, we will discuss infants' gestures toward M that serve a self-regulatory function.

This is the case of Ils, who, at 15 months, seeks M's help because his goal is far beyond his current abilities (Fig. 10.10). It involves the reading of a book. He selects the book and decides what he wants from M at each moment (Fig. 10.10, images 10.1, 10.2, 10.3, 10.4 and 10.5). This demonstrates *persistence* in his objective, as he has to compete with his peers to gain M's attention, *flexibility in the means* he employs according to the sequence of actions involved in reading in the classroom, and *sustained attention.* After the reading, he ends with a positive *evaluation* (image 10.6) by clapping (a representational gesture).

We see an analogy with what happened with A. (Fig. 10.1) when she sought her father's help to insert the ball into the box with a hammer, all while maintaining control of the situation [4].

10.7 Conclusions

Throughout this chapter, we have presented an approach to the study of the early manifestations of EF between 8 and 17 months of age. To identify executive sequences, we focused on the challenging objectives or goals that children set for themselves.

All the situations analyzed occurred in everyday contexts, specifically in the classroom during the first year of early childhood education. They revolved around specific and meaningful objectives that children independently set for themselves. All involved the use of material objects and tools provided by their teachers. Thus, the various components of EF emerged in concrete situations involving everyday objects and tools. The action with objects and tools, along with gestures, were the two central elements of the early manifestations of EF.

Based on the results presented, we can affirm that EF develop progressively, along with their components. There is a close relationship between EF's development and semiotic systems' development. In these early stages, language—traditionally considered the semiotic system par excellence for self-regulation—was absent. However, semiotic systems involving the uses of objects and gestures were central.

We categorized infants' challenges according to types of use based on their semiotic complexity. The earliest and most basic were *rhythmic-sound uses*—functional uses involving sonorous objects or musical instruments (see Chapter 4 on musical components). From the end of the first year of life, the most frequent challenges involved attempting *functional uses.* Challenges involving *symbolic uses* were the least frequent and the last to emerge, appearing well into the second year of life. These findings suggest that attempting to use objects functionally was highly motivating and meaningful for children from the last third of their first year.

Other semiotic systems widely used by children before the emergence of language included self-directed *private gestures.* These private gestures served various functions, such as "thinking", flexibly seeking solutions before returning to action, accounting for infants's inhibitory skills. Later, in the second year of life, from 13 months onward, infants began directing gestures toward adults in some sequences to include them in their action plans or to request specific help.

The central focus of our analysis and its starting point is the objective that infants set for themselves. That is, to use objects and tools effectively. Through this objective, the remaining executive components come into play. In the early manifestations of EF, from 8–10 months of age, we identified seven components working "in unison" and "coordinated" under the umbrella of the challenging goal.

The seven executive components are the *goal*, the *means* to achieve it, *inhibition, flexibility, monitoring, persistence*, and sustained *attention.* These executive components are observed when infants act and/or produce gestures to resolve the challenge. Inhibition might involve an infant ceasing a non-canonical use (e.g., sucking on an object) that distances them from their goal and replacing it with another use that brings them closer to their target. Flexibility can be observed when the child changes one use for another more appropriate (closely linked to inhibition). It can be adaptive to alternate between different types of uses to achieve the goal. Flexibility is also observed in the alternation between gestures and uses, or between gesture's types and functions. Monitoring (updating) involves controlling the course of one's actions, including uses and gestures. The intricate network of uses and gestures evolves with development. Goals and the means to achieve them differ when children are 8 months old compared to when they are 11 or 15 months old. The semiotic complexity of both uses and gestures progresses over time.

The components of EF also develop. Throughout the second year of life, in addition to the seven components already present in the earliest identified sequences, we observed sequences where new components emerged. These include the following. First, some infants *involved their teachers in their challenges*, either because they lacked the necessary skills to complete their goal independently, or because the challenge consisted of including the teacher in their action plan. In this latter case, these were symbolic executive sequences.

Further exploration is needed to understand the implications of symbolic sequences and how they differ from functional sequences.

Another novelty in the second year was that some infants *evaluated* their actions, typically positively, often through clapping. Clapping gestures were often shared with the teacher. Occasionally, clapping occurred as a private representational gesture. The final novelty observed in a 17-month-old infant was *planning*. Planning occurred before executing a symbolic sequence. These findings highlight the evolution of the complexity and range of EF components as children develop, especially as they begin to engage in symbolic actions and integrate others into their goals.

The coordination of executive components that we propose here contrasts with the three "core" EF widely accepted in the literature. This entails the segmentation of EF, where each task is used to assess a single component (inhibition tasks, flexibility tasks, monitoring tasks, etc.), despite the general agreement that EF are *interdependent but related processes* (as [46], already proposed). It also contrasts with the classical perspective in which children face external, arbitrary challenges focused on the physical and perceptual dimensions of objects or stimuli. This approach has posed significant difficulties in studying the origin and early development of EF before the ages of 2–3 years (see discussion in Chapters 8 and 9 of this volume).

We must emphasize that in the pragmatic perspective we are advocating, *the goal comes from the infant*. In this sense, the objective is meaningful. Moreover, the criteria for efficacy guide the infant's actions, not an abstract or arbitrary proposal imposed by an external individual. Conversely, the educational action of teachers promotes the pursuit of challenges. Teachers' semiotic mediation guides infants actions in constructing conventional meanings without rigidly imposing an external goal or directing the infant's actions "towards a single correct answer."

Observing infants' challenges in everyday situations has allowed us to analyze not only the challenges they set for themselves, but also the means they use to regulate and direct their behavior. We emphasize the need to seriously consider infants' actions and the processes involved, moving beyond the reductionist success/error dichotomy framework. Instead, from a microgenetic perspective, we have meticulously analyzed the "life" of the action and the uses of objects performed. We do not consider "successes" or "failures" but progressive approximations and adjustments through which infants approach their own goals.

Thus, infants' actions, their uses of objects, and gestures become *means of self-regulation.* This contrasts with the classical view of EF as *top-down* processes. Instead, EF at these ages follow a *bottom-up* (from action to representation) and a *top-down* course (from representation to action). EF would not emerge as a priori *top-down* processes. Instead, they are anchored in the construction of meanings and representations derived from action with materiality [47]. Through action directed toward meaningful goals with objects and tools, infants develop their understanding of functional/conventional uses. This understanding allows them to orient their subsequent behavior more effectively. We have observed these dialectical processes through the adjustments in uses of varying semiotic complexity, where infants seek efficacy and their articulation with self-directed private gestures that help them "think."

Moreover, the coordination of executive components and the bottom-up/top-down interplay challenges the notion of task purity, which is characteristic of standardized tests. Instead, our findings point in the opposite direction. It seems unlikely that infants can achieve their objectives without inhibition, flexibility, activation of means—even if they need correction later—monitoring or persistence. These components, along with sustained attention, are essential for tackling challenging goals.

Using objects, tools, and gestures becomes the semiotic means children employ to regulate and direct their behavior toward meaningful goals. As mentioned earlier, none of the infants in the analyzed sequences relied on language to self-regulate. It is evident that once language begins to emerge, the executive components presented here will be influenced and transformed. Further research is needed to explore how these initial forms of self-regulation through basic semiotic systems are later coordinated with language.

Additionally, we have demonstrated throughout this chapter that the earliest manifestations of EF do not occur in a material vacuum. On the contrary, they are anchored in specific situations that require concrete solutions. This again highlights the theses of the Pragmatics of the Object regarding the importance of materiality in understanding the subject (see Chapters 1 and 2 in this volume). Understanding the subject involves understanding their actions, especially during the early years of life.

In conclusion, action with objects and gestures plays a crucial role in the origin of executive functions. Agency develops from a very early age, involving the pursuit of solutions that are already creative, meaningful, and motivating. This is important for the rest of life, even though its origin lies in the everyday situations in which infants live and grow.

This has significant implications for early-years schools and early childhood education. Recognizing how materiality can be leveraged as a potential source of challenges and educational intervention is essential. Unlike controlled and structured "tasks," everyday materiality can be highly meaningful [43].

What we are proposing is not so different from what Luria, the father of the EFs concept, advocated many decades ago, as reflected in the following excerpt where Mecacci discusses his perspective:

[T]he brain [is] an instrument of regulation of behaviour [...], not [...] a 'universal' brain *abstracted from the environment* but rather [...] a *brain 'occupied' with the interaction and the environment*. Thus, it is *a 'concrete' brain*, the complete understanding of which can start only from its study as an instrument, an active system of regulation of behaviour of single individuals in relation to equally concrete and specific environmental conditions (historical, social, and cultural). (Mecacci [45], p. 139, following Luria, emphasis ours).

The proposal based on the Pragmatics of the Object that we advocate for may contribute to the paradigm shift in the approach to EF. As we discussed in Chapter 9, a growing number of authors refer to the necessity of this change. Luria, Lezak (and Piaget) can still be of great help today. They would surely align with those promoting a paradigm shift in the study of EF.

References

1. Ackermann, E. (1992). Reconstruire la même quantité ailleurs: comment procèdent les jeunes enfants? [Rebuild the same quantity elsewhere: how do young children proceed?] In In B. Inhelder, G. Cellérier, E. Ackermann, A. Blanchet, A. Boder, D. De Caprona, J.-J. Ducret, & M. Saada-Robert. *Le cheminement des découvertes de l'enfant. Recherche sur les microgenèses cognitives* (pp. 177–192). Delachaux et Niestlé.
2. Ardila, A. (2008). On the evolutionary origins of executive functions. *Brain and Cognition, 68*, 92–99. https://doi.org/10.1016/j.bandc.2008.03.003
3. Ardila, A. (2018). *Historical development of human cognition*. Springer.
4. Basilio, M., & Rodríguez, C. (2011). Usos, gestos y vocalizaciones privadas: De la interacción social a la autorregulación [Private Uses, Gestures, and Vocalizations: From Social Interaction to Self-Regulation]. *Infancia y Aprendizaje, 34*, 181–194. https://doi.org/10.1174/021037011795377593
5. Basilio, M., & Rodríguez, C. (2017). How toddlers think with their hands: Social and private gestures as evidence of cognitive self-regulation in guided play with objects. *Early Child Development and Care, 187*(12), 1971–1986. https://doi.org/10.1080/03004430.2016.1202944
6. Bates, E., Begnini, L., Bretherton, I., Camaioni, L., Volterra, V., Carlson, V., Carpen, K. Y., & Rosser, M. (1979). *The emergence of symbols: Cognition and communication in Infancy*. Academic Press.
7. Bates, E., Camaioni, L., & Volterra, V. (1975). The acquisition of performatives prior to speech. *Merrill-Palmer Quarterly of Behavior and Development, 21*(3), 205–226.
8. Belza, H., Herrán, E., & Anguera, M. T. (2020). Early childhood, breakfast, and related tools: Analysis of adult's function as mediators. *European Journal of Psychology of Education, 35*(3), 495–527. https://doi.org/10.1007/s10212-019-00438-4
9. Bochicchio, V., Keith, K., Montero, I., Scandurra, C., & Winsler, A. (2022). Digital media inhibit self-regulatory private speech use in preschool children: The "digital bubble effect." *Cognitive Development, 62*, 101180. https://doi.org/10.1016/j.cogdev.2022.101180
10. Carpendale, J., & Carpendale, A. B. (2010). The development of pointing: From personal directedness to interpersonal direction. *Human Development, 53*, 110–126.

11. Castillo, A., & López, L. D. (2022). Studying hot executive function in infancy: Insights from research on emotional development. *Infant Behavior and Development, 69*, 101773. https://doi.org/10.1016/j.infbeh.2022.101773
12. Castorina, J. A. & Barrerio, A. (2015). Contribuciones de la psicología constructivista a la comprensión del aprendizaje escolar [Contributions from Constructivist Psychology to the Understanding of School Learning]. In E. Huaire, A. Elgier & G. Maldonado (Eds.). *Psicología cognitiva y procesos de aprendizaje. Aportes desde Latinoamérica,* (pp. 197–210). Universidad Nacional de Educación Enrique Guzmán y Valle.
13. Castro-Zubizarreta, A. (2011). *El centro de educación infantil como ámbito privilegiado para promover la autonomía personal* [The Early Childhood Education Centre as a Privileged Space for Fostering Personal Autonomy]. Universidad de Barcelona.
14. Chu, J., & Schulz, L. E. (2020). Play, curiosity, and cognition. *Annual Review of Developmental Psychology, 2*, 317–343. https://doi.org/10.1146/annurev-devpsych-070120-014806
15. Consejería de Educación, Ciencia y Universidades. (2023). *Datos y Cifras de la Educación 2023–2024* [Education Data and Figures 2023–2024]. Comunidad de Madrid. ISBN: 978-84-451-4085-7.
16. Cook, S. W., Yip, T. K., & Goldin-Meadow, S. (2012). Gestures, but not meaningless movements, lighten working memory load when explaining math. *Language & Cognitive Processes, 27*(4), 594–610.
17. Correa, M., Villalobos, M. E., Cárdenas, K., Moreno-Llanos, I., Del Olmo, M. J. & Moreno-Núñez, A. (2021). Usos rítmico-sonoros de objetos e instrumentos musicales en las aulas 0-1 y 1-2 [Rhythmic and Sound Uses of Objects and Musical Instruments in 0–1 and 1–2 Year-Old Classrooms]. In C. Rodríguez & J. L. de los Reyes (Eds.), *Los objetos sí importan. Acción educativa en la escuela infantil,* (pp. 57–82). Horsori.
18. De los Reyes Leoz, J. L. (2022). A cultural viewpoint about objects: Objects that narrate cultures and emotions. In J. Bisault, R. Le Bourgeois, J. F. Thémines, M. Le Mentec, C. Chauvet-Chanoine (Eds.), *Objects to learn about and objects for learning 2. Which Teaching practices for which issues* (pp. 213–227). ISTE. Wiley.
19. Delgado, B., Gómez, J. C., & Sarriá, E. (2009). Private pointing and private speech: Developing parallelisms. In A. Winsler, C. Fernyhough, & I. Montero (Eds.), *Private speech, executive function, and the development of verbal self-regulation* (pp. 153–162). Cambridge University Press.
20. Delgado, B., Gómez, J. C., & Sarriá, E. (2010). Early functions of the gesture of private pointing: Contemplation and self-regulation through the gesture of pointing. *Action Psychological, 7*(2), 59–70.
21. Delgado, B., Gómez, J. C., & Sarriá, E. (2011). Pointing gestures as a cognitive tool in young children: Experimental evidence. *Journal of Experimental Child Psychology, 110*(3), 299–312. https://doi.org/10.1016/j.jecp.2011.04.010
22. Dimitrova, N., & Moro, C. (2012). Common ground on object use associates with caregivers' gesturese. *Infant Behavior and Development, 36*, 618–626.
23. Doebel, S. & Müller, U. (2023). The future of research on executive function and its development: An introduction to the special issue. *Journal of Cognition and Development, 24*(2), 161–171. https://doi.org/10.1080/15248372.2023.2188946
24. Doebel, S., & Lillard, A. S. (2023). How does play foster development? A new executive function perspective. *Developmental Review, 67*, 101064. https://doi.org/10.1016/j.dr.2022.101064
25. Eco, U. (1984/1990). *Semiótica y filosofía del lenguaje* [Semiotics and Philosophy of Language]. Lumen.
26. Eielts, C., Pouw, W., Ouwehand, K., Van Gog, T., Zwaan, R. A., & Paas, F. (2018). Co-thought gesturing supports more complex problem solving in subjects with lower visual working-memory capacity. *Psychological Research*, 1–12.
27. Frick, A., & Chevalier, N. (2023). A first theoretical model of self-directed cognitive control development. *Journal of Cognition and Development, 24*(2), 191–204. https://doi.org/10.1080/15248372.2022.2160720

28. García-Madruga, J. A., Gómez-Veiga, I., & Vila, J. O. (2016). Executive functions and the improvement of thinking abilities: the intervention in reading comprehension. *Frontiers in Psychology, 7*, article 58. https://doi.org/10.3389/fpsyg.2016.00058
29. Gaskins, S., & Paradise, R. (2010). Learning through observation in daily life. In D. F. Lancy, J. Bock & S. Gaskins (Eds.), *The anthropology of learning in childhood* (pp. 85–118). Altamira. ISBN 978-0-7591-1324-4
30. Goldin-Meadow, S., Levine, S., Zinchenko, E., Yip, T., Hemani, N., & Factor, L. (2012). Doing gesture promotes learning a mental transformation task better than seeing gesture. *Developmental Science, 15*(6), 876–884.
31. Guevara, I., Moreno-Llanos, I., & Rodríguez, C. (2020). The emergence of gestures in the first year of life in the Infant School Classroom. *European Journal of Psychology of Education.* https://doi.org/doi.org/10.1007/s10212-019-00444-6
32. Guevara, I., Moreno-Llanos, I., Romero, L., Zapardiel, L. & Rodríguez, C. (2022). Challenges in first-years schools: Early manifestations of executive function (Chapter 9). In J. Basault, R. Le Bourgeois, J.-F. Thémines, M. LeMentec & C. Chauvet-Chanoine (Eds.), *Objects to learn about and objects for learning* (Vol. 2). Wiley Online Library.
33. Guevara, I. & Rodríguez, C. (2023). Developing communication through objects: Ostensive gestures as the first gestures in children's development. *Developmental Review, 68.* https://doi.org/10.1016/j.dr.2023.101076
34. Gullberg, M., de Bot, K., & Volterra, V. (2010). Gestures and some key issues in the study of language development. In M. Gullberg y K. de Bot (Eds.), *Gestures in language development* (pp. 3–34). John Benjamins.
35. Hughes, C. (2023). Executive functions: Going places at pace. *Journal of Cognition and Development, 24*(2), 296–306. https://doi.org/10.1080/15248372.2023.2187636
36. Ishiguro, H. (2016). How a young child learns how to take part in mealtimes in a Japanese day-care center: A longitudinal case study. *European Journal of Psychology of Education, 31*, 13–27. https://doi.org/10.1007/s10212-014-0222-9
37. Karmiloff-Smith, A. (1992). *Más allá de la modularidad* [Beyond modularity. A Developmental perspective on Cognitive Science]. Alianza.
38. Kita, S., Alibali, M. W., & Chu, M. (2017). How do gestures influence thinking and speaking? The gesture-for-conceptualization hypothesis. *Psychological Review, 124*(3), 245–266. https://doi.org/10.1037/rev0000059
39. Konishi, H., Karsten, A., & Vallotton, C. D. (2018). Toddlers' use of gesture and speech in service of emotion regulation during distressing routines. *Infant Mental Health Journal, 36*(6), 730–750. https://doi.org/10.1002/imhj.21740
40. Korzeniowski, C., Ison M. S., & Difabio de Anglat, H. (2021). A summary of the developmental trajectory of executive functions from birth to adulthood. In P. A. Gargiulo & H. L. Mesones Arroyo (Eds.), *Psychiatry and neuroscience update. From epistemology to clinical psychiatry* (Vol. IV, pp. 459–473). Springer.
41. Kuvalja, M., Basilio, M., Verma, M., & Whitebread, D. (2013). Self-directed language and private gestures in the early emergence of self-regulation: Current research issues. *Hellenic Journal of Psychology, 10*, 168–192.
42. Lewis, C. & Carpendale, J. I. M. (2009). Introduction: Links between social interaction and executive function. In C. Lewis & J. I. M. Carpendale (Eds.), Social interaction and the development of executive function. *New Directions in Child and Adolescent Development, 123,* 1–15.
43. Lezak, M. D. (1982). The problem of assessing executive functions. *International Journal of Psychology, 17*, 281–297.
44. Lin, Y. (2020). A helping hand for thinking and speaking: Effects of gesturing and task planning on second language narrative discourse. *System, 91*, 1–10. https://doi.org/10.1016/j.system.2020.102243
45. Mecacci, L. (1977/1979). *Brain and history. The relationship between neurophysiology and psychology in soviet research.* Brunner/Mazel.

46. Miyake, A., Friedman, N. P., Emerson, M. J., Witzki, A. H., & Howerter, A. (2000). The unity and diversity of executive functions and their contributions to complex "frontal lobe" tasks: A latent variable analysis. *Cognitive Psychology, 41*, 49–100. https://doi.org/10.1006/cogp.1999.0734
47. Moreno-Llanos, I., Guevara, I., Palacios, P., & Rodríguez, C. (2024). How to study the early development of executive function? Let's put control back in the hands of children. *New Ideas in Psychology, 72*, 101049. https://doi.org/10.1016/j.newideapsych.2023.101049
48. Moreno-Llanos, I., Zapardiel, L., & Rodríguez, C. (2021). Children's first manifestations of cognitive control in the early years school: The importance of the educational situation and materiality. *European Journal of Psychology of Education, 36*, 903–922. https://doi.org/10.1007/s10212-020-00505-1
49. Moro, C. (2012). Heuristique des thèses sémiotiques vygotskiennes pour l'approche du développement des fonctions exécutives chez le jeune enfant [Heuristic of Vygotskian Semiotic Theses for Approaching the Development of Executive Functions in Young Children]. *RIFL, 6*(2), 210–223.
50. Moro, C., Dupertuis, V., Fardel, S., & Piguet, O. (2015). Investigating the development of consciousness through ostensions toward oneself from the onset of the use-of-object to first words. *Cognitive Development, 36*, 150–160.
51. Moro, C., Muller Mirza, N., & Roman, P. (2014). *L'intersubjectivité en questions. Agrégat ou nouveau concept fédérateur pour la psychologie?* [Intersubjectivity in Question: Aggregate or New Unifying Concept for Psychology?] Antipodes.
52. Moro, C., & Rodríguez, C. (2005). *L'objet et la construction de son usage. Une approche sémiotique du développement préverbal* [The Object and the Construction of Its Use: A Semiotic Approach to Preverbal Development]. Peter Lang.
53. Niebaum, J. C., & Munakata, Y. (2023). Why doesn't executive function training improve academic achievement? Rethinking individual differences, relevance, and engagement from a contextual framework. *Journal of Cognition and Development, 24*(2), 241–259. https://doi.org/10.1080/15248372.2022.2160723
54. Peirce, C. S. (1987). *Obra lógico semiótica* [Logical-Semiotic Work]. Taurus.
55. Piaget, J. (1936/1977). *La naissance de l'intelligence chez l'enfant* [The Birth of Intelligence in the Child]. Delachaux et Niestlé.
56. Ping, R., & Goldin-Meadow, S. (2010). Gesturing saves cognitive resources when talking about nonpresent objects. *Cognitive Science, 34*(4), 602–619.
57. Puche-Navarro, R. (1994). *Le développement de la bimanualité chez l'enfant de 37 à 68 semaines* [The Development of Bimanual Coordination in Children Aged 37 to 68 Weeks]. Doctoral Thesis, nº 214. Faculté de Psychologie et Sciences de l'Éducation. Université de Genève.
58. Puche-Navarro, R. (1996). Bimanualité et procédures: Développement précoce [Bimanuality and Procedures: Early Development]. *Archives de Psychologie, 64*, 41–60.
59. Real Decreto 95/2022, de 1 de febrero, por el que se establece la ordenación y las enseñanzas mínimas de la Educación infantil [Royal Decree 95/2022, february 1st, which establishes the organization and minimum teaching standards for early childhood education].
60. Rodríguez, C. (2007). Object use, communication and signs: The triadic basis of early cognitive development. In J. Valsiner & A. Rosa (Eds.), *The Cambridge handbook of socio-cultural psychology* (pp. 257–276). Cambridge University Press.
61. Rodríguez, C. (2009). The «circumstances» of gestures: Proto-interrogatives and private gestures. *New Ideas in Psychology, 27*(2), 288–303.
62. Rodríguez, C. (2012). The functional permanence of the object: A product of consensus. In E. Martí & C. Rodríguez (Eds.), *After Piaget* (pp. 123–150). Transaction Publishers.
63. Rodríguez, C. (2022). The construction of executive function in early development: The pragmatics of action and gestures. *Human Development, 66*(4–5), 239–259. https://doi.org/10.1159/000526340
64. Rodríguez, C. (2023). La acción y los gestos, protagonistas en el origen de las Funciones Ejecutivas [Action and Gestures: Protagonists in the Emergence of Executive Functions]. In M.

Orozco-Hormaza, E. Cerchiaro-Ceballos & J. C. Ossa (Eds.), *¡Sí hubo futuro en el pasado! Aportes de Rebeca Puche-Navarro a la construcción de la psicología en Colombia*. Editorial ASCOFAPSI.
65. Rodríguez, C., Basilio, M., Cárdenas, K., Cavalcante, S., Moreno-Núñez, A., Palacios, P., & Yuste, N. (2018). Objects pragmatics: Culture and communication – The bases for early cognitive development. In A. Rosa & J. Valsiner (Eds.), *The Cambridge handbook of sociocultural psychology* (2nd ed., pp. 223–244). Cambridge University Press.
66. Rodríguez, C., Estrada, L., Moreno-Llanos, I. & De los Reyes, J. L. (2017). Executive functions and educational actions in an Infant School: Private uses and gestures at the end of the first year. *Studies in Psychology, 38*(2), 385–423. https://doi.org/10.1080/02109395.2017.1305061.
67. Rodríguez, C., & Moreno-Llanos, I. (2023). A pragmatic turn in the study of early executive functions by object use and gestures. A case study from 8 to 17 months of age at a nursery school. *Integrative Psychological and Behavioral Science, 57*, 607–654. https://doi.org/10.1007/s12124-020-09578-5
68. Rodríguez, C., Moreno-Llanos, I., Cerchiario, E., Contin, L., & Guevara, I. (2021). Origen y desarrollo de las funciones ejecutivas en la escuela infantil, aula 0–1 [Origin and development of executive functions in the early-years-school, 0–1 classroom]. In C. Rodríguez & J. L. de los Reyes (Eds.), *Los objetos sí importan. Acción educativa en la Escuela Infantil*, (pp. 133–158). Horsori.
76. Rodríguez, C., Moreno-Llanos, I., Guevara, I., & Flecha, G. (2024). La acción y los gestos: primeros instrumentos de las funciones ejecutivas en la escuela infantil [Action and gestures: first instruments of executive functions in the earl years school]. In A. Barreiro & M. Carretero (Eds.), *Celebrando a Tono Castorina. Construcción de conocimientos en el campo psicológico*. Tilde Editora.
69. Rodríguez, C., & Moro, C. (1999). *El mágico número tres. Cuando los niños aún no hablan* [The Magic Number Three: When Children Still Do Not Speak]. Paidós.
70. Rodríguez, C., & Palacios, P. (2007). Do private gestures have a self-regulatory function? A case study. *Infant Behavior and Development, 30*(2), 180–194.
71. Tomasello, M. (2014). *A natural history of human thinking*. Harvard University Press.
72. Trevarthen, C., & Hubley, P. (1978). Secondary intersubjetivity: Confidence, condiding and acts of meaning in the first year. In A. Lock (Ed.), *Action, gesture and symbol: The emergence of language* (pp. 183–229). Academic Press.
73. Vygotski, L. S. (1934/1985). *Pensée et langage* [Thought and language]. Editions Sociales.
74. Winsler, A., De León, J. R., Wallace, B. A., Carlton, M. P., & Willson-Quayle, A. (2003). Private speech in preschool children: Developmental stability and change, across-task consistency, and relations with classroom behaviour. *Journal of Child Language, 30*(03), 583–608. https://doi.org/10.1017/S0305000903005671
75. Zelazo, D., & Müller, U. (2007). Executive function in typical and atypical development. In U. Goswami (Ed.), *Blackwell handbook of childhood cognitive development* (pp. 445–469). Blackwell.

Early Childhood Schools in Brasília: I Show You, and You Observe. Executive Functions, Educational Situations, and Object Use

11

Francisco Rengifo-Herrera and Gabriela Sousa de Melo Mietto

11.1 Introduction

Over the past few years, the research team of the *Infantia* Group at the University of Brasília has conducted studies based on the Pragmatics of the Object in early childhood education contexts. This chapter aims to present the results of data analysis examining the relationships between action indicators associated with object use in the classroom, executive functioning in children aged 1–4 years, and the characteristics of educational situations proposed by teachers. These observations were conducted in two classrooms from public early childhood education schools in Brasília. These data are part of the different research work we have carried out in recent years [12, 19, 25, 29, 30].

The research interest in this topic emerged from an exchange of analyses and joint activities with the DETEDUCA Group at the Universidad Autónoma de Madrid. While sharing analyses and data, we also identified particularities within the observations, prompting us to deepen our characterization of these educational situations and to identify similarities and differences in comparison to records shared during exchanges with colleagues from other countries.

To understand the approach of this analysis, we will first discuss the concept of Executive Functions (EF), with an emphasis on recent contributions by Rodríguez [36], Rodríguez et al. [38], and Moreno-Llanos et al. [21], which elucidate how infants develop these processes within the educational situations they encounter

F. Rengifo-Herrera (✉) · G. Sousa de Melo Mietto
Universidade de Brasília, Brasília, Brasil
e-mail: frengifo@unb.br

G. Sousa de Melo Mietto
e-mail: gabrielamieto@unb.br

C. Rodriguez Garrido et al. (eds.), *The Social Life of Objects in Early Development*, Social Interaction in Learning and Development,
https://doi.org/10.1007/978-3-031-87673-8_11

daily. We will also analyze the concept of educational situations, drawing on the contributions of Estrada [10, 11], Contin and Rodríguez [6], and Rengifo-Herrera [29], to establish another core theoretical foundation for our work.

When examining aspects related to EF and educational situations, our observations reveal that, in general, children demonstrated flexibility and creativity in their strategies to solve problems or carry out activities. They often sought to go beyond what teachers explicitly proposed in these educational situations [31]. However, teachers' practices frequently showed a high level of control over activities, with short (almost rushed) and minimally reflective interventions. Additionally, there was a predominant regulation of object use, with limited integration of objects into the educational situations. When objects were present, children's actions were typically restricted to observing them, with minimal opportunities for touching, manipulating, or using the objects.

Concrete interaction with everyday, culturally relevant objects is essential at this age. However, a tendency to restrict, regulate, or control these objects appears to prevail in the educational situations observed. This can hinder children's ability to self-regulate their activities, explore and analyze objects, and make inferences based on their actions. Consequently, this educational practice may limit opportunities to discover or expand relationships between objects and their conventional and symbolic uses [39].

To address this topic, we will briefly explore three concepts: (1) materiality and its relationship with psychological development and learning, (2) the development of EFs in early childhood, and (3) educational situations within the context of early childhood education.

11.2 Cultural Materiality in Psychological Development

In the creation of materiality, human beings employ various strategies rooted in historical development, as explained by Riede et al. [33]. Objects originate from the functional and pragmatic needs of different social groups, and their production and use have been transmitted across generations [27]. There is a psychological tradition that focuses strictly on the physical and perceptual aspects of objects, often leading to the assumption that materiality is self-evident. However, the mediating and regulatory roles that objects play—enabling us to achieve goals, anticipate reality, and envision the future—arise in contexts that extend beyond a purely perceptual perspective.

It is important to note, however, that materiality, on its own, does not inherently communicate the purposes for which it was created. The use of objects is not determined solely by their physical characteristics [34]. Instead, objects exist within a social and cultural framework, requiring interaction with knowledgeable individuals who understand the conventional uses associated with them. Objects are not mere gadgets; rather, they open up possibilities for thinking, relating, and regulating one's own actions and those of others. Yet, much of psychology has paid insufficient attention to analyzing, investigating, and understanding this dynamic.

Often, the conventional uses of objects can seem counterintuitive, as their intended use is not always apparent through perception alone. For instance, a spoon does not have an obvious purpose for a baby. While it possesses a concave and a convex side, the conventional use of the concave side must be demonstrated by someone who understands its context and function. Explaining how a spoon is used for feeding can be surprisingly complex. The construction of meanings and uses for objects arises through triadic interactions with adults and semiotic mediation, embedded in social dynamics where these conventional uses are shared. Rodríguez and Moro ([39]; also [34, 35]), pioneered triadic analyses of the development of conventional object uses in infants (see Chap. 3). It is during early childhood that the first intentional triadic interactions emerge, guided by adults to support children's appropriation of these conventions. Adults rely on both verbal and non-verbal semiotic systems to present, demonstrate, and share the uses and meanings of objects with children.

Through intentional and planned actions by adults, children are enabled to adopt ways of experiencing, confronting, and solving various everyday activities. This process helps children develop skills to explore, use, and ascribe meaning to culturally significant objects. A child's interaction with materiality is fundamental to learning, social relationships, and overall development throughout early childhood [26].

Moreover, materiality is deeply embedded in daily life, serving to solve problems and facilitate everyday activities that promote children's participation in, and appropriation of, cultural practices and knowledge. This process is closely linked to the development of executive functioning (EF [36, 37], see also Chaps. 9 and 10 in this volume). Analyzing children's actions allows us to infer how, through private gestures [15–17] and private uses [37], objects can become catalysts for executive functioning. Consequently, this dynamic represents a dimension that demands further understanding, expansion, and enrichment.

The triadic relationship that occurs at home is characterized by informal educational contexts. But what happens at school? How can we analyze formal contexts? Research suggests that objects play a significant role in the emergence of developmental and learning processes in school settings [11, 41, 42]. Contributing to these processes implies that educational practices and school interventions can positively impact children's development and learning during early childhood education.

11.3 The Development of Executive Functions (EF) in the Context of Early Years Schools

Executive Functions are cognitive processes that promote understanding and make it possible for children to regulate, plan and coordinate actions, promoting development and structuring the bases of any type of learning [9, 20]. EF are structural and determinant in the organization of various dimensions of the subjects. Both in the cognitive and in the relational/affective dimensions [38].

The development of EF allows children to maintain attention directed to objectives and inhibit distracting or ineffective behaviors, to be persistent in their actions, to evaluate alternative solutions in a flexible way, and to be able to follow up on actions that lead them to goals [37]. However, it is important to highlight that research on EF in the early years of life is scarce, especially when looking at the hegemonic perspectives that investigate this type of process [36, 46]. A significant part of the research on EF does not deal with children under 3 or 4 years of age, which means that these ages do not have much presence in publications. On the other hand, when studies are carried out with these ages, it seems that the focus is on more general aspects and far removed from the ecological contexts where these processes emerge and occur. There seems to be a preference for the use of standardized tasks that offer quantifications on EF [2, 4, 18] (see Chap. 8 in this volume on standardized tasks).

On the other hand, in school, studies focused on understanding EF are even less frequent. In the context of Early Childhood Education, it only seems to have a global interest as a concept to think about learning and not to understand how children organize their understanding about the world, categorize, plan, create novelties and regulate their actions based on specific goals in the daily life of the classroom, as described by Rodríguez and Moreno-Llanos [37].

In the Brazilian context, there is a document that becomes the reference for thinking about the educational processes of the country. The National Common Curriculum Base (BNCC, for its acronym in Portuguese) has as its goal the promotion of autonomy from the first years of life. This document defines that self-regulation and autonomy are definitive elements for children to develop skills for decision-making, problem solving, interactions with other people, and the relationship with nature and the environment. On the other hand, children at these ages share a good portion of their daily time in early years schools, which makes these contexts relevant to understanding the development of EF.

We have chosen to analyze and understand aspects related to EF from observation and video analysis of the challenges children face in everyday situations in early years schools. This allows us to go beyond the use of standardized tests to assess executive control indicators at these ages. In this context, it is possible to understand the trajectories followed by children's actions, the processes at play, and how teachers' interventions, as well as the educational planning proposed through the use of objects in the classroom, turn them into attractors (which direct action towards specific goals). This type of recording also allows us to understand how the processes of control, regulation, and action planning emerge in everyday activities, which guarantees ecological validity and allows us to expand contextual aspects on the understanding of EF *in loco*.[1]

[1] The Latin expression *in loco* means 'in the place itself' or 'in situ'. Its etymological origin comes from the union of *in*, meaning 'in', and *loco*, which is the singular ablative form of *locus*, meaning 'place' or 'location'.

11.4 Educational Situations in Early Childhood Education

When we refer to the concept of *educational situations*, we are discussing a category that allows us to understand that educational contexts are dense and highly overlapping in actions, meanings, practices and interactions. These contexts involve actions, intentions, meanings, purposes, and interests in understanding or learning something, all taken together. This makes them rich scenarios for analysis, but simultaneously reveals their complexity and the methodological challenges they pose for research.

Educational situations can be understood as fields of action designed to promote development and learning. They involve the planning of activities where goals and actions for children are defined to foster the emergence of knowledge. These defined areas aim to facilitate the transfer of control of the planning and action, enabling the teacher to monitor objectives, action indicators, challenges, achievements, and dynamics—both for each child individually and the group as a whole.

The goals and objectives of educational situations are tied to the teacher's understanding of the relevant educational contents and the interest of fostering children's appropriation of cultural practices and knowledge. This teaching intention drives processes that provoke changes and reorganizations in development, allowing children to internalize culturally and socially significant knowledge [5].

It is important to highlight that, given the complex network of actions and interaction dynamics that characterize educational situations, conducting a specific analysis was more challenging than in situations where just triadic interactions occur. At the same time, overly general analyses would overshadow the details of relevant microgenetic aspects recorded in observations. Consequently, this work presents records that navigate a constant tension between micro and macro levels of analysis.

This approach enables analyses rooted in collective dynamics and interactions, which manifest as learning and, consequently, as the emergence of processes related to development [23]. Educational situations involve dynamics emerging within the teacher-materiality-children triadic system during classroom activities. These situations aim to generate, promote, and transform knowledge, practices, and learning through shared interaction. This concept is further explored in the works of Estrada [10, 11], who builds on the rich discussions of didactics by French and Swiss scholars regarding the classroom as a site of problem situations [5, 22, 43, 44].

From the perspective of the Pragmatics of the Object, and particularly drawing on Estrada's work [11], it becomes evident how educational situations reveal the dynamics of triadic interactions. These interactions facilitate the circulation of semiotic layers within the flow of actions, dialogues, and gestures in the classroom. Estrada identifies three types of educational situations: semi-structured, structured, and directed.

Semi-structured educational situations are spontaneous and lack predefined goals. Children act autonomously, selecting materials and deciding what, when, and how to use them. In such situations, the teacher assumes a supportive role, remaining close to the children's actions and responding to their demands.

Structured educational situations are teacher-initiated and involve the selection of materials with specific goals. However, teachers generally refrain from explicitly directing children on what to do. Instead, they define general objectives but leave the approach open-ended, intervening only when necessary to adjust or demonstrate actions. Here, materials are offered and demonstrated, but specific actions are not imposed.

Directed educational situations are highly regulated by the teacher. They prescribe specific activities, guiding children's actions without providing alternative options. In these situations, children must follow the proposed plan.

Building upon previous research and theoretical foundations, we present data from educational situations observed in Brasília. These observations illustrate the main elements discussed in this chapter, providing concrete examples of how these dynamics unfold in practice.

11.5 What are Our Findings from Our Observations in Early Years Schools in Brasilia?

The observations and analyses conducted in Brasília focused on two age groups: children aged 1–3 years and 4–5 years. Based on these experiences, we present some of the results of our work and describe, with examples, the educational situations identified. Additionally, we characterize the actions carried out by teachers that appear to either promote or restrict the emergence of processes related to EFs. Finally, we discuss similarities and differences with studies conducted by other colleagues involved with the DETEDUCA Group.

To provide context for the reader, it is important to note that in Brazil, teacher training is designed to prepare professionals to work in both Early Childhood Education (*Educação Infantil*, mandatory for children aged 4–5 years and 11 months) and the first cycle of Basic Education (Primary Education, known in Brazil as *Ensino Fundamental 1*, for children aged 6–10 years). Despite this structure, an analysis of teacher training programs [1] indicates ongoing challenges in addressing the preparation of pedagogy students, in both, private and public universities.

> However, in some of the courses analyzed, we have observed a concern with establishing a *theoretical-methodological approach* to the content—if we may call it that—related to the preschool level, that is, the education of children aged four and older. This indicates that, despite efforts to explore alternatives aimed at formation that encompasses the specificities of Early Childhood Education, *the centrality of the schooling process and the concept of the child-as-student still prevail in teacher formation* [1], p. 22, emphasis added)

This approach results in a strong emphasis on teacher's professional knowledge relevant to Primary Education, with fewer skills tailored specifically to Early Childhood Education. Consequently, educational situations often include activities and contents that are misaligned with the developmental stages of children aged 0–3 years or 4–6 years [40]. In general, practices appear to follow principles derived from teaching focused primarily on Basic Education. A notable consequence is that teachers tend to over-rely on conventional school materials—such as pencils or pens for drawing or writing, and paper, scissors, or glue for crafting activities—which are not fully pertinent for the developmental needs and learning processes of young children.

These findings have prompted us to formulate several guiding questions for our research: What types of educational situations were planned and implemented by the teachers? What intentional actions did teachers take to promote the development of EF in the observed settings? Are there differences, and if so, what are they, compared to observations from other studies conducted in different countries and by colleagues affiliated with the DETEDUCA Group, particularly regarding educational situations?

In the group of children aged 0–3 years, we have primarily observed interactions in educational situations and the dynamics between teachers and children during mealtime [7, 32].

In their study, Rengifo-Herrera and Rodrigues [32] conducted observations in two early years schools—one private and one public—and identified two distinctly different practices. In the private school, teachers and assistant maintained control over the objects. Children did not have access to the food, which was pre-cut and served to them. The spoon remained under the teacher's control, and children were fed directly without the opportunity to feed themselves, at least during the observation periods. Conversely, in the public school, mealtime was structured as a rich interactional context. The teacher discussed the ingredients in the food and allowed children to use cutlery and eat independently. Observations suggested that the children had been given previous control of these objects in past occasions.

On the other hand, Alencar and Rengifo-Herrera [7] proposed a play-based activity involving the use of replica objects, inviting children to play at cooking. The setup included replica cooking tools (cutting boards, knives), replica fruits that could be "cut" using Velcro, and replica appliances like blenders and electric beaters. The play activity aimed to encourage children to use the objects and engage in pretend cooking with an adult. Three children aged 2.7–3 years, three mothers, and one teacher participated.

Alencar and Rengifo-Herrera [7] observed that the teacher's intervention differed from that of the mothers. The teacher encouraged exploration and use of the objects, providing direct or semi-direct assistance with the children's actions. For instance, the teacher *pointed the object*, *demonstrated the uses*, or, when necessary, handled the objects to show their (canonical and symbolic) uses. However, this was done intentionally while allowing the child to take the lead. Additionally, the teacher provided indirect guidance by pointing and offering semiotic cues about what the child could or should do. This approach enabled the children to explore, analyze the characteristics of the objects, and infer appropriate uses based on the situation.

The teacher appeared inclined to allow the children to control and use the objects independently. In contrast, the mothers seemed more focused on ensuring their child achieved the task's goal, even if it required them to take over the process and limit the child's discovery of alternatives. The mothers tended to *handle* and *control* the objects more often and frequently repeated *explanations*, including: *Type 1 explanations* (E1): explaining what the child was doing or what they should do. *Type 3 explanations* (E3): explaining what the replica objects were.

The studies by De Melo [8] have identified key aspects related to affectivity and the types of interactions between teachers and children in play contexts and shared spaces. Similarly, research has examined joint attention in neurotypical and neurodiverse children across various educational settings [13, 19, 31]. These studies demonstrate how didactic intentionality, when aligned with objectives that consider the children's specific developmental stage, generates differences in learning outcomes.

For instance, Gonçalves and Mietto's [13] research was conducted in a specialized public service known as Early Education (*Educação Precoce*), designed for children aged 0–4 who are either premature or exhibit atypical developmental indicators. Their findings emphasize the relevance of this service in fostering the emergence of early semiotic systems in pre-verbal infants, thereby impacting intentional, planned, and consistent interaction processes. Additionally, the studies by Mietto et al. [19] and Rengifo-Herrera et al. [31] further highlight the importance of intentional adult actions in interactions with young children. They underscore the value of adult observations of children's actions, including how objects are used, the types of gestures made, and the communicative behaviors that emerge in intentionally designed triadic situations.

Studies by Rengifo-Herrera [29] and Nascimento-Dias [24] offer initial analyses of educational situations and their role in promoting child agency, with a focus on EF. Nascimento-Dias [24] observed a prevalence of control and restriction by teachers, who displayed objects without allowing children to touch or use them. In contrast, Rengifo-Herrera [29] noted that teachers allowed children access to objects but did not guide or monitor their use, thus limiting opportunities to pose questions or foster deeper engagement.

In Barros [3] and Goulart-Mourão [14], it is intriguing to observe how children who select objects they are familiar with demonstrate better performance in learning phonemic awareness. These researches highlight the frequent presence of objects in classrooms. However, we have noted that teachers often seem hesitant to allow children control over these objects, preferring to regulate or constrain their use. What might drive teachers to act in this way? What types of educational situations do they plan? What intentional actions promote the development of EF? How do their approaches differ from those documented in other studies?

To illustrate the aspects we aim to analyze, we will present data collected through non-participant observations in early childhood education classrooms with children aged 1–3 years. These two sequences come from recordings made in two care day centers in Brasília between 2019 and 2022. The first sequence involves an unpublished observation that is analyzed and presented here, while the second is based on data from Rengifo-Herrera [29]. The first sequence was recorded in a classroom with children aged 10–16 months, and the second in a classroom with children aged 25–35 months.

Sequence 1 features an educational situation in which the teacher asks the children to glue paper flags onto a sheet of paper. These flags are created as part of an activity widely celebrated in many countries, including Brazil—the June festivities (*Festas Juninas* in Portuguese)—a traditional celebration that integrates pedagogical and socialization activities into daily classroom routines.

Sequence 2 follows the teacher's reading of the story The Three Little Pigs to the children. After the reading, the teacher instructs the children to choose a book from the shelves and read it while sitting on the classroom floor.

11.5.1 Sequence 1: Taking Initiative During the Activity and Transferring Control

Activity: Gluing small paper flags with adhesive. Educational Situation: Directed. Observation Duration: 34 s.

The teacher organized a structured activity involving six children aged 10 to 16 months. She selected the following materials: a glue bottle, small paper flags (rectangular colored paper cutouts with two pointed ends, typically used for decorating during *Festas Juninas*), and an A3 sheet of paper to serve as the base for gluing. The activity's objective was to glue the paper flags onto the sheet using the glue bottle. The teacher sat down and called the children to gather around her, providing verbal instructions. This sequence highlights the interactions between the teacher and a 14-month-old girl, Carol,[2] during the observation.

At the start of the activity, the teacher explained the necessary steps, outlining the goal and emphasizing the rules of the task. She demonstrated the procedure from a distance, showing the children how to do it. Additionally, she provided positive feedback by using phrases like, "That's it, Carol, exactly. Put it there, alright?" as Carol performed the task. The teacher reiterated the instructions, using phrases such as, "Put it there, on the paper," maintaining her directive tone, and reinforcing with exclamations like, "That's it!" At this point, Carol appeared to follow the teacher's commands.

Carol began gluing and then peeling the paper flags off the sheet, prompting the teacher to emphasize that the flags should not be removed. She repeated several times, "They're for gluing, Carol, don't peel them off." To *inhibit* Carol's actions, the teacher extended both arms to physically prevent her from peeling the flags. During this initial phase of the activity, the teacher maintains control of the glue

[2] All names presented in this chapter are pseudonyms.

1.1

M offers paper flags to the children (ostensive gesture of giving). Carol follows M's verbal instructions and stick the flags onto the paper (canonical use).

At this point, M maintains significant control over the activity.

Fig. 11.1 The teacher directs the children's actions

bottle, applying glue to the flags herself and then handing them to Carol to stick onto the paper (see Fig. 11.1).

The teacher's interventions seem to be aimed at getting Carol to achieve the specific goal of the activity, based on a set of instructions, both verbal and gestural (ostensive gestures of giving, gestures to inhibit Carol's action, etc.). At this point, the teacher organizes an activity where she does not offer the girl any alternatives. Carol only has to stick the flags that the teacher gives her. Even when the girl managed to stick and unstick the flags, as well as explore the material used, the teacher only allowed her to do what she thought should be done: stick them.

Later, Carol begins to take the initiative, seeking to gain more control over the activity. After more than two minutes from the start of the activity, she begins to carefully observe the bottle of glue that the teacher has and moves her hand towards it, with the intention of taking it (see Fig. 11.2, image 2.1). At this point, we can say that Carol gives herself a goal: to stick the flags autonomously. Remember that the goal is the fundamental element of EF in early development (see Chap. 10, this volume). This action indicates that there is an interest in using the object, in understanding what the adult has done with it and wanting to do it on one's own. This type of control and the definition of a goal indicate that there is a direction of attention, control over the action, and a focus to coordinate the actions.

Carol picks up the glue bottle, and it is important to note that the teacher allows her to take more initiative and control in the activity. This is evident through an ostensive gesture of giving (see Fig. 11.2, image 2.2). Carol examines the bottle closely, observing it from top to bottom (private ostensive gesture). This private gesture suggests that Carol is analyzing the object, studying its characteristics, and adjusting the bottle's orientation to use it correctly. She repeats this process twice, indicating its importance. This repetition reflects her effort to analyze the object, coordinate her actions for its use, and regulate her behavior to align with a conventional purpose: applying glue to the sheet.

The teacher then makes a crucial intervention by taking the bottle from Carol—not to hinder her, but to open the lid, an action that Carol is not yet able to perform independently. After opening it, the teacher hands the bottle back to her (ostensive gesture of giving), saying, "Take it." This intervention is significant because the

2.1 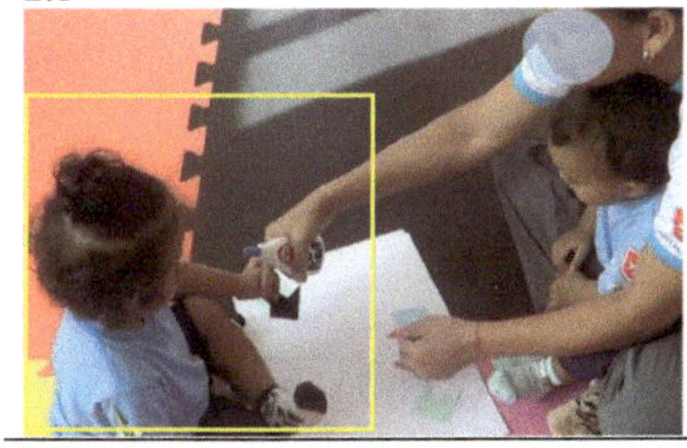	Carol gazes intently at the bottle of glue in M's hand.
2.2 	Carol picks up the bottle of glue. M acknowledges her intention and hands it to her (ostensive gesture of giving).
2.3 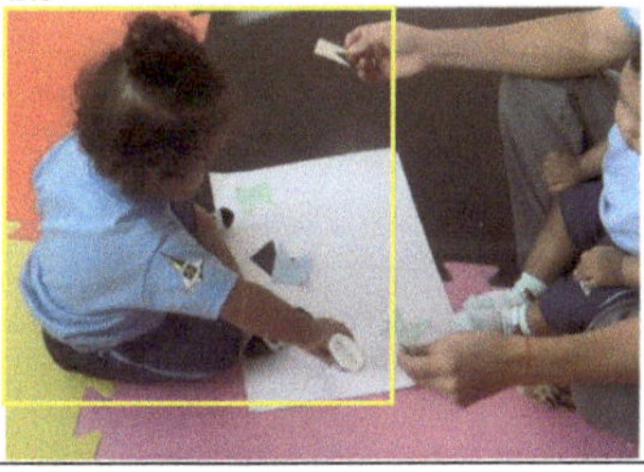	Carol applies glue to the paper (canonical use). Carol takes control of the task.

Fig. 11.2 Carol takes initiative: transfer of control

teacher recognizes the limits of Carol's knowledge and supports her in continuing her intentional action. Carol once again examines the bottle from top to bottom (private ostensive gesture) before using it conventionally, extending her arm and applying glue to the paper (see Fig. 11.2, image 2.3).

This sequence clearly illustrates the gradual transfer of control over the object from the teacher to the child. From the beginning of the scene, the teacher has been present to guide Carol's actions, though with minimal verbalization.

11.5.2 Sequence 2: Creating and Imagining as a Form of Activity Control

Activity: Canonical and symbolic uses of a book during an independent reading session. Educational Situation: Semi-structured. Observation Duration: 00:31.

After reading the story of *The Three Little Pigs* (a teacher-led activity), the teacher invited a group of children aged 25–35 months to take books from the shelves. The goal of the activity was for the children to select books, sit down, and read them independently. This was considered a semi-structured educational situation, as it did not involve completely rigid guidance; the children were free to choose the books they wanted.

In this sequence, we focus on the independent reading activity of Luiza, at 33 months old. She structured her actions to create a more complex symbolic/play-based activity than the one proposed by the teacher.

Luiza selected a book from the shelf: *O Macaquinho* (*Ciranda Cultural*). This book features a puppet—a "monkey"—that comes to life when a finger or hand is inserted to move it. Luiza showed the book to the teacher (ostensive of showing), but the teacher did not notice it. Luiza then sat next to a peer and began flipping through the book (canonical use). Afterward, she inserted her hand into the puppet's opening, pretending the monkey was biting her, exclaiming, "Ouch!" (see Fig. 11.3, image 3.1). It is clear that Luiza used the book to symbolize the act of "being bitten" (a symbolic use of the book). Here, Luiza integrated the book as a resource for creating a symbolic play scenario. This highly creative use contrasts with the teacher's somewhat vague proposal of simply "reading a book."

When Luiza symbolized being bitten, she caught her partner's attention. Noticing her partner's interest, Luiza *flexibly* adjusted her goal and actions. She used the book to simulate a new scene, pretending to read to her partner (see Fig. 11.3, image 3.2). To achieve this, she adopted a tone of voice that at times seemed to imitate the teacher. In both instances, Luiza successfully created a playful context using the book, imagining situations beyond the original intent of the educational activity.

3.1

Luiza acts as if "the monkey had bitten her" (*symbolic use*).

She moves her hand away from the book and exclaims, "Ouch!" as if it had hurt.

3.2

Then, Luiza pretends to "read" the book to her classmate.

This change in use demonstrates her *flexibility*. She adjusts her action to a new situation, including her classmate in her symbolic uses.

Fig. 11.3 Luiza establishes a goal: to engage in symbolic uses of the book for herself and a peer

It is important to note that Luiza proposed reading the book in response to her partner's attempt to take it from her. She initially avoided this by moving the book out of reach. However, rather than continuing with an avoidance strategy, Luiza used the act of pretending to read as a way to regulate her partner's actions. Instead of promoting conflict, she included her partner in the situation by transforming the interaction. This demonstrates Luiza's ability to self-regulate while using the book as a tool to influence her partner's behavior. This example highlights the role of EF in understanding the world and fostering peer relationships.

From this record, we see how Luiza leveraged the book's characteristics to incorporate symbolic actions, such as "being bitten" and "reading" to her partner. In doing so, she turned an unclear situation into an opportunity to set a goal and manage the interaction through the use of materiality. As noted, Luiza broke away from the "here and now" (*hic et nunc*), using the book symbolically in a flexible way, which opened up new possibilities for action.

The way the children interacted with the books suggests that this type of activity occurs frequently. Many children picked up books and flipped through them. However, in Luiza's case, she organized her actions around a self-defined goal. She used the book and the puppet to explore its symbolic potential. The two symbolic uses she demonstrated are evidence of her control over the situation and her ability to set concrete goals and regulate her actions beyond the teacher's initial suggestion to "read the books." Luiza oriented her actions toward simulation and the creation of a possible world through materiality [28].

11.6 Discussion: What are Our Conclusions, and What Can We Propose?

Throughout this chapter, we have described the role of intentional actions proposed by teachers and how these were implemented in various educational situations studied in Brasília. This analysis brings us back to the questions raised earlier in the text. While the educational situations were planned by the teachers, there often seemed to be a lack of clarity regarding what they were meant to promote in terms of development and learning.

Both Carol and Luiza encountered educational situations where the teacher exerted either significant control, or very little (e.g., directed or semi-structured activities). Even when the children had the freedom to use objects independently, there was little support or guidance regarding what they did, how they did it, and why. This points for two types of strategies in the design of educational activities: hyper-structured tasks (e.g., sticking the flags) versus activities with minimal support (e.g., reading books independently).

In the activity involving the flags, the teacher initially maintained control of the objects. Her primary goal for the children seemed singular: to stick the flags. When Carol reached for the glue bottle and picked it up, the teacher adapted her educational intervention, allowing the child to use the use the glue bottle as the teacher had been doing and attempting to stick the flags by herself. In this moment, the teacher recognized what the child was doing and permitted her to explore the object's use. However, verbal interactions were minimal once Carol picked up the bottle.

When adults speak, pose questions, or direct attention to specific aspects of an activity, they can spark new reflections, foster attentional control, and promote goal coordination. This approach can expand the child's cognitive functioning during the activity. However, such indicators were not consistently observed in this situation.

Regarding the use of the book, the educational situation lacked teacher intervention to question or expand the children's actions with the objects or the proposed activity. The children appeared to have no specific point of reference for what to do. Executive functions (EF) typically emerge in contexts where attention control is stimulated, when the activity encourages cognitive flexibility, and memory serves as a tool to reflect on the task at hand. In this second observation, the absence of adult guidance as a promoter of inquiry led the child to resort to symbolic uses, allowing them to regulate, learn, and imagine on her own.

If the teacher had intervened with questions, evoked information, or introduced new challenges, the activity could have been enriched further. However, instances where control of the activity was transferred to the children were rare in Brazil. This contrasts with the semi-structured and structured situations described by Estrada [11], where such practices were more explicit.

In Carol's case (sequence 1), the girl took control of the activity by attempting to take the glue bottle from the teacher's hand. This action significantly altered the dynamics of the activity. The teacher adapted her approach, enabling Carol to discover what she could do with the glue bottle and the flags. In Luiza's case (sequence 2), the activity lacked clear instructions: the children were simply told to take books, look through them, and then draw what they saw. This lack of structure led Luiza to explore symbolic alternatives, creating new possibilities beyond the original scope of the activity. For her, imagining became a necessary response to the unclear purpose of the task and the teacher's absence as a source of inquiry or guidance.

These examples highlight differences in teaching practices compared to other studies, such as those linked to DETEDUCA. For instance, Rodríguez and Moreno-Llanos [37] documented teacher actions that were carefully planned, with objects introduced at relevant moments to encourage children to explore, use, and discover independently.

This type of analysis of educational situations has provided insights into classroom practices in early childhood education. It is important to emphasize that our work does not seek to criticize teachers but to analyze how their proposed practices and educational situations are related to their professional training. Practices that allow children to explore objects freely are uncommon and are not typically part of the training repertoire for teachers in Brazil. As a result, opportunities for this type of exploration are often not facilitated. The training teachers receive often makes it difficult for them to appreciate the relevance of certain actions for children aged 0 to 6. It is essential for teachers to understand these specificities in order to design clearer objectives, goals, and activities appropriate for this developmental stage.

We have observed how certain facts and interactions may go unnoticed or be considered of lesser didactic value by teachers. However, these moments reveal how children, even in less structured educational situations, manage to use materiality to generate new actions, inferences, and ways of exploring and learning about their social and cultural reality.

To expand the understanding of the concept of Educational Situations, we propose the model presented in Fig. 11.4. For several years now [45], we have advocated for the integration of objects into daily practices in early childhood classrooms.

To achieve this, we suggest that psychological development must be understood through the relationships between Time, Context (Space), and Movement. Accordingly, Fig. 11.4 illustrates the interplay between temporality (Time 1 and Time 2), spatiality (Context), and Movement, which emerges from the interaction of these two axes. Movement is expressed in actions, activities, and situations aimed at achieving specific goals.

In these relationships, we identify what Brossard [5] terms the *Common Framework of Activity,* which is initially presented by the teacher and subsequently introduced to the children. This framework enables the identification of goals that imbue each individual's actions and the group's dynamics with meaning. The consensus established by the teacher around what is to be done is essential for ensuring

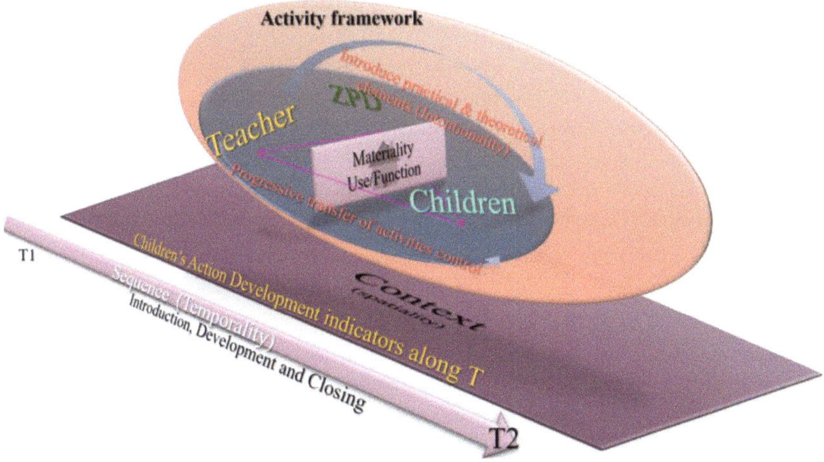

Fig. 11.4 Model of educational situations and the use of materiality. *Original in* Rengifo-Herrera [28]

that the objectives, actions, and outcomes are explicit, guiding activity toward defined procedures, focal points, and indicators for achieving the educational goals.

When planning educational situations, the teacher incorporates theoretical and practical elements with the intention of enabling children to acquire concepts, knowledge, or practices. This involves intentionally integrating objects linked to the concepts and categories the teacher aims to present. The teacher also draws on the Zone of Proximal Development (ZPD) to validate elements related to the conventionalization of practices, concepts, and knowledge that culturally shape the use of these objects within the context of the aforementioned Common Framework of Activity.

Perhaps the most significant aspect of this model is that, through these actions, the teacher progressively transfers control of the activity to the children. This transfer enables the emergence of new ways of acting, validating—through the children's actions—the proposed use, relevance, and possibilities of the objects as part of knowledge practices.

Handing control over to the children is key to fostering regulated, planned, and goal-oriented actions, which support development and relationships—the core objective of this approach. By transferring control, the teacher can monitor, promote, and encourage new ways of acting, observing children's actions, questioning uses, and channeling activity to incorporate semiotic aspects. In essence, the teacher guides the activity with intentionality, allowing children to act, make mistakes, repeat, reflect, analyze, and understand the uses and activities through their own actions.

Our focus was to observe the intentional actions of teachers aimed at promoting executive functions. Without a doubt, we found indicators related to goal-directed attention and the inhibition of distractions. In both observations, Carol and Luiza maintained consistent focus and demonstrated persistence in the activity. However, it is important to acknowledge that with more precise interventions and clearer activity objectives, the children could have expanded their cognitive possibilities beyond what the educational situations allowed.

This leads us to another question: are there differences compared to findings from other studies conducted by our colleagues associated with DETEDUCA in Madrid? In the cases analyzed—both in the educational situations observed and, in the data, collected by the *Infantia* Group—we identified a consistent tendency among teachers to control educational situations and restrict children's access to objects.

As we have previously noted, pedagogical practices predominantly focus on the use of conventional materials associated with basic schooling rather than those appropriate for Early Childhood Education. This emphasis on primary school readiness impacts how educational situations are planned, the intentionality of the proposals, and the potential to foster a freer and more fluid learning environment in early childhood education.

For the teachers observed by our team, maintaining control appears to be tied to ensuring the achievement of learning objectives. A lack of control, in their view, might result in children not learning as expected and could negatively affect perceptions of the teacher's authority over the class. It is important to note that such practices are not the result of negligence or a lack of commitment on the part of the teachers. Rather, they stem from a legacy of professional training that assumes children in early childhood education learn using the same resources and methods as adults.

The initial and ongoing professional development of Brazilian teachers must critically address these practices, drawing on recent scientific evidence in psychology and education—some of which is discussed in this chapter—to better align teaching strategies with the developmental needs of young children.

References

1. de Albuquerque, M. H. K., Rocha, E. A. C., & Buss-Simão, M. (2018). Formação docente para educação infantil nos currículos de pedagogia [Teacher training for early childhood education in pedagogy curricula]. *Educação em Revista, 34*, e183858. https://doi.org/10.1590/0102-4698183858
2. Barker, J. E., Semenov, A. D., Michaelson, L., Provan, L. S., Snyder, H. R., & Munakata, Y. (2014). Less structured time in children's daily lives predicts self-directed executive functioning. *Frontiers in Psychology, 5*, 1–16. https://doi.org/10.3389/fpsyg.2014.00593
3. Barros, V. (2023). *O desenvolvimento da consciência fonêmica de crianças em um centro de educação infantil do campo no Distrito Federal* [The development of phonemic awareness in children at a rural early childhood education center in the Federal District] [Dissertação de Mestrado, Universidade de Brasília].
4. Bernier, A., Carlson, S. M., & Whipple, N. (2010). From external regulation to self-regulation: Early parenting precursors of young children's executive functioning. *Child Development, 81*(1), 326–339. https://doi.org/10.1111/j.1467-8624.2009.01397.x
5. Brossard, M. (2001). Situations et formes d'apprentissage [Learning situations and forms]. *Revue suisse des sciences de l'éducation, 23*(3), 423–439. https://www.pedocs.de/volltexte/2011/3773/pdf/SZBW_2001_H3_S423_Brossard_D_A.pdf
6. Contín, L., & Rodríguez, C. (2021). La lectura del libro en la escuela infantil como facilitador de la atención en bebés [Book reading in early years school as a facilitator of attention in infants]. In C. Rodríguez & J. L. de los Reyes (Coord.), *Los objetos sí importan: Acciones educativas en la escuela infantil* (pp. 83–108). Horsori.
7. Correa Alencar, A. C., & Rengifo-Herrera, F. J. (2023). En educación infantil, el profesor hace la diferencia: Análisis microgenético con réplicas de objetos en situaciones lúdicas relacionadas con la comida [In early childhood education, the teacher makes the difference: Microgenetic analysis with replicas of objects in playful situations related to food]. *Diversitas, 19*(1), 238–258. https://doi.org/10.15332/22563067.9152
8. De Melo, C. (2023) *Manifestações emocionais na transição de bebês para crianças bem pequenas em creche comunitária do DF* [Emotional manifestations in the transition from babies to very young children in a community early years school in the Federal District]. [Dissertação de Mestrado, Universidade de Brasília].
9. Diamond, A. (2020) Chapter 19—Executive functions. In A. Gallagher, Ch. Bulteau, D. Cohen, & J. L. Michaud (Eds.), *Handbook of clinical neurology* (Vol. 173, pp. 225–240). Elsevier. https://doi.org/10.1016/B978-0-444-64150-2.00020-4
10. Estrada, L. F. (2021). Tipos de situaciones educativas en la escuela infantil: El rol mediador de los maestros [Types of educational situations in early years school: The mediating role of teachers]. In C. Rodríguez & J. L. de los Reyes (Eds.), *Los objetos sí importan. Acciones educativas en la escuela infantil* (pp. 159–181). Horsori.

11. Estrada, L. F. (2019). *Materialidad y prácticas educativas en la escuela infantil con niños/as entre 1 y 2 años: Una aproximación cultural, semiótica y pragmática* [Materiality and educational practices in the early years school with children between 1 and 2 years old: A cultural, semiotic and pragmatic approach]. [Tesis Doctoral, Universidad Autónoma de Madrid]. http://hdl.handle.net/10486/688559
12. Gerbassi, T. N. (2021). *Atenção compartilhada nas relações triádicas: Um estudo a partir da mãe e seus filhos* [Shared attention in triadic relationships: A study from the mother and her children]. [Dissertação de Mestrado, Universidade de Brasília].
13. Gonçalves, L. M., & Mietto, G. S. M. (2021). Educação precoce: Interações triádicas e sistemas semióticos [Early education: Triadic interactions and semiotic systems]. *Revista Educação Especial, 34*, 1–29.
14. Goulart-Mourão, I. (2023). *Relações objeto, fonema e grafema durante situações educativas de leitura compartilhada com crianças de 4 e 5 anos de uma Escola Infantil* [Object, phoneme and grapheme relationships during educational situations of shared reading with 4 and 5 year olds in a infant school]. [Dissertação de Mestrado, Universidade de Brasília].
15. Guevara, I., Moreno-Llanos, I., & Rodríguez, C. (2020). The emergence of gestures in the first year of life in the infant school classroom. *European Journal of Psychology of Education, 35*, 265–287. https://doi.org/10.1007/s10212-019-00444-6
16. Guevara, I., Moreno-Llanos, I., Romero, L., Zapardiel, L., & Rodríguez, C. (2022). Challenges in first-years schools: Early manifestations of executive function. In J. Bisault, R. Le Bourgeois, J. F. Thémines, M. Le Mentec, & C. Chauvet-Chanoine (Eds.), *Objects to learn about and objects for learning 2: Which teaching practices for which issues?* (pp. 193–209). ISTE-Wiley.
17. Guevara, I., & Rodríguez, C. (2023). Developing communication through objects: Ostensive gestures as the first gestures in children's development. *Developmental Review, 68*, 101076. https://doi.org/10.1016/j.dr.2023.101076
18. McClelland, M. M., Cameron, C. E., & Dahlgren, J. (2019). The development of self-regulation in young children. In D. Whitebread (Ed.), *The sage handbook of developmental psychology and early childhood education* (pp. 471–486). Sage.
19. Mietto, G. S. M., Cavaton, M. F. F., & Rengifo-Herrera, F. J. (2023). As deficiências do bebê têm que ser tratadas com diferença? [Do baby's disabilities have to be treated differently?]. In S. Barbato, R. Beraldo, G. Mietto, & D. Maciel (Org.), *Contribuições do desenvolvimento humano e da educação aos processos de inclusão: Princípios, ensino superior e formação de professores* (pp. 131–152). Editora UnB
20. Miller, S. E., & Marcovitch, S. (2015). Examining executive function in the second year of life: Coherence, stability, and relations to joint attention and language. *Developmental Psychology, 51*(1), 101–114. https://doi.org/10.1037/a0038359
21. Moreno-Llanos, I., Zapardiel, L. A., & Rodríguez, C. (2021). Children's first manifestations of cognitive control in the early years school: The importance of the educational situation and materiality. *European Journal of Psychology of Education, 36*, 903–922. https://doi.org/10.1007/s10212-020-00505-1
22. Moro, C., & Tapparel, S. (2012). La situation éducative comme lieu de partage, de modification et d'appropriation de significations chez l'enfant [The educational situation as a site for sharing, modifying and appropriating meanings in children]. *Prisme, 16*, 35–36.
23. Moro, C., & Tartas, V. (2013). Introduction. In J. Bernié & M. Brossard (Eds.), *Vygotski et l'école: Apports et limites d'un modèle théorique pour penser l'éducation et la formation*. Presses Universitaires de Bordeaux. https://doi.org/10.4000/books.pub.47842
24. Nascimento-Dias. (2023). *Leitura compartilhada e o uso da materialidade como estratégias para o desenvolvimento das funções executivas em crianças de 1 a 2 anos na educação infantil* [Shared reading and the use of materiality as strategies for the development of executive functions in children aged 1 to 2 in early childhood education]. [Dissertação de Mestrado, Universidade de Brasília].

25. Nascimento-Dias, P., Mietto, G., & Rengifo-Herrera, F. J. (2023). Interaction dynamics with babies during shared reading practices. *Paidéia, 33*, 10. https://doi.org/10.1590/1982-4327e3338
26. Piaget, J. (1936). *La naissance de l'intelligence chez l'enfant* [The origins of intelligence in childen]. Delachaux et Niestlé.
27. Rengifo-Herrera, F. (2021). Os signos são a "pupila" dos olhos ou como a relação sujeito/cultura emerge na semiosfera [Signs are the "pupil" of the eye or how the subject/culture relationship emerges in the semiosphere]. In J. Bizerril & A. F. Madureira (Org.), *Psicologia & Cultura: Teoria, pesquisa e prática profissional* (pp. 87–119). Editora Cortez.
28. Rengifo-Herrera, F. J. (2024a). Práticas em educação infantil em Brasília. tablets, papel e lápis ou objetos cotidianos e imaginação? *Espaço Pedagógico, 31*, 16373. https://doi.org/10.5335/rep.v31.16373
29. Rengifo-Herrera, F. J. (2024b). Quando usar objetos não é suficiente: Análise microgenética de uma situação educativa na escola infantil [When using objects isn't enough: A microgenetic analysis of an educational situation in early years school]. *Estudos de Psicologia, 42.*
30. Rengifo-Herrera, F. J., & Alencar, A. C. (2023). Na educação infantil a professora faz diferença: Análise microgenética com objetos-réplica em situações lúdicas envolvendo os alimentos [In early childhood education, the teacher makes the difference: Microgenetic analysis with replicas of objects in playful situations related to food]]. *Diversitas, 19*(1), 1–28. https://doi.org/10.15332/22563067.9152
31. Rengifo-Herrera, F. J.; Mietto, G., Nascimento-Dias, P. Gerbassi. T. & De Melo, C. (2024). Os objetos, a mediação de adultos e seu papel nos processos de desenvolvimento e educação em crianças pequenas [Objects, adult mediation and their role in the processes of development and education in young children]. En F. Negreiros & J. F. Patiño, (Orgs.), *Psicologia escolar na América Latina: rumos e desafios (pp. 18).* Átomo & Alínea.
32. Rengifo-Herrera, F. J., & Rodrigues, A. P. G. M. (2020). Quando comer não é suficiente: Tríade, cuidado/educação, desenvolvimento e uso dos objetos durante as refeições em duas creches do DF [When eating isn't enough: Triad, care/education, development and use of objects during meals in two daycare centers in the Federal District]. *Psicología desde el Caribe, 37*(3). https://doi.org/10.14482/psdc.37.3.372.21
33. Riede, F., Johannsen, N. N., Högberg, A., Nowell, A., & Lombard, M. (2018). The role of play objects and object play in human cognitive evolution and innovation. *Evolutionary anthropology, 27*(1), 46–59. https://doi.org/10.1002/evan.21555
34. Rodríguez, C. (2006). *Del ritmo al símbolo* [From rhytm to symbol]. Horsori.
35. Rodríguez, C. (2015). The connection between language and the world: A paradox of the linguistic turn? *Integrative Psychological and Behavioral Science, 49*(1), 89–103. https://doi.org/10.1007/s12124-014-9274-2
36. Rodríguez, C. (2022). The construction of executive function in early development: The pragmatics of action and gestures. *Human Development, 66*(3), 239–259. https://doi.org/10.1159/000526340
37. Rodríguez, C., & Moreno-Llanos, I. (2023). A pragmatic turn in the study of early executive functions by object use and gestures. A case study from 8 to 17 months of age at a nursery school. *Integrative Psychological and Behavioral Science, 57*(2), 607–654. https://doi.org/10.1007/s12124-020-09578-5
38. Rodríguez, C., Moreno-Llanos, I., Cerchiario, E., Mietto, G., & Guevara, I. (2021). Origen y desarrollo de las funciones ejecutivas en el aula 0-1 de la escuela infantil [Origin and development of executive functions in the 0-1 school in the early years school]. In C. Rodríguez & J. L. de los Reyes, (Coord.), *Los objetos sí importan. Acciones educativas en la escuela infantil* (pp. 133–157). Horsori.
39. Rodríguez, C., & Moro, C. (1998). *El mágico número tres. Cuando los niños aún no hablan* [The magic number three. When children do not talk yet]. Paidós.
40. Silva, J. B. da. (2021). As práticas pedagógicas de professoras de educação infantil em exercício docente na creche [The pedagogical practices of infant school teachers]. *Ensino Em*

Perspectivas, 2(1), 1–12. Recuperado de https://revistas.uece.br/index.php/ensinoemperspectivas/article/view/6043
41. Taisson, C. P. (2014). La matérialité: Une ressource pour l'enseignement-apprentissage de la lecture [Materiality: A resource for the teaching-learning of reading]. *Éducation Didactique, 8*(2), 125–138. https://doi.org/10.4000/educationdidactique.1984
42. Taisson, C. P. (2020). Conséquences de la circulation du concept de matérialité entre la recherche et la formation initiale des enseignants du primaire [Consequences of the circulation of the concept of materiality between research and the initial training of primary school teachers]. *Formation et pratiques d'enseignement en questions, 26*(1), 93–112. https://revuedeshep.ch/pdf/26/26-06-Taisson
43. Tapparel, S. (2014). Se développer en situation éducative dans une institution de la petite enfance: Le rôle de l'objet matériel en situation peinture [Developing in an educational situation in an early childhood institution: The role of the material object in a painting situation]. In C. Moro & N. Muller Mirza (Eds.), *Sémiotique, culture et développement psychologique* (pp. 141–158). Presses Universitaires du Septentrion.
44. Tapparel, S. (2015). *Situations éducatives, matérialité et développement psychologique: Étude de cas dans un Centre de vie enfantine lausannois* [Educational situations, materiality and psychological development: A case study from a childcare center in Lausanne](Doctoral dissertation, Université de Lausanne). https://serval.unil.ch/resource/serval:BIB_EBBD6BA6DDB7.P001/REF
45. Vale, V. G., Mietto, G., Cárdenas, K. & Rengifo-Herrera, F. J. (2023) *Contribuições teóricas da pragmática do objeto para a BNCC na perspectiva da Educação Infantil* [Theoretical contributions of the Pragmatics of the Object to the BNCC from the perspective of Early Childhood Education]. In F. Negreiros (Org.), Psicologia Escolar e BNCC: criticidade e análise política (pp. 139–157). Átomo & Alínea.
46. Zelazo, P. D., & Müller, U. (2011). Executive function in typical and atypical development. In U. Goswami (Ed.), *The Wiley-Blackwell handbook of childhood cognitive development* (2nd ed., pp. 574–603). Wiley Blackwell.

Part IV

Psychoeducational Intervention in Everyday Situations in the Context of Autism

Construction of Shared Meanings from the Pragmatics of the Object. Psychoeducational Experiences in the Field of Autism

12

Julia Benassi and Karina Cárdenas

12.1 Introduction

Intervention in the early development of autism challenges us in terms of how to provide support for children's participation in the world of social interactions, which not only includes the relationship with people, but also with objects. From the earliest descriptions of autism [5, 35], the alteration of the child's contact[1] with people, the *social world*, has been emphasized [6, 31], taking priority over relationships with objects, the *physical world*.

From the perspective of the Pragmatics of the Object developed by Rodríguez and Moro [63], in line with a series of works that deal with the child's interactions with objects (e.g., [42]), we support the idea that, in order to understand and analyze early communication, it is necessary to consider the object in its cultural complexity, including its public functions. In the process of constructing shared

[1] An inclusive language perspective is assumed in the writing of this chapter. Therefore, only for the purpose of facilitating reading, from now on we will use the expression: children, baby, and childhoods, without conceptual or gender distinction.

J. Benassi (✉)
Escuela Superior de Sanidad "Ramón Carrillo", Facultad de Bioquímica y Ciencias Biológicas, Universidad del Litoral, Santa Fe, Argentina
e-mail: jbenassi@fbcb.unl.edu.ar

K. Cárdenas
Pontificia Universidad Católica de Chile, Villarrica, Chile
e-mail: kcardenas@uc.cl

C. Rodriguez Garrido et al. (eds.), *The Social Life of Objects in Early Development*, Social Interaction in Learning and Development,
https://doi.org/10.1007/978-3-031-87673-8_12

meanings or understandings,[2] adults offer semiotic mediation through various systems of meaning [62], in a web of sensitive experiences. At the same time, the child requires sufficient flexibility to withstand uncertainty, tolerate changes and integrate these changes into projects aimed at anticipated goals, all thanks to the possibility of imagining or representing a future. This baggage of communicative resources is built in the triadic interactions made up by the child, the adult, and the object, opening possibilities to know, interact, understand, and feel together.

Our challenge is to accompany children with autism spectrum condition (ASC) and their families, through the process of elaboration and implementation of semiotic mediation tools [2]. This accompaniment is carried out in carefully designed experiences, aimed at the construction of shared meanings that allow children to participate in the different contexts of daily life [76].

In this chapter we will focus on three key aspects of sociocognitive development in children with autism spectrum condition. First, we will address the general aspects of this condition and explore its early development from a perspective based on a dimensional continuum. Secondly, we will carry out a comparative analysis between the development of the communicative dimension in children with autism spectrum condition and those with normotypical development, as a key to reflect on the construction of shared meanings. In this section, we will pay special attention to the role of objects and semiotic mediations generated in triadic interactions. Finally, we will analyze the semiotic qualities of the environments we design, from our psychoeducational practices, to favor the participation of children in relation to the world of objects.

Through the description of psychoeducational experiences with a child with autism spectrum condition, we will explore how multiple semiotic systems—including the material world, gestures, images, words, rhythm, and music—are set in motion in the process of meaning-making. This analysis will make it possible to highlight the dynamics between children and the adults who accompany them

[2] Building meanings to learn to participate in social life is not reduced to understanding isolated meanings, such as *If A then B*, signified/signifier relationship, in line with Saussure's proposal. *A means B for C*, that is, for an interpretant in a particular context of relations with a multiplicity of signs. Therefore, sharing the same "definition of situation", in the words of Wertsch [78], from this meaning of Peirce's three-headed sign, requires not only decoding a sign, understanding what an action, an image, a word, a gesture or how an object is used, but also implies making a reading of a network of related signs in a particular context. In this direction, Peirce's notion of interpretant is fundamental, since it proposes that the meaning of a sign is not unique or fixed, but depends on interpretation, which can vary and open up depending on experience and context, and on the relationship of that sign with others, in a network of signs. This interpretive process is open and potentially infinite, a system of chained signs, where each interpretation can generate new interpretations. For this reason, his theory can be understood as aligned with an idea of "senses", as a broad and constantly developing field of interpretation. In this chapter we adhere to this idea of the construction of meanings, as constructions of shared, situated and polysemic understandings (multiple forms of signs and functions), which involve sensory, bodily and affective experiences, what we "feel together" and not just "how we mean it together", in short, a sensory experience.

in different psychoeducational contexts, such as school, home, and therapeutic centers.

12.2 The Condition of the Autism Spectrum and the Study of Its Early Development from the Dimensional Continuum

The idea of a dimensional continuum of developmental disorders, introduced by Wing and Gould [83] and later expanded by Rivière [53] with the contribution of psychogenetic and sociogenetic studies, has been key to contemporary definitions of autism, such as the one included in the manual of the American Psychiatric Association [4]. In this version, the autism spectrum is conceptualized as a neurodevelopmental disorder of multifactorial origin, characterized by behavioral symptoms that emerge during the first year of life [38]. Unlike what was proposed by the American Psychiatric Association [3], which used the category of "Pervasive Developmental Disorders" with different subtypes, this update does not address autism in absolute terms. Instead, it defines it according to different degrees of severity, from which the necessary support is determined so that the person can function in their daily lives.

Autism spectrum disorder (ASD) affects various psychological processes, being most evident in the areas of social development, communication, and language; as well as anticipation, flexibility, and symbolization, as described by Rivière [53] in the Autism Spectrum Inventory (originally "Inventario de Espectro de Autismo (IDEA)", in Spanish). The American Psychiatric Association [4] groups these manifestations into two major areas: social communication and behaviors/interests. In addition, particularities in emotional, sensory-perceptual and motor processing [12] characterize this developmental condition, impacting to varying degrees the daily lives of people with the condition and that of their families, as well as their participation in the community [32, 85]. Research on developmental trajectories in children on the autism spectrum (e.g., [26, 36]) highlight the importance of considering the communication disorder as a continuum, in line with the previously mentioned dimensional conception. From this perspective, it is recognized that the course of development is heterogeneous and can manifest itself at different times within the first three years of life.

This understanding of the autism spectrum has influenced the approaches mostly adopted by pragmatically oriented researchers since the 1980s, broadening the analysis towards the possible interrelationships between dimensions, overcoming the limits implied on conceptualizing skills as fragmented or stagnant competencies.

However, this dimensional and holistic approach does not always translate into interventions aimed at children with autism spectrum condition, particularly into the creation of opportunities that facilitate their participation in daily life, located in the community [19]. In this regard, it is worth highlighting the CODDA approach, an acrostic proposed by Valdez [75] alluding to four key variables for the development of psychoeducational interventions in the field of autism: Contexts, Dimensionality, Development and Support (from the Spanish "*Contextos, Dimensionalidad, Desarrollo y Apoyos*").

Within the framework of studies on the genesis of nonverbal communication, Rivière and Español [20, 21, 52] analyzed the emergence of the first signs in children's interactions in their daily context. Some of these lines of research also moved to the field of developmental disorders, especially autism [54]. However, in studies related to the early development of this condition, there are few references analyzing how the uses of objects are learned, in triadic units of interaction, within the framework of the genesis of signs, and of the semiotic mediations through which the child enters the world of shared meanings [8, 10].

12.3 Keys to the Construction of Shared Meanings

12.3.1 The Development of the Communicative Dimension on the Autism Spectrum

The socio-communicative dimension follows a particular course in the development of autism, evident from the first years of life. Among the earliest warning signs are poor eye contact and the limited use of gestures with a declarative function, and even imperative in some cases [84]. One of the main effects is observed in the onset of joint attention. Especially in the use of showing (ostensive) and pointing (indexical) gestures, which are compromised from 12 months of age, both in infants with autism spectrum condition and in those with language delay [27]. In addition, a significant correlation has been reported between alterations in joint attention and difficulties in language and communication in children on the autism spectrum [15].

The absence, delay, and/or low frequency of joint attention behaviors, along with other intersubjective precursors, are some of the most characteristic signs of this developmental condition [7]. Mundy and Newell [44] found that difficulties in joint attention at 12 months were predictors of later language disturbances at 36 months. For their part, Brignell et al. [14] estimate that between 25% and 30% of diagnosed children have a significant compromise of communicative verbal language, which may be absent or reduced to less than 30 words.

On the other hand, the relationship between gesture production and typical language development has been widely studied. Infants begin to produce gestures before they develop verbal language and continue to use them throughout their lives, making gestures a privileged means of social interaction. In communication, gestures and speech are tightly integrated. Guidetti and Nicoladis [30] highlight that recent theoretical perspectives on language acquisition emphasize a functional approach to communicative development, where the use of gestures plays a central role in its learning. Some researchers even argue that spoken language may have evolved from gestures [18]. In this regard, Valdez proposes that "the revolution in the development of communication is not constituted by the appearance of the first words, but by the birth of the communicative intention in the context of human intersubjectivity" ([74], p. 206).

As a priority in early communication, gestures act as a scaffolding for the development of language skills, becoming precursors of oral language acquisition in many cases [22, 48]. However, not all types of gestures (e.g., ostensive, indexical, symbolic), nor their multiple functions (i.e., imperative, declarative, interrogative) are directly linked to language acquisition (see Chap. 7 on the development of gestures in this volume). It is known that declarative deictic gestures [17] are especially compromised in children with autism spectrum conditions. In this regard, Özçalışkan et al. [48] found that only deictic gestures predict vocabulary in children with language disorders and ASD, highlighting their importance as a means of referring to the environment before having verbal skills. Thus, gestures make it easier for the caregiver to establish a joint focus from which to communicate.

The relevance of gestures in the history of development should guide the development of early care plans and psychoeducational proposals in general. Some authors suggest that the inclusion of declarative deictic gestures in early intervention programs in autism encourages nonverbal communication, which in turn contributes to the development of verbal skills and enhances social interactions [48, 51].

From the perspective in which this chapter is inscribed, and in line with the dimensional conception of the autism spectrum, we propose that psychoeducational practices in early development not only should integrate the approach to gestures in their relationship but also the uses of objects within triadic units of interaction (adult, objects, and children) and in a network of signs. That is, gestures do not occur in a vacuum; they happen in reference to the material world. It is essential to consider them in conjunction with the objects or situations to which they refer to, whether to show, to ask another or even to ask oneself [56]. In this way, the development of gestures shares its history with that of the uses of objects in interaction with others, whether caregivers or peers [29].

Some early detection and intervention programs recognize the importance of gestures and actions with objects between 9 and 16 months of age, understanding that their consideration during interactions promotes early language learning. Therefore, attending to their presence is a tool that serves to identify possible alert signs and to promote development [24, 64].[3] These programs take into account materiality as a resource for learning, with a special focus on language, that is, from an instrumental perspective. However, from the Pragmatics of the Object perspective, for children to use that materiality for other learnings, it is first necessary for them to learn its social and cultural functions, and this happens through adults and their semiotic mediations, which include the object [62].

[3] The 16 by 16 project, developed by *the First Words Project*, provides resources to support early language and communication development. These guides make visible 16 actions with objects and 16 gestures expected to be learned by infants in their first 16 months of life.

To promote the development of the communicative dimension in those children who mainly have difficulties with verbal language, the use of augmentative and alternative communication (AAC) systems is suggested [25], thus guaranteeing the possibility of communication. Numerous studies highlight the effectiveness of implementing these systems to facilitate communication skills in children on the autism spectrum [13, 28, 46, 69]. The use of augmentative and alternative communication systems increases children's verbal repertoire and the frequency of their interactions with peers and educators [46]. However, the relevance of Augmentative or Alternative Communication should not be limited to the problems of verbal language, either due to its absence or scarce presence. Instead, it should be understood as an expansion of communicative, expressive and comprehensive possibilities, even when it also promotes the development of verbal language. Likewise, it should not be reduced exclusively to the use *of visual or voice communication devices*, but to the communicative opportunities offered by the environment with its materiality, and the interlocutors with whom the communication takes place. Therefore, environment, materiality, interlocutors and devices of multiple languages, make up an *organized system of communication.*

In this direction, some of the questions that we can ask ourselves when assessing how we communicate, and not only how the child communicates, could be: What are the occasions we provide to communicate? We allude here, on the one hand, to the *type of signs* that are deployed (visual, gestural, verbal written or oral, rhythmic, melodic, among others); on the other hand, to the *support devices or resources* used (analogue or digital); as well as to the *frequency of use of the multiple signs*; How many times do we give opportunities for the child to ask for, complete, comment? How do we implement *communicative redundancies* [63][4]?, What kind of signs do we conjugate in each communicative act?, How do we emphasize, underline, give intensity, use silences, modulate the use of signs to give them greater expressiveness? We know that imperative communication, specifically referring to pragmatic behaviors of requesting (for something), tends to predominate in children with autism spectrum condition. In this regard, it should be considered that some research, such as Nunes et al. [46] point out that communicative interlocutors do not offer sufficient conditions for the emergence of more complex semiotic functions (e.g. declarative).

On the other hand, the technological revolution in Augmentative and Alternative Communication deserves special mention. It has brought important challenges, since intervention is often reduced to providing a software program (e.g. digital communicator devices which allow the use of pictograms, images and other written or oral verbal signs), without sufficient training and support for the user and their interlocutors. Light and McNaughton [39] propose that intervention should focus not only on teaching the use of technology, but also on developing linguistic,

[4] We refer to the synchronous deployment of complementary semiotic systems, i.e., pointing rhythmically while producing the word referring to what is indicated, which facilitates understanding by the child.

social, and strategic skills to promote communicative competencies. Assessments and interventions should focus on each child's communication needs, using technology as a tool to enhance their communication skills, allowing them to express their needs, exchange information, share, relate, and engage in social interactions. The researchers argue that although technological advances have provided significant new opportunities for people with complex communicational needs, it is crucial that the intervention in alternative and augmentative communication focuses on people's needs and skills, in their context, and not only on the technology itself. In short, it is not a question of learning exclusively from the use of communication cards or technological devices, but of stablishing supports within children social relationships to promote participation.

12.3.2 The Object as Part of the Communicative Dimension

As we have mentioned, objects are part of the communication between subjects. Rodríguez and Moro [63] question the split between the so-called "physical world", referring to material objects, and the "social world", where objects are excluded, which is specially important in early development. This has lead to separate lines of research and approaches on either cognition or communication. This view has not only influenced studies of typical development, but also studies on other developmental conditions, such as the autism spectrum. In this way, autism has been linked to difficulties in social interactions (with people), dismissing its relationship with the material world. However, in recent decades, a series of studies have dealt with the interactions of children with adults, including the materiality with which they relate [49, 70, 75–81].

Williams et al. [79], also question the dichotomization between the social and material world that derives from the "Theory of Mind" approach and that still underlies many current perspectives on autism. These authors expose that, in these theories, the difficulties of intersubjective social relations are not linked to those of the material world. For this reason, they propose to challenge this duality by broadening the term "social", to include relations with objects as part of the social context in which they are introduced and used. Understanding the nature of reciprocity between the child, people, and the material world involves considering objects within the social context in which the child participates. The authors argue that this discussion does not concern only the theoretical level, but has practical consequences. In the design of inclusive and situated interventions, it is imperative to fully appreciate the interaction between different areas of development, including the child's relationship with objects and people. In fact, the findings of Ozonoff et al. [49], on atypical uses of objects at 12 months of age in children later diagnosed with ASD, were very influential on the current assessment of autism. In this regard, the ADOS Toddler Module [40] includes items related to atypical behaviors and unusual uses of objects. However, in line with what has been previously stated, these uses are not linked, at least directly, to the development of communication with other people.

In this context, from the Pragmatics of the Object, Sterner and Rodríguez [68] propose to introduce the category Uses of Objects[5] in the instruments and guides for early detection of this condition. They also highlighting that the contribution of studies in typical development is essential since it allows us to have specific references to guide the detection of possible altered uses of objects, linking them with the development of communicative signs.

The impact of social reciprocity in autism influences not only the development of the child's skills but also the level of adult involvement with them. This is evident both in the children's responses and in the quality and quantity of invitations aimed at encouraging social partners to share in the uses and interests in the environment in general, and objects in particular. Thus, the opportunities to enter and to create situations shared meanings are limited. Likewise, it is common to find that caregivers, educators, and therapists tend to become less encouraging during the interactions, affecting the quality of the offers they make to the child to participate in shared actions [67]. This situation supports the need for changes in psychoeducational teams, in order to avoid these limitations in the interventions of educators or therapists. It is equally relevant in the early monitoring of the development of populations at risk, such as siblings of children diagnosed with ASD. The previous experience of families with their children (mainly when they were firstborn), affects the way they promote interactions with their next children, as well as the level of alertness regarding the particularities of their development. These statements, arising from clinical observations, have their correlation in current research. Williams et al. [79] found that parents of children with ASD, compared to those who had typically developing children and Down syndrome, were less inviting to interact with an object. In turn, children with ASD were less likely to respond to such invitations, showing a greater tendency to be absorbed in their own uses of objects. This accounts for an interdependence between the action of the adult and that of the child, which from the Pragmatics of the Object we analyze in semiotically mediated triadic interactions.

12.3.3 Semiotic Mediations in the Fabric of Interactions

The use of objects is not carried out separately from facial expression, gestures, verbal language, gaze direction, rhythm, pauses, silences and the body at stake. This wealth of signs made up of *variety and relationships* unfolds from the earliest moments in typical development, during the interactions between adults and children. Experience allows us to assume that in cases of autism this communicative fabric could find a different quality, probably more *monochrome or devoid of*

[5] It includes the categories: non-conventional uses and conventional uses, from studies with infants with normotypical development [59, 56, 61, 63] and the category atypical uses, from the study by Ozonoff et al. [49], with children with ASD.

semiotic accompaniment, so in our educational practices we try to *build, promote and "wrap" them.*

We don't usually subject our everyday interactions, such as feeding a baby, to semiotic analysis. However, we can observe that each of these interactions presents a multiplicity of motifs, subtly woven into a plot of elements interlinked among the participants in the scene: people, objects, semiotic mediators, purposes, and details of the scenario with its unique aesthetics, which together constitute much more than just a background[6] [58, 57].

In the description of the following everyday scene, we can witness the detail of communicative interactions from a very early age:

> Paula, Amparito's mother, feeds her one of her first porridges at six months old. The girl looks at the novel object, a spoon, and her mother's hands that is carrying it. In her face, that smile is a sign that something good is happening. Amparo's eyes grow when her mother speaks to her, in continuity with a gentle body movement. Amparo follows her mother's movements, paying attention to each element deployed for her. Given her recent experience with the world of porridge, she can anticipate the meaning of this combination of movements and objects, so s*he brings her hand to the spoon and tries to grasp it.* She leans forward with her body in the chair, *leaning toward the target.* She opens her mouth and receives the porridge. Her expression is transformed accompanied by a *vocalization* that varies slightly in its form and intensity. For her part, the mother performs another series of acts, gestures and expressions. She directs her body, her gaze and asks "does this baby want more?", and then melodically comments on what Amparo does "yes, how well this baby eats....", while she carries the spoon again for an upcoming portion. She pauses, stops the action halfway between the plate and the girl's mouth, shows her the spoon, making an onomatopoeia "mmm". She moves the spoon rhythmically, repeats, and slightly varies the rhythm produced, offering it again and *helping Amparo to grasp it with her hand.*

In this way, Amparo, the spoon, her mother and each of the elements present in the scenario, weave an exquisite interactive to-and-fro. This condensation of signs, belonging to different systems, is what Rodríguez [60] calls semiotic stelae. It is a set of signs. Traces left by the adult in their interaction to demarcate a route. Amparo's mother "wraps" her baby with these *stelae* in a rich cultural fabric, giving her the possibility of entering the world of porridge. The most basic semiotic levels (looks, smiles) provide a "platform" on which other more complex sign systems (e.g., conventional uses of objects, ostensive, indexical or symbolic gestures) will be shaped and developed [43].

From the earliest uses of objects, we begin to construct meanings in terms of shapes, directions, and contents [55]. The Pragmatics of the Object offers us a perspective that facilitates the understanding of the interaction between two key elements in our psychoeducational practices: on the one hand, the *diversity of nuances present in the different signs* (e.g. variety of signs—forms and functions), and, on the other, the multiplicity of *combinations of these signs* (e.g. relations between uses and gestures), which are reflected in the concept of semiotic stelae. Thus, this perspective allows us to understand how meaning is constructed in each

[6] Alluding to Wertsch's [77] sociocultural theory of mediated action.

communicative act. This type of analysis in typical development illuminates our daily psychoeducational practices with children with autism spectrum condition and their families, motivating some of the current studies of this team.[7] For example, in an ongoing study [47], we are analyzing the semiotic interactions during the feeding scenes of infants who subsequently received a diagnosis of ASD. Our goal is to delve into the nature of these interactions, examine how semiotic trails are structured, and explore how the child participates in that communicative act, beyond the functional use of the spoon. We hypothesize that, in children diagnosed with ASD, sign patterns exhibit a smaller variety of semiotic relationships compared to typically developing children. We believe that this phenomenon should be explored in deliberate learning contexts such as early years school and Early Care.

In some disciplinary fields of health and education, the purpose of promoting "meaningful activities" has been extended, understanding this as the personal meaning that each individual gives to an activity. The priority given to meaning, in this framework, could be assimilated to the idea of following the child's interest, a relevant aspect for the design of psychoeducational proposals that demand certain conceptual reflections due to the polysemy of the term. A practice based only on the interests of children in the autism spectrum may not be aligned with the "best interests of the child", as set out in the International Convention on Children's Rights [71]. Focusing exclusively on interests, which in this population are usually restricted, could limit the possibility of opening new windows to the world [9]. The aim is to build practices that are respectful of children and, at the same time, that become facilitators of new opportunities from a rights-based perspective. These practices should allow not only the execution of tasks but also their understanding, in order for children to become agents of transformation in their daily lives.

An interaction that simply follows what the child does can be as restrictive as one that offers only structured models, based on rigid stimuli and responses, with rewards as the external engine of the activities. These rewards, being exogenous, lack the intrinsic sense of sharing with others. Rivière [54, 55] describes the meaning of activity as one of the twelve developmental dimensions involved in the autism spectrum [53]. The concept of meaning can allude to directionality, that is: where something is heading (for example, what is the direction of a street?). Here, meaning projects and therefore allows anticipation. Likewise, in its semiotic sense, the construction of meaning refers to the construction of shared meanings. For this reason, the understanding of these meanings is a critical condition for participation. This poses the challenges for us on how to listen to another when they cannot "raise" their voice, and how to communicate when the other has a voice, but their words fail to link in a network of shared meanings.

[7] DETEDUCA, Research Group: Early Development and Education. UAM.

12.4 Semiotic Qualities of Educational Environments for the Construction of Shared Meanings

The Pragmatics of the Object, with its idea of the sign's origin being in triadic interaction units, and Wertsch's [77] sociocultural theory of mediated action,[8] which highlights five key elements in the mediation of human action (scenario, actors, mediating tools, objects of action, and dialogic process), offer essential foundations for the design and analysis of our daily psychoeducational practices. The purpose of these inclusive practices, or from Najmanovich's [45] critical perspective "practices of conviviality", is to generate caring environments that promote children's participation [19]. UNICEF [71] recognizes the importance of promoting the participation of all children in the cultural life of their community as a way of guaranteeing their full development [71]. For this reason, communication and participation are presented as interdependent objectives that underpin our psychoeducational proposals. It is about designing environments at home, in early years schools or in therapeutic centers, that enable experience, "cultivating" them, as Mandoki [41] proposes. As in any crop, this task involves offering, sustaining and waiting without withdrawing. To build environments to be inhabited for organized, idiosyncratic and situated experience, instead of reproducing universal schemes. Understanding environments as semiotic trails full of signs to provide possible directions. Not one, but multiple. Not all at once or in the same space, but organized.

Children with autism spectrum conditions require these environmental supports. For example, by explaining what is expected of them or what they should do at certain times. In this direction, the TEACCH model (Treatment and Education of Autistic and related Communication-handicapped Children), offers organized and predictable environments [65] through visual materials, schedules, and routines, in order to promote autonomy, self-esteem, and self-management of children's behavior [33]. The arrangement of objects in the space, the paths proposed for their development, and the satisfaction provided by the possibility of completing tasks and participating in meaningful activities, with minimal external scaffolding by adults, are outstanding principles of the methodology. However, even if these environments are accessible, they have their limitations which relate to the promotion of social interactions and play. We are aware of the contribution of other perspectives that also deal with the organization of the environment, focusing on some specific qualities. However, the view of the environment as an external element to be structured according to the individual, is far from a sociocultural approach in which materiality is considered in its context of cultural production and action. From this approach, attention is not focused on the semiotic mediators deployed

[8] In his sociocultural theory of mediated action, Wertsch takes up the theatrical metaphor of Burke (1945), with his dramatic "pentad", composed of: (1) Act, what is done; (2) Scene, the context in which the act occurs, (3) Agent, who performs the act, (4) Agency, the means or tools used to carry out the act, (5) Purpose: The objective or reason behind the act.

by the adult, nor on how children participate with them in the co-construction of meanings.

Some aspects promoted by these perspectives, even if not specific to the study of autism, can provide valuable tools to promote accessibility and anticipation in childhood, attending to self-regulation through kinesic and sensory stimulation. Some of the guiding principles of our practices also make use of certain strategies of Waldorf pedagogies. For example, emphasizing the importance of rituals and routines, and the relevance of engaging in organized action processes. Our view integrates these and other contributions from a dimensional perspective, with special attention to the semiotic and aesthetic qualities of the environment. That is, the construction of shared meanings is sought in educational environments in which materiality is understood as part of a web of signs. This occurs through the uses that children make of the materiality and the multimodal semiotic mediations (gestures, demonstrations of the uses of objects, songs, etc.) promoted by adults. Therefore, building a shared sense *is not carrying out an activity,* but *understanding what I am doing* in order to be an agent, and *to actively participate* in social life. Therefore, psychoeducational practice *is not limited to the implementation of a predetermined program,* but involves knowing the developmental principles on which that program is structured, in order to be able to operate critically with them. From this perspective, we work in *Vaivén Infancias*[9] space, with children with various developmental conditions and their families, in the city of Santa Fe, Argentina. Francis' description, which we share below, was written drawing on experiences from more than 20 years of working in this team, as a way of illustrating our perspective.

> Our first encounter with Francis was at 2 years and 8 months of age.*The family consulted* about some behaviors that they considered the child was doing in imitation of a classmate at the early years school. According to his mother, Francis used *to turn and wave his hands on the sides of his head.* The child already said a few words and this dispelled any concerns of his parents about their child's development. However, teachers from the early years school he attended at the time, suggested turning to professionals to evaluate *some behaviors that generated concern.* The teachers perceived that the child had *stopped saying some already learned words, he looked less* at his classmates and teachers, he spent more time playing alone, and *seemed not to listen* or be interested in what the rest of the classmates were doing.
>
> We began the process of assessing Francis together with the child psychiatrist on the team and identified that the family's observations were only some of the manifestations of a behavioral spectrum that could not be explained solely by imitation of his partner's behaviors. These expressions formed a more complex web of a developmental condition that followed a particular course. A series of developmental alert indexes that were not so evident in their symptomatic production, such as self-stimulation in the absence or scarce presence of developmental milestones. We observed, for example: *gaze avoidance, absence of facial expressions and conventional gestures directed at others, instrumental use of the*

[9] The first author of this chapter is a founding member of the *Vaivén infancias project,* Santa Fe, Argentina, a transdisciplinary team of professionals in the field of health, education and art, in which she has worked since 2001 as a therapist and coordinator of psychoeducational approach devices.

other to request something (i.e., using the other's hand to access what is required instead of asking for it through a gesture or word), and *absence of verbal expressions for communicative* purposes (i.e. although he said some words, he did not do so in order to interact with another). Likewise, *he did not produce canonical uses of objects, nor did he perform actions of initiation of symbolic play*. His approach to objects was restricted not only in his interest's variety, but also in terms of the uses he made of them. On the other hand, the child tended to perform *repetitive and stereotyped actions with objects*. He did not stay with adults in a shared action such as simple circular games (e.g. interaction with a ball), reading a book, or games with puppets and dolls. In addition, Francis did not accept the interference of others in his actions and tended to become easily unregulated, wandering, running around or rattling with his feet. Some tantrums and opposition began to manifest themselves in the face of adults' refusal.

We agreed with the family that it was necessary to initiate intervention at home, regulate sleep, diet and develop play proposals. We started sharing sessions with the parents, and later we alternated with an aunt who participated in Francis' daily care. We decided to have a moment of shared reading every day, since it was one of the favorite activities of his mother, and a moment of games with musical instruments and songs with his father, a music lover. We agreed to arrange the environment to favor the requests of basic daily needs (e.g. drinking, eating, going to the bathroom, going for a walk), placing referential visual signs in the different sectors of the house, and a very simple visual agenda of the day. We *set out to promote the development of the pointing gesture*, as well as other conventional gestures that the family considered priorities. We worked with adults on the importance of stopping to maintain eye contact and other patterns of primary subjective interaction and provocation of reciprocal actions. Francis' aunt offered to reorganize the toys at home in drawers labeled with representative images, to take away scattered elements, and favor the production of communicative actions. Table 12.1 illustrates some of the orientations and resources implemented in this first period of work with Francis and his family.

We organized the toys according to the categories made with the family: (1) boxes of wheels, balls, and cars; (2) exploration and production of plastic graphs; (3) musical rhythmic exploration and production; (4) simple construction elements; (5) materials for symbolic games – game boxes – with small visual scripts to build scenarios and simple action sequences [9].

After a first period, sessions with the child and a family member in the therapeutic center were also initiated, as well as shared sessions with another therapist. In this way, the first proposed objectives were addressed: to enhance the guidelines for joint action and joint reference, the primary communication and language skills, as well as keys to the flexibility and foundations of the game. The level of behavioral rigidity was one of the main challenges for the approach. Francis tended to focus his attention on solitary actions, very restrictive interests, and opposed the adult's offers of new modes of play, especially when it came to actions shared with others.

At the same time, we began the work with the teachers in the early years school, in order to restructure the space based on Francis' needs that were jointly evaluated in that context, and the construction of mediations that facilitated Francis' participation in routine activities and involvement in other activities. They began to share in family outings the spaces of frequent circulation (e.g. market, square, among others), to which they had stopped going due to the difficulties that arose in each area. Gradually, new instances and spaces for participation were enabled for Francis and his family.

The new circuits of participation of the child and his family implied new movements: opening the house for our arrival, starting to think together, telling each other what was happening, asking each other about the process. Thus, this to-and-fro began to be woven between the child, his world of references, materiality, and actions of daily life.

Table 12.1 First orientations in Francis' home

1.1. *Library:* We set up a reading corner at home with an accessible library for Francis, and another elevated one, labeled with a reading pictogram (bottom left), to encourage requests. Every two or three weeks, we selected with his mother a cardboard song-book,[10] with a simple structure, repetitive rhythm, and good figure-ground contrast. These characteristics facilitated Francis' anticipation and participation. Whenever we introduced a new book, we kept a familiar one, balancing variety and established references. Images of the available books were placed on a selection panel on the wall, promoting interest in the material and Francis' *choice*

(continued)

[10] Three books are exhibited in the image: (1) Benegas, M., & Lalalimola. (2015). *¿Le pondremos un bigote?* Combel. ISBN 978-84-9825-970-4; (2) Rubio, A., & Villán, O. (2016). *Veo, Veo.* Kalandraka. ISBN 978-84-92608-87-4; (3) Romero, J., & Calderón, M. (2018). *Tengo, Tengo, Tengo.* Gerbera. Colección Nube de Algodón. ISBN 978-987-4071-43-9.

Table 12.1 (continued)

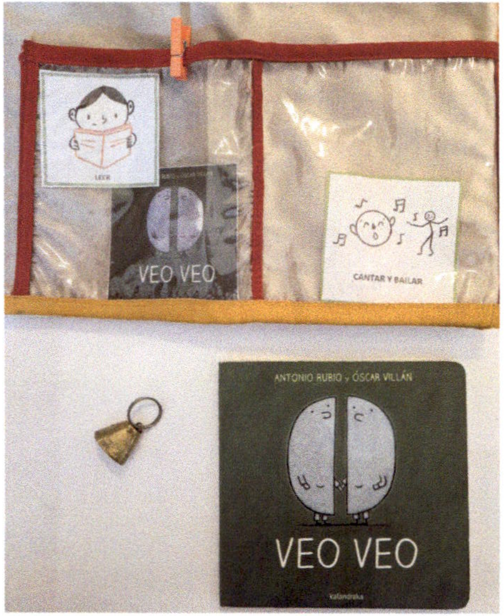

(continued)

Table 12.1 (continued)

1.2. *Shared activities at home:* We used the neighborhood children's library to expand the books available to Francis and promote participation in his community. For each book that was incorporated, we organized games and activities. During the reading moment, we anticipated the activities with cards in a pouch (image on the left), using a clothes peg to mark the present, and a small bell to open and close the interaction. We also included images with magnets and objects from the books to engage Francis through various avenues of access the fictional material

(a) (b) (c)

1.3 *Visual resources for anticipating, choosing and organizing*: (a) *Card box and pocket*: we organized in boxes the cards representing the people who refer to Francis (blue), everyday actions (green), places and objects of daily use (yellow and orange). These cards were arranged in the pouch giving a temporal order to the game session. (b) *Simple wall agenda:* the family made a very simple weekly agenda, with photos of the people or places representative of each activity of the day. (c) *Labeled drawer unit* for toys: the images on the drawer allowed Francis to choose and later store. The image of sneakers (drawing on the wall), indicated the place to leave the shoes before entering the play mat

12.4.1 The Organization of Daily Time: Routines and Transitions from One Moment to the Next

One of the aspects that must be considered when talking about the educational environment is the organization of *daily time*. From early years school, educators plan the learning experiences or activities they offer to children within an orderly context. The development of a schedule allows them to ensure that they offer different moments in which a range of varied experiences are offered to promote a balanced development. This organization is positive for both adults and children, since it allows them to anticipate what is going to happen, giving them security, but also the opportunity to learn notions of time, such as the sequence and duration of activities [37]. One of the strategies used in early childhood education is to share, through visual supports, the daily routine. This facilitates children's understanding of the activities that occur at different times in the educational environment. This also works in clinical environments and at the child's home. In these spaces, those who accompany different trajectories of development know that the use of visual supports, in an explicit way—group or personalized—constitutes a basic resource for daily work and at the same time shapes the intervention objectives. Experience confirms that routines or visual sequences are useful not only to provide structure and predictability, but also to help reduce discomfort with waiting times. This is because visual schemes provide guidance on the activities proposed at a given time, allowing an activity to be broken down, transitions to be announced, as well as to clearly represent the closures of each one [9].

On the other hand, the use of visual supports, such as daily agendas, anticipations, and agreements, from a constructivist perspective [1], are key to behavioral regulation. There is usually a tendency to reduce the instrumentation of these resources to avoid behaviors that are undesirable for the context. However, we understand that their use makes it possible to establish agreements and make conflicts and/or resolutions of social situations explicit. These tools aim to enable children to understand what is happening and what is expected to happen depending on each context [9].

Sequentiality and temporal transitions, from one moment to the next, constitute one of the keys to ordering. We have a series of *moments* within each educational session or day, specifically designed for each child and/or group, in their context of participation. For example, the comprehensive psychoeducational intervention proposal that we designed for Francis and his family is developed in different spaces: at home, at school, in the therapeutic center, and in extracurricular activities. In addition, we travel through public spaces and other everyday places that children usually attend, such as the square, the library, the markets. In each meeting, we propose routes through *moments* that do not necessarily follow a predetermined chronological order, but are arranged according to the particularities of the encounter with each child.

In other contexts, such as in early years school, routines follow a pre-established order, although always flexible to emerging situations. Some are interchangeable, depending on the way in which the child is involved in the proposal, their choices

Table 12.2 Visual resources for the selection of games with Francis: selection panel implemented in the early years school and in the therapeutic center

	*Panel with 4 game options*: Once Francis understood the dynamics of choosing between two options, we added a panel with more cards • The images[11] are arranged to encourage the request through a phrase, for example: "Give me puzzles" • Basic requests are included: "bath" and "water" (on the right) • The blackboard is another resource to promote sentence structuring. The image is placed in the center of the box and emphasizes with gestures and words: "I want X" • In the bag, the images are organized in a temporal sequence, showing the activities chosen together

and particularities of the interaction. The logic of *moments* alludes to time, to the importance of the openings and closures of each activity or sequence of activities that make up that moment, as well as to the transitions from one to another.

The description of an individual and shared play session with Francis, developed in the therapeutic center of the *Vaivén Infancias space*, 2 years after the beginning of the work, at 4 years and 9 months of age, accounts for this temporal organization:

> *After the initial moment of greeting,* Francis knows that *we will choose together the activities* we will do in the game session in *Vaivén.* To do this, he has a *selection panel* (Table 12.2) with different options. He also has his *communication folder available,* depending on the context in which we find ourselves (therapeutic center, school, square, home).
>
> Francis then organizes in a horizontal pouch the cards representing the choices made, according to the agreements he establishes with his therapist. Thus, they build together a hierarchy of activities through a freehand visual sequence that points out the great moments of the playful encounter (see Table 12.3): First, an initial routine of hand games and body massages with songs. Then, the hammock that Francis requested, to which they will add games with balls and fountains, selected among two other options offered by the therapist.

[11] The visual resources shown in Tables 12.1 (1.2.a), 12.2, 12.5 (5.5), 12.7 and 12.8, use Creative Commons BY-NC-SA 4.0 licensed pictograms from ARASAAC (https://arasaac.org).

This moment implies greater movement in space, on different planes and paths, and will lead to a subsequent period of greater attention.

They will then seek to jointly address playful objects that are located between the two, in a smaller space. This will be the moment of activity, sitting face to face, to develop a construction game that will involve a series of immediate demonstrations (the use is guided by the therapist, involving the child's body in the action) and distant (the therapist places himself as a model, without involving the child's body), scaffolding of reading visual sequences and alternating rhythms to sustain the joint action.

At this point, they will go to the reading corner, depending on the time and the possibility of extending or the need to bring it to a close, in order to choose a book (Table 12.4). Sometimes they will go to the market to buy some fruit or cookies and prepare a snack.

During the session, the therapist will go back several times to what they are doing, anticipating with a musical key that when the song ends, they will clean up to start the next proposal. They will mark in the sequence what they are doing, pointing and accompanying with brief expressions: "now" (with a word, a clip or an indicative arrow, and a gesture, articulated in a synchronous and clear choreography), and then they will go back to what they did, placing an acetate frame over the representative image to highlight it and reiterating: "we already played with the hammock." This will pave the way for what will come next: "we are going to read a story." Representative gestures will be of great help to Francis: waiting, counting, and cleaning up will be the pantomimes that will accompany a countdown and the reorganization of the elements in the space to start the next game.

Unforeseen events, more or less spontaneous, will always arise. They will require, depending on the process of each child, to solve situations, make new decisions, and make changes. During the first year of work in the different settings (home, early years school and Therapy Center) the proposals for Francis were more directed by the therapist. The time for each activity was short and the need to implement sensorimotor strategies and body support was greater. During the course of the sessions, a rhythm was built that allowed Francis to gain security, using the different supports provided for his well-being, and learning the time of waiting and projections, in a step-by-step manner, mediated by adults.

Regarding the materiality available for our playful encounters in each session, the first selection of materials was organized in boxes initialed according to categories: (a) cause-effect or action-reaction objects: cause-effect objects of rope or pop up, download banks, labyrinths, spinning tops, balloons and bubbles. With these objects we seek to build a first, more linear relationship "if I activate a, b happens", linked to the use of signs: "if I hand over or point to this card, I agree to what I ask for". Later on, we became more complex and diversified different visual representations, gestures, words, for different referent objects of the same class. For example, the ball card, or the "ball" gesture, refers not only to the red ball but to *any* ball. The process from which a sign can adopt multiple representative forms for the same referent, involves a series of planned actions where the materiality we offer plays a fundamental role. In our psychoeducational practices, this process requires a series of deliberate support from therapists, educators, and families. First, we associate an example of the sign with a copy of the object already known to that child in a particular context (e.g., the image of Francis' red ball refers to the ball he has at home). Secondly, we progressively expand the associations between different signs for the same object. For example: a visual sign, the image of any ball, not necessarily Francis', with a gesture representative of the use of the ball and/or with the word ball, segmented into movements that also accompany the segmentation of the locution: pe – lo – ta. Thus, thirdly, we will expand the reference objects (e.g. balls of different shapes, textures and sizes), for that sign that has adopted multiple possible forms (e.g. word, image and gesture). The sign will continue to be modified with different images of balls. In this way, a freehand drawing of a ball began to refer to any

Table 12.3 Freehand visual sequence[12]

[12] Freehand illustration made by Mr. Leandro Cantero, therapist of the team: *Vaivén Infancias* .

Table 12.4 The construction of the story as an aesthetic playful device[13]

	Anticipation of the proposal[14]: Francis chooses the story of *La Lora Pandora.* With the pictures in the pouch, we are telling him that: "now we are going to read the story, to sing and dance to the songs of *La Lora Pandora* and then we are going to play" (the gesture represents "play")
	Book and box/house of*La Lora Pandora* [16] Pandora receives five animals into her home who bring her a treasure of everyday life for her to keep. The repetitive, cumulative and rhythmic structure of the story, added to the illustrations and materiality favor Francis' entry into the fictional world from different points: verbal, visual, gestural, musical and material
	*La Lora Pandora Box/House*, with the different objects-artifact and objects-replica of the story This materiality allows access to the fictional world of the story. Different semiotic systems are combined: reading, singing, gestures that accompany the actions, and the unfolding of each page that allows us to discover the animal that arrives and the treasure it brings
	*La Lora Pandora book*, with the magnetic images that represent the different objects that the characters bring (e.g. blanket, toothbrush, bubble canister) When the book is opened, a finger puppet of Pandora is offered. The therapist puts it on and "makes it fly" carrying the different objects that the characters bring to keep in the house. This way, she directs Francis' attention from the illustration of the object, to the little house and then to herself, promoting joint attention

(continued)

[13] In this case, the object is presented: house—box—story of the Lora Pandora. https://www.unl.edu.ar/extension/la-lora-pandora/.

[14] Pictograms made by Camila Mallozzi, illustrator of the Colectivo Infancias Diversas.

Table 12.4 (continued)

	Francis interacting with the book *La Lora Pandora* with his therapist. While the therapist reads, Francis places the different objects in the house. For example, when Piyo el Grillo brings his brush, Francis chooses the corresponding image and sticks it on the house, which fills with objects until it "explodes". The scene is accompanied by a fold-out page illustrating the sequentiality of the outburst and a strident song. Then the therapist invites them to recreate the house with the replica objects included in the box/house

ball and not just the red ball in Francis' house. In this way, we accompany the construction of the functional permanence of various objects of daily life (see Chap. 9 in this volume).

Later the various signs were used with different functions. For example: with the same sign we could a) ask for the ball or b) ask Francis if he would throw the ball into a hoop, expecting from him not only the delivery of the object, but information that would guide the shared game. These differences show how the use of signs was expanded in its forms and functions in the communicative fabric that we were building with the child.

Just as the signs expanded their nuances and relationships in the web of communication with Francis, in each context their mode of participation was extended and more complex. The interactions were enriched through the organization of spaces and times, the use of visual cues, and the introduction of objects and their uses in small game scripts. The rhythm of the proposals, their reiteration and the arrangement of the elements in each environment, together with subtle changes that surprised within a framework of containment, helped to maintain interest and generate new dynamics of triadic interaction (child-material world-adults). In this process we accessed with Francis a shared understanding of the proposals, giving them meaning, making experience together.

12.4.2 Organization of the Physical Space: Areas, Corners or Learning Centers

The organization of the environment involves considering the time, as well as the physical space in which these psychoeducational actions take place. It is also necessary to organize the relationships located in each context between the different actors involved in it. Iglesia Forneiro [34] states that environments "speak", based on the organization of space, materials, and the interactions that occur in them. The author defines them "as an inseparable whole of objects, smells, shapes, colors, sounds, and people that inhabit and relate to each other in a certain physical framework that contains everything and, at the same time, is contained by all these elements that beat within it as if they had life" (p. 52). This proposal has its power when it comes to thinking about our work spaces. However, these environments can only "communicate" if the child has a way of interpreting them. This implies a previous history of experiences mediated by adults. From the Pragmatics of the Object, we know that in order for the environment to transmit ideas about what is or is not allowed and what is expected to happen in those spaces, it is necessary to learn to read them.

In early childhood education or in other educational instances, organizing the space into areas, corners or centers allows specific areas to promote children learning and exploration [66]. This type of organization of educational spaces invites, from its disposition of materiality and visual cues, to become involved in a shared activity. It also implies very delimited spatial conditions so that each area or learning center is well differentiated from others. With enough space between them, so that what happens in one corner, does not advance on the others. Clearly delimited areas are required so that the visual and auditory stimuli, and the materiality of one does not permeate the other, preventing the environment from becoming a multisensory chaos. Otherwise, there is a risk that what is initially proposed as a space enabled for free exploration of different proposals, ends up being an obstacle instead of an opportunity for play and participation. Let us remember that children with autism spectrum condition usually present a particular sensitivity to sensory stimuli in the environment, to certain textures, lights, visual and/or auditory overload, among others. Some studies indicate that while some children present hyposensitivity linked to the proprioceptive and visual system [11], other children tend to show tactile [50] or auditory hypersensitivity [73]. These relationships can have a substantial impact on both quality of life and social interactions [72]. Therefore, it is crucial to organize the environment so that they become safe places for all children. Thus, for example,

> when Francis enters an environment that offers multiple possibilities simultaneously, in which the material is fully accessible to him without clear visual indications of what is in each place, or demarcation of time that regulates a possible route, that environment, instead of offering possibilities of participation for him, expels him.

The organization by zones or corners requires, on the part of each child, certain self-management skills, in order to be able to prioritize environmental information and participate in the experiences or activities that are proposed. Choosing and self-managing the freedom of exploration and discovery in order to build a game is a process that is learned, in some cases incidentally, in others in a deliberate way. This process is not "natural." Denaturalizing, making aware of what is offered, proposing an organization, is a way of accompanying children with autism spectrum conditions, offering opportunities for participation, from a rights-based perspective. For this reason, dichotomizing structure *versus* freedom is a false binomial.

Free play, the possibility of taking an object and transforming it infinitely to build, for example, a symbolic game, requires a long process of semiotic mediations. It also requires a space "wrapped" with a materiality intentionally selected according to the pursued purposes. For example, using a pictogram to show a child what he or she is going to do is not the same as including that image in a sequential pattern of images, in an environment with a series of elements arranged to invite activity. For example, we offer different areas for the musical games workshop with Francis in an organized way. In Table 12.5 we describe a series of concatenated moments that occur during the musical games workshop session, in the therapeutic center, based on a theme, in this case the season of spring.

> When we finish an activity, we tell the children in the workshop group, based on the visual sequence organized at the beginning of the session, that we have already played with the proposed material and now we are going to put it away. Considering, in addition, that we have made small preparatory anticipations of the end of the game, *providing rhythmic indications,* through a snap of the fingers, an onomatopoeia, a bell or other soft sound object. This anticipatory action, which is repeated over time, is part of the codes of interaction with Francis and his classmates. These codes work as hints that allow preparation for the

Table 12.5 Musical games workshop session. Organization of spaces—time and materiality for the "spring routine"

<table>
<tr><td>5.1</td><td>5.2</td><td>5.3</td><td>5.4</td></tr>
<tr><td></td><td></td><td></td><td></td></tr>
<tr><td colspan="4">We receive Francis in an area decorated with colorful fabrics that invites us to walk around the place. Each one takes a piece of cloth, and we form a circle to the rhythm of the candombe of the greeting song (5.1). As we turn, the kite of colors takes us to the center of the room (5.2), where the flowers of the spring song invite us to dress the place (5.3). At the end of the song, Francis looks at the pouch to give way to the next moment, reading (5.4)</td></tr>
<tr><td>5.5</td><td>5.6</td><td colspan="2">5.7</td></tr>
<tr><td></td><td></td><td colspan="2"></td></tr>
<tr><td colspan="4">We read the story of colors, where a puppet paints landscapes, integrating flowers, fabrics and objects with which we create the symbolic world of spring (5.5). After reading, we build puzzles with the landscapes of the story. The blackboard and a round of cushions invite us to do so (5.6). Finally, the spring song is played in another area of the room, where the relationship between the visual sequence, the arrangement of the drums and the maraca guides the rhythm in a succession of movements from left to right and in different planes of space (sitting in a chair, kneeling and then standing) (5.7)</td></tr>
</table>

end of each moment. In addition, we try to include this story in a melody, singing that this game is about to end. The story, the narrative and the time constitute the memory of what we are doing, the music and the rhythm are part of a shared and multimodal biographical construction.

12.4.3 "Wrapping" the Spaces: Visual Keys, Segmentation of Materiality, and Semiotic Mediation

Promoting practices from the perspective of "conviviality" [45] is related to attending to the multiplicity of possibilities of participation. This implies, among other things, co-creating polysemic educational environments. We are often faced with the paradox of environments overloaded with information, but stripped of semiotic structures that organize meanings, where verbalistic communication prevails. "Wrapping" these environments is the first step in our interventions, whether at home, school or other spaces of child participation. The greater the diversity of forms of access we offer, the more opportunities for participation we will provide. However, this semiotic "wrapping" requires an order, according to increasing complexity, to avoid juxtapositions and overlaps.

To promote understanding as a basis for participation, we propose to consider a series of actions that lead us to establish a common reference. We understand that it is necessary to carefully observe what our children do, how they do it, what they look at, how they relate to objects, etc. Likewise, we have to perceive the child's rhythm, try to follow it, and sustain it on a basis of repetitions, incorporating subtle variations to open new lines of action (as if it were a musical composition). From there, we make explicit, with different signs, what we are doing, what we did, and what we will do, inviting the child to get involved in the proposals based on the arrangement of the materials in the space and their temporal organization.

Along these lines, at the beginning of the intervention with Francis it was necessary to reduce the objects and other stimuli available, and to increase the visual cues representing the spaces, actions, and offerings of the environment (i.e. a picture indicating the place to leave the shoes, a circuit of objects in the space indicating a route, posters indicating with word and image the proposal for that play corner). In this way, we sought that each element available in the space could be a clear sign for the child (i.e. what can be done here?). Likewise, it was also necessary to reduce auditory or audiovisual stimuli such as the television and other screens, agreeing with Francis' family to use all electronic devices in interaction, exclusively at the time of preparing to do something together.

Children often get caught up in the digital world, losing mobility and connection to the analogue world. The proposal is to replace the times of exposure to screens with shared moments of action with the material world. The experience of making different uses with objects, transforming them into their tangible reality, in interaction with others, is fundamental for development. The mediation of an adult, through words, gestures, images, and rhythms, while proposing and responding to the child's actions, fosters a reciprocity that screens cannot offer.

We know that the possibility of establishing social relations with another implies various regulations and agreements that are not exclusively semiotic, at least for the child. These agreements can, over time, be transformed from ritualization into signs that allow the construction of thought. They are formed at the intersections of multiple elements, combining a kind of "grammar" of rituals and routines, sensory strategies adapted to each child and context. This grammar is composed of a variety of signs with their polymorphisms and polysemy (visual, gestural, verbal, oral, written, rhythmic-musical, with their cadences and silences), the organization of the body and the arrangement of materiality in space.

In this way, in a dialogic process, the setting of each scenario, the availability and offers of the actors on the scene, as well as the use of mediating tools, seek to promote sensorimotor experience, communication and the possibility of anticipation in the co-creation of shared understandings. Thus, for example, since we received Francis and his family during the first years of treatment, we have been "wrapping" the environments of his home, therapeutic center and school, according to the needs of each moment of his development and according to the psychoeducational objectives agreed with the family and the teachers. In this process we deploy the different semiotic resources that we mention throughout this chapter and that we present below in a list following an order of ascending complexity:

> From the beginning of the work we used (a) *visual anticipators* (i.e. pouches—Table 12.1) and musical anticipators (i.e. songs for openings and closings of activities or for transitions from one moment to another, rhythms to guide the time and sequentiality of an activity); (b) The *sequential organization of the objects or materials* for the game, in plain sight, but out of his direct reach, was always key to favoring Francis' disposition. First, we use the object on display in hand, showing off two options for the child to choose from. The selection palettes, created by his mother, were very relevant to this objective (Table 12.6). The arrangement of the objects in a horizontal line, either on a shelf or drawers uncovered from the front, allowed Francis to see the objects in the order in which we would use them, thus indicating each moment of play as if it were a material agenda (i.e. 1st ball, 2nd stories, 3rd, blocks). Even when we initially relied on materiality to communicate, we incorporated a representative image next to each object to build the relationship between the object, the visual sign (the card), gestural sign (pantomime), the word that names that game or toy and the concrete action of playing. This allowed for a back and forth through different semiotic systems, and Francis could request the required object using some of the representative signs even in its absence. (c) We gradually introduced resources of greater semiotic complexity, such as *selection panels for* toys, games, books and songs (i.e. support in which the images of the activities and/or materials to be selected are arranged—Table 12.2); (d) we incorporated visual sequences in each space of daily activities (e.g., in the bathroom to wash hands, placemats with instructions for setting the table, among others), (e) later we incorporated *visual communication devices*: *leaflets* (Table 12.7), *communication* folders (Table 12.8), semi-structured sequences of activity, with spaces to complete, and activity scripts of increasing complexity (Table 12.9); (f) we used *visual agendas* for the session or class and subsequently, daily and weekly agendas.

Providing support for the *construction of meaning* implies rethinking what mediations adults offer in our interactions, how *we wrap* environments so that they facilitate communication, in short, what conditions we promote to favor shared

Table 12.6 Selection device: choice paddles

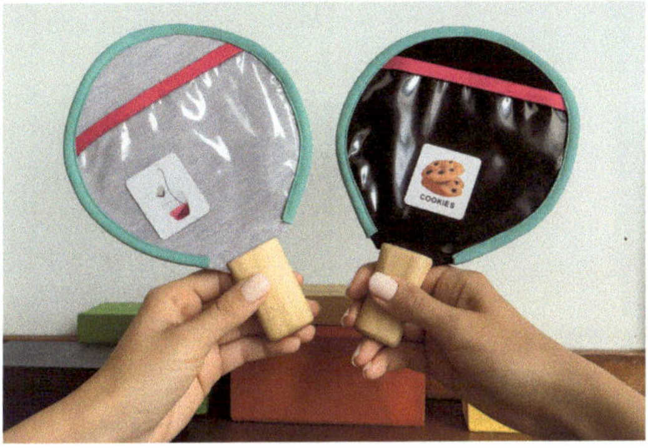	To help him understand the choice at the start of treatment, Francis' mom adapted ping-pong paddles as movable selection panels. Thus, he could show him the options one by one and help him point out his choice. Then they placed the images in the pouch to organize the sequence temporarily. In this case, Francis chose what to eat and what to drink

Table 12.7 Visual communication device: triptych

	**Visual communication leaflet**: At 5 years and 6 months, a foldable triptych was designed for Francis with images organized by colors: subjects, actions, and objects Although Francis was not yet literate, written text was included as a reference for the adults guiding him and for him to gradually become familiar with the written code. This analogue resource has a digital correlate with more visual signs and a voice reader However, technology was avoided due to the child's tendency to attach rigidly to screens

understandings. Thus, we understand that the responsible deployment of the communicative keys that we have described through some everyday scenes with Amparo and Francis, promotes opportunities for social participation, practices based on a rights-based perspective.

12.5 Conclusions

In this chapter we proposed a conceptual journey on the construction of shared meanings that we promote from different contexts: families, teachers and therapists of children with autism spectrum conditions. We underline how semiotic mediations that include the material world play a relevant role as facilitators of participation in everyday life. We promote the production of rhythms, gestures,

Table 12.8 Conversation folder

<table>
<tr>
<td>
</td>
<td>The folder includes photos, icons, and questions to start interactions and encourage dialogue during group meetings. It was created for the reading group in the baby library, which Francis attended when he was 5 years old
*The red line crossed over the photo indicates who did not attend, and the children drew the therapist who joined, freehand</td>
</tr>
</table>

uses of objects, and demonstrations of those uses, songs, words, in order to scaffold psychoeducational processes. We have proposed the Pragmatics of the Object as a lens that allows us to look at the richness of that network of signs, or *semiotic trails,* in which we welcome children from an early age. We emphasized two key aspects: a variety of signs and semiotic systems and a multiplicity of semiotic relationships, of which materiality is a very important part. From this perspective, we proposed that in our practice, we recapitulate the genesis of development to promote the construction of shared meanings. We make it explicit that with this concept we intend to encompass not only the understanding of meanings: that the object becomes a sign of its use, that the gesture, the image and the word represent a social world, but also that the context guides participation, that the spatial arrangement and temporal organization are an invitation to be part of it, a guide for experience, and that all this is understood as part of a cultural fabric. This is especially relevant in pedagogical or therapeutic contexts where the environment and the educational intention generate a learning and communication experience that goes beyond the transmission of meanings.

Throughout this chapter, we weaved together some basic principles that guide our accompaniment of children in their diversity. These are especially relevant for children with autism spectrum condition, their families, and educators. We highlight the *communication tools* we use to generate *conditions conducive to play and participation* in daily activities, always in a context of *care.* We understand that just as a sign cannot be reduced to a meaning and play cannot be "boxed in". Play always open, multiplies and generates relationships. Psychoeducational practices cannot be restricted to a box, a recipe or a program. The "box" is only the container of a world of possibilities. In the words of Najmanovich [45], it

Table 12.9 Activity script

	On Christmas Eve, materials and a guide were provided in the waiting room of the therapeutic center to participate in the construction of the tree.[15] In this way, families, children and therapists are invited to be part of the process. Francis, at 5 years old, still does not read words, but the images help him to understand the process

[15] Freehand illustration made by Camila Sarmiento, therapist of the team: *Vaivén Infancias* .

is necessary to "get out of the boxes", the instruction, the therapeutic center, the classroom, the desk and the chair, to rethink how we inhabit the environments, how we reinvent the nearby space, to make a socially significant cultural experience, located in each community. In this way, we bet that our children can become authors [23] of their own actions and those of us who accompany them become good mediators to make this possible.

Acknowledgements We thank the generosity of the children, their families and the professionals from the teams: "*Vaivén infancias*", "Colectivo Infancias Diversas", "*Fono y Alma*" (Santa Fe, Argentina), for the shared work that this chapter attempts to describe and for the photographs and drawings that illustrate it.

References

1. All, M., & Benassi, J. (2010). *Comunicación y comprensión en procesos de integración educativa con alumnos con trastornos del espectro autista* [Communication and Understanding in Educational Integration Processes with Students with Autism Spectrum Disorders]. [Crongress paper]. Actas de las XIX Jornadas Nacionales de Cátedras y Carreras de Educación Especial de las Universidades Nacionales RUEDES y XIII Jornadas Nacionales de la Red de Estudiantes de Cátedras y Carreras de Educación Especial RECCEE, Buenos Aires, Argentina.
2. All, M., Benassi, J., Allevi, M., Colombero, F., & Maina, S. (2019). *Tejido comunitario de tramas psicoeducativas en torno a las infancias con Condición del Espectro Autista [Community Tapestry of Psychoeducational Frameworks Surrounding Childhoods with Autism Spectrum Condition].* [Poster]. I Simposio de Autismo del Litoral, Entre Ríos, Argentina. Organizado por TEA MyD.
3. American Psychiatric Association. (1994). *Diagnostic and statistical manual of mental disorders* (4ª). American Psychiatric Association.
4. American Psychiatric Association. (2013). *Diagnostic and statistical manual of mental disorders* (5th ed.). American Psychiatric Publishing.
5. Asperger, H. (1944/1991). Die 'autistischen Psychopathen' im Kindesalter. *Archiv für Psychiatrie und Nervenkrankheiten*, 117, 76–136. En U. Frith (Ed.), *Autism and Asperger Syndrome* (pp. 37–92). Cambridge University Press.
6. Baron-Cohen, S., & Nuñez, M. (1998). ¿Son los niños autistas mejores físicos que psicólogos? [Are Autistic Children Better Physicists than Psychologists?]. *Journal for the Study of Education and Development, 21*(84), 33–43. https://doi.org/10.1174/021037098760378775
7. Belinchón, M. (2019). Alteraciones asociadas al autismo: ¿Qué nos enseñan sobre cómo los bebés adquieren el léxico? [Autism-Related Alterations: What Can They Teach Us About Lexical Acquisition in Infants?]. *Llengua, Societat i Comunicació, 17*, 52–63.
8. Benassi, J. (2012). *Las concepciones de signo en los estudios de detección y desarrollo temprano de los Trastornos del Espectro Autista: Revisión teórica a la luz de una perspectiva pragmática del desarrollo temprano del niño* [Conceptions of the Sign in Early Detection and Development Studies of Autism Spectrum Disorders: A Theoretical Review from a Pragmatic Perspective on Early Child Development]. [Unpublished Doctoral Thesis]. Facultad Latinoamericana de Ciencias Sociales, Argentina-Universidad Autónoma de Madrid.
9. Benassi, J., & Valdez, D. (2011). Ayudas para construir significados compartidos [Aids for Constructing Shared Meanings]. In D. Valdez & V. Ruggieri. (Eds.), *Autismo: Del diagnóstico al Tratamiento [Autism: From Diagnosis to Treatment]* (pp. 241–271). Paidós.
10. Benassi, J., Rodríguez, C., & Valdez, D. (2013). Los usos de los objetos en la génesis de la comunicación de los niños con TEA. Análisis de criterios de valoración para la construcción de prácticas psicoeducativas tempranas [The Use of Objects in the Genesis of Communication

in Children with ASD: Analysis of Assessment Criteria for the Development of Early Psychoeducational Practices]. In: Primera Conferencia Latinoamericana del Espectro Autista. Santiago de Chile. *Revista chilena de Psiquiatría y Neurología de la Infancia y Adolescencia, 24*(3), 267.
11. Blanche, E. I., Reinoso, G., Chang, M. C., & Bodison, S. (2012). Proprioceptive processing difficulties among children with autism spectrum disorders and developmental disabilities. *American Journal of Occupational Therapy, 66*, 621–624. https://doi.org/10.5014/ajot.2012.004234
12. Boucher, J. (2009). *The autistic spectrum. Characteristics, causes and practical issues.* SAGE.
13. Branson, D., & Demchak, M. (2009). The use of augmentative and alternative communication methods with infants and toddlers with disabilities: A research review. *Augmentative and Alternative Communication, 25*(4), 274–286. https://doi.org/10.3109/07434610903384529
14. Brignell, A., Chenausky, K. V., Song, H., Zhu, J., Suo, C., & Morgan, A. T. (2018). Communication interventions for autism spectrum disorder in minimally verbal children. *The Cochrane Database of Systematic Reviews, 11*, CD012324. https://doi.org/10.1002/14651858.CD012324.pub2
15. Charman, T., Baron-Cohen. S., Swettenham, J., Baird, G., Drew, A., & Cox, A. (2003). Predicting languaje outcome in infants with autism and pervasive developmental disorder. *International Journal of Languaje and Communication Disorders, 38*(3), 265–285.
16. Colectivo Infancias Diversas. (2023). *La Lora Pandora* [Pandora the parrot] (C. Mallozzi & A. Ilari, Ilustradoras; M. Allevi, M. D'Angelo, J. Benassi, R. Brasca & F. Colombero, Coord.). Programa de Lecturas, Ediciones UNL. ISBN 978-987692308-8.
17. Colonnesi, C., Stams, G. J., Koster, I., & Noom, M. J. (2010). The relation between pointing and language development: A meta-analysis. *Developmental Review, 30*, 352–366. https://doi.org/10.1016/j.dr.2010.10.001
18. Corballis, M. C. (2002). *From hand to mouth: The origins of language.* Princeton University Press.
19. D'Angelo, M., Benassi, J., Allevi, M., & Brasca, R. (2022). Infancias diversas: Construcción colectiva de modos de acompañamiento y comunicación en tiempos de COVID–19 [Diverse Childhoods: Collective Construction of Support and Communication Approaches in Times of COVID-19]. *Revista de extensión universitaria, 17*, 14–14.
20. Español, S. (2001). Creación de símbolos y ficción durante el segundo año de vida [Symbol Creation and Pretend Play During the Second Year of Life]. *Estudios de Psicología, 22*(2), 207–226.
21. Español, S. (2004). *Cómo hacer cosas sin palabras. Gesto y Ficción en la infancia temprana* [How to Do Things Without Words: Gesture and Fiction in Early Childhood]. Machado libros.
22. Esteve-Gibert, N., Igualada, A., & Prieto, P. (2019). El gest com a facilitador i precursor del desenvolupament del llenguatge [Gesture as a Facilitator and Precursor of Language Development]. *Llengua, Societat i Comunicació, 17*, 26–41.
23. Fernández, A. (2002). *Poner en juego el Saber: propiciando autorías de pensamiento* [Putting Knowledge into Play: Fostering Thought Authorship]. Nueva Visión.
24. First Words Project. (2018). 16 by 16: *First Words Project.* https://firstwordsproject.com/about-16by16/
25. Fortea-Sevilla, M. S., Escandell Bermúdez, M. O., Castro-Sánchez, J. J., & Martos-Pérez, J. (2015). Desarrollo temprano del lenguaje en niños pequeños con trastorno del espectro autista mediante el uso de sistemas alternativos [Early Language Development in Young Children with Autism Spectrum Disorder Through the Use of Alternative Systems]. *Revista de Neurología, 60*(Supl 1), S31–S35.
26. Fountain, C., Winter, A. S., & Bearman, P. (2012). Six developmental trajectories characterize children with Autism. *Pediatrics, 129*(5), 1112–1120.
27. Franchini, M., Hamodat, T., Armstrong, V. L., et al. (2019). Infants at risk for autism spectrum disorder: Frequency, quality, and variety of joint attention behaviors. *Journal of Abnormal Child Psychology, 47*, 907–920. https://doi.org/10.1007/s10802-018-0471-1

28. Ganz, J. B., Earles-Vollrath, T. L., Heath, A. K., Parker, R., Rispoli, M. J., & Duran, J. (2012). A meta-analysis of single case research studies on aided augmentative and alternative communication systems with individuals with autism spectrum disorders. *Journal of Autism and Developmental Disorders, 42*, 60–74. https://doi.org/10.1007/s10803-011-1212-2
29. Guevara, I. & Rodríguez, C. (2023). Developing communication through objects: Ostensive gestures as the first gestures in children's development. *Developmental Review, 68*, 101076.
30. Guidetti, M. & Nicoladis, E. (2008). Introduction to special issue: Gestures and communicative development. *First Language, 28*(2), 107–115. https://doi.org/10.1177/0142723708088914
31. Gómez, J. C. & Núñez, M. (1998). Dossier documental sobre la mente social y la mente física. *Infancia y Aprendizaje, 84*, 85–98. https://doi.org/10.1174/021037098760378801
32. Hodgetts, S., Nicholas, D., Zwaigenbaum, L., & Mc, C. D. (2013). Parents' and professionals' perceptions of family-centered care for children with autism spectrum disorder across service sectors. *Social Science and Medicine, 96*, 138–46.
33. Howley, M. (2015). Outcomes of structured teaching for children on the autism spectrum: Does the research evidence neglect the bigger picture? *Journal of Research in Special Educational Needs, 15*(2), 106–119.
34. Iglesias Forneiro, M. L. (2008). Observación y evaluación del ambiente de aprendizaje en educación infantil: dimensiones y variables a considerar [Observation and Assessment of the Learning Environment in Early Childhood Education: Dimensions and Variables to Consider]. *Revista Iberoamericana de Educación, 47*, 49–70. https://rieoei.org/historico/documentos/rie47a03.pd
35. Kanner, L. (1943). Autistic disturbances of affective contact. *Nervous Child, 2,* 217–250.
36. Landa, R. (2007). Early communication development and intervention for children with autism. *Mental Retardation and Developmental Disabilities Research Reviews, 13*(1), 16–25.
37. Lavanchy, S. (1993). La educación pre-escolar: desafío y aventura [Preschool Education: Challenge and Adventure]. Universitaria.
38. Lewis, J. D., Evans, A. C., Pruett, J. R., Botteron, K., Zwaigenbaum, L., Estes, A., Gerig, G., Collins, L., Kostopoulos, P., McKinstry, R., Dager, S., Paterson, S., Schultz, R., Styner, M., Hazlett, H., & Piven, J. (2014). Network inefficiencies in autism spectrum disorder at 24 months. *Translational Psychiatry, 4*, e388. https://doi.org/10.1038/tp.2014.24
39. Light, J., & McNaughton, D. (2013). Putting people first: Re-thinking the role of technology in augmentative and alternative communication intervention. *Augmentative and Alternative Communication, 29*(4), 299–309. https://doi.org/10.3109/07434618.2013.848935. PMID: 24229334.
40. Luyster, R., Gotham, K., Guthrie, W., Coffing, M., Petrak, R., Pierce, K., & Lord, C. (2009). The Autism diagnostic observation schedule-toddler module: A new module of a standardized diagnostic measure for autism spectrum disorders. *Journal of Autism and Developmental Disorders, 39*(9), 1305–1320. https://doi.org/10.1007/s10803-009-0746-z
41. Mandoki, K. (2008). *Estética cotidiana y juegos de la cultura* [Everyday Aesthetics and the Play of Culture]. *Prosaica I.* Siglo XXI.
42. Manzi, F., Savarese, G., Mollo, M., & Iannaccone, A. (2020). Objects as communicative mediators in children with Autism spectrum disorder. *Frontiers in Psychology, 17*(11), 1269. https://doi.org/10.3389/fpsyg.2020.01269.PMID:32625148;PMCID:PMC7311758
43. Moro, C., & Rodriguez, C. (1994). Prelinguistic sign mixity and flexibility in interaction. *European Journal of Psychology of Education, 9*, 301–310 (1994). https://doi.org/10.1007/BF03172903
44. Mundy, P., & Newell, L. (2007). Attention, joint attention, and social cognition. *Current Directions in Psychological Science, 16*(5), 269–274.
45. Najmanovich, D. (2020). Ni adentro ni afuera de las cajas: De la inclusión a la convivencialidad Neither Inside nor Outside the Boxes: From Inclusion to Conviviality]. In: G. Untoiglich y G. Szyber (comps.), *Las promesas incumplidas de la inclusión: Prácticas desobedientes [The Unfulfilled Promises of Inclusion: Disobedient Practices]* (pp. 125–162). NOVEDUC.

46. Nunes, D., Barbosa, J., & Nunes, L. (2021). Comunicação Alternativa para Alunos com Autismo na Escola: Uma Revisão da Literatura [Alternative Communication for Students with Autism at School: A Literature Review]. *Rev. Bras. Educ. Espec, 27*, e0212.
47. Ocampo, S. (in prep.). Las interacciones triádicas en las escenas familiares de alimentación, en bebés entre los 5 a 15 meses de edad que posteriormente recibieron diagnóstico de condición del espectro autista y en bebés con desarrollo típico. Un estudio retrospectivo desde la Pragmática del Objeto [Triadic Interactions in Family Feeding Scenes in Infants Aged 5 to 15 Months Later Diagnosed with Autism Spectrum Condition and in Typically Developing Infants: A Retrospective Study from the Perspective of Object Pragmatics]. [Unpublished Masters' Thesis]. Facultad Latinoamericana de Ciencias Sociales, Argentina-Universidad Autónoma de Madrid.
48. Özçaliskan, S., Adamson, L. B., & Dimitrova, N. (2016). Early deictic but not other gestures predict later vocabulary in both typical development and autism. *Autism, 20*, 754–763. https://doi.org/10.1177/1362361315605921
49. Ozonoff, S., Macari, S., Young, G. S., Goldring, S., Thompson, M., & Rogers, S. (2008). Atypical object exploration at 12 months of age is associated with autism in a prospective sample. *Autism: The International Journal of Research and Practice, 12*(5), 457–472. https://doi.org/10.1177/1362361308096402
50. Puts, N. A. J., Wodka, E. L., Tommerdahl, M., Mostofsky, S. H., & Edden, R. A. E. (2014). Impaired tactile processing in children with autism spectrum disorder. *Journal of Neurophysiology, 111*(4), 1803–1811. https://doi.org/10.1152/jn.00890.2013
51. Ramos-Cabo, S., Vulchanov, V., & Vulchanova, M. (2019). Gesture and language trajectories in early development: An overview from the autism spectrum disorder perspective. *Frontiers in Psychology, 10*, 1211. https://doi.org/10.3389/fpsyg.2019.01211
52. Rivière, Á., & Español, S. (2003). La suspensión como mecanismo de creación semiótica [Suspension as a Mechanism of Semiotic Creation]. *Studies in Psychology, 24*(3), 261–275. https://doi.org/10.1174/021093903770411184
53. Rivière, A. (2002). *IDEA: Inventario de espectro autista* [IDEA: Autism Spectrum Inventory]. Fundec. (Original work published in 1998).
54. Rivière, A. (2003). Actividad y sentido en autismo [Activity and Meaning in Autism]. In M. Belinchón, A. Rosa, M. Sotillo & I. Marichalar (Comps.), *Ángel Rivière. Obras escogidas, Vol III. Metarrepresentación y semiosis* [Ángel Rivière. Selected Works, Vol. III: Metarepresentation and Semiosis] (pp. 123–131). Médica Panamericana. (Original work published in 1996)
55. Rivière, A. (2003). Comunicación, suspensión y semiosis humana: Los orígenes de la práctica y de la comprensión interpersonal. En M. Belinchón, A. Rosa, M. Sotillo e I. Marichalar (comp.) *Ángel Rivière. Obras Escogidas* [Communication, Suspension, and Human Semiosis: The Origins of Practice and Interpersonal Understanding]. *In M. Belinchón, A. Rosa, M. Sotillo e I. Marichalar (comp.) Ángel Rivière. Obras Escogidas [Ángel Rivière. Selected Work] (Vol, III, pp.181–201)* (Vol, III, pp.181–201). Original work published in 1999.
56. Rodríguez, C. (2009). The "circumstances" of gestures: Proto-interrogative and private gestures. *New ideas in Psychology, 27*(2), 288–303. https://doi.org/10.1016/j.newideapsych.2008.04.002
57. Rodríguez, C., Estrada, L., Moreno-Llanos, I., & de los Reyes, J. L. (2017). Executive functions and educational actions in an infant school: Private uses and gestures at the end of the first year. *Estudios de Psicología, 38*(2), 385–423. https://doi.org/10.1080/02109395.2017.1305061
58. Rodríguez, C., & Moreno-Llanos, I. (2023). A pragmatic turn in the study of early executive functions by object use and gestures. A case study from 8 to 17 months of age at a nursery school. *Integration Psychological Behavior, 57*, 607–654. https://doi.org/10.1007/s12124-020-09578-5
59. Rodríguez, C. (2006). *Del ritmo al símbolo. Los signos en el nacimiento de la inteligencia* [From Rhythm to Symbol: Signs in the Birth of Intelligence]. Horsori.

60. Rodríguez, C. (2007). El ojo de Dios no mira signos. Desarrollo temprano y semiótica [God's Eye Does Not See Signs: Early Development and Semiotics]. *Infancia y Aprendizaje, 30*(3), 343–374.
61. Rodríguez, C. (2012). The functional permanence of the object: A product of consensus. In E. Martí, & C. Rodríguez (Eds.), *After piaget* (pp. 123–150). Transaction Publishers.
62. Rodríguez, C., Basilio, M., Cárdenas, K., Cavalcante, C., Moreno-Nuñez, A., Palacios, P., & Yuste, N. (2018). Object pragmatics: Culture and communication—the bases for early cognitive development. In A. Rosa, & J. Valsiner (Eds.), *The Cambridge handbook of sociocultural psychology* (2da ed., pp. 223–244). Cambridge University Press. https://doi.org/10.1017/9781316662229
63. Rodríguez, C., & Moro, C. (1999). *El mágico número tres. Cuando los niños aún no hablan* [The Magic Number Three: When Children Still Do Not Speak]. Paidós.
64. Rogers, S. J., & Dawson, G. (2010). *Early start denver model for young children with autism: Promoting language, learning, and engagement*. The Guilford Press.
65. Sanz-Cervera, P., Fernández-Andrés, M. I., Pastor-Cerezuela, G., & Tárraga-Mínguez, R. (2018). Efectividad de las intervenciones basadas en metodología TEACCH en el trastorno del espectro autista: Un estudio de revisión [Effectiveness of TEACCH-Based Interventions in Autism Spectrum Disorder: A Review Study]. *Papeles del Psicólogo, 39*(1), 40–50. https://doi.org/10.23923/pap.psicol2018.2851
66. Schickedanz, J. A. (2008). *Increasing the power of instruction. Integration of language, Literacy, and Math Across the Preschool Day.* NAEYC.
67. Soukup-Ascençao, T., D'Souza, D., D'Souza, H., & Karmiloff-Smith, A. (2016). Parent-child interaction as a dynamic contributor to learning and cognitive development in typical and atypical development. *Journal for the Study of Education and Development, 39*(4), 694–726.
68. Sterner, A., & Rodríguez, C. (2012). Valoración de signos de alarma en autismo entre los 9 y los 16 meses de edad [Assessment of Early Warning Signs of Autism Between 9 and 16 Months of Age]. *Psicología Educativa, 18*(2), 145–158. https://doi.org/10.5093/ed2012a15
69. Syriopoulou-Delli, C. K., & Eleni, G. (2022). Effectiveness of different types of augmentative and alternative communication (AAC) in improving communication skills and in enhancing the vocabulary of children with ASD: A review. *Review Journal Autism Developement Disorders, 9*, 493–506. https://doi.org/10.1007/s40489-021-00269-4
70. Taylor Brukner, C., & Yoder, P. (2007). Restricted object use in young children with autism. *Autism. The International Journal of Research and Practice, 11*, 161–171.
71. UNICEF (2006). *Convención sobre los derechos del niño. UNICEF Comité español* [Convention on the Rights of the Child. UNICEF, Spanish Committee]. https://www.unicef.org/es/convencion-derechos-nino/texto-convencion
72. Uchoa Sena, B., & de Souza Barros, T. (2023). Hypersensitivity in children with Autism spectrum disorder (ASD). In I de Souza (Ed.), *Health of tomorrow: Innovations and academic research* (pp. 428–442). https://doi.org/10.56238/sevened2023.007-036
73. Urízar-Sánchez, C., Sariego, R. H., Walker, J. K., & Gomez, G. M. (2022). Hiperacusia en trastornos del espectro autista: una revisión de la literatura [Hyperacusis in Autism Spectrum Disorders: A Literature Review]. *Revista de Otorrinolaringología y Cirugía de Cabeza y Cuello, 82*, 258–269.
74. Valdez, D. (2012). Desarrollo comunicativo [Communicative Development]. In J. A. Castorina & M. Carretero (Eds.), *Desarrollo cognitivo y educación I* [Cognitive Development and Education I] (pp. 195–213). Paidós.
75. Valdéz, D. (2019). *Autismo: Cómo crear contextos amigables* [Autisms: How to Create Friendly Contexts]. Paidós.
76. Valdéz, D., Benassi, J., & Rodriguez, C. (2018). Uses of semiotic objects and mediation in early triadic interactions in siblings of children diagnosed with autistic spectrum disorder. Poster presented at the Annual Meeting International Society for Autism Research (INSAR), May. Rotterdam, Holland. http://www.autism-insar.org/page/2018AnnMtg

77. Wertsch, J. V. (1991/1993). *Voces de la mente: Un enfoque sociocultural para el estudio de la acción mediada* [Voices of the Mind: A Sociocultural Approach to the Study of Mediated Action]. Visor.
78. Wertsch, J. V. (1984). The zone of proximal development: Some conceptual issues. *New Directions for Child and Adolescent Development, 7–18.* https://doi.org/10.1002/cd.23219842303
79. Williams, E., Costall, A., & Reddy, V. (2018). Autism and triadic play: An object lesson in the mutuality of the social and material. *Ecological Psychology, 30*(2), 146–173. https://doi.org/10.1080/10407413.2018.1439140
80. Williams, E., Kendall-Scott, L., & Costall, A. (2005). Parents' experiences of introducing everyday object use to their children with autism. *Autism, 9*(5), 521–540. https://doi.org/10.1177/1362361305057869
81. Williams, E., Reddy, V., & Costall, A. (2001). Taking a closer look at functional play in children with Autism. *Journal of Autism and Developmental Disorders, 31*(1), 67–77. https://doi.org/10.1023/A:1005665714197
82. Williams, E. (2003). A comparative review of early forms of object-directed play and parent–infant play in typical infants and young children with autism. *Autism: The International Journal of Research and Practice, 7*(4), 361–377. https://doi.org/10.1177/1362361303007004003
83. Wing, L., & Gould, J. (1979). Severe impairments of social interaction and associated abnormalities in children: Epidemiology and classification. *Journal of Autism and Developmental Disorders, 9*, 11–29.
84. Ye, Q., Liu, L., Lv, S., Cheng, S., Zhu, H., Xu, Y., Zou, X., & Deng, H. (2021). The gestures in 2–4-year-old children with autism spectrum disorder. *Frontiers in Psychology, 12*, 604542. https://doi.org/10.3389/fpsyg.2021.604542
85. Zaidman-Zait, A., Mirenda, P., Duku, E., Szatmari, P., Georgiades, S., Volden, J., Zwaigenbaum, L., Vaillancourt, T., Bryson, S., Smith, I., Fombonne, E., Roberts, W., Waddell, C., & Thompson, A. (2014). Examination of bidirectional relationships between parent stress and two types of problem behavior in children with autism spectrum disorder. *Journal of Autism and Developmental Disorders, 44*(8), 1908–17. https://doi.org/10.1007/s10803-014-2064-3

MIX
Papier aus verantwortungsvollen Quellen
Paper from responsible sources
FSC® C105338

If you have any concerns about our products,
you can contact us on
ProductSafety@springernature.com

In case Publisher is established outside the EU,
the EU authorized representative is:
Springer Nature Customer Service Center GmbH
Europaplatz 3, 69115 Heidelberg, Germany

Printed by Libri Plureos GmbH
in Hamburg, Germany